The A to Z of WORLD DEVELOPMENT

For Reference

Not to be taken from this room

D0514593

"The A-Z of World Development is an excellent reference tool for secondary school students. The short, clear articles and superb illustrations provide a quick and balanced explanation on many relevant topics, institutions and significant people in world development. This book should be on the shelves in every History, Geography and Social Studies Department. It is a handy reference work for students of international relations in history, politics, geography, economics and law courses."
ALLAN HUX, Co-ordinator of Social Studies, Toronto Board of Education

"The book makes fascinating reading and clearly fills a gap in reference works for Development Studies. Every school Geography Department should have at least one copy."
DAVID POTTS, Head of Geography, The Cherwell School, Oxford

"Thanks to *The A-Z of World Development* **for guiding us on our way to better understanding the world. A rattling good book!"**
PROFESSOR NORMAN MYERS, editor, The Gaia Atlas of Planet Management

The A-Z of World Development
First published in 1998 in the UK by
New Internationalist Publications Ltd
Oxford, England

Copyright © Andy Crump/New Internationalist 1998

Copyright © for photographs and art rests with the individual or agencies.

The book is sold subject to the condition that it shall not, by way of trade or
otherwise, be lent, re-sold, hired out or otherwise circulated without the publisher's
prior consent in any form of binding or cover other than that in which it is
published and without a similar condition including this condition being imposed
on the subsequent purchaser.

Production editor/Picture research: Troth Wells
Design by the New Internationalist

Printed by C&C Offset Printing Co. Ltd., Hong Kong

British Library Cataloguing-in-Publication Data
A catalogue record for this book is available from the British Library
ISBN 1-869 847-46-6

New Internationalist Publications Ltd
Registered office:
55 Rectory Road
Oxford OX4 1BW

Front cover photo:
Children in the Grenadines, Netherlands Antilles *Amedeo Vergani*

6/00

DISCARD

The A to Z of
WORLD
DEVELOPMENT

Compiled by Andy Crump **NI** Edited by Wayne Ellwood

R&F
338.9
A111

ACKNOWLEDGEMENTS

PUTTING THIS BOOK TOGETHER has been a genuine exercise in trans-Atlantic co-operation. I would especially like to thank Andy Crump in Geneva whose meticulous research skills and encyclopedic knowledge of development issues form the backbone of this project. I also want to give special thanks to my colleagues at the **New Internationalist** in Oxford, Troth Wells and Dexter Tiranti.

Troth provided much-needed encouragement from beginning to end, adding valuable editorial comments and overseeing the final production and design of the book – a major task in itself. Dexter's tireless enthusiasm helped to give the book life and convince others of its importance. Thanks, too, to Dinyar Godrej in Holland who was enlisted to turn his copy-editing talents to the manuscript and did so with his usual aplomb.

I would also like to thank our designers Alan Hughes, Andrew Kokotka and Ian Nixon for a visually splendid book, and Diana Senior, our painstaking proof-reader. Thanks to to the rest of the staff at the **New Internationalist** for their patience and unstinting support – Vanessa Baird, Chris Brazier, Fran Harvey, Ian McKelvie, David Ransom, James Rowland, Richard Swift, Véronique Szerauc, Nikki van der Gaag and Michael York.

Wayne Ellwood
Toronto, 1998

DEVELOPMENT – WHAT'S THAT?

ISN'T IT SOMETHING we keep telling developing nations to jolly well get on with? Soft, let's say with Hamlet, that would be scanned. Fortunately we have here a rattling good book to help us with our scanning. Thanks to the **NI** for guiding us on our way: we certainly need it.

For opening instance: which nation shall we say is developed in worthwhile fashion? The United Kingdom likes to think its economy has been steadily expanding for years. In conventional terms, it has: per-capita Gross National Product (GNP) has been climbing steadily, occasional blips apart, for a full half century. But when we look at Net Economic Growth (NEG), also known as Sustainable Economic Welfare, we find that it peaked in the early 1970s and has been declining since 1980. NEG is economic growth with deductions made for environmental problems and other downside factors. When an oil spill is cleaned up, the many activities involved are counted as economic endeavours just as worthy as growing food or educating children. In fact, they are merely getting us back to where we were before the oil spill occurred. It is absurd to add them to GNP; they should be deducted – they are not.

The same applies to many social ills. If you are mugged, the costs of police help, plus possibly medical care, court activities and even imprisonment for the offender, are all reckoned to be improvements to the economy and as muggings increase, so GNP expands. Foolishness compounded. A finance whiz in Japan has calculated that the Kobe earthquake was marginally good for his country's economy. In the past quarter century, the British economy has expanded by one and a half times but road traffic has doubled, the incidence of asthma has tripled, the number of workless households has tripled, and violent crime has quadrupled.

So wherein lies development? And does it have to be centred on economic development, even where that is all beneficial? Brazil has per-capita GNP of $3,640 but life expectancy is 67, and its average family size is 2.4 children. Sri Lanka, with a much more social and egalitarian cast to its economic system, has figures of $700, 73, and 2.3.

The United Nations Development Programme has assembled a set of criteria by which to measure 'human development', including health, education, income/employment, women's status, social security, social fabric and environment. On this composite index, Saudi Arabia with its autocratic regime and dismal human rights record ranks 73rd, by contrast with its per-capita GDP (Gross Domestic Product, similar to GNP) ranking of 41st. Most of the oil-rich Arab countries are similarly at odds. The United States is fourth on the human development index list and third on the other. Switzerland shows the greatest divide of all the industrialized countries, 16th and 4th. The top country worldwide in terms of human development is Canada, which is in 7th place on the per-capita GDP index.

Finally, can we say that any country is truly developed as long as the world tolerates 840 million people semi-starving, 1.3 billion people with cash incomes of less than $1 per day, and a gap between the richest one fifth and poorest one fifth that is around 60:1, the widest ever and growing ever wider?

Ultimate development, where art thou? *The A-Z of World Development* makes an excellent starting point for those wanting to find out more about this complicated concept.

*Professor **Norman Myers**, Green College, Oxford, 1998*

CONTENTS

Entries in **bold** indicate a cross-reference

Gathering fuelwood
A boy in Benin, West Africa, with a bundle of firewood. Gathering
wood is a daily task undertaken by women and younger members
of the family in many parts of the Third World.
Photo: Claude Sauvageot

Heavy burden
Coming home in the evening sun this peasant in Yunan, China,
carries a yoke of baskets, while in the background corn cobs dry
against the house walls.
Photo: Claude Sauvageot

INTRODUCTION

Making a splash
Bathed in sunlight, three children in Nicaragua scoop up a drink of water from a standpipe – just over half the population there has access to clean water.

THERE IS NO SHORTAGE of worthy reference books available. A brief trip to a good local bookstore will quickly turn up dozens. However, you're not likely to come up with another one quite like this. Why? Because the book you hold in your hands is not an ordinary reference book – although, admittedly, it does have the *appearance* of one. First of all it's organized alphabetically (the title gives it away). And secondly, the entries are succinct and buttressed with lots of supporting data. You can look up a particular concept or phrase in an instant. Or you can meander idly at your own pace: read about the life of Che Guevara; get a quick introduction to solar cells or an instant briefing on the Ogallala Aquifer.

In fact, there are 624 entries in total in this 'dictionary' of world development. Read them all and you'll have a comprehensive overview of the main ideas and issues of concern to social activists and non-governmental organizations involved with Third World development over the last quarter century.

But you'll also have more than that. Because this is definitely *not* a reference book which calmly attempts to straddle the middle ground. In fact, our original conception was that this compendium would reflect the editorial position of those of us who published it – the editors at the **New Internationalist** magazine. For those of you who don't know the **New Internationalist**, let me explain. We are a collective of writers, editors and designers who publish the **NI** magazine, widely considered the magazine of record on issues of international development, social justice and the relationship between rich and poor nations.

The **NI** has been in the business of packaging information for over 25 years. During that time we've become practised at the art of sifting, sorting and editing for our readers. Because, as many people are beginning to realize, the value of information is determined by more than just quantity.

That's a notion that runs counter to one of the shaping myths in this age of high-speed electronic communications: the more information that is available the better for everyone. It is widely believed that freedom of information is the grease that lubricates the machinery of democracy.

While the basic premise may be true, the issue is complex – mainly because all information does not carry the same weight. The yapping of your television set and the flashy images of the advertising industry dominate public discourse in a much more powerful way than the marginal messages of

Gates of perception
More information may not mean more knowledge: information can be filtered, flattened, and packaged to reinforce a particular worldview.

the alternative press or the isolated critique of corporate power floating around in cyberspace.

In terms of sheer quantity there is more data zapping around the globe than ever before. But the reality behind the hype is of course much different. For most of us there is not too *little* information, but too *much*. Most of us don't have the time, the inclination or the technology to wade through it all. The demands of work, family, leisure, friends, children and community means time is limited. There are only so many books, magazines and newspapers we can read, only so many TV shows we can watch, and only so many Web sites we can 'surf' in the course of a normal week. In fact, given this glut, some brave souls are beginning to ask whether information for information's sake complicates and confuses an understanding of where power lies in the world and who benefits from its exercise.

Media critics like American linguist Noam Chomsky worry not about a shortage of information but about the ideological conformity which unites the major media, so that information is filtered, flattened and packaged to reinforce a particular worldview. Voices which challenge the dominant ethos of liberal capitalism are marginalized and contained, while 'freedom of speech' and 'freedom of information' are offered as proof that democracy works. Meanwhile, as

Snow on top
Outdoor cooking in Peru's cold highlands: about 40 per cent of Peru's population – 8 million people – are indigenous groups such as Aymara and Quecha indians who live in the Andes region.

poverty grows, the gap between rich and poor widens and the global environment is desecrated in the name of economic growth, fundamental questions about the market system, commodity production or the powerful role of Western corporations are ignored.

It is this kind of concern which sparked the editors of the **New Internationalist** magazine to think about publishing this *A-Z of World Development*. We wanted to produce a reference book on the major themes, ideas and personalities that have shaped relations between rich and poor worlds over the last 50 years. But we wanted to do that in a way which

What the world wants today?
The flashy images of the advertizing industry appear to erase years of apartheid on this hoarding in Johannesburg, South Africa.

avoided the orthodox and bogus notions of objectivity which pervade mainstream journalism. In short we wanted to produce a reference work 'with attitude'. And I think we've managed more or less to do that.

This *A-Z of World Development* has the illusion of being comprehensive. But of course it is not. We could have easily produced a set of entries two or three times the size because the list of *potential* entries is virtually limitless. (I'm sure you will wonder immediately why we didn't produce an entry on tubewells, the telephone or Tierra del fuego.) Like all information in the modern media age, our choice of what to include is both subjective and politically charged – since choosing what entries *not* to include is as much a subjective decision as choosing those which we *do* include. This list of entries reflects our concerns at the **New Internationalist** and to a lesser extent the interests of our researcher, Andy Crump, who compiled most of them. Of course, there are lots left out. Nonetheless, the entries here cover a huge range of issues and ideas. There is lots to fascinate and more to intrigue.

All the entries are cross-referenced in **bold** in the text. In this way you can follow a thread of interest from entry to entry adding to the picture as you go. Or you can simply read entries as they stand. As is the case in any dictionary the entries are generally succinct, enough to give you a basic overview, a few key statistics and, I hope, an appetite for more.

We've also given this book our unique **NI** stamp in more ways than by just adding our own editorial spin. As you'll see when you dip into the book we've spiced up the standard reference work format. We've included an impressive selection of wonderful photographs, and dozens of colourful graphs, charts and illustrations to complement the usual columns of grey text. In that way we're confident this book will take pride of place on your bookshelf.

Of course this *A-Z of World Development* is a research tool and we hope it will be used in that way. But it is also a reference book to be seen, to peruse, to read to your kids (or to have them read themselves) and to enjoy. So dig in. And happy reading.

Wayne Ellwood
Toronto, 1998

Aral Sea
Rusting hulks lie like beached whales in Uzbekistan's inland Aral Sea. Since 1960, the Sea's surface area has shrunk by half as river water has been diverted to feed irrigation schemes.

Bold indicates a cross-reference

ABORIGINES

The descendants of the original inhabitants of any country or region are called aborigines or **indigenous people**. Today, however, the term is commonly used to describe the native inhabitants of Australia. It is widely believed that Australian Aboriginal society is the oldest on Earth (dating back some 40-60,000 years) and that it provides a prime example of how it is possible to live in harmony with the natural environment. It is unclear where the Aborigines originated, but after migrating to Australia they soon

First people

Aboriginal society is probably the oldest in the world, dating back over 40,000 years. Today Aborigines make up about one per cent of Australia's 18 million population. **ABORIGINES**

spread to every part of the island and to neighbouring Tasmania, living as semi-nomadic hunter-gathers. Men fashioned weapons from wood and stone, while women used rudimentary wooden and stone utensils. Weaving was common but there was no pottery and no beasts of burden were used. With only a few basic tools, Aborigines lived and flourished from fertile coastal areas to the inhospitable, almost waterless deserts of the interior. Before contact with Europeans there were around 500 separate Aboriginal tribes, each with a complex social organization and language. Today about 30 such languages survive.

Society was based on a rich and elaborate mythology known as 'The Dreamtime' which governed every aspect of life. Political affairs were conducted by male elders and male initiation rites were common. Men hunted while women and children gathered food with everyone receiving equal shares.

Despite material **poverty**, Aborigines have a rich artistic heritage of storytelling, graphic arts, music and dramatic rituals. When English colonists first stepped ashore in the late 1700s, they concluded that the **land** did not belong to anyone and so declared it *terra nullius*.

Aboriginal people were denied basic **human rights**, including citizenship and title to land. Whole families were killed and children abducted from their parents. Western diseases wiped out thousands more so that the original population soon fell by 80%. Aborigines suffer from the usual problems that commonly affect disadvantaged and marginalized groups: they have few prospects for either **employment** or integration into society without losing their traditional culture. It is estimated that less than 1% of Australia's 18 million people are of Aboriginal descent.

Since 1967 the Australian

Government has been forced to recognize Aboriginal grievances. From 1970 onward the state began to return large areas of (usually barren, unproductive) land to the Aborigines. However, the Government has generally retained the rights to all minerals on this land. Nonetheless, there has been some progress. The country's first Aboriginal Member of Parliament was elected in 1971 and in 1992 the Government finally recognized native land rights.

ABORTION

The expulsion or removal of a foetus from the womb of an expectant mother before it is capable of independent survival. Abortion may occur naturally in the form of a miscarriage. Or it may be induced for therapeutic or social reasons – to protect the life, health or social standing of the mother. Induced abortion is one of the world's most contentious issues. While it is fully legal and state-funded in some countries, it is strictly prohibited in others.

Abortion prevents birth but it is viewed generally as a 'last resort', both socially and ethically. A major problem is that relatively few women have access to safe abortion, even in countries where the practice is legal. Unsafe abortion is a serious concern in **developing countries**. For example, it accounts for 31% of recorded maternal deaths in Bangladesh and is a key factor in 30% of maternal deaths in Ethiopia, India, Tanzania and Zambia. In the West the problem is less serious. However, women face growing difficulties in terminating unwanted pregnancies in countries like the US and Germany. 'Right To Life' movements and groups campaigning for the 'rights of the unborn child' have staged violent protests. Women attending abortion clinics have been aggressively harassed by demonstrators. In the US several abortion clinic workers have been murdered.

ACACIA

A genus of evergreen trees and shrubs with 800 different species. Acacias are found throughout the tropics and subtropics. They are particularly abundant in savannahs and arid regions in Australia, Africa, India and the Americas. They are leguminous and consequently help to improve or maintain **soil** fertility. Most species are fast-growing, robust and grow well in unfavourable conditions; they are now widely used in **land** reclamation and **agroforestry** projects. They are grown as shade trees and soil-improvers as well as to control **soil erosion**.

In several regions acacias are indispensable as a prime source of forage for livestock. The leaves and nutritive pods can be browsed or the trees lopped for fodder. Acacia trees also yield a variety of useful products including gums (especially the commercially important Gum Arabic), tannins, dyes and wood which is suitable for both construction and furniture-making. Gum Arabic comes from *acacia Senegal*, a tree native to North Africa where it is grown commercially. The gum is used to make jellies and candies, with more than 90% of world supplies coming from Sudan.

ACID RAIN

Industrial pollutants like **sulphur dioxide** and nitrogen oxide are absorbed into the atmosphere and then fall to earth as dilute sulphuric and nitric acid in the form of acid rain. Most of the pollutants come from burning fossil fuels (vehicle exhausts contribute a significant amount) but smelting of **copper** and other non-ferrous metals is also a key source, releasing an estimated 6 million tonnes of sulphur dioxide yearly. Acid rain damages trees, plants and crops, acidifies lakes, rivers and **groundwater** and corrodes buildings. It is also believed to be a major factor behind the world-wide decline in frogs, toads and other amphibians. Atmospheric sulphur dioxide also aggravates respiratory conditions like bronchitis and asthma and contributes to heart disease. In parts of Europe acid rain has been falling for more than a century, decimating forests and destroying lakes – especially in Scandinavia.

Now acid rain is affecting the **Third World** too: extensive forest damage has recently been discovered in China, which is now the world's leading burner of **coal**. Even the famed Taj Mahal is slowly being eroded by acid rain.

The problem of acid rain was one of the first examples of damage from trans-boundary pollution: those countries where acid rain falls are not necessarily those creating it. For example, acid rain in Japan is thought to originate in China while most Canadian acid rain comes from the US. Attempts to control industrial and vehicle emissions have been hampered by a lack of international agreement on both cause and effect and on the problems and expense of implementing and enforcing any clean-up directives. In the US, until recently the world's largest burner of coal, the impact of acid rain led to the 1990 Clean Air Act, which forced industries to reduce their emissions of sulphur dioxide. It is estimated the US will spend $2.4 billion by 2010 to control sulphur dioxide emissions. But the reduced effect of acid rain on the environment and human health should save the country some $12-40 billion.

ACP COUNTRIES

The name applied to the countries of Africa, the Caribbean and the Pacific (hence ACP) that are signatories and contracting parties to the **Lomé Convention**, an agreement which attempts to promote economic co-operation between those countries and the **European Community**. The 70 members are: Angola, Antigua and Barbuda, Bahamas, Barbados, Belize, Benin, Botswana, Burkina Faso, Burundi, Cameroon, Cape Verde, Central African Republic, Chad, Comoros Islands, Congo, DR Congo (former Zaire), Djibouti, Dominica, Dominican Republic,

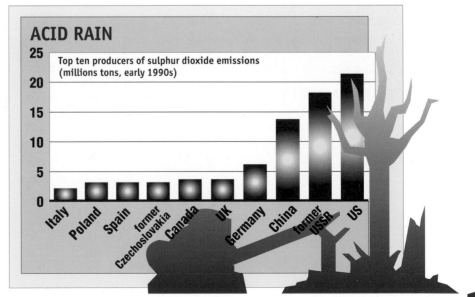

ACID RAIN

Top ten producers of sulphur dioxide emissions (millions tons, early 1990s)

25
20
15
10
5
0

Italy | Poland | Spain | former Czechoslovakia | Canada | UK | Germany | China | former USSR | US

UNEP, OECD, UN Economic Commission for Europe.

Equatorial Guinea, Eritrea, Ethiopia, Fiji, Gabon, Gambia, Ghana, Grenada, Guinea, Guinea-Bissau, Guyana, Haiti, Ivory Coast, Jamaica, Kenya, Kiribati, Lesotho, Liberia, Madagascar, Malawi, Mali, Mauritania, Mauritius, Mozambique, Namibia, Niger, Nigeria, Papua New Guinea, Rwanda, St Kitts-Nevis, St Lucia, St Vincent and the Grenadines, São Tome and Principe, Senegal, Seychelles, Sierra Leone, Solomon Islands, Somalia, Sudan, Surinam, Swaziland, Tanzania, Togo, Tonga, Trinidad and Tobago, Tuvalu, Uganda, Vanuatu, Western Samoa, Zambia and Zimbabwe.

ACQUIRED IMMUNO-DEFICIENCY SYNDROME (AIDS)

An incurable disease first identified in 1980. AIDS results from infection by the **Human Immuno-deficiency Virus** (HIV). But it is more correctly a term used to describe a large variety of opportunistic infections that occur as a consequence of HIV infection. AIDS is generally marked by weight loss, diarrhoea and swollen glands following an incubation period of at least 6 years.

The long incubation period is significant because it allows individuals the opportunity to infect others. HIV is essentially a sexually transmitted infection but can be passed in other ways: through contaminated blood or blood products, contaminated hypodermic needles, and from mother to baby during childbirth. AIDS was originally identified within homosexual communities and was cruelly dubbed by some as the 'Gay Plague'.

Today over 90% of newly infected adults contract the virus during heterosexual intercourse. An estimated 25 million people have been infected with HIV, with the vast majority in Africa, Southeast Asia and in the Americas. Of the total more than 8 million may have developed AIDS.

By the year 2000 an estimated 26 million people may be living with HIV. The illness is likely to have a huge impact as it incapacitates and kills young and middle-aged adults who are in their most productive years. It has already become a leading cause of death in urban areas of the United States, sub-Saharan Africa and parts of Europe.

AEDES (see also Dengue, Yellow Fever and Mosquito)

A widely-distributed genus of mosquitoes found throughout the tropics and subtropics which transmits several serious diseases. Most species are easily recognized: they are black with white or silvery-yellow markings on the legs and thorax. *Aedes aegypti*, a coastal and riverine species that breeds close to human habitations, is the most important.

It is responsible for spreading **dengue** and **yellow fever** which are transmitted by the bite of female mosquitoes.

Females lay their eggs in stagnant **water** which includes anything from puddles to old tins, discarded **coconut** shells and tyres that have filled up with water. Some species of Aedes spread filariasis and other viruses which cause several forms of encephalitis.

AFLATOXINS

Poisonous substances produced in the spores of the fungal mould, *aspergillus flavus*. Aflatoxins can damage the immune system and cause liver **cancer**; they are also mutagenic, causing chromosomal damage in a wide range of animals. Aflatoxins were first identified in the 1960s, after 100,000 turkeys mysteriously died on a farm in the UK. It was later found that the birds had been fed meal contaminated with aspergillus mould.

In general, moulds grow best in warm, moist conditions – so aflatoxins are a major problem in the humid tropics and subtropics where stored cereals and nuts are frequently contaminated.

Peanuts (**groundnuts**) are especially at risk. Modern farming techniques tend to increase the water content of crops which encourages the growth of moulds. This may account for aflatoxin contamination which is on the increase around the world. Acute aflatoxin poisoning is fatal and malnourished children are most at risk since they lose the ability to excrete the poisons.

The majority of cases are in India and eastern Africa. Surveys in the Sudan have found aflatoxins in 80% of raw foods.

AFRICAN DEVELOPMENT BANK

The African Development Bank is one of four 'multilateral development banks' (MDBs). Its headquarters are located in the Côte d'Ivoire (Ivory Coast) and it has been in operation since 1966. The bank aims to contribute to the economic development and social progress of its regional members by

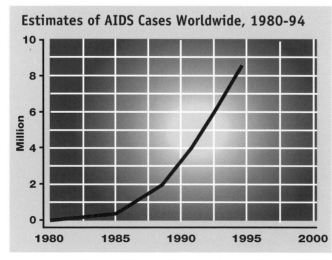

Estimates of AIDS Cases Worldwide, 1980-94

Global AIDS Policy Coalition, in Vital Signs 1995/1996, Worldwide Institute, Earthscan.

encouraging partnerships to be formed between African and non-African countries. Membership was originally restricted to African countries but this restriction was removed in 1982. The bank now has 51 African members and 26 non-regional members, although loans are available only to African nations. In 1973, an African Development Fund was set up as a 'concessional' loan arm of the bank (ie with softer repayment terms and lower interest rates). Most major Western donor nations are members of the Fund.

AFRICAN NATIONAL CONGRESS (ANC)

An organization formed in South Africa in 1912 to fight against racial discrimination and extend the franchise to black Africans. In the early 1940s the ANC first adopted a policy of non-violence to try and overturn segregationist laws. Then in 1943 the ANC Youth League introduced a more aggressive programme proposed by its leaders **Nelson Mandela** and Oliver Tambo. In 1958 some members of the Congress grew tired of multira-cial democratic ideals and left to form the more radical Pan Africanist Congress (PAC).

At a PAC-organized protest in Sharpeville in 1960 police opened fire on demonstrators, killing 69 people. Soon afterwards, the ANC, PAC and the Communist Party were outlawed by the South African Government. When the ANC's leaders were imprisoned the organization went underground with a strategy of controlled but accelerating **guerrilla** violence. The offshoot Pan Africanist Congress was less restrained and employed a campaign of terror.

After years of struggle and international pressure the ANC's exiled leaders began talks with the Government in 1988. In 1990 ANC leader Nelson Mandela was finally

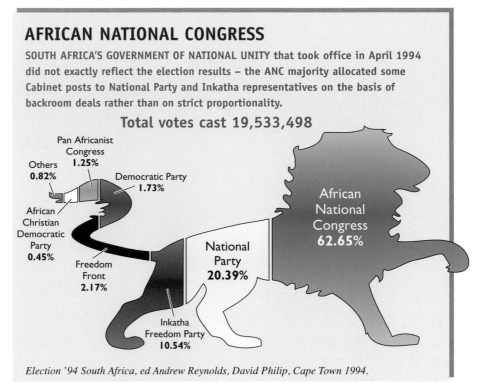

AFRICAN NATIONAL CONGRESS

SOUTH AFRICA'S GOVERNMENT OF NATIONAL UNITY that took office in April 1994 did not exactly reflect the election results – the ANC majority allocated some Cabinet posts to National Party and Inkatha representatives on the basis of backroom deals rather than on strict proportionality.

Total votes cast 19,533,498

Pan Africanist Congress **1.25%**
Others **0.82%**
Democratic Party **1.73%**
African Christian Democratic Party **0.45%**
Freedom Front **2.17%**
Inkatha Freedom Party **10.54%**
National Party **20.39%**
African National Congress **62.65%**

Election '94 South Africa, ed Andrew Reynolds, David Philip, Cape Town 1994.

released after 27 years in jail. His high profile on the global stage, coupled with the ANC's consistent promotion of the principle of non-racial democracy, created an environment in which all political parties could gather to negotiate a transitional constitution. This was carried out from 1991 to 1993 and led to the Government of National Unity. The country's first democratic election followed in April 1994 when Nelson Mandela became the country's first black President.

AGRIBUSINESS

Farming has become industrialized in many parts of the world and is now under the control of a relatively small number of multinational corporations. Agribusiness is the term used to describe these companies and their activities in the field of agriculture. The influence of these multinational businesses extends to every aspect of agriculture, including ownership of **land** and plantations, agrochemical factories, shipping companies, marketing organizations,

research facilities, banking institutions and even the outlets through which produce is sold to the consumer. They can dictate where, what and when crops are grown. In addition, they control the quality and price of food and can even shape consumer tastes.

Corporations like Unilever, Tate and Lyle, Hoechst and British American Tobacco (BAT) promote expensive, complex technology and farming methods to increase and maximize yields in the pursuit of profits. Traditional, more ecologically-sound farming practices recycle nutrients back into the **soil**, use crop rotations to avoid the build-up of pests and grow leguminous crops to help replace nitrogen in the soil. Today these time-honoured methods have been replaced by industrial agriculture which uses expensive inputs of **fertilizers**, **pesticides** and herbicides – most of which are produced and sold by agribusiness firms.

In the US, a handful of companies produce 75% of all **agrochemicals** while a similar number supply half of all hybrid seeds. A select few cor-

ACP Countries – Agribusiness

porations dominate processing, manufacturing and distribution. As a result, the number of family farms in the US has fallen by half in the last 25 years.

Corporate-controlled farming also tends to make farmers assume all the risks of production. Nestlé, a Swiss-based multinational, provides a good example. The company derives half of its turnover from raw materials such as milk, **coffee** and **cocoa**. But it does not own a cocoa **plantation** or a cow. It simply contracts with local farmers throughout the **Third World** who must provide a fixed amount of produce by a certain date at a price set by the company. Third World farmers are increasingly pressured into growing **cash crops** for export, meaning that less of their land is available to produce food for themselves and their families.

Agribusiness companies have been remarkably successful in persuading governments to support their operations. For example, the Common Agricultural Policy of the **European Community** forces member governments to pay $21 billion each year to farmers to produce surpluses and then store them. In the US, farmers receive $26 billion worth of subsidies. The subsidies help to arti-

Fly spray
Agrochemicals include insecticides and herbicides as well as pesticides and fertilizers. Every year an estimated 5,000 people die from the effects of agrochemical poisoning – mainly in the Third World where people are less well protected. AGROCHEMICALS

ficially reduce the price of produce to a level which farmers from developing countries may not be able to match. This surplus food can then be dumped as cheap produce in **developing countries**, where it competes unfairly with local farmers' produce, driving many of them out of business.

AGROCHEMICALS
Any chemical used in modern industrialized agriculture is called an agrochemical. They include both **pesticides** and **fertilizers**. New high-yielding crop varieties depend on large amounts of fertilizers. Yet the overuse and abuse of agrochemicals imposes heavy costs on national economies and can quickly destabilize the ecosystem in farming communities.

The period from 1950 to 1990 was the golden age of agrochemicals. Global **fertilizer** use increased ten-fold in 40 years to 140 million tonnes. However, when farmers

realized that much of the fertilizer was not being absorbed by crops and was polluting the ecosystem, they cut back their purchases. Consumption levelled off at around 122 million tonnes in 1995, but is now increasing once more.

On the other hand, pesticide use continues to increase. Annual sales are now worth more than $34 billion. But there is a growing awareness that pesticides can be toxic to both animals and humans. As a result of this some farmers have begun to switch to more natural farming methods. Between 1987-1993, organically cultivated **land** in the **developed countries** expanded four-fold.

AGROFORESTRY
Agroforestry is basically the combined production of crops and/or livestock together with trees. The term refers to all systems where trees are either deliberately left or planted on **land** where crops are

THE WORLD'S TOP 12 AGRIBUSINESSES

Philip Morris	United States
Cargill	United States
Nestlé	Switzerland
Unilever	UK/Netherlands
Pepsico	United States
Coca-Cola	United States
Conagra	United States
RJR Nabisco	United States
Grand Metropolitan	United Kingdom
Elders IXL	Australia
Anheuser Busch	United States
BSN Group	France

Agrodata.

grown or animals grazed. This mixture helps to recycle nutrients, prevent **soil erosion** and improve crop yields. It also produces **biomass** for energy and fodder for livestock as well as controlling **water** run-off. Leaf litter from the trees adds organic matter to the **soil** and acts as a mulch, retaining soil moisture and preventing erosion. Leguminous trees improve soil fertility directly through nitrogen fixation.

Tree roots also help bind the soil and increase aeration. Mixtures of trees and crops provides more complete ground cover which helps to prevent soil erosion and weed invasion. Multipurpose trees can provide fodder for livestock, edible fruits and nuts as well as fuel, timber and supports for climbing vegetables.

Previously, closely integrated agroforestry programmes were followed for centuries around the world. But agroforestry has attracted increasing attention over the past decade as a sustainable form of land use, especially capable of meeting people's **basic needs**. Agroforestry systems have now spread to Asia, Africa and Latin America.

AID

A term referring to the net flow of official development assistance (ODA). This is the transfer of capital, usually in the form of loans or grants, from governments, international agencies and public institutions of the industrialized world to governments of the **Third World**. The costs of other forms of assistance, technology transfer or provision of materials may also be included in the totals.

The goal of the aid system is for wealthy nations to help those less well off. But it is a complex, controversial and inequitable system with several major failings. The global community has agreed to a number

of aid 'targets' over the years and the **United Nations** has also set aid goals, but few have ever been achieved. In 1968 the UN Conference on Trade and Development (UNCTAD) recommended that rich countries should channel at least 1% of their **GNP** in aid to the developing world.

The UN's second Development Decade Strategy (1971-80) called on donor countries to devote a minimum of 0.7% of GNP to official development assistance and the Paris Conference in 1981 suggested donors direct at least 0.15% of their official development assistance to the **least developed countries** (LDCs). Only 4 industrialized countries (Norway, Denmark, Sweden and the Netherlands) currently meet the 0.7% GNP target.

Around 75% of all 'official aid' registered with the **Development Assistance Committee** (DAC) of the **OECD** is bilateral (country-to-country) aid, much in the form of grants. The rest is channelled through multilateral agencies like the **World Bank**, the **International Monetary Fund** (IMF) and various regional development banks. Traditionally, over half of all bilateral aid is to finance specific projects; 10% is **food aid** and 2% goes to **disaster** relief. However, in the early 1990s the balance began to shift with more aid directed towards emergency relief and **debt service**.

From 1970-80, official aid rose by 50% and by the early 1990s, Western nations were giving well over $50 billion annually in aid to **developing countries**.

However, even though total aid spending has grown, OECD members were still averaging only 0.3% of GNP in 1994. Aid from the wealthy petroleum-exporting countries also continued to drift downward with a continued depression in world **oil** prices.

According to the **World Bank** the three biggest recipients of official development aid were: China ($3.2 billion), Egypt ($27 billion) and India ($2.3 billion).

Net aid: The amount of assistance allocated under overseas aid

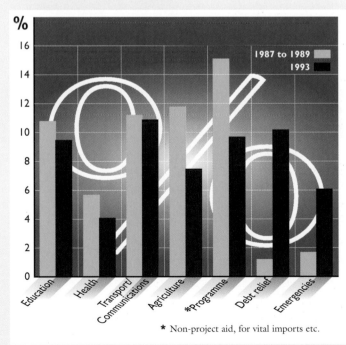

AID'S MOVING TARGET

%

16

14

12

10

8

6

4

2

0

Education Health Transport/ Communications Agriculture *Programme Debt relief Emergencies

1987 to 1989
1993

* Non-project aid, for vital imports etc.

THE CHART shows how aid has shifted away from spending on health and education – the core tasks of poverty reduction – towards debt 'relief' and emergencies. Overall, considerably more than half the total is not 'aid' at all, but returns to the donors in interest payments and purchases of goods and services.

The Reality of Aid 1996, Earthscan.

WHO GETS WHAT?

Comparison of per capita share of Gross National Product (GNP) and Official Development Assistance (ODA). South Asia with average GNP per capita of under $500 receives less than $5 per head in ODA, compared with the Arab States which receive $20 per head while their average per capita GNP is almost $2,000.

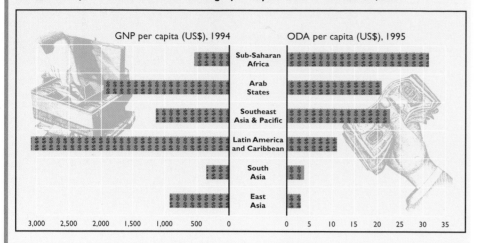

Human Development Report, 1997, UNDP.

schemes. Net flows of official development assistance count towards the UN target of 0.7% of GNP.

Gross aid: The amount in the net aid package before deductions have been made for **debt** repayments and interest payments on past aid loans.

Bilateral aid: Aid provided on a country-to-country basis.

Multilateral aid: Contributions made to international institutions for use in or on behalf of a developing country. This includes contributions to the budgets of certain multilateral organisations like the World Bank. The term also refers to the aid provided by these multilateral organisations.

Aid and Trade Provision: A small proportion of a bilateral aid programme set aside to give higher priority to a restricted number of commercial and industrial development projects.

Budgetary aid: Financial assistance given to the government of a developing country to help its annual budget.

Financial aid: All financial flows (bilateral and multilateral) other than the cost of technical co-operation. It includes both project and non-project aid.

Non-project aid: All financial aid other than project aid, including programme aid, budgetary aid, **debt relief**, food aid and disaster relief.

Programme aid: The main form of non-project aid; includes non-specific support to finance vital imports and is usually provided to assist countries with particularly acute balance of payments problems.

Project aid: Grants or loans to finance production and infrastructure. In contrast to programme aid, project aid is generally tied to a specific investment.

Sector aid: Assistance intended to benefit a designated sector of the economy, using a flexible mix of capital goods, project aid and technical co-operation.

Tied and Untied aid: Aid is 'untied' when it is not subject to any geographical limitations on procurement. Aid is 'tied' when procurement is limited to the goods and services of the donor country.

Technical assistance: Aid can also be given as technical co-operation, especially common with the various specialized agencies of the UN.

In 1974, **EF Schumacher** described overseas aid as 'a process where you collect money from the poor people in the rich countries and give it to the rich people in the poor countries'. This is still true today: it is estimated that 20-30% of aid never actually reaches the poor. It is either siphoned off into private bank accounts or absorbed into administrative costs. In addition, billions of dollars in aid has also been swallowed up by ill-considered mega-projects that provide little real benefit to the poor majority, serving instead to improve the living standards of the élite and relatively well-off urban dwellers. Many of these large-scale projects were initiated because they served the interests of the donor nations. The folly of this has now been recognized and smaller-scale projects are becoming more commonplace.

Critics argue that aid has been used as a political and economic weapon in the interests of the donor countries. In fact, most Western aid is 'tied' to the purchase of goods and services from the donor nation and is primarily a subsidy to domestic exporters. Much official aid never leaves the shores of the donor nation. Of the aid that does, the bulk of it is directed to improving exports of unprocessed food crops and raw materials to the benefit of the industrialized world. More shameful still, by the mid-1990s, 70% of official aid was being used by poor nations to pay their debts to multilateral agencies like the World Bank and International Monetary Fund.

Development aid is given as often for political and commercial reasons as it is for humanitarian reasons. The US, the major aid donor in the post-World War II era, often gave aid for blatant geopolitical reasons in an attempt to outflank the Soviet bloc. Now Japan – which enjoys a massive trade surplus (over $300 billion in 1992) – is the world's largest aid donor. By 1995, Japan's ODA stood at slightly over $14.4 billion, most of it being used to shore up Japanese business and consolidate Japanese power within the Asian region. On the other hand, European governments like France and Britain tend to favour their ex-colonies.

Despite massive amounts of Western aid, since 1982 the **Third World** has actually received less in aid from the industrial world than it has paid back in interest and loan repayments. Between 1983-1990, more than $160 billion was transferred from the developing world to donor countries in the **North**. In 1989, the net transfer of financial resources from developing countries peaked at $52 billion. Various plans to reverse the flow of funds and alleviate the debt problem faced by the Third World have been proposed but none have been implemented with any major degree of success. In 1990, debt relief and increased aid led to an overall net flow back to the **South** of around $9 billion.

AIR POLLUTION

The atmosphere is subject to a wide array of natural pollutants as well as those produced by human industry. Natural sources can include smoke from forest fires, wind-blown dust and emissions from volcanic activity. Poisons released by human activity include oxides of sulphur and nitrogen, particulate matter, hydrocarbons, **lead** and a variety of other chemicals. On a global basis millions of tonnes of sulphur oxides, particulate matter (mostly soot), nitrogen-based oxides, **carbon dioxide** and ammonia are vented into the atmosphere every year. Member nations of the **Organization for Economic Co-operation and Development** (OECD) account for more than half of this pollution.

People breathe in polluted air and consequently the respiratory tract is the organ that suffers most damage. For example, the former German Democratic Republic produced 5.5 million tonnes of **sulphur dioxide** annually and had the highest air-pollution rate in the world. As a

London gasping
In 1996 pollution caused by motor vehicles in towns and cities added $5 billion to the UK's health bill. AIR POLLUTION

result 40% of the population suffered chronic breathing difficulties.

Industrialized nations recognized that air pollution was a serious public health issue decades ago and many have introduced strict clean-air legislation to ease the problem. Yet the real problem is that air pollution crosses national borders and therefore requires international co-operation. More than a billion people around the world regularly breathe air that is now so polluted that it breaches internationally-recognized safety limits.

About 3 million deaths each year are attributable to air pollution. Cities are worst affected. In Athens, on the most polluted days, death rates increase six-fold. Breathing the

ALLENDE GOSSENS, SALVADOR (1908-1973)
A Chilean politician who became the first Marxist head of state elected by a democratic vote in the Western world. He became president of Chile in 1970 as the candidate of the Popular Front Alliance and quickly nationalized the **copper** industry, the nation's biggest income earner. He also initiated major social reforms to bring some measure of social and economic justice to the country, including **land reform** and co-operative production.

However, under constant pressure from the media, local elites, foreign corporations and the US Government, he was unable to solve the nation's economic problems or to deal effectively with his political opponents. Eventually in 1973 the armed forces led by **Augusto Pinochet** staged a coup, backed by the United States Central Intelligence Agency (CIA) and some major **transnational corporations** involved in the copper trade. Allende and many of his supporters were brutally murdered and thousands more were tortured and imprisoned during the period of vicious military dictatorship which followed.

air in Bombay is equivalent to smoking 10 cigarettes a day. Capital cities in developed nations, including London, Brussels and Madrid, regularly breach safety limits set by the **World Health Organization** (WHO).

Globally, 625 million city dwellers are exposed to unhealthy levels of sulphur dioxide from the burning of fossil fuels. In addition to threatening human health, air pollution also harms agricultural productivity and damages forests, **water** supplies and buildings. Estimates of annual damage from air pollution are difficult to quantify and calculations are scarce. However, one 1985 OECD report estimated the cost of air pollution at 1% of the **Gross Domestic Product** (GDP) in France and 2% in the Netherlands.

In the US the price tag is estimated at $40 billion annually in health care and lost productivity. In 1996 the UK Government reported that air pollution caused by motor vehicles in urban areas added $5 billion to the national health bill.

ALLIANCE FOR PROGRESS
(see also Organization of American States)

Founded by US President John F Kennedy at Punta del Este, Uruguay in 1961. The Alliance was set up in the wake of the Cuban revolution and in the midst of growing political unrest throughout Latin America.

The US saw the organization as a bulwark against creeping **communism** and as a vehicle for bolstering American economic interests in the region. Its stated policy concerns are to help accelerate economic progress, improve co-operation and improve living standards throughout Latin America.

Yet most economic integration attempts in Latin America have met with limited success. Today there is a growing feeling the Alliance has been dominated by US self-interest.

ALTERNATIVE ECONOMIC INDICATORS

WEALTH AND WELL-BEING ARE NOT THE SAME THING. The United Nations Development Programme (UNDP) has produced a different measure of 'wealth' called the 'Human Development Index' (HDI).

This index measures levels of education and health while discounting the value of incomes beyond a certain point. Points are deducted for high levels of inequality – so some countries that seem to have a lot of money, like Saudi Arabia and Luxembourg, do relatively badly on the HDI because they neglect general welfare in favour of the rich and super-rich.

The HDI doesn't show wealth differential within countries: black South Africans taken separately would rank 123 on the Index whilst whites would rank below Spain. And the North/South divide persists – the top 20 ranked countries HDI are all in the North; Barbados, ranked 24, is the highest from the South.

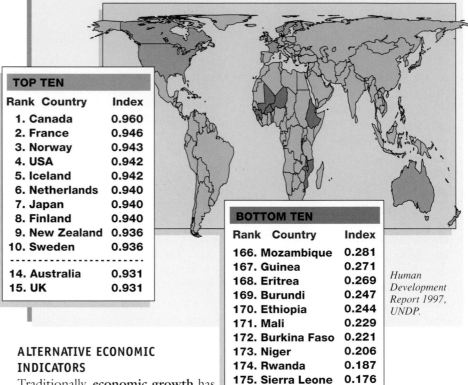

TOP TEN	

Rank Country	Index
1. Canada	0.960
2. France	0.946
3. Norway	0.943
4. USA	0.942
5. Iceland	0.942
6. Netherlands	0.940
7. Japan	0.940
8. Finland	0.940
9. New Zealand	0.936
10. Sweden	0.936
-----------------------	
14. Australia	0.931
15. UK	0.931

BOTTOM TEN	

Rank Country	Index
166. Mozambique	0.281
167. Guinea	0.271
168. Eritrea	0.269
169. Burundi	0.247
170. Ethiopia	0.244
171. Mali	0.229
172. Burkina Faso	0.221
173. Niger	0.206
174. Rwanda	0.187
175. Sierra Leone	0.176

Human Development Report 1997, UNDP.

ALTERNATIVE ECONOMIC INDICATORS

Traditionally, **economic growth** has been equated with improved living standards and social progress. But often this is not the case and there are several social and environmental factors which are ignored in the conventional measure of economic growth. The main way of gauging economic prosperity until the 1990s was **Gross National Product** (GNP), a basic measure reflecting the prices for which a country sells its goods and services. Increases in GNP indicate economic growth which is assumed to be good by definition. But GNP fails to take into account social and environmental costs. **Disasters**, **automobile** accidents, fires and environmental clean-ups are counted as good growth because they are given a

financial value. For example, the 2 billion dollars spent cleaning up the **Exxon Valdez** oil spill off the coast of Alaska perversely counted as boosting the GNP.

In an attempt to measure more accurately the economic and social wealth (or poverty) of a nation, several alternative indices have been devised. These include the UN's **Human Development Index**; the **Index of Sustainable Economic Welfare**, the **Physical Quality of Life Index**, the Genuine Progress Indicator, the Per Capita Grain Consumption Index and the Elementary Living Conditions Index. The 1992 UN Conference on Environment and Development formally recognized the insufficiency of indicators such as GNP. The resulting blueprint for future action, Agenda 21, included a proposal to develop integrated systems of national accounts which would include social, economic and environmental aspects.

ALTERNATIVE ENERGY
(see Renewable Energy)

ALUMINUM/ALUMINIUM

Aluminum is the most abundant metal in the Earth's crust and comes mainly from **bauxite** ore. It is silvery-white and remarkably light. It is also easy to work with, forming alloys with several other metals and plastics.

It is used for everything, from saucepans and foil wrapping, to aircraft, electrical conductors and sheathing for nuclear fuel rods. Aluminum production is extremely energy-intensive and can be economically extracted only via the direct application of electrical current. Modern aluminum smelters use 13-18 kilowatt-hours of electricity to produce a kilogram of metal. In total, aluminum production accounts for around 1% of annual global energy use.

Levels of aluminum in **water** supplies are increasing from natural causes and through contamination caused by humans. **Acid rain** releases aluminum into the **soil**. Aluminum in water supplies is thought to cause kidney damage and leads to increased incidence of Alzheimer's disease, a form of senile dementia.

World-wide over 18 million tonnes of aluminum are produced each year. The US (3.9 million tonnes), the former Soviet Union (2.4 million tonnes) and Canada (1.5 million tonnes) are the major producers. Mineral use is now growing more rapidly in **developing** countries than in the **North**. From 1977 to 1987 the **Third World's** share of aluminum use grew from 10% to 18% with the greatest growth in use in the newly-industrializing countries.

AMAZONIA

The Amazon River in South America is the world's second longest river (6,516 kilometres) and the largest by volume. The waterways of the Amazon Basin (6 million square kilometres) drain half the continent and provide a vast array of differing habitats, including grasslands, **wetlands**, shrublands and lakes. The region's **tropical forests** range from swampy **mangroves** in the east to high mountain forests in the Andes. The wide mix of trees includes **acacia**, rosewood, Brazil nut, palm, mahogany, cedar and **rubber**. Rainforests cover 40% of Brazil and produce an estimated 25% of the world's oxygen. In addition, the area has the greatest bio-diversity on Earth.

The number of species of plants, insects, vertebrates, freshwater **fish**, amphibians and primates in Amazonia exceeds any other part of the world. Despite this unique situation, Brazil's rainforests are being cleared for timber and agriculture at an alarming rate and an incalculable number of wildlife species are disappearing as a result.

Economic development and exploitation of Amazonia began in earnest in the 1960s, fuelled by tax incentives and the construction of the Trans-Amazonia Highway, the Belém-Brasilia Highway and 2 railway lines. The area has large deposits of **natural gas**, **oil**, iron,

Top 5 largest watersheds
in million sq kms

Amazon 6.0
Zaire 4.1
Nile 2.6
Yangtze 1.7
Ganges 0.98

Amazing Amazon

Snaking through the Brazilian rainforest, the Amazon is the world's largest river by volume. But the Nile just beats it for length – 6,695 kilometres compared to the Amazon's 6,516.
AMAZONIA

bauxite, gold, nickel, **copper** and tin, as well as timber.

Figures on the extent of clearance of the Amazonian forest are notoriously difficult to establish, but best estimates suggest that 5-7% of the total forested area has been lost. From 1960-1970, at least 10 million hectares of **land** in Brazil, together with 1.5 million hectares in Colombia and 500,000 hectares in Peru was cleared for pasture.

Clearance has continued virtually unabated since, although a mixture of government policies and the clamour of the international community has managed to halt the rate of increase of **deforestation**. By the early 1990s, around 2 million hectares of Amazonian forests were being destroyed each year.

By destroying the Amazonian ecosystem, the world is losing millions of species of plants and animals. In addition, the lives and cultures of **indigenous peoples** in the area are also under threat. Some 500 years ago, Amazonia was home to 230 native groups totalling around 2 million people. Today, the number of groups has been halved and there are fewer than 50,000 native people left.

As the forest is cleared new and old diseases spread. **Malaria** in particular is now a major concern. In 1970, 51,000 cases were reported in the region. By the mid-1990s the figure had rocketed to over 1.5 million. Billions of dollars in overseas **aid** have been used to persuade Brazil and other governments to protect Amazonia and its indigenous peoples.

Several initiatives, such as the demarcation of a huge reserve for **Yanomami** indians, announced at the 1992 Earth Summit, have been planned. Yet the battle over exploiting the Amazon continues. In 1996, a new Brazilian decree allowed **cattle** ranchers, loggers and mining companies to issue legal challenges to the integrity of Indian forest reserves.

AMNESTY INTERNATIONAL (AI)
This is an international organization founded in Britain in 1961 which aims to defend **human rights** around the world. It is concerned principally with freedom of speech and the right of individuals to express their own religious or political beliefs. AI is politically unaligned and campaigns world-wide for the release of 'prisoners of conscience' and against all forms of torture.

It also aims to improve the welfare of **refugees**. The organization is funded by voluntary contributions and now has more than 100,000 members in over 75 countries. Amnesty International was awarded the Nobel Peace Prize in 1977.

ANAEMIA
A disease brought about by a reduction in the quantity of haemoglobin, the oxygen-carrying pigment, in the blood. The main symptoms are fatigue, breathlessness following even the slightest exertion, pallor and poor resistance to infection.

Widespread in many countries, anaemia afflicts up to 15% of adult men and even higher proportions of women and children. The condition is particularly dangerous in pregnant women as it multiplies by a factor of 4 the risk of death during childbirth.

The disease can arise from the loss of blood caused by an accident or through chronic internal bleeding from an ulcer. It can also be caused by a lack of iron in the diet. Iron is essential for the production of haemoglobin. An estimated 900 million people suffer from anaemia due to iron deficiency.

Anaemia is also caused when red blood cells are destroyed by **toxic chemicals** or the action of parasites. Certain hereditary conditions which cause deformities in red blood cells can also bring on anaemia, as can leukaemia which suppresses the production of red

AMIN DADA, IDI (1925-   )
A former Ugandan heavyweight boxing champion who became a politician and served as the nation's president from 1971-79. Following military training in the UK he rose rapidly in the Ugandan army and led a bloody coup which deposed Milton Obote in 1971. He exercised a reign of terror over his own people but his outlandish and eccentric behaviour made him a laughing stock in the West.

In 1972 he expelled 80,000 Asians from the country and confiscated **land** owned by Jews. He became President of the **Organization of African Unity** in 1975. Under his regime the Ugandan environment was exploited to the full and has yet to recover. In 1978 Amin annexed parts of northern Tanzania, a move which was to lead to his downfall. An offensive launched by the Tanzanian army backed by 'rebel' Ugandan troops toppled Amin in 1979 and he fled to exile in Saudi Arabia.

THE **A** TO **Z** OF WORLD DEVELOPMENT

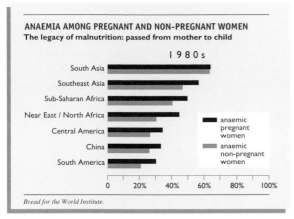

ANAEMIA AMONG PREGNANT AND NON-PREGNANT WOMEN
The legacy of malnutrition: passed from mother to child

1 9 8 0 s

South Asia
Southeast Asia
Sub-Saharan Africa
Near East / North Africa
Central America
China
South America

■ anaemic pregnant women
■ anaemic non-pregnant women

0   20%   40%   60%   80%   100%

Bread for the World Institute.

blood cells in the bone marrow. Successful treatments for most forms of anaemia exist but vary depending on the cause of the complaint.

ANCESTOR WORSHIP

A religious attitude to deceased members of a group or family, commonly found in societies other than Christian, Jewish or Muslim. Adherents believe that the souls of the dead remain influential in this world and may exert their powers on behalf of their descendants.

Ancestor cults can be socially important in reinforcing the authority of living elders who, as guardians of ancient shrines, are effectively the mouthpiece of the spirits. Festivals of the dead were regular features of Greek and Roman religions. Ancestor worship also formed a significant part of traditional Chinese religion and survives in the Buddhist family altar in Japan.

ANDEAN GROUP

A sub-group of the Latin America Free Trade Association (LAFTA) founded following the Cartagena Agreement in 1969. It was initially formed by Colombia, Peru, Chile, Ecuador, Venezuela and Bolivia to promote economic co-operation and tariff integration between member countries. Chile withdrew from the Group in 1977 and Peru left in

1997. Panama is now an associate member. There are 26 observer countries.

ANIMISM

The belief that the physical world is permeated by an invisible spirit, sometimes referred to as the *anima mundi*. The term is also used to describe all forms of belief in which natural objects, phenomena and the universe itself possess souls or spirits.

ANOPHELES
(see also Malaria and Mosquito)

A widely-distributed genus of **mosquito** responsible for the spread of **malaria**, with some 350 species occurring in both tropical and temperate regions. These insects have a huge impact on human health. The malarial parasite, plasmodium, is transmitted to humans solely through the bites of females. Male anopheles mosquitoes feed on nectar and other plant juices.

ANTARCTICA

The southernmost continent (14.2 million square kilometres) which surrounds the South Pole and consists mainly of a vast ice-covered plateau. The prevailing climate is the most severe and inhospitable in the world and although the continent contains almost 90% of the world's fresh water, it is mostly in the form of ice. The continent supports a small range of plants and animals, while the surrounding sea has a rich flora and fauna. Despite the ice and snow, Antarctica is one of the world's greatest deserts. The average precipitation is about 50 millimetres. Antarctica's specialized flora must survive cold, lack of **water** and lengthy winter periods of almost total darkness. Of the 800 species found on the continent, 350 are slow growing lichens. The indige-

nous **land** animals are wholly invertebrate. Many, such as lice and fleas, are parasites of the millions of sea birds which visit the continent.

Antarctica forms part of the 'global commons' – land and **resources** which are not legally owned but deemed to be the heritage of all humanity. Some nations have made political claims to territory in Antarctica, with several claims overlapping and therefore under dispute. Semi-permanent scientific research stations were first established on the continent during the International Geophysical Year (1957-58).

The nations involved agreed to respect the terms laid out in the Antarctic Treaty, signed the

Cold comfort
A cave in the Great Ice Barrier beckons while brave birds circle above in the world's most inhospitable climate, shown in this 1911 illustration to Captain Scott's last expedition. ANTARCTICA

following year, which put a halt to all territorial claims and provided freedom for future scientific experimentation and observation.

The continent could prove to be of enormous economic value as significant quantities of **coal**, iron ore and **oil** have already been discovered. Extensive coal deposits under the Transantarctic Mountains are reported. However, the problems of recovering these under the severe conditions which exist most of the year may prove insurmountable. Global concern over the environmental impact of any such mining or oil exploration has also prevented any resources from being exploited.

In the late 1980s, several nations, led by Australia and France, opted to press for Antarctica to be turned into a 'World Park' free from exploitation of its mineral wealth. As yet no international agreement has been reached as to how the resources in this 'common heritage' should be shared. Nor has it been decided who would pay for consequent environmental damage that may arise.

Despite this, nations like the US and Japan continue to explore for oil, in violation of a moratorium agreed under the 1980 Convention on the Conservation of Antarctica Marine Living Resources (CCAMLR). In addition, the 1991 Madrid Protocol for Protection of the Antarctic Environment prohibits mineral exploration, other than for scientific purposes, for a period of 50 years.

Concern over possible pollution problems are well founded. Oil spills in Antarctica would be disastrous since oil takes far longer to decompose in cold temperatures. An oil spill would also increase the capacity of ice to absorb heat and thus cause it to melt.

Further legislation is also needed to manage stocks of **fish** and krill – the tiny sea creatures at the base of the food chain. Fleets from Russia, Japan, Poland and Germany are **fishing** extensively in Antarctic waters, mainly for krill which is used for **fertilizer** and animal feed.

ANZUS TREATY

A security treaty concluded in 1951 by Australia, New Zealand and the United States which required them to provide mutual **aid** in the event of aggression by foreign powers. It was temporarjly replaced by the South East Atlantic Treaty Organization (SEATO) from 1954-77.

The treaty was effectively sabotaged in 1985 when New Zealand adopted a non-nuclear policy and refused to allow US warships into the country's ports because of the possibility that they might be carrying nuclear-weapons.

APARTHEID (see also African National Congress and Mandela, Nelson)

A policy adopted by the South African Government which called for the segregation and separate development of the white and black populations. The word 'apartheid' was coined by the South African Bureau for Racial Affairs in the late 1930s.

The policy was introduced by the ruling Afrikaner National Party in 1948. Under the system, inhabitants were classified into 4 racial categories: African, Coloured, Indian and White. The original apartheid system had 7 major components:

Group Areas Act: People were forced to live in areas restricted to their particular racial category.

Separate education: Children could only attend schools allotted for their own **race**.

Homelands: All blacks were deemed to have a tribal homeland which became their official home, even though they may never have been there.

Voting rights: Blacks were not eligible to vote, except for candidates of their own racial group in elections for virtually powerless local authorities.

Separate amenities: Entertainment, shopping and public transport were all segregated according to race.

Mixed marriage: Marriage between people of different racial groups was prohibited.

Immorality Act: Sex between people from different racial groups was prohibited.

The inequalities of apartheid prompted an international outcry which eventually forced South Africa to withdraw from the **Commonwealth** in 1961. After years of national and international pressure, limited reforms began to emerge during the 1980s. In 1985 both the Mixed Marriage and Immorality Acts were repealed. About that time, non-whites began to win limited constitutional reforms. Meanwhile internal unrest grew and internation-

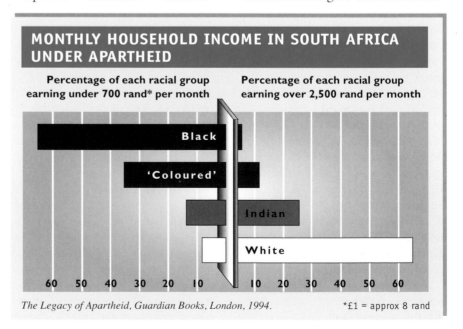

MONTHLY HOUSEHOLD INCOME IN SOUTH AFRICA UNDER APARTHEID

Percentage of each racial group earning under 700 rand* per month

Percentage of each racial group earning over 2,500 rand per month

Black

'Coloured'

Indian

White

60 50 40 30 20 10   10 20 30 40 50 60

The Legacy of Apartheid, Guardian Books, London, 1994.   *£1 = approx 8 rand

High hopes
The ending of apartheid in 1990 promised a brighter future for these youngsters, just two of South Africa's 30 million black people. APARTHEID

al pressure on the apartheid regime increased. This led eventually to further concessions and a commitment by more liberal white politicians to remove the inequalities. However, conservative members of the white community refused to accept reforms.

In 1990 the Government relaxed the Separate Amenities Act, which opened up such facilities as swimming pools and cinemas to mixed race use. In response, conservative local leaders either banned non-whites or imposed a *de facto* ban by simply introducing exorbitantly high entrance fees which the majority could not afford.

But change was inevitable and the Government finally released the imprisoned black leader **Nelson Mandela** in 1990. After Mandela's release, democratic multi-party elections were held in 1994 and a new constitution was drafted in 1996.

Although apartheid has now been officially abolished, the country's black majority are still severely handi-capped. The richest 5% of South Africans (mostly white) owns 88% of all private property while half the population (mostly black) lives below the **poverty** line. A third of all blacks (some 3 million people) are illiterate.

APPROPRIATE TECHNOLOGY

Low-cost technology designed for small-scale use. The idea originated with **Mahatma Gandhi** as a means of improving living standards in rural regions of India. The concept was taken up and developed by **EF Schumacher** who founded the Intermediate Technology Group which helps put some appropriate technology ideas into practice.

Northern technology, based on Northern needs and infrastructures, social patterns and skills is not always relevant in the **South**. Appropriate technology can be sustained and maintained by local people without needing to import parts and supplies that may be either difficult to obtain or prohibitively expensive. The term is usually applied to small-scale, decentralized development using locally-available **resources**. Southern critics have, however, pointed out that the term should not be used to mask the transfer of second-rate technology or to impose differing standards for **North** and South.

AQUACULTURE
(see also Fish Farming)

Aquaculture is the controlled cultivation and harvest of freshwater or marine aquatic species of plants and animals. Rearing of freshwater **fish** has been practised in Asia for over 4,000 years, usually on small farms of less than a hectare each. These farms generally produce over 4 tonnes of fish per hectare, 5 times more protein than any agricultural crop. Fish have a food-to-flesh conversion rate of 1.5:1 — better than beef, pigs or chickens. As wild species are fished out the intensive farming of fish and other aquatic species is growing. The global aquaculture industry was worth almost $30 billion in 1994, a threefold increase over the previous decade.

Prawn cocktail
One out of every five fish eaten today comes from a fish farm like this one for prawns in Bangladesh. World aquaculture production rose to 23 million tons in 1996, up from 7 million tons in 1984. AQUACULTURE

Marine fisheries traditionally provide the bulk of the world's fish – around 90 million tonnes. But by the year 2000 demand will outstrip marine supplies. At present, aquaculture accounts for around 22% of global fish production. This is likely to rise to 40% within 15 years as 13 of the world's 15 main marine **fishing** grounds are in serious decline.

More than half the fish in Israel and a quarter of the fish in China and India now come from fish farms. The Chinese, mostly using species of **tilapia**, have developed a system of fish-farming in which bottom-feeding fish and surface feeders, together with fish which feed at five other levels, are reared in the same ponds. China produces more than half the world's aquaculture output. In Kuwait, where freshwater is scarce, tilapia are reared in brackish **water**.

Elsewhere, other forms of aquaculture are being developed.

Seaweed is grown as food for humans and livestock. And shellfish like oysters and mussels are reared in controlled conditions in sheltered coves and bays.

The Giant Clam, native to **coral reefs** in the Pacific Ocean, has long been a delicacy for the Chinese and Pacific islanders. Large specimens can yield up to 25 kilograms of meat and they are now being farmed in coastal waters off several islands in the region.

Despite the attraction of aquaculture there are major ecological concerns, including pollution from concentrated fish wastes and the dilution of wild gene pools through inter-breeding of escaped farmed fish. In coastal areas of the **Third World**, thousands of hectares of **mangroves** have been raised to construct breeding ponds and thousands of small farmers have been made landless as wealthy land-owners scramble to get into the lucrative prawn-export business, such as in Bangladesh.

AQUINO, CORAZON 'CORY' (1933-)

Filipino politician and former President of the Philippines (1986-92). Corazon Cojuangco was born into a wealthy and politically active family. After schooling in the Philippines and college in the US, she married a promising young Filipino politician, Benigno Aquino, in 1955. He became the chief opposition leader during the martial law era of President **Ferdinand Marcos**. Her husband was assassinated when he returned to the Philippines from exile in 1983.

When Marcos called elections in 1986 Corazon Aquino became the main opposition candidate. 'Official' results declared Marcos the victor. However, Mrs Aquino's supporters claimed widespread fraud and military officials quickly overturned the results. Corazon Aquino was declared President on February 25, 1986. Later that day Marcos fled to Hawaii. Mrs Aquino called for a new constitution which was ratified by a massive popular vote in 1987. Her term of office was plagued by frequent charges of fraud and corruption, and suggestions that her economic policies were ineffective in tackling the nation's widespread **poverty**. In addition, continuing skirmishes between Leftist guerrillas and the Filipino army undercut her administration's stability.

ARAB BANK FOR ECONOMIC DEVELOPMENT IN AFRICA (ABEDA)

An institution formed by the **Arab League** states in 1974 with the intention of promoting the economic development of African countries not members of the Arab League. The bank also aims to encourage the participation of other Arab funding agencies to help the development process in Africa.

In addition to funding projects the Bank provides administrative and technical assistance to other Arab funding agencies. It has 18 members, all of which are also members of the Arab League except Comoros Islands, Djibouti, Somalia and Yemen.

ARAB LEAGUE (LEAGUE OF ARAB STATES)

An organization formed in 1945 to promote unity and co-operation among all Arab countries, with a secretariat in Cairo. Member states are Egypt, Iraq, Jordan, Lebanon, Saudi Arabia, Syria, North Yemen, Algeria, Bahrain, Djibouti, Kuwait, Libya, Mauritius, Morocco, Oman, Qatar, Somalia, Tunisia, United Arab Emirates and South Yemen.

The **Palestine Liberation Organization** (PLO) is also a member. The League's activities have been limited by contradictory political stances adopted by member states. Egypt was expelled in 1979, following the signing of a peace treaty with Israel. It was re-admitted again in 1990.

ARAL SEA

The Aral Sea is surrounded by Afghanistan, Iran, Kazakhstan, Kyrgyzstan, Tajikistan, Turkmenistan and Uzbekistan. Only 40 years ago the Aral covered 67,000 square kilometres and was the world's fourth largest inland body of **water**. Today it is one of the planet's greatest environmental

ARAFAT, YASSER (1929-)

Palestinian politician. Arafat was born in Cairo, the son of a merchant from the Gaza Strip, where he lived during the 1948 Palestine War. He graduated as a civil engineer in 1955 and worked as an engineer with the Egyptian Army during the 1956 Suez War before taking up a post in Kuwait. In 1958 he formed the clandestine Fatah group based in Algiers. Its goal was to create a liberated Palestinian homeland.

In 1968, Fatah emerged as the leading force in the **Palestine Liberation Organization** (PLO) and Arafat was elected chairman of the executive committee. The same year he visited Moscow and convinced Russia to back the PLO cause. In 1970 the PLO moved from Jordan to Beirut.

In 1974 the Arab community recognized the PLO as the sole legitimate representative of the Palestinian People and Arafat was called to address the UN General Assembly where the PLO had been granted observer status. Following the Israeli invasion of Lebanon in 1982, Arafat was forced to move the PLO headquarters to Tunis.

Negotiations at the 1991 Middle East Peace Conference eventually led to the signing of an accord in 1993 which required Israel to vacate the Gaza Strip and the West Bank town of Jericho as a first step in granting Palestine autonomy in the Occupied Territories.

Arafat return to the Gaza Strip in 1994 as President of the Palestinian Authority. He was awarded the Nobel Peace Prize, jointly with Yitzak Rabin and Shimon Peres, in 1995.

ARMS CONTROL

Several arms limitation and reduction treaties were agreed between the United States and the former Soviet Union after the first effort to reduce the risk of nuclear **war** (the 'Hot Line' agreement) was concluded in 1963. However, most did little to prevent the proliferation of armaments or to halt the development of newer and deadlier forms of nuclear, chemical or biological weapons.

Since 1945 only two multilateral agreements governing actual **disarmament** have been reached. The first (the Biological Weapons Convention of 1972) not only prohibits the production of biological weapons, it also provides for the destruction of existing stockpiles. The second (the Conventional Forces in Europe Treaty of 1990) called for the Soviet Union to give up its superiority in conventional arms and for the 16 members of the **North Atlantic Treaty Organization** (NATO) and the 6 members of the former **Warsaw Pact** to destroy large numbers of tanks, combat aircraft and other non-nuclear weapons in Europe.

Although the Hague Peace Conferences of 1899 and 1907

---

disasters. A massive, long-standing scheme to irrigate large areas of the Central Asian desert has caused the Sea to shrink drastically.

For the last 30 years the **irrigation** scheme has diverted water from 2 major rivers flowing into the Aral. From 1981-1990, the combined outflow of the 2 rivers dropped from 55 billion cubic metres to 7 billion cubic metres. Since 1960, the Aral has lost 70% of its water and 55% of its surface area. It shrank more than 96 kilometres from its original boundaries and the water level dropped some 13 metres over a 25-year period. The Sea is now split into 2 separate basins each with bitter, salty water.

The **ecology** of the surrounding area has suffered. Violent dust storms sweep the southern and eastern shores. The Sea is now too saline for **fish** and too shallow for ships to navigate. Some 20 of the 24

indigenous fish species have disappeared and the annual fish catch, which totalled 44,000 tonnes in the 1950s and supported 60,000 jobs, has dropped to zero.

In the desert areas, water in the irrigation channels is now badly polluted, drinking water is of poor quality and **soil erosion** is increasing rapidly. Each year, 150 million tonnes of toxic dust and salt from the dry sea bed is picked up by winds and dumped on surrounding farmland, decimating harvests.

In addition, the accumulation of agricultural chemicals in local water supplies in the former Soviet regions is causing birth defects, miscarriages, kidney damage and **cancer**. Rates of **anaemia** in pregnant women are the highest in the world; infant mortality is higher than in any other former Soviet republic and **life expectancy** is 20 years shorter.

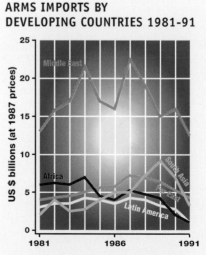

ARMS IMPORTS BY DEVELOPING COUNTRIES 1981-91

World Military and Social Expenditures, Ruth Leger Sivard, World Priorities, 1992.

Aquaculture – Arms Control

made efforts towards disarmament, the first treaties to specifically focus on arms control were the Washington Conference on the Limitation of Armaments (1921) and the London Naval Treaties (1930, 1935 and 1936). Since the 1920s, several other multilateral arms control treaties have been negotiated, each of which is supported by a varying number of countries. They mostly concern nuclear weapons though none of them calls for the destruction of all nuclear weapons.

Geneva Protocol (1925): Prohibits the use of asphyxiating, poisonous or toxic gases and all bacteriological forms of warfare. Does not restrict research or development and build-up of chemical weapons.

Antarctic Treaty (1959): Declares **Antarctica** a demilitarized zone, the first nuclear-free zone on the Earth.

Partial Test Ban Treaty (1963): Bans the testing of nuclear weapons in the atmosphere, outer space and underwater. Does not prevent nuclear testing underground.

Outer Space Treaty (1967): Prohibits nuclear weapons in space or around the Earth's orbit. Does not legislate against weapons which enter space and return to Earth.

Latin America Nuclear Free Zone Treaty (1967): Bans all states and territories in the region from testing, possessing or deploying all forms of nuclear weapons.

Non-Proliferation Treaty (1968): Prohibits the transfer of nuclear weapons and technology outside the 5 major countries recognized as having nuclear weapons. Also commits these states to stop further arms production and development.

Seabed Treaty (1971): Bans the deployment of nuclear weapons on the seabed beyond the limit of territorial waters. No ban on mobile underwater weapons systems.

Biological Weapons Convention (1972): Outlaws the development, production, stockpiling and use of all **biological warfare** agents and toxins and requires the destruction of any existing stocks.

Environmental Modification Convention (1977): Bans hostile use of technology to change weather patterns, ocean currents, the **ozone** layer or to alter the ecological balance in any way for military purposes.

Inhumane Weapons Convention (1981): Places restrictions on weapons held to be particularly injurious. Bans fragmentation bombs and prohibits the use of mines, booby traps, napalm and incendiary devices against civilians.

South Pacific Nuclear Free Zone Treaty (1985): Bans testing, manufacture, acquisition and stationing of nuclear weapons in the region. Requests the 5 major nuclear weapons states to sign a protocol banning the use or threat of nuclear weapons and nuclear testing.

Conventional Forces in Europe Treaty (1990): Requires NATO and former Warsaw Pact members to reduce their tanks, artillery and other offensive weapons so there is a balance between both sides. Agreement covers Europe from the Atlantic to the Ural mountains.

ARMS SPENDING

In 1995 the world spent $864 billion on armaments, representing 3% of global **GNP** – the lowest level since 1967 – roughly $150 for every person. Despite this welcome reduction, about a quarter of the entire global scientific research and development budget is spent on defence and armaments and around half a million scientists are working on the development of new weapons. In total some 70 million people are engaged in military activities worldwide. The cost of weapons is soaring. A single test of a nuclear weapon costs over $12 million. Developed nations now spend 30 times more on arms than on overseas **aid**. But developing countries also spend lavishly on arms – $200 billion annually. While national budgets have been cut in health and education, arms spending has remained relatively stable. Major weapons systems continue to be imported by 90 developing countries and the traffic in arms accounts for a large proportion of the total overall trade in these countries. More than 90% of all the weapons traded come from 6 countries: the US, Russia, France, the UK, Italy and Germany.

The arms trade is a major economic activity and the **South** provides a major and growing market for the **North**, accounting for over half of all purchases and 15% of the market value. More than half the **Third World** arms trade is in the Middle East. In 1991, the Pentagon announced that annual sales of US arms would reach a record $33 billion, half of which would be destined for the Middle East.

The money spent on arms could be diverted to much better causes. For example, what was spent in one

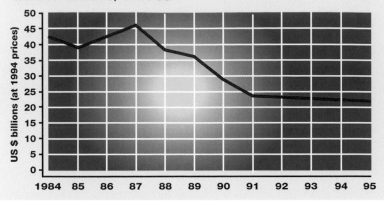

AGGREGATE VALUE OF DELIVERIES OF MAJOR CONVENTIONAL WEAPON SYSTEMS, 1984-95

SIPRI Yearbook 1994, Stockholm International Peace Research Institute, OUP 1994; Human Development Report 1997, UNDP.

day during the 1991 war in Kuwait could have funded an **immunization** programme for a million children for 5 years.

ASBESTOS

There are three distinct types of asbestos, a group of naturally occurring fibrous mineral silicates. These are crocidolite ('blue' asbestos), chrisotite ('white') and amosite ('brown'). Once mined, asbestos fibres are separated and spun into a cloth. Asbestos is highly resistant to heat and is a poor conductor of electricity. In the past it has been used for a variety of fireproof materials and in the building industry.

Asbestos fibres range in size from 30 centimetres down to a few thousandths of a centimetre in length. If inhaled they lodge in the bronchial tubes and cause a disease of the lung known as asbestosis. Victims are unable to breathe properly. Asbestos is also known to cause **cancer** in the lung, the gastro-intestinal tract and the inner lining of the chest cavity. Since 1982, the use of asbestos has been restricted or prohibited in many industrialized nations. As a result companies have opened new factories in **Third World** countries like India and Mexico and in South Africa and South Korea where regulations governing production and use are less restrictive. Canadian manufacturers, with government backing, are actively promoting sales abroad. More than 95% of Canada's asbestos is exported, mostly to developing countries.

ASIA PACIFIC ECONOMIC CO-OPERATION (APEC)

Established in 1989 and based in Singapore, APEC aims to promote trade and investment within the Pacific Basin. There are 18 members from Southeast Asia as well as Australia, Canada, Chile, China, Hong Kong, Japan, South Korea, Mexico, New Zealand, Papua New Guinea, Taiwan and the United States. APEC members represent more than a third of the world's **population** and account for over 50% of the world's economic production and 40% of the global **oil** trade.

ASIAN DEVELOPMENT BANK

A multilateral development bank (MDB) located in the Philippines which began operating in 1966. It aims to promote economic and social development in the Asian and Pacific region by lending funds and providing technical co-operation. The bank has 40 regional and 16 non-regional members. Membership is open to countries which are members of the **United Nations** Economic and Social Commission for Asia and the Pacific (ESCAP) as well as to other member states of the UN.

ASSOCIATION OF SOUTH EAST ASIAN NATIONS (ASEAN)

A regional alliance of countries (Brunei, Indonesia, Malaysia, the Philippines, Singapore, Burma, Laos and Thailand) established in 1967. Based in Jakarta, Indonesia, its stated goals are to 'foster **economic growth**, social progress and cultural development in the region; bring about peace and stability; promote collaboration and mutual assistance in matters of common interest; and maintain close and beneficial co-operation with existing international and regional organizations with similar aims'. The Philippines and Thailand have strong defence links with the US while other ASEAN members take a non-aligned stance.

ASWAN HIGH DAM

Egypt's Aswan High Dam was built on the Nile River to prevent flooding and provide **water** for **irrigation**, domestic and industrial needs. Construction began in 1960. The building costs were largely met by the Soviet Union and the **dam** opened in 1971. The dam is 114 metres high and the artificial lake behind it is one of the largest in the world, extending over 560 kilometres upriver. It is capable of holding over 2 years of the Nile's average annual flow. The dam's hydroelectric

Dam power

Egypt's Aswan High Dam, built with Soviet aid, opened with great fanfare in 1971 to provide irrigation water and hydro-electricity – but the downside has been water salinity, and disease in the dam lake. ASWAN HIGH DAM

Arms Control – Aswan High Dam

ATATURK, KEMAL (1881-1938)
Born Mustafa Kemal. He was a Turkish soldier, politician, founder and first President of Turkey. An admirer of the European way of life, he modernized the nation's legal and education system.

After graduating from military college he became an active supporter of independence. He then resigned from the army in 1919 and was elected to head the National Congress. When the British occupied Turkey in 1920 and dissolved the Chamber of Deputies, he established the National Assembly and took on the roles of President and Prime Minister.

Two years later he proclaimed a republic and was elected President in 1922. In 1924 he abolished the 'caliphate' (the traditional system of political rule) and instigated sweeping changes to Turkish politics, law, education and culture. In 1934, he was given the name Ataturk ('Father of the Turks') by the National Assembly.

plant contributes significantly to the nation's energy needs and has helped to reduce Egypt's fuel import bill.

However, the project has created problems too – including a drastic increase in waterborne diseases. **Schistosomiasis** (**bilharzia**) is now commonplace in villages around Lake Nasser. Poorly-managed irrigation schemes have also led to widespread **salinization**.

Before the Aswan Dam was built, annual flooding washed away salts that accumulated in the **soil**. Now 35% of all irrigated **land** is affected by salinization. Downstream, soil fertility has been sharply reduced.

The Nile used to deposit 100 million tonnes of organically-rich sediment on 10,000 square kilometres of land. The dam has reduced the total to a few tonnes per year. The resultant loss of fertility is countered by the addition of expensive chemical **fertilizers**. Silt is rapidly building up behind the dam and may eventually curtail electricity generation altogether.

Further downstream the reduction of silt flow has also led to coastal erosion and damaged the **fishing**

industry along the Mediterranean coast. Following the opening of the dam, annual sardine catches in coastal waters virtually collapsed, although there is now a 36,000 tonne fishery in the dam's reservoir.

The river delta, essential to Egypt's economy, is falling into the sea as silt is trapped upstream. Most of the northern delta lies only 3 metres above sea level. Rising levels caused by **global warming** could result in Egypt losing up to 19% of its habitable land within 50 years. That would displace about 16% of the nation's population and destroy 15% of the country's economic activity in the process.

AUSTERITY MEASURES
(see also Structural Adjustment)
Rigid controls on the economy adopted by **Third World** governments – usually imposed

as a condition of taking loans from developed nations or multilateral agencies such as the **International Monetary Fund** (IMF). These measures come in the guise of structural adjustment policy and often lead to reduced government spending on health and education though not on things like **arms spending** or luxury imports. Increased **unemployment** and price rises in basic foods often follow. Several developing countries have been faced with riots as the local population has expressed its anger at the measures.

AUTOMOBILES
According to the **Organization for Economic Co-operation and Development** (OECD) motor vehicle numbers increased globally from 246 million in 1970 to about 427 million in 1980. In 1990 there was one motorized vehicle for every 10 people on the planet and in 1995, 36 million cars were built. Today, 100,000 cars roll off the world's production lines daily and there will be an estimated 650-700 million passenger cars alone by the year 2000. Three out of every four of the

There are 680 million vehicles on the planet, increasing at the rate of more than one every second or one new car for every two babies born

Fossil Fuels in a Changing Climate, Greenpeace International, Amsterdam, 1993.

world's 680 million vehicles are found in the industrialized countries, but the number in developing countries is increasing rapidly.

The US, with 41% of the world's vehicles, has 1 car for every 2 people. In Germany, France and Italy, the average is 1 car for every 3 people, with Britain and Japan not far behind. Compare this to Brazil which has 1 car for every 16 people or Mexico with 1 for every 21 inhabitants.

Although most motor vehicles are found in the developed world, their impact is global. Millions die or are injured in road accidents every year. Around 250,000 people died in officially reported car accidents in 1985 and the number of casualties in the developing world, where reporting is lax, is

increasing. Fatality rates in the **Third World** are 10 times worse than the developed nations. Automobiles are energy-intensive and a major source of pollution. On average, cars account for half of all **oil** use. Modern vehicles use only 20% of the potential energy in their fuel, the rest is converted to pollutants and heat.

Catalytic converters have been developed to control exhaust pollution, but this technology does not effect the emission of carbon gases. Engines which burn 'lean' fuel, which is far less polluting than ordinary fuel, are under development but will not replace the millions of 'dirty' engines presently on the road for decades to come. Most vehicles run on **rubber** tyres and there is no environmentally

sound way of disposing of them, with the result that 'tyre mountains' now appear throughout the world. Motor vehicles also swallow vast amounts of **land** and public funds for roads and parking lots. Construction costs for new roads in the US in 1988 alone totalled $22 billion.

The global auto industry is gearing up for the growth of developing country markets. Asia, with its fast-growing economies, is the most promising region. Car sales in China, India, Indonesia, Malaysia, Thailand and Vietnam are growing faster than the nations' economies. Between 1979 and 1995, the number of cars in China vaulted from 150,000 to 1.9 million.

The result could be catastrophic: many cities in Asia already have terrible **air pollution**, congestion and noise with little or no protective legislation. In Bangkok, 500 new cars enter the city's notoriously congested and polluted streets daily, where traffic already crawls along at average speeds of less than 1.5 kilometres per hour at peak periods.

AYURVEDIC MEDICINE

A form of alternative, non-Western medicine. Ayurveda is the science of life, health and healing of the ancient Aryans. The science is based on the 3,000 year-old *Atharva veda* – an ancient Hindu encyclopedia of medical wisdom. Ayurvedic medicine is mainly herbal-based and is used by about a billion people around the world. It has gained many converts in the West in recent decades partly because it is comparatively cheap.

Ayurvedic medicine rectifies any imbalances that may occur of the 3 essential elements – *vata* (air), *pitta* (bile) and *kapha* (phlegm). These 3 elements comprise the *tridosh* from which the human body originates and which regulates normal bodily functions.

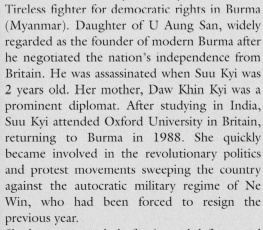

AUNG SAN SUU KYI (1945-   )

Tireless fighter for democratic rights in Burma (Myanmar). Daughter of U Aung San, widely regarded as the founder of modern Burma after he negotiated the nation's independence from Britain. He was assassinated when Suu Kyi was 2 years old. Her mother, Daw Khin Kyi was a prominent diplomat. After studying in India, Suu Kyi attended Oxford University in Britain, returning to Burma in 1988. She quickly became involved in the revolutionary politics and protest movements sweeping the country against the autocratic military regime of Ne Win, who had been forced to resign the previous year.

She became a symbol of unity and defiance and her National League of Democracy (NLD) won a majority of 80% in the 1990 election – despite the fact that many NLD leaders, including Suu Kyi, were arrested and disqualified from taking part in the election.

The military barred the NLD from taking power and repudiated the election results in 1991. Suu Kyi has remained under house arrest in Rangoon (Yangon) since 1989 and was denied contact with her British husband and two sons from 1990 on. She was awarded the Nobel Peace Prize in 1991, but was not allowed to leave Burma to accept it. In 1995, the Burmese military junta released Suu Kyi after 6 years of house arrest. But it rejected her call for talks, kept in place all martial law regulations prohibiting political debate and continued to imprison hundreds of political dissidents.

Buddhism

This magnificent Buddha is in Burma where the religion became established in 1044. Today about 80 per cent of Burma's population is Buddhist, while worldwide there are 500 million Buddhists.

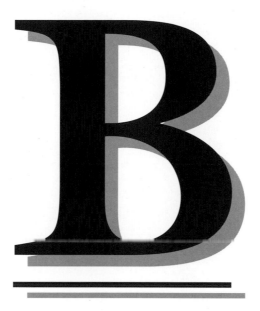

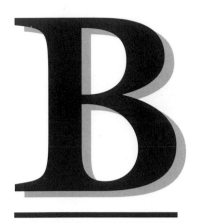

Bold indicates a cross-reference

BABYMILK
(see also Breast-Feeding)

Dried, powdered milk or any other substitute for breast-milk can have a devastating effect on **infant mortality rates** in the developing world. A new-born child becomes totally dependent on reconstituted bottle-milk within a week because the mother's breast-milk dries up when the suckling stimulus is removed. In addition, cash to pay for the milk powder, and clean **water** to mix it with, are not readily available. Five million babies die from diarrhoea each year and the **United Nations Children's Fund** (UNICEF) says that a million lives could be saved if powdered babymilk was discouraged and **breast-feeding** promoted.

By the early 1990s the global market for babymilk was worth $8 billion. More than a quarter of that is sold to the **Third World**. Nestlé, the world's largest food company, controls over half the market. In 1984, in response to an international consumer boycott of the firm's products, Nestlé agreed to abide by **World Health Organization** (WHO) recommendations in the International Code for the Marketing of Breast Milk Substitutes. These were designed to stop the promotion of powdered milk at the expense of breast-feeding. However, in 1989 Nestlé again began supplying vast quanti-

ties of free powdered milk to hospitals in the Third World – in contradiction of the WHO Code which called for such supplies to stop. As a result, the Nestlé boycott was re-imposed. In 1992 supporters in 20 countries succeeded in limiting free babymilk distribution and forced the company to halt all bottle-feeding promotion.

BANANAS

The edible fruit of the *musa* plant which includes both bananas and plantains. The fruit of these plants can either be cooked, made into

Banana bunch
Like an inquisitive bird, the banana flower peers down from its eyrie in the tree, its exotic green 'feathers' made from a 25-kilo bunch of bananas. BANANAS

flour or eaten fresh. Most commonly-grown varieties of bananas and plantains are cultivated in humid tropical lowlands. In optimal growing conditions, they mature 12-15 months after planting. Average yields are in the region of 750 bunches per hectare.

Throughout temperate zones, imported bananas are usually eaten raw or used in baking. The fruit is sugary and easily digested. Both bananas and plantains contain carbo-

hydrates, iron and vitamins A, B_1, B_2 and C. Plantains contain considerably more starch than bananas and are usually boiled, fried or roasted. There is virtually no taste for plantains outside of the tropics and they do not enter into export trade.

Bananas, however, are a major source of foreign exchange in many **Third World** countries. They are harvested early and ripened in transit under controlled temperature, humidity and ventilation. The fruits remain in good condition for 2-3 weeks.

In Ecuador, a leading banana producer, nearly 3 million people are involved in the banana business. In Panama, banana production employs 21% of the labour force and in Somalia 17% of workers depend on the crop.

Two-thirds of the global market is controlled by 3 Western-based multinational corporations. Exporting countries receive only 11% of the price paid for the fruit by Northern consumers.

In addition to the fruit, the large green leaves of the banana plants are widely used as a roofing material, to produce makeshift umbrellas and as wrapping for goods sold at market. Fibres from the stems can be used for making bags and ropes. In Africa, beer which has a low alcohol content but is high in vitamins is made from bananas.

Global banana production is around 41 million tonnes. Brazil (5 million tonnes), India (4.6 million tonnes), the Philippines and China (both 2.4 million tonnes) are the major producers. The annual production of plantains is around 21 million tonnes.

BAND AID

The Band Aid Trust was established in 1984 by the Irish pop singer **Bob Geldof** and others, originally as a response to media reports of a **famine** in Ethiopia. In the summer

Bob's bonanza
Shocked by Ethiopia's 1984 famine, Bob Geldof (above) and other musicians raised millions through Band Aid, Live Aid and events like Sport Aid. BAND AID

of 1985, Geldof helped to organize Live Aid, two huge concerts performed simultaneously by pop groups in Britain and the US. The concert was broadcast to the world's largest ever television audience. As a result, the Band Aid trust raised $160 million. Band Aid had no development programmes of its own, but simply passed on funds for projects submitted by other **aid** and relief agencies.

BANDUNG CONFERENCE

In 1955, representatives of 29 African and Asian countries, including China but excluding Japan, met at Bandung in Indonesia to voice their individual and collective opposition to **colonialism**. It was the first attempt of Afro-Asian nations to collectively oppose colonialism and call for neutrality between East and West. A subsequent conference held in Algiers in 1965 foundered due to conflicting interests. Many developing nations then joined the emerging **Non-Aligned Movement**.

BANK FOR INTERNATIONAL SETTLEMENTS (BIS)

An intergovernmental banking institution located in Switzerland which aims to promote co-

BANDARANAIKE, SIRIMAVO (1916-)

Sri Lankan politician. She succeeded her husband Solomon as leader of the Sri Lankan Freedom Party after his assassination and shortly afterwards was appointed head of government. In 1960 she became the first woman in the world to hold the position of Prime Minister. During her term she nationalized **oil** deposits and several US companies. Her socialist coalition with the Marxist Party was defeated in 1965, but she returned to power in 1970 following a landslide election victory. She forcibly crushed a **guerrilla** uprising and maintained an anti-imperialistic stance.

She presided over the creation of the Sri Lankan Republic in 1972 and served as its first Prime Minister until 1977. During this term in office she promoted a **land reform** programme which nationalized British-owned **plantations**. She was also active in the international **Non-Aligned Movement** and was appointed its President in 1976. She was eventually expelled from Parliament in 1980 for alleged abuse of power while in office.

operation among central banks in international financial settlements. The central banks of the 33 member countries are all from **developed countries**, with the exception of South Africa. They include a majority of European countries as well as Australia, Canada, Japan and the United States.

The BIS itself is governed by representatives from several of these central banks. It was originally set up in 1930 to co-ordinate financial dealings and reparations arising after the end of the World War I. Most of its functions are now carried out by the **International Monetary Fund** (IMF), although the BIS maintains an important role as a trustee. Its main activities are the purchase and sale of gold, foreign currency and bonds for its member central banks.

BANDARANAIKE, SOLOMON DIAS (1899-1959)

Sri Lankan politician. An ardent nationalist, he founded the Sri Lanka Freedom Party (SLFP) in 1951 and eventually rose to fill the post of Prime Minister. He pledged himself to carry out a socialist programme and follow a strictly neutral foreign policy. He was a strong nationalist and attempted to substitute Sinhalese for English as the official language. His failure to resolve growing tensions between ethnic Tamils and the Sinhalese led to a series of problems and unrest. The Tamil minority in the country staged secessionist uprisings throughout the late 1950s. Bandaranaike was assassinated by a Buddhist monk in 1959.

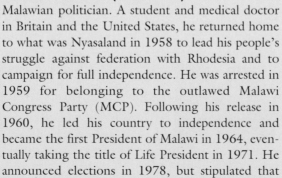

BANDA, HASTINGS (1905-1997)

Malawian politician. A student and medical doctor in Britain and the United States, he returned home to what was Nyasaland in 1958 to lead his people's struggle against federation with Rhodesia and to campaign for full independence. He was arrested in 1959 for belonging to the outlawed Malawi Congress Party (MCP). Following his release in 1960, he led his country to independence and became the first President of Malawi in 1964, eventually taking the title of Life President in 1971. He announced elections in 1978, but stipulated that candidates had to be MCP members and pass an English test, thus ruling out 90% of the population. When journalists reported electoral fraud, all foreign press were expelled from the country. When Banda was finally forced to step down in the late 1980s, he controlled a third of Malawi's businesses. In 1995, he was arrested and charged as an accessory in the 1983 murders of 3 former cabinet ministers.

BAREFOOT DOCTORS

A term used originally to describe a system of medical care established in China under the Communist regime of **Mao Zedong**. Men and women with little formal training provide basic medical services and help to educate local communities on preventative health care issues like a healthy diet, good hygiene and **family planning**. The system was a huge success and has been widely imitated in other **Third World** countries where the use of health educators is now widespread. Over the past two decades, government-run health services in the **South** have begun to tap into the rich reservoir of skills found among traditional healers and traditional birth attendants, to help offset the shortage of trained doctors. China has 15-20 times more homeopathic doctors than it has conventionally-trained medics. In Africa there is one traditional healer for every 500 people, compared to one doctor for every 28,000.

BARTER

The practice of exchanging goods without the intermediate stage of money. At the international level most barter is in **primary products** and takes place between developing nations, that lack the foreign exchange for conventional trading. For example, **rubber** can be exchanged for timber, **cocoa** for copra. It is estimated that bartering may account for more than 20% of world trade. Encouraging the barter system may help promote South-South trade.

BASIC NEEDS

The essential items of private consumption and basic services needed by every individual to maintain a reasonable standard of living. These include adequate food, shelter, clothing and household equipment, together with essential community services such as safe drinking **water**, sanitation, health services, education, transport and cultural facilities. The term was largely originated by the **International Labour Office** (ILO) and is sometimes held to include the right to work. An estimated 1.4 billion people are so poor that they cannot meet their basic needs for food or shelter.

BAUXITE

The chief ore of **aluminum/ aluminium,** bauxite is formed through the weathering of aluminum-rich rocks and clays under tropical conditions. Approximately 4 tonnes of bauxite are needed to produce a tonne of aluminum via a process that requires large inputs of energy. For this reason aluminum is mainly produced in **developed countries** like the US, Japan and Canada rather than in **Third World** countries where most bauxite ore is mined. The annual global production of bauxite is approximately 100 million tonnes. Australia (36 million tonnes), Guinea (17 million tonnes) and Jamaica (7.4 million tonnes) are the leading producers. About 18 million tonnes of aluminum are produced annually, led by the US with 3.9 million tonnes. Jamaica is particularly vulnerable to global trends to replace or recycle aluminum since bauxite represents 58% of the nation's export earnings.

BERI-BERI

Beri-beri is an inflammation of nervous tissue which occurs mainly among people living in the tropics. The disease is caused by a deficiency of vitamin B1 (thiamine) in the diet. It is most prevalent in areas where

Basic needs

Percentage of people with access to health services

Region	Percentage
Sub-Saharan Africa	66%
Middle East & North Africa	82%
South Asia	77%
East Asia and Pacific	87%
Latin America and Caribbean	74%

The State of the World's Children, 1996, UNICEF.

BEGIN, MENACHEM (1913-1992)

Israeli politician. Born in Poland, he qualified as a lawyer before fleeing the country on the eve of the German invasion in 1939. Following a spell in a Soviet prison, he was released. He then joined the Free Polish Army and was sent to Palestine. In 1943 he became leader of the extremist Irgun Zvai Leumi organization in Palestine.

Following several years of armed struggle, he was elected to the Israeli Parliament in 1949 and remained a member until 1984. As head of the right-wing Likud Party he was Prime Minister of Israel from 1977-83. In 1978 he shared the Nobel Peace Prize with President **Anwar Sadat** of Egypt for their efforts in achieving the **Camp David Peace Agreements** and subsequent peace treaty between the 2 countries. He twice ordered invasions of Lebanon, in 1978 and 1982. Growing public criticism of the invasions coupled with high **inflation** in the Israeli economy led to his resignation in 1983.

the staple diet is polished rice; thiamine occurs mainly in the rice husks which are discarded. Treatment with vitamin supplements brings about total recovery.

BERNE CONVENTION

Common name for the Convention on the Conservation of European Wildlife and Natural Habitats which is designed to protect all forms of endangered wildlife in most parts of the European continent.

BETEL NUT

The seed of the palm, *areca catechu*, which is commonly chewed in several countries, mainly in Asia and mostly by men. In India, chewing betel is a habit for more than 20 million people and betel-chewers outnumber smokers. There are more than 20 brands of betel 'quid', also called *pan masala*, commercially available. The seed is usually chewed together with the leaves of the betel tree, along with pepper or lime and a variety of spices. The nut contains a mild narcotic and red dye. Studies have shown that continued chewing of betel can cause oral **cancer**.

BHOPAL DISASTER

One of the world's worst industrial accidents which re-emphasized the differences between **human rights** in the developed and developing worlds. As a result of a leak of deadly methyl-isocyanate gas at the Union Carbide factory in Bhopal, India in 1984, thousands of people died. Exact figures were impossible to obtain – the bodies of many victims were cremated while others died later, having left the area. In 1988, the Indian Government estimated that in the area surrounding the factory 1 person a day was dying as a result of injuries or illness caused by the leak. The Indian Government acknowledged that 521,262 people

Chemical catastrophe
Workers at Union Carbide's Bhopal plant demand an end to the company's activities in India – and an end also to chief executive Warren Anderson. BHOPAL DISASTER

were 'exposed' to the gas leak. Estimates of casualties range from the official Government figure of 1,754 dead and 200,000 injured to as high as 15,000 dead and 300,000 injured. A week-long investigation by **UNICEF** found that at least 10,000 had died. In 1989, researchers found that more than 70% of people in the worst-affected areas around the factory were either ill or disabled.

Half of all women were experiencing menstrual problems and the number of spontaneous abortions, stillbirths and babies born with genetic defects had risen markedly. Post-traumatic stress disorder, a deterioration in mental health commonly associated with wars and disasters, was also discovered in 57% of those examined. In addition, 40% of those living in areas that had received only mild exposure to the gas cloud were also found to be ill. Diseases of the eyes and gastro-intestinal tract were commonplace.

Following lengthy legal battles, the Indian Government and Union Carbide agreed to a $470 million settlement, although Union Carbide continued to deny liability. The company claimed the leak was deliberately caused by a disgruntled employee. The $470 million final

settlement amounted to a mere $793 for each of the 592,000 victims who had filed compensation claims.

The Indian Supreme Court also brought criminal charges of culpable homicide against Union Carbide and against Warren Anderson, chief executive of Union Carbide at the time of the disaster. To date, the company and its executives have avoided coming to trial.

BICYCLE

The world produced 109 million bicycles in 1995, 3 million more than the previous year. Asia accounts for over two-thirds of global production. China is the world's leading manufacturer producing over 40 million bicycles annually, a quarter of which are for export. Bicycles are by far the healthiest form of modern transport, both for people and for the environment.

With an acute shortage of **oil**, the Cuban Government has been encouraging bicycle use and there are now more than 700,000 bicycles in the nation's capital. In the Netherlands there is an extensive network of dedicated cycleways and bicycles are used for half of all travel in some cities. In California, workers

World production of bicycles and cars in millions

In 1965 the number of bikes and cars produced was comparable. By 1995, three times more bikes than cars were being produced.

1965	1995
Bicycles: 21	Bicycles: 109
Cars: 19	Cars: 36

Vital Signs 1997/1998, Worldwatch Institute, Earthscan.

in Palo Alto are reimbursed for business trips in the city that are made on bicycles.

Over 400 police departments around the US and Canada have implemented bicycle patrol sections. In Uganda, bicycles have become the most common method of moving agricultural produce to markets in Kampala and other cities. Conversely, in many Asian cities bicycles are seen as symbols of **poverty**.

BILHARZIA

Common name for **schistosomiasis**, a tropical disease most prevalent in Africa though it is also found in the Americas, Asia and the Pacific. At least 200 million people are infected and a total of 600 million in 74 countries are at risk. Of those infected, 20 million suffer some form of clinical morbidity or disability.

BIO-GAS
(see also Alternative Energy)

A methane-rich gas produced by the fermentation of animal dung, human sewage or crop residues. In addition to gas, the slurry formed is rich in nutrients and can be used as an organic **fertilizer** which is particularly useful as food in fish-farm ponds. The gas can be used to light lamps, run machinery or produce electricity. **Methane** has a high octane rating and burns cleanly. It can also be used in diesel engines. However, the methane produced by treatment of

wet **biomass** like manure or sewage sludge is not ideal for vehicles. Biogas plants are currently being used to supply millions of homes in 46 **developing countries**.

BIOLOGICAL CONTROL

The control of pests like insects and fungi through the use of natural or biological means rather than by chemical **pesticides**. This can include: breeding pest-resistant crops; reducing fertility in the pest

species; disrupting breeding patterns by releasing sterilized animals; breeding viruses that attack the pests; or using natural or exotic predators to control pest outbreaks.

In nature, all pests are controlled by natural forces. The methods used in bio-control programmes attempt to recreate those forces in an infested area. When successful, a balance between pest and predator is established and the need for **toxic chemicals** is decreased.

Biological control methods tend to be self-regulating. The number of

BIKO, STEVE (1946-1977)

South African founder and leader of the 'Black Consciousness' movement in the struggle against **apartheid**. Following his schooling, he enrolled at the University of Natal Medical School. There he became involved with the National Union of South African Students, a moderate movement fighting for the rights of blacks. Disenchanted with the lack of progress, he established the South African Students Organization (SASO) in 1968 aimed at raising black self-esteem and awareness. He became especially active with youth groups and his increasingly high-profile activities soon brought him into conflict with the authorities.

Along with several other SASO members he was put under a banning order in 1973, restricting his political activity, movements and public statements. Biko then began to operate covertly, founding the Zimele Trust fund for political prisoners and their families. He was arrested and held for almost 5 months without trial in 1975. He was arrested again at a roadblock in Port Elizabeth in 1977 and for the next 24 days was held naked and manacled. He died of injuries caused by 'application of force to the head' after being trucked 1,000 kilometres to Pretoria. The police were initially absolved of responsibility for his death though later testimony before the Truth and Reconciliation Commission in 1996 revealed that Biko had been beaten to death by his captors.

predators falls in tandem with the pest population. Bangladesh is an interesting example. In the 1970s, Bangladesh began exporting frogs' legs to Europe. The sharp fall in the country's frog population led to a boom in both agricultural pests and waterborne diseases. Pesticide imports jumped by 25%. By 1989, yearly spending on pesticides had increased by more than $30 million – 3 times what was earned from exporting frogs legs.

One of the earliest forms of bio-control occurred in the 1890s when 'cottony cushion scale' was accidentally introduced into California. In the absence of natural predators the disease quickly decimated citrus orchards. A natural predator of the insect carrying the scale disease was eventually discovered in Australia and within 2 years the State's citrus groves were once again healthy.

Another well-known example of bio-control was the use of the 'myxamotosis' virus (which is native to America) to control rabbit populations in Australia and Britain. Within 3 years of the virus being introduced into Australia, over 99% of the nation's 100 million-strong rabbit population was wiped out.

Current examples include efforts to combat **cassava** pests and pine aphids in Africa and the screw-worm fly in the US. All these pests were accidentally introduced by humans.

Natural ecosystems are extremely complex and biological control programmes should only be introduced after careful research and study or there is great risk that 'solutions' may end up causing their own secondary problems.

BIOLOGICAL DIVERSITY

A measure of species richness and natural genetic variation which can apply either within or between species of wildlife. Species diversity is vital to the proper functioning of ecosystems and is the basis of bio-

logical wealth and adaptability. Well over 90% of all species that have ever lived have already disappeared. Species loss is difficult to calculate, but estimates suggest that we are currently losing 50-100 species daily of the 5-30 million thought to exist. If current rates of habitat destruction continue, the stock of species may be diminished to the point where natural selection will be unable to operate properly.

Though current losses are cause for concern, future losses may be critical. Worse still, current figures are misleading because they tend to measure only the loss of entire species. A species with a million members could be reduced to 10,000 and that may still be enough to ensure survival. However, half of its genetic diversity will have disappeared in the process.

Humans have long taken advantage of natural genetic variation, selecting out plants or animals with characteristics that

are preferable. Genetic diversity has had its most noticeable impact in agriculture. Between 1930 and 1975, over half of the yield increases in cereal crops, sugar cane, **cotton** and peanuts could be attributed to selective breeding. Improved genetics also accounted for 25% of increased milk yields in cows over the same period.

Resource depletion and the intro-

■ Between 70 and 95% of the earth's species are contained in the world's disappearing tropical forests. Today we are losing 50 species a day. By 2020, 10 million species are likely to become extinct.

The Passenger Pigeon
Last seen in 1889, flocks of these bright-eyed wild pigeons once darkened the skies of eastern North America, recorded in groups three or four miles wide. Unfortunately they proved easy prey for commercial hunters. Sheer population size was no insurance against extinction.
BIOLOGICAL DIVERSITY

duction of foreign plants or animals are leading to the destruction of wild and semi-domesticated plants whose genes are essential to allow our major crop plants to survive. Of the estimated 80,000 edible plants, only 150 have been cultivated on a large scale. Less than 20 provide the bulk of the world's food. The same is true of livestock. In Europe, 118 **cattle** varieties are under threat due to 'homogenized breeding'.

The more these organisms are manipulated to suit our needs, the more vulnerable they become. Because of the loss of potato varieties, a **potato** blight destroyed European harvests in the 1840s and well over one million people died as a result. As recently as 1970 a fungus threatened to destroy 80% of the US corn (**maize**) harvest. A rare perennial corn found growing on a few hectares in Mexico has genes that may convey resistance to 4 of the 7 most important corn diseases. It offers hope of disease-resistant plants worth billions of dollars. But only 2,000 specimens of this variety exist.

The loss of unique habitats which hold the greatest genetic diversity is depleting the world's pool of genetic material, weakening the ability of plants to evolve and adapt to changes. Many anti-cancer drugs come from organisms found in **coral reefs** or in **tropical forests**, two of the natural habitats most under threat.

The Biodiversity Convention was adopted at the UN Conference on Environment and Development (UNCED) in Brazil in 1992. It urges industrialized nations to assist **developing countries** to conserve areas of species richness through the transfer of both finance and technology. Poor nations are to be responsible for setting up and maintaining protected areas. The first beneficiaries should be the **indigenous people** and rural populations who have lived successfully in many

Potato plight
Irish peasants' dependence on one potato variety made them vulnerable to the blight which devastated the potato crops in the 1840s. Many died, and many emigrated, like this couple, to England and America. BIOLOGICAL DIVERSITY

of these fragile ecosystems for centuries. The Convention also examines ways of regulating the movement across borders of living organisms that have been genetically modified.

BIOLOGICAL WARFARE

The use of living micro-organisms, or of infectious material derived from them, to bring about death or disease in humans, animals or plants. The practice, sometimes referred to as germ warfare, has been around for a long time. During World War I the Germans infected cavalry horses of the Allied Powers with bacteria. Several other bacteria, such as *bacillus anthracis* which causes anthrax and *pasteurella pestis* which causes plague, have been tested as possible biological weapons. The Japanese reportedly used plague bacteria against the Chinese army in the 1930s. Organisms used in weapons need to be highly virulent, but not necessarily lethal. They may be used in an aerosol form, in bombs or added to **water** supplies.

Biological warfare was officially condemned by the **Geneva Convention** in 1925. The 1975 Biological Weapon Convention officially bans biological warfare and

prohibits the development, production and stockpiling of biological and toxic weapons. However, research continues into developing new strains of hazardous organisms, because they are both cheap and easy to produce. Botulin, the toxin produced by the bacterium *clostridium botulinum*, is the most poisonous substance in the world. It is still being produced, ostensibly for medical purposes, at Porton Down, the former germ warfare centre in the United Kingdom.

There is no hard evidence that biological weapons have been used during the 20th century. Although the Chinese accused UN forces of using germ warfare during the **Korean War**, the charge was never substantiated.

BIOMASS
(see also Renewable Energy)

A scientific term used to describe an amount of living cellular matter. Biomass is composed of both plant material (phytomass) and animal matter (zoomass), though 99% of the world's biomass is plant material. The oceans contain about a third of the planet's biomass. In **developing countries**, biomass, in the form of wood, crop residues and animal dung provides over 40% of the fuel needs.

BIOSPHERE

The thin covering of the planet that contains and sustains life. It includes the **soil**, the **water** and the atmosphere in an area extending 6,000 metres above to about 10,000 metres below sea level. The biosphere concept was first introduced by the French naturalist Jean Lamarck and was developed by the Russian scientist Vladimir Vernadsky. The biosphere approach has recently been refined by British scientist, James Lovelock. He proposes that the global ecosystem, which he calls **Gaia**, is able to creatively maintain its own equilibrium by responding to disruptive changes through a system of natural feedback mechanisms.

BIOTECHNOLOGY

The application of biological organisms and systems to industrial processes. Living organisms can be manipulated to produce food, drugs or other products. For example micro-organisms have been used for centuries to make bread, convert milk to cheese and brew alcohol. Today antibiotics and vitamins are manufactured through manipulation of microbial organisms.

Over the past 20 years **genetic engineering** has allowed an unprecedented degree of flexibility and control in these industrial processes. Genetic engineering is a form of biotechnology in which single-celled organisms have their DNA modified so that they can be used to produce useful substances such as insulin or new vaccines.

Engineered micro-organisms are also used in the fermentation of **sugar** to produce **methane** and alcohol. Bacteria are used to remove heavy metals from polluted areas, to produce proteins from **oil** residues and to separate precious metals from mining waste. The agricultural biotechnology business alone is worth some $100 billion a year.

Fermentation of bacteria or the cross-breeding of plants may appear relatively harmless. But the release of unique, genetically-engineered organisms poses a potentially dangerous situation. 'Transgenic' crops, engineered for disease resistance, are being planted on thousands of hectares in China each year. In the US, 1,300 transgenic crops have already been field-tested. There is a possibility that genes with pest or disease resistance could escape into wild populations and pass on the same traits to weeds, upsetting the natural balance and causing millions of dollars worth of damage.

Genetic engineering is now seen as a major business opportunity. An American biotechnology company has patented several extracts from the Neem tree which had been used as a source of natural medicine for centuries by Indian doctors and farmers. Another company took out US patents covering all genetically-engineered **cotton** varieties until the year 2008. And the patent is pending in Europe, Brazil, China and India.

The patents cover methods of inserting genes into cotton, such that virtually all transgenic cotton products would have to be licensed through the company before they could enter world trade. Several **transnationals** have also taken out patents on bacteria, plants, animals – and even humans. One such human patent is the 'human t-lymphotropic virus type 2' obtained from Guaymi indians in Panama. Critics have called these activities bio-piracy.

BIRTH CONTROL

The limiting of human births, either by reducing the number of offspring or lengthening the interval between pregnancies. The term was originally coined in 1924 by US reformer Margaret Sanger. Basic birth control techniques including **contracep-tion**, sexual abstinence, induced **abortion**, sterilization and **breast- feeding** have been around for thousands of years. By 1900, all the commonly-used methods of birth control, apart from oral contraceptives, were understood if not widely available.

The birth control pill, based on synthesized derivatives of natural steroid hormones, was discovered in the 1920s. It did not become available until the mid-1950s and then only in North America and Europe. Today over 100 million women around the globe use or have used oral contraceptives. Although remarkably effective, if taken over a lengthy period the pill can jeopardize a woman's health. Users are more likely to suffer from heart attacks, strokes and embolisms than non-users.

Research on chemical contraceptives for men has progressed slowly. This could be because men, who have dominated scientific research, may not have been especially motivated to find a male contraceptive; and men generally have been content to let women take responsibility for birth control, and risk possible side-effects. It was not until 1990 that a highly-effective male contraceptive was developed. The contraceptive, which is reversible and has minimal side effects uses a hormonal drug, *testosterone enanthate*, which is administered in the form of weekly injections. However as yet this is not widely used. Despite advances in birth control, it has taken a long time for information and materials to reach poor rural areas of the developing world. In 1988, only half the population in 40% of **developing countries** had easy access to

Genes Means Money
Biotech Sales, selected items 1995

Pharmaceuticals $197 billion

BIOTECH is big business – and big money. The same big corporations often have a stake in pharmaceuticals, agrochemicals, seeds and animal health. They wield more power than some nation-states.

Agrochemicals $29 billion

Seeds $15 billion

Animal health $15 billion

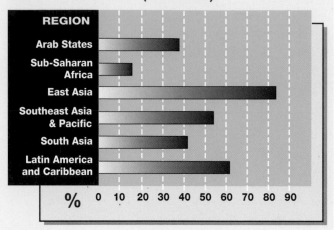

AVERAGE PERCENTAGE OF COUPLES USING CONTRACEPTION (1987-1994)

REGION	
Arab States	
Sub-Saharan Africa	
East Asia	
Southeast Asia & Pacific	
South Asia	
Latin America and Caribbean	

% 0 10 20 30 40 50 60 70 80 90

Human Development Report 1997, UNDP.

modern methods. Yet the example of China, the most populous country on earth, shows that **family planning** can be successful on a nation-wide scale and in resource-poor rural areas if the commitment and political will is there. China adopted a sustained national birth control programme during the early 1970s.

The Government urged all couples to stop at 2 children. In 1979 it launched a 'one-child-family' programme with the aim of limiting the population to 1.2 billion by the year 2000. The plan was supported by extensive and readily-available family planning services. Social acceptance of the programme was difficult because families in China are traditionally large and in rural areas there is a strong prefer-ence for sons. Despite these constraints, the programme met with a fair degree of success, but this was largely due to the coercive measures adopted by the Government.

By the year 2000 China is expected to have a population of 1.25 billion. This is 50 million people more than the target figure, but still a considerable achievement. Most world leaders agree that there is a pressing need to regulate human fertility, although how this should be done is extremely contentious – especially among religious groups.

BIRTH RATE

The number of live births in any given year divided by the mid-year **population** of the country in question gives the birth rate. It is used for comparative purposes and is usually multiplied by 1,000 and expressed as the Crude Birth Rate (births per thousand population). Since 1965, the global birth rate has shown a general decline, falling from 33.9 in 1965-70 to 26 in 1985-90. As living standards improve, the birth rate tends to decline. The critical factor is not the average national income, but the extent to which that income improves the lives of families and more especially, women. China, Sri Lanka, Costa Rica, Singapore, Thailand, Malaysia and other countries have demonstrated that virtually all birth-rate reducing factors can be provided to most families at low-cost, but only if the government decides to make it a major policy focus.

Africa, with 40 births per thousand has the highest rate, while Europe with 11 has the lowest. All of the poorest nations experience annual crude birth rates between 20 and 50; average birth rates in the industrial-ized nations are around 20 per thousand.

BLACK SEA

Large inland sea bounded by Bulgaria, Romania, Turkey and the former Soviet Union and the site of a unique coastal energy project. The Black Sea has the world's largest reserves of several mineral gases, an estimated 75 billion tonnes of high-calorie fuels like hydrogen sulphide, ammonia, **methane** and ethane.

Hydrogen sulphide, naturally-produced from decayed animal or vegetable matter, is toxic to all living organisms A layer of debris contain-ing this deadly gas has been rising steadily over the past 7,000 years and it is thought that the layer may reach the surface within the next 50 years.

A proposed power station is to harness the potential offered by the Black Sea's deposits of mineral gases. The plant will generate an estimated 80 billion kilowatt/hours of energy per year.

A series of pumps will siphon **water** saturated with the gases. Once pressure from deep-sea water is removed, the combustible gases are released. The gases will be separated from the water and sulphide will be recovered to manufacture **fertiliz-ers** and sulphuric acid for industrial purposes. The cost of pumping and purifying the sea water is estimated at about 20% of the power to be generated.

The clean water will be returned to the sea. In 1966, 6 countries sharing the Sea formed the Black Sea Environmental

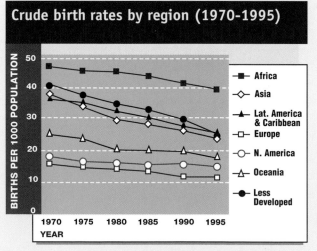

Crude birth rates by region (1970-1995)

BIRTHS PER 1000 POPULATION

- ■ Africa
- ◇ Asia
- ▲ Lat. America & Caribbean
- □ Europe
- ○ N. America
- △ Oceania
- ● Less Developed

1970 1975 1980 1985 1990 1995
YEAR

United Nations Population Division, World Prospects: the 1994 Revision.

Programme with the aim of reducing pollution from **oil** spills and other industrial sources.

BLACKWATER FEVER

A rare, but extremely serious complication from **malaria** in which the malarial parasite causes widespread destruction of red blood cells, leading to the excretion of blood pigment in the urine.

The dark brown urine formed gives rise to the disease's name. Sufferers from the complaint develop a high fever and jaundice and a reduced flow of urine caused by a blockage of the kidneys.

The condition can also be caused by improper use of the malaria drug, quinine. Blackwater fever can be treated successfully with regular blood transfusions coupled with prolonged rest and careful nursing.

BOREHOLES

A narrow well which taps a subterranean source of **groundwater**. The water is often pumped to the surface by a windmill. These wells are sunk in semi-arid areas to allow farming or the rearing of livestock. Starting in the 1950s, the **World Bank** and other organizations supported borehole drilling in dry areas to open up **land** for **cattle** ranching. In

Well women

As women draw water, pigs wallow idly in overspill puddles near this well in Burkina Faso, West Africa. Today, over two-thirds of people in the developing world have access to safe water.
BOREHOLES

Botswana and Senegal boreholes doubled the amount of land available for grazing.

But with uncontrolled access to the wells, cattle stripped the surrounding land of vegetation, making it resemble deserts or moonscapes. Rings of windswept sand extended more than 10 kilometres from boreholes in the Kgalagadi district in Botswana. Similar situations have occurred in fragile ecosystems such as the **Sahel** where traditional pastoralists have been encouraged to use boreholes to intensify their animal husbandry.

BOTTOM-UP DEVELOPMENT

A theory of development that calls for funds and projects to be aimed directly at the rural poor in an effort to reduce **poverty** and meet basic human needs. It is the opposite of

'trickle-down' development which was the main theory behind foreign **aid** until the late 1960s.

Aid was allocated to specific projects, mostly large-scale industrial, energy and transport projects with the assumption that improved industrial productivity would provide economic benefits which would eventually 'trickle-down' to those most in need.

In reality, the aid usually benefited a wealthy minority in urban areas. But rich nations continued to provide aid in this form because it allowed them to sell machinery and equipment and to charge fees for providing the essential technical assistance needed to operate it. Moreover, donors could maintain a degree of control over the way in which the aid was spent.

As the failings of the 'trickle-down' approach became clear there has been an increasing swing towards 'bottom-up' development, with the emphasis on **rural development** and small-scale projects.

BORLAUG, NORMAN (1914-   )
(see also Green Revolution)

American scientist and plant breeder who was instrumental in developing the new high-yield strains of **wheat**, **maize** and rice that formed the basis of the **Green Revolution** in underdeveloped countries. He graduated from the University of Minnesota in 1941 and went to work at the Rockefeller Foundation's Co-operative Mexican Agricultural Programme in Mexico. He developed strains of wheat that increased crop yields dramatically – production in Mexico tripled during the time he was there. The 'dwarf' wheat he helped produce increased harvests in Pakistan and India by 60%. He served as director of the Inter-American Food Crop Programme (1960-63) and as Director of the International Maize and Wheat Improvement Centre in Mexico (1964-79). He received the Nobel Peace Prize in 1970 for his role in the Green Revolution.

BOVINE SPONGIFORM ENCEPHALOPATHY (BSE)

Also referred to as 'mad cow disease'. BSE came to prominence during the late 1980s following a major outbreak in the UK. Herds in various parts of Europe were also affected. The main concern was that the disease could spread to humans through the consumption of contaminated meat. **Cattle** with BSE lose their balance and stumble about as if intoxicated. The disease causes cavities to appear in their brains, the tissue of which becomes spongy in texture. BSE was first discovered in 1986 and is believed to be related to Scrapie – a disorder first identified over 200 years ago that affects sheep and has similar symptoms to BSE.

To boost production, cattle were fed ground-up carcasses of sheep. In a cost-cutting move, the treatment used to process the carcasses was made less stringent and it is believed this is what led to the appearance of BSE.

By 1990 no evidence had been found proving that BSE could pass to humans – although several other animals, including pigs, mice, cats and antelopes – did develop a disease similar to BSE. However by 1996 over 167,000 cases of BSE had been reported in the UK and at least 4 farmers and 2 teenagers had died from Creutzfeldt Jakob Disease (CJD) which causes similar symptoms in humans. In addition, 350 new cases of BSE were being reported each week. There are strong indications that those who died contracted something from the infected cattle. It is impossible to estimate how many people will be affected in the long-term, but with 10% of the British herd infected, numbers could be massive. Some forecasts put the total as high as 80,000.

BRAIN DRAIN

Wealthy nations frequently favour the immigration of technically and highly-skilled people. This encourages an exodus of talented and well-educated people – commonly known as a 'brain drain'. The skills of these people are then lost to the immigrant's home country. In addition, the country responsible for the costs of education and training gathers no return on it's investment, nor any compensation for the possible loss in productivity.

Africa is the hardest hit in this respect. Between 1985 and 1990 the continent lost around 60,000 middle and high-level skilled workers. In Ghana, 60% of the doctors who qualified during the 1980s have reportedly left the country.

Latin America also loses a high proportion of its university graduates, up to 20% in some cases. However, the greatest loss of brainpower, especially scientific brains, is in Asia. From 1972-1985, India, the Philippines, China and Korea saw more than 145,000 scientists emigrate, most of them to the United States.

Several suggestions have been made to minimize this transfer of skilled and educated labour. One idea is that emigrants should repay any education subsidy that they receive; another is that subsidies should be allocated at different levels, with the higher level requiring the recipient to work in the home country for an agreed period of time following qualification. Another proposal is for the country receiving the immigrant to make a payment to the home nation.

BRANDT COMMISSION

The common name of the Independent Commission on International Development established in 1977 under the Chairmanship of **Willy Brandt**, a former Chancellor of the Federal Republic of Germany. The 18-member commission was to examine the economic and social disparities within the global community and to suggest ways to solve the dilemma of global **poverty**.

In 1980 the findings of the Commission were published in *North-South: A Programme for Survival* (also known as the *Brandt Report*). It called for urgent action to improve relations between the rich **North** and the poor **South** and made specific recommendations in 4 main areas:

Aid: The Commission called for $4 billion in extra aid annually to the

World meat production 1950-1996

Million tons

200 –
160 –
120 –
80 –
40 –
0 –

1950 1960 1970 1980 1990 2000

Vital Signs 1997-1998, Worldwatch Institute, Earthscan.

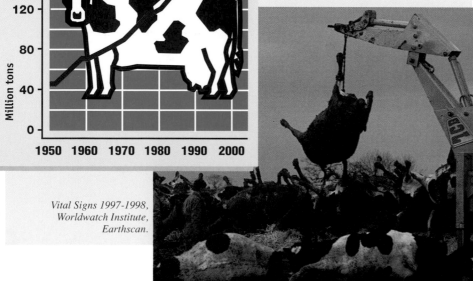

What's the beef?

UK annual meat consumption at about 70 kilos per head is one of the highest in the world. BSE or 'mad cow disease' reduced consumption of beef, and thousands of cattle were culled. BSE

BRANDT, WILLY (1913-1992)
German politician. He was active in the anti-Nazi resistance movement during World War II and became mayor of West Berlin in 1957. In 1966 he was appointed West German Minister of Foreign Affairs. Three years later he became Federal Chancellor, serving until his resignation in 1974. His 'Ostpolitik' policy led to treaties with the Soviet Union and Poland and between East and West Germany. He was forced from office when one of his aides was found to be spying for the former German Democratic Republic (East Germany). He was awarded the Nobel Peace Prize in 1971 and became Chair of the Independent Commission On International Development Issues in 1977. He also served in the European Parliament from 1979-83.

least developed countries, on grant or concessional terms, for a period of 20 years. This would require all governments in the North to increase their official development aid to 1% of **Gross National Product** (GNP) by the year 2000. The Commission also called for a new international system of taxation and proposed that **developing countries** should be allowed greater access to funds available from global financial institutions at preferential terms. In addition, those countries classified as 'Least Developed' should be allowed more say in the world's multilateral financial institutions such as the **World Bank** and **International Monetary Fund** (IMF).

Food: The Commission recommended that a further $8 billion should be spent every year until the year 2000 to improve agricultural development and that specific aid should be given to assist with **land reform**. A further annual fund of $200 million should be set aside to ensure both the availability of cereal stocks and the provision of emergency food supplies as and when required. International agreements should also be concluded to stabilize world food supplies and prices and ensure the dismantling and removal of all protectionist barriers erected by the North to

safeguard their agricultural markets.

Trade: More equitable trading regimes would be produced if the North removed all protectionist measures which discriminate against exports from the South. The Commission also called for funding and **resources** to allow the South to process and market more of its own raw materials. Commodity prices were to be stabilized through a system of international agreements and a 'Common Fund' was proposed to finance buffer stocks and other measures through which commodity prices could be guaranteed.

Energy: The Commission urged that a long-term financing facility should be made available to promote energy resources in the South. Meanwhile, **oil** producing nations

should maintain production levels and consumer countries should do their utmost to meet strict energy-conservation targets.

Despite making specific recommendations on how development in poorer countries could be improved the report stimulated disappointingly little international action. A second report, *Common Crisis* (1983) was issued after the Commission was disbanded.

BREAST-FEEDING
(see also Babymilk)
After the birth of a child, a yellowish fluid called colostrum is produced in the mother's breast. This fluid contains protective proteins and antibodies which provide babies with increased resistance to a variety of infections, parasites and diseases – especially **respiratory infections**, allergies and diarrhoea. Most infants require no other food or liquid other than breast milk during the first 4 to 6 months of life. Breast milk is always clean, pure and the correct temperature.

Breast-feeding also inhibits menstruation. Suckling is estimated to prevent more births every year than all other forms of **birth control** put together. On average, women in **developing countries** who breast-feed have 4 fewer children than if they had not breast-fed. Breast-

Breast is best!
That seems to be the view of this contented baby in Burkina Faso, West Africa.
BREAST-FEEDING

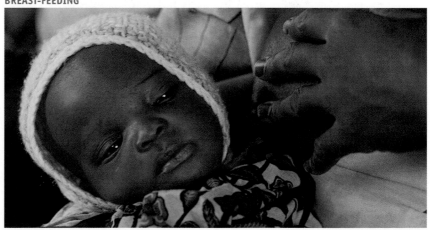

B SE – Breast-Feeding

BREAST-FEEDING

The percentage of babies receiving only breastmilk for the first four months after birth (selected countries).

Sub-Saharan Africa	%
Rwanda	90
Burundi	89
Ethiopia	74
Zaire	68
Botswana	41
Tanzania	32
Nambia	22
Kenya	17
Ghana	8
Senegal	7
Angola	3
Burkina Faso	3
Nigeria	2
Niger	1

Central Asia	%
Kazakhstan	12

Middle East & N Africa	%
Morocco	65
Iran	48
Egypt	38
Jordan	32
Yemen	15
Sudan	14
Turkey	14
Tunisia	12

Asia & Pacific	%
China	64
Bangladesh	54
India	51
Indonesia	47
Nepal	36
Philippines	33
Pakistan	25
Sri Lanka	24
Thailand	4

Americas	%
Bolivia	53
Peru	40
Mexico	38
Costa Rica	35
El Salvador	20
Nicaragua	11
Trinidad/Tobago	10
Brazil	4
Haiti	3

The Progress of Nations 1996, UNICEF.

feeding also increases the intervals between births, thus giving smaller babies more time to benefit from the nourishment of their mother's milk.

Large companies that produce **babymilk** are trying to persuade millions of women, particularly those in the **Third World**, to cease breast-feeding and use artificial milk instead. In the developing countries around 10 million cases of infant **malnutrition** and diarrhoea occur each year as a direct result of mothers who stop breast-feeding. Babies fed on bottled milk are twice as likely to die as those who are breast-fed. In the **developed countries** in Europe and North America the trend away from breast-feeding reached a peak in 1970 when

only 30% of mothers breast-fed their children. Since then, a growing realization of the value of breast-feeding has seen the figure rise again to reach 90% in some countries.

BRETTON WOODS CONFERENCE
(see also IMF and World Bank)

The Conference, held during World War II, aimed to design the rules for a revitalized global economy after the expected defeat of Germany and Japan. It was held at Bretton Woods, New Hampshire in 1944 and was attended by representatives from 44 states and governments, including the Soviet Union. But the governments of the United States, the

United Kingdom and Canada were the main actors. In 1945 they established a system of international financial rules which ultimately led to the foundation of the **International Monetary Fund** (IMF) and the **International Bank for Reconstruction and Development** (IBRD), now commonly known as the **World Bank**. The IBRD was set up to make long-term capital available to countries in urgent need of foreign **aid**. The IMF's primary role was to finance short-term imbalances in international payments in order to stabilize **exchange rates**. Efforts to launch an International Trade Organization at the Conference were stymied, but were instrumental in leading to the formation of the **General Agreement on Tariffs and Trade** (GATT) in 1948.

BRUNDTLAND COMMISSION

Popular name for the **World Commission on Environment and Development** (WCED) which was chaired by the then Norwegian Prime Minister, Gro Harlem Brundtland.

BUDDHISM

A non-theistic religion and philosophical system founded in northern India in the 6th century BC by Gautama Siddartha (the Buddha). He left his wife and son to seek spiritual truth and after 6 years of austerity became enlightened under a banyan tree near Buddha Gaya. Followers seek to emulate his example of perfect morality, wisdom and compassion, culminating in a transformation of consciousness into 'enlightenment'. Buddhism teaches that greed, hatred and illusion separate the individual from a true perception of the nature of things. Buddhism's central beliefs are based on the Buddha's 'Four Noble Truths':

1 To exist is to suffer.

San survival
Few San Bushmen today coax flames from dry twigs – most have had to abandon their hunter-gatherer way of life and work on farms instead.
BUSHMEN/SAN

2 Suffering is caused by attachment to 'impermanent' earthly things.

3 Suffering ceases once attachment ceases.

4 There is a 'way' to escape earthly suffering.

This prescription varies with different strands of Buddhism, but the most commonly held is the 'Eight-fold Path' to enlightenment. Some Buddhists believe that the steps in the Eight-fold Path can only be obtained through long meditation and by leading a strict moral life. Others believe that the Buddha helps those who turn to him for help and guidance.

Buddhism spread through southern and eastern Asia as a creed of righteousness and non-violence. Two distinct forms developed, *Theravada* and *Mahayana*. In India, the country where the Buddha began his search for inner peace, Buddhism had virtually died out by the 13th century. Today, there are more than 500 million followers in Sri Lanka, Nepal, Japan, Thailand and Burma. Buddhism has a small but growing number of followers in the West.

BUSHMEN (SAN)

The name given to the **aboriginal** people of Southern Africa, also known as the San. Once widespread across the savannah region south of the Zambezi river, the San have been decimated by Bantu and European encroachment since 1700. Their population has fallen by 80% and their **land** base by 85%. There are estimated to be only 50,000 surviving in the Kalahari Desert in Botswana and Namibia. Traditionally hunter-gatherers, most now lead sedentary lives as hired farm workers. Only a handful of nomadic Bushmen still exist, restricted to parts of the Kalahari in western Botswana. The women collect roots and berries while the men hunt with bows and poisoned arrows. In the 1980s, some 2,500 San returned to the desert to create a modified version of their old hunter-gatherer lifestyle. Bushmen are typically of small stature with dark, yellowish skin. Their language is based on the same 'click' sounds found in several other languages in southern Africa.

BUTHELEZI, CHIEF MANGOSUTHU (1928-)

Zulu leader of the semi-independent KwaZulu region in South Africa from 1970. He is a direct descendant of two of the most distinguished Zulu kings. He attended Fort Hare University, recognized as a nursery of black **nationalism**, and later began his political career as a member of the **African National Congress** (ANC). He was a close friend of its leaders, **Nelson Mandela** and Oliver Tambo, but later fell out with both over his opposition to economic sanctions and armed resistance to **apartheid**. He initially opposed KwaZulu becoming a nominally independent 'homeland', but hoped it would lead to a confederation of black 'homelands', with eventual majority rule over all of South Africa under a one-party socialist system.

Buthelezi founded *Inkatha* in 1975, an organization set up to fight for a non-racial, democratic political system. (Inkatha is a grass coil used by Zulu women to support loads carried on their heads; the many strands give the coil its strength). In 1990, he contested the leadership of South Africa's black community following the un-banning of the ANC. Prior to that Inkatha had been in violent conflict with a major ANC ally, the Congress Of South African Trade Unions (COSATU), which had challenged his leadership of the country's 4.5 million Zulus.

Although he was invited into the post-apartheid government of Nelson Mandela, the two remained at odds. Buthelezi's Inkatha Freedom Party (IFP) originally boycotted the elections and clashes broke out between the ANC and the IFP.

Buthelezi finally agreed to join the Government only after the new constitution recognized his nephew, Goodwill Buthelezi, as King of the Zulus. In 1994, Inkatha received 10% of the vote. Then in 1996, Buthelezi accused the ANC of trying to completely control the nation's politics. He withdrew from Parliament in protest.

Cocoa
The golden pod of cocoa is cracked open to reveal the seeds that,
when fermented and roasted become the dark delight of chocolate.
The Central American Mayan indians thought cocoa a divine gift – a
sentiment many chocoholics might agree with today.

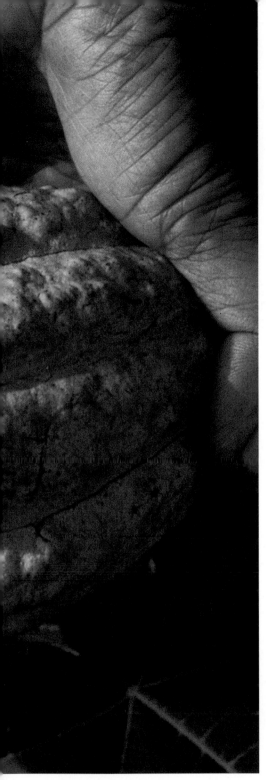

C

Bold indicates a cross-reference

CALORIE CONSUMPTION

The average daily requirement of calories for human beings is estimated at around 2,500. Most people in the developed world receive around 40% more than they need, while the average person in the **Third World** consumes 10% less. An intake of less than 1,500 calories a day is likely to result in severe **malnutrition**. It is estimated that by the year 2000, some 588 million people will be seriously undernourished.

CAMP DAVID AGREEMENT

In 1978, US President Jimmy Carter, Egypt's **Anwar Sadat** and Israel's **Menachem Begin** met at Camp David (the official country retreat of the US President) to establish a peace treaty between Israel and Egypt. Egypt was to regain the Sinai Peninsula in exchange for the Agreement (signed in 1979) which effectively made Egypt neutral in the conflict.

The treaty also called for the Palestinians to elect a 'self-governing authority' in the West Bank and Gaza Strip over a 5-year transition period. This was finally achieved in 1995. To encourage the accords, the US agreed to provide $10 billion worth of economic and military **aid** to Israel and Egypt, with two-thirds of this going to Israel.

CABRAL, AMILCAR (1921-1973)

Agronomist and politician. Born in Guinea, he was educated in Portugal where he established the Centro de Estudos Africanos (Centre for African Studies) in 1948. After returning home, Cabral became involved in the independence struggle on the islands of Cape Verde off the coast of Guinea-Bissau.

In 1956 he founded the African Party for the Independence of Guinea and Cape Verde (PAIGC), both Portuguese colonies. Cabral planned that the two nations could go their own ways once independence was achieved.

The same year he co-founded a national independence movement in Angola with Agostinho Neto. In 1963 Cabral launched a **guerrilla** war against Portugal and became leader of those regions of Guinea not controlled by the Portuguese Army. In 1972 he established the People's National Assembly of Guinea. He was assassinated outside his home in 1973 and so did not live to see his country's independence a year later.

CANCER

Cancer is a breakdown of the normal process of cell growth. It begins with the genetic mutation of a single cell. Transformed cells then divide without restraint, eventually giving rise to billions of aberrant cells. These cancerous cells can invade and destroy nearby tissues or be transported in the blood or lymph to other parts of the body.

Cancers of epithelial tissue (such as skin, breast and lung) are called 'carcinomas'; those in connective tissue (bone, muscle and cartilage) are known as 'sarcomas'; and cancers in cells of the blood system are 'leukaemias'. The aberrant cells may give rise to a tumour, sometimes evident as a palpable lump or a mass. A tumour is benign if it remains in place. But tumours can be life-threatening if they impinge on the normal functioning of body organs. Malignant tumours have the capacity to spread around the body, migrating via the blood or lymph fluid and establishing secondary tumours at other sites or in other organs.

Cancer can be caused by a wide variety of factors, including exposure to chemicals, dietary content and viruses. But socio-economic factors

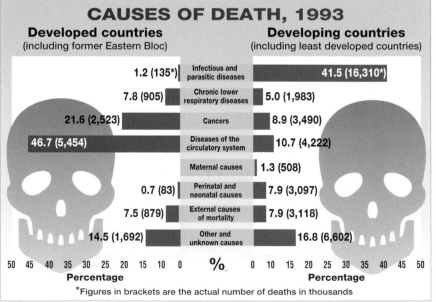

CAUSES OF DEATH, 1993

Developed countries (including former Eastern Bloc)	Cause	Developing countries (including least developed countries)
1.2 (135*)	Infectious and parasitic diseases	41.5 (16,310*)
7.8 (905)	Chronic lower respiratory diseases	5.0 (1,983)
21.6 (2,523)	Cancers	8.9 (3,490)
46.7 (5,454)	Diseases of the circulatory system	10.7 (4,222)
	Maternal causes	1.3 (508)
0.7 (83)	Perinatal and neonatal causes	7.9 (3,097)
7.5 (879)	External causes of mortality	7.9 (3,118)
14.5 (1,692)	Other and unknown causes	16.8 (6,602)

Percentage ... % ... Percentage

*Figures in brackets are the actual number of deaths in thousands

World Health Report 1995: Bridging the Gaps, WHO.

like stress and habits like smoking and drinking appear to be major causes. It is now widely believed that 85% of all cancers are caused by environmental factors, with the remainder having a hereditary basis or arising from spontaneous metabolic disturbances.

Cancer is an increasing health problem in **developing countries**: 3.5 million of the 6 million annual cancer deaths now occur in the **Third World**. The number of cases in developing countries is expected to double over the next quarter century. It is also becoming more apparent that many cancers are caused by some kind of infection. Of the 10 million new cancer cases in 1995, 15% were attributable to an infectious agent.

CANCUN SUMMIT

Cancun, a coastal resort on Mexico's Yucatan Peninsula, was the site of a **North**-**South** Summit meeting held in 1981, following proposals put forward by the **Brandt Commission** in 1980. One of the largest Summit meetings ever held, the 8 industrialized and 14 **developing countries** attending discussed the widening gap between rich and poor nations and ways to reduce it.

CAPITAL FLIGHT

Every year the **International Monetary Fund** (IMF) calculates the total purchases of goods and services around the world and all interest payments paid internationally. This is then compared with a similar calculation for goods and services *sold* and the interest *received*.

There has always been a regular discrepancy in these accounts, which shows on a global scale that up to $100 billion annually is unaccounted for. Much of this money is lost through what is called 'capital flight' – the transfer of vast sums of money out of a country, often illegally. The removal

from power of President **Marcos** of the Philippines and President Mobutu in former Zaire served to focus attention on the enormous wealth that is often deposited abroad illegally. Vast sums are transferred by wealthy businesspeople, corrupt bureaucrats and venal politicians to secret bank accounts in the West. Much of the money is siphoned off from foreign **aid** grants or loans, seriously damaging the recipient nation's economy in the process.

Recent figures show that Mexico suffers worst from capital flight. More than $53 billion was siphoned out of the country from 1976-85. During the same period Venezuela 'lost' $30 billion, Argentina $26 billion, South Africa $17 billion, India and Malaysia $12 billion each, and Brazil, Nigeria and the Philippines $10 billion each. For Mexico, Argentina and Venezuela, three of the largest debtor nations, an amount equal to half the money borrowed over the last 15 years has vanished. In the Philippines, during

the reign of the Marcos family, it is estimated that capital flight amounted to 80% of the outstanding national **debt** from 1962-86. But unscrupulous **Third World** élites are not the only problem. Commercial banks in tax-haven countries, where much of the capital flight funds end up, are also to blame for actively promoting tax-free, high-interest investments.

Tax reforms are needed to combat the problem. In Latin America all interest earned overseas is tax free. Repatriation of money that has 'fled' is a possibility, but unlikely. In the Philippines for example, little of the vast wealth that Marcos spirited out of the country has been recovered.

CAPITALISM

An economic system dominant in the Western world since the break-up of feudalism, under which most of the means of production are privately owned, preferably with minimal state intervention. It encompasses

Playboy of the Western World

With 'drab' Communism's collapse in the late 1980s, 'colourful' capitalism quickly captured the hearts, minds – and bodies – of East Europeans with consumerist items like *Playboy* magazine, seen here advertised on a tram in Prague, Czech Republic. CAPITALISM

Servant of capital

Free-wheeling capitalism needs a cheap workforce – if it's not available locally you either export your factory or import labour. This Italian migrant worker builds Volkswagens in Germany. CAPITALISM

freedoms of ownership, production, exchange, acquisition, employment, movement and open competition. Production is determined and income distributed through the operation and impact of markets. The term 'market' describes an economic system defined by the existence of private capital and wage labour.

According to the economic theories developed by German philosopher and political scientist Karl Marx, capitalism was characterized by the formation of capitalist and labour classes. In Marx's view the 'bourgeoisie' accumulate all surplus value while the workers (also called the proletariat) receive nothing apart from wages, accumulate no capital and remain without property.

The development of modern capitalism was sparked by the growth of the English textile industry during the 17th century and the term is used today to define the economic and political system that developed following the industrial revolution. The ideology of classical capitalism was expressed in Adam Smith's Inquiry into the Nature and Cause of the Wealth of Nations (1776), which advocated leaving economic decisions to the free play of self-regulating markets. The policies of 19th

century capitalism included free trade, secure money based on a gold standard, balanced budgets and minimum levels of social spending.

World War I was a turning point. After the war global markets shrank, the gold standard was abandoned, the control of banking was moved from Europe to the US and trade barriers multiplied. The basic features of the modern system are uncontrolled free markets based on the profit motive and unrestricted ownership of the means of production (capital).

If the system is allowed to develop without restriction it has certain undesirable attributes including a marginalized, permanently impoverished underclass. This has led Western nations to curb the worst excesses of capitalism by establishing 'mixed economies', characterized by substantial government regulation. Communist countries opted to follow the doctrine of Karl Marx who maintained that capitalism contained the seeds of its own destruction. So they abolished capitalism

and the free-market system, replacing them with centrally-planned economies controlled by government functionaries.

Many economists contend that democracy in its purest form can only occur under capitalism, while others argue that capitalism erodes democracy and makes government the servant of capital. Socialists claim that capitalism is inherently unjust and exploitative as it involves the accumulation of wealth in the hands of someone other than the producer. Capitalism is nothing if not flexible and there are many variations including: commercial capitalism (in which large-scale operators control exchange), industrial capitalism (dominated by large-scale private production), finance capitalism (controlled by bankers and creditors), and state and welfare capitalism (in which the state intervenes in the interest of social welfare).

CARBON DIOXIDE

A colourless, odourless, non-toxic, non-combustible gas which is naturally present in air and which is a vital part of the carbon cycle. It is produced when animals breathe and when any material containing carbon is burned. The atmospheric concentration of the gas has risen

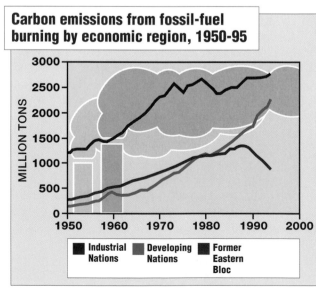

Carbon emissions from fossil-fuel burning by economic region, 1950-95

MILLION TONS

3000 · 2500 · 2000 · 1500 · 1000 · 500 · 0

1950   1960   1970   1980   1990   2000

■ Industrial Nations   ■ Developing Nations   ■ Former Eastern Bloc

Vital Signs 1996/1997, Worldwatch Institute, Earthscan.

markedly over the past 100 years from 280 parts per million (ppm) in 1850 to 361 ppm today, a 30% increase. This increase is almost solely due to the burning of organic, carbon-based fuels such as coal, oil, natural gas and wood. It is known that carbon dioxide (CO_2) contributes more than any other gas to the Greenhouse Effect.

Most experts accept that concentrations of atmospheric CO_2 will at least double in the long-term due to continuing use of carbon-based fuels. Global emissions of CO_2 are forecast to grow by 2.7% annually over the next 40 years. If current trends continue, emissions from the burning of fossil fuel could reach 7 billion tonnes by the year 2000.

Of the current total, the US contributes 23%, followed by China, Russia and Japan. The pollution from these countries is still increasing, whereas other nations such as France and Germany have managed to reduce their emissions. The contribution of developing countries is growing fast – up from 30% of the total in 1990 to 40% in 1994. Under the Framework Convention of Climate Change industrial countries are supposed to cut their carbon emissions back to 1990 levels by the turn of the century. But many, including Australia, Canada and the US will fail to reach their targets. In 1989, a Japanese study predicted that global emissions of CO_2 in 2030 would be 18 billion tonnes – over three times what they were in 1986. And in 1997 the International Energy Agency predicted that carbon emissions from fossil fuels would exceed 1990 levels by nearly 50% by the year 2010.

CARIBBEAN COMMUNITY (CARICOM)

CARICOM came into effect in 1973. It is made up of ex-British colonies in the Caribbean and superseded the Caribbean Free Trade Association (CARIFTA). The main aim of the organization is to promote economic integration and development among member states through a common market to which all members belong. CARICOM also helps operate common services like shipping and weather monitoring. The Community is based in Guyana and is controlled by a Heads of Government Conference with 14 members, 2 associate members and 9 observer countries.

CARIBBEAN DEVELOPMENT BANK (CDB)

A regional development bank launched in 1970 and located in Barbados. The bank aims to stimulate and improve the economic growth and development of member countries in the Caribbean, with particular regard to the needs of the less developed nations in the region. Membership is open to all states and territories in the Caribbean Basin and non-regional countries which are members of the United Nations. The Bank has 20 regional members. There are also 5 non-regional contributing governments – Canada, France, Germany, Italy and the United Kingdom. Three of the regional members (Mexico, Colombia and Venezuela) are non-borrowing members. The CDB has established a Special Development Fund which makes loans at concessionary rates. Canada, Colombia, Venezuela, the United Kingdom and the United States have made contributions to the Fund.

CARRYING CAPACITY

A term used in ecology to describe the maximum number of plants or animals (including humans) that a particular area can support. When the carrying capacity is exceeded, there are insufficient natural resources to maintain an environ-

CARSON, RACHEL LOUISE (1907-1964)

Visionary American genetic biologist, writer and editor. She became well known for her books on environmental pollution and the natural history of the oceans. Carson's books The Sea Around Us (1952) and Silent Spring (1962) were groundbreaking texts which greatly increased public awareness of world-wide threats to the natural environment. She warned of the dangers of industrial pollution, the senseless proliferation of deadly chemicals and the need for environmental monitoring and protection.

mental balance and various species may be threatened. Most species oscillate in number, fluctuating just above and just below the carrying capacity of the environment. Some, like lemmings and snowshoe hares, increase numbers far in excess of carrying capacity. This is then followed by a catastrophic reduction in numbers caused by mass starvation or, in the case of lemmings, mass migration. The carrying capacity is thus undersubscribed, at which point numbers begin to increase and the cycle is repeated.

As the world's population pushed past 4 billion, human demands began to outstrip the sustainable supply of natural resources. The global per capita production of several basic commodities peaked in the late 1970s. Per capita wood production peaked in 1967, fish in 1970, oil in 1973, beef in 1976 and grains in 1978 – and all have been declining ever since.

There is now strong evidence that human beings have already exceeded the Earth's carrying capacity. Approximately 40% of the what ecologists call the 'net primary production' (NPP) of the Earth's ecosystem is currently diverted to human activities. If global **economic growth** continues at the current pace and the Earth's population doubles in the next 35 years, human beings will monopolize 80% of NPP for their own use. Growth-centred economics is pushing the regenerative capacities of the Earth ecosystems to the brink. In addition, rich countries are consuming far more resources per person than people in poor countries. It takes 4-6 hectares of **land** to maintain the average consumer lifestyle in the **North**, yet the total available productive land globally is 1.7 hectares per person. For example, Holland consumes the output of a productive land mass 14 times its size. This unequal claim on the Earth's resources is known as 'appropriated carrying capacity'. Most governments are unwilling to admit to problems of carrying capacity because this implies a limit to growth and if growth is limited then issues of **poverty**, including redistribution of wealth and population control, must be confronted head-on.

CASH CROPS

Crops which generate revenue for the producer through their sale or export, as opposed to crops grown to provide food for a farmer or for local sale. They can be divided into two categories. Export food crops such as cereals and **legumes** are mainly grown in the **North** and traded all over the world. Other crops like **coffee**, **cotton**, **tea**, **oil palm**, **rubber** and jute are predominantly produced in the **South** for export to the North.

Cash crops grown in the South for export to the industrialized nations are a major source of foreign exchange, especially for poor nations with no **oil** or mineral

CRAVING FOR CASH

Cash crops are the only things some countries can export. But such crops take up land which could be used for growing food for local consumption. This would not matter if the terms of trade were fair and cash-crop prices were higher. Cocoa shows how poorer countries provide for a hunger for chocolate in the rich world.

COCOA

TOP 10 PRODUCERS		Income (GNP per capita in US$, 1995)	TOP 10 CONSUMERS		Income (GNP per capita in US$, 1995)
	'000 tonnes			'000 tonnes	
1 Ivory Coast	747	660	1 United States	593	26,980
2 Brazil	290	3,640	2 Germany	264	27,510
3 Ghana	243	390	3 United Kingdom	180	18,700
4 Malaysia	220	3,890	4 France	160	24,990
5 Indonesia	180	980	5 Japan	111	39,640
6 Nigeria	110	260	6 Brazil	73	3,640
7 Cameroon	105	650	Italy	73	19,020
8 Ecuador	85	1,390	8 Spain	60	13,580
9 Colombia	50	1,910	9 Belgium	57	24,710
10 Dominican Rep.	48	1,460	10 Canada	49	19,380

The State of the World's Children 1998, UNICEF; Pocket World in Figures 1995, The Economist.

wealth. But both production and prices are fickle, open to disruption by natural forces or manipulation of commodity markets.

For example, Honduras depends on **bananas** for 70% of its export earnings and Dominica also earns more than half its foreign earnings from bananas. When crops were devastated by hurricanes in 1979 and 1980, national income plummeted. Unfortunately, even when harvests are good and prices favourable, the purchasing power of cash crops rarely keeps pace with the price of manufactured goods or grain.

Critics argue that growing cash crops uses up **land** that could be used to grow food and therefore cash crops are a major cause of world **hunger**. For example, in Brazil soya beans for export displaced black beans, the staple diet of the poor. Food riots followed and Brazil was forced to import black beans from Chile.

Cash crops also tend to be grown by the richest landowners who gradually buy out smaller farmers and take over more and more of the best farmland. Throughout the **Third World** peasant farmers are forced to use marginal land to grow food for their families. In Mali more land is used to grow cotton and

peanuts for export than is used to produce food for local consumption. During the devastating **famine** in the African **Sahel** in the 1970s and 1980s, production of cash crops for export actually increased.

Globally cash crops now absorb almost 750,000 square kilometres of land. Approximately 5% of the world's cultivated land is used to grow cotton, much of it once provided a livelihood for peasants. Cotton is prone to a variety of pests and has an extremely high demand for nitrogen, quickly exhausting soils. Land used to grow groundnuts intensively requires a minimum fallow period of 6 years to recover fertility.

Small-scale farms, which are usually the most productive, have virtually no incentive to produce cash crops since they rarely benefit from increased export earnings. For example, the **United Nations** reported that when coffee prices rose 58% from 1968 to 1973, prices paid to producers in Rwanda remained fixed. Similarly when the world price for groundnuts rose in 1968-69, the Senegalese government's price to farmers actually fell.

In the fickle growing conditions faced by most farmers in the developing world it makes more sense to follow a pattern of diversified cropping that produces food around the year. Even where conditions are ideal, cash crop producers become vulnerable to the fluctuations of global commodity markets which are primarily manipulated by the richer consumer nations. Some countries simply lack the infrastructure needed to get crops from field to market.

CASSAVA

A shrubby flowering plant, also known as manioc, which is native to tropical America. Many varieties are cultivated for their edible starchy, tuberous roots. These can be processed into tapioca, ground into meal, used as animal fodder or cooked and eaten as a vegetable. Cassava is a staple food in many areas in the tropics, especially for poor people. It produces high yields where soils are poor and rainfall low and provides more calories per hectare than most other staple crops. It is the principal source of carbohydrates in Latin America and parts of the Pacific.

World-wide, 400 million people have a daily diet based on cassava. It contains no protein, so those who depend on cassava frequently develop **kwashiorkor** or other protein-deficiency diseases. The plant's tubers are almost pure starch and contain a poison, hydrocyanic

Cassava crop
Sturdy but starchy tubers from this plant, also known as manioc, feed almost half a billion people in Africa, Asia and Latin America. CASSAVA

acid, which must be removed before they are eaten. Cassava is being used increasingly as a livestock feed and for industrial starches. Global production is around 137 million tonnes per year. Brazil (25 million tonnes), Thailand (19 million tonnes) and Democratic Republic of Congo, formerly Zaire (16 million tonnes) are the major producers.

CASTE SYSTEM

A system of social stratification which has existed for at least 2,000 years. In its most developed form it is found in India's Hindu community, where social groups are separated from each other by religious rules of ritual purity.

They are ranked on a scale from pure to impure. Contact between castes is prohibited on the grounds that lower castes will pollute higher ones. Membership of a caste is inherited and Hindus regard this as divinely ordained.

Members must marry within their own caste. Social mobility within a rigid caste system is impossible. Each caste is traditionally associated with a specific type of work, reinforcing segregation.

In India the main castes and their occupations are Brahmin (priests), Kshatriya (soldiers and landlords), Vaishya (farmers and traders), Sudra (labourers) and Harijans or 'untouchables' who undertake the most menial of tasks. In addition to these main castes, there are several thousand sub-castes at the village level.

CASTRO, FIDEL (1927-   )

Cuban revolutionary and politician. He became a political activist as a student in 1947, before graduating as a lawyer in 1950 and then becoming a candidate for elections to the House of Representatives in 1952. When General Fulgencio Batista took power in 1953, Castro began to organize an armed opposition to the dictatorship. He was jailed from 1953-55 for his political activities. He then went to Mexico from where he led an invasion of Cuba in 1956. With a **guerrilla** group of 5,000 supporters, he waged a continual war against Batista, finally emerging victorious in 1959.

He became the country's leader and attempted to establish a revolutionary socialist state built on egalitarian principles and democratic participation. He nationalized foreign companies and seized the **land** of large estate owners. The US, goaded by Cuban exiles in Miami, continued to harass the Castro regime with an escalating series of economic blockades.

Meanwhile, Cuba lent its support to revolutionary efforts elsewhere in the **Third World** and formed a strong alliance with the Soviet Union. Under Castro's charismatic leadership Cuban education and health care reached Western standards and the country's social progress became an example for other Latin American countries. Education and health services were free and citizens were guaranteed **employment**.

However, Castro was unable to break the economy's dependence on **sugar**. When the Soviet Union collapsed, subsidized sugar exports to the Communist Bloc stopped and the country lost access to Soviet **oil**. The US economic blockade tightened, living standards began to deteriorate and the Cuban economy was thrown into a deep crisis. Castro then moved tentatively towards a market economy, allowing free agricultural markets, turning state farms into **co-operatives** and encouraging foreign investment, especially in **tourism**. At the moment the country is at a crossroads. Ordinary Cubans are concerned and confused, though there is still considerable popular support for both Castro and the revolution.

Cattle camp

These cattle are herded in southern Sudan by Dinka people. The Dinka are nomadic pastoralists whose lifestyle has been disrupted many times – from boundary lines drawn up in the late 1890s to civil war a hundred years later. CATTLE

There have been vigorous attempts to abolish the system, most notably by Mahatma Gandhi. Discrimination based on caste was abolished in India in 1947. Over the past 50 years greater social mobility and opportunities for individual advancement have weakened the caste system, but prejudice remains strong.

CATTLE

Large ruminant mammals of the family *bovidae*, most of which have been domesticated, including bison, buffalo, yak, and zebu. People began to domesticate cattle at the same time as they began to cultivate plants. It was convenient to herd them close to settlements since the animals were a source of high-quality protein (milk and meat) as well as supplying hides and other items.

Over the past 50 years cattle industries have surged in many countries as booming grain yields made it relatively inexpensive to feed cereals to animals. In 1995 global meat production from livestock was 190 million tonnes, or about 33.4 kilograms per person. Beef production, at 46 million tonnes, saw a steady rise with China accounting for over half the increase. The nation raised its beef consumption from 1 kg per person in 1990 to 3.6 kilos per person in 1995. From 1990-1995, India's beef production rose 12% to 1.1 million tonnes. The demand for beef also rose in most Asian nations with the result that Australia switched from grass-fed to grain-fed beef to supply that growing market. Over the same period beef consumption in the US also rose, but marginally at 1%, while in Europe demand fell. Globally, the US is the world's leading beef producer (11.5 million tonnes annually). The **European Union** is second (8 million tonnes), followed by Brazil (4.6 million tonnes). However, prices for grain to be used as cattle feed jumped by a third in 1995 so it is unlikely that beef production will continue to rise.

Rearing cattle is environmentally destructive, causing extensive degradation of drylands, destruction of forests and worsening the concentration of **greenhouse gases** in the atmosphere. Moreover, meat-rich diets cause heart-disease, strokes and several types of cancer. In both the developed and developing world, cattle-rearing has had devastating effects.

In Africa expansion onto fragile lands has reduced the area for traditional pastoralists. In Latin America ill-conceived, government-subsidized development projects have encouraged private companies to clear rain forest for raising beef cattle.

Cattle were originally domesticated in Asia and Africa where some 80% of agricultural **land** is still worked with draught animals. Their manure is also a precious source of fertiliser and fuel, providing up to 30% of rural energy requirements in some areas. Modern industrial-style agriculture has introduced intensive rearing techniques. But the majority of cattle still spend most of their time grazing outdoors, browsing over half the planet's land area. Beef cattle consume vast quantities of the **water** devoted to agriculture and huge amounts of the world's grain harvest.

In the US half the grain and hay fed to cattle is grown on irrigated land. The result: more than 3,000 litres of water is needed to produce a kilogram of beef. Roughly 40% of the world's grain is fed to livestock. The land on which animal feed is grown is know as 'ghost acreage'. In the US 40 million hectares of land are used this way.

Modern cattle are notoriously poor food converters; it takes at least 10 calories of feed to produce 1 calorie of grain-fed steak. The impact has been considerable. From 1950-1990, Taiwan increased its beef consumption six-fold. To produce the extra meat meant a doubling of per capita grain use. In 1950, Taiwan was a grain exporter; by 1990, it was importing 74% of its grain – most of it for cattle feed. The **Third World** was a net grain exporter until the early 1960s. For the past decade or so it has been a net importer with 75% of cereal imports used to feed animals. In total about a third of the world's grain is used as animal feed.

Cattle waste is also a global problem. The Netherlands, Belgium and parts of France are classified as 'manure-surplus', meaning that they produce more manure than the land can absorb. Nitrogen from this manure escapes into the atmosphere as gaseous ammonia, contributing to the build up of **acid rain**. **Methane** is the worst of the so-called 'greenhouse gases' and cattle account for 15-20% of global methane emissions by belching and farting.

Weeds, depleted soils and erosion are also commonplace on land where cattle are grazed. The land eventually loses all its productivity and agricultural potential. The great cattle boom of the last century in the US destroyed native mixed-grass ecosystems. In Australia, 13% of grazing land is 'severely degraded'. In South Africa, overgrazing has rendered 3 million hectares of land unfit for cattle.

The **Sahel** disaster in the 1970s was caused partly by drought and partly by the decades of better-than-average rainfall that preceded it. Desert land that had not been used for centuries was cultivated and pastoralists herded livestock onto small areas of pasture. This worsened the process of **desertification** and when drought struck it was devastating. Over 3.5 million head of cattle perished.

Forests, too, are being converted into rangeland. India has 196 million cattle so its remaining forests are under intense pressure. In Latin America since 1970, over 20 million hectares of moist tropical forest have been converted to pasture – even though the **soil** is poor and unsuitable for long-term grazing. In Mexico 18 million hectares of pasture were once forest and nearly 70% of deforested land in Panama and Costa Rica is now pasture.

Governments continue to subsidize cattle production despite criticism. In 1990 the **Organization for Economic Co-operation and Development** (OECD) gave $120 billion worth of support to the beef industry. From 1963-1985 the **World Bank** channelled $1.5 billion to Latin America alone, mostly for beef cattle projects. In Australia and the US, the governments continue to allow low-cost grazing on public lands. Until such support is rethought, the destruction of the environment and human health by large-scale cattle production will not change. The practice is not even economically productive. In Costa Rica from 1969-1985 the cattle sector generated less income than it received in loans.

CENTRALLY PLANNED ECONOMIES

A term usually applied to communist states that looked to the former USSR for leadership. Most are now moving toward market-oriented systems. Until the late 1980s, this group included Albania, Bulgaria, Cambodia, China, Cuba, Czechoslovakia, East Germany, Hungary, North Korea, Laos, Mongolia, Poland, Romania, USSR, Vietnam and Yugoslavia.

CHAGAS DISEASE

An untreatable disease caused by infection spread in the faeces of blood-sucking bugs. It is endemic in Central and South America where

CHAVEZ, CESAR (1927-1993)

An inspirational leader of migrant Hispanic farm workers in the US. After serving in the US Navy during World War II he became a farm labourer. He quit his job to organize Mexican-American migrant farm workers into the United Farm Workers of America (UFAW), the nation's first agricultural workers union.

He came to international attention in 1965 when he led a 5-year strike by California grape-pickers strike. In 1968 he orchestrated a North America-wide boycott of California table wines.

By 1970, 17 million people supported the boycott and growers were forced to recognise the union and its demands. He continued to fight for the rights of fruit and vegetable farm workers until his death.

17 million people are infected and 100 million people are at risk.

There are 2 stages: an acute stage which develops within 3 weeks of infection and may last up to 2 months. Symptoms include fever, lymph node swelling and enlargement of the spleen and liver. The chronic stage can last for years. Parasites invade vital internal organs. Once in the muscles of the heart and in the central nervous system,

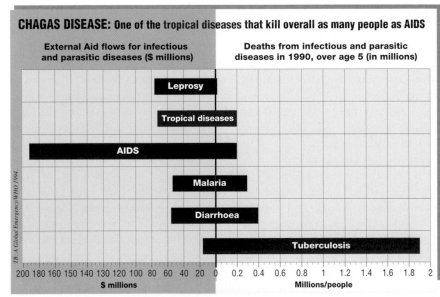

CHAGAS DISEASE: One of the tropical diseases that kill overall as many people as AIDS

External Aid flows for infectious and parasitic diseases ($ millions) | Deaths from infectious and parasitic diseases in 1990, over age 5 (in millions)

Leprosy
Tropical diseases
AIDS
Malaria
Diarrhoea
Tuberculosis

200 180 160 150 140 130 120 100 80 60 40 20 0   0.2 0.4 0.6 0.8 1 1.2 1.4 1.6 1.8 2
$ millions   Millions/people

TB: A Global Emergency/WHO 1994

Victors and victims

Iraqi prisoners in the Gulf War of 1991. Saddam Hussein was condemned for his alleged use of chemical weapons – but he wasn't the first. 'I am strongly in favour of using poisoned gas against uncivilized tribes,' said Winston Churchill in 1919, threatening to use chemical weapons on the Iraqis who were revolting against British domination. CHEMICAL WARFARE

potentially fatal inflammation and lesions can occur. It is especially prevalent in children. In 1991, Argentina, Bolivia, Brazil, Chile, Paraguay and Uruguay (which account for 60% of all cases) launched a co-ordinated plan to eliminate the disease.

CHEMICAL WARFARE

The military use of toxic substances to kill or disable, to pollute food or to poison **water** supplies. The first large-scale use of chemical weapons took place during World War I when chlorine, phosgene and mustard gas were all used. These gases killed around 100,000 soldiers and injured 1.3 million. They were rendered ineffective through the development of gas-masks and were not used in World War II.

Toxins have now been developed which penetrate the skin. Binary toxic weapons have also been produced in which two harmless chemicals are fired in the same artillery shell. On explosion, these mix to provide a lethal aerosol. It is alleged that these types of chemical weapons were used during the Iran-Iraq conflict in the 1980s and may have played a part in

causing the mysterious **Gulf War** syndrome suffered by many troops who fought against Iraq.

Many nations have developed the technology for chemical weapons because most of the chemicals are similar to common **pesticides**. Even though their use is prohibited under the Geneva Protocol of 1925 the production and stockpiling of chemical weapons continues. The US and Russia have considerable stockpiles and France is also believed to have supplies. The United Kingdom reportedly destroyed its stockpiles in the 1960s. In 1990, following the end of the **Cold War**, the US removed its chemical weapons from Europe to Johnson Atoll in the Pacific for disposal.

A 40-member UN Conference on Disarmament met in Geneva in 1980 with the intention of negotiating a complete ban on chemical weapons and in 1986 a group of experts gathered in Berne to begin discussing means to curb the proliferation of chemical weapons. The main stumbling block to progress was the problem of verification. The West argued for compulsory inspection of chemical plants; the former Soviet Union steadfastly maintained

that any inspection system should be voluntary.

In 1988 two American companies refused to supply the US Government with thionyl chloride – used in the production of nerve gas. In 1993, 120 countries, including the US and Russia, signed a treaty outlawing the manufacturing, stockpiling and use of chemical weapons.

CHERNOBYL
(see also Nuclear Power)

A **nuclear power** station in the former USSR which in 1986 suffered the world's worst nuclear accident. The accident resulted from an experiment involving the switching off of safety systems and caused the deaths of 31 people. At least 129 others suffered acute radiation sickness and many thousands are expected to die prematurely as a consequence of radiation exposure. The explosion and fire produced more radioactive fallout than the atomic bombing of Hiroshima and Nagasaki and irradiated an area of 200,000 square kilometres in parts of Ukraine, Russia and Belarus.

Conservative estimates of the cost of the disaster have already reached $340 billion and are expected to rise. An estimated $13 billion has already been spent including the cost of encasing the ruptured reactor in steel and concrete. Clean-up and repair costs will include: resettling 116,000 people in safe areas; 13,500 new dwellings; compensation for the loss of property and crops and the cost of long-term medical treatment for those with radiation sickness.

Efforts to reduce high radiation levels near Chernobyl have failed and another 100,000 people may have to be resettled. Officials in Belarus believe that 20% of the nation's farmland has been poisoned. By 1990, **tuberculosis** in the vicinity of Chernobyl had risen by 14% and the incidence of common illnesses in the worst affected areas had increased by 70% due to a weakening of immune systems caused by radiation exposure. Around a quarter of the region's children have thyroid deficiencies and the **cancer** rate is rising.

The high level of **radioactivity** was caused by rain when the Soviet Government decided to 'seed' the strontium-caesium radioactive clouds to prevent them drifting toward Moscow. In 1993, researchers documenting the massive increases in thyroid cancer in the region estimated that as many as 2.3 million children may have been exposed to radioactive iodine.

Radiation from the Chernobyl plant drifted across much of Europe, polluting vast areas of countryside and poisoning numerous animals. Estimates suggest that a minimum of 2,000 people in the **European Community** are likely to develop cancers over the next 50 years as a result.

CHILD LABOUR

The UN Convention on the Rights of the Child adopted in 1989 affirmed the rights of the world's children to be protected against all forms of abuse, neglect and exploitation. By 1995, it had been ratified by 185 nations, making it the most widely-adopted **human rights** convention. Many countries have adopted legislation stipulating minimum ages below which children cannot legally be employed and specifying conditions under which children can work. The **International Labour Office** (ILO) Minimum Age Convention of 1973 sets 13 as the lowest age when children can work, and then for light work only. Yet official figures produced by the ILO indicate that at least 200 million young children under the age of 15 are working to support themselves and their families. The actual total may be twice as high.

In India alone there are an estimated 16 million children

working. The ILO says 75 million children between 8 and 15 are forced to work, some to pay off family debts. Wages are frequently paid in advance so the children are in 'debt bondage' to their employees. Most child workers cannot go to school. But since education has no significant bearing on **employment** opportunities in most of the **Third World**, there is little incentive to go to school anyway.

Children are generally docile, fast, agile and above all cheap and dispensable. Consequently, millions of children in **developing countries** toil long hours for little reward with no fringe benefits, insurance or security. Working children are more likely to suffer occupational injuries because of unsafe working conditions, inexperience, fatigue and the fact that most work places and machinery have been designed for use by adults.

In Africa, 20% of children work and in Latin America the figure is 25%, including more than 7 million in Brazil alone. Children also work in some industrialized countries: 100,000 children work on farms in Spain and tens of thousands work in Italy's leather industry.

CHIPKO MOVEMENT

A grassroots, community-led movement in India opposing indiscriminate **deforestation**. The movement originated among village women in the Himalayan foothills of the Indian state of Uttar Pradesh in 1974. 'Chipko' means 'to embrace' in Hindi. The movement took its name from women who embraced trees to prevent them from being felled. Chipko owes a great deal to the philosophy of **Mahatma Gandhi** in its commitment to non-violent resistance and its village-oriented approach to economic development.

The Chipko campaign in India resulted in a 15-year ban on com-

Legal minimum ages for different types of work, selected countries

AGE	COUNTRY	TYPE OF WORK
18	Peru Bolivia Luxembourg United States	– Ports and seafaring – Construction – Abattoirs, meat rendering – Construction
17	Pakistan Burma Austria Canada	– Mining, circular saws – Mining – Tanneries, glass manufacture – Maritime work
16	Peru Ivory Coast Mexico United Kingdom	– Deep-sea fishing – Mining – Work with acids – Noxious substances
15	Thailand Dominican Rep. Italy Costa Rica	– Night clubs, bars – Mining – Machinery in motion – Street trades
14	India Cyprus Belize Sri Lanka	– Explosives, carpet weaving – Construction – Electrical work – Street trades
13	Germany Switzerland Denmark Tunisia	– Light agricultural – Non-industrial light – Shop assistant – Non-industrial light
12	Egypt Benin Senegal Burkina Faso	– All work – Light agricultural – Seasonal work – Domestic service

Most countries have laws against child labour. But those laws kick in at different ages, are routinely abused – and the very definition of exploitative child work varies the world over.

The International Labour Organization's Minimum Age Convention sets a basic minimum age for employment of 15 years while allowing light work at 13 and prohibiting hazardous work until 18. But only 49 countries have ratified the Convention and none of these are countries considered to have the highest incidence of hazardous child labour.

The State of the World's Children 1997, UNICEF.

mercial logging in Uttar Pradesh and saved 12,000 square kilometres of sensitive watershed. Its success spawned similar movements elsewhere. Chipko was concerned from the beginning with the just allocation of rights to exploit forest **resources** – based on the view that forests support both human communities and wildlife. Over the years the Chipko campaign has gradually evolved into a full-fledged **conservation** movement.

CHITTAGONG HILL TRACTS

Forests covering the Chittagong Hills on the border between Bangladesh and Burma are home to many *adivasis* or tribal people. Since the 1970s, the Bangladesh Government has forcibly moved over 400,000 Bengali settlers from the plains to the Chittagong Hill Tracts. Thousands of hill people, mainly Jumma, have been displaced, killed or forced to adopt Bengali culture. Jumma people who were repatriated from Burma to Bangladesh in 1981 and 1984 were treated violently and inhumanely, despite government assurances of safety. In 1992, Bangladeshi soldiers and settlers burned alive over 1,200 Jumma people and caused thousands to flee to neighbouring India.

CHLOROFLUOROCARBONS (CFCs)

Chemical compounds in which hydrogen atoms in a hydrocarbon are replaced by atoms of chlorine and fluorine. These synthetically-produced chemicals are used as aerosol propellants, refrigerants, solvents in the electronics industry and in the production of insulating foam for packing. Although there are several such compounds CFC-11 (trichlorofluoromethane) and CFC-12 (dichlorodifluoromethane) account for 80% of global CFC production.

These human-made chemicals build up and persist in the environment. They are broken down only by the action of ultraviolet radiation when they have risen into the upper atmosphere. CFCs are **greenhouse gases**, which means they allow incoming solar radiation but block outgoing radiation reflected from the Earth's surface. This effectively heats up the planet. CFCs are amongst the worst of the greenhouse gases and are thought to be responsible for between 14-25% of **global warming**. CFCs are also responsible for the depletion of the stratospheric **ozone** layer. Chlorine is released when CFCs break down and then reacts with ozone – destroying it in the process.

Concern over CFCs led to a ban on their use in certain countries and to the Vienna Convention of 1985 which took the first steps towards a global ban. To prevent a further rise in the concentration of atmospheric CFC, emissions would have to be cut by 85%. The Vienna Convention called for CFC production to be frozen at 1986 levels, with the aim of reducing total emissions by half by the end of the century.

Eighty governments signed the subsequent **Montreal Protocol** and pledged to phase out CFCs by the year 2000. Pressure on wealthy governments to help developing nations like China and India curtail their CFC production and find suitable alternatives eventually led to a $6 billion fund which was set up in London in 1991. So far the fund has received 80% of the amount pledged by the industrialized nations, leaving a shortfall of $115 million.

In 1995, global CFC production declined by 20%, falling for the seventh consecutive year. However, in **developing countries** CFC production actually rose by 87% from 1986-1993, while exports rose 17-fold. Evasion of controls is widespread. At least 10,000 tonnes of CFCs entered the US illegally in 1995, with a similar amount entering the **European Union**. There is also a burgeoning black market in Russia, India and China. Russia has opted out of the Montreal Protocol and has facilities to produce 100,000 tonnes of CFCs, even though domestic demand is much lower.

CHOLERA

An acute bacterial infection of the intestines which is transmitted in drinking **water** contaminated by faeces from an infected person or via contaminated food. Cholera is closely linked to **poverty** and is still prevalent in tropical countries. Epidemics occur

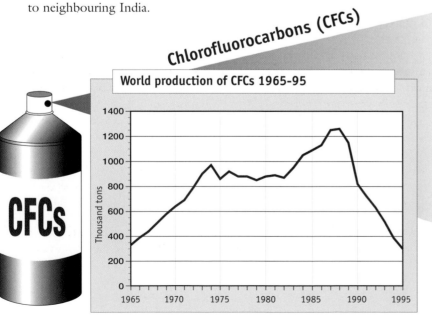

Chlorofluorocarbons (CFCs)

World production of CFCs 1965-95

Thousand tons

Vital Signs 1996/1997, Worldwatch Institute, Earthscan.

where sanitation is poor and safe drinking water is scarce. The mortality rate in untreated cases is over 50%. After an incubation period of 1-5 days, symptoms begin suddenly. Victims suffer severe vomiting and diarrhoea, which can lead to dehydration and death. In extreme cases, an imbalance in the concentration of body fluids can cause death within 24 hours. In 1996, there were cholera epidemics in Asia, Africa and Latin America. Treatment consists of replacing lost body fluids and salts. Vaccinations against the disease provide only temporary immunity.

CHRISTIANITY

A religious faith based on the teachings of Jesus Christ, a Jew born in Bethlehem about 2,000 years ago who is held by believers to be both human and divine. The significance of Jesus, known as the Christ, is shown by the fact that the Western calendar recognises his birth as marking the beginning of the modern era. Followers of Jesus are known as Christians. They believe that God is the creator of the universe and of all life. Jesus is the only son of God and was sent to reconcile humanity with God after human sinfulness had broken the relationship. Jesus' death was a triumph over sin and evil; his resurrection from the dead showed the triumph of life over death and gave the promise of everlasting life to those who believe in him.

Christians first believed that Jesus would return soon, 'at the end of time', to establish God's rule on Earth. When this did not happen, the 'Second Coming' became an event for the distant future, when all would be judged. Christianity was originally combined with Judaism. It spread rapidly through the Roman Empire, despite persecution by Nero and later emperors. Orthodox Christianity was spread around the world by European colonial powers until it began to be challenged by materialism, atheism and agnosticism in the 19th and 20th centuries

The total number of Christians is estimated at more than a billion. In 1900, about 80% of the world's Christians lived in Europe or North America. Today, 55% live in the **Third World**. As the proportion in the **developing countries** continues to rise, the number of Christians in the West is falling. One characteristic of modern Christianity is the increased understanding and co-operation between Christians in different parts of the world. The word 'ecumenical', meaning 'world-wide', is used to describe this spirit

CIRCUMCISION

In males, the removal of all or part of the foreskin on the penis. In many primitive societies, circumcision is part of a ceremony initiating youths into adulthood. Among some Islamic people it is performed just before marriage. Jewish boys are circumcised when they are 8 days old. Its origins are unknown, although it does have some health advantages, especially in hot climates. **Cancer** of the penis occurs infrequently in men who have been circumcised. Female circumcision, where the clitoris is removed, is also commonly practised in some Islamic cultures. It forms part of the **genital mutilation** experienced by many girls as a means of enforcing virginity.

COAL

A carbon-containing mineral deposit which is widely used as fuel and as a raw material in the plastics, steel and chemical industries. Coal is formed through prolonged pressure on

God zone
A statue of Jesus in the Roman Catholic cathedral at Betancuria, Canary Islands. The Spanish brought Christianity to the Canaries in the 16th century, when they conquered – and effectively wiped out – the local population. CHRISTIANITY

partially-decomposed vegetable matter over millions of years.

There are several types of coal. The simplest form is peat where **water** and volatile compounds are bound together and the carbon content is relatively low. Lignite (brown coal) contains more carbon, and anthracite has the highest carbon content. A tonne of anthracite produces the same energy as 3 tonnes of lignite.

Coal began to be used as a fuel around 1800, during the Industrial Revolution. By 1920, coal accounted for 80% of the world's total commercial energy consumption. **Natural gas** and petroleum gradually replaced coal until **oil** prices began to skyrocket in the 1970s. Coal still accounts for around 30% of commercial energy production and its use increased steadily from 1950 to 1995.

Over 4 billion tonnes of coal are mined each year: China (950 million tonnes) and the United States (830 million tonnes) are the major producers and users. Known reserves of anthracite could last for another 200 years at current rates of consumption, while supplies of lignite could meet demand for nearly 400 years.

Pit stop
This miner works in the Onyeama pit in Nigeria's Enugu region. Although Nigeria is the world's sixth largest producer of oil, coal is used in most households. COAL

Burning coal produces soot and other particulate matter, as well as **carbon dioxide** (CO_2) and other gases which add significantly to the **greenhouse effect**. Coal-fired power stations produce around 10% of all **greenhouse gases**. Concern is also growing about emissions of **sulphur dioxide** (SO_2) and oxides of nitrogen which are emitted when coal is burned. Both contribute to the production of **acid rain**. Emissions can be reduced by the use of scrubbers and by fluid-bed technologies. However, these technologies are expensive.

In industrial countries coal is mainly used for smelting iron ore and in electric power stations. **Economic growth** in **developing countries** accounted for most of the increase in coal use during the 1990s. In China the use of coal has recently increased by 4% annually and the country now accounts for 25% of total world use. The cost of **air pollution** in China is estimated at $95 billion and it will take a $20 billion investment in pollution control over the next decade to stop the problem from worsening. Alternatives to coal are being developed in response to growing concern over SO_2 and CO_2 emissions. The use of **renewable energy** sources such as solar, wind and wave power may prove to be the best and most ecologically-sound alternative.

COCAINE

A white powder processed from the leaves of the coca bush, commonly found in the Andes mountains in South America, which is a major narcotic in the global **drug trade**. Coca leaves have been chewed by local inhabitants in the Andes for centuries. The bush grows wild in Peru, Bolivia and Ecuador. The leaves are rich in nutrients but they also dull the appetite and act as a stimulant, enabling people to work long hours with little food. Coca is also used in hospitals as a local anaesthetic and in some areas it is the only anaesthetic available.

Cocaine stimulates the nervous system, producing a short-lived feeling of euphoria but the drug itself is not physically addictive. Ingested in small amounts, it decreases appetite, relieves fatigue and increases mental alertness. Cocaine can be injected in solution or smoked in a chemically-treated form known as 'freebase'.

In the 1980s, a new form of cocaine appeared called 'crack'. This gives a more intense euphoric state and is extremely addictive. Use, possession and trade of cocaine is illegal in most nations but the cocaine trade offers huge rewards and is growing despite internationally co-ordinated efforts to prevent it.

The UN Fund for Drug Abuse Control co-operates with governments in Latin America to curb cocaine production. Millions of dollars are being spent to persuade farmers to grow alternate crops like **coffee**, fruit and vegetables. However, demand in the **North**, which fuels the cocaine trade, has not been significantly lessened by government efforts.

The economies of indebted Latin American nations indirectly benefit from the cocaine trade and a handful of drug lords have become billionaires. In Colombia drugs are the nation's most profitable export, worth twice as much as coffee. In Bolivia the drug trade brings in $2.5 billion a year, almost 4 times the total value of all the country's legal export earnings. In Peru the income of $600 million from illegal drug exports makes it the nation's biggest export earner.

Cocaine manufacture causes severe pollution, **deforestation** and **soil erosion**. Paraffin, sulphuric acid, acetone, toluene, lime and carbide are all used in the process. All are dumped or discharged into **water** courses during production of powdered cocaine. In addition, large sections of tropical forest are cleared for coca cultivation. In response, governments and local authorities spray vast tracts of land and local inhabitants with defoliants and other hazardous chemicals. In 1989, a caterpillar was found that feeds exclusively on the leaves of the coca plant and the US Government is now examining plans to use the insect in biological-control programmes.

COCOA

Cocoa comes from the bean-shaped seeds of a tree which grows in warm, humid lowland areas throughout the tropics. The crop requires high rainfall (over 1,200 millimetres annually) distributed evenly throughout the year, with no dry season. Commercial production also needs average temperatures of 30°C. Cocoa is a suitable crop for small farmers and can be grown under an

Van Houten's
-the cocoa that for a century has charmed MILLIONS with its perfect flavour

Best & goes Farthest

'umbrella crop' such as **coconut**. Seedlings must be raised under a shade crop as intense sunlight damages the leaves. Trees begin to bear fruit 3-5 years after planting. Harvested pods are split open and the beans are then fermented and dried until the halves separate easily, a process which takes 7-10 days.

Cocoa has a high food value, containing 10% protein and over 50% fat (cocoa butter). It is used to produce a variety of sweets, baked goods and drinks.

Cocoa has become one of the world's major primary **commodities** and is an important **cash crop**, particularly in West Africa. It is produced solely in the **Third World** mainly for export to Northern consumers. World consumption continues to rise, though price fluctuations make it a risky and unpredictable business. Cocoa prices reached a peak in 1977 and have fallen since. World production is around 2.2 million tonnes: Ivory Coast (747,000 tonnes), Brazil (290,000 tonnes) and Ghana (243,000 tonnes), are the main growers.

COCONUT
The coconut palm tree is grown at low elevations in wet tropical lowlands. The fruit of the tree is one of the most important of tropical crops. Coconuts have a thick, fibrous husk surrounding a single-seeded nut. The hollow core contains coconut milk. The white kernel can be eaten raw or dried to produce copra from which coconut oil is extracted. Coconuts are grown primarily for oil production. The dried flesh (copra) is a rich source of vegetable oil which is used for making soaps, creams, synthetic rubbers, sweets and for cooking. The leftover coconut 'cake' is used as a livestock feed and the coarse husk fibre (known as coir) is used to make matting, brushes, furniture and water-resistant ropes.

Two varieties of coconut palm, tall and dwarf, are cultivated commercially. Tall trees, which reach a height of 30 metres, take longer to mature and do not begin to yield until 6 or 7 years after planting. Nuts usually require 12 months to reach maturity.

Harvesting takes place about 6 to 8 times a year. Harvesting is done by skilled climbers, although trained monkeys are sometimes used. Knives attached to long bamboo poles may also be used. The average annual yield is about 50 nuts per tree which will produce around 10 kilograms of copra. Freshly-harvested nuts are husked and split into halves which are then dried in the sun or in kilns.

The meat or kernel becomes detached from the shell after 2-3 days. The copra is collected and stored. Globally, some 4.8 million tonnes of copra are produced annually. In addition to its commercial uses, the shells of coconuts are used as a fuel in drying kilns. The sap of the palm ('toddy') is used to make wine and the trunks of older trees may be cut down and used for house construction or boat-building.

COFFEE
Coffee is one of the most important **Third World** export crops. Two varieties, *arabica* and *robusta,* are grown commercially. Arabica beans are the most sought-after. Robusta, although easier to grow, produces lower quality coffee. The plants need average temperatures of 20-28°C and rainfall of around 1,700 millimetres and so grow best in equatorial regions. Coffee must be picked when ripe and the surface of the fruit is red. Harvesting takes place every 12 days during the season. Once the pulp has been removed, the coffee beans are dried and stored.

Coffee was 'discovered' by Europeans who began to grow it throughout distant tropical colonies. The crop was introduced into Brazil in the 1870s but quickly became the nation's leading export. Coffee is the most important internationally-traded commodity after **oil**. It is grown almost exclusively in the Third World and the economies of **41 developing countries** now depend on it. Coffee growers in developing countries receive less than 10% of the final selling price;

INSTANT PROFIT
Nine-tenths of the price you pay for your instant coffee goes to the powerful companies who ship, roast and retail the product. Just one-tenth reaches the people whose lives are spent growing and harvesting it.

Growers 10%
Exporters 10%
Shippers and Roasters 55%
Retailers 25%

The Oxfam Chain Game, Oxfam, 1995.

Coal – Coffee

the rest is retained by the companies which control the trade. In 1978, when coffee prices were at record highs, Brazil produced a quarter of the world's coffee. A decade later trade was still worth $8.5 billion and over 50 developing countries were growing coffee beans for export.

The US imports over a million tonnes annually (a third of the global crop) and is the world's largest coffee consumer, followed by Germany. Annual production is 5.6 million tonnes. The leading producers are Brazil (1.3 million tonnes), Colombia (780,000 tonnes) and Indonesia (390,000 tonnes).

Several attempts have been made by producers and consumers to stabilize the coffee trade. The International Coffee Agreement (ICA) established export quotas to smooth out the fight for market share and stabilize prices. But it collapsed in 1989 when the US pushed to change quotas and allow more top-quality arabica coffee onto the world market. Brazil, with 30% of global exports, mostly the cheaper robusta coffee, refused to agree to the change.

COLD WAR

After World War II, the US and the Soviet Union emerged as the world's superpowers. The 'Cold War' (roughly 1945-90) is the name given to the confrontation between these superpowers and their respective allies. The term was first coined by Bernard Baruch, an adviser to US President Truman. The superpowers were never in direct military conflict, partially for fear of nuclear war. Instead, there was a conflict of ideologies – Western **capitalism** versus Soviet **communism**. In 1947, President Truman re-affirmed the US intention of resisting communist expansion, a doctrine which was followed by all subsequent US governments. Several major confrontations between the super-

Cold warrior
The Berlin Wall – symbol of the Cold War – claims another victim: an 18-year-old man shot dead as he attempted to cross to West Berlin. COLD WAR

powers occurred: the blockade of West Berlin (1948), Communist victory in China (1949), the **Korean War** (1950) and the Cuban missile crisis (1962).

The tense relationship between the superpowers began to ease with the Vietnam peace talks in 1968. However, it was not until Mikhail Gorbachev emerged as the Soviet leader in 1985, that the pace of détente increased. He introduced liberal reforms at home and moved to reduce arms stocks.

He also pressured old-guard Communist leaders in Eastern Europe to make way for younger reformers. Within 5 years all Soviet satellite states were on the path to multiparty democracy. The Cold War's central symbol, the Berlin Wall, was torn down in 1989 and East and West Germany were unified in 1990. In November 1990, the Charter for a New Europe was

signed in Paris by 34 countries from both East and West and this marked the official end of the Cold War.

COLOMBO PLAN

Signed in Sri Lanka in 1951, the Plan was designed to foster co-operative economic and political development in the countries of south and southeast Asia. There is an annual meeting of a Consultative Committee and financial arrangements are negotiated and administered bilaterally rather than through a central fund.

There are 24 member countries: Afghanistan, Australia, Bangladesh, Bhutan, Burma, Cambodia, Fiji, India, Indonesia, Iran, Japan, South Korea, Laos, Malaysia, Maldives, Nepal, New Zealand, Pakistan, Papua New Guinea, the Philippines, Singapore, Sri Lanka, Thailand and the United States.

COLONIALISM
(see also Neo-Colonialism)

A process of political and economic domination which started around 1500 when European nations began to conquer, settle and exploit vast areas of the world beyond their own geographical frontiers.

A 'colony' was the name given to a group of people who established social and economic lives overseas but retained the language, customs and allegiances of the 'mother country'. The impetus for colonialism can be traced to the opening of a navigable sea route around southern Africa in 1488 and the 'discovery' of America in 1492. The Portuguese and the Spanish were most active in the early colonial era. The Portuguese began exploiting the native peoples and natural **resources** in parts of Brazil and Africa shortly after 1500. And the Spanish, after looting gold and silver

Raj rage
Indians protest to the British colonial officials about the 1897 famine. COLONIALISM

by the ton in Mexico, quickly established an empire which stretched from Chile in the south to California and Florida in the north.

In the 16th century, the Dutch pushed into parts of China, Japan, India, Persia and Indonesia. But France did not fare particularly well in its early colonizing efforts, mainly due to problems in Europe. England's East India Company led the conquest of India in the early 1600s. Then, following wars with Spain and France, Britain made huge territorial gains in North America. Eventually, the British Empire emerged as the wealthiest of all European colonial systems.

In the late 19th and early 20th centuries several new colonial powers emerged, including Germany, the United States, Japan, Russia and Italy. Africa was the main target. Prior to 1880 there were few colonies in Africa but by the turn of the century almost the whole continent was controlled by European powers.

Colonialism had a profound impact both on the colonized and the colonizers. For the most part Europeans saw their tropical dependencies as mere suppliers of raw materials. Despite the rhetoric about civilizing and educating the natives every European power treated its colonies in much the same manner – as a way of transferring wealth to Europe. Gold and silver from the Americas also provided a catalyst for global **capitalism**. In 1500, Europe had $200 million worth of gold and silver. A century later the amount was 8 times

greater. **Third World** peoples and cultures were distorted and brutalized by the colonial experience. Millions were enslaved, millions more died from violence or from imported diseases. Local economies were changed irrevocably. And foreign religious and political institutions were introduced which created new traditions in place of indigenous knowledge and tradition.

In the period between the two World Wars most colonial systems began to disintegrate as **nationalism**, revolution and economic modernization began to erode the influence of colonial powers.

From 1945 on, **decolonization** occurred at an ever-increasing pace. Britain began to disband its empire. India and Pakistan were finally granted independence in 1947 after years of struggle and agitation. In the 1950s, many African colonies followed suit. Britain withdrew from the Persian Gulf and Singapore in 1971 and from Hong Kong in 1997.

The French were more reluctant to abandon their colonies. France was eventually forced into decolonization by violent wars in Indochina and North Africa. The remaining European colonial powers (Belgium, Portugal and the Netherlands) gradually gave up their overseas possessions during the 1950s, 1960s and 1970s, often unwillingly.

COMMODITIES

A commodity is anything that is produced for sale or that enters into trade. However, the term is commonly used to refer to the raw materials and **primary products** which are traded internationally. These include food crops like **bananas, cassava, cocoa, coffee, maize, wheat, sugar** and **tea**; fibre crops such as **cotton, sisal**, wool and jute; base metals including **gold,** silver, **copper**, tin, **lead** and **aluminium/aluminum**; oilseeds such as soya, olive and **groundnuts**; fuels, like **coal**, **oil** and **natural gas**; and certain other **cash crops** like **tobacco** and **rubber**.

In real terms, the price of most commodities drifted downward through the latter half of the 1980s and early 1990s. Using 1985 prices as 100, the index had fallen to 71 by 1994. **Third World** commodity exporters have lost millions of dollars during the last two decades because of low prices. Protectionist measures implemented by the United States, the **European Community** and other importing countries exacerbated the situation.

There were hopes that producer/consumer co-operation would stabilize global commodity prices. Instead, treaties on coffee, cocoa, wheat, tin and sugar all collapsed by 1990, causing prices to fall with them. Only the pact on natural rubber was still operating.

Through the early 1990s, the wholesale prices of tea, vegetable oils, rubber, grains and base metals continued to fall, some reaching their lowest point since the early 1980s. Fourteen countries in Asia, 19 in Latin America and 37 in Africa rely on a single commodity for at least 20% of their export earnings.

The purchasing power of these commodities has been steadily falling. In 1975, a tonne of coffee bought 290 barrels of oil. In 1983, it could purchase just under 100 barrels. From 1975 to 1990, the price of cocoa declined by half and the price of sugar by 80%.

There appears to be little hope for immediate improvement. Commodity price increases in the short term are expected to be slow and gradual, with the result that those poor nations which depend heavily on a few commodities could become even worse off.

COMMON FUND

At the third **United Nations Conference on Trade and Development** (UNCTAD) in 1972 delegates decided to establish a Common Fund to help stabilize the income of **Third World** nations dependent on the export of 18 basic **commodities**. Agreement was reached in 1979 on the structure and operation of the Fund.

Through its 'First Window' it provides support for **International Commodity Agreements**, lending money to strengthen existing agreements and stabilizing prices through the creation of international buffer stocks. The fund's 'Second Window' finances efforts to improve both the quantity and the quality of commodity production, concentrating on support for agricultural goods which are unsuitable for stockpiling.

It took a full 15 years of lengthy negotiations before enough countries had ratified the agreement for the Fund to be finally launched in 1990. However, with starting capital of $750 million well below the $6 billion UN target, the Fund's impact will be limited.

COMMONWEALTH

A loose association of 53 independent nations which were all once part of the British Empire. The Commonwealth's aim is to foster multinational co-operation and assistance among its member states who hold nearly 25% of the world's **population**.

Commonwealth government leaders meet every 2 years while finance ministers meet annually. The organization is serviced by a permanent Secretariat based in London. Since it was set up, only 3 countries have withdrawn from the organization. Ireland left in 1949, South Africa withdrew in 1961 (but has now returned) and Pakistan in 1972. Nigeria has been suspended since November 1995.

Full members include Antigua and Barbuda, Australia, the Bahamas, Bangladesh, Barbados, Belize, Botswana, Brunei, Cameroon, Canada, Cyprus, Dominica, Fiji, Gambia, Ghana, Grenada, Guyana, India, Jamaica, Kenya, Kiribati, Lesotho, Malawi, Malaysia, Maldives, Malta, Mauritius, Mozamique, Namibia, Nauru, New Zealand, Papua New Guinea, St Kitts-Nevis, St Lucia, St Vincent, Seychelles, Sierra Leone, Singapore, Solomon Islands, South Africa, Sri Lanka, Swaziland, Tanzania, Trinidad and Tobago, Tonga, Tuvalu, Uganda, Vanuatu, Western Samoa, Zambia, Zimbabwe and the United Kingdom.

The Commonwealth Secretariat

Educating Rita... and Rajan... and Thembi...
Education ministers from the Commonwealth countries pose during their 1997 conference held in Gaberone, Botswana. COMMONWEALTH

was established in 1965 by the Heads of Government Conference and based in London. It serves the Commonwealth collectively, providing the central administration for joint consultation and co-operation in many fields. It services the Commonwealth Prime Ministers' meetings. It also collects and disseminates information for use by member countries and co-ordinates, via various Commonwealth institutions, technical co-operation for economic and social development.

COMMONWEALTH OF INDEPENDENT STATES (CIS)

A group of states from the former Soviet Union, formed to co-ordinate relations and to provide a mechanism for orderly dissolution of the USSR. There are 12 members: Armenia, Azerbaijan, Belarus, Georgia, Kazakhstan, Kyrgyzstan, Moldova, Russia, Tajikistan, Turkmenistan, Ukraine and Uzbekistan.

COMMUNISM

A movement based on the principle of communal ownership of all property. More specifically, it is based on the *Communist Manifesto* published by **Karl Marx** and Friedrich Engels in 1848, according to which the capitalist, profit-based system of private ownership is replaced by a classless communist society in which the means of production and all property are communally owned. This involves the revolutionary overthrow of those who control capital and the means of production (the 'bourgeoisie') by those who must sell their labour in order to live (the 'proletariat' or working class). No-one owns significantly more than any other – either because all property is held in common or because the institution of private property does not exist.

'Have you volunteered?'
Words from a Red Army soldier in his ardent call to defend the Russian Revolution, shown on a 1920 Soviet poster by one of the genre's most famous artists, Dimitry Moor (1983-1946). Moor's political awareness and clarity of expression made his posters some of the most striking of the period. COMMUNISM

According to Marxist theory, **socialism** is a stage in an evolutionary process which leads to communism. Advocates claim it is the true economic expression of democracy, summed up in the slogan 'from each according to his [*sic*] ability, to each according to his need'. In the second half of the 19th century Marxist theories spawned social democratic parties throughout Europe, although the result was the reformation of **capitalism** rather than its overthrow.

The first flawed attempt at communism was led by the Russian Social Democratic Labour Party which destroyed the Tsar's regime in the 1917 Revolution. In 1918, the party changed its name to the Communist Party of the Soviet Union and so made clear the distinction between communism and socialism. Subsequently, many socialist parties in Eastern Europe followed the Russian example, usually with Soviet encouragement. The Russian Communist party enjoyed

unchallenged authority over international communism until 1948, when Yugoslavia rejected its influence. In 1949 the Soviets supported communists in China when they overthrew the centuries-old feudal regime and founded the People's Republic of China. But in 1960, under **Mao Zedong**, a deep rift developed between the two states.

Since the Russian Revolution a handful of small communist states have developed in the **Third World**. All were opposed by Western powers and most were actively undermined by the US Government. Politically, they have been characterized by one-party rule, corrupt and inefficient bureaucracies, brutal and repressive policing, strict censorship and the inability to accept political opposition. Most have been able to provide little more than **basic needs** for their citizens. In 1987 the Soviet Union and many Communist states in the Soviet sphere began to admit their failings and to restructure their governments along capitalist and

Commodities – Communism

pluralist lines. Following the break-up of the Soviet Union, only a few countries now describe themselves as communist: these include China, North Korea, Mongolia, Cambodia, Vietnam and Cuba.

COMPENSATORY FINANCING FACILITY

A division of the **International Monetary Fund** (IMF) through which nations can obtain a quick loan to cover a temporary shortfall in export receipts. It was designed for countries where a deficit occurs because of unforeseen circumstances like a natural disaster. It can also be used to cover the costs of temporary food imports caused by similar circumstances.

CONFERENCE ON SECURITY AND CO-OPERATION IN EUROPE (CSCE)

An organization which includes all European countries with the exception of Albania. In 1975, Conference members signed the Helsinki Agreement promoting freedom of contact and movement between their countries, including exchanges between East and West. In fact the Agreement had little success, with the Soviet Bloc reluctant to keep their promises. In 1989 the Communist governments in Eastern Europe began to be replaced and the CSCE was proposed as an instrument of collective security, eventually to replace both the **North Atlantic Treaty Organization** (NATO) and the **Warsaw Pact**.

In 1990 leaders of 34 Western and Eastern European nations, plus the US and Canada, met to decide a charter for a new Europe. The summit was held in recognition of the end of the **Cold War** and the re-unification of Germany and to discuss security implications for the changing face of Europe. The proposed 'Charter for a New Europe' included

commitments to improve regional security, individual liberties, the rule of law and Western-style capitalist democracy. Several agreements were reached including a decision to 'insti-tutionalize' the CSCE by establishing a small secretariat in Prague. Future summits will be held every 2 years with foreign ministers meeting on a more frequent basis. In 1992, 10 states of the former-USSR were admitted, bringing the total number of countries to 52. In 1994, the CSCE became the **Organization for Security and Co-operation in Europe** (OSCE).

CONSERVATION

'Conservation' is a term used to describe the exploitation of natural **resources** without jeopardizing the long-term viability of the resource base or inflicting undue or excessive environmental damage. It is distin-guished from 'preservation': maintaining the pristine state of nature as it is or might have been *before* the intervention of either anthropogenic or natural forces.

Critics charge that 'conservation' is a mask for a form of 'green imperialism' orchestrated by Western governments that have already destroyed much of their own native flora and fauna. The culture and needs of local popula-tions tend to get short shrift.

Biodiversity is richest in tropical regions where most **developing countries** are located. In response to the burgeon-ing global market for **eco-tourism** and in response to national and international pressure, many developing countries have introduced

extensive programmes to conserve their unique habitats and indigenous species to 'preserve them for posterity'. Frequently this has been done with support from Western-based conservation agencies.

As a result some **Third World** critics level charges of **neo-colonial-ism**. In Africa, for example, species conservation is sometimes described by locals as white people making rules to protect animals that they want to see in parks when they visit.

Often conservation policies tend to benefit foreign **tourism** and tend to ignore local needs, traditions and cultures. Africans do not generally use the parks and rarely receive any significant benefits from them. Yet they pay the costs in several ways. Indirectly, when government funds go to establishing and maintaining parks rather than schools or health services; and directly, when local people are banned from hunting or prevented from following their normal routines such as gathering **fuelwood**.

Conserving what and for whom?
The 200,000 Masai in East Africa may not benefit from 'conservation' which can mean game parks for foreign tourists rather than health or education services for local people.
CONSERVATION

Space is another basic problem. Many animals, especially the big game species idolized by Europeans and North Americans, need large swathes of **land**. Tigers for example, may need up to 100 square kilometres.

The larger the animal the greater the number of individuals that are needed to make the species viable and the more space needed. But the developing world, with its booming human **population**, does not have the space. Or does not have the space in the right place – removed from human settlements and in the habitat needed by the species at risk.

In India, only 6 wildlife reserves existed when the nation gained independence in 1947. Now, there are over 400, covering some 4% of the country. Some Indians have also pointed out that although Hindus revere the cow, they do not call for the world to follow suit. They compare this with the demands by those who love animals like elephants and whales and who call for a global protection of these species.

The *World Conservation Strategy* (1980) proposed that conservation and **sustainable development** were mutually interdependent and that you could not have one without the other. In 1991 an updated version, *Caring for the Earth,* named conservation of the Earth's natural resources and biodiversity as core principles. The report called for all countries by the year 2000 to introduce a plan to safeguard their **biological diversity** and to set up a system of protected areas covering at least 10% of each of the nation's main ecological regions.

CONSUMERISM

A term used to describe societies whose central purpose has become the acquisition of mass-produced consumer goods. As people find their value and meaning in **commodities** the dominance of consumerism imposes huge strains

Global Consumerism

◆ **The world's poor** – some 1.1 billion people – includes all those households that earn less than $700 a year per member. They are mostly rural Africans, Indians and other South Asians.

◆ **The 3.3 billion people** in the world's middle-income class earn between $700 and $7,500 per member and live mostly in Latin America, the Middle East, China and East Asia. This class also includes the low-income families of the former Soviet bloc and of Western industrial nations.

◆ **The consumer class** – the 1.1 billion members of the global consumer society – includes all households whose income per member is above $7,500. They live mainly in North America, Europe and Australasia.

Category of Consumption	Consumers (1.1 billion)	Middle (3.3 billion)	Poor (1.1 billion)
Diet	meat, packaged food, soft drinks	grain, clean water	insufficient grain, unsafe water
Transport	private cars	bicycles, buses	walking
Materials	throwaways	durables	local biomass

Worldwatch Institute.

on earth's natural **resources** and an untenable burden on the planet's ecosystem.

The term is also used to describe a kind of citizen activism which attempts to reform the worst excesses of consumer society. The idea is that consumers should influence the design, quality, service and price of goods and services provided by commercial enterprises. Movements promoting this idea have sprung up in Europe and North America following the concentration of economic power in huge global corporations and the increased technical complexity of many consumer goods.

Organizations like the UK Consumers Association allow independent tests on goods and services, the findings of which can be passed to consumers and producers alike.

CONTADORA GROUP

A regional group of Central and South American countries formed in 1983 to promote development and co-operation between member states and to reduce conflicts among Central American nations. The Group was named after an island in the Gulf of Panama and consisted of Panama, Colombia, Mexico and Venezuela. It has now evolved into the Rio Group.

CONTRACEPTION

The prevention of unwanted pregnancy, also referred to as **birth control** or **family planning**. Contraception is now an accepted means of preventing pregnancies in most **developed countries** and, increasingly, in **developing countries** – even those where the Catholic church forbids the practice.

Today there are several methods of contraception. The 'birth control pill' is the best known. Tens of millions of women have used it since it became widely available in the 1960s. It is highly effective and may protect some women against some forms of **cancer**.

Either sex can also opt for sterilization. In women this involves cutting or tying the fallopian tubes. Male sterilization, known as vasectomy, involves cutting the *vas deferens* which transports sperm.

Several barrier methods are also used. Male condoms are worn over the male penis; female condoms fit inside a woman's vagina; a diaphragm covers a woman's cervix. All these are less reliable than the 'pill' but have no effect on body chemistry. Some barrier devices also stop infections from sexually transmitted diseases, most notably **AIDS**.

Intra-uterine devices (IUDs) are small objects made from plastic or **copper** wire which are inserted into

'Planned Family – Happy Family'
That's the message from this family-planning poster at a clinic in Burkina Faso, West Africa. CONTRACEPTION

the uterus. IUDs lost popularity when they became associated with infections and infertility in some women.

One of the oldest contraceptive methods is the rhythm method, which involves restricting intercourse to the days in a woman's menstrual cycle when she is least likely to conceive.

By 1990, more than half of married couples were using family planning compared to less than 10% in 1965. Globally, 18% of couples opt for female sterilization and 4% for male. Some 15% of married women use the 'pill' while IUDs account for 20% of contraceptive use and condoms around 8%.

CONVENTION ON BIOLOGICAL DIVERSITY

A global agreement adopted by the UN Conference on Environment and Development (UNCED) in Brazil in 1992. The convention aims to conserve the world's biodiversity and to achieve a sustainable use of its **resources**, including a fair and equitable sharing of the benefits arising from the exploitation and use of genetic resources.

There are 169 signatories, though only a quarter of them have ratified the convention. In many industrial-ized nations business leaders have lobbied governments not to sign, claming that its provisions on intellectual property rights would jeopardize their patents and profits.

CONVENTION ON THE CONSERVATION OF MIGRATORY SPECIES OF WILD ANIMALS (BONN CONVENTION)

A specialized global convention which lists **endangered species** of migratory animals and insects and their habitats. The Convention began in 1983 and applies to the entire population of any animal species whose members cyclically and predictably cross one or more national boundaries. The 42 parties to the Convention agreed to conserve those species by restricting harvesting, conserving habitats and controlling other adverse factors.

Appendix I of the Convention covers all migratory species deemed to be endangered. Appendix II covers endangered migratory species which require international agreements to maintain their numbers. Subsidiary

◆ 50 plant species become extinct every day.
◆ Small islands in the Pacific, Atlantic and Indian Oceans contain larger numbers of rare and threatened plants. ◆ The numbers of species threatened are seriously underestimated – probably only 50% of mammals and 20% of reptiles have been reviewed.
◆ Two-thirds of the world's bird species are endangered and one out of ten faces extinction. CONVENTION ON BIOLOGICAL DIVERSITY

agreements have been concluded to conserve seals in the Wadden Sea, bats in Europe and small cetaceans in the Baltic and North Seas.

CONVENTION ON THE CONTROL OF TRANSBOUNDARY MOVEMENTS OF HAZARDOUS WASTE (BASEL CONVENTION)

Adopted in 1989 in Basel, Switzerland, after discussions involving 100 countries plus the **European Community**. After 18 months of negotiations the Convention was signed by only 35 countries, over half from the **Third World**.

The Convention attempts to limit and control the international transport and disposal of hazardous wastes. But it also attempts to minimize its production and to assist **developing countries** in the environmentally-safe management of any **hazardous waste** they generate.

The Convention allows for waste shipments between signatory states following the 'prior informed consent' principle – all waste exports which a recipient state has not authorized in writing are prohibited. Waste exports are only allowed if the country of origin does not have the technical means or suitable sites for disposal and the recipient nation can dispose of them in an environmentally sound and efficient manner.

Where waste is shipped illegally, the country of origin is liable to reclaim the waste. Ironically, the Convention did not define what constitutes hazardous waste. But it does list more than 40 classes of materials which have to be controlled, not including nuclear waste or waste destined for **recycling**.

Industrial society produces vast amounts of hazardous waste. Countries from the **Organization for Economic Co-operation and Development** (OECD) produce an estimated 300 million tonnes annually, 10% of which crosses international borders.

Around 20 million tonnes of hazardous waste is exported to the Third World each year from Europe alone. And the OECD exports another 600,000 tonnes of toxic waste, 20% of which is shipped to the Third World for disposal.

Over 40 developing countries have imposed a total ban on waste imports and continue to press for a ban on trade in all waste products. Most African states are in favour of a total ban. Following the appearance of so-called 'leper ships' in 1988, 16 West African states agreed to set up Dumpwatch, a body to monitor dumping and prosecute offenders.

The 'leper ships' were loaded with hazardous waste which no country would accept. Two ships, the *Karin B* and the *Deep Sea Carrier* contained unidentified toxic waste which Italian companies had dumped in Nigeria. The contents of the ships, together with that of the *Zanoobia*, which had been sailing around the world for over 12 months in search of a resting place for its cargo, were all eventually returned to Italy.

In 1994, 120 parties to the convention decided to make it illegal to ship any hazardous waste from OECD countries to the **South**, including toxic waste destined for recycling. The US (which has not ratified the convention,) attempted to undermine the agreement claiming that categorical trade bans were undesirable – a view supported by Canada, France and Australia.

CONVENTION ON INTERNATIONAL TRADE IN ENDANGERED SPECIES OF WILD FAUNA AND FLORA (CITES)

CITES was launched in 1975 to control the global trade in **endangered species**. It prohibits trade in the rarest 600 or so species of animals and plants and monitors trade in a further 200 groups through a system of import, export and re-export permits. Appendix I forbids trade in all listed animals or any products derived from them. Appendix II restricts trade in separately listed species at risk of becoming endangered. Appendix III allows individual nations to announce their own domestically endangered species and trading regulations.

Parties to CITES also examine ways to conserve and exploit wild animals and occasionally remove animals from the appendices. For example, trade in vicuna wool was

TRADE IN WILDLIFE
BY 1993, 123 COUNTRIES belonged to the Convention on International Trade in Endangered Species (CITES) – an increase of 26 per cent since 1900.

CACTI
FIFTEEN PER CENT of the cacti traded comes from the wild. Chile, Mexico and the US are major exporters of illegal cacti, while the main importers are Europe, Japan and the US.

re-introduced following an increase in their numbers. Similarly, some species like the American alligator are now out of danger so their listing has changed accordingly. In addition, any nation can declare a 'reservation' which exempts it from CITES trade restrictions. Data compiled by the Wildlife Trade Monitoring Unit of the World Conservation Union (IUCN) indicates that trade is prohibited for about 680 species on Appendix I and is regulated for a total approach-

Contaception – CITES

Your place or mine?
Two white rhinos get together in Kenya – their future may be brighter now thanks to controls on the illegal trade in rhino horn. CITES

ing 30,000 on Appendix II.

Parties to the Convention are required to submit annual reports and records of trade to the CITES Secretariat in Switzerland. Enforcement of the treaty is about 60% effective. Illegal trade is monitored by the Trade Records Analysis of Flora and Fauna in Commerce (TRAFFIC), a network of offices with 11 branches, affiliated with the **Worldwide Fund for Nature** (WWF) and the IUCN.

With 110 members, CITES is one of the most widely-supported international conventions. However, it has several weak points. Some nations like Japan simply ignore the Treaty. It is also difficult to police and enforce the regulations. And the fact that participating nations are allowed to register 'reservations' according to their national priorities also hampers its effectiveness. The worth of the convention is further undermined by non-participating nations who are effectively free to trade in all endangered species.

CONVENTION ON THE LAW OF THE SEA (UNCLOS)

Around 70% of the Earth's surface is covered by salt **water**, most of which is 'open' sea not under any country's legal jurisdiction. These seas and oceans contain vast natural **resources** including **fish** and sea-bed minerals. The UN Convention on the Law of the Sea was signed in 1992 by 131 countries after 8 years of lengthy negotiations. UNCLOS aims to promote peaceful use of the sea, rational resource use, **conservation** of living organisms and the study and protection of the marine environment. It also aims to establish international rules and principles to govern these issues and the means to enforce them.

The Convention placed more than 40% of the world's oceans under the jurisdiction of coastal states and defined 4 specific zones: a territorial sea which extends 12 nautical miles from the coast; a contiguous zone which extends 24 miles from the coast; an extended economic zone which extends 200 miles more; and the continental shelf.

Under this system, the whole of the Caribbean and the Mediterranean come under the jurisdiction of various coastal states. Tiny developing island states in the Pacific Ocean now control sea zones over 335,000 square kilometres. The Law of the Sea upholds the right of free navigation within all Extended Economic Zones (EEZ) and gives nations stronger powers to regulate pollution and the exploitation of natural resources in their waters. In its 320 articles the Convention defines maritime zones, legal rights and establishes a mechanism for settling international disputes.

Traditional 'freedom of the seas' remains for 60% of the world's oceans. Almost half of this (mostly deep, sea-bed) is designated as the 'common heritage' of humankind and is to be controlled by an International Seabed Authority. The Authority would oversee the mining of the seabed and distribute any proceeds among the landlocked and least developed nations.

However the United States, the United Kingdom and Germany disagreed with this approach and withheld their signatures. As a result the Convention has been virtually becalmed. By 1994, only 60 nations had ratified the Convention and nearly 100 signatory states have not fully approved it.

CO-OPERATIVES

Organizations set up to manufacture, buy or sell produce, either without the aim of making profits or with profits equally distributed to members as dividends. The co-operative movement was inspired by the British philanthropist Robert Owen in the early 19th century and was seen as an alternative to the competition inherent in **capitalism**.

Co-operatives attempted to introduce an equitable, communal economic system within capitalist society. This concept of co-operative organizations working for mutual benefit is now common throughout the world.

Co-operative societies in agriculture, in which farm machinery is shared and produce is marketed jointly are common in both the developed and the developing worlds. For example, the wholesale distribution of agricultural produce in both Italy and France is often handled by co-operatives.

COPPER

A reddish metal which has extensive industrial uses. Most copper deposits are low-grade ore and at least 10 different copper-containing ores are mined. Copper is used widely in the electrical industry and for cables, wire and pipes. It is also important in alloys such as bronze and brass and is an essential component of anti-fouling paints, algaecides and wood preservatives.

Copper is a naturally-occurring element which is part of the biological cycle; 18,000 tonnes of the metal are emitted into the atmosphere each year from natural sources. Human activity is responsible for a further 56,000 tonnes. Copper dust and fumes are unhealthy and can lead to respiratory diseases.

There are an estimated 560 million tonnes of copper reserves around the world – enough to last 66 years at current rates of consumption. Some 10.7 million tonnes of copper is mined annually. Chile (2.2 million tonnes), the US (1.8 million tonnes) and Canada (617,000 tonnes) are the major producers.

CORAL REEFS

Coral are small, sedentary marine animals which live in dense colonies and are found in all oceans, usually in warm, shallow **water**. The 'stony' corals, of which there are about 1,000 species, secrete a rigid external skeleton made of calcium carbonate (limestone). Coral reefs are formed by millions of stony corals, each building on the hard skeleton of the previous generation. The main reef-building occurs at depths of less than 50 metres and in waters where the temperature is around 20°C. Within this zone, symbiotic algae are present in the tissue of the corals and these stimulate the secretion of limestone, accelerating the growth of the reefs. Reefs play a major role in protecting coastal **land** from erosion by lessening the force of tides and waves. They also act as a 'sink' for carbon and will play a major role in slowing **global warming** by absorbing excess atmospheric carbon. Coral reefs currently form a sink for 111 million tonnes of carbon annually, equivalent to around 2% of present emissions of **carbon dioxide**.

Coral reefs are one of the most diverse, productive ecosystems in the world, rivalling tropical rain forests in diversity. They are the planet's oldest ecosystems and appear to be the only ones that have survived intact since the emergence of life.

The broad range of corals secrete a vast number of differing chemicals which are used by humans for a multitude of purposes, most significantly in the field of medicine. In their limited expanse they harbour one-third of all **fish** species. The potential yield of fish from coral reef waters is estimated to be in the region of 9 million tonnes – about 11% of the current global marine fish catch. Yet coral reefs everywhere are under threat of destruction. Over-fishing and the use of dynamite to harvest reef fishes is destroying both fish stocks and the reefs themselves. Reefs elsewhere are threatened by pollution that either kills the coral directly or causes algal blooms which cut off light. Similarly, silt run-off caused by **deforestation** and poor farming practices on land

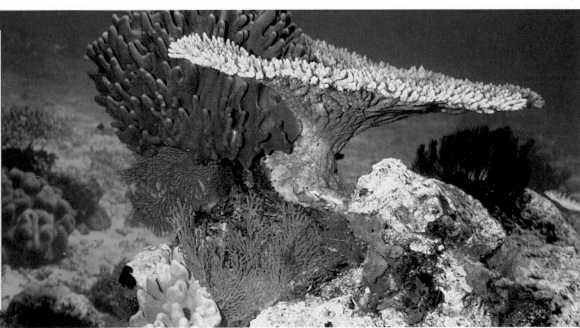

Coral reefs

Coral reefs are the marine equivalent of tropical rain-forests – a single reef may hold over 3,000 species of coral, fish and shellfish. Over 85 per cent of the world's coral reefs are already damaged by pollution, mining, tourism, blast fishing, shipping and ocean warming.

clouds coastal waters and kills the tiny coral polyps which must have light to photosynthesize.

Increasing amounts of human sewage, produced in coastal regions throughout the tropics by the booming tourist industry, is also posing a serious threat to coral reefs. **Tourism** causes damage in other ways too. In 1996 the Egyptian Government detained a Cunard cruise ship, the Royal Viking Sun, until the company paid a $15 million fine for damage that it had caused to a local reef.

In Sri Lanka, coral reefs are being quarried for their limestone which is used in the building industry. In the Maldives and Comoros, large chunks of coral are taken for use as building stone or mortar. Reef damage is extremely bad in the Philippines where most of the coral is collected and exported to US markets.

In 1989 the Filipino coral curio and souvenir trade was estimated at about 2,000 tonnes annually, with nearly 75% of this shipped to the US. Belgium, the United Kingdom, France and Japan have all imported significant quantities of coral from the Philippines, despite a law passed by the Filipino Government in 1977 which banned the collection and export of coral.

COTTON

Cotton is a small, drought-tolerant tropical and sub-tropical shrub which grows to a height of 1-2 metres. It is the most significant vegetable fibre in the world in terms of commercial trade. The fibres are mainly used to produce textiles. Wild species of cotton are native to arid and semi-arid zones in Australia, South America, northern and southern Africa and desert regions in Arabia and Southeast Asia. Several varieties are grown commercially.

The plant is a perennial but is usually replanted each year to avoid the build-up of pests. Commercial production depends heavily on intensive pest-control methods. Cotton usually matures 5-8 months after sowing. The fruits of the plant, called bolls, contain about 10 seeds, each with soft fibres (or lint) extruding from the seed coat which can be spun into yarn for cloth. During the height of the dry season, the bolls burst open exposing the lint which is then harvested, usually by hand. The seeds are dried and the lint separated in a ginning mill. It is then baled and shipped to factories where it is spun into thread for manufacturing textiles. Seeds may also be exported as they contain a high degree of edible oil which is used to produce margarine, salad oils and

soaps. The by-products of oil-extraction also provide valuable food for livestock. Gossypol, the pigment derived from cotton, has potential as a safe and effective male contraceptive.

Global production is increasing with annual production now around 60 million tonnes. China and the US (around 4.3 million tonnes each) and India (2.3 million tonnes) are the leading producers. Growth is stalled by competition from synthetic fibres, virtually all of which are produced by industrialized countries. In addition, the US, Japan and the **European Union** all place import quotas on cotton. In producer nations, erratic weather can play havoc with the crop. In Pakistan heavy rains in 1995 destroyed half the cotton crop and farmers lost an estimated $4 million. The same year, drought in southern Africa ruined cotton crops in South Africa and Zimbabwe.

COUNCIL FOR MUTUAL ECONOMIC ASSISTANCE (CMEA)

An association of communist countries (also known as COMECON) founded in 1949 in opposition to the **Marshall Plan**. It sought to promote economic co-operation and development between member states through the creation of a common market, but had no real central organization and no effective **free trade** between members. The Council was based in Moscow and linked the Soviet Union with Bulgaria, Czechoslovakia, Hungary, Poland, Romania, the German Democratic Republic, Mongolia, Cuba and Vietnam.

In 1990, the collapse of Communist regimes in Eastern Europe coupled with movement towards free-market economies led to the rapid demise of the CMEA. The dissolution rocked the already fragile economies of many Eastern European countries which were heavily dependent on intra-CMEA

Bursting out all over
It might not look much but cotton – seen here on the plant in Khiva, Uzbekistan – is the most significant vegetable fibre traded commercially. COTTON

THE **A** TO **Z** OF WORLD DEVELOPMENT

trade. In 1989, intra-CMEA trade made up 40-80% of member states' total trade. The CMEA was abolished in early 1991 and was replaced by the Organization for International Economic Co-operation, a body incorporating the ex-Warsaw Pact countries along with Vietnam, Cuba and Mongolia.

COUNCIL OF EUROPE
An association of European states founded in 1949 and based in Strasbourg. The Council's goals are to improve living conditions, uphold the principles of parliamentary democracy and to promote the economic and social progress of its members. It is organized to provide a framework for intergovernmental co-operation in culture, education, health, social welfare, crime prevention, youth affairs and relations between developed and **developing countries**. A mainly consultative body, the Council has negotiated a number of conventions including one on **human rights**, which resulted in the formation of the European Court of Human Rights in 1959.

Since the sudden upheavals in Eastern Europe during the late 1980s, the Council has expanded considerably. It now has 32 members: Austria, Belgium, Bulgaria, Cyprus, Czech Republic, Denmark, Estonia, Finland, France, Germany, Greece, Hungary, Iceland, Ireland, Italy, Liechtenstein, Lithuania, Luxembourg, Malta, the Netherlands, Norway, Poland, Portugal, San Marino, Slovakia, Slovenia, Spain, Sweden, Switzerland, Turkey and the United Kingdom. There are 9 'guest' member states, mostly former Soviet Bloc countries. Israel has observer status.

CULTURAL REVOLUTION
After the 1949 Chinese Revolution the People's Liberation Army (PLA) was sent into the countryside to promote the 'Great Leap Forward'.

de CUELLAR, JAVIER PEREZ (1920-   )
Peruvian diplomat and fifth Secretary-General of the **United Nations**. He joined Peru's foreign ministry in 1940 and the diplomatic service in 1944. He served as ambassador to France, the United Kingdom, Bolivia, Brazil and Switzerland before becoming Peru's first ambassador to the Soviet Union (1969-71). He was subsequently appointed as his country's permanent representative to the UN, a post he held until he was elected Secretary-General in 1982. He was seen as a 'hands-off' leader, advocating use of the Security Council for **peacekeeping** and negotiations. He was re-elected for a second term in 1986. As Secretary-General he kept a relatively low profile at a time when the **World Bank** and **IMF** increasingly began to set global agendas. Nevertheless, his diplomatic skills brought some personal victories. He helped resolve the civil war in El Salvador and personally negotiated the ceasefire in the Iran-Iraq war in 1988. He left office in 1991.

This ambitious plan of **land** collectivization and education initially met with little success. Chairman **Mao Zedong** revived the programme again in the late 1960s, ostensibly to spread more radical ideas to the people. This process became known as the 'Cultural Revolution'.

The movement reached its peak from 1966-68. It was designed as an attack on bureaucracy and an attempt to re-invigorate revolutionary ideas. But the movement soon had a life of its own. Many leading officials were dismissed, the formal education system was abolished and reforms were introduced to foster

On guard
This young Red Guard was one of many during Mao Zedong's Cultural Revolution.
CULTURAL REVOLUTION

'correct' political views. Militant students formed groups of 'Red Guards' to attack the existing hierarchy which they viewed as 'bourgeois' and too Westernized. The country bordered on anarchy as marauding band of youths set out to destroy cultural objects symbolic of the 'old order'. Priceless art objects and buildings were plundered. Thousands of bureaucrats and intellectuals were sent to work in the countryside while industrial production stagnated and the institutions of government were left to drift. Mao, backed by the PLA, was fortunate to survive the uprising. The Cultural Revolution wound down in the early 1970s as a power struggle developed over which faction would succeed Mao. But the country has yet to recover from the massive human and economic dislocation of the period.

CUSTOMS UNION
An agreement whereby customs duties are abolished between member countries and all goods can be freely imported and exported without quotas. A common external tariff is also established for goods imported from non-member nations.

Desertification

Changes in climate and human activities can squeeze the last drops of moisture from arid ground, turning it into desert. Over a third of the world's land surface is 'dryland' and home to 850 million or so people and their animals.

D

Bold indicates a cross-reference

DAMS

Dams are used to restrict or divert the normal flow of **water** in rivers and streams for a variety of purposes. These include: raising the water level for navigation; storing and providing water for **irrigation** and industry; and producing a high-pressure source of water to generate hydro-electricity.

There are many types and sizes of dam, but two forms are commonly used for large-scale projects. *Gravity dams* depend on their sheer weight to hold back water and have a flat,

Dam damage

Straightening out and dyking rivers increases the speed and volume of the river's flow creating serious flooding in very wet years when dykes might not hold. Deforestation increases damaging erosion and destroys a river's watershed.

Silt is trapped behind dams, reducing fertility downstream as well as the capacity and life-span of the dam. Downstream silt must be replaced by expensive chemical fertilizer.

New Internationalist, No. 273, Nov 1995.

Dyking cuts off wetlands which are natural absorbers of flood and provide a wildlife habitat.

Reservoirs flood the often-fertile land ato the bottom of valleys and displace thousands of people to less suitable land or overcrowded urban areas. Large reservoirs, particularly in hot climates, have enormous losses of precious water through evaporation. Irrigation channels spread disease, particularly malaria (300 million sufferers) and bilharzia (200 million affected).

Dams always carry the danger of collapse due to earthquakes, flooding or sabotage. Casualties from dam collapse will be much higher than those from normal flooding.

Riverine fisheries are destroyed as nutrients (fish food) become trapped behind dams and fish are unable to move up rivers to spawn. Downstream agriculture, with reduced water and silt flow is subject to much higher dangers of salinization (salt-poisoning).

vertical face. *Arch dams* consist of curved concrete structures with a convex face upstream. They are less bulky than gravity dams and are cheaper to build. There are 13,000 dams more than 15 metres high. The highest, on the Vaksh River in the Soviet Union, reaches 300

metres. All but 7 of the world's 100 largest dams have been built in the last 50 years. Construction costs keep rising. The price tag of the Yacreta Dam between Argentina and Paraguay jumped to $6 billion, more than 3 times the original prediction.

In **developing countries**, dams are usually funded by agencies like the **World Bank**. But the Bank's record has not been good. It invested $2.3 billion in sub-Saharan Africa from 1976-96 on 41 hydropower projects but concluded that poor performance of power utilities adds to public deficits and diverts scarce funds from basic education and health care.

Many dams are built to generate hydro-electricity, a relatively cheap, non-polluting, renewable source of energy. Dams produce 20% of the world's electricity but it is estimated that less than 10% of the potential hydropower is currently being tapped; the remainder could be exploited with little technical difficulty.

But dams are not without serious problems. Over 350,000 square

DALAI LAMA (1935-   )

The religious and political leader of Tibet. The current Dalai Lama was born in 1935, the son of Tibetan peasants. At the age of 5 he was chosen by Buddhist monks and taken to Lhasa, the nation's capital. Ten years later in 1950, China invaded and occupied Tibet. When Chinese troops crushed an uprising in 1959, murdering thousands of Tibetans in the process, the Dalai Lama and around 100,000 other **refugees** fled to India. He then set up a government-in-exile in the Himalayas and has campaigned ever since to end Chinese domination of his homeland. He was awarded the Albert Schweitzer Humanitarian Award in 1987 and the Nobel Peace Prize in 1989.

In 1994 the Chinese government held an elaborate religious ceremony during which a six-year-old child, was declared the 11th Panchen Lama, a revered Tibetan Buddhist leader who is second in importance to the Dalai Lama. This was a deliberate move by the Chinese to undermine the authority of the Dalai Lama who had earlier certified a different child as the Panchen Lama.

kilometres of **land** around the world is already under water as a consequence of dam building. When a dam's reservoir is filled, valuable and often unique wildlife and habitats are lost and people are displaced from their homes and land.

Downstream ecosystems are disrupted. Silt and valuable nutrients are trapped behind the dam. Fisheries are also severely depleted. Reduced silt deposits downstream means that **soil** fertility is severely reduced. Coastal erosion can also increase as a result of silt-load loss.

Large dams contribute to earthquakes because of the weight of the enormous quantities of water which build up behind them. They provide perfect habitats for a variety of parasites and insects. A further potential problem is the possibility of collapse. Most of the world's large dams have yet to stand the test of time. From 1970 to 1983, 3 major dams burst in Colombia, India and the US while Argentina, Nepal, Liberia and Mozambique recorded dam breaches during the period.

In 1996, the International Commission on Large Dams (ICOLD) reported a rise in the number of large dams under construction. In January 1994, 1,164 dams over 15 metres high were being built compared to 1,116 in 1991. Over 60% of them were in China, Turkey, Japan and South Korea. ICOLD also reported that the average height of dams was continuing to rise.

DDT (see also Agrochemicals)

Common name for *dichloro-diphenyl-trichloroethane*, an organochlorine compound which became widely used as a contact insecticide and is now regarded as the most extensively applied of all **pesticides**. It was first synthesized in the late nineteenth century but entered into wide-scale use in the 1930s. DDT works against **mosquitoes**, flies, fleas, lice and cock-

roaches specifically attacking the insects' central nervous system. It has been used widely in **malaria** eradication programmes. However, uncontrolled use has enabled many insects to develop resistance to it.

DDT is a fat-soluble, stable compound and is essentially non-biodegradable. It is highly toxic to some species of **fish** and also poses an extreme hazard to birds. It is now a common contaminant of **groundwater**. Its impact on wildlife has been disastrous mainly because of bio-accumulation. DDT builds up in the fatty tissues of all animals and its toxic effects get concentrated as it passes to animals higher up the food chain.

Due to its widespread use, DDT is present in virtually all foods and living organisms. In humans, it has been found in significant and sometimes dangerous levels in mother's milk and is particularly potent in areas where the diet is deficient in protein. In the 1960s, DDT was found to be strongly carcinogenic. It is now prohibited in many industrialized countries but continues to be used throughout the **Third World**. Even though it's banned in the US, American companies still produce about 18 million kilograms a year, most of which is shipped to developing nations.

Deadly Dangerous Toxin

Once hailed as the key to eradicating malaria, DDT is now reviled by many as a persistent poison which lingers in many foods and organisms. DDT

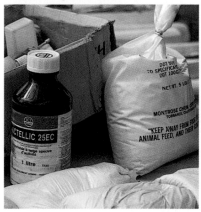

DEATH RATE

The number of deaths in a given year divided by the mid-year **population** of the country in question gives the death rate. It is used for comparative purposes and is usually multiplied by 1,000 and expressed as the 'crude death rate' (deaths per thousand population). For almost 40 years, the global death rate has continued to fall, from 16.5 per thousand in 1960 to 9.1 per thousand in 1996. As standards of living improve and health services get better, crude death rates can be expected to decrease, despite ageing populations. Oddly, Europe has shown an increasing death rate for the past 20 years, up from 10.3 in 1965 to 10.8 in 1990. The rate is highest in Africa (as a result of low life expectancy) and second highest in Europe (as a result of the high proportion of elderly people).

DEBT

The global debt crisis emerged following the **oil** shocks of 1973 and 1979 when several **developing countries** were unable to repay or service their debts. Oil-exporting countries were overflowing with money which they placed on deposit with Western banks. The banks then put the money into large prestige projects in the **Third World**. At the same time global interest rates soared as the US borrowed money to finance its huge budget deficit. A global recession coupled with weak commodity prices caused Third World debt to balloon.

At least 15 countries fell behind in **debt-service** payments, including Argentina, Bolivia, Brazil, Costa Rica, Democratic Republic of Congo (formerly Zaire), Dominican Republic, Ecuador, Honduras, Ivory Coast, Liberia, Nigeria, Panama, Peru, Tanzania and Zambia. In the case of Zambia, the nation's debt was three times as large as its **GNP**.

At the start of the 1980s, 109

developing countries owed a collective debt of $579 billion. By 1986 the total had risen to $1.02 trillion, climbing to $1.9 trillion at the end of 1994.

The **World Bank** says the rate of increase is slowing down though it forecasts a further $30 billion rise in total debt by the year 2000. Of the total, $1.24 trillion (87%) is held by countries belonging to the **Organization for Economic Co-operation and Development** (OECD), either directly or through international organizations.

The sheer size of the debt of many developing countries has become a useful lever in negotiations with donor governments and agencies who have often relaxed repayment terms in order to protect their own commercial banks. Most of the increased debt in the latter half of the 1980s was from new loans to developing countries from 'official' sources, mainly governments. This helped to offset the fall in loans from private banks and contributed to repayments on previous loans.

Official loans accounted for just 14% of the debt of 19 severely-indebted 'Upper Middle-Income' countries in 1982. But by 1988 this figure had risen to 30%. In the mid-1990s, Brazil, Mexico and China were among the worst debtor nations, each owing over $100,000 million.

Developing country debts remain at the mercy of fluctuating interest rates and export earnings. Every 1% rise in US interest rates adds about $4 billion to the debt bill. Latin America already owes $487 billion and the debt is growing at a faster rate than export earnings. Many developing countries have been forced into more borrowing simply to service their debts. However, the 'conditionality' accompanying the loans (strict measures to cut consumption and boost exports) often worsens the plight of the indebted nation.

Providing further loans to pay off debts seems an unlikely way out of

EXTERNAL DEBT – selected countries 1995
Expressed as total (million $) and as percentage of Exports of Goods and Services

Country	Total external debt (million $)	External debt as % of Exports of Goods and Services
Low-income economies		
Mozambique	5,781	1,192.5
Ethiopia	5,221	458.2
Bangladesh	16,370	298.2
Vietnam	26,370	396.0
Nigeria	35,005	274.5
China	118,090	77.3
Low-middle-income economies		
Bolivia	5,266	410.1
Indonesia	107,831	202.9
Russian Federation	120,461	126.7
Upper-middle-income economies		
Mexico	165,743	170.5
Brazil	159,130	269.8
Argentina	89,747	320.2

World Development Report 1997, World Bank.

the crisis: countries simply fall deeper into debt and enter a downward 'debt spiral'. The best way out would be to write-off some of the debt, a move proposed by the former Soviet Union and European creditor governments, led by France. Other nations try to 'reschedule' their debts.

This means they are unable to meet their payment obligations and must negotiate new terms. By 1995, some 80% of the funds owed to commercial banks were covered by 'rescheduling'.

In the years immediately following the debt crisis, repayments tended to be far larger than new loans and there was a net annual flow of money from the Third World to the developed world. In 1989, countries in Latin America, Africa and Asia paid $133 billion more to Northern creditors than they received. From 1983-1989, a surplus of $165 billion flowed from 'recipients' to 'donors'.

In 1990, the trend was reversed and the amount of money flowing into developing countries in the form of **aid**, new investment and loans, finally edged higher than the

interest charges, debt repayments and profits flowing out. But by 1994, the position had changed again and the less developed countries were paying $112 billion more than they were receiving.

Loans from multilateral banks, the World Bank and the **International Monetary Fund** (IMF) carry stricter terms than normal bank debt. The World Bank and the IMF steadfastly refuse to forgive or restructure debt, claiming it would jeopardize their 'preferred status' in capital markets and force them to raise interest rates. Their 'preferred' status means that payments to them take precedence over all other creditors.

DEBT RELIEF

Easing the burden on debtors by refinancing, rescheduling or cancelling repayments. A loan is refinanced when the creditor country makes a new loan to enable the debtor nation to meet the **debt service** payments on an earlier loan. A loan is rescheduled when the interest payments on the outstanding portion of the loan are rearranged to make payments easier.

Most of the high-profile, debt-relief initiatives, including the Baker and Brady plans (see below) have been aimed at the so-called **middle-income countries** (MICs) like Argentina, Brazil and Mexico which owe most to commercial banks.

Low-income countries whose debts tend to be with donor governments and some MICs such as Jamaica, Egypt and Ivory Coast which also owe the bulk of their debt to governments have separate arrangements. Large debts have only been forgiven when politically expedient. For example, Poland's debt was halved in 1991 to allow its pursuit of a market-based economic system. Egypt's debt was also halved in return for its support for the US-led coalition in the **Gulf War**.

The governments of Canada, Germany, the UK and the US have forgiven over $6 billion worth of loans to Sub-Saharan African countries, mostly for humanitarian and practical economic reasons. But commercial loans will need to be gradually written off too in a way which does not threaten an already rocky global banking system.

Baker Plan: Proposed in 1985 by James Baker, then Treasury Secretary of the United States. The plan was based on the willingness of commercial banks to increase lending and the provision of new, strictly-controlled loans from the **International Monetary Fund** (IMF), **World Bank** and the other regional development banks. New financial arrangements were suggested that would allow voluntary exchanges of debt for other obligations, or for equity between banks and debtor nations. The plan failed to have much of an impact, primarily because commercial bank lending continued to decline and multilateral lending stagnated.

Brady Plan: Proposed in 1989 and named after incumbent US Treasury Secretary, Nicholas Brady. It called for $70 billion in debt relief to reduce the amount owed by MICs. The World Bank and IMF agreed to provide about $13 billion each over the following 3 years to support debt reduction. Japan pledged about $4.5 billion.

The plan recommended a $29 billion debt-conversion scheme, a paltry amount considering 39 nations were potential users. If the money was used to buy back debt at the average market discount price of 36 cents per dollar, commercial debt would be reduced by a mere $80 billion: the majority of the $221 billion owed to commercial institutions would remain untouched. Furthermore, debtor nations would have to pay interest on the $29 billion. The plan also called for $30-35 billion of public money to be used to guarantee low-interest bonds that could be exchanged for commercial bank debt. This would cut the amount debtors had to pay each year by $6 billion. Public guarantees on the new bonds were meant to stimulate banks to accept a reduction in the amount they were owed.

By the end of 1990, the plan had produced savings of $22 billion for the MICs and another $5 billion worth of loans were cancelled for the poorest members of the group. Multilateral banks provided the financing for bonds needed to restructure the debt of **middle-income countries** such as Brazil, Mexico and Argentina. However, these bonds were not made available to the poorest countries. Neither the Baker Plan nor the Brady Plan appreciably reduced **Third World** debt, although they did give the commercial banks time to reduce their risk of default. The Brady Plan was significant in that it recognized that many Third World debts will never be repaid.

DEBT SERVICE
A loan repayment composed of interest and amortization. Often expressed as the ratio of debt service payments to earnings from exports of goods and services in any particular period (debt service ratio). In 1975, the collective debt service of the **Third World** amounted to 9% of export earnings. By 1985 it had climbed past 20%. By 1994, debt service was almost 3 times the value of all developing country exports. Debt service payments by **developing countries** exceeded loan disbursements from 1983 to 1989,

Banking on debt
Banks in the 1970s grew sleek on oil money; they then encouraged developing countries to borrow – and so the millstone of debt was hung around many Third World economies. DEBT

resulting in a net transfer to the **North** of $163 billion. In Africa, debt-service payments consume around 14% of export revenues, about the same as before the debt crisis began in 1982.

In Sub-Saharan Africa, debt service payments amount to $10 billion annually, about four times what the region spends on health and education. Latin America is in the worst position – 30% of Third World debt is concentrated in the region and debt service is around 30% of exports.

DEBT SWAP

Several ingenious methods to help alleviate the debt burden of **Third World** countries appeared during the 1980s, mainly making use of discounted debt. The **United Nations Children's Fund** (UNICEF) proposed a plan of Debt Relief for Child Survival. Under the plan, banks would be encouraged to turn over a portion of their high-risk loans to UNICEF in return for beneficial tax deductions. UNICEF would then assume the claim on the developing country; repayments would be made in local currency which could be used to finance

UNICEF projects in the country concerned.

In a so-called 'debt-for-nature' swap, Bolivia agreed to exchange $650,000 of its $4 billion external debt for an agreement to preserve 1.5 million hectares of forest and a 122,000 hectare wildlife reserve. The US-based Conservation International group purchased the debt from an American bank at an 85% discount and gave it to the Bolivian Government.

In return, the authorities agreed to protect the rainforest and set up a $250,000 trust (using local currency) to administer and maintain the reserve. In the world's largest 'debt-for-nature' swap the **Worldwide Fund for Nature** (WWF) agreed to pay off $5.4 million of Ecuador's $11 billion national debt. WWF was to buy the debt cheaply from a New York bank.

Three million dollars of the money saved would be used to finance projects in the Galapagos Islands, the rest would be spent on projects on mainland Ecuador. Similar deals were negotiated with Bolivia, Costa Rica, Peru, the Philippines and in Africa with Zambia and Madagascar. WWF (US) has agreed to buy $2.1 million of Madagascar's national

debt at a 55% reduction.

By 1996 Madagascar had managed to cut its $100 million commercial bank debt in half through debt-for-nature swaps. An anonymous Swiss donor provided the WWF with the funds necessary to buy $2.27 million of Zambia's debt from a group of European banks at an 80% discount. The local currency equivalent will go toward protection of elephants and rhinoceroses in Zambia.

In debt-for-equity swaps foreign investors buy up discounted Third World debt in international markets and exchange the debt with the debtor country in return for shares in local companies. Commercial banks are now taking advantage of this idea and establishing special debt-for-equity funds. Creditor banks form a company and become indirect investors, maintaining an interest in the country to which they had originally made the loan.

Three of these funds have been set up in Brazil, 2 in Chile, and 1 each in the Philippines and Venezuela. In 1990, a debt-for-equity fund was set up in Argentina with $1 billion in funding. Fourteen banks from Europe, North America and Japan were amongst the institutions buying shares. Argentinian debt is converted into shares in Argentinian companies with 3 dollars of debt exchanged for every dollar of shares acquired.

In one of the most innovative debt-swaps, the Dutch football club PSV Eindhoven acquired discounted Brazilian debt and used it to pay for the transfer of a Brazilian soccer player, Romario Farias. Despite these initiatives, between 1985 and 1992, debt swaps accounted for only about 2% of debt conversions.

DECOLONIZATION (see also Colonialism)

At the end of World War II there were about 70 independent, sovereign states. Vast tracts of Africa,

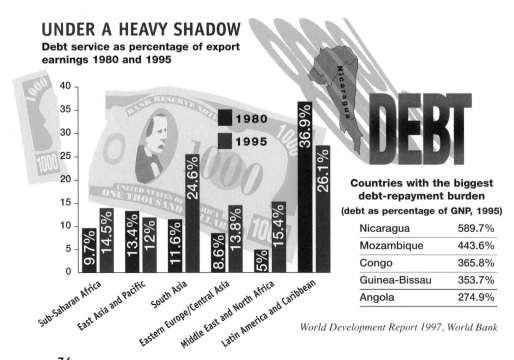

UNDER A HEAVY SHADOW
Debt service as percentage of export earnings 1980 and 1995

■ 1980
■ 1995

Sub-Saharan Africa: 9.7% / 14.5%
East Asia and Pacific: 13.4% / 12%
South Asia: 24.6% / 11.6%
Eastern Europe/Central Asia: 8.6% / 13.8%
Middle East and North Africa: 5% / 15.4%
Latin America and Caribbean: 36.9% / 26.1%

Countries with the biggest debt-repayment burden
(debt as percentage of GNP, 1995)

Nicaragua	589.7%
Mozambique	443.6%
Congo	365.8%
Guinea-Bissau	353.7%
Angola	274.9%

World Development Report 1997, World Bank

Logging off
Under Dutch colonial rule, the forests of Kalimantan (then Dutch Borneo) were just one of the resources plundered in what is now Indonesia. Indonesia shook off the colonial shackles in 1954, setting an important example for other developing countries. DECOLONIZATION

the Indian subcontinent, Asia and the Middle East were still controlled by European powers, either as colonies and protectorates or as 'mandates' from the then **League of Nations** (now United Nations). Thirty years later the age of formal European **colonialism** was over and there were more than 170 independent states.

European powers slowly abandoned their colonies partly due to the rise and spread of **nationalism** within the colonies themselves and partly as a result of increasing domestic opposition. Britain, with the largest overseas empire, began to decolonize in the late 19th century, granting independence to the countries where white Europeans were in the majority – Canada, Australia and New Zealand – and also to South Africa.

Then in 1947 the largest non-white territory, India, became independent. Colonies in Asia and Africa, the Caribbean and Oceania quickly followed suit.

In the 1960s the British Empire was effectively replaced by a multiracial **Commonwealth**. However, the independence struggle was not without violence. There were violent

clashes in Malaya, Kenya, Cyprus and Borneo where Britain fought to install pro Western governments open to foreign investment.

The French reluctantly withdrew from their colonies, following bitter disputes in Indochina and Algeria. The Netherlands, Belgium and Spain all relinquished their colonies during the 1960s. The Portuguese were the last to relax their grip, finally giving up their colonies in 1974-75 after prolonged fighting in Angola, Mozambique and Guinea-Bissau.

Despite formal political independence, many **Third World** countries continue to be politically and economically dependent on their former colonial rulers or on one of the superpowers. This situation is sometimes referred to as neo-imperialism or economic **imperialism**.

DECOMMISSIONING
(see also Nuclear Power)

A term used to describe the process of dismantling and disposing of old nuclear reactors, the full costs and dangers of which are unknown. Decommissioning involves disposing of whole nuclear plants including the reactor itself. Large

volumes of radioactive waste are produced and the problem of disposal has yet to be solved.

The **International Atomic Energy Agency** (IAEA) reported in 1990 that 143 nuclear facilities in 17 countries were at some stage of decommissioning. Moreover, 64 nuclear reactors and 256 research reactors may need decommissioning in the next few years. A typical commercial reactor produces 6,200 cubic metres of low-level nuclear waste over a 40-year lifetime. Demolishing the plant creates an additional 15,480 cubic metres.

Despite its urgent need to decommission, the UK has fallen behind in the technology needed to dismantle reactor core chambers. Japanese engineers are in the lead, having already used robotic tools to dismantle a small experimental pressurized-water reactor.

The costs of decommissioning are astronomic, if not prohibitive. It would cost an estimated $480 million to decommission a single pressurized-water reactor. In 1989, experts in the UK calculated that the costs of decommissioning and dealing with spent fuel would be in the region of $960 million per nuclear plant.

The Worldwatch Institute in the United States estimates that decommissioning costs will average $1 million per megawatt of generating capacity. No decommissioning costs were calculated during the planning and building of any nuclear reactors.

In Germany, critics point out that the estimated $100 million needed to dismantle the Karlsruhe plant could maintain it in a moth-balled state for 200 years. Britain has abandoned the idea of dismantling nuclear plants and is now considering entombing them instead.

DEFORESTATION

By 1950 more than 100 million hectares of the world's forests had been cleared but forests still covered a third of the world's **land** surface. By 1975 the amount of cleared forest had doubled to more than 200 million hectares. Each year an additional 17-18 million hectares of **tropical forests** and woodland disappear and forested land is expected to cover only a sixth of the Earth within a decade.

Today all forests, coniferous, temperate and tropical, are under threat. But it is the destruction of tropical forests which is currently having the greatest impact.

Tropical rainforests play a critical role in regulating the global climate. They cover less than 12% of the land surface of the planet but contain at least half of all species. Since 1945 over 40% of the world's rainforests have been destroyed. During the 1980s, 7.3 million hectares of tropical forest were being cleared annually for agriculture.

Another 4.6 million hectares were selectively felled each year for timber. Logging has increased in all tropical regions. However, commercial logging is directly responsible for only 20% of rainforest deforestation. The landless poor who invade the forests, burn and clear land and cultivate a plot for a short while before moving on, are the main cause of forest destruction.

The impact of their actions is global. Burning forests means there are fewer trees to suck up **carbon dioxide** (CO_2). Nearly 2 billion tonnes of CO_2 are spewed into the atmosphere each year through forest burning, increasing **global warming** in the process.

Forest cover in tropical nations like Brazil, Colombia, Indonesia, Mexico, Thailand, Ivory Coast, Nigeria, Peru and Malaysia is disappearing at an average rate of 80,000 hectares a year. Deforestation in the Brazilian Amazon increased 34% in the period 1991-94.

Yet forests play an important role in protecting watersheds, restricting

soil **erosion** and **recycling** nutrients. They are also a source of wood and food for local people and a repository of germplasm for pharmaceutical research and crop-breeding.

Third World politicians often point out that the same industrialized nations that want to save tropical rainforests destroyed their own indigenous forests decades ago. Northern temperate forests have declined by a third since pre-agricultural times. Meanwhile tropical forests which the world's conservationists are now trying to protect have declined by only 5%.

Northern governments continue to subsidize the destruction of what little remains of their own forests. The US loses $300-400 million annually by subsidizing the forestry industry. In the Tongas National Forest in Alaska, the world's largest remaining temperate rainforest, the US spent $357 million between 1982-88 building roads and providing other services to private logging operations.

Southern governments also subsidize the timber industry. In parts of Brazil and Central America, forests have been cleared for **cattle** ranching to produce beef allegedly for hamburger outlets.

The revenue from beef production covers approximately 35% of the cost of the ranches, the rest is provided by the Brazilian Government in the form of tax concessions and subsidized credit at a cost of more than $5 billion.

Critics say that the major organizations charged with saving the tropical rainforests (the International Timber Treaty Organization, the **World Bank** and the FAO) offer solutions which benefit the rich and powerful, the very people who stand to gain from the short-term, unsustainable exploitation of the forests.

In economic terms, rainforests are worth more standing than felled. A hectare of forest in Peru used for harvesting fruit and latex, together with a restricted amount of logging, was found to produce a sustainable yield of $7,000 per hectare, 7 times what would have been earned from logging alone.

BURNING AND LOOTING

The world is losing almost 10 million hectares of forest land each year, an area about the size of South Korea. This rate of destruction has remained unchecked despite international initiatives like the 1992 Earth Summit.

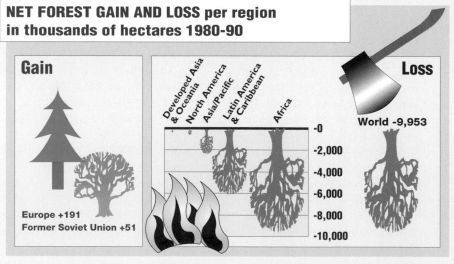

NET FOREST GAIN AND LOSS per region in thousands of hectares 1980-90

Gain: Europe +191, Former Soviet Union +51

Loss: Developed Asia & Oceania, North America, Asia/Pacific, Latin America & Caribbean, Africa. World -9,953

-0, -2,000, -4,000, -6,000, -8,000, -10,000

Forest Resources Assessement 1990; Global Synthesis, FAO, 1995.

DENGUE FEVER
(see also Mosquito)

Also known as 'Breakbone' fever. A disease of the tropics and sub-tropics, dengue fever is transmitted to humans by mosquito bites. Some 2.5 billion people are at risk of infection in more than 100 countries outside Europe. An estimated 20 million cases occur annually, of which 500,000 need to be hospitalized. The disease is characterized by painful joints, fever and an irritating rash. Symptoms begin a week or so after the bite and recur in milder form after a few days. There is no specific treatment; the disease usually runs its course in a week. It is rarely fatal but patients need lengthy convalescence.

In the haemorrhagic form, for which there is no cure, there is bleeding from the mouth and nose, excessive thirst and difficulty in breathing. There is no cross-immunity, meaning that someone who has recovered from one form is still susceptible to the other three. The haemorrhagic form most often occurs in people who have recovered and are then re-infected with one of the other viruses.

DEPENDENCY THEORY

A theory developed in the 1960s and 1970s by a group of radical economists, including André Gunder Frank and Samir Amin, to explain why the majority of **Third World** nations remain poor and underdeveloped. The core of the theory is that **colonialism** warped Third World economies so that all economic benefits flowed back to the colonial powers. Even after political independence this economic pattern remained – making Third World countries dependent on international finance and Western money markets.

The theory argues that modern foreign **aid** serves merely to reinforce this hierarchical relation-ship and maintain the dominance of Western-based **transnational corporations** in a form of economic neo-imperialism. Third World **resources** and labour are consistently undervalued and poor nations are kept in misery and systematically 'underdeveloped', to the benefit of the capitalist West.

In addition, wealthy nations reinforce Third World dependency by using their economic power and superior market position to gain unfair advantage in international trade. The theory is similar to the exploitation theory proposed by **Karl Marx** and much of the analysis has proven accurate.

DENG XIAOPING (1904-1997)

Chinese Communist leader. Deng studied in France and the Soviet Union from 1921-26 before returning to China and becoming active in politics. He participated in the 'Long March' in 1934 when the Chinese communists retreated to their new base in northwest China and he fought in the resistance army against the Japanese invasion during World War II. Following the Communist victory in the revolution of 1949 he became a Vice Premier. In 1954 he became Secretary General of the Communist Party, taking a seat on the ruling Politburo in 1955. From then on he was a major policymaker in both foreign and domestic affairs. His views on individual self-interest clashed with Chairman **Mao Zedong**. Deng believed people needed material incentives and that China needed a cadre of skilled personnel and competent managers.

During the mid-1960s he was stripped of his posts and disappeared from public life. With support from Premier Zhou Enlai, he was reinstated as Deputy Premier in 1973. Two years later he became Vice Chairman of the Party's Central Committee, a member of the Politburo and Chief of the General Staff, acting as effective head of government in the months preceding the death of Zhou Enlai in 1976. At this point he was once again purged only to be again reinstated following Mao's death later that year. In the ensuing power struggle two of his protégés became Premier and General Secretary of the Communist Party.

He then proceeded with his own reform policies – decentralizing management, building up a corps of skilled technicians and increasing individual responsibility, with material incentives as rewards. He also strengthened China's trade and cultural ties with the West and opened up foreign investment. He was China's main policy maker throughout the 1980s and remained firmly in control even though ill-health forced him to step down from the Party's Central Committee and Politburo in 1987. His leadership was put to the test in 1989 when young people began clamouring for a more democratic government. Deng's ruthless suppression of the students in Beijing's Tiananmen Square and the subsequent trials and executions of some student leaders and sympathizers forced many Western governments to rethink their relations with China.

DESALINATION

The removal of salt from brine to produce fresh **water** fit for human consumption, **irrigation**, industry and other uses. Desalination is an energy-intensive, expensive process which is used only where there is no alternative supply of fresh water. It is used to produce irrigation water in arid regions where there is sea water aplenty but little fresh water, notably in the wealthy Gulf States. Of several methods the most common is the evaporation of sea water by heat. The water vapour is then condensed to produce pure water, while the dissolved salts are left behind. A huge amount of energy is needed, hence its large-scale use only in oil-rich, water-poor desert countries.

The most promising new desalination method is a solar-powered still, which will drastically reduce the costs of power needed for evaporation. With water shortages looming everywhere, desalination may become a necessity in the future. Already some 8 million cubic metres of fresh water are produced daily from sea water. Middle Eastern countries account for 75% of the total, the US 10% and Africa and Europe 5% each.

DESERTIFICATION

The process by which arid or semi-arid land becomes desert through climatic change or human action. Removal of the top-soil layer results in a lowering of the ground's water-storage capacity and fertility, leading to crop failure.

Over-intensive farming and the destruction of trees and vegetation helped to create the 1930s 'Dust Bowl' in the US and have caused deserts in Africa and southwest Asia to spread by several kilometres a year. Traditional peasant agriculture does not usually lead to desertification and places minimal pressure on the **land**. But when peasants are forced into repeated use of marginal lands, desertification becomes unavoidable. Public awareness of desertification rose as a result of the drought in the **Sahel** from 1968-73. The 1977 UN Conference on Desertification (UNCOD) drew attention to the problem and a decade-long programme to counter desertification followed.

The **UN Environment Programme** (UNEP) claimed that desertification was causing a $26 billion loss in food production every year. Then during the late 1980s, critics from the **World Bank** and the Institute of Development Studies (IDS) in Britain charged that UNEP's figures were inaccurate. In 1977 UNEP claimed the Sahara desert was irreversibly extending southwards every year. Those figures were based on a 1975 study that concluded the Sahara had moved south 100 km between 1958 and 75.

In 1989 geographers from University College, London pointed out that the 1958 data was limited and that the 1975 figures were taken in the midst of a drought. Comparative satellite studies of the Sahara during the 1980s do not show an advancing desert and several researchers on long-term projects in the Sahel report little irreversible degradation.

When the rains return productivity recovers. During the dry years of 1982-84 the vegetation front did move south but it moved north again during 1985-87 when the rains returned. Researchers in Australia report similar cyclical findings.

Over a third of the world's land surface is semi-arid or arid. These drylands support some 850 million people and produce substantial quantities of meat, cereals and fibres.

DEVELOPED COUNTRIES

A term used to describe the northern, industrialized nations, sometimes also referred to as the 'First World'. The list of developed countries varies according to the organization which is compiling the tables. However, it almost always includes the 35 market-oriented countries of the **Organization for Economic Co-operation and Development** (OECD) as well as Bermuda, Israel and South Africa. Generally, nations having a per capita income of over $10,000 are included in the group.

DEVELOPING COUNTRIES

A loose term used to identify poor **Third World** nations, using criteria based almost exclusively on per capita income. The 172 countries in this group include states which are variously labelled as developing countries, underdeveloped countries, **low-income countries**, Majority World, the **South** or the Third World. These nations generally have low levels of technology, basic living standards and little in the way of an industrial base. Their economies are mainly agricultural and are characterized by cheap, unskilled labour and a scarcity of investment capital.

Per capita incomes are below $5,000 and often less than $1,500. Around 70% of the world's **popula-**

DESERTIFICATION

◆ More than 900 million people in the world live under the shadow of desertification and drought – usually they are among the poorest people.

◆ Since 1950, 11 per cent of the planet's vegetation (approximately 1.2 billion hectares) has suffered land degradation. About three-quarters of this damage has occured in drylands which cover one-third of the world's land area. Already 70 per cent of these drylands are degraded to some degree.

◆ Drylands are rich in genetic diversity where species have adapted. Because dryland species are adaptable to environmental stress they are a vital source of genetic material to improve crop varieties and increase their drought tolerance and disease resistance. They are also a source of valuable pharmaceutical products.

◆ It is estimated that desertification results in more than $42 billion per year in lost income.

UNSO Office to Combat Desertifiaction and Drought, UNDP.

tion live in the developing countries, almost all of which are in Africa, Asia, Oceania and Latin America. Many communities outside the major towns are poverty-stricken and **hunger**, disease and **illiteracy** are still commonplace. The **Development Assistance Committee** of the **Organization of Economic Co-operation and Development** (OECD), the **UN**, the **International Monetary Fund** (IMF) and the UN **Conference on Trade and Development** (UNCTAD) all produce listings of developing countries.

DEVELOPMENT ASSISTANCE COMMITTEE (DAC)

A specialized committee of the **Organization for Economic Co-operation and Development** (OECD), the DAC provides a forum for consultation among the OECD's 17 main donor countries and the European Commission. It aims to increase the **resources** channelled to **developing countries** by OECD members. The DAC's role is to improve, harmonize and co-ordinate the **aid** policies and programmes of its members. Around 75% of all official aid registered with the DAC is bilateral, much of it in the form of grants. DAC members are: Australia, Austria, Belgium, Canada, Denmark, Finland, France, Germany, Italy, Japan, the Netherlands, New Zealand, Norway, Sweden, Switzerland, the United Kingdom, the United States and the European Commission.

DIELDRIN
(see also Agrochemicals)

Dieldrin (and the closely related aldrin) are chlorinated hydrocarbons that have been widely used as insecticides, both in the home and outdoors. Like other synthetic chemicals, dieldrin persists in the environment and accumulates in food chains. Dieldrin has been found in rain water, ground and surface **water**, **soil** and food crops and is extremely toxic to birds, insects, **fish** and mammals. It is also carcinogenic. In 1976, dieldrin and aldrin were banned in the US. In Europe the regulations over the use of dieldrin vary enormously, ranging from a comprehensive ban in France, to voluntary restrictions in the UK and Germany. The **World Health Organization** (WHO) classifies dieldrin as 'extremely hazardous' and the **World Bank** recommends against its use. Chemical companies in Europe, particularly Belgium, continue to manufacture and export it to the **Third World**.

DIOXINS (see also Agrochemicals)

A family of 210 closely related chemicals, the most notorious of which is tetrachlorodibenzo para dioxin (TCDD). They have no industrial uses and are not deliberately manufactured. Instead they occur as contaminants in several industrial processes, most notably during the production of the herbicide 2,4,5-T. They are also formed as waste-products in industrial and waste-treatment processes.

TCDD is one of the most **toxic chemicals** ever produced. In mammals it is 70,000 times more poisonous than cyanide and it is also carcinogenic. TCDD was a contaminant in Agent Orange, a defoliant sprayed liberally during the **Vietnam War**. From 1961-1971, 18 million gallons of Agent Orange were sprayed over South Vietnam. As a result there were massive increases in birth defects, liver **cancer** and chloracne – a serious skin disease. TCDD was also found in drinking **water** in the Love Canal area in the US, the site of a massive chemical-waste dump. In several industrialized nations, buildings have been contaminated by dioxins following fires in which electrical insulating equipment containing

polychlorinated biphenyls (PCBs) has been burned. Incomplete incineration of chlorinated wastes, domestic rubbish and plastics also releases dioxins.

In 1984 the Carcinogenic Assessment Group of the US Environmental Protection Agency (EPA) labelled dioxins 'highly carcinogenic'. Meanwhile, industries responsible for the production of dioxin insist that its worst effect is the skin disease, chloracne.

DISARMAMENT
(see also Arms Control)

The Geneva Protocol of 1925 (observed by 120 nations) was the first time that methods or weapons of war were regulated in a way that was acceptable to the majority of the world's **population**. The agreement banned poison gases and bacterial agents for use in war. In 1930 the **League of Nations** (the forerunner of the **United Nations**) attempted, unsuccessfully, to reduce weapons of war. Since World War II the UN has made several attempts to introduce binding legislation to reduce weapons.

The goal has been complete disarmament, but in practice most measures have been for 'arms control'. Only three agreements: two multilateral and the third bilateral, have brought about actual dismantling and destruction of weapons. Despite 50 years of dialogue between the former USSR and the United States, it was not until 1987 that they finally agreed to destroy some nuclear weapons.

Biological Weapons Convention, 1972: A multilateral agreement recognized by 99 states that prohibits the development, production, stockpiling and use of biological agents and toxins in armed conflicts. It also calls for the total destruction of any stocks accumulated.

Elimination of Intermediate-Range Nuclear Forces Treaty, 1987 (INF): The INF Treaty bans all Soviet and American ground-launched ballistic and cruise missile systems with a maximum range of 500-5,500 kilometres and provides for their destruction over a period of 18 months to 3 years. For the first time this treaty included a process of verification acceptable to both sides, one of the major stumbling blocks to all previous attempts at arms reduction. The treaty does not include sea-launched or air-launched missiles and cuts nuclear arsenals by only 4%.

Conventional Forces in Europe Treaty, 1990 (CFE): A landmark multilateral agreement between the 16 members of the **North Atlantic Treaty Organization** (NATO) and the 6 ex-Warsaw Pact countries, covering the reduction of conventional forces in Europe. Both sides are pledged to destroy large numbers of tanks, combat aircraft and other non-nuclear weapons.

The INF treaty (also known as START I) was signed by US President **Reagan** and Russian Premier Gorbachev in 1987. A further treaty (START II) was signed by Presidents Bush and Yeltsin following the end of the **Cold War**. Three years later it was ratified by the US Congress but faced strong opposition in Russia. Once in force it will limit the number of nuclear weapons deployed to 3,500 each. Both Russia and the US continue to dismantle nuclear warheads and launchers. During the past decade, Russia has destroyed about 20,000

warheads and the US some 10,000. However, the US intends to keep a 'hedge' stockpile, warheads removed from deployment but kept in reserve, not dismantled. Russia is considering doing the same with their 12,000 warheads currently in storage. Dismantling is a lengthy and costly process: Russia can manage only 1,500 warheads per year. Still, there is scepticism about the real commitment to actual disarmament – with good reason. The US tested a nuclear device underground just a day after the Bush-Yeltsin agreement in 1992.

DISASTERS

A term used to describe accidents that cause either massive loss of life or economic damage. The **UN** defines a 'disaster' as an event that kills at least 10 people or seriously injures or affects at least 100.

The severity and frequency of global disasters has increased significantly over the past 40 years. In the 1960s, there were 16 major disasters.

In the 1970s, there were 29 and in the 1980s, 70. Over the same period economic losses from disasters jumped from $10 billion to $93 billion. From 1967-91, the major causes of death from natural disasters were droughts (1.3 million), cyclones (0.8 million), earthquakes (0.6 million) and floods (0.3 million). All these figures are likely to be significant underestimates.

The increase can be linked to a growing human **population** and the impact of human activities which help cause or worsen natural disasters. Population growth is forcing people to live and work in more dangerous places, such as low-lying flood plains or steep mountain slopes. And **deforestation**, over-grazing and **air pollution** have increased the frequency and severity of droughts and floods.

Disasters in **developing countries** inflict greater human suffering and loss than those in the rich world. From 1967-1991, 15% of global disasters were in Africa and 22% in the Americas. Yet 60% of the total

Number of natural disasters by region and type over 25 years (1970-1994)

	AFRICA	AMERICAS	ASIA	EUROPE	OCEANIA	TOTAL
Earthquake	41	135	252	165	85	678
Drought & Famine	296	53	88	16	16	469
Flood	184	382	653	154	135	1,508
Landslide	12	90	99	21	10	232
High wind	84	454	685	228	199	1,650
Volcano	9	33	46	16	6	110
Other	205	90	189	94	6	593
TOTAL	831	1,246	2,012	694	457	5,240

Numbers of people affected by natural disasters (annual average over 25 years 1970-1994)

	AFRICA	AMERICAS	ASIA	EUROPE	OCEANIA	TOTAL
Killed	76,485	8,988	55,922	2,240	94	143,728
Injured	1,017	15,180	37,288	3,475	135	57,096
Affected	11,450,827	4,481,691	111,473,882	561,580	653,580	128,621,807
Homeless	256,871	308,359	4,334,807	64,965	14,077	4,979,080
TOTAL	11,785,200	4,814,218	115,901,899	632,260	668,133	133,801,711

World Disasters Report 1997, International Federation of Red Cross and Red Crescent Societies.

deaths were in Africa and only 6% in the Americas. There is a clear reciprocal link between **poverty** and natural disasters. Poverty tends to cause disasters and disasters tend to cause or exacerbate poverty. The human impact of a disaster often starkly illustrates the gap between rich and poor.

DIVISION OF LABOUR

In modern manufacturing the production of any item may be subdivided into several tasks carried out in a repetitive fashion by many people, with none of them responsible for producing the final product. Each worker becomes highly efficient in performing a specific, limited task.

Division of labour is a way of maximizing productivity and is seen as a symbol of development and modernization. However, such a division frequently results in lack of job satisfaction: workers become bored with repetitive work and have no pride in the final product.

The **globalization** of the economy has also opened up the possibility of individual tasks being farmed out to countries with the cheapest labour or some other form of economic advantage. The **World Bank** proposes that Latin America should extend its advantages in mining and agriculture and start producing technologically-intensive goods. Meanwhile, East Asia should focus on the manufacture of labour-intensive, low-skill products while Southeast Asia is to concentrate on medium and high-technology goods. Africa's proper niche is said to be producing basic **commodities**. This will create a division of labour which will reinforce current global inequalities. The industrialized **North** will have valuable high-tech industries, countries with the cheapest labour will produce low-end consumer goods and 'less developed' economies will concen-

trate on the export of basic commodities or on **tourism**.

DOMESTIC LABOUR

Women typically work about 25% longer than men. In both rich and poor nations women usually do the work and chores involved in raising a family and running a household. Even those women working for wages usually do most of this domestic labour. They prepare and process food, carry **water**, collect fuel, grow subsistence crops and provide child care and nursing for the whole family.

In terms of national and global accounting this work is invisible. Women's work, especially household work, is unpaid and therefore not counted in official economic statistics. Yet the contribution to the national economy is significant. For example, in Nepal women directly contribute about 22% to household income. When their unwaged domestic labour is estimated their contribution to household income rises to 50%. It is estimated that the 'invisible' unpaid household work by women is equivalent to a third of total global production.

DRUG TRADE

The international drug trade is one of the largest, most profitable businesses, despite years of attempting to stamp it out. Drug trafficking generates an estimated $500 billion a year of business. The **Organization for Economic Co-operation and Development** (OECD) estimates that some $85 billion of that is laundered through financial markets. The key producer countries are in the developing world, although most of the profits end up in the industrialized countries where most of the demand lies. Burma is the leading exporter of heroin while Colombia, Peru and Bolivia are the largest suppliers of **cocaine**. Pakistan comes

Belize breeze
Hidden at the back of the exports ledger, away from the entries on 'bananas' and 'sugar cane' might be written 'Belize breeze' (marijuana) – reckoned to be the country's main money-spinner.
DRUG TRADE

first in cannabis exports. An estimated 300 tonnes of cocaine are produced annually, along with 250 tonnes of heroin and more than 25,000 tonnes of cannabis. These crops will be eliminated only if farmers are given an incentive to grow something of similar or higher value. Given the high price of drugs this is unlikely. Many millions in the developing world now depend on growing narcotics for their livelihood. In some countries the drug trade has become a pillar of the economy. In Bolivia for example, cocaine accounts for around 20% of the **Gross National Product**.

In Western nations, many people use small amounts of marijuana/cannabis and cocaine for 'recreation' as they would alcohol or **tobacco**. And in both rich and poor countries, millions of poor and desperate people use addictive drugs to try and escape from the hopelessness of **poverty** and **unemployment**. Pakistan and Thailand are thought to have 1.5 million heroin addicts between them.

One radical solution is to decriminalize drug use. This may reduce the violence and crime associated with trafficking and allow drug sales to be taxed to the benefit of everyone rather than only lining the pockets of individual drug dealers.

Endangered Species
A fine silverback gorilla in the Virunga national park, Rwanda – one of an endangered species whose survival is threatened by poachers and war in the region

THE **A** TO **Z** OF WORLD DEVELOPMENT

Bold indicates a cross-reference

EAST TIMOR

The eastern half of the island of Timor located in the Timor Sea just north of Australia. An independence movement began on the island in the early 1970s when Portugal was trying to divest itself of its few remaining colonies. When the Government in Lisbon was overthrown in 1974 a struggle in East Timor began among the Portuguese administration, Indonesians who wished to annexe the territory, and the independence movement.

In 1975 a failed coup prompted the Portuguese to leave and the Revolutionary Front for the Independence of East Timor (FRETILIN) gained control, declaring independence in November 1975. Indonesia invaded nine days later and claimed East Timor as its 27th province. Response from the international community was muted.

The Indonesian Army then began to exterminate any Timorese who opposed its rule. In 1988, the **European Union** supported East Timor's right to **self-determination** and the UN followed suit in 1989. Nevertheless, the oppression has continued. The Timorese language is not allowed in schools and thousands have been harassed, imprisoned and murdered. At a pro-independence demonstration in 1989 the Indonesian Army fired on an unarmed crowd killing 200 people and injuring many more. An estimated 20% of the nation's population have been killed so far.

In 1993, Xanana Gusmao, the East Timorese resistance leader was sentenced to life imprisonment after a trial which **Amnesty International** said was rigged. Gusmao had criticized Indonesia since the invasion. In 1996, the Nobel Prize was awarded to Bishop Carlos Belo and Jose Ramos Horta, two long-time campaigners for independence in East Timor. This was a major public relations blow to the Indonesian Government's illegal occupation of the tiny nation.

EBOLA

A deadly haemorrhagic fever. It is caused by infection from one of the new 'hot' viruses, so called because they cause virtually untreatable diseases in humans and animals. Those ill with the ebola virus have fever, vomiting and bloody diarrhoea, and others can be infected from the body fluid of patients. Ebola first appeared in Zaire (now Democratic Republic of Congo) and Sudan in 1976 and has since surfaced in Ivory Coast (1994 and 1995), Liberia (1995) and again in Zaire (1995). The number of cases in each epidemic has been relatively small, due to swift medical intervention, but the disease has a 77% fatality rate.

The natural carrier of the ebola virus and its method of transmission is unknown. In 1989, a fatal disease in laboratory monkeys imported into the US from the Philippines was linked to an ebola-like virus. And in 1995, French scientists isolated a new strain from a researcher who became infected while performing an autopsy on a chimpanzee, indicating that monkeys may well be the source of the virus. This has not been confirmed and similar conjecture surrounds the means of transfer to humans of the **HIV** (AIDS) virus.

ECOLOGY

The study of the relationship between living organisms (plants, animals and humans) and the environment, including the ways in which human activities affect wildlife populations and alter natural surroundings. Ecology is concerned with the relationship of different species to each other – and with biological, physical and chemical components of the environment (or habitat) in which they live. A community of organisms

Arms tirade
A UK poster protests the sale of British arms to Indonesia, which has occupied East Timor since 1975.
EAST TIMOR

84

and their habitat is called an ecosystem. The full effect of human intervention on the earth's ecosystems is unpredictable because these natural systems are both highly complex and interdependent. Ecologists argue that we need to proceed slowly and carefully monitor the impact of human actions on the natural world. Their warnings have been mostly ignored.

ECO-TOURISM (see also Tourism)

The World Tourist Organization estimates there will be 937 million tourists annually by the year 2010, almost double the 500 million recorded in 1993. Mass commercial **tourism** began after World War II, primarily between North America and Western Europe. When high-speed, wide-bodied aircraft appeared in the 1970s, far off locations came within easy reach of large numbers of Western tourists. With the backing of multilateral agencies and foreign investors, many **Third World** governments began to chase the tourist dollar, exploiting their 'exotic' cultures, sun, sea, and wildlife.

By the late 1980s, many Northern companies were promoting 'green', 'environmentally-friendly' holidays to the **South**. In 1991, almost 500 US tour operators were offering these kinds of holidays and eco-tourism accounted for 10% of the global tourism market.

However, 'green' tourism in most cases proved to be a sham. Costa Rica, for example, was touted as one of the top eco-tourism destinations and massive resorts were built. However, most of the investment came from foreign companies and it was they who garnered the profits.

In Belize, an 'integrated, ecologically sound resort' was built on an island rich in wildlife and Mayan artefacts without consulting the local population. Elsewhere, the sheer volume of tourists began to

ECO-TOURISTS!

BEFORE BOOKING YOUR HOLIDAY ASK YOURSELF THE FOLLOWING QUESTIONS:

 What's the environmental impact of tourism on the country I want to visit? (eg tourist hotels mean less water available for local people)

 Are people forcibly resettled to make way for tourist developments? (land clearance or local people banned from Nature Parks)

 By travelling to this country am I supporting a repressive regime?

 Are my tastes increasing demands for goods/services from the North? 'I want to eat what I can get at home'

 How much have my attitudes to a culture/society been changed by the experience of being there? ('I came to escape all of the above. Where's the beach?')

threaten the natural environment. In the Caribbean, treatment facilities were unable to cope with the increase in sewage from tourists. Untreated sewage was flushed into the sea, damaging the fragile **coral reefs** that many tourists had come to enjoy. In the Antarctic the international community has drafted 'guidelines for visitors' to minimize damage caused by the growing number of cruise ships in the region.

ECONOMIC EXCLUSION ZONES (EEZs)

Established under the Law of the Sea, EEZs allow coastal states to control an area which extends 200 nautical miles seawards from their own coastlines. Within this zone, nations exercise control over all economic activity, especially **fishing**, pollution control, scientific research and environmental preservation. International shipping has right of passage but rights over seabed mineral **resources** in the EEZs remain a matter of debate.

Ocean areas claimed under EEZ regulations total 24.5 million square nautical miles and cover 99% of living marine resources commonly exploited by world fisheries. Most of the world's major fishing grounds lie within EEZs and several small island states have benefited substantially from the introduction of the zones. As a result of EEZs, areas of 'open ocean' were reduced by approximately 30%.

The Law of the Sea has yet to be officially ratified by the requisite number of states for it to become **international law**. The US is the only nation not to recognize exclusive fishing rights within declared EEZs.

ECONOMIC GROWTH

An expansion in output of a nation's economy, traditionally measured in purely economic terms, usually determining the increase in the **Gross National Product** (GNP). Economic growth is regarded as desirable because many politicians and business leaders see it as the best way of raising the standard of living. However, drawbacks include increased pollution from greater industrial activity, depletion or despoliation of natural **resources** and environmental degradation, all of which are not taken into account at present when GNP is calculated. For comparative purposes and to allow an evaluation of improvements in living standards, economic growth is measured in per capita terms. In a developing country, the growth rate may be high while the actual rate of growth *per person* is

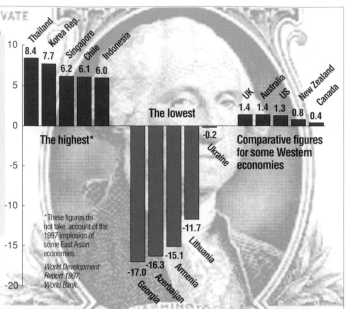

FAST GROWTH AND SHARP DECLINE

Economic growth 1985-1995, shown as average annual growth/decline in the Gross National Product (GNP) per capita.
(Selected countries)

VATE

The highest*

Thailand	Korea Rep.	Singapore	Chile	Indonesia
8.4	7.7	6.2	6.1	6.0

The lowest

Ukraine -0.2
Georgia -17.0
Azerbaijan -16.3
Armenia -15.1
Lithuania -11.7

Comparative figures for some Western economies

UK	Australia	US	New Zealand	Canada
1.4	1.4	1.3	0.8	0.4

*These figures do not take account of the 1997 implosion of some East Asian economies.
World Development Report 1997, World Bank.

much lower if the **population** is increasing at a rapid rate.

The world's economy has continued to grow since 1950. In 1995 the global economy grew by 3.7% and income per person increased by more than 2%. The robust growth of the 1990s was due to the performance of a handful of **developing countries** whose output of goods and services rose by 6%, more than double that of the industrialized countries.

The best performances were in Asia. Between 1991 and 1996 the Chinese economy grew by well over 60%, raising income per person by 50% in just 4 years. Over the same period, economic growth in Latin America more or less stagnated, mainly due to the poor performance of Mexico. Africa continued to expand, up 3% in 1995. Nearly all the East European economies expanded in 1995, while Japan completed a third year in a row with no growth.

Measured in per capita dollars, the Gross World Product rose annually from $1,487 per capita in 1950 to $3,629 per person in 1995. But this average distorts the true picture. Millions of people saw no rise in their income or standard of living and for millions of others any increased income was absorbed by **inflation** and higher prices.

Recently there have been calls to re-evaluate the concept of economic growth. In 1990 the **United Nations Development Programme** (UNDP) began producing a **Human Development Index** which takes into account social and demographic as well as economic factors.

ECONOMIC AND SOCIAL COUNCIL OF THE UNITED NATIONS (ECOSOC)

One of the main **United Nations** bodies, responsible to the General Assembly, which determines the economic and social activities of the UN. The 54-member council seeks to improve living standards and to help solve economic and social problems throughout the world – by initiating studies, preparing reports, organizing international conferences and co-ordinating the activities of specialized agencies. It has 6 commissions covering statistics, **population**, social development, **human rights**, the status of women, and narcotic drugs. There are also 5 regional economic commissions.

Economic and Social Commission for Asia and the Pacific (ESCAP): Originally launched as the Economic Commission for Asia and the Far East (ECAFE) in 1947. Activities include the establishment of regional centres for training and research purposes, the promotion of schemes and projects for regional co-operation, the distribution of information and the provision of advisory services over a wide range of subjects. It has 49 members and 10 associate members.

Economic Commission for Africa (ECA): Established in 1958 to assist in Africa's social and economic

No vote

New Zealand was the first country to give women the vote, in 1893. Now, over 100 years later, women in Kuwait are still waiting. ECOSOC

development. Activities include collecting information and research, recommending national government and inter-government action and providing advisory services. Also promotes economic and technological development in the region. It has 53 members and 2 associate members.

Economic Commission of Europe (ECE): Established in 1947 to assist in the reconstruction of Europe and to maintain European economic relations with other countries in the world. It has become a central agency for trade promotion, the exchange of technical information and research and analysis of economic development in the region. It has 54 members.

Economic Commission for Latin America & the Caribbean (ECLAC): Established in 1948, ECLAC aims to assist in the economic development of the region. Activities include the collection of information for research, recommending government and inter-regional action and co-ordination of advisory services. It was strengthened in 1962 by the creation of the Latin American Institute of Economic and Social Planning (ILPES). It has 41 members and 4 associate members.

Economic & Social Commission for Western Asia (ESCWA): Established in 1973 to initiate and participate in the process of economic reconstruction and development in the area. Aims to raise economic activity, promote trade, and maintain and strengthen the economic relations of member countries with themselves and with the outside world. It has 13 members.

EL NIÑO

A poorly-understood recurrent climatic phenomenon that affects the Pacific coast of South America but which appears to have a dramatic influence on weather patterns much farther afield. The process starts with

CLIMATE CHANGE

CLIMATE RESULTS FROM INTERACTION between the atmosphere, the oceans, the land surface, the polar ice caps and biological life (plants, animals and humans). Our climate is constantly changing, but most of the change takes place over generations and goes unnoticed. However, a sudden extraordinary event in one place can bring about rapid change all over the globe. For example:
• Dust in the atmosphere from volcanic explosions can result in cooling due to increased reflection of solar energy. A huge volcanic eruption in Indonesia in 1815 has been linked to the 1816 'year without a summer' in the eastern US and Canada.
• In 1983 El Niño, a warm ocean current off the Peruvian coast, was 7°C warmer than usual. Weather across the world was altered – including floods along the west coast of North and South America and droughts in southern Asia, Africa and Australia.

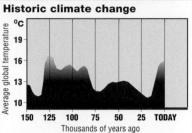

Historic climate change

a surge of warm ocean **water** in the eastern Pacific, along the coast of Peru. The effects are generally first felt in December (El Niño is used in Spanish to mean 'Christ Child').

It is not solely oceanic but couples with an atmospheric phenomenon called the Southern Oscillation. A complete cycle lasts from 3-6 years, with the most intense El Niño component lasting about a year. No two cycles are alike and 11 have been identified since 1950.

The warm phase of the most recent cycle lasted from 1990 to 1995. It is thought the phenomenon is triggered by a reduction in the trade winds in the tropical South Pacific. This slows the pushing effect on surface waters in the ocean allowing warm surface water in the eastern Pacific to accumulate.

Where warm water accumulates, the upwelling of colder water is prevented. Starved of the nutrients that the upwelling normally produces, the surface waters are impoverished. Many seabirds starve and thousands of **fish** die, dramatically affecting commercial fisheries as a result. Recent research indicates that salinity and an exchange of heat from the ocean's water to the air in a region to the north of Papua New Guinea, where El Niño is thought to originate, could also be an important factor. Salt water has a greater density than freshwater and an incoming block of salt-dense water could deflect the warm current off-track

and so trigger the El Niño effect. A wide variety of **disasters** have been blamed on El Niño, including a **famine** and fires in Indonesia, bush fires in Australia, rainstorms in California and the destruction of the anchovy fishery off the coast of Peru. Climatic changes in Central and North America and in parts of Africa are also blamed partly on El Niño

ELECTROMAGNETIC RADIATION

The world now boasts a wide range of sources emitting low-level electromagnetic radiation, including high-voltage power lines, electric blankets, microwave ovens, radar dishes, portable telephones and radios. Minute electrical currents are also generated by all living organisms – in animals they are important regulators of the central nervous system. The brain and all other organs have very low-level magnetic fields.

Deep in the brain, the pineal gland is sensitive to all magnetic fields, produced internally or externally and alters its output of neuro-hormones according to any changes. These hormones govern brain activity and glands that are responsible for controlling normal growth and other functions. The 'electromagnetic smog' created by modern-day electrical devices exposes individuals to higher radiation levels than normal and may have significant biological effects, especially the low-frequency radiation (microwaves) produced by high-voltage power lines.

A study at the US embassy in Moscow, which was receiving a regular bombardment of microwaves as part of Soviet surveillance operations, found that 40% of employees had blood cell disorders. In 1981 the **World Health Organization** (WHO) reported that exposure to microwaves can 'lead to the appearance of autonomic and central nervous system disturbances'.

Exposure to abnormal magnetic fields can also disrupt biological cycles and produce symptoms similar to chronic stress syndrome. This can lead to weight loss, a weakened immune system, decline in fertility, low-birth weight, diminished resistance to infections and serious psychological disorders.

Normal cell division is also affected, increasing the risk of **cancer**. A US study found that cancer rates are 5 times higher among children living near high-voltage electricity pylons.

The strength of magnetic fields produced by power lines depends on a variety of factors including the voltage, local topography and weather conditions. Voltages in overhead power lines vary from country to country. The US and Russia use up to 765 kilovolts (kv) while the UK uses 400 kv.

Despite using microwaves to 'bug' foreign embassies, the former Soviet Union regarded all forms of low-intensity radiation as harmful and set exposure limits 10,000 times stricter than those in the US. Legislation was also introduced specifying a one-kilometre safety corridor for all power lines.

'Pulsed' microwaves can be highly psychoactive and can cause neurological changes. As a result the US hopes to develop electromagnetic weaponry which will produce low-level microwave beams capable of immobilizing and disorienting opposing soldiers.

EMPLOYMENT

At least a third of the world's workforce is unemployed or 'underemployed' (ie working below the level of their training, abilities and needs). The right to work is a basic human right but employment opportunities in most **developing countries** have lagged well behind **population** growth. Globally, the labour force is increasing at around 2% per year. The **International Labour Office** (ILO) in Geneva suggests that 20-25% of adults in **Third World** cities are without regular work. Furthermore, the total labour force in the developing world will rise dramatically – up from 1.2 billion in 1980 to over 2 billion by the year 2000. To reach an acceptable level of employment in the Third World, more jobs will have to be created than currently exist within the entire industrialized world – an average 50 million per

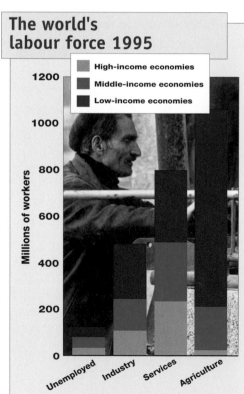

The world's labour force 1995

High-income economies
Middle-income economies
Low-income economies

Millions of workers
1200
1000
800
600
400
200
0

Unemployed   Industry   Services   Agriculture

World Development Report 1995, World Bank.

year. One of the traditional solutions to this dilemma has been for workers to move to where there is paid work. Remittances from Third World nationals working overseas doubled from 1970-82 and now stand at around $22 billion a year. Estimates for Africa and Asia show that only 10% of adults work for regular wages. The rest rely on subsistence agriculture, payment in kind or some form of bartering of goods or services in order to survive. Additionally, the role of women is often belittled or overlooked entirely. In many Third World countries women do the bulk of the agricultural work. But since the work is unpaid it is not considered 'real' work and thus rendered invisible.

In rich and poor nations alike many people are forced to work under appalling conditions, for pitifully low wages. Discrepancies in pay and working conditions may worsen over the next few decades, despite the best efforts of **trade unions** and others campaigning for equality. Around 300 years ago it took 90% of the world's work force to feed a much smaller **population**. In many **developed countries**, the number of people working on the **land** has fallen to well below 10%. The introduction of new technology and corporate 're-structuring' in the West has boosted **unemployment** and left many with unmarketable job skills.

Over the next century, hundreds of millions of people will lose their jobs as industries become more and more automated, with only jobs in the service industries likely to increase significantly. As the developed nations come to terms with a shrinking workforce, an ageing population and growing dependence on machines, a complete change in the work ethic may be necessary. Meanwhile in the **South**, countries will be facing an ever-increasing number of young people clamouring for work. Newly industrializing

THE **A** TO **Z** OF WORLD DEVELOPMENT

nations such as Brazil and Mexico may well have potentially more jobs and markets than other countries, but they will have to concentrate on labour-intensive, low-technology industries to provide jobs and decent living standards for the majority of the population.

ENDANGERED SPECIES

Any plant or animal whose survival in the wild is threatened by habitat destruction or direct harvesting of the species itself. The following categories are used by the World

Dead as a ....
When does 'endangered' become 'extinct'? It's too late to ask the North American Mastodon which bowed out centuries ago.
ENDANGERED SPECIES

Conservation Union (IUCN) and are accepted for use by international bodies such as the Convention on Trade in Endangered Species of Flora and Fauna (CITES).

Extinct Species: Not definitely located in the wild during the past 50 years.

Endangered Species: In danger of extinction, survival unlikely if situation remains unchanged.

Vulnerable Species: Likely to move into the 'endangered' category in the near future if situation remains unchanged.

Rare Species: Small populations that are not at present 'endangered' or 'vulnerable'.

Indeterminate Species: Known to

be 'endangered', 'vulnerable' or 'rare' but not enough information available to determine which category is appropriate.

Insufficiently Known Species: Suspected of belonging to one of the above categories but not definitely known due to lack of information.

Threatened: A general term used to denote species which are in any of the above categories.

The first comprehensive UN report on bio-diversity issued in 1995 estimated that the world was home to 15 million animal and plant species, of which only 1.75 million had been identified. A minimum of 5,400 animals were considered to be 'endangered'.

ENROLMENT

Over a billion young people are enrolled in formal education worldwide, compared to 300 million in the 1950s. School enrolment is increasing everywhere. The number of children in primary and secondary

education in the developing world tripled between 1960 and 1980. An estimated 545 million students are enrolled and the pace of enrolment has doubled over the last decade. Sub-Saharan Africa and South Asia alone have enrolled 33 million new students since 1990. Nonetheless there are still many millions unable to attend.

In 1995, a comparative survey of the 21 **OECD** members found that over half of the adult population had completed secondary school. The **World Bank** reported that the number of children attending school in the developing world had risen from below half in 1960 to 76% in 1995 and urged all governments to provide at least 6 years of education as a means of stimulating **economic growth**.

According to **UNESCO**, annual attendance in post secondary institutions around the world grew from 28 million in 1970 to 65 million in 1991 and was projected to reach 97 million by 2015. In the less developed countries, enrolments

The State of the World's Children 1997, UNICEF.

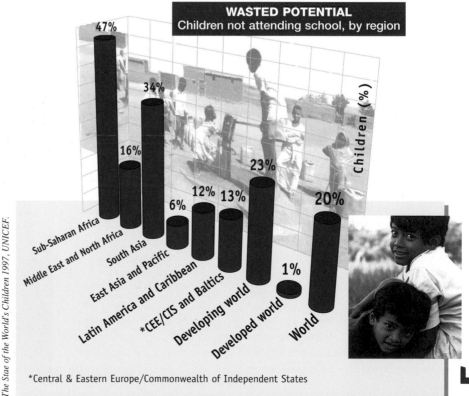

WASTED POTENTIAL
Children not attending school, by region

Children (%)

- Sub-Saharan Africa: 47%
- Middle East and North Africa: 16%
- South Asia: 34%
- East Asia and Pacific: 6%
- Latin America and Caribbean: 12%
- *CEE/CIS and Baltics: 13%
- Developing world: 23%
- Developed world: 1%
- World: 20%

*Central & Eastern Europe/Commonwealth of Independent States from 1970-1991 tripled to reach 30 million.

Meanwhile problems of language, religion, culture and cost are also influencing enrolment. In the US, one child in 6 entered school speaking a language other than English. And in Mexico 9 million children spoke only an indian dialect. Several nations began to take steps to solve this. The number of Canada's aboriginal people enrolled in higher education quadrupled from 1985-1995 due to government financial **aid** and programmes designed specifically for native people.

Despite improvements, educational opportunities for women are still significantly below those of men. In **Third World** countries, female enrolment at secondary level is only half that of men, although female enrolment increased from 225 million in 1990 to 250 million by 1996. In industrialized countries, enrolment at the primary and secondary levels is similar for men and women. But differences are marked at the tertiary level, particularly in science and technology. In countries such as Italy, Austria, Canada, the Netherlands and the United Kingdom, women account for just a third of the students in those fields.

ESPERANTO

An artificial language invented by a Polish philologist, LL Zamenhof in 1887. It was intended as a universal medium of communication and is recognized as the most successful of all artificial languages, now spoken by over 100,000 people. Zamenhof's *Fundamencio de Esperanto* (1905) lays down the basic principles of the language which has regular grammar and pronunciation in line with spelling. Esperanto is easy for Europeans to learn as its words are derived from roots commonly found in European

Niente Parlez
'Esperanto' means 'hopeful' in Esperanto and its founder, Ludwig Zamenhof, was just that when he launched his hybrid language in 1887. Today about 100,000 people can speak it. ESPERANTO

languages. More than 30,000 books have been published in Esperanto.

ESSENTIAL DRUGS

In 1977 the **World Health Organization** (WHO) launched a policy on 'Essential Drugs' (EDP) which stressed that most serious health problems could be treated using relatively few drugs. The number of prescription drugs varied wildly from country-to-country. In Norway in the late 1970s there were over 1,000 branded prescription drugs while in India there were more than 15,000. From the tens of thousands of drugs produced around the world, the WHO put together a list of 250 'essential' drugs.

The UN agency argued that adopting an Essential Drugs Policy would lead to the elimination of undesirable drugs, curb over-medication and promote the use of cheaper 'generic' drugs. Brand-name drugs usually cost considerably more than the basic, generic preparation.

In Britain, for example, doctors commonly prescribe the drug frusemide which costs up to 9 times more than the generic version. As a result the National Health system loses almost $10 million a year. However, major pharmaceutical companies oppose the Essential Drugs scheme, claiming it will severely restrict their operations and profits. The world's leading drug-producing nations (France, Germany, Italy, Japan, the UK and US) control about 75% of the global trade in drugs. They also contribute over half of the WHO's budget. As a result the agency has been handcuffed and unable to promote the EDP since it is merely an agent of its member governments. The WHO spends under $5 million on the programme each year, less than is normally spent on the promotion of a single new drug.

ETHANOL

Ethanol (*ethyl alcohol*) is produced by fermentation and is the active ingredient in alcoholic drinks.

A lot of bottle
The Chinese have become the world's leading beer drinkers, knocking back both their own brews and the imported designer brands from the West. ETHANOL

Alcohol abuse annually kills an estimated 1.3 million people worldwide usually through prolonged heavy drinking. Most die from damage to the liver, others from drink-related accidents like drunk-driving or violent crime.

Russians are the world's leading drinkers; an estimated 100,000 people there die yearly from alcohol-related illnesses. On a global scale, alcohol causes nearly 3 times as much disease and disability as **tobacco**. It also exacts a massive toll on public spending. In the United States in 1990, alcohol was responsible for $98 billion in combined medical bills and lost productivity. Global consumption of alcohol is grossly underestimated as many people brew their own. This 'home-brew' is usually more potent and dangerous than commercial products.

In many **developing countries**, women turn to brewing as a means of earning an income. Some governments like China, Mexico and the Czech Republic consider alcohol production economically beneficial and encourage it. China has become the world's leading beer drinking nation.

The relatively untapped markets in the developing world are now being targeted increasingly by the major alcohol companies. If these countries wish to avoid problems seen elsewhere, a tax on sales could be the answer. A 1988 study concluded that a 20% tax on beer in the US would cut traffic fatalities by a third and save millions of dollars in medical costs.

Ethanol also has widespread industrial uses. It can be used directly as a fuel or mixed with ordinary gasoline (petrol) to produce 'gasohol'. Many crops like corn, **rice** or **sugar** cane can be converted into ethanol. Six tonnes of corn grown on a hectare of **land** will yield about 2,200 litres of alcohol. Car engines need no modi-fication if the gasohol mixture contains less than 20% ethanol. When added to gasoline, alcohol increases the octane rating and elim-inates the need for **lead** additives. Engines running on alcohol are 18% more powerful than those running on petrol, and emissions of hydro-carbons and carbon monoxide are significantly reduced.

Gasohol is widely used in the US and in several developing countries, notably Brazil, Kenya and the Philippines. Brazil's PROALCOOL programme is the largest, producing around 11 million cubic metres of ethanol annually using **biomass** from its vast supplies of sugar cane. More than a million vehicles in the country run on pure alcohol and virtually all passenger cars run on gasohol. In 1996, price controls on alcohol and gasoline ended and the programme was put at risk. Till then gasohol had remained competitive due to heavy government subsidies. Brazil's 4.5 million cars running on gasohol are rapidly ageing and only 1% of new cars are being fitted with alcohol engines. The Brazilian Government is set to continue the programme which employs 1.3 million people, mostly sugar-cane workers. Fermenting surplus sugar could produce enough fuel to satisfy 2% of the current global market for petrol.

ETHNIC CLEANSING
(see also Genocide)
A term first used during the 1992 war in the Balkans. It describes a policy where ethnic groups are expelled from the territory in which they reside by use of force, threat or terror so that it can be exclusively occupied by the aggressor. Ethnic cleansing has occurred elsewhere, but under different names. In 1974, Turkey expelled the Greek popula-tion from the northern part of Cyprus replacing it with the Turkish population from the south. In

Death's dominion
Bitter fighting in former Yugoslavia in the early 1990s led to macabre scenes like this, where a body lies like a shadow fading into the ground.
ETHNIC CLEANSING

Rwanda from 1994-97, Hutus attempted the same with their Tutsi neighbours (see **Genocide**). In the Balkan conflict 250,000 were killed and 3 million people displaced.

EUCALYPTUS
A genus of tropical and subtropical evergreen trees containing almost 600 species, native to Australia but now widely planted elsewhere. Also known as gum trees, they are fast-growing, drought-resistant and important sources of timber and other products. The wood can be used for fuel and building and the bark for paper. All parts of the tree contain essential oils – the oil-of-eucalyptus commonly used in proprietary medicines as an inhalant comes from the leaves of the blue gum tree. In their natural habitat eucalyptus forests prosper on poor **soil**, are adapted to frequent fires and support a wide range of wildlife.

In Australia, where they are logged extensively, the timber is converted to wood chips for paper pulp. Approximately 5 million tonnes are exported to Japan annually. Commercial eucalyptus

Koala connection
Eucalyptus leaves are the staple food for koalas. But koalas are a sidebar in the commercial eucalyptus story – the trees are grown widely in the world and supply woodpulp used in rayon fibre, and medicinal oils. **EUCALYPTUS**

forests are long-term investments and are harvested every 40-80 years.

The trees absorb a great deal of **water** and can be used to reclaim marshy **land**. They are also used extensively in **reforestation** projects with 40,000 square kilometres around the world now under euca-lyptus. However, outside their natural range they can cause serious environmental damage. They are used to protect areas threatened by **desertification**. But their thirst for water inhibits the growth of other plants, depriving farmers of fodder and preventing the replenishment of **groundwater**. Eucalyptus trees also produce toxins. In areas of low rainfall when these are not flushed from the soil they destroy nutrients and the trees return less in leaf litter than they absorb through their roots.

EUROPEAN BANK FOR RECONSTRUCTION AND DEVELOPMENT (EBRD)

Following the disintegration of the Soviet Bloc, the EBRD was estab-lished to promote economic reforms and democratization in Eastern Europe and in the former-USSR itself. Sixty per cent of its loans are earmarked to **privatization** initia-tives in these countries. With headquarters in London, the Bank began operating in 1991. It has 59 members, including all 25 members of the **OECD**. The 12 member states of the **European Community**,

in conjunction with the European Investment Bank and the European Commission, own 51% of the new bank. The US, Japan and Russia are the major participating nations. The Bank's structure, aims and functions are similar to the **World Bank** which was set up to help rebuild Europe after World War II.

EUROPEAN COMMUNITY (EC)

Established in 1965, the EC (formerly EEC – European Economic Community) is an organi-zation of western European states whose purpose is to foster economic co-operation – with the eventual aim of economic and monetary union and a measure of political unity. Agreements have been reached on the removal of customs tariffs, the setting of common tariffs for non-member states and the abolition of barriers to free movement of labour, services, and capital. The organiza-tion incorporates the European **Coal** and Steel Community (ECSC), the European Atomic Energy Community (EURATOM) and the European Economic Community (EEC).

The 6 original members (Belgium, France, Germany, Luxembourg, Italy and the Netherlands) adopted a common agricultural policy in 1962

which has since undergone several revisions. These countries were joined in 1973 by Ireland, Denmark and the United Kingdom, followed by Greece (1981), then Spain and Portugal (1986). These 12, with a population of 345 million, formed the European Community. Austria applied for membership in 1989 and several newly-democratic Eastern European nations have since indicated their desire to join. Movement toward fuller European integration led to **European Union** (EU) in 1992 following the signing of the Maastricht Treaties of political and monetary union. Attempts to develop a common foreign policy have met with only limited success.

The EC has a highly developed set of rules governing trade and economic agreements with non-member countries. **Aid** to the signatories of the **Lomé Convention** and to the dependen-cies of EC member states is channelled through the European Development Fund. The EC has also been criticized for its agricultur-al policy, especially the effects on world food markets of heavily-subsi-dized food exports under the EC's controversial Common Agricultural Policy. In addition, continued pro-tectionist measures work against imports of some foods from the

Flagging spirits
Two youngsters display the European flag, each star a symbol of the 12 original member states, the circle a symbol of unity. **EUROPEAN COMMUNITY**

developing countries. At the same time, the EC has also run world-wide **food aid** programmes in cereals, dairy and other products using its surplus production.
Institutional Organization:

European Commission: The Commission, situated in Brussels, is made up of 17 members appointed by individual governments (2 each from France, Germany, Italy, Spain and the UK) and is supposedly independent of any national interest. Members are elected for a 4-year term. The Commission, whose members are duty-bound to act in the interests of the Community rather than their own nations, acts as an advisory body and is responsible for implementing policies decided by the Council of Ministers.

The individual EC governments can exert influence on the decision-making process through the Council of Ministers via the Commission, or through the Committee of Permanent Representatives which is also based in Brussels. The Commission, which is answerable to the European Parliament, meets weekly. Decisions are taken by a simple majority.

Parliament: Initially the European Parliament was merely consultative but has since assumed increasing power. Members have been directly elected since 1979. It is still not a true legislative body but has the authority to dismiss the Commission and reject the Community budget in its entirety. The full Parliament meets in Strasbourg, most specialized committees meet in Brussels and the Secretariat is sited in Luxembourg. There are 567 parliamentary seats, elected members serve 5-year terms. Socialists form the largest single political group, but they are outnumbered by the combined strength of the centre and the right. The allocation of seats per country is determined by population ratios.

Council of Ministers: Meets in Brussels and Luxembourg and is

Mountains of fat
Critics of the EC's Common Agricultural Policy, which subsidizes European famers, point to butter mountains (pictured above), wine lakes and grain mountains as the reprehensible results.
EUROPEAN COMMUNITY

composed of 1 minister from each of the member states who has responsibility for the subject under discussion. These ministers represent national interests but are supposed to reach a unanimous decision. The Council decides on Commission proposals and is the Community's principal decision making body. It passes on its decisions to the Commission. Heads of States meet twice a year in the European Council to discuss policy matters and foreign affairs.

Judiciary: The European Court of Justice, based in Luxembourg, hears disputes which fall under EC legislation. Thirteen judges rule on questions of Community law and the validity of actions taken by the Commission, the Council of Ministers and individual governments. Judgement is by majority vote and is binding on all parties. A Court of Auditors is also located in Luxembourg and reviews matters of a financial nature.

EUROPEAN FREE TRADE ASSOCIATION (EFTA)

An association founded in 1960 to promote economic development and foster **free trade** in industrial goods between its 7 member states and to lobby for liberal, non-discriminatory practices in world trade. Tariffs on non-farm trade between members was abolished in 1967. By 1973, free-trade agreements had

been negotiated between all EFTA members and the European Economic Community (EEC) and by 1984 tariff-free trade in industrial goods was achieved between all 18 members of the two groups. Individual countries are free to negotiate independent trade agreements with non-member states. EFTA's main goal was the formation of a European Economic Area (EEA) through negotiation with the **European Community**. Most members have now left to join the **European Union**. Only Iceland, Liechtenstein, Norway and Switzerland remain.

EUROPEAN MONETARY SYSTEM (EMS)

The EMS established an exchange rate mechanism (ERM) in 1979, a voluntary system of semi-fixed **exchange rates** to stabilize the currencies of member countries of the **European Community**. An earlier attempt at economic and monetary union had foundered in the mid-1970s. In the EMS the devaluation or revaluation of any country's currency requires the agreement of all the other member nations.

The system is based on the European Currency Unit ('Ecu'), which has now entered global markets in its own right. The Ecu is a weighted average of all the different currencies of the member states. In 1990, most member countries of the EC were members of the EMS, which was viewed by many as being the first step towards full monetary union within the EC and the eventual adoption of a single European currency.

The EMS opens the way to economic and monetary union. But members states first have to meet a number of stiff economic conditions. These include: a steady and low **inflation** rate; national **debt** less than 60% of **GDP** and a government deficit less than 3% of GDP; set exchange rates for at least 2 years with no currency devaluation; and long-term interest rates no more than 2 points higher than those of the 3 nations with lowest inflation.

A single currency was planned for 1999. This is now in doubt as several nations look unlikely to meet the economic requirements. Movement towards full monetary union will now be staggered.

EUROPEAN UNION (EU)

The **European Community** (EC) changed its name to the European Union (EU) in 1992 following the signing of the Treaty on European Union in Maastricht, Holland. The EU aims to co-ordinate policy among its 15 member states in 3 areas: economics, defence and home affairs. Economic policies are designed to establish a common market and common currency. Defence policies will be based on developing a 'common foreign and security policy'. Justice and home affairs policies will cover such topics as immigration, drugs, **terrorism** and improved living and working conditions.

The goal of the European Community, set out in the 1957 Treaty of Rome, was to lay the foundation for an ever-closer union between the peoples of Europe. The Single European Act of 1986 amended the Rome Treaty and established a single Community market. In 1992 the **Maastricht Treaty** extended the concept of union to include a single European currency and give broader powers to the European Parliament. In 1994, Finland, Sweden, and Austria also joined the European Union.

EUTROPHICATION

Eutrophication occurs when **water** becomes enriched with nutrients which then stimulate plant and algal growth. The process normally takes thousands of years but increased

nutrient loading as a result of human activities can cause eutrophication in a matter of years. Rains wash nitrogen-laden **fertilizers** and **phosphates** from detergents into municipal sewage systems. In addition, human and animal wastes in sewage, industrial wastes and phosphates from water-softeners all promote eutrophication. This waste water is flushed directly into rivers, streams or lakes. The increased presence of nitrogen and phosphates encourages the rapid growth of algae and plants, eliminating oxygen from the water in the process. 'Algal blooms', a common sign of eutrophication, make the water uninhabitable for **fish** and other forms of aquatic life.

Scientists have now discovered that chemically-enriched run-off also leads to eutrophication in tropical coastal seas. At first, coral flourishes from the extra nutrients. But the algae soon start to win out, the corals die and tropical reefs are threatened. The number of algal blooms or poisonous 'red tides' in coastal ecosystems has doubled over the past 20 years. These can damage fish stocks, accumulate toxins in shellfish and be deadly to humans.

Bureau de change...Wechsel...
Trade and tourism make it vital for currencies to be convertible at a more or less stable rate of exchange. EXCHANGE RATES

EXCHANGE RATES

The value of one nation's currency in terms of another's. International trade and **tourism** make it essential for currencies to be convertible at a more or less stable rate of exchange. In 1947 the **International Monetary Fund** (IMF) fixed member currencies in terms of gold at a rate which could not be changed without full IMF agreement. Exchange rates are 'fixed' when countries use specific measures, such as gold or another agreed standard, to define how much the currency is worth.

Alternatively, when supply and demand determines the value of a currency, it is said to be 'floating'.

In 1971, faced with huge deficits from spending on the **Vietnam War**, US President Richard Nixon decided to suspend the convertibility of the US dollar into gold. This led to floating exchange rates and constant fluctuations in the value of one currency against another.

The exchange rate of many **developing countries** is fixed to a major currency (mainly the US dollar) or to a basket of currencies. So the value of major currencies used in international commerce float and there is constant uncertainty about the real value of exports and imports. The aim of systems such as European Monetary Union is for countries to fix currencies in terms of each other and so limit fluctuations.

EXPANDED PROGRAMME ON IMMUNIZATION (EPI)

A programme co-ordinated by the **World Health Organization** (WHO) which attempted to vaccinate 80% of the world's children against the 6 major childhood diseases by the end of 1990.

Tetanus kills 800,000 new-born children every year and whooping cough kills 600,000 of the 5 million who contract the disease annually. A child dies from **measles** every 15

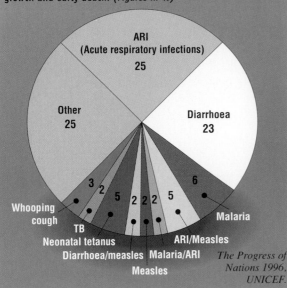

The child-killer diseases

Causes of death in children under 5, in the developing world. About half of child deaths are associated with malnutrition and it is the conspiracy between malnutrition and infection which draws many children into the downward spiral of poor growth and early death. *(Figures in %)*

ARI (Acute respiratory infections) 25

Other 25

Diarrhoea 23

3
2
5
2 2 2
5
6

Whooping cough
TB
Neonatal tetanus
Diarrhoea/measles
Measles
Malaria/ARI
ARI/Measles
Malaria

The Progress of Nations 1996, UNICEF.

seconds. **Tuberculosis** claims up to 10 million victims. And there are 270,000 cases of **polio in the world** each year – most of those in the **Third World**. All of these diseases can be prevented by vaccinations. The EPI began in 1974 when **immunization** coverage for children in the developing world was below 5%. By 1989, two-thirds of the world's children were immunized and over 2 million lives a year were being saved.

The EPI is one of the world's best-supported international programmes with institutions like **UNICEF**, the **World Bank**, **United Nations Development Programme** (UNDP), the Rockefeller Foundation, Rotary International and the Save The Children Fund all playing major roles. Nevertheless, in the early 1990s, around 46 million infants every year were still not being fully immunized against the 6 childhood killer diseases. Some 2.8 million children were dying yearly and another 3 million were disabled, yet it cost only $10 dollars per child to vaccinate them. In Africa, 19 countries were still vaccinating fewer than 50% of children for all 6 diseases. The programme now aims to provide immunization for 90% of the world's children by the year 2000.

EXPORT-LED GROWTH

An expansion of an economy partly driven by an increase of exports over imports. Exports are considered to have a positive economic impact by increasing investment which in turn leads to more manufacturing and greater **employment**.

EXPORT PROCESSING ZONES

These areas, also known as Free Trade Zones, are designated by governments for the duty-free entry of imported goods or materials. Merchandise can be stored, displayed or used for manufacturing within the zone. Goods can also be re-exported without duties being levied. Customs duties are only applied to the goods, or items manufactured from the goods or materials, when they pass into an area of the country outside the export-processing zone which is subject to the customs authority.

EXXON VALDEZ

A supertanker, laden with 1.2 million barrels of crude **oil**, which ran aground in Prince William Sound in Alaska in 1989. The ship, which was being piloted illegally, had just left Valdez, the southern terminal of the Alaska Oil Pipeline, when it spilled 267,000 barrels of oil. It was 10 hours before the first containment booms and oil-removing equipment reached the scene. The oil eventually covered 25,000 square kilometres of coastal and offshore waters and the environmental impact was devastating.

By mid-1990, 35,000 dead sea birds from 89 species had been found and these were believed to represent only 10-30% of the total killed. Some 10,000 sea otters, 16 whales and 147 bald eagles were amongst the larger animals killed by the spill. Salmon, black cod and valuable herring spawning grounds were also decimated. The massive clean-up was believed to have cost the company which owned the stricken vessel well over $2 billion. Wildlife in the region will continue to suffer the effects of the spill well into the next century. Public concern aroused by the accident has cast doubts over the further exploitation of oil and gas **resources** under the Arctic National Wildlife Refuge in Alaska. In 1993, a US

Midnight fiasco

At four minutes past midnight on 24 March 1989 the Exxon Valdez tanker ran aground in Prince William Sound, Alaska, spilling 42 million litres of oil into the sea. Some 3,840 kilometres of shoreline were oiled, and thousands of workers were involved in the clean-up. EXXON VALDEZ

federal judge in Alaska fined the oil company a record $5 billion in punitive damages. The money was used to compensate 34,000 fisher-people whose livelihoods had been damaged as a result of the spill. The company appealed against the judge's decision.

Fishing
As the dawn breaks, these fishers in Bangladesh cast their circular nets onto the water. The nets fall; the men will draw them in and take their silvery, slippery catch aboard.

Bold indicates a cross-reference

FAMILY PLANNING
(see also Contraception)

The process of deciding the number and spacing of children in a family. Hundreds of millions of women would like to be able to choose whether or not to become pregnant. In **developing countries** an estimated 100 million women (1 in every 5) want to avoid pregnancy but are not using any form of contraception and have no means of spacing or limiting births. The 45 million induced abortions around the world attest to this unmet need for family planning. If all women who wished to avoid childbirth were able to, births would fall by 27% in Africa, 33% in Asia and 35% in Latin America and the number of women who die during pregnancy or childbirth would be halved.

It could be you

'Family Planning – could it have helped us? It's for you too. Don't wait until it's too late!' entreats this poster from Burkina Faso, explaining the glum expressions of the couple. FAMILY PLANNING

FAMINE

A prolonged shortage of food which causes widespread and persistent **hunger**, starvation, ill health and a substantial increase in the **death rate**. Famines can occur when crops and food supplies are destroyed by natural causes such as droughts, floods, torrential rains, cold, hurricanes, vermin, plant disease or insect infestations. Drought is the most common cause of famine in arid and semi-arid areas.

The earliest recorded famine was in Egypt around 4,000 BC. Asia has been the region hardest hit in recent centuries. This is partly due to the huge numbers of people in China and India who work the **land** in drought- or flood-prone areas.

Famines in India have been recorded from the 14th century. The Deccan famine (1702-04) claimed 2 million lives, while an estimated 9-13 million people died during a famine in northern China from 1876-79. The **potato** blight which devastated Western Europe in the mid-1840s caused a million deaths in Ireland alone and initiated a massive migration to North America. Ironically, despite the failure of the potato crop, English landowners continued to export food from Ireland during the famine while thousands of Irish died from hunger. This illustrates the point that there is almost always food available even during the most severe famine. However, it usually goes to those who have the money to buy it, rather than those who most need it.

More recently, a famine in Ethiopia killed 1.5 million people from 1971-73. The Ethiopian famine galvanized the global community as painful images of the hungry and the dying flashed across the world's television screens. Huge cargo planes were able to despatch food from existing stocks and the scale of lives lost was significantly reduced.

Famines due to natural causes

Famine fury
Until recently India's history was scarred with devastating famines, many of the worst occurring during British rule. In this 1900 painting, some Indians are blaming the British for food shortages and deaths of friends and family. FAMINE

continue to occur – severe food shortages threatened 150 million human lives in drought-stricken Sub-Saharan Africa in the mid-1980s. But famines often have more to do with human actions than nature. Over the centuries, warfare has been the most common cause. For centuries, armies have destroyed enemy crops and blocked food supply routes. From 1967-69, Nigeria cut supply routes to Biafra, a tiny territory fighting for its independence, and over 1.5 million Biafrans died as a result. Similarly, during World War II the 3-year siege of Leningrad by the Nazis led to more than a million Russian deaths from starvation.

Human greed rather than conflict can also lead to famine. In 1943, in India, the price of **rice** was driven up by speculators even though there was only a small shortage in the overall supply. As a result the poor were priced out of the market and nearly 1.5 million people died from **hunger** and hunger-related diseases.

FANON, FRANTZ OMAR (1925-1961)

Black, French-speaking psycho-analyst and social philosopher of West Indian background. He wrote lucidly and passionately on the national liberation of colonial peoples. He joined the Algerian National Liberation Movement (FLN) in 1954 and became editor of its newspaper in 1956. In 1960 he was appointed Ambassador to Ghana by the FLN Government. He was bitterly opposed to racism and wrote *Black Skin, White Masks* in 1952. In a later work, *Wretched of the Earth* (1961), he urged blacks to purge themselves of their degradation through a 'collective catharsis' to be achieved by violence against the European oppressors.

FERTILITY RATE

An estimate of the number of children that an average woman would bear during her reproductive lifetime, assuming that age-specific fertility rates prevailing at the time of the calculation remained constant. The fertility rate has fallen steadily in recent decades. Between 1950 and 1970, women had an average of 4.7 babies. The average fell rapidly to 3.7 births by 1980, to 3.2 by 1990 and to just under 3 by the mid-1990s.

There are marked regional differences: fertility rates range from 5.3 in the **least developed countries**, to 3.2 in **developing countries** and 1.7 in industrialized nations. In Europe, women now have less than 2 children each, which is below the **population** replacement level. If this trend continues, national populations will begin to decline.

In 1996, Yemen's fertility rate of 7.6 was the highest in the world, closely followed by some nations in Africa with rates of over 7. Meanwhile, the fertility rate in the most populous countries began to stabilize. In India it stood around 3.2 and in China at 1.8 – the latter in part due to the Government's wide-ranging **birth control** policies. Kenya, which had the world's highest fertility rate during the 1980s, exhibited a sharp decline down to an average 5 children per woman. Other countries with traditionally high fertility rates were also showing marked declines. In 1995 Bangladesh reduced its fertility rate to 3.2, a huge drop from 6.4 in 1981.

Although the global fertility rate fell by more than a third over the last 30 years, the annual number of births has actually risen. It jumped 12% between 1980 and 1995, largely due to the increase in the number of women of reproductive age.

FERTILIZER

Any substance containing 20 or so chemical elements essential for plant growth that can be added to **soil** to maintain or improve soil fertility. Both nutrients and humus are needed to maintain the physical structure and overall productivity of soil. Fertilizers are essential components of most modern intensive farming systems. They may either be organic – in the form of manure, compost, bonemeal, blood or fishmeal; or inorganic – usually compounds of nitrogen, phosphorus and potassium.

Nitrogen is generally added as industrially-manufactured ammonium nitrate, **phosphates** are derived from naturally-occurring rocks and potassium is mined from potash deposits. Globally, the average consumption of fertilizers multiplied 10-fold from 1950 to 1989. From 1989 to 1995 this trend suddenly and unexpectedly reversed. Per capita use fell by 25% – from 28 kilograms per hectare to 21 kg/hectare. This drop was accompanied by a drop of 8% in per capita grain production. However it is now increasing again.

The amount of fertilizer used varies widely. In 1989, India was applying 57 kg/hectare compared

---

ARE CHILDREN BAD FOR YOU?

The theory goes that children keep you on your toes, in touch with the younger generation as you grow older. But it is also the case that too many children drain your health as well as your pocket. The fewer children you have, the longer you are likely to live. Declining fertility rates in many countries in Asia and Latin America are reflected here in increased life expectancy.

	1981		1995	
	Number of babies born to each woman	Life Expectancy at Birth (in years)	Number of babies born to each woman	Life Expectancy at Birth (in years)
Bangladesh	6.4	48	3.2	57
Morocco	6.9	57	3.4	65
El Salvador	5.6	63	3.8	67
Vietnam	5.1	63	3.7	66
Egypt	4.8	57	3.7	65
India	4.8	52	3.2	62
Brazil	4.0	64	2.8	67
Colombia	3.7	63	2.6	70

The State of the World's Children 1997 and 1998, UNICEF; World Development Report 1997, World Bank.

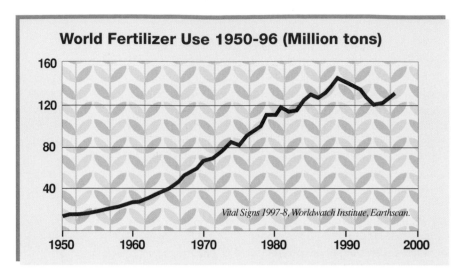

World Fertilizer Use 1950-96 (Million tons)

Vital Signs 1997-8, Worldwatch Institute, Earthscan.

to Japan's 427 kg/hectare. In Africa, an average of 32 kg/hectare was used compared with 386 kg/hectare in Europe. Only half of all fertilizer is actually used on crops. The rest runs off into streams and lakes causing **eutrophication** of surface waters and nitrate contamination of drinking water.

FIRST WORLD
(see also Third World)

A rarely used term which usually refers to the developed or industrialized countries of North America and the democratic states of Western Europe, together with Japan, New Zealand and Australia. Several traditionally neutral countries including Austria, Finland, Ireland, Sweden and Switzerland are often included in the category.

FISH

Fish have been around for 450 million years and are one of the oldest forms of life. They have been extensively hunted or cultivated by humans for nearly 5,000 years.

Of the 20,600 known freshwater and marine species, about 9,000 are currently used by humans. However, only 22 marine species are routinely harvested in quantities exceeding 100,000 tonnes per year and just 5 groups (herrings, cods, jacks, redfish and mackerels) account for half the annual catch.

Fishing provides work for over 25 million men and women and global fish exports earn well in excess of $17 billion annually. Fish are a major source of food and many industrial goods like lubricants, paints and glues are produced from fish by-products. Fish oils and fats are also used in the manufacture of margarine and soaps. Of the commercial fish catch, 20% is eaten fresh, 22% is frozen, 14% is cured and 13% is canned. Around 30% of the world catch is directly reduced to **oil**, fertilizer or fishmeal for use as a high-protein livestock feed. In total, roughly half of the world's fish catch ends up as animal feed.

In nutritional terms, fish is the primary source of protein for a billion people around the world – including half the people in Asia. Fish and fish products have a protein content of 15-20% and some fish contain more protein per gram than almost any other food. Fish also have a high content of the amino acid lysine which makes it an extremely beneficial supplement to the low-protein, high-carbohydrate diets commonly found in **developing countries**. Fish contain a variety of other nutrients too, including vitamins A, B, D, calcium, phosphorus, iron, iodine and fluorine. Fish oil has been shown to be an important factor in helping to prevent heart attacks.

Although seas and oceans cover around 70% of the world's surface, fish provide only 23% of all animal protein consumed. The place of fish in the diet varies widely around the world and the reasons for this are not just the proximity of good fishing grounds. For example per capita fish consumption in Russia is twice that of the US, because in the 1950s and 1960s the Soviets decided it would be easier to provide protein by investing in deep-sea fisheries. They were among the first to develop factory ships, exploiting all ocean stocks and causing national fish consumption to rise accordingly.

Fish is a staple of the Japanese diet because the Japanese decided to use their scarce arable **land** to grow rice and to obtain animal protein from the sea.

Taste preferences are also important in determining the role fish plays in a nation's diet. Americans for example eat over 35% of the world's tuna catch, whereas the Japanese consume around 50%

Protein packed
Fish like these, drying in stone pots in Ghana, are the protein base for one billion people in the world – including half of Asia's population. FISH

of the global squid catch. Although in general people in the **Third World** eat less fish per person than those in **developed countries**, it represents a much larger proportion of their total animal protein supply. Poor people in the developing nations tend to spend proportionately more of their household budget on fish than on all other kinds of meat.

Due mainly to over-fishing, fish consumption in the West has been falling since the early 1970s. Nevertheless, according to the **Food and Agriculture Organization** the global demand for fish will rise from 92 million tonnes in 1990 to 113 million tonnes by the year 2000 – with over half this coming from Third World countries.

FISH FARMING

Fish farming, the breeding of **fish** in a controlled environment, is the major form of **aquaculture**. In the 1980s, 10% of the fish eaten in the world, mainly carp, trout, salmon, and shellfish were raised on fish farms. Fish farming is a long-established tradition among rural populations in East Asia. In China over half the fish eaten, some 4 million tonnes, is produced on fish farms which occupy over 10 million hectares of **land**. Fish are raised alongside pigs or poultry and the animal waste is used to fertilize the fish ponds. The fish eat harmful insects, destroy weeds and improve **soil** quality, improving grain yields by up to 10% in the process. Following active promotion by international development agencies, the **Food and Agriculture Organization** (FAO) has decided to dedicate half of its fisheries budget to aquaculture. Fish farming is increasing worldwide by about 5% a year. Globally, aquaculture produced around 17 million tonnes of fish in 1994.

FISHING

Since 1950, global yields of **fish**, both marine and freshwater, have risen almost 5-fold, from 20 million tonnes in 1950 to around 100 million tonnes today – exceeding global beef production by a wide margin. In 1994, the total fish harvest was 109 million tonnes, up from 102 million tonnes in 1993.

The per capita fish harvest reached 19.3 kg in 1994, higher than 1993 but below the peak set in 1988.

However, 13 of the world's 15 major fishing grounds are now in serious decline. Throughout the 1970s the spectacular growth-rate of catches slowed dramatically due to over-fishing by high-tech factory trawlers. The productivity of many traditional marine fishing grounds plummeted and 11 key fish stocks became severely depleted. Although the overall size of catch remained more or less constant annual increases slowed to 1-2%, below the rate of population increase.

Saltwater sources provide over 80% of the world's total fish catch. In total, marine fish catches rose from 18 million tonnes in 1950 to around 84 million tonnes in the late 1980s, remaining at this figure throughout the early 1990s.

Developing countries, with extensive coastlines, accounted for just 27% of global marine fish catches in the 1950s. Today, they account for around half of all catches, thanks mainly to the effect of the 200 mile **Economic Exclusion Zones** (EEZ) which protect their fishing grounds. There are 3 main fisheries:

Deep Sea Fishing: Largely monopolized by a handful of industrial nations up to the early 1970s. Since the introduction of EEZs, developing countries have been building up fishing fleets to exploit their fisheries potential. Licensing has been introduced allowing industrialized nations to fish in **Third World** EEZs, bringing in much needed foreign exchange. However, several poor nations are faced with the problem of how to stop poaching. Mauritania has an EEZ of around 130,000 square kilometres containing what is regarded as one of the richest fishing grounds in the world. In 1981, 120,000 tonnes of fish were 'officially' caught in the area, while the actual total catch was estimated at

nearer 1.25 million tonnes.

Artisanal fishing: Mostly in freshwater and off-shore coastal marine fishing grounds by small family-owned boats. In 1982, approximately 25% of the total world fish catch was contributed by artisanal fisherfolk. Small-scale fishing is of prime importance in

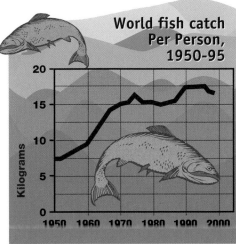

World fish catch Per Person, 1950-95

Vita Signs 1997-1998, Worldwatch Institute, Earthscan.

developing countries, supplying at least three-quarters of domestic demand. In the 1980s, artisanal fish catches represented two-thirds of the total catch in Asia and 85% of the African catch. Catches of freshwater fish rose from 2.2 million tonnes in 1950 to over 13 million tonnes by 1989, then declined to 6.6 million tonnes by the mid-1990s.

Aquaculture: Fish **farming** has been growing in importance over the past decade or so but still accounts for only 10% of the total global fish catch. It is an especially important source of protein in China, India and other Asian countries where millions of tonnes of fish, shellfish and prawns are produced annually. In most developing countries the water temperature is ideal for aquaculture and the **UN Food and Agriculture Organization** estimates that yields from fish farming could be raised to around 40 million tonnes per year. However, critics say marine aquaculture benefits Third World élites, damages delicate coastal habitats and

Fertilizer – Fishing

risks diluting the genetic strength of wild fish stocks.

The maximum sustainable yield from the oceans of 'conventional' fish (excluding squid and octopus) is estimated at about 100 million tonnes. As with all forms of food production, there is a serious problem of waste. A significant portion of all fish is inedible and around 40% is wasted.

Commercial fishing is also notoriously wasteful. Trawlers and especially shrimp-boats throw overboard an estimated 10 million tonnes of unwanted fish, many of which do not survive. Shrimp fishers in the Gulf of Mexico lose 80% of their catch through killing, damaging, or discarding fish. Post-harvest losses are also enormous. Some 10-40% of catches are lost, mainly due to spoilage.

The global fishery is in the grip of a serious crisis: protests, disputes and violent confrontations have been commonplace since the early 1990s. Spanish trawlers have been seized by Canadian Government vessels in Canadian waters.

Iceland and Norway have fought over fish in the Barents Sea and Arctic waters. Members of the European Union stage continual fights over fishing quotas. And millions of Indian fisherpeople have protested against proposed joint ventures with fleets from other countries.

FOOD AID (see also Aid)

The gap between food needs and aid deliveries from donor nations widened in 1995. During the year, poor countries required 14 million tonnes of food aid, an increase of 12% over 1994.

The UN Food and Agriculture Organization reported that 36 million people faced severe food shortages during 1995, with more than 23 million of them in Sub-Saharan Africa. Many more faced

Who's helping whom?
'Donated by the People of the United States of America' proclaims the can of soybean salad oil. No doubt the People's beneficence is gratefully received by recipients like this man in Guatemala. Or is it? FOOD AID

scarce and uncertain food supplies – including North Korea, the former Soviet republics, Bosnia-Herzegovina and parts of Central America. Despite the demand, food aid shipments fell by a third in 1995, mostly as a result of cut-backs by the United States. Total food aid commitments were the lowest since the mid-1970s and fell well below the minimum target of 10 million tonnes established by the World Food Conference in 1974.

Food aid is not necessarily positive. It can depress food prices in local markets and be a disincentive to farmers. In addition, countries can produce a food surplus and still require food aid if production is geared to exports.

Even though the 1995 harvest in Ethiopia was average, the country still needed over a million tonnes of food aid. Moreover, much food aid is in the form of wheat.

Introducing this grain into countries where it is not a staple can change taste preferences and force farmers to grow a crop which is inappropriate or unsuited to the environment. From 1993-96, the international budget for food aid was halved and the amount of available grain dropped to 7.6 million tonnes.

FOOD AND AGRICULTURE ORGANIZATION (FAO)

Founded in 1945, the FAO is the largest of the specialized agencies of the UN with a membership of 170 countries (plus 1 associate member). Its aims are to increase the efficiency of the production and distribution of all food and agricultural products, to improve the condition of rural populations and to raise levels of nutrition in the developing countries. The FAO collects, analyses and disseminates information, advises governments on policy and planning and provides opportunities for governments to meet and discuss food and agriculture problems. It carries out a major programme of technical advice and assistance predominantly in the developing world giving direct, practical help on behalf of governments and development funding agencies. By 1989, more than $33 billion had been channelled to more than 100 developing countries.

The FAO's governing Conference, composed of all member nations, meets every 2 years and elects a Council of 49 member nations which serve 3-year rotating terms. The Council oversees the day-to-day running of the organization, working together with the Director-General who is head of the Secretariat based in Rome. The constitution allows all member countries to have an equal say in determining the FAO's programme and activities. Funding comes from contributions by member nations, from Trust Funds set up by member countries and from the United Nations Development Programme (UNDP).

FOOD IRRADIATION

Ionizing radiation can alter the chemical structure of biological material and may be used to preserve food. The chemical alterations allow food, especially fresh fruit, vegetables and other perishable produce, to be kept for a much longer time than ordinary preservation methods.

Only low-energy ionizing radiation is used. Provided the irradiation is properly controlled, food should not become radioactive though it is possible that some trace metal compounds in the food could do so. Bacteria are less sensitive to radiation than people so the dose needed to kill them is much higher. As a result there is a health risk for people who work in irradiation factories.

Irradiation allows food that has been contaminated or spoiled to be made fit for human consumption. The opportunities for taking advantage of unwary consumers that this offers upsets many opponents of irradiation. They also claim that the appearance, feel, texture taste and smell of food is altered as a result of irradiation. Milk and fatty foods are particularly susceptible to change. Radiation also damages at least 6 vitamins, especially A, C, D, E and K. Toxins and hazardous chemicals may also be produced in the food as a result of irradiation. For example, aflatoxins (carcinogenic chemicals produced by moulds) were found to be stimulated by irradiation at approved dose levels.

FOUR TIGERS

A name given to the Asian nations of Hong Kong, South Korea, Singapore and Taiwan, all of which have experienced extraordinary economic growth over the past few decades, coupled with remarkable increases in living standards. Their success has been held up as a model for other Third World economies. However, critics note that each of these countries is a special case and that similar conditions do not exist elsewhere. Hong Kong was, until 1997, a colony of the UK, and the economic progress of the other 3 Tigers was achieved by restricting labour rights and imposing rigid

authoritarian political regimes. South Korea's economic collapse in 1997 called the whole Tiger model into question.

FREE TRADE

Trade between countries which is theoretically free of legal or other restrictions that may interfere with its flow. International trade, free of all tariffs or quotas, was first proposed in Britain in 1846. According to orthodox economic theory, free trade allows nations to specialize in those commodities which can be produced most efficiently, so world production is maximized. The idea was revived in 1947 with the General Agreement on Tariffs and Trade (GATT).

However, the unrestricted free flow of goods and services has always been a chimera. In the 1980s the global recession led to protectionist measures to discourage foreign imports by pricing them out of the market. Some economists argue that free trade between developed and developing nations is impossible. Others claim that government intervention is necessary to protect domestic producers.

Nonetheless, over the past two decades, 'free trade areas' have been established in which states, usually neighbouring countries, enter into a common agreement to remove all tariffs, quotas and other regulatory trade barriers. Each state usually retains the right to trade with non-member states on their own terms.

FREIRE, PAULO (1921-1997)
Brazilian educator. Born into a poor family, Freire was awarded a scholarship which allowed him to complete his schooling and attend the University of Recife. In 1958 he began working to improve literacy rates among impoverished sugar-cane cutters. During this time he developed revolutionary ideas about using literacy programmes to help the poor understand and take control of their own lives. He believed that culture was used as an instrument of oppression through which the elites could impose their values on the uneducated masses.

He began to design literacy programmes with the participants' own day-to-day living experiences in mind. Freire used literacy teaching as part of a process of 'conscientization' through which the poor gained a new awareness of society, their role in it and their power to transform it. His ideas were embraced by radical Catholics in Brazil who were beginning to set up Christian 'base' communities across the country. In 1961 a left-wing government was elected in Brazil which supported Freire's approach. In 1963 his literacy teams worked all across Brazil in a national literacy project aimed at making 5 million people both literate and politically aware. Then in 1964, a military coup toppled the Government and Freire was jailed. He later went into exile in Bolivia and Chile. Five years later he accepted an invitation to become visiting professor at Harvard in the US, where he wrote his best-known work Pedagogy of the Oppressed.

Many governments in Africa, Asia and Latin America tried to implement Freireian literacy programmes, with varying degrees of success. In 1979, he returned to Brazil where he founded the Workers' Party and was elected to municipal government in São Paulo in 1988. He resigned 3 years later but his work continued. Freire's approach to literacy training and adult education has had a major impact on a global scale.

However, even in the longest-surviving of these areas, such as the **European Free Trade Association (EFTA)**, governments have become adept at using non-tariff barriers to subvert free trade when it becomes politically necessary.

A Free Trade Area is where a number of countries have entered into reciprocal **free trade** agreements within which most goods can be traded free of quotas and customs duties or reduced tariffs.

FRELIMO

The **Frente de Liberação de Moçambique** (Mozambique Liberation Front). A political and military movement formed to gain independence for Mozambique from its colonial ruler, Portugal. Established in Tanzania in 1962 by Mozambican exiles, Frelimo was originally headed by Eduardo Mondlane. His **guerrilla** army of several thousand soldiers began their campaign in northern Mozambique with support from both the Soviet

Freedom fighter
In 1967 the Women's Detachment of Mozambique's Frelimo liberation movement was born. Women received military training and fought against the Portuguese colonialists. FRELIMO

Bloc and Western governments. Mondlane was assassinated in 1969 and was succeeded by Samora Machel, a military man who extended Frelimo's activities deeper into Mozambique. Following the

military coup in Portugal in 1974, Mozambique was granted independence and Machel became the head of government in 1975. Frelimo subsequently became a Marxist-Leninist party and tried to rebuild the nation's shattered economy. The Government's efforts were hampered by peasant resistance to collective agriculture but even more so by the disruptive activities of the South African-backed Renamo dissidents.

FUELWOOD

Two billion people who live mainly in poor rural communities rely on wood for their primary source of energy. Of these, 70% do not have access to secure supplies. It is estimated that 2.7 billion people (half the population of the developing world) will be unable soon to satisfy their fuelwood needs. In parts of Africa, Asia, and Latin America the annual average consumption of wood is 1 tonne per person. Over 1.7 billion cubic metres (m³) of wood are burned each year in the

FRIEDMAN, MILTON (1912-   )

American economist. He graduated from Columbia University with a doctorate in economics and joined the University of Chicago. He soon became a leading advocate of **monetarism**, claiming that the business cycle is determined mainly by money supply and interest rates, not by the fiscal policy of the government.

In 1962 he published *Capitalism and Freedom* in which he proposed a negative income tax or guaranteed income to replace centralized, social welfare services which were too bureaucratic and which, to his mind, were harmful to the traditional values of individualism and work.

Friedman's monetarist doctrine became a dominant economic theory from the 1970s on. His followers, known as the 'Chicago School', were an important influence on conservative economic policies in both the US and Britain. Under the military regime in Chile after the 1973 coup, Friedman's acolytes were a major force in the radical restructuring of the Chilean economy.

He is regarded as one of the leading *laissez-faire*, conservative economists of the 20th century and was awarded the Nobel Prize for economics in 1976.

THE **A** TO **Z** OF WORLD DEVELOPMENT

developing countries. The largest fuelwood user is India (222 million m³), followed by China (171 million m³) and Brazil (168 million m³).

Those who rely on fuelwood use an average of only 3 kilogrammes per day but still supply cannot meet demand. This fuelwood crisis is caused by an increasing **population** coupled with the degradation of woodlands by commercial forestry operations and the clearing of forests for **plantations** and **cattle** ranching.

The situation is most acute in Sub-Saharan Africa where fuelwood accounts for 80% of the total energy consumed. Due to over-exploitation and recurrent droughts, wood is in short and rapidly diminishing supply. The result is that women in rural communities now may have to spend a whole day collecting wood, venturing further and further afield in order to satisfy their needs. In towns and cities, people are spending up to a third of their income on firewood.

In the arid and semi-arid areas of Africa, Asia and the mountainous areas of Latin America, collecting fuelwood can take 100 300 days a year and may use up 25% of an urban family's income. Despite its widespread use, fuelwood is a major health hazard. Between 300-400 million people suffer from respiratory diseases caused by breathing smoke from wood fires.

FUNDAMENTALISM

A mind set that can affect almost any belief system. It is not confined to religious beliefs but encompasses secular forms too. Any obsessive pre-occupation with a single explanation of the cosmos or a single 'answer' to the problems of society can slip easily into fundamentalist belief.

Fundamentalists venerate the authority and wisdom of the past. They use the vocabulary of revolution but hark back to a mythical golden age that must be recovered in order to set things right. Fundamentalism is not the same as extreme opinion. Movements of religious revival and social orthodoxy have erupted throughout human history. But they usually arise in defence of an existing and unquestioned truth rather than as deeply-estranged reactions to an era where no-one knows what to believe any more. Fundamentalism reasserts an old truth as the answer to modern doubt. It is thus a by-product of the modern age.

FUTURES MARKET

Trade in **commodities** (from soybeans to sow bellies) takes place in three related kinds of markets: the spot market, the forward market and the futures market. Futures markets are especially common for commodities whose prices are volatile and for which the link between future price and supply is uncertain. They are organized for the purchase and sale of enforceable contracts to deliver a commodity such as **wheat**, **cotton** or gold (or a financial instrument like treasury bills) at some future date for a specified price. These 'futures' are bought and sold by auction. The seller does not normally intend to deliver the commodity, nor does the buyer intend to accept delivery. Each will at some future point cancel the obligation by an offsetting purchase or sale. They simply wish to engage in risk-taking, hoping to make a profit from the fluctuating prices.

Futures markets are thus ancillary to the markets where commodities are actually bought and sold. They were originally set up to provide insurance to growers against the risk of price changes by passing that risk to speculators. In fact there is now concern that speculators artificially distort the market and determine the prices at which commodities are traded, avoiding the classic laws of supply and demand. The world's largest futures exchange is the Chicago Board of Trade.

MARKET MADNESS

'Futures' markets are intended to secure the price of commodities in advance. In practice they are highly speculative. Prices can move very quickly, partly because of the huge amounts of money involved. Such short-term fluctuations make it difficult to plan, invest in, or earn a reliable living from coffee production.

On the London Commodity Exchange during 1994 a tonne of Robusta coffee-bean 'futures' for delivery in January 1995 would have cost you:

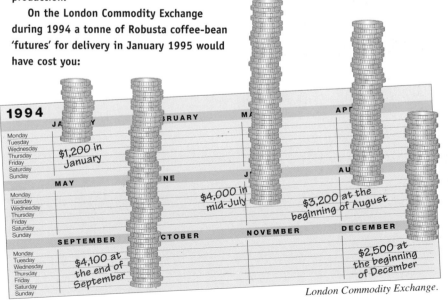

$1,200 in January

$4,000 in mid-July

$3,200 at the beginning of August

$4,100 at the end of September

$2,500 at the beginning of December

London Commodity Exchange.

Free Trade – Futures Market

Ganges

In Varanasi, India, the *ghats* (steps) of the holy river Ganges are washed with colour as Hindu pilgrims make their way into - and onto - the waters. From dawn to dusk on a single day, as many as 30,000 people may visit this sacred site.

G

Bold indicates a cross-reference

G7/G8

A label used to describe the 7 governments of the wealthiest, most industrialized nations, plus Russia, that attend the annual Western Economic Summit. The Summit was set up in 1975 as an emergency response to the decision by the **Organization of Petroleum Exporting Countries** (OPEC) to increase **oil** prices. It discusses all forms of economic problems. Nations attending are the United States, Canada, Japan, the United Kingdom, France, Germany, Italy (and Russia). The **European Community** also sends a representative.

G10

Also known as the **Paris Club**. A group consisting of the wealthiest members of the **International Monetary Fund** (IMF) who act as an informal steering committee for the Fund. The 10 original members are Belgium, Canada, France, Germany, Italy, Japan, Netherlands, Sweden, the United Kingdom and the United States. Switzerland became the eleventh member in 1984.

G15

A term used to describe a group of 15 developing nations that gather to discuss development and **Third World** issues. The group was formed at the Non-Aligned Summit meeting in 1990. Member states promote South-South co-operation and develop a common strategy towards the **North**, acting as the main political organ for the **Non-Aligned Movement**. Members are: Algeria, Argentina, Brazil, Chile, Egypt, India, Indonesia, Jamaica, Malaysia, Mexico, Nigeria, Peru, Senegal, Venezuela and Zimbabwe. A three-nation steering committee of Malaysia, Senegal and Venezuela (one representative from each of the continents in the South), guides and stimulates the activities of the group.

G77

Began as the 'Caucus of 75', a group of **developing countries** which first met at the **UN Conference on Trade and Development** (UNCTAD) in 1964. The organization was formed to express a unified **Third World** position on global economics and development affairs. It eventually issued a joint declaration supported by 77 developing countries. There are now 128 countries and its membership overlaps considerably with the **Non-Aligned Movement**. The G77 argues its case at the UN and attempts to pressure the developed world to provide further **aid** and other assistance to the Third World. The Group of 77 was the forerunner of 2 similar groups: **G8** (the industrialized countries) and **G15** (mainly semi-industrialized nations), all of which meet to discuss global economic issues and promote the interests of their member states.

GALBRAITH, JOHN KENNETH (1908-)

Canadian-born economist who has spent most of his working life in the US. Galbraith was a brilliant scholar and obtained his doctorate in 1934. He then taught at Princeton and Harvard universities until World War II. Following duties in various government posts he resumed teaching at Harvard, establishing himself as a politically active, liberal-minded academic with good communications skills. He held his post at Harvard from 1949-75. He was also a key adviser to President John F Kennedy and from 1961-63 served as US ambassador to India.

He became known for his finely-crafted, witty writing and his people-centred economics. His first major work was *American Capitalism: The Concept of Countervailing Power* (1951) in which he questioned the goal of competition in industrial society. In *Affluent Society* (1958) he called for less emphasis on production and more support for social welfare and public services. He was a stinging critic of uncaring corporations and unwieldy bureaucracies and was adamant about the need to reign in the power of big business. In his later works he drew parallels between the rigidity of centrally-planned economies and the anti-democratic nature of what he called 'managerial' capitalism.

GAIA

Gaia was the name given to the Earth in ancient Greek mythology, the mother goddess who sprang from primordial chaos. The Gaia Principle is a theory, proposed by British scientist James Lovelock, that the **biosphere** is a 'super-organism'. He argues that the earth, like all living organisms and systems, is capable of self-regulation. Stimulated by the possibility of life on other planets Lovelock suggests that our planet is in a sense 'alive' and capable of manipulating conditions to suit its own needs. The Gaia Principle regards the biological and geological aspects of the earth and

GANDHI, INDIRA (1917-1984)

Indian politician. A daughter of **Jawaharlal Nehru**, independent India's first Prime Minister, Gandhi entered politics as a young woman and rose to become leader of the Congress Party. She served two terms as Prime Minister (1966-77 and 1980-84) and had two sons, Sanjay and Rajiv, both of whom also became active in politics. In 1975 she was accused of electoral malpractices and was threatened with the loss of her seat in parliament. She responded by creating a state of emergency and imposing strict authoritarian government. Her social and economic programme was devised by her son Sanjay and included a ruthless **family planning** policy which contributed significantly to her electoral defeat in 1977. Sanjay also played a role in masterminding her return to power in 1980, but he was killed in a plane crash the same year. Indira Gandhi was assassinated in 1984 by a Sikh bodyguard, following her use of soldiers to clear malcontents from the Sikh Golden Temple at Amritsar. She was succeeded as Prime Minister by her other son, Rajiv.

GANDHI, MOHANDAS MAHATMA (1869-1948)

Indian activist and philosopher, leader of the nationalist movement which led India to independence from the United Kingdom in 1947. Also known as the 'Mahatma' (Great Soul). Gandhi studied in England and in 1893 moved to South Africa to practice law. He became famous for championing the rights of the Indian community. He believed that individuals had the right to practice civil disobedience in the face of unjust laws. Gandhi's political philosophy had a religious basic, reflecting the Hindu and Buddhist conceptions of human destiny.

He returned to India in 1914 and became leader of the Indian National Congress and a key figure in the struggle against British rule. His policy of non-cooperation with civil authorities began in 1919 and was then extended into civil disobedience. Following 3 years of imprisonment Gandhi withdrew from politics in 1924 and travelled around India. He campaigned on behalf of India's lowest caste, the 'untouchables' and promoted indigenous craft industries, endearing himself to the majority of the population in the process.

In 1927 he returned to politics and 3 years later made his famous walk from Ahmedabad to the sea, where he distilled salt from sea water in protest against the government's salt monopoly. In 1932, he began his first 'fast unto death' to protest against the government's attitude towards untouchables. In 1942 Gandhi asked that Britain withdraw from India immediately and was jailed. He was released in 1944 and took part in independence discussions.

Although initially opposed to partition, he finally accepted the establishment of Pakistan. He was appalled by the Hindu/Muslim conflicts that followed and started another fast hoping to stop the carnage. His policy of non-violence and pleas for friendship between Muslims and Hindus enraged many religious zealots and he was finally assassinated by a Hindu fanatic. Although Gandhi was never a member of the Indian Cabinet, he is regarded by many as the most influential of all Indian leaders.

its atmosphere as a single, interacting system. The system has a built-in ability to create the environment that most favours its own stability – and to maintain it in the face of pollution and other forms of environmental change or stress. Lovelock also notes that for the first time in history the speed of change being forced on the earth by human action may threaten the future of humankind.

GANGES

The River Ganges rises in the Himalayas in Nepal and northern India and flows 2,700 kilometres into the Bay of Bengal through the world's largest delta in Bangladesh. Boasting a highly seasonal **water** flow, the river is used to irrigate the Ganges plain, which contains several of India's major cities and which forms the world's second largest agricultural area, after China's Yangtze Valley. The Ganges supports a farming industry that sustains well over 300 million people. The river is also a major conduit for pollution – at least 114 major towns and cities discharge raw sewage into it.

The Ganges is sacred to India's Hindus who seek to bathe in its waters and be cremated on its banks. Today many cadavers are thrown directly into the river as the rising cost of firewood takes cremation beyond the price of most. **Deforestation** in the Himalayas and along the river's banks has accelerated topsoil loss and boosted siltation levels in the Ganges, causing regular, severe flooding in the low-lying Bangladesh delta.

In 1978, for example, flooding caused $2 billion worth of damage in India and hundreds of people lost their lives. India's control of the river's flow, most notably the construction of a **dam** at Farakka, has caused bitter controversy with neighbouring Bangladesh. So much water is now diverted from the river that during the dry season only a trickle reaches the Ganges' natural outlet in the Bay of Bengal. The decrease in fresh water has caused a rapid advance of salty sea water across the western portion of the delta in Bangladesh, damaging precious **mangrove** forests and the local economy. In 1966 India and Bangladesh agreed to share the waters of the Ganges with each country guaranteed at least 900 cubic metres of water per second during the driest 6 weeks of the year.

GANJA

Another name for marijuana or cannabis. Ganja is a non-addictive drug derived from the hemp plant (*cannabis sativa*). It is usually smoked in the form of dried leaves and flowers but can also be sniffed or taken in food. It is mainly valued for the mild euphoria it produces, although it also enhances awareness and improves memory. Other effects include loss of muscular co-ordination, increased heart rate, drowsiness and hallucination.

Marijuana has been the subject of much medical and social debate. Its use is still widely prohibited, although several countries in Europe began to ease restrictions in the late 1980s. In the medical field, it is considered to be beneficial in the treatment of glaucoma. Mexico is the world's leading producer.

GAY LIBERATION

Also referred to as the 'Gay Rights' or 'Homosexual Rights' movement. A civil rights movement that seeks to eliminate laws barring homosexual acts between consenting adults and that calls for an end to discrimination against homosexuals in any shape or form. The ultimate goal is to encourage society to accept homosexuality.

There were virtually no efforts to promote homosexual rights up until

GELDOF, BOB (1954-   )

Irish rock musician with the 'Boomtown Rats' group. He was the inspiration and driving force behind **Band Aid** and Live Aid (1984-86) and an abrasive and vigorous campaigner for improvements in the way **aid** is given to **developing countries**. Band Aid produced a record and Live Aid featured two concerts, one in London and one in New York, performed on the same day and broadcast one after the other to the world's largest ever television audience.

Both were charity events raising huge sums of money for **famine** prevention and relief, especially in Ethiopia. The Band Aid record raised $11 million and the Live Aid concert brought in a further $27 million. Several other similar fund-raising events, arranged by musicians, sports people and professionals from a variety of fields were initiated following Band Aid. Although an Irish citizen, Geldof was appointed a Knight Commander of the British Empire in 1988 for his efforts to improve living standards in the developing world.

the beginning of the 20th century. In 1933, the German-based World League of Sexual Reform was stifled by Hitler's rise to power. In the US, the Mattachine Society was formed in 1950 in Los Angeles. The Daughters of Bilitis, founded in San Francisco in 1955, was the first organization for lesbians. In Europe the Culture and Recreation Centre (CRC) founded in Amsterdam in 1966 has become a major international centre for gay activism.

Militant gay activism first appeared in 1969, following a clash between gays and police at the Stonewall Inn, a gay bar in New York City. That protest led to a proliferation of gay rights movements and the June date of the riot is commemorated yearly by Gay Pride

Week in the US and elsewhere.

Opposition to homosexual activity is greatest in countries where Roman Catholicism is the predominant religion, such as Ireland or Austria, or in Latin American countries like Mexico where 'machismo' is widespread. In Europe and North America gay rights are becoming more accepted. In 1961, Illinois became the first US state to repeal laws prohibiting sexual acts between consenting adults. By the mid-1990s, legislation had been passed in several countries to legalize homosexual marriages and domestic partnerships, bestowing many of the rights and responsibilities accorded to conventional marriages. Over the past 2 decades, the gay rights movement has become even more

Glad to be Gay

'I can't even march straight!' - the humorous T-shirt slogan matches the light-hearted mood of this gay pride march in South Africa. GAY LIBERATION

visible by fighting for increased research into **AIDS** which has disproportionately struck gay communities around the world.

GENDER

Feminists distinguish between sex and gender. They draw attention to the fact that masculine and feminine genders are shaped by society and culture, whereas the male and female sexes are biological facts. Individuals can theoretically choose to change their gender. Many feminists don't argue for women's rights in a man-made world. Instead they say the world should change so that women are seen no longer as child-bearing, home-makers dependent on men, but as free agents capable of setting their own agenda and determining their own lives.

It is commonly believed that both men and women benefit equally from **economic growth**, that increasing a man's income will improve the welfare of an entire family and that within a family the benefits and burdens of wealth or **poverty** will be shared equally.

Development policies and programmes everywhere have mostly been run by men and have been built on this premise and the vision of the male 'breadwinner'. But this bias is especially harmful in the **Third World**, where most of a woman's work takes place in the non-wage economy for the purpose of raising a family. In most societies, gender bias is compounded by discrimination based on class, caste or **race**. It is especially harmful in poor areas of Africa, Latin America and Asia where it means that women are denied equal access to **basic needs** such as food, education, jobs, information and credit. This form of gender bias and discrimination consequently assists in maintaining, if not exacerbating, poverty.

GENERAL AGREEMENT ON TARIFFS AND TRADE (GATT) (see also World Trade Organization)

An international, negotiated series of contracts setting out a code of practice and rules to orchestrate fair trading in global commerce. GATT had its origins in the first tariff-

negotiating conference held in Geneva in 1947 and was established the following year at the urging of the US.

The GATT agreement centred on four principles of 'good conduct'. These are: commercial non-discrimination; reciprocity; the prohibition of quantitative restrictions on imports; and the prompt and equitable settlement of commercial disputes and conflicts. Negotiations took the form of 'rounds' of which there have been eight: Geneva (1947) when GATT was established; Annecy (1949); Torquay (1950-51); Geneva (1955-56); Dillon (1960-61); Kennedy (1964-67); Tokyo (1973-79); and Uruguay (1986-1994).

The original GATT membership of 23 has now ballooned to 123 states – 107 nations took part at the final meeting of the **Uruguay Round**. Member countries account for over 80% of world trade (around $4,000 billion).

GATT was initially dominated by the **developed countries** and focused heavily on the protection of tariffs and trading advantages. This led **Third World** nations to seek another forum for negotiations, eventually leading to the creation of the **United Nations Conference On Trade and Development** (UNCTAD) in 1964.

During the Kennedy Round, (1964-67) GATT's Committee on Trade and Development was set up to review the application of the provisions of the Round IV agreement, which contained special measures to help promote the trade and development of the less-developed countries. The principle of a single tariff for all industrial manufactured goods was also first agreed upon during these discussions.

The major concerns at the Uruguay Round were: developed country subsidies for both agricultural exports and farm-support; the opening up of markets in the industrialized world to textiles from the

Gender inequality starts young

In many countries if there has to be a choice about who goes to school, parents may often send sons rather than daughters as the rewards from boys' future prospects are deemed greater than from girls – who may marry and settle elsewhere.

% of primary school age boys and girls out of school

	Boys	Girls
Sub-Saharan Africa	44	50
Middle East and North Africa	13	22
Asia and Pacific	15	22
Americas	8	7
Europe	8	7

The Progress of Nations 1996, UNICEF.

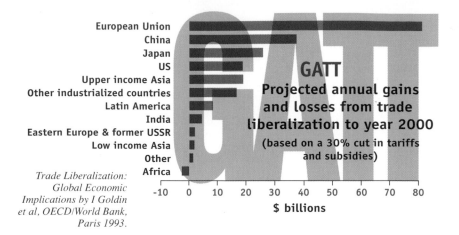

GATT
Projected annual gains and losses from trade liberalization to year 2000
(based on a 30% cut in tariffs and subsidies)

European Union
China
Japan
US
Upper income Asia
Other industrialized countries
Latin America
India
Eastern Europe & former USSR
Low income Asia
Other
Africa

-10 0 10 20 30 40 50 60 70 80
$ billions

Trade Liberalization: Global Economic Implications by I Goldin et al, OECD/World Bank, Paris 1993.

Third World; rules governing foreign investment; and global trade in services. In addition, delegates attempted to clarify the rules governing 'intellectual property'. Continuing discussions on how to strengthen GATT led to its demise and the creation of the **World Trade Organization** in 1995.

GENERALIZED SYSTEM OF PREFERENCES (GSP)
A system adopted by the **European Community** in 1971 whereby **developing countries** are given preferential access to certain markets for some of their products. Preferences are not reciprocal. **Developed countries** importing manufactured and processed goods from developing countries give the latter certain tariff advantages in their markets (either duty-free or reduced duty access). Limits for the GSP goods are set and when that limit is reached, customs duties can be applied again.

The GSP encompassed around 90% of industrial products but just over half of the world's agricultural-trade products. The original aim of the GSP was to encourage industrialization in the developing world and to reduce the **Third World** dependence on the export of raw, unprocessed materials.

At present there are more than a dozen such schemes in operation including those of the European Community, United States, Japan and Canada.

GENETIC ENGINEERING
A scientific technique used to transfer genes from one organism to another or to change genetic materials within an organism. By altering its genetic make-up scientists can induce an organism to make proteins quite unlike anything it would normally produce.

Typically, a sequence of genes is inserted into the DNA of a host bacterium. The altered DNA instructs the bacterial cell to synthesize the desired product. For example, if the piece of genetic DNA responsible for producing growth hormone in humans is inserted into cells of a certain bacterium, the bacterium will make the human hormone as it reproduces. It can then be extracted and used to treat children who suffer from a lack of the hormone. As bacteria can be cultured quickly and easily, large quantities of such products can be obtained. The same methods can be used to produce many other products such as insulin for diabetics.

Some large animals like sheep have also had their genetic material engineered so that they can produce substances commonly used as blood-clotting agents. The substance is produced in the milk of ewes and can be regularly harvested. Genetic engi-

Gene jargon

There is a lot of jargon in this field. Some of it is scientific; some is designed to confuse or put people off. Here are some basic terms you may come across:

BIOSAFETY: The impact of genetic engineering on the environment and health.

BIOTECHNOLOGY: The industrial use of biological processes. Sometimes used by the industry instead of 'genetic engineering'.

GENETIC ENGINEERING: A technique used to transfer genes from one organism to another or to change genetic material within an organism.

GMO (Genetically modified organism): Any plant, animal, micro-organism or virus which has been genetically engineered.

NOVEL FOOD: A term (usually used by the food industry) to describe genetically engineered food.

PHARMING: A word developed by the industry for the production of medicinal products from genetically engineered plants and animals.

TRANSGENIC: Used in the context of animals, it means something which contains genes from another species.

neering can also be used to improve crop plants and yeast strains used in brewing or to produce micro-organisms to help extract minerals.

Many 'transgenic' organisms have already been field tested. These are organisms like **fish**, plants, or animals which contain genes from another species. There are already pigs with human genes, mice that

glow green in the dark and tomatoes with fish genes. Some of these things have been done to find a cure for diseases, others to improve crops or give foods we eat a longer shelf life. Some experiments are done just to see what's possible. The question is: who decides what is permissible? By 1995, over 2,700 field tests of genetically-engineered organisms had taken place in the US alone.

Critics continue to warn of potential dangers. Most transgenic crops have been bred to incorporate greater herbicide tolerance or increased resistance to pests. As crops interbreed with wild relatives, it is possible that these traits may be passed to wild plants, leading to major ecological disruptions. In addition, Northern corporations are searching for new genes from places relatively untouched and unexplored by the West.

Indigenous people are especially upset since they see companies making money out of their plants and their own genes without receiving anything in return. In the process, corporations are patenting genes for private gain, a move which is vigorously opposed on ethical grounds by a growing citizens' movement in both the **North** and the **South**.

GENEVA CONVENTION

An international agreement first reached in 1864 which established rules to govern the treatment of those wounded in war. The first conference was attended by 16 countries who agreed to rules covering the care and protection of non-combatants and the wounded. It was later extended to cover prisoners of war and the protection of civilians during conflict. Prisoners of war are entitled to food on the same scale as the captor country's rear-line troops. They also have the right to adequate clothing, footwear and medical attention. They may also send and receive letters, food parcels and reading matter. Those permanently incapacitated may be repatriated.

A 1949 revision also extended protection to guerrillas fighting wars of **self-determination** or civil wars in which they exercised control over large tracts of territory.

Over 150 nations agreed to the 1949 Convention but only about half that number signed the protocols of 1977. Most countries accept the convention as morally binding although it cannot be legally enforced. Neutral nations and the International Red Cross play a supervisory role in seeing that the terms of the convention are respected.

GENITAL MUTILATION

More than 100 million girls and women live with the results of genital mutilation. So-called 'female circumcision' is practised in 26 African countries and also occurs in Malaysia, Indonesia, Yemen and in parts of Brazil, Mexico and Peru. In Europe and North America many immigrants from these regions still maintain the practice. For many men and women it is a symbol of their heritage. Others undergo the operation as a religious requirement, although neither the Bible nor the Qu'ran prescribe female **circumcision**.

The practice involves the removal of parts of the external female genitalia. Approximately 15% of affected women undergo 'infibulation', the most severe form, in which the clitoris, all of the labia minora and all or part of the labia majora are removed. The vulva is then stitched together, leaving only a small opening for urine and menstrual blood to pass through. The age of circumcision varies from infancy up to the sixth month of pregnancy. The operations are carried out in several ways. In isolated areas, traditional birth attendants use a razor blade, knife or piece of glass, stitching the sides or holding them in place with thorns. The health impacts are severe ranging from pain, haemorrhage, infections and tetanus, to pelvic infections, urinary tract problems and infertility. One study in West Africa found that 83% of circumcised women had a circumcision-related problem which required medical attention at some point during their life.

GENOCIDE
(also see Ethnic Cleansing)

The deliberate and systematic extermination of a racial, religious, political or ethnic group – most commonly used to describe the Nazi persecution of Jews during the World War II. The word was coined after World War II to establish a

Human Development Report, UNDP, Information Bulletin, UNHCR, Survival International.

STRIFE and GENOCIDE

Half of the world's states have recently experienced inter-ethnic strife.

The result has been:

● In Afghanistan one in six people has been disabled by a landmine.

● In Congo (former Zaire) more than 800,000 people have been displaced.

● In Sri Lanka more than 14,000 have died in clashes between Tamils and the Sinhalese.

● In former Yugoslavia more than 130,000 people have been killed since 1991.

● Up to 50,000 people were killed in Burundi in 1993.

● In Rwanda the attempted genocide of Tutsis has resulted in an estimated 200,000 - 500,000 deaths.

● In Brazil an average of one tribe a year has been wiped out since 1900.

G ATT – Genocide

THE **A** TO **Z** OF WORLD DEVELOPMENT

113

legal framework through which the international community could prevent the mass destruction of large groups of people.

In 1946 the UN General Assembly affirmed that 'genocide is a crime under **international law** which the civilized world condemns, and for the commission of which principals and accomplices are punishable'. In 1948 the UN approved the Convention on the Prevention and Punishment of the Crime of Genocide.

Genocide is distinguished from 'crimes against humanity' because it can occur in times of peace or war. It is defined as: killing members of a racial, religious or ethnic group; causing serious bodily or mental harm to members of the group; deliberately inflicting conditions on the group designed to bring about its physical destruction; imposing measures intended to prevent births within the group; or forcibly removing children from the group. Genocide is considered an international crime so that any nation can act on what it considers a violation of the UN Convention.

In 1995, the International War Crimes Tribunal for ex-Yugoslavia indicted Serb leaders Radovan Karadizic and Ratko Mladic on charges of genocide and crimes against humanity.

In 1994, Hutus in Rwanda systematically slaughtered the Tutsi people. Half a million died in the bloodbath. In 1995, one defendant alone admitted to having killed 900 people. Rwanda's prisons now contain 47,000 people accused of genocide.

GEOTHERMAL ENERGY

The use of heat generated in the earth's interior to produce power or heat. The earth's temperature increases by 1°C for every 30 metres of depth. This rate is higher in geologically active areas. To capture this energy subterranean hot **water** is pumped to the surface, converted to steam or run through a heat exchanger. Naturally-occurring steam may be used to drive turbines to produce electricity. Volcanoes, geysers and hot springs can also be tapped. Hot rocks are drilled and cold water pumped in, which then fills underground fractures and cavities, turns to steam, becomes pressurized and finally emerges from other **boreholes**.

The geothermal energy in the upper 5 kilometres of the earth's crust is 40 million times more than is contained in all the world's crude **oil** and **natural gas** supplies. Although only a fraction of the total is economically exploitable, use is growing.

In Iceland geothermal energy is the most important source of power. Italy, New Zealand, the Philippines and the United States are also users. Geothermal power currently produces the equivalent of 50 million megawatts of electricity a year, accounting for about 0.1% of the world's energy requirements. There are geothermal plants in 27 countries and vast untapped **resources** in countries like the Philippines and Indonesia. Some countries like Djibouti and St Lucia are currently investigating ways to best harness the heat and steam produced by volcanoes.

Geothermal energy has to be managed properly as steam can be removed at a rate faster than it is replaced. At the world's largest geothermal-power field in northern California, natural steam pressure has dropped 20% because of over-exploitation.

GLOBAL WARMING

Global warming results from a build-up of **carbon dioxide** (CO_2) and other **greenhouse gases**; it has been identified by scientists as a major threat to the global environment. Initial computer models are being steadily refined and the dire forecasts have improved somewhat. Models adjusted to compensate for the effects of cloud cover suggest that warming due to the 'greenhouse effect' may be only half as intense as previously predicted. However, scientists still believe the level of atmospheric CO_2 will double through the continued burning of fossil fuels.

Since the last Ice Age 10,000 years ago, the earth's ambient temperature has risen by 4°C. However, the rate at which the temperature is rising has increased dramatically since the beginning of the Industrial Revolution. In 1990, the Intergovernmental Panel for Climate Change (IPCC), a group of experts from around the world, concluded that glaciers were melting at increasing rates and snow cover had decreased significantly since 1980. The IPCC also agreed that, if no steps were taken by the global community to reduce emissions of greenhouse gases, the average temperature would rise by 1.8°C by 2020, causing corresponding rises in sea levels of 20 cm. Even if greenhouse gases were reduced by 80% immediately, temperatures during the 1990s would still rise by 0.1°C

Blowing in the wind
Like the funnels of a giant steamer, these cooling towers loose off their clouds of steam. GLOBAL WARMING

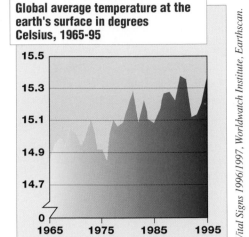

Global average temperature at the earth's surface in degrees Celsius, 1965-95

15.5
15.3
15.1
14.9
14.7
0

1965　1975　1985　1995

Vital Signs 1996/1997, Worldwatch Institute, Earthscan.

per decade – twice as fast as during the rest of the century.

Scientists agree that natural ecosystems can cope with a 1°C rise in temperature without being seriously disrupted, provided that the rate of change does not exceed 0.1°C per decade.

In 1995, the average temperature at the earth's surface rose to a record high. It was the hottest year on record, despite an unusually cold December in Europe and North America. In addition the 1995 high average temperature occurred without the influence of natural phenomena such as **El Niño**, that occasionally contribute to global warming. It also represented a 0.3°C increase since 1992, a year after the **Mount Pinatubo** eruption which spewed millions of tonnes of dust into the atmosphere, blocking solar radiation and lowering global temperatures for about 2 years.

GLOBALIZATION

Economic globalization is said by its supporters to be the next stage in the natural expansion of the capitalist system. In recent years there has been a significant move to increase the clout of global corporations at the expense of national governments. The result has been to further open up Southern markets to Northern commercial interests. State-owned enterprises have been privatized, sectors of the economy deregulated, tariffs and trade barriers removed and restrictions on the flow of capital liberalized.

The current scale of globalization differs from anything that has gone before and there is little pretence that the development process will benefit anyone but the wealthy.

Economic globalization forces labour to compete internationally, pushing down wages and jeopardizing job security. Companies relocate production to countries where labour is cheap while retaining control and research and development in the home country.

Globalization has also sparked what critics call 'a race to the bottom' as countries strip away social programmes like welfare and **unemployment** insurance in order to appear competitive and win the favour of corporate investors. Globalization is part of a package of neo-liberal economic policies which use the rhetoric of open markets and **free trade** to mask a growing gap between rich and poor both within and between countries.

GOLD STANDARD

A monetary system in which the standard unit of currency is a fixed quantity of gold or a currency whose value is kept at a fixed quantity of gold. The gold standard began in Britain in 1821. Prior to this silver had been the principal monetary metal. For the next 50 years a bi-metallic system operated outside Britain, until Germany, France and the United States adopted the gold standard in the 1870s. The stimulus for the change was the discovery of significant amounts of gold in the western US. The system collapsed after the World War I and attempts to revive it were thwarted by the economic depression of the 1930s.

Following World War II, the values of all currencies of member countries of the **International Monetary Fund** (IMF) were fixed in terms of either gold or the US dollar. This gave a certain predictability to international trade since member countries could freely convert gold or US dollars into their own currency. In 1971, dwindling gold reserves coupled with an increasing balance of payments deficit led the United States to suspend free convertibility of dollars into gold at fixed rates of exchange. From then on the global monetary system was based on the dollar and other paper currencies and not gold. Although the price of gold fluctuates

Gold
World reserves 43,030 metric tonnes

South Africa 20,000 metric tonnes	47%
Former Soviet Union 6,220	14.6%
USA 4,770	11.1%
Canada 1,780	4.1%
Australia 1,400	3.2%
Brazil 940	2.2%
Other 7,290	17.8%

US Bureau of Mines 1996

on the world market, holdings of gold are still retained by every country because gold is an internationally recognized symbol of wealth which cannot be easily manipulated by interested parties. South Africa (584 tonnes in 1994), the US (331 tonnes) and Australia (256 tonnes) are the world's leading producers.

GRAMEEN BANK
(see also Microcredit)
A bank started in Bangladesh to assist the rural poor. Small amounts are loaned, mostly to women, without collateral and without the need for guarantors. So far loans have been made to more than 500,000 people. Even though money is lent without collateral the Grameen bank reports a 98% repayment rate, far in excess of most conventional banks.

The founder of the Bank, economist Muhammad Yunus, started the project in 1977 with funds borrowed as a personal loan. He believed that conventional banking was 'anti-poor' and that rural families knew how to solve their own problems if given the **resources** to do so. He also confirmed that women were better money managers than men. The bank has now spread throughout Bangladesh, operating in 35,000 villages with a staff of 14,000. It lends out $500 million annually and its education programmes reach more than 12 million people. The Grameen Bank's success has sparked a global boom in **microcredit** with dozens of similar operations now being set up in other countries. In 1996 there were 168 such ventures in 44 countries.

GREENBELT MOVEMENT
A movement founded in Kenya in 1977 by biologist Wangari Maathai. Under her leadership the movement organizes efforts to manage local **resources** and works towards the preservation of the nation's topsoil, stabilization of climate and the sustainable use of tree crops and products. It began with a project to involve people in planting and caring for native trees and has proved so successful that it now receives support from the **United Nations** and the US National Council of Negro Women.

Under the guidance of foresters, local people learn to recognize and find the seeds of local trees, germinate and then transplant them into the open. As an incentive, a small fee is paid for each seedling that survives. The movement has spread throughout the country at the request of local women's groups who apply for and then oversee a nursery. Thanks to the project, several million trees have already been successfully planted in small lots across Kenya.

GREENHOUSE EFFECT
(see also Global Warming)
The atmosphere, like the glass of a greenhouse, lets much of the sun's visible and near ultraviolet radiation pass through it to warm the planet's surface. The warm earth re-radiates electromagnetic radiation but of a far lower frequency (infra-red). Molecules of **carbon dioxide** (CO_2) and water in the atmosphere absorb this radiation which then cannot escape. As in a greenhouse the heat energy is trapped, raising the temperature. Human activities such as burning fossil fuels, which increases the concentration of CO_2 and other similar **greenhouse gases** in the atmosphere, tends to promote the heating effect, as does the burning of forests which contributes 25% of all greenhouse gases.

CO_2 has been increasing in the atmosphere at 0.4% annually and if this continues, atmospheric concentrations will be double those of pre-industrial times within 80 years. The concentration of CO_2 alone could raise temperatures by 1.5-4.5°C over the next 50 to 100 years. Yet changes of only fractions of a degree can cause glaciers to melt.

Sea levels around the world could rise up to 77 centimetres due to melting polar ice and thermal expansion of sea **water**. Coastal areas could be devastated and low-lying countries like the Maldives and Tuvalu would disappear. Fifteen million people in Bangladesh alone would lose their homes and most of the nation's farmland would be submerged. Recent estimates of a possible rise in sea-level have been revised downward but the threat is nonetheless real.

Limiting the use of fossil fuels to reduce CO_2 levels will cost an estimated $350 billion over the next 10 years. Irrespective of the costs, the global community cannot agree on

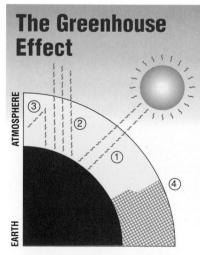

The Greenhouse Effect

A layer of gases in the atmosphere acts like an insulating blanket trapping solar energy that would otherwise escape into space. Without these 'greenhouse gases' the earth would be frozen, barren and lifeless.

HOW IT WORKS

1. Solar energy enters the atmosphere unaffected by greenhouse gases.

2. The sun's rays are absorbed by the earth, then reflected back at longer heat wavelengths.

3. Greenhouse gases absorb this heat, then send it back to the surface.

4. When greenhouse gas concentrations increase, more heat is captured causing temperatures in the lower atmosphere and surface to rise. This affects both weather and climate.

ATMOSPHERE

EARTH

the specific measures to reduce or switch to less polluting forms of energy. Most effort has been spent on cutting CO_2 emissions. Yet proposals for a 20% reduction in emissions by 2005 were vetoed by the United States, the former Soviet Union, Japan and the United Kingdom – countries which between them account for half of global emissions.

Extensive tree **plantations**, acting as 'carbon sinks', have been proposed as one solution to absorbing the 5 billion tonnes of carbon generated each year. Other proposals include growing algae or issuing 'carbon permits'. Algae, grown in either fresh or saline water, are 10 times more efficient at CO_2 uptake than trees. Another proposal is for the allocation of 'carbon permits' to individual countries based on their **population** size. Countries wishing to exceed their permitted level of carbon emissions would have to acquire permits from other countries to cover the excess production.

GREENHOUSE GASES

Gases, generally produced as a result of human activities, which contribute to the 'greenhouse effect' and so cause the ambient temperature of the world to rise. The worst of the gases is **carbon dioxide** (CO_2) which contributes half the effect of all greenhouse gases. Other major greenhouse gases include **chlorofluorocarbons** (CFC-12 is 5,400 times more powerful as a greenhouse gas than CO_2), **methane** (21 times more potent than CO_2) and nitrous oxide (290 times more potent).

If all greenhouse gas emissions were stabilized today their concentration in the atmosphere would continue to increase as they are being vented at a rate faster than they are being destroyed. By 1995, the concentration of CO_2 in the atmosphere had reached 360 parts per million, higher than at any time in the past 150,000 years.

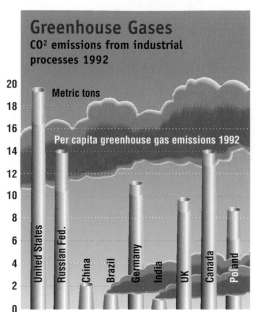

Greenhouse Gases
CO_2 emissions from industrial processes 1992

World Resources, 1996/1997, World Resources Institute.

GREEN MOVEMENT

The word 'green' was adopted in the 1970s by environmentalists to identify key issues, policies and actions that a modern society or individual must consider to help protect the environment and so make development sustainable. The German Ecology Party which rose to prominence in the late 1970s called itself *Die Grunen* (the Greens). *Die Grunen* arose from the merger of about 250 ecological and environmental groups.

Critics inaccurately portray the green movement as having a 'single-issue' focus when in fact the protection and preservation of the natural resource base effects all aspects of life. Nevertheless, 'green' issues were taken up by all mainstream political parties in Europe, after the UK Green Party captured 15% of the popular vote in the 1989 European elections. In 1984, an umbrella group, the European Greens, was founded in Brussels to co-ordinate the activities of the European parties. In the late 1980s and early 1990s, environmentally-friendly 'green' organizations sprang up everywhere.

Many people now favour 'green' trust funds. This investment backs companies whose production does not harm the environment and

avoids companies that have links with the arms trade, repressive regimes, or the exploitation of animals. The 'green' consumer has had a significant effect on shaping industry, particularly with regard to packaging and **recycling**. Consumers are increasingly opting for 'green' products and are prepared to pay extra for them.

GREEN REVOLUTION

A term applied to the development and widespread adoption in the **Third World** during the 1960s and early 1970s of high-yield variety (HYV) strains of cereals – notably **wheat**, **corn** and **rice**. The **Food and Agriculture Organization** (FAO) launched the World Plan for Agriculture and Development at the World Food Congress in 1963. It involved the introduction of HYV cereals, primarily those developed at the International Rice Research Institute (IRRI) in the Philippines and the International **Maize** and Wheat Improvement Centre (CIMMYT) in Mexico.

HYV plants were short-stemmed to avoid wind damage and quick-maturing, making it possible to raise 3 crops a year if conditions were favourable. However, HYV seeds must be used with high inputs of fertilizers, **pesticides** and **water**.

HYV seeds immediately boosted food production in **developing countries**. Cereal yields rose by 2% annually between 1961 and 1980; wheat yields jumped by 2.7% and rice yields rose by an average 1.6%. In nations like Indonesia and the Philippines, where **irrigation** was available and conditions favoured the new **high yield varieties (HYVs)**, yields rose by over 3% a year.

From the mid-1960s, impressive increases became commonplace in several parts of Asia and Latin America. India doubled its wheat yield in 15 years and rice yields in the Philippines rose 75%. The area

Revolutionary cassava

'High-yielding, disease-resistant, drought-tolerant' cassava like this, at a tropical-agriculture institute in Nigeria, is one of the jewels in the crown of the Green Revolution. Yields may be higher but the super-plants require expensive fertilizers and chemicals that put them out of the reach of peasant farmers. GREEN REVOLUTION

devoted to HYVs in the developing world rose from 60,000 hectares in 1960 to 50 million hectares by the late 1970s. In Asia alone, output in 1976 was 15 million tonnes, double the 1971 harvest. By 1980, some 27% of all seed used in the developing world was derived from HYVs, although there was a massive geographic imbalance. Only 9% of seeds in Africa were from improved varieties compared to 44% in Latin America.

Despite raising yields, the Green Revolution also had its down side. Only cereals which could be stored easily and which were traded on the world market were the focus of research. Crops grown by small farmers in Africa and Latin America, like **cassava**, sorghum and **millet**, were essentially ignored. The storage of the harvest from HYVs is difficult because their high moisture content makes them much more vulnerable to moulds. In addition HYVs do not perform well on marginal soils. They are also extremely vulnerable to pests and disease, having little or no natural resistance. Worse, they only produce high yields when used with large amounts of expensive agro-chemicals and irrigation water. During the 1970s world consumption of **fertilizers** almost doubled, pesticide use

increased 5-fold, and irrigated **land** rose from around 160 million hectares to over 200 million hectares, mostly as a result of HYV use.

Increased mechanization also had negative environmental effects, mostly as a result of **soil** compaction in ecologically fragile areas. The use of tractors to replace draught animals is expensive and leads to a loss of animal manure, a valuable low-cost organic **fertilizer**. Also the costs of irrigation and chemicals encourages exports in order to recoup the cash outlay. Many

farmers were convinced by promises of profits to stop planting indigenous crops in favour of HYVs. This led to a jump in the price of traditional crops and to forced changes in diet. In addition, farmers who could afford the chemicals needed to grow HYVs prospered, while poorer farmers and peasants were unable to make use of the new varieties and their plight worsened. Global food supplies doubled between 1950 and 1980, but grew by just 20% from 1980-1990. It is estimated that food production will need to increase by 60% within the next 30 years simply to maintain current nutritional levels. Most HYVs have now reached their biological limits and experts are now touting a so-called 'Gene Revolution' as the next way of increasing global food production.

GROSS DOMESTIC PRODUCT (GDP)

The total monetary value of goods and services produced within a country over a year. It may be used to determine the wealth of a country, but is less widely used than the **Gross National Product** (GNP). By the mid-1990s, the global GDP was around $26 trillion, with the industrialized countries accounting for $20 trillion of the total.

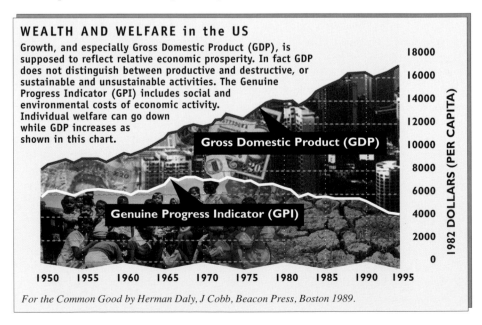

WEALTH AND WELFARE in the US

Growth, and especially Gross Domestic Product (GDP), is supposed to reflect relative economic prosperity. In fact GDP does not distinguish between productive and destructive, or sustainable and unsustainable activities. The Genuine Progress Indicator (GPI) includes social and environmental costs of economic activity. Individual welfare can go down while GDP increases as shown in this chart.

Gross Domestic Product (GDP)

Genuine Progress Indicator (GPI)

1950 1955 1960 1965 1970 1975 1980 1985 1990 1995

1982 DOLLARS (PER CAPITA)

18000 16000 14000 12000 10000 8000 6000 4000 2000 0

For the Common Good by Herman Daly, J Cobb, Beacon Press, Boston 1989.

Luxembourg, Switzerland and Japan have the highest GDP per capita ($34,000) while Sudan, Somalia and Mozambique have the lowest ($80).

GROSS NATIONAL PRODUCT (GNP)
(see also Alternative Economic Indicators)

The most commonly used measurement of the wealth of a country. The GNP is the total value of goods and services produced within a country together with income received from other countries (notably interest and dividend payments, minus similar payments made to other countries). For many **developing countries**, interest and dividend payments to foreigners are normally more than similar receipts. In these circumstances, the national product is less than the domestic product.

The concepts may be expressed either in gross or net terms. For the latter, a deduction is made for the capital assets used up in producing the goods and services sold. Net national product is often referred to as National Income, the sum of all income received in a given year. It is equal to GNP less depreciation. For comparative purposes GNP is frequently expressed as a per capita figure, the total GNP divided by the number of people in the **population**.

GROUNDNUT/PEANUT

Also commonly known as peanuts, groundnuts are low-growing plants native to tropical South America. They push their developing seed pods underground to avoid drying out in the sun. Consequently, they grow best on light, sandy soils which can be penetrated easily. Each pod contains up to 5 seeds or nuts and the crop is now cultivated from the tropics to warm temperate regions.

Groundnuts require 400 millimetres of rain and temperatures of 23°C during their 4-5 month

Warm smiles and sharp hoes
Women farmers in Kenya make ready to hoe the weeds away from their groundnut plants. The peanuts, which are legumes, grow in clusters under the earth. GROUNDNUT

growing season. They are best grown in rotation with other crops such as **cotton** or **maize**, or inter-cropped with **millet**, sorghum or cowpea. Harvesting should be carried out in dry conditions otherwise aflatoxin-producing fungal moulds may develop on the nuts making them dangerous to eat. Average yields are around 600 kilograms per hectare. The nuts are highly nutritious and are used in cooking, eaten raw, roasted and made into peanut butter. They also produce an excellent cooking oil. Two-thirds of world production is processed into edible oils or into protein-rich animal feed. The world's leading producers are: China (9.6 million tonnes), India (7.6 million tonnes) and the US (1.7 million tonnes), with around 25 million tonnes being produced globally each year.

GROUNDWATER

Water that has percolated into the **soil** or rock and become trapped. Groundwater is extensively used in many parts of the world. In the United States more than half the nation's drinking water and 80% of rural livestock-needs come from groundwater. Global supplies are being depleted and polluted at alarming rates. Excessive **deforestation** causes increased water run-off, hastening the reduction of underground supplies. As a result, aquifers shrink and **land** subsides. In coastal areas, over-exploitation of groundwater leads to intrusion of salt-water from the sea.

Ill-considered applications of agricultural chemicals and uncontrolled landfill dumping also contribute to the pollution of groundwater supplies. Water moves relatively slowly through the ground, so many of the

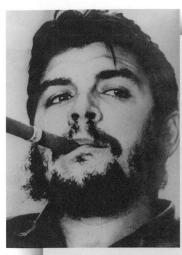

GUEVARA, ERNESTO 'CHE' (1928-1967)

'Che' Guevara was a revolutionary Latin American guerrilla leader. Born in Argentina, he excelled at sports and studied medicine. He travelled widely in the region and was appalled by the poverty he saw. He came to believe that the only way to achieve radical social change was through violent revolution. He visited Guatemala in 1954 where he witnessed the overthrow of the mildly-socialist regime of Jacobo Arbenz in a coup supported by the US Central Intelligence Agency. This set Guevara permanently against the US and convinced him that socialism through global revolution was the only path to follow. He then travelled to Mexico where he met Fidel and Raul Castro. He later joined them when they returned to Cuba to overthrow the dictatorship of Fulgencio Batista. He remained on the island until Castro's forces eventually ousted the dictator in 1959. Guevara then became a Cuban citizen and a prominent member of Castro's administration. He also became well-known in the West for his staunch opposition to all forms of imperialism and neo-colonialism.

In the 1960s he documented Cuba's policies and his own thoughts in many speeches and writings, most notably in El socialismo y el hombre en Cuba. He also wrote several books on the theory and tactics of guerrilla warfare. In 1965 he and other Cuban revolutionaries travelled to Africa to help guerrilla fighters in the Congo. Then in late 1966 he travelled incognito to Bolivia to create and train a guerrilla army. A year later, the group was almost annihilated by the Bolivian army. Guevara was wounded, captured and later shot.

chemicals sprayed or dumped decades ago have yet to filter into underground supplies. Nonetheless, in Denmark the concentration of nitrates in groundwater has trebled over the last 30 years due to the effects of fertilizers and animal manure.

Groundwater is notoriously difficult to cleanse once polluted. It contains no micro-organisms and flows so slowly that dilution or dispersal of contaminants is impossible. Overuse of groundwater is now widespread in parts of China, India, Mexico, Thailand, the United States, North Africa and the Middle East. Non-renewable, so-called 'fossil' aquifers are being depleted at ever-increasing rates. Saudi Arabia mines fossil groundwater to meet 75% of its water needs. Renewable sources of water, those replenished by normal rainfall or snow melt, are faring no better. In Beijing, water tables have been dropping by 1-2 metres annually and many wells have gone dry, while in Mexico groundwater pumping exceeds recharge by 50-80%.

GUERRILLA

A member of an irregular military force usually engaged in small-scale conflicts against conventional military forces. Traditionally, guerrilla fighters take up arms against a ruling government or foreign invaders who they deem to be exploiting the population. Guerrilla tactics include sabotage, terrorism and shifting points of attack. The basic premise is to harass the enemy until enough military strength is amassed for victory, or enough political and military pressure is brought to bear to cause the enemy to sue for peace.

The Chinese General, Sun-tzu, devised the essentials of guerrilla tactics in 350 BC even if he did not use the word and the Chinese have been role models ever since. Most of the revolutionary wars waged since World War II have been based on the teachings of Mao Zedong, himself a noted guerrilla leader and tactician.

'Guerrillas must swim among the people like the fish in the sea,' Mao wrote. He meant that guerrillas must have a political goal and must gain and hold the support of the populace who provide them with supplies, information and shelter. However, the use of terrorist tactics has to be carefully managed. Guerrilla fighters may lose the support of the people if government forces retaliate and non-combatants are punished in an effort to 'flush out' the rebels.

Mao's thoughts
'Guerrillas must swim among the people like fish in the sea', said Mao Zedong, meaning that fighters' success depended on the support of local people – as in the Vietnam War. GUERRILLA

GULF WAR

The Gulf War took place following Iraq's invasion of Kuwait in August, 1990. The Iraqis wanted to gain control of Kuwait's valuable oil fields to help pay off $80 billion in debts the country had run up during its war with Iran which ended in 1988. Following an invitation from Saudi Arabia and a request from the Kuwaitis, the United States led a multinational alliance to oust the Iraqis. The operation was code-named Desert Storm and included forces from several NATO countries as well as from other Arab nations.

The US-led forces threatened to attack if Iraq did not comply with a UN Security Council resolution ordering the country to withdraw from Kuwait by January 15, 1991. The Iraqi leader Saddam Hussein refused and the War began on January 17.

Iraq had the world's fifth largest army, some 950,000 soldiers, most of whom had extensive combat expe-

Undermined

Clearing landmines in Kuwait: one deminer is killed and two are injured for every 5,000 mines cleared. **GULF WAR**

rience from the recently-concluded conflict with Iran. The Iraqis were also well-equipped with arms, including both chemical and biological weapons. However, they were no match for the technically-sophisticated US weapons. The 6-week long campaign provided a valuable testing-ground for a new generation

of American computer-based weapons. The War also boosted public support for the administration of US President Ronald Reagan who shamelessly exploited American patriotism against the 'evil Saddam'.

The Iraqis were tenacious but they were eventually routed by the American-led Allied Forces: 100,000 Iraqis were killed and 65,000 captured. On the Allied side, 234 died and 479 were wounded.

The retreating Iraqi forces set fire to virtually all Kuwait's major oil wells. This resulted in a major ecological disaster which cost millions. There were also millions of landmines indiscriminately laid during the War, many of which have yet to be removed. In 1998 conflict threatened again as Saddam denied UN weapons inspectors access to putative production sites.

THE REAL COST

The Gulf War may have been short but it was one of the most violent, brutal few weeks in human history.

FINANCIAL

Every year the world spends about $900 billion on arms. To this the Gulf War added the expenditure needed to replace all the military hardware: the bombs, rockets and ammunition used, and the tanks, planes and ships destroyed. About one million foreign military personnel and their equipment were deployed in the Gulf. Added to this is the cost of reconstruction after the War.

	$ billions
Cost of Coalition forces	70
Reconstruction costs in Kuwait	70
Iraq	110
Saudi Arabia	1
Total	**251**

● These costs are at least seven times greater than total annual official development assistance to the Third World and five times greater than the $50 billion needed – though not provided – to implement the environmental recommendations of the Rio 'Earth Summit'.

THE SOUTH

The world's poorest countries paid heavily for the War.

● 40 Third World countries suffered losses as serious as if they had been hit by a 'natural disaster'. Increased oil prices, reduced trade and lost remittances from migrant workers in the Gulf cost them about $12 billion.

● Enormous losses were incurred by foreign nationals, mostly from Third World countries, who became refugees. Palestinians in Kuwait lost assets estimated at $8 billion; the average income of Palestinians living in the Occupied Territories is estimated to have halved as a result of the War.

THE ENVIRONMENT

The long-term cost to the environment is still being counted.

● Every day noxious pollutants from burning oil wells in Kuwait produced the equivalent of ten times the daily emissions from the whole of US industry and all its power plants.

● The cloud from the burning oil wells reached two miles high, 400 miles south and 60 miles east to west. Acid rain spread as far as southern Turkey, western Pakistan and, later, the Himalayas.

● Some 20,000 birds were killed by oil slicks.

HEALTH AND WELFARE

The destruction of Iraq's electricity, health care, water and food-supply systems has caused unemployment, hunger, disease and suffering for millions of ordinary people in Iraq which continues today.

● Real earnings have fallen to less than 7% of pre-War levels.

● Absolute poverty levels have risen to equal those of India.

● Mortality rates among under five-year-olds have increased to four times pre-War levels.

● Within one year of the end of the War a minimum of 20,000 deaths from preventable diseases occurred, particularly among children in the refugee populations.

REFUGEES

Millions of people living in and around Iraq were forced to flee their homes.

● Some 2.5 million Iraqi nationals (mostly Kurds in the North and Shia in the South) became internal refugees after the uprisings that followed Desert Storm.

● 400,000 foreign nationals (mostly Arab) left Iraq.

● 1.6 million people left Kuwait after the Iraqi invasion, most of them from the foreign resident population which included 625,000 Arabs (of which 350,000 were Palestinians), 600,000 Asians (mostly from Sri Lanka, India, South-East Asia and the Philippines), 60,000 Iranians, 3,000 Turks and 11,700 Westerners.

● 800,000 Yemeni citizens were expelled from Saudi Arabia.

CASUALTIES

The War was an unequal contest. Iraqis suffered almost 200 times more casualties than the coalition.

IRAQI DEATHS

Iraqi armed forces during Desert Storm	100,000
Iraqi civilians from coalition bombing	7,000
Iraqi soldiers assassinated by Kuwaitis	100

COALITION DEATHS

Coalition forces	479
Israeli civilians (Scud attacks)	2

WOUNDED

There are no detailed figures. The military still estimate the number of wounded at three times the number of deaths, which places the number of Iraqi soldiers wounded by Desert Storm at 300,000.

Map labels: TURKEY, CAIRO, EGYPT, ISRAEL, JORDAN, SYRIA, BAGHDAD, IRAQ, SUDAN, RED SEA, ETHIOPIA, DJIBOUTI, SAUDI ARABIA, RIYADH, YEMEN, KUWAIT, ARABIAN GULF, UNITED ARAB EMIRATES, ABU DHABI, IRAN, OMAN, SOMALIA, ARABIAN SEA, India Pakistan Sri Lanka the Philippines

New Internationalist No. 236.

Homeless

Over half of Mumbai (Bombay) city's people live on pavements or in squatter dwellings like this, set against a backdrop of wealthy high-rise housing. But spirits are hard to crush, and from the slums come some of the most beautiful jewellery, pottery, glassware, woodwork and fabrics.

Bold indicates a cross-reference

HABITAT LOSS

Until 1950, exploitative hunting by humans was the most important cause of species depletion. The American Bison, the Quagga, Passenger Pigeon, Dodo and Great Auk were among those animals hunted to extinction. Human predation is still responsible for the slide toward extinction of the great whales and fur seals as well as numerous other land-based species.

However, loss of natural habitat has now become the greatest threat to wildlife. Human activities have destroyed forests, coral reefs, mangroves, estuaries and wetlands. Vast tracts of grasslands have been turned into farmland while other areas have been paved over, dug up, drained or poisoned.

Tropical forests are one of the two main storehouses of biodiversity, containing 40% of all the planet's species Humankind has destroyed nearly 30% of the world's 'moist' tropical forests. A quarter of Brazil's forests are gone and 80% of Thailand's have disappeared. Countless varieties of wildlife have suffered in the process. Over a third of the planet's swamplands have been drained. In Britain over 80% of the flower-rich lowland has been cultivated or built on.

Virtually all forms of human activity can alter natural habitats: overgrazing of livestock can lead to soil erosion; deforestation can

cause siltation of water courses; and non-indigenous wildlife species can alter the natural balance irrevocably. Conversion of land to cropland, grazing pasture or tree plantations destroys natural eco-systems. And whole habitats can be replaced by human settlements, harbours or roads. Specialized habitats, especially island sites, are irreversibly altered by mining and quarrying.

There has been no global tally of habitat loss. However, in 1987 the Sierra Club in the US reported that only a third of the Earth's total land mass remained in a wild state, devoid of human settlements, roads or other signs of permanent presence. Of this total, 42% was in Antarctica or the Arctic, 20% was mainly desert and the rest primarily mountain ranges. Tropical forests which support the greatest diversity of wildlife make up a small and rapidly declining percentage of the total. A World Conservation Union (IUCN) study in the late 1980s found that 68% of original habitat had been lost in Southeast Asia and 65% in Sub-Saharan Africa. Globally, virtually all remaining natural habitats have been degraded from their original state.

HAMMARSKJÖLD, DAG (1905-1961)

Swedish politician and international civil servant. The son of a Swedish Prime Minister, he served as deputy Foreign Minister from 1951 to 1953 and headed the Swedish delegation to the United Nations. In 1953, he succeeded Trygve Lie as UN Secretary General. During his term of office he dealt with the Suez Crisis (1956) and the civil war sparked by the granting of independence to the Congo (1960). He was credited with introducing the UN's peacekeeping role, which is not in its charter. He was killed in a plane crash while trying to resolve the crisis in the Congo and was posthumously awarded the Nobel Peace Prize in 1961.

LOSS OF WILD HABITAT (percentages of original area lost, selected countries 1980s)	%
Vietnam	80
Ivory Coast	79
Philippines	79
Madagascar	75
Ethiopia	70
Cameroon	59
South Africa	57
Indonesia	49
Malaysia	41

International Union for the Conservation of Nature.

HAZARDOUS WASTE

Any waste that has the potential to inflict damage on either human health or the natural environment. Over 400 million tonnes of hazardous waste are generated world-wide each year – more than 90% of it by industrialized countries. The substances that make up most hazardous waste are acidic resins, arsenic residues, compounds of lead and mercury, organic solvents, pesticides and radioactive materials.

American industry generates around 250 million tonnes of toxic waste each year and the European Community produces another 30 million tonnes. Norway recently discovered 7,000 sites where the soil is contaminated with hazardous waste and the Government estimates that it will cost billions of dollars to clean them up.

Several ways of disposing of hazardous waste, each with varying degrees of safety and expense, have been developed. These include landfill, incineration, underground injection and the detoxification of wastes by bio-engineered organisms. Advanced plasma arc furnaces can destroy toxic wastes (including Polychlorinated Biphenyls PCBs and dioxins) almost instantly by producing temperatures four times as hot as the surface of the sun. But the preferred method of disposal has been to dump where it is cheapest, either at sea or in the Third World.

In Europe, disposing of hazardous waste can cost up to $500 per tonne. In Africa it can cost as little as $2.50 a tonne. Since 1986 approximately 3 million tonnes of toxic waste have been shipped from Western Europe and North America to other countries. Europe 'officially' sends about 120,000 tonnes of toxic waste to the Third World each year.

Experts believe as much as 30 million tonnes of hazardous waste crosses national borders each year, with a high proportion going to poorer countries. Many developing countries have attempted to profit by disposing of wastes from industrial countries including Angola, Benin, Congo, Guinea and Guinea-Bissau.

Many other Third World nations have tried to prevent hazardous wastes from being dumped in their countries. Members of the Organization for African Unity (OAU) set up a 'Dumpwatch' body for this specific purpose.

In Europe, Britain remains the major sink for hazardous wastes. In 1990, 200 barrels a week of highly toxic chemical waste were transported by road from Italy. A 1990 study found that the illicit trade in toxic waste in the UK was 3 times as great as the legal trade. Less than 25% of the waste was incinerated or disposed of safely. The majority was simply dumped in landfill sites.

Hazardous wastes pose a significant long-term danger. Persistent chemicals in landfill sites can cause surface and groundwater pollution, contamination of land and mass exposure of whole communities to highly-toxic chemicals. Love Canal in the US is a famous example, although there are now numerous similar sites in Europe and North America where clean-up bills total billions of dollars. Germany alone has estimated landfill clean-up costs at $10 billion. If properly treated, most wastes can be rendered harmless. But the long-term solution lies in reducing waste rather than safe disposal.

HELSINKI CONFERENCE

The 80 nations attending the 1989 Helsinki Conference agreed to phase out chlorofluorocarbons (CFCs) as soon as possible and not later than the year 2000. They also promised to phase out the use of other chemicals that damage the ozone layer – such as halons, methyl chloroform and carbon tetrachloride. The decision, taken in view of the growing evidence of damage to the world's stratospheric ozone layer, tightened up the terms of the 1987 Montreal Protocol which focused on the removal of 5 major CFCs.

At the follow-up conference in London in 1990, delegates agreed to a more specific timetable for phasing out CFCs by the year 2000. The donor nations also agreed to provide technology and funding to help non-industrialized countries to develop or produce safe alternative chemicals and laid down specific guidelines for removal of other gases harmful to the ozone layer.

POISON
HAZARDOUS WASTE

OECD

MAJOR EXPORTERS
of hazardous waste (thousand metric tons per year, early 1990s)

Germany	522
Netherlands	195
Canada	175
US	157
Switzerland	121
UK	83
Austria	68
Hungary	25
Sweden	25
Finland	24
Italy	20
Norway	17
France	16
Denmark	13

HEPATITIS

Inflammation of the liver which can cause ill health and death. Hepatitis A is an acute infection usually contracted through eating contaminated food. Hepatitis B is a chronic viral infection transmitted through blood, semen, other body fluids or via contaminated needles and syringes.

Of the world's infectious and parasitic diseases, Hepatitis B is the most prevalent. More than 2 billion people have been infected and some 350 million are chronically infected and at serious risk. Every year some 1-2 million deaths occur from the disease. It can be passed from mother to new-born, from child to child and from child to adult. In 1989 scientists discovered 2 more viruses (Hepatitis C and D) both of which are blood-borne. Up to 100 million people are infected with Hepatitis C. Interferon is the only effective drug but it is extremely expensive.

In 1990 researchers isolated the virus for Hepatitis E which is believed to cause one of the most lethal forms of the disease. It is spread through **water** contaminated with faeces from infected people and is estimated to affect up to a million people each year. It is especially prevalent in Asia, with pregnant women most at risk. Around 20% of pregnant women who contract the virus die.

HIGH YIELD VARIETIES (HYVs)
(see under Green Revolution)

Modern hybrid crops (mainly rice, **wheat** and maize) developed through plant breeding techniques, that produce higher than normal yields when grown under specific conditions. From the early 1960s to the early 1970s global grain yields doubled as a result of planting HYVs. Asia benefited the most with increased yields worth around $1.5 billion. However, such high yields require up to 90 kilograms of nitrogen per hectare. HYVs also

Super soya
Yellow Jewel, Great Treasure—these are some names given to the bountiful soya bean. HYVs

need lots of **water** and have low resistance to pests. This means **irrigation** and repeated applications of costly **pesticides** if elevated yields are to be realized. HYVs therefore tend to be planted by relatively wealthy farmers who can afford the expensive **agrochemicals** and irrigation. New varieties are also vulnerable to insect attack. Plant breeders are turning to wild stock to try and breed in resistance. But their task is difficult because varieties generally display resistance to only a few pests and the loss of wild stock is exacerbating the situation.

Approximately 55 million hectares, about a third of all cultivated land in the **developing** countries, are now planted with HYVs of wheat or rice. For example, over half the wheat grown in India today comes from HYV seeds.

The shift to HYVs and away from traditional food crops has ironically led to a rise in the price of locally-grown food on occasion. Although they have boosted overall crop production HYVs are not a magic solution to the world food shortage. Even with HYVs, only an estimated 25-40% of the potential yield in temperate zones is being realized. In the tropics the situation is even worse, with only 10-20% of the potential yield being harvested. World food production must rise by 60% by the year 2025 if current nutritional levels are to be maintained.

HINDUISM

The world's oldest religion dating back as far as 2,750 BC. Hinduism encompasses a number of diverse traditional beliefs and practices. Unlike other religions it does not have a formal creed. One of the central concepts is the belief that one's

Sacred ceremony
In the glow of a candle s flame, a bridegroom bows to the *puja* borne by the young Brahmin priest as part of the Hindu wedding. HINDUISM

THE **A** TO **Z** OF WORLD DEVELOPMENT

HO CHI MINH (1890-1969)
Vietnamese nationalist, politician and Marxist leader. Born Nguyen Tat Thanh, the son of a poor country scholar, he managed to travel and work his way around the world. During a stay in France from 1917-23 he became an active socialist, demanding that France give equal rights to its subjects in Indochina. He left France for Russia where he strengthened his belief in the significance of a revolutionary role for oppressed peasants.

In 1924 he went to China and formed the first Vietnamese Nationalist Movement. In Hong Kong in 1930 he presided over the formation of the Indochinese Communist Party. Ten years later when Germany invaded France, he saw his chance for Vietnamese independence.

He adopted the name Ho Chi Minh ('he who enlightens') and entered the country to form the League for Independence of Vietnam. In 1940, the Japanese invaded Indochina and imprisoned or killed all French officials. When the Japanese were defeated by the Allied Forces, Ho negotiated with the United States and declared Vietnam independent. Under the agreement, Chinese troops were to occupy territory north of the 16th parallel.

But France refused to accept the agreement and sent troops to Vietnam to regain control. The Indochina War began in 1946 leading to the defeat of the French in 1954. Accords reached in Geneva determined that Vietnam should be divided at the 17th parallel until elections could be held to establish a unified government. Ho had become established in North Vietnam, the poorer region of the two and he was forced to seek **aid** from China and Russia in order to survive. His regime became more repressive and rigidly totalitarian.

Throughout his life Ho Chi Minh managed to skilfully maintain the backing and support of both Russia and China. In 1959, Ho's Vietcong **guerrillas** began an armed revolt against the US-backed government in South Vietnam. Soon afterwards the North decided to fight for unification with the South and the **Vietnam War** began. 'Nothing is as dear to the heart of the Vietnamese as independence and liberation,' He wrote at the time. He died before the War was won.

---

actions in life lead to a reincarnation at a higher or lower level of life. Hinduism teaches a profound respect for all forms of life and is based on a **caste system**, a hierarchical system of social and religious stratification.

The goal of Hinduism is to find a release from the cycle of 'rebirth' and return to the ultimate, unchanging reality. Release may be sought through good works, meditation or devotion to a particular god. Hindus believe that the divine can be manifest in any number of gods, objects or people, which then become worthy of worship. Most of the world's 700 million Hindus are found in India and surrounding countries.

HIZBOLLAH
A Lebanese political-religious movement: the name in Arabic means Party of Allah. Hizbollah emerged under the leadership of Shia cleric Shaikh Muhammad Hussein Fadlallah in opposition to the Israeli invasion of Lebanon in 1982. It was believed to have been the brainchild of Ali Akbar Mohtashemi, the Iranian ambassador in Syria. Hizbollah carries out **guerrilla** attacks on Israeli targets in southern Lebanon, receiving military and financial **aid** from Iran. In the 1980s, Hizbollah began taking Western hostages in Lebanon, especially Americans, as a ploy to inhibit US involvement in the Iran-Iraq war and to secure clandestine supplies of US arms for Iran. In 1991, a three-way swap involving Lebanese, Palestinian and Israeli detainees ended Hizbollah's hostage-taking activities.

HOMELESS
There are two common definitions of the homeless: a person who has no shelter and is forced to sleep outdoors; or those people whose shelter is inadequate, lacking in **water**, power and sanitary facilities.

The right to shelter has been

REASONS FOR HOMELESSNESS
Detailed analysis reveals that 40% of those officially homeless in Britain became so because parents, relatives or friends were no longer willing or able to accommodate them.

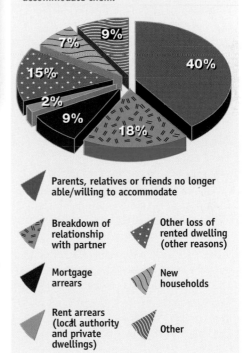

- ◤ Parents, relatives or friends no longer able/willing to accommodate
- Breakdown of relationship with partner
- Other loss of rented dwelling (other reasons)
- Mortgage arrears
- New households
- Rent arrears (local authority and private dwellings)
- Other

Who Says There's No Housing Problem? by Jill Mann, Alastair Smith, Shelter, London 1993.

No place to go
In Britain the number of homeless households more than doubled from around 62,920 in 1980 to 148,250 in 1992 according to the charity Shelter. HOMELESS

do sleeping at friends' or relatives'. There were an estimated 200,000 of these 'hidden' homeless in Britain in 1991 and another half million people 'living rough' on the streets.

HUMAN DEVELOPMENT INDEX (HDI) (see also Alternative Economic Indicators)
An annual assessment of the progress of nations in improving living standards. The indices are produced by the **United Nations Development Programme** (UNDP) and follow the assumption that **economic growth** does not necessarily equate to human development and improved well-being. The reports assess the actual impact of development on people, rather than using the **Gross National Product** (GNP) which is based purely on financial information like income and savings, commodity production and the accumulation of capital.

The HDI includes factors like **life expectancy** and access to education, in the belief that human development requires both economic growth and an equitable distribution of income and **resources**. The HDI is a basic aggregate of 3 indicators: life expectancy is used to determine longevity; adult **literacy** and years of schooling to estimate knowledge; and **GDP** per person as a means of gauging command over resources.

enshrined in the **Universal Declaration of Human Rights**. Yet more than a billion people are without adequate shelter or housing. Of these, 100 million have no shelter whatsoever. This problem is global, but most acute in the developing world. In a study of 14 cities in Africa, Asia and Latin America, between 32% and 85% of the residents were living in 'informal' slum and squatter settlements. This housing is often built in the worst areas, on flood-prone, low-lying **land** or on unstable hillsides. Residents rarely own the land or pay any property **taxes**. Initially constructed using temporary materials such as cardboard or corrugated iron, the housing gradually becomes more permanent. Such dwellings are always overcrowded with multiple occupancy commonplace.

Today 37% of the population in **developing countries** lives in urban areas. By the year 2000 this will have risen to 57%. Accompanying this growth is a widespread expansion of slums and squatter settlements on the periphery to accommodate newcomers, most of whom are too poor to afford proper housing. Since the mid-1970s Mumbai (Bombay) has doubled in size, while its squatter population has increased by 1,000%.

In all these settlements life is dire and conditions unhealthy, with little or no water, sanitation, power, waste removal or transport. Moreover, the residents live in permanent fear of eviction. Authorities arrive, often without warning, to bulldoze and torch settlements. People lose not only their homes, but often all their possessions. 720,000 people were evicted in Seoul, South Korea, to make the city more 'respectable' when it hosted the Olympic Games.

In industrial countries where the illegal occupation of land is rare, those unable or unwilling to afford accommodation end up on the streets. In Europe, more than 3 million people are homeless. Many more have no fixed address and make

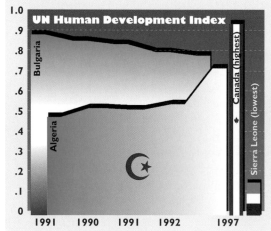

UN Human Development Index

EVERY YEAR the UN calculates a 'Human Development Index' (HDI) for all the countries of the world, for which points are deducted for high levels of inequality. The chart shows that the biggest decline in HDI rating from 1991 to 1997 came in Bulgaria, suffering as it replaces state control with the free market.

- The biggest improvement surprisingly came in Algeria, despite the war between the repressive government and the fundamentalist FIS.
- In both Bulgaria and Algeria the change arose due to shifts in gross national product rather than the education or health components of the Index.
- Sierra Leone has the lowest HDI in the world while a rich country, Canada, has the highest.

Human Development Report 1997, UNDP.

The initial report discovered that some countries, including Costa Rica, Jamaica and Sri Lanka achieved a high level of human development with modest levels of per capita income. Others, including Brazil, Oman and Saudi Arabia failed to translate their rapid economic growth into commensurate levels of human development.

Many oil-producing nations, particularly those in the Middle East and North Africa, also failed to translate their wealth into improved living standards. The countries of Western Europe, North America and Japan have the top HDI while African nations occupied the bottom 10 places. As the HDI evolves it will include other aspects of human development. Enough data already exists for 30 countries to include **gender** inequalities in the HDI. When equality for women is included Japan, which is usually close to the top of the index, plummets to around number 20.

HUMAN GENOME PROJECT

An ambitious international effort to identify and analyze the 100,000 or so genes that make-up the human body. Laboratories in Europe and North America are collaborating to produce detailed maps of the human

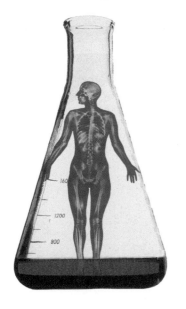

genome. By 1996, the approximate location of about 75% of human genes had been identified and more than 50% had been broken down into their constituent parts. It is estimated that 99% of the genome should be sequenced by the year 2002.

The work is being carried out in parallel with research to isolate specific disease-related or disease-causing genes. By the mid-1990s, genes responsible for Alzheimer's disease and a predisposition to breast **cancer** had already been discovered. However, pioneering gene therapy activities have produced mixed results. Some rare conditions have been improved, but cystic fibrosis and muscular dystrophy have not responded to gene therapy.

Critics say the Project gives 'property rights' over human genes (often from indigenous people) to Western scientists.

HUMAN IMMUNO-DEFICIENCY VIRUS (HIV) (see also AIDS)

HIV is a retrovirus which leads to Acquired Immuno-deficiency Disease Syndrome (**AIDS**) in humans. HIV destroys the body's natural defences against disease by multiplying in the cells that are sent by the immune system to destroy it, making infected individuals susceptible to a wide range of opportunistic infections. Many of these infections are not normally serious, but HIV gives them the opportunity to have a lethal impact.

The virus is spread through sexual contact, intravenous drug use and blood transfusions as well as from an infected mother to her infant in utero or during birth. AIDS takes at least 6 years to develop after the initial infection.

Around 30 million people in total have been infected with the virus. The first cases of infection are thought to have occurred in the mid-1950s. But the origins of the outbreak are still not known and sci-

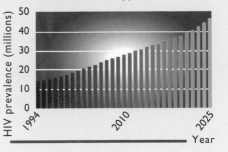

PREVALENCE OF HIV
If projected world figures for hiv-infected adults alive in the year 2000 are extended to 2025, this is what happens:

World Health Organization.

entific opinion has shifted many times. There are three main theories: HIV developed from an old human disease unknown to science; it developed from a natural virus of some other species, probably monkeys or apes; or it was deliberately or accidentally manufactured. Each theory had its supporters and detractors though nothing has been proven. With no curative drugs or a vaccine available, it is better to find out where HIV is going rather than where it came from. In recent years speculation has also increased that the link between HIV and AIDS is not as straightforward as has been widely accepted.

HUMAN RIGHTS

Privileges claimed or enjoyed by every human being by virtue of being human. The concept developed from the Roman idea of 'natural law'. Early milestones in establishing human rights in Britain were the Magna Carta (1215), the Habeas Corpus Act (1679) and the Bill of Rights (1689). None of these were as fundamentally comprehensive as the US Bill of Rights (1788) or France's Declaration of the Rights of Man (1789). During the 19th century, human rights began to be enshrined in **international law**, best illustrated by the **Geneva Conventions**, a series of treaties which governed the humane treatment of civilians, soldiers and prisoners during times of war.

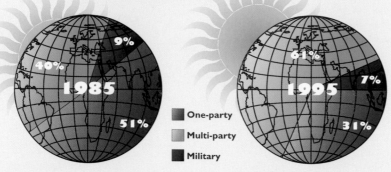

DYING DICTATORSHIP

PERCENTAGE of the world's population living under multi-party, one-party or military systems.

1985
9%
40%
51%

1995
61%
7%
31%

■ One-party
■ Multi-party
■ Military

THE IMPROVEMENT IS GENUINE but the figure for multi-party democracy should still be treated with caution since it includes countries like Mexico and Russia where the democratic practice is far short of ideal.

World Human Rights Guide, Charles Humana, Pan 1995, NI.

The UN **Universal Declaration of Human Rights** was adopted in 1948. It stated that people have the right to life, liberty and education; to freedom of movement, religion, association and information; to a nationality and to equality before the law. Although not a binding code, the UN declaration has spawned subsequent agreements, such as the Covenant on Civil and Political Rights (1966) and the Covenant on Economic, Social, Civil and Political Rights (1966), both of which have been accepted as binding by 35 countries.

In 1950 the **Council of Europe** founded the European Commission of Human Rights which investigates grievances and complaints laid by states or individuals. The findings of the Commission are examined by the European Court of Human Rights, whose jurisdiction has been recognized by a number of European countries. In countries like Britain, basic rights are not protected by statute but are rights by common law. Many nations still deny their citizens basic rights. Under South Africa's **apartheid** system, blacks were denied many basic rights. Many Soviet Bloc countries prevented freedom of expression; and racial and sexual discrimination are still prevalent in most nations. In addition, social and economic rights (the right to work, to decent housing, to food and health care), which involve direct challenges to the economic status quo, rarely receive the same attention as civil and political rights.

HUNGER

The average person needs about 2,500 calories a day to survive. People in the developed world consume 40% above this figure daily, while the average **Third World** citizen gets by on 10% less. During the first half of the 1980s the number of 'hungry' people in the world reached 512 million. Every year another 40 million people are added to the total. By the year 2000, an estimated 588 million men, women and children will be seriously undernourished. Each year, some 40 million people die from hunger and hunger-related diseases. It is difficult to attach numbers to hunger and starvation. The UN **Food and Agriculture Organization** defines 'undernourishment' as a daily caloric intake of around 1,650 calories but that figure varies according to human characteristics, age and environmental conditions. For example, 800 calories a day are needed by infants under one year of age, while 3,600 calories daily are required to sustain an adult male leading an active life. In the 1960s, half the global **population** had a daily intake

HUSSEIN, SADDAM (1937-   )

Iraqi dictator. Born to a peasant family in northern Iraq, Hussein joined the country's Ba'ath Party in 1957. He spent several years in exile in Egypt following a failed coup attempt in Iraq in 1959. He became Iraq's President in 1979 and immediately had 500 of his party's top members executed. The following year he launched an attack on Iran. When the Iran-Iraq War finally ended in 1988, over 120,000 Iraqi soldiers had lost their lives. With Iraq some $80 billion in **debt** as a consequence of the War, Hussein looked for support from neighbouring Arab countries. Instead Kuwait and Saudi Arabia frustrated his bid for higher **oil** prices, stepping up their own production. They also pressed Iraq to repay billions of dollars borrowed to finance the War.

In response, Hussein decided to invade Kuwait in August 1990, with a veiled threat to do the same to Saudi Arabia. This in turn led to Saudi Arabia inviting the United States to liberate Kuwait and remove the Iraqi threat to the Gulf's oil supplies. This confrontation turned into the short-lived Persian **Gulf War** of 1991. Following Iraq's defeat by the combined power of the Allied forces, Hussein began to rebuild Iraq and establish an even more brutal regime. He ruthlessly suppressed rebellions by Shia Muslims in southern Iraq and by Kurds in the north of the country and rotated senior military personnel in order to reduce the risk of a military coup.

Pumping power
Water bursts through the turbines, free falling into the river once more at the Tucurui Dam in Brazil where some 24,000 people had to be relocated. HYDRO-ELECTRIC POWER

of less than 1,900 calories. By 1990, one in 10 people still had a daily consumption of 1,900 calories or less.

Estimates suggest that 950 million people, about 20% of the world's population, consume too few calories each day to support an active working life. If food was distributed evenly around the world, everyone would have enough to satisfy their needs. Unequal distribution means that hunger and **malnutrition** are commonplace. The hungry are mostly those people who lack the cash to buy or the land to grow food for themselves and their families. This is true even in the richest of countries.

The majority of the world's hungry and undernourished live in Asia and about 85% of those live in rural areas. A 1987 UN report ranked hunger and malnutrition in Asia as 'one of the world's most serious issues of human welfare'. At the same time at least 30% of adults over the age of 40 in the US are classified as obese. And in Britain $200 million was spent annually in the early 1980s on slimming aids.

HYDRO-ELECTRIC POWER/ HYDROPOWER (see also Dams)

Electricity generation using the power of falling **water**, often referred to as hydropower. The falling water turns a turbine and the higher the reservoir of water the less water is needed for the same output. It is a relatively cheap source of power, particularly in mountainous areas where rainfall is high. It is also non-polluting compared to electricity generated by burning **coal** or **oil**. A single 10-kilowatt hydropower plant is estimated to save 21 tonnes of fuel oil per year, as well as reducing the release of **carbon dioxide** by 70 tonnes.

Hydropower supplies around 20% of the global electricity (or 6% of global energy), with North America producing more hydro-electricity than any other region. By 1990, a total capacity of 550 gigawatts of

hydropower had been installed worldwide. Much of the world's potential hydropower remains untapped with most of it in the developing world. By 1990, Europe and North America had developed almost half of their hydropower potential whereas less than 10% had been exploited in Asia, Africa and Latin America. The large **dams** needed to produce effective hydropower plants carry heavy environmental and social costs, especially in the tropics. Nonetheless, the **World Bank** projects that 223.5 gigawatts of hydropower will be installed in **developing countries** by the year 2000 with more than half the total in Brazil, India and China.

As the high cost of large-scale hydropower projects sinks in, mini-hydro-electric schemes have received more attention. China has built some 90,000 such plants since 1968. These produce over 5,000 megawatts of electricity, the equivalent of 6 **nuclear power** stations. These projects are cheap and relatively simple to build. Electricity is generated close to the point of need and they are ideal for powering rural industries, schools and hospitals.

Indigenous Peoples

'I do not want gold prospectors here. I do not want my forest destroyed,' said Esmeraldo Tisibora-u-theri, a Yanomami from Brazil. Since 1987 over 50,000 small prospectors have moved into Yanomami land, polluting rivers with mercury and destroying the indigenous peoples' way of life.

Illiteracy – Ivory

I

Bold indicates a cross-reference

The State of the World's Children 1998, UNICEF.

ILLITERACY

According to the **United Nations Educational, Scientific and Cultural Organization** (UNESCO), some 25% of the world's adult **population** is illiterate. Average rates of **literacy** vary from 50-70% in the **Third World** to nearly 99% in industrialized countries. In total, there are more than 900 million illiterate people in the world, nearly 98% living in **developing countries**. Over the past four decades, literacy rates for people of 15 years and over have improved everywhere, most notably among women. But women still account for two-thirds of the world's

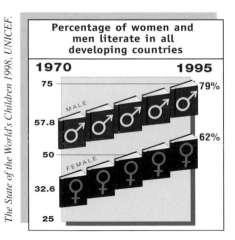

illiterate adults (some 565 million people), concentrated mainly in developing countries.

More than half of today's illiterate adults live in India (291 million) and China (166 million). In India 57% of adult males are literate compared with

only 29% of women. **UNESCO** is leading the campaign against illiteracy, aiming to reduce it to 15% of 1990 levels by the year 2000.

IMMUNIZATION

A means of providing immunity to diseases by artificial means. This can be done by injecting antibodies against specific diseases (passive immunity) or by **vaccination** (the injection of disease-causing microorganisms to stimulate the body to form its own antibodies without producing the disease).

Immunization against diphtheria, pertussis, tetanus. **measles**, **tuberculosis** and **polio** has saved millions of children from death and disability. **Hepatitis** B and **yellow fever** vaccines have also proved invaluable. Since 1960, child and infant mortality rates have been more than halved by vaccination.

In 1980, only 20% of the world's children were protected against the major immunizable diseases. By 1995, the figure had risen to 80%. More than 70 **developing countries** reported that 80% of all children had been immunized. However, 25 countries (18 of them in Africa) still reported coverage below 50% for the 6 major vaccines.

IMPERIALISM

The extension of one nation's power over another either through

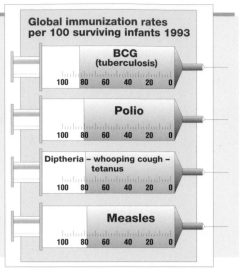

World Health Report 1995: Bridging the Gaps, WHO.

conquest or in the pursuit of 'empire' – an influence so dominant as to amount to virtual sovereignty. Apologists defined imperialism as 'a search for captive markets'. Others, like Marxist theorist **VI Lenin**, claimed that imperialism was the 'final stage' of **capitalism** when international competition grows in order to secure markets and exploit **resources**.

The rapid development of commerce in 19th century Europe coincided with newly-discovered ocean passages and improved seafaring technology. Western traders and missionaries saw overseas colonies as potential treasure troves of both raw materials and souls. New industries in **oil**, **rubber**, chemicals and iron and steel were developing and depended on resources extracted from abroad.

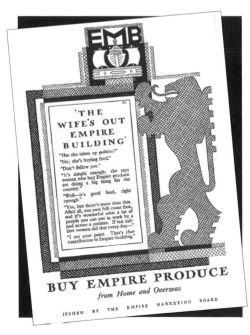

Copper was needed for a new electrical industry and **coffee**, **tea** and **sugar** were sought to meet the growing appetites of Northern consumers. Among European nations this led to a desperate scramble for colonies in the last half of the 19th century. In 1800 most people in the world were self-governing. Within a hundred years, a quarter of the globe had been taken over as colonies by half a dozen European states.

IMPORT SUBSTITUTION

A policy often adopted by **developing countries** to protect domestic industry and natural **resources**. Imports are blocked by tariffs and/or quotas. This allows a nation to develop its own local manufacturing ability and eventually to develop an export trade. Sometimes a more expensive domestic product may be substituted for a less expensive import as a way of improving trading balances.

INDEX OF SUSTAINABLE ECONOMIC WELFARE (ISEW)

A method for estimating the economic and social progress of nations which was created as an alternative to the most commonly used indicator, **Gross National Product** (GNP). GNP is seen as a poor indicator of a nation's true development because it gives a positive value to *any* economic activity whether it is productive, unproductive or destructive.

The ISEW takes into account previously ignored factors such as income distribution, environmental destruction and natural resource degradation, including long-term environmental damage. According to the ISEW the welfare of US citizens grew 42% from 1950-1976. After that it began to decline steadily, dropping 12% by 1988. In simple terms, the ISEW shows that

for over 15 years the net benefits of **economic growth** in the US have fallen below the growth of the population, leading to a decline in individual welfare.

There are two major problems with the ISEW. First, it requires data that is hard to come by – such as quantitative figures of environmental degradation. And second, it can only be used where vast amounts of information are regularly collected and accessible. This limits its use to a handful of countries.

INDIGENOUS PEOPLES
(see also Aborigines)

Indigenous peoples (also called 'native' or 'tribal' people) are found on every continent and in most countries. All indigenous peoples have ancient ties to the **land**, water and wildlife of their ancestral domain. Traditionally, their sustainable lifestyles cast them as guardians and stewards of their natural environment.

Most indigenous peoples now live under conditions where their **human rights** are abused and under the constant threat of extinction. Colonists, explorers, missionaries and developers from majority cultures

have brought both violence and deadly diseases. Peoples have been annihilated, their cultures eroded. One third of North American Indians have disappeared since 1800. In South America, in the first half of this century, Brazil alone lost 87 tribes. As a result, vast repositories of ancient knowledge have disappeared. Sustainable subsistence lifestyles have been cast aside in the name of development as indigenous homelands have been invaded and natural **resources** plundered.

Most indigenous peoples face a bleak future. Industries and governments want to exploit resources on native lands to pay off debts and modernize economies. Sometimes governments wage a form of war on indigenous people who control their own territories. Such wars receive little publicity. Little is heard of the Indonesian Government's attack on the people of **East Timor** and West Papua; or Guatemala's extermination of 100,000 Mayans; or the Indian Government's actions against the Nagas; or of the mass killings and torture in the **Chittagong Hill Tracts** of Bangladesh.

By means of force or indoctrination,

Home on the range
Leaning against his modern-day horse a Sioux of the Cheyenne River Reservation in South Dakota ponders an uncertain future (below), and a fully-beaded, Sioux cradle (right) based on traditional designs. INDIGENOUS PEOPLES

indigenous people are being absorbed into the cultural mainstream everywhere. Only a small fraction of the Penan hunter-gatherers continue their traditional lifestyle in the rainforests of Borneo. Only 10% of Sami (Lapp) people in northern Scandinavia still forage with their herds of reindeer. Half of North America's Indians and New Zealand's Maories live in cities.

Where indigenous people have been granted rights to their own land, they have often suffered unwanted intrusions. In Ecuador, the Government gave the Huaorani rights to protect their land while granting **oil** exploration concessions on the same land to foreign companies. In Brazil in 1992, the government was forced to expel 40,000 gold prospectors from the remote lands of the **Yanomami** indians – the last large, isolated group of indigenous peoples in the Americas.

Over the past 25 years, indigenous peoples from around the world have begun to work together stimulated by a mixture of modern communications, the **decolonization** process and the American civil rights movement. From humble beginnings in Australia, North America and Scandinavia the indigenous people's movement has begun to make its voice heard in Central and South America, Asia, the Pacific islands, Africa and Russia.

INFANT MORTALITY RATE (IMR)
The IMR is the number of deaths of children aged 0-12 months per 1,000 live births in a given year. This includes 'neonatal mortality' (death occurring within the first four weeks of life) from such causes as asphyxia and injuries sustained during the birth process. Neonatal deaths account for two-thirds of all infant mortality in **developing countries**, mainly due to a lack of good medical facilities.

The world's IMR fell by 37%

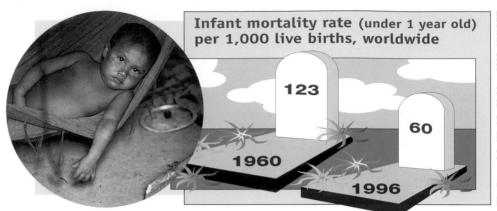

Infant mortality rate (under 1 year old) per 1,000 live births, worldwide

123 1960
60 1996

The State of the World's Children 1998, UNICEF.

between 1970 and 1996 – from 97 to 60 deaths per 1,000 live births. But this still means that some 8.4 million infants die before their first birthday. Despite dramatic improvements over the last 20 years, there is a huge gap between the developed and developing worlds. In rich countries the average is 6.9 infant deaths per 1,000 live births, compared to an average 106.2 deaths per 1,000 live births in developing countries.

The infant mortality rate is regarded as a measure of social affluence rather than simply a reflection of the quality and availability of ante-natal and obstetric care. The countries with the lowest IMRs are among the wealthiest. In 1996 Japan, Sweden and Finland had the lowest rates with 4 deaths per 1,000 live births, closely followed by Iceland with 5 deaths per 1,000. By comparison, the worst rates are in Angola (170), Afghanistan (165), Sierra Leone (164), Malawi (137) and Mali (134).

The infant mortality rate is often accompanied by figures for child or 'under 5' mortality – the number of children who die under the age of five. In 1995 the global average child mortality rate was 81.7 per 1,000 live births, down 40% from the 1970 figure.

INFLATION
A steady rise in prices which results in a steady fall in the value of money. Inflation can occur when demand for goods exceeds supply (demand-pull inflation); or when costs of production increase independent of the state of demand (cost-push); or

when governments expand the money supply by printing more money (monetary inflation).

Deflation is the opposite process and causes a reduction in both output and **employment**. Inflation and deflation occurred regularly in 19th century Europe. The abnormal, prolonged and severe deflation of the 1930s was followed in the post-war years by a protracted period of inflation, reaching 10% per year and more in many countries. Inflation creates instability for business, labour and consumers. Whereas the rich can often ride out short-term periods of inflation, the poor, those on fixed incomes and those with little bargaining power suffer greatly. Unchecked inflation is a threat to the entire monetary system. Remedies vary but can include wage and price controls, reduced government spending and a tightly-controlled money supply.

INFORMAL ECONOMY
Businesses and workers operating outside the officially-recognized sector of a nation's economy. The informal sector is quasi-legal, so regulations governing trading licences, minimum wages, property titles and **taxes** are generally ignored. In sub-Saharan Africa, some 60% of urban workers are employed in the informal sector, producing 20% of annual output – worth $15 billion. Approximately half the workforce in Latin America is employed in the informal sector, in what are sometimes referred to as micro-enterprises.

This area is now expanding rapidly in the developing world and attracting official recognition. The **Inter-American Development Bank** has established a separate department to co-ordinate loans and support to these micro-enterprises. In the past, **aid** agencies allocated **resources** only to the modern, formal sector – usually large-scale industry owned by the state or wealthy élites.

The **International Labour Office** (ILO) reports that the informal sector is much more efficient and cost effective in promoting development and improving a nation's economic performance. In Latin America every $1,000 lent to the informal sector creates a job, compared with the $12,000 needed in the formal sector.

Most job seekers in the **Third World** end up finding work in the informal sector. In India, the informal manufacturing sector has produced twice as many new jobs over the past 20 years as has the formal sector. ILO studies have also found that even though informal enterprises are not strictly legal, most of them pay taxes in some form.

Large companies on the other hand tend to exploit legal loopholes and ultimately pay a smaller proportion of gross income in taxes.

INFORMATION TECHNOLOGY (IT)

A wide-ranging term used to describe the various technologies

Well heeled
Mickey Mouse holds the key on this colourful shoe-and-key cutting workshop facade in Tunisia, North Africa.
INFORMAL ECONOMY

TOP INTERNET COUNTRIES
Hosts/100,000 population (Jan 1996) and % increase from July 1995

Country	Hosts	% increase
Finland	42	86%
USA	23	42%
Norway	22	33%
Australia	17.5	49%
Sweden	17	40%
Aotearoa/NZ	15	22%
Canada	15	42%
Switzerland	13	35%
Netherlands	12	29%
Denmark	11	40%
Britain	9.5	55%
Austria	9	30%
Israel	8	62%
Taiwan	2	56%
South Africa	2	17%
South Korea	1	23%

Network Wizards, www.nw.com

involved in the collection, processing and transmission of information. These include computing, telecommunications and microelectronics.

The IT revolution, based firmly in the **North**, is proceeding in a rapid, mostly unregulated manner. The **South** has comparatively poor basic communications: 9% of people have a radio, 3% have access to newspapers and only 1 in 500 has a television. Nonetheless Western companies flood the world with television programmes and films altering tastes and cultural values in the process.

The press influences people everywhere, but 90% of foreign news in newspapers is provided by only 4 Western news agencies. In 1990, Northern countries accounted for over 90% of the data-processing industry and controlled virtually all communications satellites. **Transnational corporations** (mostly Western-based and Japanese) control telecommunications and electronic networks, as well as the production of electronic components and computers.

The first generation of computers began in the 1950s, but by the mid-1990s many people in the North regularly used desk-top or lap-top models. Commerce, banking and industry were revolutionized by computer technology. Hundreds of millions of virtually instant financial transactions now take place daily. Computers can be programmed to buy and sell stocks and companies can now send huge sums of money around the globe electronically to maximize profits.

By the early 1990s, the South had begun to benefit slightly from the IT revolution, but in an indirect way. Many Northern companies were moving their electronics and computer production to countries where labour is cheaper. And major banks and airline companies were turning to countries like India for low-cost computer programming. Even data entry, such as the translation of 3 million British criminal records into computerized format, was contracted to clerks in **developing countries** to save money.

In 1996, 5 new satellites were launched by Northern companies to add to the 3,600 existing ones, as part of a $3.4 billion project to create a 66-satellite network capable of delivering voice, data, fax and paging services to anywhere in the world. Sub-Saharan Africa, where the majority of people may never make a telephone call in their life, is one of the target markets.

The exponential growth of the Internet during the 1990s also left out much of the South. Only 10% of the global **population** can afford access to the Internet. Well over 90% of all Internet sites are located within **OECD** countries, the operating language is English and the main companies controlling the technology are all based in the North.

INTEGRATED PEST MANAGEMENT (IPM)

There are four basic ways of controlling agricultural pests: cultivation to discourage the build-up of pest populations; control using chemicals; crop breeding and the selection of resistant varieties; and encouraging the natural enemies of pests (so-called biological control).

IPM is a combination of all these. The goal is not to eradicate pests but rather maintain populations at acceptable levels. A form of IPM has been practised in China for

Prickly pear pest
Prickly pear comes from Mexico and was taken to South Africa as a fodder crop – but it ran riot and grew out of control. The woolly grey cochineal bugs were introduced to destroy the cactus. IPM

centuries. Farmers flood paddy fields early in the season to kill off the yellow stem-borer without the need for costly chemicals. Ducks are also allowed into the fields where they eat plant hoppers, leaf-rollers and army worms. IPM programmes in India have cut pesticide use by 40% and improved yields. Similar results have occurred with Brazilian soybeans and Nicaraguan **cotton** crops. It is estimated that widespread adoption of IPM methods could reduce pesticide use by 50-75% cent world-wide. And it generally saves money: in 1987 farmers in the United States using IPM earned $579 million more in profits than they would have otherwise.

INTEGRATED PROGRAMME FOR COMMODITIES (IPC)

A global trading measure designed to regulate the cost of raw materials (or basic commodities) through the creation and maintenance of international pricing arrangements. The IPC was originally established by the fourth **United Nations Conference on Trade and Development** (UNCTAD) in 1976.

INTER-AMERICAN DEVELOPMENT BANK (IDB)

A multilateral development bank founded in 1959 to provide assistance to **developing countries** in Latin America and the Caribbean by providing low-interest loans and technical co-operation. Membership was originally restricted to 21 members of the **Organization of American States** (OAS), but was extended to include Canada in 1972. In 1976, 12 other non-regional members, mostly from Europe, were admitted. Today the bank has 46 members. The Bank's funds are replenished every 4 years. The Bank also operates a Fund for Special Operations which provides soft loans.

Perfect harmony
Maize, squash and beans growing together in South Africa. Maize takes up nutrients from the soil which the beans replenish: yields can be greater thanks to such practices. INTERCROPPING

INTERCROPPING

Intercropping is a technique of growing of two or more crops in the same field – in sequence, in combination or both. Crop and animal production may also be mixed in even more complex, ecologically-sound systems designed to maximize production. The process has been commonly practised by millions of farmers in the tropics for centuries and can be particularly beneficial to cash-poor farmers and smallholders.

Most **subsistence** farmers prefer to plant at least two crops in the same field to minimize the risk of total crop failure. A typical Nigerian farmer may grow up to 8 crops on the same plot, including **bananas**, beans, **cassava**, melons and yams. While in India over 80 crops are grown in a variety of mixed-crop combinations. In Africa, 98% of the continent's most important legume, the cowpea, is grown in combination with other plants. Combining crops often yields more than when crops are grown alone (**monoculture**).

Planting early-maturing crops together with plants that may take a year or longer to mature (such as sugar-cane or cassava) means the early-maturing ones can use **land**, water and light while the main crop is still small. It also helps spread the harvest throughout the year, alleviating storage problems. Tall plants can also be combined with shorter shade-tolerant crops. For example, plants like sweet potato can be raised between **maize** rows. And 'multi-storey' combinations such as **coconut**, black pepper, **cocoa**, **pineapple** are now more common as farmers try and coax as much food as possible from limited land holdings.

Intercropping increases the volume of post-harvest debris (often an important source of fodder for livestock) as well as improving **soil** fertility. In **rubber** and **tea** intercroppings, plant debris has been found to take the place of thousands of kilograms of chemical **fertilizers** (see **Agrochemicals**). The effects of diseases, fungi, weeds and pests can all be diminished by intercropping. One study found 60% fewer plant-feeding insects in mixed-crop fields. Several disease-resistant plant combinations have also been identified. For instance, mixing cassava and beans reduces both the incidence and severity of powdery mildew on cassava and angular leaf spot on beans. Cowpea viruses are diminished when the legume is grown beside cassava or plantain. Intercropping encourages the efficient use of light, **water** and nutrients and helps prevent weed invasion and growth. The only drawback is that it is labour-intensive – it is difficult to mechanize weeding when crops are so close together. This is a serious obstacle to the technique being adopted in the **North**.

INTERNATIONAL AGRICULTURAL RESEARCH INSTITUTES

The Consultative Group on International Agricultural Research (CGIAR) was founded in 1971 to guide international research on a wide range of topics associated with agriculture and farming. It is an informal association of governments, international and regional organizations and private foundations. The origins of the system lie in collaborative research on raising crop productivity by the Rockefeller Foundation and the

INTERNATIONAL AGRICULTURAL RESEARCH INSTITUTES

International Maize and Wheat Improvement Centre (CIMMYT): Located in Mexico. Aims to improve varieties and production of **maize**, **wheat**, barley and triticale (a small-grained rice).

International Rice Research Institute (IRRI): Based in the Philippines. Mandated to develop improved **rice** varieties and rice-growing systems and maintain a germplasm bank.

International Centre of Tropical Agriculture (CIAT): Based in Colombia. Emphasis on improving the production of beans, **cassava**, rice and beef.

International Institute of Tropical Agriculture (IITA): Based in Nigeria. Aims to improve varieties and production of cowpea, yam, cocoyam, sweet potato, **cassava**, maize and beans, paying close attention to the needs and conditions in Africa.

International Potato Centre (CIP): Located in Peru. Develops improved varieties of **potatoes**.

International Crop Research Institute for the Semi-Arid Tropics (ICRISAT): Based in India. Aims to improve the quality and reliability of food production in semi-arid tropical regions.

International Centre for Agricultural Research in Dry Areas (ICARDA): Based in Syria. Develops rainfed agricultural systems in arid and semiarid regions, particularly in northern Africa and western Asia.

International Service for National Agricultural Research (ISNAR): Based in the Netherlands. Provides guidance, information and expertise to help strengthen individual national agricultural research programmes.

International Food Policy Research Institute (IFPRI): Based in the United States. Identifies, examines and evaluates governmental and international agency intervention in national, global and regional food problems.

West African Rice Development Association (WARDA): Based in Liberia. Promotes self-sufficiency in rice in West Africa and develops improved rice varieties for the area.

International Board for Plant Genetic Resources (IBPGR): Based in Italy. Co-ordinates an international network of germplasm banks.

Centre for International Forestry Research (CIFOR): Based in Indonesia. Research and development of sustainable forest management systems.

International Centre for Living Aquatic Research Management (ICLARM): Based in the Philippines. Aims to develop sustainable management of aquatic resources.

International Centre for Research in Agroforestry (ICRAF): Based in Kenya. Mandated to research and develop all forms of agroforestry.

International Irrigation Management Institute (IIMI): Based in Sri Lanka. Charged with researching existing **irrigation** methods and techniques and developing new systems which will be sustainable.

International Livestock Research Institute (ILRI): Based in Ethiopia and Kenya. A merger of the **International Laboratory for Research on Animal Diseases** and the **International Livestock Centre for Africa:** This new institute will work on livestock production methods, disease control and improving rearing methods.

Mexican Government in 1941. There are 16 research centres in the CGIAR system. The CGIAR supports and influences all the individual centres. It is funded mainly by the **World Bank**, the **United Nations**

Development Programme (UNDP), the **Food and Agriculture Organization** (FAO) and donor governments including the United States, United Kingdom, Canada, Germany, and Sweden. Substantial contributions also come from private organizations, notably the US-based Rockefeller Foundations and the Ford Foundation. Funding fell by 22% between 1990-94 to $215 million with the World Bank making an abortive attempt to take over full control.

INTERNATIONAL ATOMIC ENERGY AGENCY (IAEA)

Founded in 1957, the IAEA's mandate is to 'accelerate and enlarge the contribution of atomic energy to peace, health and prosperity throughout the world; to apply safeguards over nuclear materials and ensure that they are used only for their intended peaceful purposes'. The agency is based in Vienna and has 2 main roles: to act as an international information exchange on civil nuclear applications; and to administer the **Nuclear Non-Proliferation Treaty**. It has 121 members and has a special relation-

Still a force to be reckoned with
Nuclear power provides about 6 per cent of the world's energy, and most new stations like this one in Brazil are constructed in the South. **IAEA**

ship with the **United Nations**. The agency has close ties to the **nuclear power** industry and is seen to be an uncritical supporter of nuclear expansion. In 1990, the IAEA concluded that up to 500 new nuclear power stations should be

commissioned world-wide between 2001 and 2010 to provide a quarter of anticipated global energy needs.

INTERNATIONAL BANK FOR RECONSTRUCTION AND DEVELOPMENT (IBRD) (World Bank)

The IBRD was set up following the 1944 **Bretton Woods** agreements to facilitate economic and infrastructure reconstruction following the World War II. It is commonly known as the World Bank, although it is only a wing of the World Bank group.

Based in Washington, the IBRD is an independent body. It has 178 members, all of whom must also belong to the **International Monetary Fund** (IMF). The Bank is the largest of the **Multilateral Development Banks** (MDBs) and finances development projects in member countries by making loans to governments or under government guarantee. The Bank's original capital was set at $10 billion. All members make a capital subscription in accordance with a formula related to their economic strength. The US is the largest contributor with Japan rapidly approaching parity. The Bank's main resources are obtained by direct borrowing in international capital markets and from governments. It lends on near commercial terms.

Since 1948 most of its loans have been to spur **economic growth** in **developing countries**, though it has also made loans for educational and social schemes, including **family planning** and resettlement programmes. It plays an important role in appraising and advising on the development programmes of developing countries, as well as producing several influential annual statistical publications.

Shares in the bank are allocated according to contributions, the biggest shareholders getting the most votes on the Executive Board. Loans recommended by the IBRD

President rarely come to a vote. Each member nation is represented on the Bank's Board of Governors but most decisions are taken by a group of 22 Executive Directors. Five are appointed (from France, Germany, Japan, the UK and the US) and the rest are elected from country groupings.

The World Bank group consists of the IBRD, the **International Development Association** (IDA) and the **International Finance Corporation** (IFC). All use common services and staff and all are responsible to the President of the IBRD who is always from the United States.

Today more and more people are questioning the Bank's credibility and activities. Critics charge that the Bank is a tool of **neo-colonialism** controlled by rich, Western countries to force **Third World** nations to take a subservient place in the global economy. In 1993, US civil rights leader Jesse Jackson endorsed this view in an address to the leaders of 11 African states, when he said, '[the industrial nations] no longer use bullets and ropes, they use the World Bank and IMF'.

INTERNATIONAL COMMITTEE OF THE RED CROSS (ICRC)

An organization founded under the 1864 **Geneva Convention** to provide care for all casualties of war. Inspired by Swiss philanthropist Henri Dunant, the ICRC is based in Switzerland with branches in countries throughout the world. It is part of the International Red Cross movement (see box). The Red Cross emblem represents the Swiss national flag with the colours reversed.

In Muslim nations, the crescent has been adopted instead of the cross. The ICRC is active in a variety of areas associated with war or armed conflict. Red Cross activities now involve dealing with **refugees**, the disabled and the alleviation of

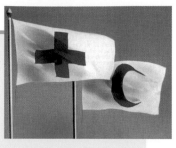

INTERNATIONAL COMMITTEE OF THE RED CROSS

THE RED CROSS began on 24 June 1859 in Solferino, a town in Northern Italy, where French and Italian troops were engaged in a fierce battle against occupying Austrian forces. The medical services of the armies involved were quite inadequate to deal with the situation and the wounded were abandoned to their fate.

A visiting Swiss entrepreneur, **Henry Dunant**, was so appalled by their suffering he called on the local population to join him in helping them.

On his return to Switzerland Dunant convinced politicians, military officers, philanthropists and friends of the need for wounded soldiers to be treated and cared for.

Eventually they formed the **International Committee of the Red Cross.** They adopted a distinctive sign – a red cross on a white background – to identify and thereby protect those who assisted wounded soldiers.

Right: The battle for Solferino in Northern Italy, 1859. Below right: Henry Dunant, founder of the Red Cross.

The ICRC is the founding institution of the **International Red Cross and Red Crescent Movement (also known as the 'International Red Cross')**, which now has the following components:

 The **International Committee of the Red Cross**

 The **International Federation of Red Cross and Red Crescent Societies** (founded in 1919, this is the world federation of National Societies)

 The **National Red Cross and Red Crescent Societies,** duly recognized by the ICRC; in October 1989, there were 149 Societies with more than 250 million members

human suffering and misery caused by epidemics, floods, earthquakes and other natural or human-made **disasters**.

INTERNATIONAL COMMODITY AGREEMENTS (ICAs)

Agreements between producers of primary, unprocessed **commodities** to regulate their production and sale in order to stabilize prices and conserve supplies. Examples include the Tin Agreement (1956), **Coffee** Agreement (1962) and **Rubber** Agreement (1976). Natural factors

such as crop failures and the discovery of new mineral deposits cause considerable fluctuations in the supply of commodities and prices oscillate accordingly. Under the agreements, producers, mainly **developing countries**, agree to limit production. Minimum prices are fixed, marketing systems established and buffer stocks built up by purchasing surpluses. The surpluses are then sold to stabilize prices when prices exceed a specific ceiling.

Several ICAs have been negotiated through the **Integrated Commodity Programme of the** United Nations Conference on Trade and Development (UNCTAD). Those concerning tin, **rubber**, **coffee** and **cocoa** were designed to stabilize prices at a level fair to both producers and consumers, using buffer stocks and export controls via a quota system. Other ICAs were agreed to cover jute and tropical timber and were concerned primarily with research and development. A purely administrative International Sugar Agreement was also negotiated.

By 1990, the system had more or less collapsed. Today the prospects for developing countries which rely on a single commodity for the bulk of their export earnings are not good. The Coffee Agreement collapsed in 1989. Export quotas were suspended for 2 years and the price of coffee fell by almost half as a result. The inability of the 74 producer and consumer nations involved in the pact to agree on a new arrangement followed the collapse of the International Cocoa Agreement and the failure of the International Tin Council. The failure of similar commodity pacts on **wheat** (1979) and **sugar** (1984) consigned both to the free market.

INTERNATIONAL CONFERENCE ON POPULATION AND DEVELOPMENT

In 1994, representatives from 175 countries gathered in Cairo for the third conference on Population and Development, following those in Bucharest (1974) and Mexico City (1984). The delegates discussed a 20-year Programme of Action which had been drafted by the UN Population Fund (**UNFPA**), organizers of the conference.

To reduce global fertility and put a lid on global **population**, conference delegates agreed it was essential to concentrate on improved access to contraceptives; reduced child mortality; and promotion of women's rights to reproductive health. The language of the original draft document espousing the empowerment of women was strongly criticised by fundamentalist regimes and some Muslim countries boycotted the conference. Several Catholic countries and the Vatican

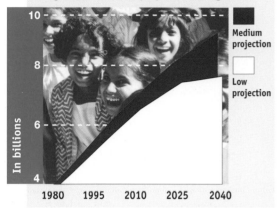

Projected world population growth

The State of World Population 1995, UNFPA.

campaigned against the provisions regarding **contraception**.

INTERNATIONAL COURT OF JUSTICE (ICJ or World Court)

The **League of Nations** established the Permanent Court of International Justice in 1920. Its successor, the International Court of Justice (ICJ) was founded in 1945 and is the major judicial body of the **United Nations**. Based in The Hague, the Court is meant to maintain **international law** and peace. In reality, it is effectively impotent since more than 110 UN member states refuse to recognize its jurisdiction.

Only sovereign states may take disputes to the Court. But the ICJ's ultimate authority depends on both parties agreeing to accept its ruling – not always guaranteed. For example, in 1974 France refused to accept the Court's jurisdiction when Australia and New Zealand attempted to ban French nuclear testing in the South Pacific. The Court has 15 judges, elected by the UN **Security Council** and the **General Assembly**. The 15

seats are distributed in the same way as membership on the Security Council – the 5 permanent members of the Council have always been represented on the World Court bench, except for China which has not nominated a judge since 1967.

INTERNATIONAL DEVELOPMENT ASSOCIATION (IDA)

An affiliate of the **World Bank** established in 1960 to provide soft loans to **developing countries** which are too poor to service loans on conventional terms. Credits are approved interest-free for 50 years with a 10-year grace period. The bulk of IDA's resources are provided by the 24 richest World Bank members with the fund replenished at 3-year intervals. In 1992, over half of IDA loans were tied to purchases of goods and services from donor countries. Britain heads the list of the rich countries benefiting from this 'aid'. Over $400 million went to UK suppliers in 1992, more money than was loaned out to Bangladesh.

INTERNATIONAL ENERGY AGENCY (IEA)

The IEA is an autonomous, 23-member body established in 1974 to set up an international energy programme. The agency operates within the framework of the **Organization for Economic Co-operation and Development** (OECD). Its basic objectives include encouraging member countries to reduce their dependence on **oil** by adopting energy **conservation** and using **alternative energy** sources. Members agree to share oil supplies in emergencies. The IEA also aims to stabilize the international energy trade and develop a rational management programme for use of world

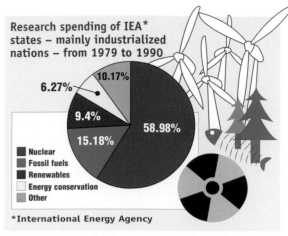

Research spending of IEA* states – mainly industrialized nations – from 1979 to 1990

6.27%
10.17%
9.4%
15.18%
58.98%

- Nuclear
- Fossil fuels
- Renewables
- Energy conservation
- Other

*International Energy Agency

A Solar Manifesto by Herman Scheer, James and James, London 1994.

energy **resources** in the interest of the global community.

INTERNATIONAL FINANCE CORPORATION (IFC)

A **World Bank** affiliate established in 1956. The IFC was set up to encourage and assist private sector investment in **developing countries** by providing loans to private companies and financial intermediaries (ie investment and development banks) where sufficient capital is not otherwise available on reasonable terms. Finance is always provided alongside funds from private investors; the IFC reinforces rather than competes with private capital. The agency has 161 members and total authorized capital of over $1 billion.

INTERNATIONAL FUND FOR AGRICULTURAL DEVELOPMENT (IFAD)

IFAD evolved from a 1974 World Food Conference resolution which stressed the need for a new financing on concessional terms for agricultural projects in **developing countries**. IFAD's role is to mobilize **resources** for agricultural development – specifically to focus on food production, rural **poverty** and the creation of **employment** for the landless poor. The Fund was launched in 1977, with an initial funding of $1 billion, as the 13th specialized agency of the **United Nations**. OECD and **OPEC** members provide the bulk of IFAD's funds. Low-interest loans to small farmers and the rural poor put seeds, **fertilizer** and tools in the hands of those who have previously had little outside help. Although IFAD is widely recognized as a highly effective agency and one that helps those most in need, it has had trouble convincing members to fulfil their financial obligations.

INTERNATIONAL LABOUR OFFICE (ILO)
Founded in 1919 when it was affiliated to the **League of Nations**, the ILO became a specialized agency of the **UN** in 1946. Its stated goals are to improve working conditions and living standards around the world. Based in Geneva, the 171-member agency advocates a World Labour Code to protect the interests of workers; supports labour research projects; monitors labour legislation; and provides technical assistance to developing nations. The ILO's main goals are to establish international labour standards and to develop ways of ensuring fair labour conditions on an international scale. It is especially concerned with the conditions under which young people and women are employed; the protection of workers outside their native

Tinkering with cans
Under an African sun, two Ugandans fashion watering cans out of metal roofing sheets. Many workers like these are not protected by laws covering wages or safety – issues covered by the International Labour Office. ILO

countries; the activities of **transnational corporations**; industrial relations; and **human rights**. In 1977, the US withdrew from the ILO on the grounds that it had become dominated by political interests but later rejoined in 1980.

INTERNATIONAL LAW
Present international law evolved from regulations drawn up to govern relations between European Christian states in the 16th and 17th centuries. Formation of the **League of Nations**, later the **United Nations**, allowed member states access to this global legal framework. Since then international law has significantly broadened its scope to include the oceans, **Antarctica** and space. However, laws cannot be enforced unless they coincide with the aims of one or more of the major powers. In effect **Third World** countries have little opportunity to press for their rights or seek redress for unjust treatment. Public international law (also called the Law of Nations) is administered by the **World Court**. It is based on: 1) natural law or laws recognized by sovereign nations; 2) codified agreements between states, including international conventions; 3) customs followed in practice and; 4) the writings and opinions of respected legal figures.

Private international law, also called Conflict of Laws, determines the laws a country should apply and in which courts jurisdiction lies. This can prove crucial for the fair treatment of claimants, as shown by the case of industrial poisoning in **Bhopal**, India. It also highlights the inequalities within the world's differing legal systems. With the growing recognition of 'common heritage' issues such as transboundary pollution and the exploitation of Antarctica, space and the high seas, there is an increasing interest in the role of international

law. The 1990s have been declared the Decade of International Law by the UN General Assembly.

INTERNATIONAL MARITIME ORGANIZATION (IMO)
The IMO was set up in 1959, originally as the International Maritime Consultative Organization, a specialized **UN** agency with headquarters in the United Kingdom. The IMO now has 149 member nations and 2 associate members. Its main objectives are the development of internationally acceptable ways of improving safety at sea; the prevention of marine pollution from ships; and means of improved navigation for maritime traffic.

The IMO facilitates the drafting and adoption of international conventions, protocols and codes of practice. It also arranges seminars and workshops and produces publications and conference proceedings. As part of its general programmes the IMO also provides technical assistance in the form of personnel and training facilities, mainly for the less-developed countries.

INTERNATIONAL MONETARY FUND (IMF)
The IMF is a specialized financial agency of the **United Nations** established under the 1944 **Bretton Woods** agreements. Along with the **World Bank**, **General Agreement on Tariffs and Trade** and the **Marshall Plan** it formed part of a system designed to stabilize the global economy. The Fund now has 179 members. Its stated aims are to promote international monetary co-operation and the growth of world trade, to stabilize foreign **exchange rates** and to smooth financial arrangements amongst member states. The ultimate goal is to provide a secure global financial base that will support a liberal trading system and avoid the protectionist policies which

contributed to the global economic depression of the 1930s.

Each member country contributes to the Fund in both gold and national currency, in accordance with pre-set quotas which also determine the amount they may withdraw. The higher a member's contribution, the greater its voting rights. The upshot is that the IMF is controlled by the wealthiest nations.

Having originally operated in US dollars linked to gold, the IMF switched to **Special Drawing Rights** (SDRs) as a standard unit of account in 1972. Countries receive SDRs in proportion to their national quotas and these may be exchanged for foreign currency to buy imports. The IMF provides standby loans to members with balance-of-payment problems; the amount of the loan is limited by the quota system and is normally repayable within 5 years. If the loan is large, conditions are attached and the recipient country has to adopt economic and fiscal policies recommended by the Fund and follow IMF advice on how to resolve its financial problems (see **Structural Adjustment Programmes**).

Measures usually include reducing expenditure in so-called 'non-productive' areas like health, education and food subsidies. Attempts by some members in 1996 to force the sale of part of the IMF's gold reserves (90% of the Fund's reserves are in gold) to help ease Third World **debt** and ease conditionality on new loans were unsuccessful.

The IMF operates special facilities for developing nations. These include the **Compensatory Financing Facility** which makes additional cash available to compensate for unexpected shortfalls in export earnings and a facility which makes financing available for the setting up of buffer stocks agreed under **International Commodity Agreements**. The IMF is based in Washington and the head is always a European (as the head of the World Bank is always an American). Power resides, in theory, with 21 executive directors. In fact, control is exercised by the major quota nations – Japan, the United Kingdom, France, Germany and the United States which has the largest quota.

INTERNATIONAL PROGRAMME OF CHEMICAL SAFETY (IPCS)

An international co-operative set up in 1980 to monitor and oversee the safe use and management of industrial and agricultural chemicals. Initially proposed by the **International Labour Office**, the **World Health Organization** and the **United Nations Environment Programme**, the IPCS brings together 27 countries and 67 participating institutions concerned with chemical safety standards.

There are over 7 million known chemicals and thousands of new ones are introduced each year. At least 80,000 chemicals in regular use are potentially hazardous to humans. The IPCS reports on the effects of these different chemicals on the human body; sets guidelines for exposure limits; proposes means to standardize measurements used in exposure and toxicity testing; and provides information on methods for coping with chemical accidents and the treatment of poisoning.

In 1996 some 60 top international scientists wrote an open letter to the IPCS expressing their concern at the 'improper' and 'excessive' influence of business interests. The scientists claimed that the IPCS had deviated from accepted procedures for scientific objectivity by giving representatives of industry undue influence in the programme's assessments of chemical hazards.

INTERNATIONAL ORGANIZATION FOR STANDARDIZATION (ISO)

An organization founded in 1946 and based in Geneva which is concerned with establishing, controlling and making uniform all international scientific, industrial and commercial standards of measurement and design. There are 76 national Standards Institutes around the world and another 23 associate members.

INTERNATIONAL REGISTER OF POTENTIALLY TOXIC CHEMICALS (IRPTC)

A centralized register of data on hazardous chemicals, established in 1976, following a recommendation of the 1972 UN Conference on the Human Environments in Stockholm. The IRPTC is located in Geneva and run by the **United Nations Environment Programme** (UNEP). Although more than 65,000 industrial chemicals are now in commercial use, little data is available on their dangers to human health or the environment. The IRPTC disseminates data on these chemicals, locates and publicizes the lack of knowledge in specific areas and encourages research where necessary.

INTERNATIONAL TROPICAL TIMBER ORGANIZATION (ITTO)

An organization established in 1983 to promote the sustainable production and **conservation** of tropical timber and to oversee the International Tropical Timber Agreement (ITTA). It is composed of representatives from 23 producer and 27 user countries and from the timber industry. ITTO members account for 75% of the world's **tropical forests** and more than 95% of trade in tropical timber. It's task is to promote the timber trade and ensure that it becomes viable in the long-term. Its 'Target 2000' programme aims to ensure that all

Walking on water
In Kalimantan, Indonesia, a woman picks her way carefully over logs which have been hewn from the tropical forests. ITTO

tropical timber entering international trade by the year 2000 is derived from forests under sustainable management.

Global trade in tropical timber amounts to around $6 billion annually, with virtually all trees harvested from natural forests in an unsustainable fashion. Trade is falling as forests are exploited. Research by the ITTO in 1990 found that less than 0.1% of tropical logging was being done sustainably. Progress towards Target 2000 has been painfully slow.

INTERNATIONAL WHALING COMMISSION (IWC)
Set up in 1946 under the International Convention for the Regulation of Whaling, the IWC governs **whaling** operations by member governments. It regulates the hunting of 12 species of great whales and the minke whale. Its mandate is to promote whaling on a sustainable basis rather than curtailing or abolishing the industry. It sets catch and size limits and provides information on whale numbers and whaling operations.

The IWC has been the main focus of the international anti-whaling campaign. In 1988 it introduced a three-year moratorium on whaling which most nations respected, although some whaling was carried out for purported 'scientific' purposes. In 1996 the IWC's Scientific Committee estimated there were at least 750,000 minke whales in the southern oceans and a further 110,000 in the north Atlantic. With these revised numbers, Japan and Norway, the world's leading whaling nations, are free to take their full quota under the IWC system.

INTIFADA
An Arabic word meaning 'rebellion' or 'uprising'. In 1987 several Palestinian labourers were killed by an Israeli military vehicle in the Gaza Strip, part of the territory captured by Israel during the Six Day War of 1967. The funerals of the labourers turned into protests at the Israeli occupation. A general strike followed, along with civil protests. In response, Israeli repression increased. The clamp-down exacerbated an already volatile situation, leading to more confrontations and deaths. The balance of power and peace in the Middle East was rocked by this uprising of an unarmed grassroots population.

INUIT
Indigenous people who live in the far north of Canada, Alaska and Greenland. Traditionally, Inuit fished and hunted seals, whales, walruses and caribou. Clothing was made from animal skins and the main social units were small family bands. Native people to the south called them 'Eskimos', a Cree word meaning 'eaters of raw meat'. There are now about 70,000 Inuit in total.

In 1975, Inuit in Canada called for the creation of an autonomous state. In 1992, the Government announced the creation of the territory of 'Nunavut', meaning 'Our Land' in the Inuit language. The 2.2 million square kilometre territory includes the northern part of Hudson Bay and the Arctic archipelago and represents about 20% of the Canadian landmass. Inuit leaders were initially scornful, claiming the area represented only a portion of the Inuit's historical lands. Eventually, however, they approved the agreement in a plebiscite.

Nunavut will become a quasi-independent state within Canada and the 17,500 Inuit who live there will obtain political autonomy and property rights over the **land**.

'Revolution of stones'
So PLO leader Yasser Arafat dubbed the 1988 *Intifada* (Uprising) where Palestinian youths defied the might of the Israeli Army with Molotov cocktails, sticks and of course, stones. INTIFADA

The new territory is not considered a Canadian province but the federal government will retain administrative control. In return for renouncing territorial claims in the future, the Inuit were to receive almost $1 billion over a 12-year period.

INVISIBLE TRADE

This is trade which does not involve the direct sale of material goods – including services like transport, **tourism**, banking and insurance as well as income from interest, dividends and returns on investments. Western countries, especially the United States and the United Kingdom, earn the most from this form of trade.

IRRIGATION

A means of providing otherwise unavailable **water** to farmers to enable crops to be grown. Irrigated farming is one of the most productive forms of agriculture known. The world's irrigated farmlands produce 40% of the total global crop yield. Of the 1.5 billion hectares of total cropland, around 250 million hectares are irrigated.

Irrigation may involve the flooding of whole fields (as in **rice** growing) or the water may be run in channels between rows of plants. High-pressure sprinklers may also be used. Traditional systems incorporating earth banks, channels and lifting devices are still used by farmers throughout the **Third World**. Modern methods are frequently large-scale and expensive. They usually involve building **dams**, artificial reservoirs, canals and pumping systems.

From 1950 to 1970 the irrigated area of the world doubled. But the industrial-scale irrigation projects responsible for this are expensive – it can cost up to $10,000 to irrigate a single hectare of land in some areas. Ironically, irrigated land is often used for **cash crops** to raise the foreign exchange needed to repay the installation costs of the irrigation equipment.

Irrigation has been practised for centuries, especially in the Third World where 75% of all irrigated **land** is still found. In 1985 Third World countries had invested $250 billion in irrigation. By the year 2,000 another $100 billion will have been spent.

China has over a third of the

MORE THAN 10% of the world's irrigated land suffers from yield-suppressing salt build-up which is spreading at the rate of 1.5 million hectares a year. Currently less than 40% of water used in irrigation ends up benefiting crops.

world's irrigated land, with India not far behind. Indian authorities have spent $20 billion on irrigation over the past 40 years. However, much of the world's land is badly waterlogged and plagued by **salinization**. Productivity on these lands is falling. Almost 10 million hectares of irrigated land in India is in danger of becoming infertile.

The amount of irrigated land world-wide grew from 163 million hectares in 1968 to 271 million hectares in 1985. However, by 1990 a growing awareness of the environmental costs of irrigation were beginning to hit home and the amount of irrigated land was increasing at just 1% annually, less than half the increase seen in the 1970s.

Irrigation is extremely water intensive: it can take as much as 1,700 cubic kilometres of water to grow half a tonne of grain – sufficient to supply half of a person's diet for 3 years. Around a quarter of water withdrawn for irrigation is lost during storage or transport. Although more is being pumped from the ground than ever, less and less of it is being used to grow crops. Industrial and domestic demands for water are increasing everywhere, especially in Asia. Competition for water between rural and urban uses means that irrigation water for agriculture will fall 15-30% short of projected demand in parts of India, Indonesia and Malaysia if urban needs are fully met. On the Arabian peninsula 75% of the water for farming is drawn from deep aquifers that are not replenished by rainfall.

Excessive or ill-managed irrigation can also leach **soil** nutrients, leaving soils drenched with salts and can threaten public health. In

Simple magic

The graceful Egyptian *shaduf* is one of the earliest forms of irrigation. Its simple movement fills a bucket of water which is tipped into a channel from where it flows to give life to thirsty plants. **IRRIGATION**

THE **A** TO **Z** OF WORLD DEVELOPMENT

pursuit of maximum production and short-term financial gain, modern schemes are large-scale and intensive – often 3 crops are grown on the same piece of land. Drainage is usually inadequate and salinization is common. By 1990, 30-40% of the world's irrigated cropland was thought to be either waterlogged or suffering from salinization.

Irrigation also provides new homes for creatures carrying water-borne diseases like **malaria**, filariasis and **schistosomiasis**. Crop-destroying insects and pests like rats thrive in newly-irrigated areas when year-round supplies of food suddenly become available. It is now generally recognized that irrigation projects are most likely to succeed where projects are small, fallow periods are observed and management is left up to local communities. Research has found that irrigating every other furrow in fields can save a third of water with only minor reductions in yields.

Similarly, intermittent rather than continuous flooding of rice paddies could save 40% of water with minimal loss of output. In the 1990s new, highly-efficient micro-irrigation systems were introduced. These include drip irrigation, where water is literally dripped at the base of plants. By 1991, Israel was using drip irrigation on more than half its irrigated land.

ISLAM

The Muslim religion originated in Arabia in the 7th century AD and was spread by Arab conquests 1,300 years ago. Its scriptures are detailed in the Koran which is the basis of Islamic belief, practice and law. Its holiest shrine is Mecca in Saudi Arabia. Hundreds of thousands of Muslims make the pilgrimage there every year. The majority of the world's 850 million Muslims are not Arabs. More live in India, Pakistan and Bangladesh than in all the Arab countries combined. Within Islam there are deep sectarian divisions,

Islamic majesty
'None to be worshipped but Allah. Muhammad is his prophet' reads the inscription on this mosque in Nairobi, Kenya – so there can be no excuses for ignorance. ISLAM

primarily between the Shias and the Sunni. The Islamic Conference, founded in 1969, is an organization with 45 member states.

Most members agree on issues like the Palestinian struggle against Israel. But the Iran-Iraq war caused serious divisions and several Islamic nations are concerned about Libya and Iran using religion to extend their influence in the Islamic world.

Over the past 50 years there has been an growing interest in Islam by black Americans in the United States seeking an alternative to the racial attitudes of many white Christians.

IVORY

Close-grained, calcified tissue which forms the tusks of elephants, walruses and the teeth of hippopotamus. It is used to make piano keys, jewellery and ornaments. The Japanese alone currently import around 130 tonnes each year. In 1989, the African elephant, the main source of ivory, was declared an **endangered species** by the **Convention on Trade in Endangered Species of Flora and Fauna** (CITES), effectively preventing global trade in the commodity. In response, ivory-producing countries Botswana, Burundi, Malawi, Mozambique, Zambia, Zimbabwe, South Africa and China said that they would continue to trade ivory with other countries doing the same or with countries who were not CITES members. China later agreed to the global ban in 1991.

At the 1994 meeting of CITES, South Africa raised the possibility of exploiting the ivory from the hundreds of elephants culled annually in Kruger National Park. The proposal was withdrawn when no backing was received. In 1995 Kenya burned 10 tonnes of confiscated ivory to reaffirm its commitment to saving the elephant. As the trade in elephant ivory winds down, there is growing concern about the slaughter of other ivory-bearing animals like the walrus.

Jumbo catch
Spears at the ready, a group of African hunters surround an elephant in this 1860 engraving - ivory and meat were the prizes they sought. IVORY

Landmines
Generals and warlords are spoiled for choice in this deadly weapon.
There are some 350 types of landmines, supplied by over 50
countries. Danger, Mines – *Perigo Minas!*

JKL

J ayewardene – Low-Income Countries

JKL

Bold indicates a cross-reference

JINNAH, MOHAMMED ALI (1876-1948)

Indian Muslim politician, founder and first governor-general of Pakistan. The eldest of 7 children, Jinnah went to school in India, then attended law school in Britain where he qualified in 1895. He returned the following year and started his own law practice in Bombay. Ten years later he entered politics. His main goal was to establish some form of Hindu-Muslim unity. Opposed to Mahatma Gandhi's pacifist stance, Jinnah left both the All-India Muslim League and the Congress in 1920.

His efforts to overcome Hindu-Muslim tensions in India led him to work with legislative assemblies in India and Britain and he attended the Round Table Conferences in London from 1930-32. He was originally opposed to the idea of an independent Pakistan, but he soon became convinced that a Muslim homeland on the Indian subcontinent was the only way to safeguard Muslim interests and the Muslim way of life.

His energy revitalized the Muslim League which in 1940 adopted a resolution to form a separate Muslim state. Overcoming the opposition of **Mahatma Gandhi**, **Jawarhalal Nehru** and the British colonial administration, an agreement was finally reached to establish Pakistan as an independent country in 1947. Jinnah became the country's first Prime Minister and was regarded as the father of the nation until his death in 1948.

JAYEWARDENE, JUNIUS RICHARD (1906-1996)

Sri Lankan politician. After graduating from law college, he became a significant national politician in the years before Ceylon (now Sri Lanka) gained its independence in 1948. He was initially socialist-leaning, favouring elements of both **Buddhism** and Marxism. He joined the United National Party (UNP) of Ceylon and held several political and ministerial posts before becoming party leader in 1970.

In 1976, the UNP initiated a series of national strikes which led to a state of emergency being imposed by Prime Minister **Srimavo Bandaranaike**. When this was lifted in 1977, the UNP won the subsequent election and Jayewardene became Prime Minister. The following year the constitution was changed and he was made President.

Meanwhile in the North, Tamil separatists continued to demand independence, despite Jayewardene's concession to recognize the Tamil language in the new constitution. Unrest and general strikes continued, fuelled by IMF-approved economic measures which caused thousands to lose their jobs and prices to rise. Nonetheless, the UNP won the next election in 1981, primarily because of a boycott by opposition parties.

In Sri Lanka's first Presidential election in 1982, Jayewardene won 53% of the vote. He then moved to turn the country into a 'duty free zone'. Despite a traditional policy of non-alignment, he moved the country closer to the United States.

In 1987, he signed an accord with India's Prime Minister Rajiv Gandhi in an attempt to calm the ethnic crisis in Sri Lanka, although groups on both sides continued to clash. When the UNP won the elections again in 1988 the 82-year-old Jayewardene ceded power.

THE **A** TO **Z** OF WORLD DEVELOPMENT

JUNK FOOD

A term used to describe modern, industrially-processed food which is either unhealthy or of poor nutritional quality. It forms a significant and growing part of national diets, especially in North America and Europe. Americans now eat a third less fresh fruit and vegetables than they did at the turn of the century. Over the same period their diet of processed food has tripled. This rise has been accompanied by a large increase in the consumption of saturated fats and refined carbohydrates. More than 75% of what Americans eat is processed in some fashion. This costs more than $10 billion a year, 70% more than it costs to grow the food. Globally, advertising pressure to promote junk food is growing at an alarming rate. Less than 50 US-based corporations account for over two-thirds of all food processing.

KAUNDA, KENNETH (1924-)

Zambian leader. Kaunda was the leading African politician opposed to the Federation of Rhodesia and Nyasaland under the British colonial administration. The proposed union was eventually called off and he was appointed Prime Minister in 1964 of what was then called Northern Rhodesia. Ten months later the country's name was changed to Zambia and Kaunda became the independent nation's first President.

Kaunda strove to keep in check militants opposed to Ian Smith's white-led regime in Rhodesia and found himself in conflict with Britain over several issues, including his opposition to racism. In 1972 he assumed authoritarian powers to preserve national cohesion, but was confirmed as the people's choice after a new constitution in 1973. He garnered international respect as a leader, but in the 1990s internal opposition to his government was growing in the face of economic malaise and corruption. He was voted out in 1991 and replaced by Frederick Chiluba.

KENYATTA, JOMO (1895?-1978)

First President of Kenya (1964-78). A member of the majority Kikuyu tribe, he entered public life by joining the Kikuyu Youth Association in Nairobi. In 1929 he travelled Europe to protest against British encroachment upon Kikuyu land. He returned for a 15-year stay in Europe in 1931 that included study at the London School of Economics.

In 1946 he became head of the New Kenya African Union, a nationalist group seeking political rights for blacks. In 1952 he was jailed by the British for 7 years. He went on to head the Kenya African National Union (KANU), which won a majority in elections for an independent Kenyan parliament in 1962. In December 1963 Kenya became independent and Kenyatta assumed the role of Prime Minister. The following year he proclaimed Kenya a republic and became its president. KANU became the sole legal political party and opposition was silenced. Kenyatta followed a pro-West course in his leadership of Kenya, encouraging capitalist growth and promoting foreign investment.

KHOMEINI, AYATOLLAH RUHOLLAH (1900-1989)

Imam (spiritual leader) of Iran from 1979 to 1989. Born Sayyid Ruhollah Moussavi, Khomeini studied Islamic theology and law, going on to become a teacher and author of over 20 religious books. In the 1950s he earned the title of ayatollah for his Islamic scholarship. In the early 1960s he emerged as a leader of the Shia clergy's opposition to Shah Reza Pehlavi's regime, organizing demonstrations against the Shah's modernization programs. Khomeini underwent jail and house arrest after calling for the Shah's overthrow in 1963. He then spent 13 years in Iraq and issued several proclamations denouncing the Shah which were secretly circulated in Iran. In 1978 when the Iranian Government tried to attack his character in a newspaper article, Muslim riots broke out across the country. Iran then put pressure on Iraq to expel him, and he resettled in Paris. In France he had greater access to the international media and gave instructions to his followers in Iran over the telephone. On February 1, 1979 Khomeini returned to Iran (after the Shah had fled into exile) and declared it an Islamic republic and himself its supreme religious and political leader for life.

Under his regime thousands of people were executed, women's rights minimized and Western music banned. From November 4, 1979 to January 20, 1981 militants held the US embassy staff in Teheran hostage. Khomeini called the US the 'Great Satan' and did not order the release of the hostages until US President Jimmy Carter was leaving office.

The Iran-Iraq War (1980 – 1988) consolidated popular support for his regime, but left hundreds of thousands dead and the economy in ruins. In 1989, Khomeini famously issued a *fatwa* ordering the death of British author Salman Rushdie for alleged blasphemy in his book *The Satanic Verses*.

KING, MARTIN LUTHER, Jr. (1929-1968)

US civil rights leader. Born to a family of black Baptist ministers in Atlanta, Georgia, he graduated from Morehouse college in 1948, received a divinity degree from Crozier Theological Seminary in 1951 and a doctorate in 1955 from Boston University where he met Coretta Scott, whom he married. Accepting a ministry at the Dexter Avenue Baptist Church in Montgomery, Alabama, he formed the Montgomery Improvement Association to change the climate of racial tension which was maintained by segregated bus seating. This was the first of many organizations he formed to pursue non-violent resistance along the lines of the Indian leader **Mahatma Gandhi**. The Montgomery buses were desegregated in 1956.

King first gained national recognition for his civil rights demonstrations in Birmingham, Alabama, in 1963 which led to his arrest. On August 28, 1963, he led the March on Washington, delivering his famous 'I Have a Dream' speech to 250,000 civil rights supporters. The following year he was awarded the Nobel Prize for peace.

In 1965 he led another march to Selma, Alabama, for voting rights. The next year he took his campaign to the northern US. As a pacifist he opposed the **Vietnam War**. On April 4, 1968, he was assassinated in Memphis, Tennessee, where he had gone to lead a strike of sanitation workers. James Earl Ray, his white assassin, later claimed there was a wider conspiracy to the shooting. King's birthday, January 15, is a public holiday in most US states.

KOREAN WAR (1950-1953)

At the end of World War II, the Allies established the 38th parallel as a temporary dividing line between Soviet-occupied North Korea and US-occupied South Korea. The goal was to disarm the Japanese forces that had controlled the territories since 1904. Subsequent **UN** efforts to reunite the country failed.

On June 25, 1950, North Korean troops launched a surprise invasion of South Korea. The **UN** gathered an international force from 15 countries under the command of US General Douglas MacArthur to halt the invasion of South Korea. By November 24, 1950 the North Koreans were driven back to the Yalu River and UN forces planned to reunite Korea under control of the (pro-capitalist, pro-American) South. But two days later a large Chinese army invaded the North and helped the North Koreans push back the **UN** forces. By January 1, 1951, MacArthur's 485,000 strong UN army was driven back to the 38th parallel. A 'talking war' began with both sides trying to reach an accord, while fighting continued around the dividing line. MacArthur, who was given to making inflammatory pronouncements, was replaced by General Matthew B Ridgway. Offensives and counter-offensives resulted in heavy casualties.

Finally an armistice was signed on July 27, 1953, but before that prisoners were repatriated. UN negotiators insisted that the over 70,000 prisoners taken by the UN forces be allowed to choose whether to return to the North or not. Three-quarters did not. No formal peace treaty has been signed in the region.

KWASHIORKOR

A form of **malnutrition** caused by severe protein deficiency. It mainly occurs in young children under the age of 5. It develops soon after breast-fed babies are weaned and occurs commonly in poor countries, especially parts of West Africa where the normal diet lacks protein and families are large. It is especially common in young children weaned to a diet of cereal, **cassava**, plantain and sweet potato or other similar starchy foods.

The name kwashiorkor is derived from a Ghanaian word meaning 'the sickness that the elder children get when the next baby is born'. Affected children are apathetic, have swollen stomachs and ankles, diarrhoea and enlarged livers. A reddish-orange discoloration of hair is frequently seen and associated gastric infections are also common. Any infection usually proves to be fatal. Recovery is rapid and complete when children are supplied with a healthy, nutritionally-balanced diet.

Hands up

The war is over for this North Korean soldier as he is caught by his enemies – a US marine and his South Korean ally. **KOREAN WAR**

LAISSEZ-FAIRE

A term (literally meaning 'leave things alone') coined by Colbert, Finance Minister to Louis XIV of France, it was adopted by those who believe the state's role is to protect property rights and to interfere as little as possible in the free play of market forces which are based on self-interest and the profit motive.

The concept was also advocated by British economist **Adam Smith** and widely accepted until the beginning of the 19th century when the failings of unrestrained **capitalism** became clear: the rise of monopolies; the unjust distribution of wealth; and the gross exploitation of labour. *Laissez-faire* is now used to describe the economic thinking of neo-conservatives and the 'New Right'. They contend that there should be no controls on capital flows within or between any economy. The theory is still offered as a justification for unhampered free markets, though in practise there has never been a pure *laissez-faire* economy. Today most nations have 'mixed' economies with varying degrees of involvement by the state.

LAND

There are an estimated 13 billion hectares of land above sea level. Approximately 1.5 billion are being used to grow crops. This total has increased by 9% since 1965, whereas pasture lands and wood lands have both been declining steadily over the same period.

In Asia, an estimated 82% of cropland is already being cultivated. In Africa, 30% of the continent's 840 million hectares of land is potentially cultivable but only a third of it is being used.

As the world's **population** grows the amount of land available per person decreases. Per capita cropland has fallen by a third since 1945 and a further fall (to around

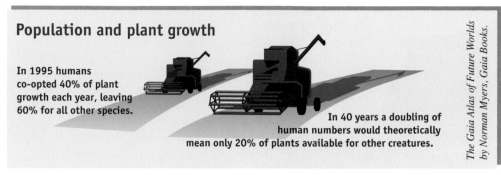

Population and plant growth

In 1995 humans co-opted 40% of plant growth each year, leaving 60% for all other species.

In 40 years a doubling of human numbers would theoretically mean only 20% of plants available for other creatures.

The Gaia Atlas of Future Worlds by Norman Myers, Gaia Books.

0.17 hectares per person) is expected by the year 2000. It is estimated that on average a hectare of land is required to feed one person.

As much as 15% of all global farmland may have been destroyed since 1945 as a result of **salinization**, waterlogging, compacting from heavy machinery, erosion and pollution from **agrochemicals**. Nearly two-thirds of the most degraded land is in Africa and Asia.

LAND REFORM

The break-up of large agricultural estates, farms or ranches, followed by redistribution to landless peasants or small farmers of both the land and the legal title to the land. Reforms may be initiated by governments, individuals or by revolution and may include assistance and credit for the new landholders. The most common political goal of land reform is to abolish feudal or colonial forms of ownership and prevent exploitation of peasants. Economic goals include encouraging more intensive cultivation and a better integration of agriculture into the national economy.

A clear example of land reform took place during the French revolution when feudalism was abolished and land owned by the aristocracy and the clergy was seized and sold at public auction. In Britain, the pressure for land reform was eased by the exodus of the rural population to the cities during the industrial revolution. The Russian Revolution of 1917 introduced collective ownership of

all agricultural land. In Latin America, land reform has been violently resisted by land-owning élites whose political clout and power far outstrips the ability of *campesinos* (peasant farmers) to force changes in land-holding patterns.

The most successful example was in Mexico in 1911 when **Emiliano Zapata** succeeded in turning over a third of all privately-held land to the peasantry. In Africa reforms have been painfully slow. Ethiopia and Mozambique have carried out the most radical reforms, vesting title of the land in the state and guaranteeing rights to cultivate the land to farmers and their descendants.

Land redistribution in communist countries like China and Cuba was successful in reducing widespread **hunger** and in giving peasants control over their immediate future. Many Pacific islanders believe they have an inalienable right to their land and that even if others claim 'legal' ownership, it will always revert back to them or their descendants.

LANDLESS LABOURERS

In 1988 the **UN Food and Agriculture Organization** (FAO) warned that landlessness is 'the single largest agrarian problem' facing the **Third World**. Three-quarters of the Earth's **population** live in **developing countries** and 70% of these people are small-scale farmers, though many are effectively landless. Millions of subsistence farmers own no **land**. In Peru, 75%

Luther King – Landless Labourers

of the rural population are either landless or have too little land to sustain their families. In India, 40% of rural households are landless. It is estimated that 220 million rural households (some 938 million people) will be landless by the turn of the century.

Tenant farmers work land owned by someone else. Shifting cultivators clear land that has no apparent owner, until it becomes unproductive, then move on. Many other people are 'functionally landless'. They may have legal title or customary right, but not enough land to support themselves. Or else their tenure may be worthless because they lack water rights. In some countries women have no legal right to own land.

In many countries land-holding patterns from colonial days continue and small-scale farmers are excluded from the best and most fertile land. Governments have favoured large farms in order to develop **cash crops** for export. Meanwhile **population** pressure causes overuse and destruction of already marginal areas. As good land is exhausted by generations of misuse, the total number of landless people swells.

The average size of family-held units is shrinking throughout the developing world. In 1970, throughout Africa and Asia farms averaged just under 2 hectares. By 1980 this had shrunk to around 0.5 hectares as the population grew. Landless and functionally landless farmers tend to have no collateral and are therefore denied access to the credit needed to buy seeds, **fertilizers** and equipment that may improve their situation. The result is a downward spiral into deepening **poverty** and **malnutrition**, or migration in search of paid **employment**. Many low-paid, unskilled urban workers in the developing world are from a landless, rural background.

LANDMINES

Around 2,000 people are involved in landmine accidents every month. Of these, around 800 will die as a result while the others will have been maimed for life. Countries like Angola and Cambodia have a very high rate of disability with around 30 amputees per 10,000 inhabitants. (The US which has no mine problem has an amputations rate of 1 per 22,000 people.) In many cases the vast majority of casualties have been civilians, often children. It is estimated that 85% of children who encounter landmines die before reaching hospital.

There are more than 110 million active landmines scattered in over 70 countries, or 1 for every 17 children or 52 humans in the world. A further 110 million have been stockpiled. The most commonly used mines are cheap, costing between $3 and $30 each. But removing them can cost 50 times as much. One deminer is killed and two are injured for every 5,000 mines cleared. About 100,000 mines are removed

each year, but until recently 2 million more were being planted annually. In 1996 the UN Secretary General increased his estimate of the resources needed to clear all existing mines from $33 billion to over $50 billion. In the same year funding for demining was less than $150 million.

By the 1990s, the global community had begun to tackle the problem. A broad-based coalition of **non-governmental organizations**, united as the International Campaign to Ban Landmines (ICBL). Their lobbying efforts were successful in raising the profile of the problem and got politicians talking about the issue. In 1997, with a ban on landmines signed by over 90 countries imminent, they were awarded the Nobel Peace Prize. The initiative to ban landmines took the name of the Ottawa Process, after a historic conference in Ottawa where Canadian Foreign Minister Lloyd Axworthy boldly challenged delegates from other countries to bypass consensus politics and agree

LANDMINES – THE WORST AFFECTED

Number of mines (millions)	Country	Amputees per 10,000 inhabitants
	Angola	
	Cambodia	
	Afghanistan	
	Iraq (Kurdistan)	
	Vietnam	
	Eritrea	
	Mozambique	
	Sudan	
	Ethiopia	
unknown	Burma	
	Bosnia &	not available
	Herzegovina	not available
	Croatia	not available

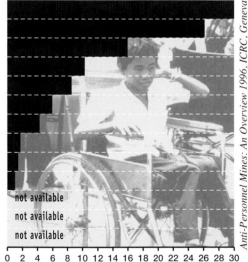

20 18 16 14 12 10 8 6 4 2 0   0 2 4 6 8 10 12 14 16 18 20 22 24 26 28 30

Anti-Personnel Mines: An Overview 1996, ICRC, Geneva.

Under normal circumstances amputations are very rare. In the US, which does not have a landmines problem, the rate is 1 per 22,000 people.
The leader in sheer number of mines in the ground is Egypt with 23 million (a mixture of anti-tank and antipersonnel), many left over from World War II, but they have not caused large-scale havoc because they are confined to border regions.

on a treaty to ban mines regardless of opposing positions. Activists argue that a ban is just the first step towards ameliorating the landmines problem. Attention needs to focus on the mammoth task of mine-clearance world-wide and destroying existing stockpiles.

LASSA FEVER

A rare but fatal viral disease endemic to West Africa, named after the village in Nigeria where it was discovered in 1969. It is transmitted to humans by rats. After an incubation of 1-3 weeks, headache, high fever and acute muscular pains develop. Those afflicted often experience difficulty in swallowing. Death, mainly from kidney or heart failure, results in over half of the cases. Lassa fever can kill within 7 days. The worst recorded outbreak of the disease was in 1997 when 23 people in Sierra Leone died.

Treatment with blood plasma from patients who have recovered is the best available therapy. The only known cure (Ribavirin) is produced by a US-based company which holds the patent rights. Costs of the drug skyrocketed to $1,000 per dose when it was falsely believed that it could prove useful in treating **HIV** infection. Two unlicensed Chinese producers of the drug have offered to donate a consignment to the Sierra Leone government at a price of around 50 cents a dose.

LATIN AMERICAN FREE TRADE ASSOCIATION (LAFTA)

LAFTA was formed in 1960 to remove all restrictions on trade among member countries: Argentina, Brazil, Bolivia, Chile, Colombia, Ecuador, Mexico, Paraguay, Peru, Uruguay and Venezuela. The Association worked to promote regional economic development in Latin America but made little progress towards a common market. In 1980, the same 11 states agreed to re-launch their efforts, replacing LAFTA with the Latin American Integration Association devoted to achieving the same end.

LEAD

A dense, soft, blue-grey metal. Lead is poisonous but extremely resistant to corrosion. It is malleable and has been used since Roman times for pipe work, especially for plumbing. It is a powerful neurotoxin, even in trace quantities. Lead pipes, particularly in soft-water areas, have become a major health problem and are gradually being replaced by plastic piping.

Lead is used for a variety of industrial purposes — in shields to protect against X-rays; in batteries; in paints; in glass production; and as an additive to gasoline.

The addition of tetra-ethyl lead to gas in order to prevent engine knocking has pumped massive quantities of lead into the environment, with extremely high concentrations in urban areas that have dense traffic flows. Each year 450,000 tonnes of lead are released into the atmosphere by human activities, compared to 3,500 tonnes from natural sources.

Acute lead poisoning is characterized by abdominal pain, muscle pains, **anaemia** and nerve and brain damage. Lead retards the development of young children, lowering mental function and learning ability.

Lead pollution has been dramatically curbed in industrial nations since the 1970s. But this has not happened in the developing world mainly because cars and industrial machinery are often old and poorly maintained. Most gasoline sold in Africa has a lead content between 0.5-0.8 grams per litre. Gasoline in Europe contains less than a third of that and, in the United States, less than a twentieth. More than 90% of children in some African cities have

LEAD
World reserves 120 million tons

TOP PRODUCERS: (1996)

Australia	20%
United States	15%
Canada	10%
China	8%
Mexico	4%
Other	30%

USBM 1991

lead levels in their blood high enough to cause neurological damage. Around 5.7 million tonnes of lead are produced each year for industrial purposes. Australia, with 465,000 tonnes, is the leading producer followed by the US, Canada and China.

LEAGUE OF NATIONS
(see also United Nations)

An international organization created in 1920 with the goal of maintaining world peace. The League's covenant was incorporated in post-war peace treaties at the end of World War I. However, the US was excluded when it refused to ratify the Treaty of Versailles. The League settled minor disputes and organized international conferences.

But in the 1930s it was unable to deal effectively with major international incidents such as the Japanese intervention in China and Italy's invasion of Ethiopia. Germany withdrew from the organization in 1933 and the League gradually became less effective. It was replaced by the **United Nations** after World War II.

LEAST DEVELOPED COUNTRIES (LDCs)

A category developed by the UN to describe poor, commodity-exporting **developing countries** with little industry. In 1968, 24 developing countries were recognized by the **UN Conference on Trade and Development**

LEE, KUAN YEW (1923-)

Singaporean politician and lawyer. Born into a wealthy English-speaking, Chinese family. After schooling in Singapore he went to university in England where he became a socialist and in 1950 received a degree in law. He returned to Singapore to become legal adviser to the Postal Union. He was opposed to Britain's colonial rule of his country and in the early 1950s founded the People's Action Party (PAP). In 1958 he helped negotiate a self-governing status for Singapore and in 1959 his party won a massive election victory. But Lee refused to form a government until Britain released members of his party who had been imprisoned. He became Prime Minister in 1959 and immediately proposed a 5-year plan of slum clearance, the emancipation of women, expansion of education services, industrialization and a comprehensive public housing programme.

In 1963, he took Singapore into the newly-created Federation of Malaysia. But this resulted in intense rivalry between Chinese and Malays in Singapore and eventually caused him to withdraw from the Federation. As a result, Singapore became a sovereign state under Lee's leadership. He soon came to dominate the nation's political activities. After the main opposition party boycotted parliament in 1966, his party won the next 4 elections unchallenged. His rule began to become more authoritarian, often threatening civil liberties and resorting to press censorship to silence dissent. Nonetheless, by the 1980s, Singapore followed Japan in per capita income and was a major manufacturing economy on the global scene. Lee Kuan Yew resigned from his post of Prime Minister in 1990, but retained his leadership of the PAP.

(UNCTAD) as LDCs. The criteria were: per capita **Gross Domestic Product** (GDP) of $1000 or less (at 1970 prices); manufacturing that contributed 10% or less of GDP; and a **literacy** rate of 20% or less. The category was adopted by the UN General Assembly in 1971.

At a conference in 1981 donor nations pledged to double their official development assistance to LDCs countries. By 1989, the category included 42 countries: Afghanistan, Bangladesh, Benin, Bhutan, Botswana, Burkina Faso, Burma, Burundi, Cape Verde, Central African Republic, Chad, Comoros Islands, Djibouti, Equatorial Guinea, Ethiopia, Gambia, Guinea, Guinea-Bissau, Haiti, Kiribati, Laos, Lesotho, Malawi, Maldives, Mali, Mauritania, Mozambique, Nepal, Niger, Rwanda, Samoa, São Tomé and Principe, Sierra Leone, Somalia, Sudan, Tanzania, Togo, Tuvalu, Uganda, Vanuatu, Western Samoa, Yemen and Yemen Democratic Republic.

In 1990, a second UN Conference on the Least Developed Countries was attended by 150 nations. Only 8 countries had met their 1981 pledge to double official development assistance. The Conference adopted a new Programme of Action which stressed **human rights** and democracy, the role of the private sector, the potential role of women in development and the need for stringent **population** policies.

LEGUMES

Leguminous plants are found throughout the world with the greatest variety in the tropics and subtropics. Of the 18,000 legumes, fewer than 20 are cultivated extensively. These include **groundnuts** (peanuts), soybeans, various peas and beans, and several varieties of clover. In addition, several species of leguminous trees are widely used. The most important feature of legumes is their ability to convert nitrogen from the air into inorganic nitrogen compounds which enrich the **soil** and can be readily used by other plants. The nitrogen-fixing contribution of legumes can be vital for maintaining soil productivity over long periods and a legume crop can add up to 500 kilograms of nitrogen annually to a hectare of **land**. Cultivated legume crops add more nitrogen to the soil world-wide than chemical **fertilizers**.

In Australia, over 100 million hectares of land have been brought into cultivation thanks to leguminous plants. Legume seeds, in the form of beans or pulses, are second only to cereals as a source of human and animal food. Before the **potato** was introduced into Europe, beans constituted the bulk of the diet of most people. Legume seeds remain a major source of food for millions of people in Latin America, India and throughout Asia. Several species of leguminous trees like **acacia** and leuceana are also able to fix nitrogen. They yield protein-rich foliage, pods and seeds. And since they tolerate drought conditions they are a valuable source of fodder for livestock in arid regions. Despite the chronic deficiency of protein in virtually every developing country there has been little research into increasing the yield of pulses.

LEPROSY

A chronic disease affecting the skin, mucous membranes and nerves which is particularly prevalent in tropical countries. Leprosy is caused by a bacterium related to the organism that causes **tuberculosis**. It is only contracted after close personal contact with an infected person, usually transmitted via sneezing or skin contact. After infection, the incubation period is usually 1-3 years and symptoms appear slowly. For many years leprosy could be controlled with potent sulphone drugs. Dapsone, developed in the 1940s, stopped bacteria from multiplying but dapsone-resistant strains of leprosy soon began to appear. However, treatment with a mixture of dapsone and two potent anti-leprosy drugs (rifampicin and clofazimine) proved to be a permanent cure. Over a million people have been cured by this combination. There are an estimated 1.8 million cases of leprosy in the world. But the total number of cases has dropped by 67% from an estimated 5.5 million in 1991. Improvement in living standards has seen the disease disappear from most industrialized countries but it is still prevalent in the **Third World** and in regions of the developed world where living conditions are poor. **Aboriginal** people in Australia are one example of this. Today, most people with leprosy (1.26 million) are in Southeast Asia. Multi-drug therapy is helping to eliminate leprosy as a public health problem, unthinkable even 10 years ago when there were still 12 million cases of the disease.

LENIN, VLADIMIR ILICH (1870-1924)

Russian revolutionary, born Vladimir Ilich Ulyanov. Lenin was born into a middle class family but became a strong advocate of Marxism while studying for a law degree which he was granted in 1891. Following graduation he was arrested as a subversive in 1895 and sentenced to exile in Siberia. From 1900 onward he lived mostly in Western Europe where he emerged as leader of the communist ('Bolshevik') section of the Russian Social Democrats.

When the Russian tsar was overthrown in 1917, Lenin returned to his homeland where he helped organize and direct the Bolsheviks to power in the October Revolution later that year. The new Soviet Government established a 'dictatorship of the proletariat', abolished all newly-won political and civil liberties and took the Communist Party as its official name.

Lenin was appointed head of state. He amended Marxist theory and persuaded many to accept his own revolutionary ideology which became known as Leninism. In 1920, Leninism became a world-wide movement when Lenin imposed his '21 conditions' which stipulated that communist parties everywhere should organize themselves according to the principles that he had laid down for the Russian party. He originally attempted to introduce a socialist system of economics, by abolishing markets, foreign exchanges and money, but in 1921 reversed this policy and allowed a market economy to be adopted.

In order to achieve a Communist revolution in the absence of a large industrial working class, Lenin had to rely heavily on the support of the peasantry, many of whom were only interested in increasing the size of their land holdings. His new economic climate led to a marked increase in the size of the rich peasant class known as Kulaks. The sweeping and draconian reorganization of the agricultural sector of Soviet society, begun shortly before Lenin's death and mostly carried out later under Stalin, was referred to as 'collectivization'. Efforts were made to ensure that agricultural workers were employed in the same way as industrial workers in the state-controlled sector. To achieve this, violent and oppressive actions were taken leading to a massive forced relocation and the murder of up to 6 million Kulaks and peasants.

LIE, TRYGVE HALVDAN (1896-1968)

Norwegian politician and international civil servant. He was appointed first Secretary General of the **UN** in 1946 and served until 1952. He was an outspoken leader and championed China's right to take a seat on the UN Security Council after the 1949 revolution. During his term of office he dealt with the Arab-Israeli War and the UN involvement in the **Korean War**. He favoured armed support for South Korea against Communist North Korea, a policy which echoed the American position. This alienated the Soviet Union and eventually led to his resignation.

LIBERATION THEOLOGY

A movement within Roman Catholicism which began at the second Latin American Bishops' Conference in Colombia in 1968. The participants issued a document affirming the rights of the poor and asserting that industrialized nations were enriching themselves at the expense of **developing countries**. The text, *Teología de la liberación*, was written by a Peruvian priest, Gustavo Gutierrez.

The movement aims to apply religious faith and the power of the church to assist the poor and oppressed through involvement in political and civil affairs. It identified some of the socio-economic factors leading to inequality and called for active participation. Liberation theology insists that the church take an active role in helping the poor to gain power and dignity in their struggle against wealthy élites. Followers have been heavily criticized by the Roman Catholic hierarchy and clergy advocating liberation theology have been accused of supporting Marxism and **socialism**. In the early 1990s, the Vatican began to take steps to try and curb the movement.

LIFE EXPECTANCY

Most published figures refer to life expectancy at birth. This is the number of years a new-born child will live, given the range of mortality risks in their country of birth. Modern medicine, science and technology all act to prolong lives. Consequently life expectancies for most people in the world have been steadily increasing. In 1950 the average life expectancy was a mere 46 years. By 1996 average life expectancy had risen to 65 years. The success brought about by improvements in living standards,

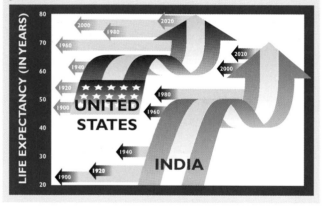

THE CENTURY GAP

People in the North still live longer than those in the South. But the gap is narrowing as the century draws to an end, and will continue to narrow into and beyond the year 2000.

Ageing in Developing Countries by Ken Tout
OUP/Help Age International, 1989.

health services and medical advances over the last 40 years has been reflected in rising life expectancies everywhere. Even in the **Third World** average life expectancy has risen from 41 to almost 60 years and is expected to reach 71 years by 2020.

The place of an individual's birth has a profound influence on determining the age of death. For example the average life expectancy in Africa is now 51 years, whereas a child born in Europe is likely to live to 74. Longevity still tends to correlate with per capita income levels. Inhabitants of poor countries have the shortest life expectancy: Rwanda, at 36 years, has the lowest. Meanwhile, the

average Japanese citizen will live till at least 80. Women everywhere live on average 5% longer than men.

LIMITS TO GROWTH

A report published in 1972 which provided an in-depth investigation of the relationship between **population** and the **resources** people depend on for survival. Sponsored by the Club of Rome and the Massachusetts Institute of Technology, researchers used a series of computer models to project future trends. *Limits to Growth* warned of finite resource limits and described problems of supporting a rapidly-increasing human population. The gloomy forecast prompted a wave of debate about the future.

The publication of the report followed a decade or more of growing environmental awareness about the place of the human race within the natural world. **Consumerism**, technology, profit, growth and power began to be seen as negative factors which destroyed and degraded the Earth's natural resources and threatened the long-term survival of both the environment and human beings.

Although *Limits to Growth* aroused considerable controversy by concluding that 'the limits to growth on this planet will be reached in the next hundred years', detailed work published later in a little-heralded technical report showed that it was possible to choose parameters through which population, capital and material growth could all be sustained well past the year 2100.

In 1992 the authors produced *Beyond the Limits,* a reworked version in which the basic conclusions of the first report were upheld and strengthened. The conclusions were:

● The rates of use of essential resources and pollution have already passed physically sustainable limits. Without significant reductions in material and energy flows there will be an uncontrollable decline in food output, energy use and industrial production.

● This decline is not inevitable. It can be avoided by a reversal of policies and practices that perpetuate growth, combined with a massive increase in the efficiency with which materials and energy are used.

● A sustainable society is still technically and economically possible.

LITERACY (see also Illiteracy)

The overall adult literacy rate in **developing countries** increased from 68% for men and 46% for women in 1990, to 79% (men) and 62% (women) in 1995. In most of the developed world the adult literacy rate is close to 99%. Nevertheless, nearly two-thirds of all non-literate adults in the **Third World** are women. World literacy rates among women increased slightly to 66% by mid-decade but still remain significantly behind men in all developing countries. The

Adult literacy rate % 1995

NORTH 98% ● Canada 97%

WORLD

71% SOUTH

◄ 75%

The State of the World's Children 1998, UNICEF.

● Niger 14%

world's least literate countries are predominantly in Africa, with Niger (14% adult literacy), Burkina Faso (19%), Sierra Leone (31%) and Afghanistan (32%) 'topping' the list. The world's most populous nations including China, India, Indonesia,

Bangladesh, Brazil and Mexico account for around 70% of the world's illiterate adults.

LOCUST

A dozen or so species of grasshoppers which have swarming or migratory characteristics. When environmental conditions are favourable, immature forms of the insects called nymphs or hoppers crowd together. As numbers increase, the insects change their behaviour, shape and colour and mature into a gregarious migratory phase. Migratory locusts form swarms which travel over long distances and devour all crops and vegetation en route.

The most damaging variety is found in Africa and Southwest Asia. When conditions are right prodigious swarms assemble. One of the largest ever covered 1,000 square kilometres (km) and contained 40 billion locusts which ate up to 80,000 tonnes of food per day. This swarm had a bio-mass equivalent to a million people.

Swarms can move 3,000 km in a month devastating vast tracts of **land**. In a single day, an average swarm can eat enough food to feed an estimated 400,000 people for a year. Every year locusts cause $10 billion worth of damage to crops in Africa and the Middle East. In 1988 the worst locust outbreak in 30 years swept across North Africa and spread as far as Iran, southern Europe and the Caribbean. Over $200 million was spent on anti-locust operations.

For a week before they take to the air, locusts 'march' along the ground, covering 1-2 km per day and consuming all the vegetation as they proceed. During this period control measures can best be applied, though this depends on international co-operation and an early warning system. Once the young hoppers have undergone the final moult into winged adults, it is too late. In 1997 a new biological

A plague of locusts
Fire, smoke and beaters cannot stop the march of the locust hoppers or *sauterelles* in this 1891 picture of Algeria. LOCUST

pesticide was discovered which killed locusts when sprayed from the air and offered new hope for control.

LOMÉ CONVENTION

A convention first signed in 1975 which provides for trade concessions between countries of the **European Community** (EC) and 46 African, Caribbean and Pacific (**ACP**) countries. The Lomé Convention creates duty-free access to the EC for a wide range of goods and tropical products. Part of a $3.2 billion **aid** package from the European Community (EC) was also set aside to finance a system to stabilize exports (Stabex) which was designed to compensate ACP nations for loss of export earnings on key **commodities**.

Lomé II offered improved access to the EC for different ACP agricultural products, extended Stabex and established Sysmin, a similar system of compensation to assist those ACP states whose economies were heavily dependent on mineral exports. New provisions on industrial and agricultural co-operation were also included as well as commitments on the promotion and protection of investments and recommendations on the **fishing** industry. Sixty-four ACP states signed Lomé II.

Lomé III further liberalized trade and improved the effectiveness of $8 billion of EC aid. Lomé IV outlined measures to alleviate drought and curb **desertification** and emphasized social and cultural projects. Lomé IV will run for 10 years compared with

the previous conventions which had 5-year terms. It offers improved access to the EC for ACP products and suggests that **debt** problems can be met by converting some loans into grants. There were 70 ACP member countries in 1996.

LOW-INCOME COUNTRIES

Another term to describe countries with a below-average per capita income and part of a system used to rank countries based on national economic performance. The **World Bank** originally defined any country having an annual per capita **Gross National Product** (GNP) of less than $400 as a Low Income country. The exact figure and number of countries varies with annual updates.

The **World Bank** ranks all nations with populations of more than a million on their economic performance. In 1996, 64 nations were in the low-income category ($725 or less), 65 in the lower middle-income ($726-$2,895) and 35 countries in the upper middle-income group ($2,896-$8,955).

The **Organization for Economic Co-operation and Development** (OECD) uses slightly different criteria, classifying any country with a per capita income of less than $700 as low-income. The OECD Middle-Income group is also split into 'lower' and 'upper', the former having a per capita **GNP** of $700-1,300 and the latter a per capita GNP of over $1,300.

The State of the World's Children 1998, UNICEF.

Low-income countries In 1996, the lowest income countries were all in Africa.	
GNP per capita (US$) 1996	
Mozambique	80
Ethiopia	100
Tanzania	120
Burundi	160
Malawi	170
Switzerland *For comparison*	40,630

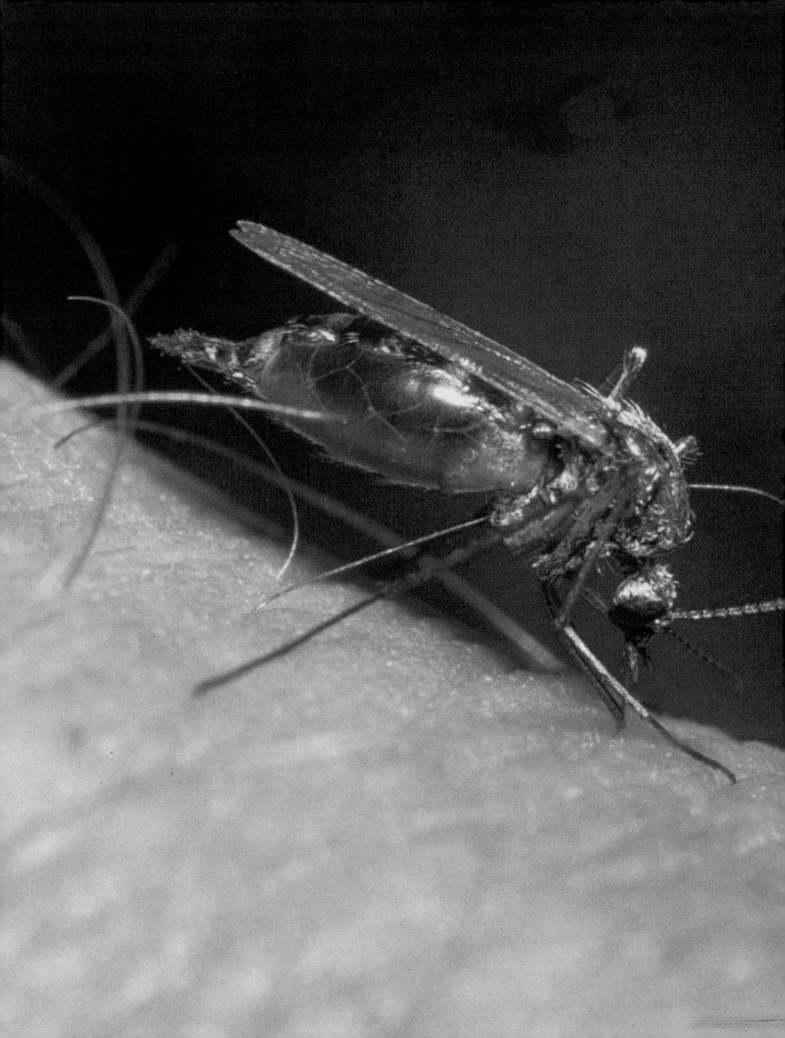

Mosquito

A blood-thirsty mosquito makes the most of a fleshy arm before taking to the air in search of the next victim. In tropical regions, mosquitoes carry infections such as malaria and dengue fever.

Maastricht – MIGA

Bold indicates a cross-reference

MAASTRICHT TREATY

Common name given to the Treaty On **European Union** signed in Maastricht, Holland in 1992. The Treaty, together with the Single European Act signed in 1986, paved the way for strengthening and deepening the **European Community** (renamed the European Union in 1993). Maastricht introduced EU citizenship with rights to vote in local and European elections in a person's country of residence.

It also strengthened the democratic nature of the European institutions and enshrined a new principle of 'subsidiarity', which means that what can be done locally, regionally or nationally should not be pursued at the Community level. It specified the procedures and timetable to follow on the path towards monetary union.

The Treaty reaffirmed the common foreign and security policy practised informally since 1970. It also enhanced co-operation in justice and home affairs (especially customs and immigration) and provided a broadening of the EU's role in the environment, social policy, research and development, telecommunications, health, culture and consumer protection.

MAIZE

An annual cereal grass also called corn. Cultivated as a grain crop in Central America for 3,000 years, maize is now the staple food for over 220 million people in 18 countries in Latin America and Africa. In terms of world production, it is the third most important cereal crop after **rice** and **wheat**. However, maize has less protein than wheat and also lacks the full range of necessary vitamins. People who eat a lot of maize with few other foods can develop *pellagra*, a vitamin-deficiency disease characterized by dry, scaly skin.

In poor countries maize is used to produce meal or porridge-like dishes. In **developed countries** it is eaten directly as a vegetable or processed into flour, canned corn or breakfast cereals. In North America and Europe maize is used extensively as an animal feed. Maize has industrial uses too, including corn oil, starches, alcohol, dextrin and adhesives.

Some maize matures in a little over 2 months while other varieties take more than a year. The ideal growing temperature is over 19°C, although it will tolerate temperatures ranging from 14-30°C. A rainfall of 600-1,200 millimetres is needed and should be evenly distributed throughout the growing season.

The development of hybrid strains has allowed yields to rise dramatically. In the 1930s, just 1% of all maize grown in the United States

was hybrid, now it is virtually all hybrid. The US produces between a third and a half of the world's maize, although the bulk of it is used for livestock feed. Globally, 482 million tonnes are grown each year. The United States (194 million tonnes), China (91 million tonnes) and Brazil (24 million tonnes) are the world's largest producers.

MALARIA (see also Mosquito)

An infectious disease caused by the presence of parasitic protozoa in the red blood cells. The disease is transmitted via blood-sucking, female **Anopheles** mosquitoes and is confined to tropical and subtropical areas. It is the most prevalent and devastating parasitic disease to afflict the human race.

There are 300-500 million new cases reported annually, 90% of them in Africa. About 270 million people are believed to be infected at any one time. Up to 2 million people die every year from malaria and its complications and over 2.4 billion people, almost half the world's **population**, are at risk of getting the disease.

When a mosquito bites, parasites are injected into the blood stream and migrate to the liver and other organs, where they multiply. After incubating for up to 10 months, parasites return to the blood stream and invade the red blood cells. Rapid multiplication of the parasites ruptures the cells, causing fever, shivering and sweating. **Anaemia** also develops and the patient may become nauseous. When the next batch of parasites is released symptoms reappear.

The intervals between bouts of fever vary with the different types of malaria. Severe forms cause both liver and kidney failure and brain and lung complications. Malaria can be cured at low cost if drugs are given during the initial stage of infection. Widespread programmes

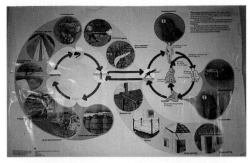

What to do – and what not to do
This poster in a health clinic in Ghana shows the life-cycle of the malarial mosquito, and how to avoid being bitten.
MALARIA

to control malarial mosquitoes, mostly using **DDT**, have been in place since the 1930s. However, the mosquitoes' resistance to DDT and similar chemicals is growing.

Despite malaria's impact on global health, and the vast **resources** being used to combat the disease, the situation has shown little improvement over the past 30 years. Large-scale forest clearance, particularly in **Amazonia**, has led to a marked rise in mosquito numbers. Extensive, ill-managed **irrigation** schemes throughout the tropics have produced numerous ideal breeding sites. Favourable conditions for mosquitoes to breed are also created in urban slums throughout the tropics.

No cost-effective, safe alternative has been found to replace the hazardous DDT in anti-malarial spraying programmes. Chloroquine a safe, cheap drug widely used to combat malaria is now becoming ineffective as the parasite has developed resistance to it. Quinine, produced from the bark of a tree, still remains the front-line drug for malaria – although resistance to it is also spreading. A new class of drugs developed from an ancient Chinese herbal remedy offers hope for the future. Although development of a new vaccine is underway, the resistance of mosquitoes and malaria parasites to insecticides and commonly-available drugs means that 470 million people, mainly in tropical Africa, live where there are no measures to control the disease.

MALNUTRITION

A condition caused by an imbalance between what an individual eats and what is required to maintain health. The word literally means 'bad feeding' and can result from eating too little, but may also imply dietary excesses or an incorrect balance of basic foodstuffs such as proteins, fats and carbohydrates. A deficiency (or excess) of one or more minerals, vitamins or other essential ingredients in the diet may arise from the inability to digest food properly as well as from actually consuming an unbalanced or inadequate diet. An unbalanced diet can cause a variety of nutritional disorders including **beri-beri**, rickets and pellagra. Chronic under-feeding leads to listlessness, immune system damage, impairment of mental functions and, eventually, death. Excess eating leads to obesity, heart disease and also hastens death.

There are two forms of malnutrition. In the **Third World** tens of millions starve to death each year; while in the developed world illnesses caused by overeating increase annually. This phenomenon of simultaneous **hunger** and glut also appears within countries.

Malnourished people are more vulnerable to infection, disease and general ill health. Today it is estimated that there are almost 800

million severely malnourished people around the globe. At least 20 million underweight babies are born each year simply because their mothers are malnourished.

In the Third World, 60% of deaths in children under 5 are related to malnutrition caused by underfeeding. In such cases, doctors measure the degree of malnutrition by assessing a child's weight in relation to height. A moderately malnourished child is one whose weight is 70-80% of the norm for its height.

Children exhibiting less than 70% of the norm are labelled as severely malnourished. A child with less than 60% of the expected weight is unlikely to survive without immediate treatment.

Poverty is the most immediate indirect cause of malnutrition in both the developed and developing worlds. In industrialized countries the money available to low-income families is frequently spent on food of dubious nutritional quality. In poor countries 40 million people die from hunger and hunger-related diseases annually, many of them infant children. It is a cruel irony then that in the United Kingdom over $250 million is spent on slimming aids each year and in the United States at least a third of people over 40 are obese.

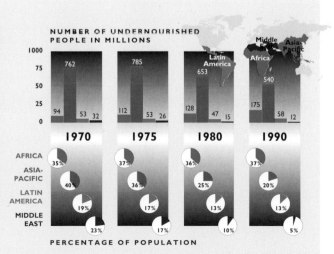

THE SCALE OF HUNGER

THE NUMBER of hungry people in the world has actually fallen in recent years, despite overall population increases. But nearly 800 million people still face persistent, everyday hunger. Much larger numbers suffer from malnutrition and seasonal or temporary hunger.

NUMBER OF UNDERNOURISHED PEOPLE IN MILLIONS

	1970	1975	1980	1990
Total	762	785	653	540
Africa	94	112	128	175
Asia-Pacific	53	53	47	58
Latin America	32	26	15	12

PERCENTAGE OF POPULATION

	1970	1975	1980	1990
AFRICA	35%	37%	36%	37%
ASIA-PACIFIC	40%	36%	25%	20%
LATIN AMERICA	19%	17%	13%	13%
MIDDLE EAST	23%	17%	10%	5%

Hunger 1995: Causes of Hunger, Bread for the World Institute, Silver Spring 1994.

Maastricht Treaty – Malnutrition

MANGROVES

Trees and shrubs which form dense thickets and low forests on coastal mudflats, salt marshes and estuaries throughout the tropics. Mangroves cover at least 14 million hectares, fringing over half of all tropical shores and are typically associated with river mouths where the **water** is shallow and the sediment levels high.

They form one of the most diverse of all ecosystems and provide a unique habitat for 2,000 species of **fish**, invertebrates and plants. In

MALTHUS, THOMAS ROBERT (1766-1834)

English priest, economist and demographer, famous for his theories regarding human **population** and food supply. He was born into a wealthy family, graduating from Cambridge University in 1788 and taking holy orders in 1797. In his essay *The Principle of Population as it affects the Future Improvement of Society* (1798) he argued that population growth was one of the major problems facing the world because population increased in a geometrical ratio whereas food increased in a mathematical ratio.

Malthus was an economic pessimist and viewed **poverty** as the inescapable lot of humankind. He concluded that the human race was doomed to ultimate starvation if population was not regulated. Later in life he proposed that 'moral restraints', sexual abstinence and delayed marriages could keep human numbers from increasing too quickly and that **birth control** should be introduced and made compulsory.

His work had a great influence on the theory of population and social policy. He continued to publish and in 1820 wrote *Principles of Political Economy* in which he addressed the problems of gluts, slump and depression. His writings anticipated the economic theories proposed by John Maynard Keynes in the 1930s.

MANDELA, NELSON (1918-   ) (see also African National Congress and Apartheid)

South African lawyer, politician and nationalist. Mandela was the son of a Tembu chief and attended university in South Africa, qualifying as a lawyer in 1942. He practised law in Johannesburg and in 1944 became a member of the **African National Congress** (ANC). He soon became a leader of the black liberation group and a vociferous opponent of **apartheid**. He was arrested and tried for treason, a lengthy process which lasted from 1956 to 1961. During this extended trial he divorced his first wife and married Nomzamo Winifred (Winnie Madikizela Mandela).

After the Sharpeville massacre in 1960 and the subsequent banning of the ANC, Mandela abandoned his non-violent stance. In 1962 he was arrested again and jailed for 5 years. While still incarcerated he and several others were tried for sabotage, treason and conspiracy. This followed a police raid at the headquarters of *'Umkhonto We Sizwe'* (Spear of the Nation), the military wing of the ANC that Mandela had been instrumental in forming. He admitted that some of the charges were true and in 1964 was sentenced to life imprisonment. During his imprisonment he retained wide support among South Africa's black community. He also became a cause célèbre among the international community opposed to apartheid. His wife, Winnie, became a prominent spokesperson for the ANC and was placed under house arrest several times.

Mandela was eventually released in 1990 and assumed the role of leader of the black majority, succeeding Oliver Tambo as head of the ANC in 1991. He continued his efforts to dismantle apartheid and push for majority rule. In 1992 a referendum of the white population approved continued reforms and agreement was reached for a multiracial election in 1994. The result was an emphatic victory for the ANC and Mandela, who was sworn in as President.

Despite several setbacks he oversaw rapid changes including the introduction of a new constitution and the final dismantling of apartheid. By 1995 his honeymoon with the black majority was over. The Government's reconstruction and development programme was proceeding very slowly. He announced that people must rid themselves of the 'culture of entitlement' and instituted a campaign to try and break a boycott of rent payments which was supported by 80% of black township residents. Tensions worsened between parties in the government of national unity. His estranged wife Winnie was dismissed from her deputy minister post, won an appeal against the dismissal and then promptly resigned. Mandela also admitted that he had given 'shoot to kill' orders to guards at ANC headquarters during an Inkatha Freedom Party demonstration the previous year, during which several people died. He was succeeded as head of the ANC in 1997 by Thabo Mbecki.

Indonesia, mangrove forests have been farmed for fish since the 15th century. Today, milkfish are raised in 35,000 hectares of mangrove ponds.

Mangrove forests or swamps are a valuable source of timber, pulpwood, fuel and charcoal. The timber from the trees is impervious to water and resists attack by marine worms and the trees also provide raw materials used in making dyes, glues, rayon and tannin. Mangrove swamps act as breeding-grounds for a variety of commercially important fish, shrimps and crabs as well as being a source of other useful products such as wax and honey.

LOSS OF MANGROVE FOREST

Thailand Original area (sq km) 1,469 — LOSS 87%

India Original area (sq km) 12,624 — LOSS 85%

Bangladesh Original area (sq km) 10,778 — LOSS 73%

Philippines Original area (sq km) 1,992 — LOSS 61%

Guatemala Original area (sq km) 1,250 — LOSS 60%

Ghana Original area (sq km) 2,100 — LOSS 70%

Nigeria Original area (sq km) 24,400 — LOSS 50%

Indonesia Original area (sq km) 38,200 — LOSS 45%

World Resources 1993, World Resources Institute OUP.

Mangroves also play an important role in desalinating sea water and are one of the major factors in stabilizing shorelines. In addition, they are able to reclaim **land** from the sea. A network of horizontal roots anchor trees to soft mud, trapping sediment. This process slowly extends the shoreline and mangroves can move seaward at a rate of up to 100 metres a year.

Throughout the tropics mangroves are under threat from clear-cutting, charcoal production, sand and shale mining, land reclamation for agriculture or **aquaculture** and coastal pollution.

Mangroves in Asia are being felled to provide wood chips for Japan to make paper and rayon. The Sunderbans in Bangladesh, the most extensive mangrove forest in the world, is being threatened by a reduced flow of water in the River **Ganges** due to various **dam** projects and **irrigation** systems. Around 45% of the mangroves in Indonesia and Malaysia have disappeared and Africa has lost 55% of its mangrove forests. Globally, only about 165,000 square kilometres of mangroves remain.

MAQUILADORAS

Export-assembly plants that are being set up in Central America and along the US-Mexico border. Large foreign-based corporations have transferred their assembly operations to the region to take advantage of low wages thus reducing production costs. Workers, mostly women, tend to have few or no labour rights.

Following **free trade** agreements between Mexico, the United States and Canada in the late 1980s, several US-based companies moved their pro-

MANLEY, MICHAEL NORMAN (1924-1997)

Jamaican socialist politician. Following his education in Jamaica, Manley attended the London School of Economics. He was a pilot in the Canadian Air Force and worked briefly as a journalist before returning to Jamaica in 1952 where he became active in the People's National Party (PNP). Manley also held several major posts in the **trade union** movement, including Sugar Supervisor of the National Workers Union (1953-54) and vice-president of the Caribbean **Bauxite** and Mineworkers Union (1955-72). He was elected to Jamaica's parliament in 1962 and became PNP leader in 1969, serving for 3 years as leader of the opposition.

The PNP won the election of 1972 and Manley became Prime Minister. He immediately raised the bauxite export tax and began to challenge the foreign companies which ran many of the large-scale operations on Jamaica. He was a strong advocate of democratic **socialism** and put great emphasis on social reform and economic independence. Manley also campaigned vociferously for Caribbean unity and was a strong supporter of the **Non-Aligned Movement**. He supported all anti-

colonial struggles and liberation movements, and was an outspoken critic of the white supremacist regime in South Africa. In 1978 Manley was awarded the UN Gold Medal for his work in the anti-apartheid struggle.

His activities brought him into conflict with the United States and American companies began to withdraw from Jamaica resulting in cutbacks in government spending and widespread economic hardship. In the early 1970s, Jamaica was beset with street violence and crime, eventually causing Manley to declare a state of emergency in 1976. But despite the unrest, high **unemployment** and economic stagnation, the PNP was returned to power. In 1979 Manley rejected the severe conditions which the **International Monetary Fund** (IMF) attempted to impose during loan negotiations. The following year he was voted out of office and replaced by the pro-American leader of the Jamaican Labour Party, Edward Seaga.

In 1984 Jamaica was again forced to go to the IMF and social welfare spending was slashed. Two years of popular discontent followed, after which Manley's PNP was again returned to power. Relations with the US changed as Manley toned down his socialist rhetoric. A co-operative anti-drug programme was set up to halt the $750 million annual marijuana trade. Free enterprise was encouraged, IMF loan conditions were respected and the Jamaican currency was devalued. Manley resigned as Prime Minister and PNP leader in 1992 due to ill health.

Mangroves — Maquiladoras

Mangroves — Maquiladoras

MAO ZEDONG (1893-1976)

Born into a peasant family he became a Marxist politician and helped form the Chinese Communist Party in 1921. In 1927, he led an uprising which was quickly crushed by the Nationalist forces led by General Chiang Kai-Shek. Mao fled to the mountains where he built up the Red Army. In 1934, the Communists were forced to undertake the 'Long March' across the central part of China to escape the Nationalist army. The rigours of the march united the Communists and in 1937 he entered into an uneasy alliance with Chiang Kai-Shek to fight the Japanese.

After World War II, Mao expelled Chiang Kai-Shek and his followers to Taiwan. Communist strength had grown from 30,000 to 3 million in just 10 years. Mao then proclaimed the People's Republic of China in 1949. As Chairman of the Communist Party, he provided the pattern and direction for the development of the country through such events as the 'Hundred Flowers' campaign and the 'Great Leap Forward' of 1959 (supposedly to promote industrial growth). He ignored the advice of experts and put into action audacious and sometimes ludicrous plans such as building thousands of back-yard steel furnaces to try and boost steel production.

The Great Leap Forward was a spectacular failure: heavy-handed, inflexible and dogmatic. The **famine** which followed killed as many as 20 million people, one of the greatest human tragedies of the century. As a result Mao stepped down as Party Chairman, though he remained Party leader. He was a populist who attempted to adapt the theory of Marxist revolution to China, where the peasantry rather than the proletariat was the focus of social discontent. His philosophy and thinking was published in the famous 'Little Red Book'. In steering China away from the Soviet Union, Mao had great influence in the **Third World**. He was regarded as a brilliant military strategist and published extensively on the role of **guerrilla** armies in 'people's wars'. He also understood the need to keep the Red Army on his side to reinforce his leadership. During the 'Cultural Revolution' which began in 1966 he attacked the new Party Chairman, creating widespread unrest which consolidated his own power. The 'Cultural Revolution' had a devastating impact on China, creating social and economic chaos for nearly a decade and causing the deaths of up to 10 million people. However, this did not stop Mao from being idolized by many socialists around the world. He initiated contact with the West in the early 1970s, finally meeting US President Richard Nixon in 1972. He died in 1976, an icon whose policies were largely ignored by the new leadership.

also avoid having to install equipment necessary to satisfy US health, safety and environmental regulations. As a result they can supply the US-market with goods at the same price but at a much lower production cost, thereby maximizing profits. Meanwhile, people living in the shantytowns which have sprung up near the maquiladoras lack basic services like clean **water** and sewage and are sur-

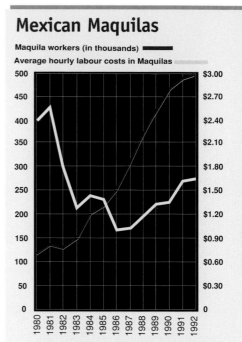

Mexican Maquilas

Maquila workers (in thousands) ▬▬▬
Average hourly labour costs in Maquilas ▬▬▬

Runaway America by Harry Brown and Beth Sims, Resource Center Press, Albuquerque, NM, 1993.

rounded by ever-increasing pollution and a rapidly-degrading natural environment. Maquiladoras generated more than $3 billion of value-added income for Mexico in 1991.

MARITIME LAW

The world's oceans and seas cover 362 million square kilometres, almost 72% of the Earth's surface. They contain natural **resources** of incalculable wealth. Not surprisingly, disputes over ownership have been common. Since the formation of the **United Nations**, several attempts have been made to establish an international agreement governing the oceans and the

duction plants across the border into Mexico. Then during the early 1990s, over 1,500 US, Canadian, Japanese and European companies set up *maquiladoras* inside the border. Many of these are multinational companies like General Motors and IBM.

Well over 2,000 maquiladoras have been established and the number is growing by 15% annually. They employ 500,000 Mexicans at an average of under $2 a day. Generally speaking, they qualify for benefits such as exemption from income **taxes**, preferential interest rates and export incentives. Special trade agreements exempt the companies from paying American tariffs and from meeting other restrictions on both trade and production. The companies

MARCOS, FERDINAND (1919-1989)

Controversial Filipino politician. During his studies at law school in 1939 he was convicted of murdering a political opponent of his father, but eventually managed to secure his own acquittal. During World War II he was a **guerrilla** fighter and survived terms in prison camps. He became President of the Philippines in 1965 and his regime, backed by the United States, became increasingly repressive. His presidency was continually threatened by civil unrest and claims of financial irregularities and fraud. In 1972, he declared martial law and assumed dictatorial powers. Although controls were relaxed during the early 1980s, the suspicious murder of opposition leader Benigno Aquino Jr caused further unrest and the controls again tightened.

Marcos was eventually overthrown in 1986 after massive public demonstrations. He went into exile in Hawaii and was succeeded as President by **Corazon Aquino**, widow of the murdered opposition leader. During the Marcos era the Philippines ran up a $3.9 billion dollar **debt** while the President's family fraudulently diverted vast sums overseas.

In 1993, a US federal jury in Hawaii, ordered his estate to pay more than $1.2 billion to 10,000 plaintiffs. However, it is unlikely that any of the money will appear – the Philippines Government has still not managed to trace the billions of dollars that Marcos allegedly looted from the nation's treasury.

---

resources they contain. The **International Law** Commission struggled for 7 years to produce articles which were put before the UN Conference on the Law of the Sea in 1958. However, these conventions proved totally inadequate and less than a quarter of the world's nations agreed to them.

In 1970 the UN declared the seabed and ocean floor 'the common heritage of mankind' and this initiative eventually led to the third Conference on the Law of the Sea in 1973. **The Convention on the Law of the Sea** (UNCLOS), adopted in 1982, deals with issues of peace and security; the allocation of natural resources; navigation; access and transport; and scientific research in the marine environment. It also provides a framework for resolving any disputes.

Shipping lanes

The world s oceans and seas cover more than 70 per cent of the earth s surface and disputes over who owns what are common.
MARITIME LAW

Several other initiatives protect specific oceans such as the North Sea and the Mediterranean.

The 1972 London Dumping Convention prohibits the disposal of radioactive waste at sea. In 1987 the 'precautionary principle' was applied to the treaty protecting the North Sea. This means that lack of full scientific proof should not be used as a reason for postponing the implementation of environmental protection measures. The principle has since been adopted by the **United Nations Environment Programme**, the Nordic Council, and the Barcelona Convention for protection of the Mediterranean.

MARPOL CONVENTION

Common name for the International Convention for the Prevention of Pollution from Ships, adopted under the auspices of the **International Maritime Organization** in 1973. The convention contains 5 annexes. The first 2, which cover pollution by **oil** and noxious liquids, came into force in 1983. The last 3 are optional and need at least 15 countries whose combined merchant fleets total at least half of world tonnage to ratify them in order to make them effective.

In 1988, Annex V finally came into force. The annex bans the dumping of all plastics including **fishing** gear made from synthetic materials, but allows the disposal of other forms of refuse under controlled conditions. In 'special areas' like the Mediterranean, Baltic and Black Seas, only food wastes can be dumped into the sea but not within 19 kilometres of **land**.

All contracting parties to the Convention are obliged to provide adequate waste-disposal facilities within their ports to allow shipping to dispose of wastes.

Annex III dealing with **hazardous waste** in packaged form and Annex IV covering disposal of sewage have still not received the support required to bring them into force.

MARSHALL PLAN

Also known as the European Recovery Programme (named after **George Marshall**). A post-World War II, US-financed scheme to rehabilitate the economies of the 17 western and southern European nations. The US was fearful that the **poverty**, **unemployment** and war-ruined economies in Europe would encourage the spread of **communism**. From 1948-51, $13 billion in **aid** was channelled to the war-shattered European economies (including those under Soviet occupation) helping to rebuild

MARSHALL, GEORGE C (1880-1959)

American general and politician; Army Chief of Staff and strategic adviser to the US President during World War II.

After the War, he served as Secretary of State (1947-49) and devised the European Recovery Programme (more commonly known as the **Marshall Plan**) in which the United States undertook to provide economic **aid** to Europe to repair the structural and economic damage inflicted by the war. He was awarded the Nobel Peace Prize in 1953.

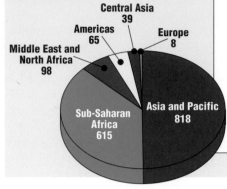

Maternal deaths per day in pregnancy and childbirth (by region)

Central Asia 39
Americas 65
Europe 8
Middle East and North Africa 98
Sub-Saharan Africa 615
Asia and Pacific 818

Countries with the highest annual number of maternal deaths per 100,000 live births

1.	Sierra Leone	1800
2.	Afghanistan	1700
3.	Bhutan	1600
	Guinea	1600
	Somalia	1600
6.	Angola	1500
	Chad	1500
	Mozambique	1500
	Nepal	1500
10.	Yemen	1400

The Progress of Nations 1996, UNICEF.

infrastructure and boost both industrial and agricultural production. The Plan was a huge success and European economies expanded 15-25% during the period. In fact, it was so successful that US President Truman thought the idea should be extended to the less developed countries around the world. The first US foreign aid followed with the 'Four Point Plan' of 1949.

MATERNAL MORTALITY

The **World Health Organization** (WHO) defines maternal mortality as death during or within 42 days of a pregnancy from causes related to or aggravated by pregnancy. Every year 585,000 women around the world die during pregnancy or childbirth. Over 99% of these deaths occur in the **Third World**. Lack of medical attention, poor education, housing, sanitation and nutrition contribute to the risk of women dying as a result of complications arising from pregnancy.

In the **developing countries**, death during childbirth accounts for 20-45% of all deaths of women of childbearing age. In the US and most of Europe, the figure is less than 1%. The risk of maternal death is frequently 100 times greater in the Third World than in industrial countries.

In Africa, women face a 1 in 21 chance of succumbing to a pregnancy-related fatality in their lifetime. This compares with a 1 in 9,850 chance in Northern Europe. Haemorrhage, infection, toxaemia, obstructed labour and unskilled **abortion** account for 75% of all maternal deaths in poor nations.

The vast majority of women in developing countries deliver their offspring at home. In much of Asia and Africa only 20-35% have any form of antenatal care and only a third of births are attended by people with medical training. Despite the best efforts of **primary health care** workers and 'traditional birth attendants' these fatalities will only be avoided when medical

MARX, KARL (1818-1883)

German political theorist, economist and sociologist. During his student days in Berlin, he was influenced by the works of the German philosopher Hegel. He received a doctorate in 1841 and began to work as a journalist shortly afterwards, and married in 1843. His newspaper was suppressed and he emigrated to Paris where he began a long association with the British-based industrialist Friedrich Engels.

The two published the *Manifest der Kommunistischen Partei* in 1848. Commonly known as the 'Communist Party Manifesto', it was written as the platform for the Communist League and contained a summary of his whole social philosophy. Its appearance coincided with the revolution in France in which **socialism** was prominent.

A revolutionary climate in Germany allowed Marx to return to restart his newspaper. But in 1849 he was expelled, eventually settling in London where he spent most of the rest of his life, more or less poverty-stricken, studying in the British Museum. His most famous theoretical work, *Das Kapital* (1867), was a critical analysis of **capitalism**. His works formed the basis of much of late 19th century socialism in Europe. His philosophy of human nature, history and politics gave authority to the communist cause. Marx believed that at a certain point of development the economic structure of capitalism would no longer be able to contain the ever-increasing forces of production. The crisis of capitalism world then have to be resolved by revolution which should transfer power to the proletariat (the labouring masses). This would be followed by a movement towards an economy that would be 'communist' and classless. Marx was noted for his attacks on 'utopian' socialism and described his own work as 'scientific' socialism.

supplies and specialized medical attention become widely available to women at risk.

MAU-MAU

Militant African nationalist movement that originated among the Kikuyu people of Kenya in the 1950s. The Mau-Mau advocated violent opposition to British rule. In 1952, following a campaign of terror and sabotage, the British began a military offensive to combat the Mau-Mau. Four years later over 11,000 rebels had died in the fighting and 20,000 more Kikuyu were imprisoned in detention camps. Despite the efforts of the British authorities, the Kikuyu resistance became the backbone of the Kenyan independence movement, led by the charismatic Jomo

Softly, softly
Peering left and right, guns and pangas at the ready, the African Home Guard move stealthily in search of Mau-Mau 'terrorists' – one of whom, Jomo Kenyatta, later became first President of independent Kenya.
MAU-MAU

Kenyatta. Although jailed as a Mau-Mau leader in 1953, Kenyatta was later released and went on to negotiate independence. He became first President of an independent Kenya in December, 1964.

McNAMARA, ROBERT (1916-   )

McNamara graduated from Harvard University and became a faculty member. He was disqualified from active duty in World War II due to poor eyesight. When the war ended, he was hired by Ford Motors to revitalize the company. He proved so successful that he quickly rose up the corporate ladder and in 1960 became the first person outside the Ford family to become company president.

Less than a month later he resigned to take the post of Secretary of Defence in the administration of John F Kennedy. His term of office saw massive cost-cutting and he favoured 'flexible response' rather than the more hawkish 'massive retaliation'. He initially supported US involvement in the **Vietnam War** but later began to doubt this decision and eventually opposed the continued bombing of North Vietnam. As a result he gradually lost influence in the Johnson administration and resigned in 1968 to become President of the **World Bank**.

During his 13 years at the Bank his rhetoric showed strong sympathy towards the problems and needs of the developing world. In 1978 he defined absolute **poverty** as 'a condition of life so limited by **malnutrition**, **illiteracy**, disease, squalid surroundings, high infant mortality and low **life expectancy** as to be beneath any reasonable definition of human decency'. Unfortunately some 1.2 billion people now satisfy that definition.

In 1990, McNamara called for a massive reduction in global military spending, noting that the **Third World** arms expenditure in 1988 totalled around $170 billion, close to what was spent on health care and education combined. He urged that military spending be reduced 50% by the year 2000.

MEASLES

A highly-infectious viral disease especially common in children. Measles is acquired through personal contact and is spread by infected people coughing and sneezing. It tends to appear in epidemics every 2-3 years. After an incubation of 8-15 days, patients develop severe catarrh, small spots

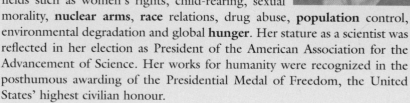

MEAD, MARGARET (1901-1978)

American anthropologist best known for her studies on the peoples of Oceania. A graduate of Columbia University, she went on a field trip to Samoa in 1925 and collected material for the first of her 23 books, *Coming of Age in Samoa* (1928). She received her doctorate a year later. In addition to being a respected anthropologist, she was well known for her activities in a broad range of social and humanitarian fields such as women's rights, child-rearing, sexual morality, **nuclear arms**, **race** relations, drug abuse, **population** control, environmental degradation and global **hunger**. Her stature as a scientist was reflected in her election as President of the American Association for the Advancement of Science. Her works for humanity were recognized in the posthumous awarding of the Presidential Medal of Freedom, the United States' highest civilian honour.

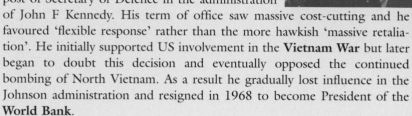

inside the mouth and a raised, blotchy red rash on the body which lasts for 3-5 days. During the whole of this time the patient remains infectious. Those infected are susceptible to pneumonia and middle ear infections. Complete recovery may take 2-4 weeks after which time the body develops a persistent immunity. A vaccine provides effective immunity although evidence is beginning to emerge that it may not provide lifelong protection. A single dose should be given 12-15 months after birth.

In the developed nations measles is no longer a serious concern. However, in the **Third World** the disease is a major killer of small children: as many as a million children a year in the **developing countries** die of the disease. Due to greater risk of infection and a lower level of general health, children in poor countries need to be immunized earlier. Measles is the main killer disease among the 6 **vaccine-preventable diseases** targeted under the World Health Organization's **Expanded Programme on Immunization** (EPI).

MENDES, CHICO (1947-1988)

Mendes was a Brazilian **rubber** tapper and union activist who was brutally murdered in December 1988 because of his outspoken activism on behalf of the country's poor. Mendes led a movement of **rubber** tappers and **indigenous people** in their struggle to live and work in the Amazonian forest and to protect its survival.

His vision combined the principles of **ecology**, social justice and **human rights**. His goal was to protect his fellow rubber tappers' right to earn a livelihood by stopping the wholesale destruction of the rainforest at the hands of rich **cattle** ranchers. Instead, he advocated selectively harvesting the natural bounty of the forest: extracting latex from **rubber** trees, gathering nuts when the rubber was not flowing and doing so in a sustainable way which would protect the forest for future generations.

Chico Mendes was an important grassroots leader and his murder made global headlines. Darli Alves, a landowner and cattle baron was eventually arrested for the murder. He and his son were convicted and sentenced to 19 years in prison. They escaped from prison soon afterwards (with help from the police) but were recaptured in 1996.

In recognition of Mendes' tireless work on behalf of the landless and the forest itself, the Brazilian government established the Chico Mendes Extractive Reserve, a tract of almost a million hectares of protected rainforest.

MEIR, GOLDA (1898-1978)

A founder and Prime Minister of Israel (1969-74). Her family emigrated from Russia to the United States in 1906. She joined the Milwaukee Labour Zionist Party and in 1921, together with her husband, emigrated to a kibbutz in Palestine. She became active in politics and during World War II emerged as a forceful spokesperson for the Zionist cause in negotiations with Britain. In 1946, following the British arrest of many Jewish leaders, she became a leading advocate of an independent Israeli state. In 1948 she was a signatory of Israel's independence declaration and was then appointed ambassador to Moscow.

She was elected to the Israeli Parliament in 1949 and served as Labour Minister until 1956. She was responsible for major housing and road construction programmes. A strong advocate of unrestricted Jewish immigration, she was appointed Foreign Minister in 1956, at which time she changed her name from Myerson to Meir. After retiring from her post in 1966, she helped to form the Labour Party and was elected Prime Minister as a compromise candidate when Levi Eshkol died in 1969. Her term of office was marred by the outbreak of the Yom Kippur War in 1973. Israel's apparent lack of readiness shocked the nation and she was fortunate to be able to form a coalition government in March 1974 to retain power. A month later she resigned.

MERCURY

A unique metal, liquid at normal temperatures, that usually comes from cinnabar, a sulphide of mercury found sparsely in volcanic rock. The few known reserves of cinnabar may be exhausted within a decade. Mercury has a number of uses. In metallic form it is used in switches and thermometers. Compounds of mercury are widely used in anti-fungal agents and as detonators for explosives, while mercury amalgams are extensively used for dental treatment.

Mercury is highly toxic and is fatal in large doses: it can be swallowed, inhaled and is easily absorbed through the skin. The human body cannot excrete it and so it has a cumulative effect.

Mercury damages the kidneys and the nervous system. Symptoms include tremors in the limbs and loss of mental faculties. In the 19th century, hat makers who used mercury developed these symptoms, giving rise to the phrase 'mad as a hatter'. Most cases of mercury poisoning now arise through the inhalation of mercury vapour, usually among workers in mercury-refining factories or those who involved in the manufacture of thermometers and barometers.

There have also been several examples of mass-poisoning.

All that glitters

Shiny mercury globules in the hand of a gold-panner at Diwalwal, Philippines. Mercury is used to refine gold, but in this process it pollutes the waters used with its highly toxic properties.

Global mercury production in metric tonnes: 2,890 (1996)

MAJOR PRODUCERS

Spain	1,500
Kyrgyzstan	580
China	300
Algeria	240

USBM 1991

Mercury-based compounds are commonly used on seeds to prevent moulds from growing and hundreds of people in Iraq were poisoned when dressed seeds were cooked and eaten. In Japan, effluent discharged from a mercury-refining factory polluted an area of coastal waters and **fish** became contaminated. Local inhabitants who consumed large quantities of fish developed **Minamata disease**, a name taken from the town where the factory was located.

Mercury poisoning has become a serious concern and governments are enacting legislation to deal with the problem. Switzerland now requires warning labels on all batteries which contain mercury. France has launched a scheme to encourage people to discard used batteries in collection boxes. Similar battery-collection points are commonplace in other European countries too. In Sweden, health authorities have advised dentists not to use mercury amalgam when filling the teeth of pregnant women.

The worst levels of mercury pollution were in the Amazon basin in Brazil. In 1979 when the price of gold soared to $850 an ounce, hundreds of thousands of inexperienced miners poured into the area in search of gold. Mercury used in gold-extraction releases as much as 100 tonnes of the deadly metal into the ecosystem each year.

METHANE

A colourless, odourless flammable gas that is the main constituent of **natural gas**. It is used as a fuel and plays a significant part in influencing **global warming** and **ozone** destruction.

Atmospheric methane concentration increased markedly around 150 years ago and has continued to rise at a rate of 1% per year. Molecule for molecule, methane is 20 times more effective at warming the globe than **carbon dioxide** (CO_2). The total amount of methane added to the atmosphere annually has been estimated at 550 million tonnes, about half of which comes from human actions.

Most is removed through oxidation, and temperate and boreal forests play an important role in absorption. Clearing forests and using nitrogen-based **fertilizers** sharply reduces the amount of methane absorbed by soils. The concentration of atmospheric methane in the northern hemisphere is almost 10% higher than that in the southern hemisphere.

Methane is produced naturally by a variety of sources including marshes and bogs, termites, enteric fermentation in ruminant animals and the burning of **biomass**. Leaky natural gas pipelines in Russia are responsible for 5% of emissions. Termites can release up to 150 million tonnes of methane each year as they digest vegetative matter. They prefer tropical grasslands and as **tropical forests** are replaced with pasture, termite numbers increase. The global livestock herd is estimated to vent between 50-100 million tonnes annually. In addition, 5 million square kilometres of marshland and 1.5 million square kilometres of rice paddies release an estimated 150 million tonnes.

Over the past 2 decades, landfill sites have also been found to release around 70 million tonnes a year, more and more of which is being used as fuel. The amount of methane in the air is now increasing at a rate 50 times faster than any other time in the past 160,000 years.

The Intergovernmental Panel on Climate Change (IPCC) warns that a 15-20% reduction in emissions is required by the year 2000 merely to stabilize atmospheric concentrations at 1990 levels.

MICROCREDIT

Credit in the form of small loans to the rural and urban poor as a means of escaping the **poverty** trap. Usually given to individuals and small, local enterprises even though they have little or no collateral — a situation which prevents them from borrowing through the conventional banking system. The best known example of the microcredit system is the **Grameen Bank** in Bangladesh which has made over 2 million loans since 1983.

The number of people around the world benefiting from microcredit institutions rose from 1 million in 1985 to 10 million in 1997, when a Microcredit Summit meeting was held in an effort to extend credit to as many as 100 million of the world's poorest families by 2005. Although the **World Bank** has pledged $200 million for funding micro-enterprises, it has been proven that such funds are best administered and controlled at the local level.

MIDDLE-INCOME COUNTRIES (MICs)

A term used to describe **Third World** nations that are relatively far along the development path, as measured by orthodox economic indicators. These include Brazil, Chile, Kuwait, Korea, Malaysia and Mexico. The **World Bank** classifies 55 nations as Low-Income, 71 as Lower-Middle-Income and 43 as Upper-Middle-Income. The Bank's criteria are a **GNP** of less than $725 (Low-income), $726-$2,895 (Lower-middle-income) and $2,896-$8,955 (Upper-middle-income).

Those countries most seriously in **debt** to the commercial banks are in the Latin American middle-income group. Together they account for around half the total Third World debt. Most debt-reduction plans, including the Brady Plan, have been aimed at reducing the debt of Upper MIC countries. However, debt repayments of these countries still account for 26% of their export earnings.

MIGRANT LABOUR

Casual and usually unskilled workers who move systematically from one place to another offering their services on a temporary, often seasonal basis. In North America, migrant labour is used in farming for planting, weeding and harvesting. Wages, working conditions and living standards tend to be low. Migrant workers lack organization and so are easily exploited by middlemen, job brokers, labour contractors and the like. They may be treated as outsiders in the communities where they work and they have little or no access to schools, medical care or welfare facilities. In the US some 500,000 people work as migrant labourers.

Migrant labour is also used on a large scale in South Africa. Black workers are drawn from rural areas to work in towns, although under the **apartheid** regime they were not allowed to live in the towns. As a result, huge satellite townships sprang up around the predominant-ly white urban centres.

Migrant workers are also common in Europe. After World War II, Germany's rapid industrial growth created a severe labour shortage. As a result, several million unskilled workers were imported from Turkey, Greece, Italy and Yugoslavia. The same phenomenon was seen elsewhere in Europe, where the migrants were often referred to as 'guest workers'. France and Britain imported migrant workers from their respective former colonies and their cheap labour was used as a tool to drive down wages.

Malians and Senegalese went to work in Sicily as the Sicilians moved north to Germany. Spaniards moved to France. Egyptians and Pakistanis arrived in Greece as Greeks went to work in Germany, Scandinavia and Britain. Egyptians also worked Jordanian farms when Jordan's Palestinians went off to work in the Gulf.

As free market labour policies weaken job security, migrant workers are being used more and more, especially in jobs deemed to be 'dirty' or demeaning. When recession came to Europe in the 1970s, the huge numbers of guest workers created tension and proved to be fodder for racist nationalist movements who targeted migrant labourers as the source of national ills. A similar situation arose in the Middle East during the 1970s when millions of workers from Egypt, Yemen, Jordan, Pakistan and other Muslim countries flocked to the oil-rich Arab states whose economies were expanding rapidly.

Remittances sent home by migrant labourers have become a major source of income for many **Third World** nations. Mexicans in the US now send back an estimated $3 billion a year and that money has become one of Mexico's largest sources of foreign exchange.

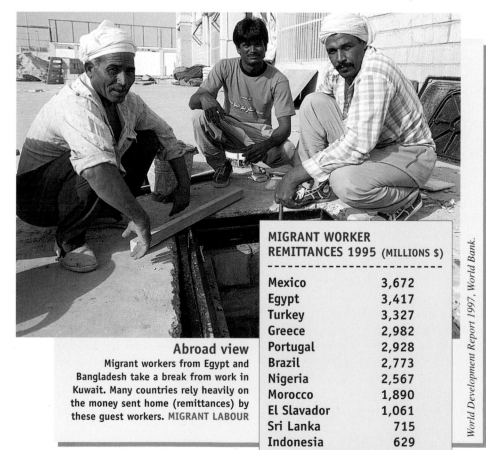

Abroad view
Migrant workers from Egypt and Bangladesh take a break from work in Kuwait. Many countries rely heavily on the money sent home (remittances) by these guest workers. MIGRANT LABOUR

MIGRANT WORKER REMITTANCES 1995 (MILLIONS $)	
Mexico	3,672
Egypt	3,417
Turkey	3,327
Greece	2,982
Portugal	2,928
Brazil	2,773
Nigeria	2,567
Morocco	1,890
El Slavador	1,061
Sri Lanka	715
Indonesia	629

World Development Report 1997, World Bank.

THE **A** TO **Z** OF WORLD DEVELOPMENT

MILLET

Millet is a name applied to several distinct, small-grained cereal species which grow in a range of environments. Of all the commonly-grown cereal crops 'bullrush' millet is one of the most drought-resistant and can withstand much hotter conditions with far less rainfall than **maize**. However, it is relatively low-yielding and is particularly prone to attack from birds.

Several species of millet are cultivated in areas with extremely low rainfall. The grain grows well on poor soils and is the staple crop for many of the world's rural poor in arid regions. Together with sorghum, millet is the staple food for almost 200 million people in 13 arid countries in East and West Africa. Millet is often inter-cropped with sorghum, **groundnuts** or cowpeas to avoid complete crop loss if growing conditions are bad. At harvest time, the heads of the plant are cut off by hand. Yields of 450 kilograms per hectare are average. Millet is used to make flour. It can also be cooked as porridge or fermented to produce alcoholic drinks. Around 32 million tonnes of millet are produced world-wide each year. India (11 million tonnes), Nigeria (5 million tonnes) and China (4 million tonnes) are the world's leading producers.

MINAMATA DISEASE

A form of **mercury** poisoning that killed 43 people in the Japanese town of Minamata between 1953 and 1956 and injured many more. Minamata is a company town of the Nippon Chisso Hiryo firm whose main products are **fertilizers** and vinyl chloride. People developed the disease by eating **fish** contaminated with di-methyl mercury derived from the effluent of a local plastics factory. Symptoms include tremors, impaired hearing, severe **anaemia** and bone deformities. In acute cases

Taken for a ride
Former British Prime Minister Margaret Thatcher embraced monetarism with open arms, keeping inflation low, regardless of the resultant unemployment. MONETARISM

people suffered brain damage, delirium and paralysis and eventually died. Many women in the area gave birth to deformed babies and the incidence of genetic deformities also rose.

MONETARISM

An economic doctrine emphasizing the role of money in the functioning of a nation's economy. Monetarists advocate the 'quantitative theory of money' which suggests that govern-

ment intervention in the economy should be limited to managing the money supply. The theory is that excessive increases in money supply will cause **inflation**. Consequently, the amount of money in the economy used to purchase goods and services must be balanced with the economy's ability to produce the goods and services. Monetarist concern with inflation has meant keeping interest rates at historically high levels in order to regulate **economic growth**. Consequently,

unemployment has become a major worry across the industrialized world as governments adopted monetarist policies and focused on inflation at the expense of jobs.

MONOCULTURE

The cultivation of a single crop on large tracts of **land**. It is a typical feature of modern, large-scale agriculture as it reduces labour costs and maximizes machine use and marketing efficiency. The alternative is **intercropping** (or polyculture), growing a mixture of crops, either together or in sequence.

Fewer than 100 plant species provide most of the world's food and within these genetic diversity has been drastically reduced. Of the 8 major crops in the United States, only 9 varieties account for 50-75% of the total harvest. In monoculture, **soil** fertility, soil structure and soil moisture are reduced while susceptibility to pests is increased.

Monoculture uses mostly **high-yield variety** (HYV) plants which increase the need for chemical nutrients and **pesticides**. Although massive growth in agricultural production has been achieved using monoculture, such agro-ecosystems are more artificial, unstable and prone to collapse.

The perils of monocropping were illustrated in the 19th century when a blight wiped out the **potato** harvest in Europe, leading to the Irish Potato **famine**. Today genetically-uniform crops cover much of the world's crop land. Across Asia a single rice variety covers nearly 4.5 million hectares.

All commercial **banana** varieties have been bred from the Cavendish banana which has no resistance to the 'black sigatoka' fungus. In 1975, 15 million hectares of winter **wheat** were planted in the Soviet Union using a single variety which proved susceptible to a harsher than usual winter, wiping out the entire crop.

Blowing a gale
India has two monsoon seasons: the south-west monsoon starts on the west coast in June, heading northwards, while the north-east one blows from October to December. In between the sudden downpours are periods of clear brilliant sunshine and the plants and flowers burst into spectacular colours. MONSOON

MONSOON

A seasonal, large-scale reversal of winds in the tropics, chiefly occurring as a result of differential heating of the oceans. It exerts greatest effect in India, China and Southeast Asia. The term is derived from the Arabic word *mawsim* and is commonly used to describe the intense rainfall that generally accompanies the wind reversal. Monsoons bring rain during the summer as they blow inland from the sea. The rest of the year is dry with the winds blowing in the opposite direction.

MONTONEROS

A left-wing Peronist group best known for urban **terrorism**, political kidnappings and assassinations in Argentina. The group was primarily composed of young, middle-class men and women dedicated to overthrowing the Argentinean Government. They funded themselves through bank robberies and ransoms paid for the release of hostages. The group was originally established as a quasi-military force by **Juan Peron**. However, when Peron returned to Argentina in 1973 after an 18-year exile in Paraguay, he condemned the group.

In retaliation they became leftist revolutionaries, intensifying their terrorist actions. From Peron's return until his widow's overthrow in 1976, the Montoneros attempted to overthrow the Argentine state. In response the military Government and right-wing terrorists carried out a brutal counter-campaign against them.

MONTREAL PROTOCOL

An 1987 agreement reached in Canada to review the role of **chlorofluorocarbon** (CFC) gases in the destruction of the **ozone** layer. The meeting was a follow-up to the Vienna Convention on the Protection of the Ozone Layer held 2 years earlier. The Protocol was signed by 30 governments, together with the **European Community** (EC), although some CFC-producing **Third World** countries, notably China and India, withheld their agreement until assurances on compensation or technology-transfer for production of alternatives were agreed. The agreement aimed to freeze CFC production at 1986 levels. It also called for consumption to be reduced gradually to 50% of 1986 levels by 1999.

At follow-up conferences in London, Copenhagen and Vienna the industrialized world finally agreed to fund the transfer of technology to the developing world to help meet CFC phase-out timetables. Delegates agreed to set up a special fund worth $240 million over 3 years.

They also decided to implement much stricter and swifter moves to curb CFC production, including a total ban on the chemicals by the year 2000. Restrictions on halons, which are up to 10 times more destructive than CFCs, were also tightened.

Two other key ozone-depleting chemicals, carbon tetrachloride and methyl chloroform, were added to the Protocol during the London meeting. Carbon tetrachloride use is to be ended by 2000 and methyl chloroform production is to be phased out by 2005. **Developing countries** will be allowed up to 10 years leeway on the phasing out of certain chemicals.

Two months after the 1995 Vienna agreements, scientists announced the discovery of a 40% loss of ozone over **Antarctica**. Most industrial countries were failing to live up to their CFC phase-out obligations. In 1995, Russia announced that it could not meet the phase-out date either and requested a four-year extension, applicable to Poland, Belarus, Bulgaria and Ukraine as well.

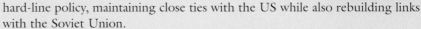

MUBARAK, HOSNI (1928-)

Egyptian military leader and politician. Son of a court functionary, Mubarak graduated from the Air Force Academy in 1950. After serving as a fighter pilot he went to Russia to take further courses. After the 1973 Arab-Israeli War he was appointed Director-General of the Air Force Academy. In 1975, President **Sadat** appointed him Vice President, ostensibly on the grounds that he had no power base and would thus be no threat. Following Sadat's assassination Mubarak became President in 1981, also becoming leader of the ruling National Democratic Party. He pursued a hard-line policy, maintaining close ties with the US while also rebuilding links with the Soviet Union.

He worked hard to regain Arab community support and in 1989 Egypt was allowed to return to the **Arab League**. He supported the **Palestine Liberation Organization** (PLO) and opposed the 1990 Iraqi occupation of Kuwait. Egyptian forces fought on the side of the Allied Forces, but were careful not to enter Iraqi territory. Despite the boycott by opposition parties of elections in the early 1990s and the continuing rise and influence of Islamic **fundamentalism** in Egypt, Mubarak was re-elected President in 1993. He played a significant role in brokering various peace accords between Israel and the PLO.

MOSQUITO (see also Aedes, Anopheles and Malaria)

More than 3,000 species of small, biting insects with almost world-wide distribution. Mosquitoes are especially abundant in the tropics and are viewed by many as humankind's greatest pest. In most species, males feed on plant juices while females, who must have blood to reproduce, bite and suck the blood of animals often transmitting serious diseases to humans and livestock in the process.

Mosquitoes are intermediary hosts for many parasites and can infect humans with **malaria**, **yellow fever**, filariasis, **dengue** and a variety of other diseases.

MOUNT PINATUBO

A volcano 90 kilometres northwest of Manila in the Philippines which erupted in 1990 after lying dormant for 600 years. Smoke and ash rose 25 kilometres into the air. An

Mosquito-ridden
Virologists test for malaria at a refugee camp in northern Thailand. Female mosquitoes suck blood, and in tropical areas pass on potential killers like malaria and dengue fever.
MOSQUITO

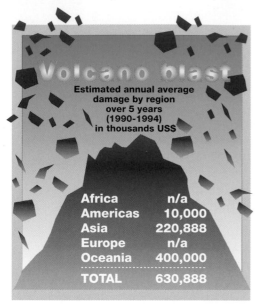

Estimated annual average damage by region over 5 years (1990-1994) in thousands US$

Africa	n/a
Americas	10,000
Asia	220,888
Europe	n/a
Oceania	400,000
TOTAL	**630,888**

World Disasters Report 1996, International Federation of Red Cross and Red Crescent Societies, Geneva.

estimated 200 people lost their lives and 100,000 were made **homeless**. The ash and dust produced by the eruption were so great they blocked out solar radiation, contributing to a lowering of average global temperatures for more than 2 years.

MUJAHADIN

An Iranian political party founded secretly in 1965 which stressed the importance of religion and believed that Shia **Islam** would guide the masses to join the revolution and sweep to victory. Severe repression by the Iranian Government annihilated all the founding members, resulting in an influx of new recruits, many of whom were Marxist. This led to an organization with a mixture of viewpoints.

In 1975, a Mujahadin manifesto described Islam as the ideology of the middle class and Marxism as the ideology of the working class and concluded that Marxism was the true revolutionary creed. This split the party into 2 factions, each of which carried out **guerrilla** actions.

In 1978, yielding to popular pressure, the Shah of Iran released most Mujahadin prisoners including Masud Rajavi, the only surviving member of the original central

committee. Both factions became stronger and helped overthrow the Shah in 1979. However, they soon fell foul of **Ayatollah Khomeini** when they refused his instruction to surrender arms.

An armed struggle against the Khomeini regime followed, with the guerrillas targeting parliamentarians and revolutionary guards. In 1981, a Mujahadin bomb killed President Muhammad Ali Rajai and Premier Muhammad Javad Bahonar.

The Government responded by killing 10 central committee members and executing any found guilty of violence. By 1982 the Mujahadin claimed to have killed over 1,200 religious and political leaders while the Government claimed to have executed 4,000

Mujahadin members.

When the war with Iraq began, the Khomeini regime accused the Mujahadin of being agents of Iraq. Later Masud Rajavi set up his new headquarters in Baghdad and from there joined with the Iraqis in the war against the Teheran regime. When Khomeini died, Iraq stopped all anti-Iranian activities, but the Mujahadin continued to maintain its base in Iraq with some 4,500 troops.

The name mujahadin has also been used by warriors of the Islamic group *Taliban* in Afghanistan.

MULTIFIBRE AGREEMENT (MFA)

A complex system of bilateral quotas which protect rich countries from

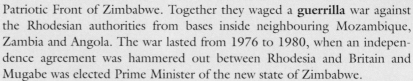

MUGABE, ROBERT (1925-   )

Zimbabwean politician. The son of a carpenter, he trained as a teacher before attending university in South Africa and Ghana. In 1960 he returned to colonial Rhodesia and, together with Reverend Ndabaningi Sithole, founded the **Zimbabwe African National Union (ZANU)**, a breakaway group from Joshua Nkomo's Zimbabwe African People's Union (ZAPU).

Mugabe was imprisoned in 1964 for 'subversion' and given a 10-year sentence. While in prison, he gained a law degree and managed to depose Sithole as ZANU's leader. After his release, he and Joshua Nkomo formed the Patriotic Front of Zimbabwe. Together they waged a **guerrilla** war against the Rhodesian authorities from bases inside neighbouring Mozambique, Zambia and Angola. The war lasted from 1976 to 1980, when an independence agreement was hammered out between Rhodesia and Britain and Mugabe was elected Prime Minister of the new state of Zimbabwe.

He formed a coalition between ZANU (mostly Shona people) and ZAPU (mostly minority Ndebele people) and implemented wide-ranging policies to improve the living standards of black Zimbabweans. In 1982 he ousted Nkomo from the coalition and strife between the Shona and Ndebele grew. In 1984 his ZANU party set up a new one-party state structure composed of a Central Committee and a Politburo. In 1987, ZANU and ZAPU merged and Mugabe became the nation's first President. Pressure from within ZANU and from abroad forced him to accept a multiparty system again and in 1990 he was re-elected to the presidency after running against weak opponents in multiparty elections.

Since then **IMF**-imposed liberalization measures have slashed public expenditures causing widespread suffering. Meanwhile, the Mugabe administration has become more autocratic and intolerant. A majority of the electorate and several opposition parties boycotted the 1996 elections which returned Mugabe with 93% of the vote.

Third World competition in textiles by limiting imports. Quotas and tariffs are levelled against imports from **developing countries** but not from other industrialized nations. The MFA contradicts the principles of **free trade** and calls to scrap the MFA have been steadily growing.

Textiles and clothing are a sector where **developing countries** have a comparative advantage and have a trading surplus with the industrialized world. World trade in textiles and clothing was worth over $200 billion in 1992, with the developing nations exporting about $60 billion worth of goods.

The **World Bank** reported that if quotas were removed poor countries could gain an estimated $3 billion through increased sales. Most of the benefits would go to South Korea, China and Brazil, the three biggest exporters.

The World Bank also calculated that if all import tariffs on textiles were removed it would generate an additional $15 billion in trade, with the developing countries receiving $8 billion of this amount.

In 1992, restrictions still covered 67% of clothing and textile exports from developing countries. It is estimated that textile exports would rise by 82% and clothing by 93% if trade is completely liberalized.

MULTILATERAL DEVELOPMENT BANKS (MDBs)

The MDBs are major banks set up by international treaties that lend money to **Third World** governments and government agencies to fund development projects. There are four MDBs: the **World Bank**, the **Inter-American Development Bank**, the **Asian Development Bank** and the **African Development Bank**. Policy decisions in these banks are made by a board of governors representing individual member nations. The number of voting shares of each

government depends on their financial contribution to the bank. The MDBs are the largest public development lenders in the world.

Each bank operates a two-tier structure of lending. Funds are lent at close to commercial interest rates through a programme referred to as a 'hard loan window'.

Loans are also made at little or no interest through a 'soft loan window'. At the World Bank, the **International Bank for Reconstruction and Development** (IBRD) is the hard loan window and the **International Development Association** (IDA) is the bank's **soft loan** window.

An MDB's financing is provided by member countries in two forms. 'Paid-in' capital is money that is actually *transferred* to the banks when the governments purchase capital stock. 'Callable' capital is money that is *pledged* by the member governments but not actually paid to the bank. Callable capital acts as a guarantee allowing MDBs to borrow on the open market. It could, theoretically, be collected if required. In general, the paid-in capital of major donor governments is only 10% of that outstanding as callable capital.

As well as receiving paid-in capital and pledges of callable capital from donor governments, money for the MDB's hard-loan windows is obtained by selling securities to investors and raising money from the commercial market. The funds for soft loan windows come exclusively through contributions by donor governments.

The MDBs are supposed to make only enough profit to cover administrative costs and maintain high credit ratings. In fact profits are much larger: the World Bank has made a profit every year since 1947. Its 1990 net income of $1.1 billion represented an 86% increase over its

income at the start of the decade.

In addition, MDB funds are often of dubious value to the recipient. From 1982 to 1985, the MDBs disbursed $76 billion to Northern companies in contracts for such things as goods and equipment, construction and consultancy fees.

MULTILATERAL INVESTMENT GUARANTEE AGENCY (MIGA)

An agency formed in 1985 to offer insurance for multilateral investments. The MIGA is now the fastest-growing institution within the **World Bank** system. It aims to promote private investment in less-developed countries by offering insurance against non-commercial risks – primarily war, expropriation, nationalization and currency-exchange restrictions.

It also offers long-term political risk insurance, covering investors

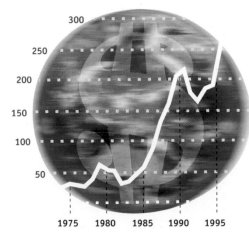

Foreign Direct Investment
1975-1995 ($ billions)

World Trade Organization, Annual Report 1996, Geneva.

against future take-overs by governments following civil war, revolution or changes in economic policy. MIGA is designed to complement national schemes like Britain's Export Credit Guarantee Department or Canada's Export Development Corporation – both government-funded schemes designed to support private investment.

Mount Pinatubo – MIGA

Nationalism

'The Bosnian people decided to leave former Yugoslavia because of the rise of nationalism in other areas', said Bosnian Osman Sinanovic. But these refugees from Serb aggression paid a high price as they fled to UN safe haven Tuzla in 1995: 10,000 of their friends and family were unaccounted for.

N

Bold indicates a cross-reference

NARMADA VALLEY PROJECT

One of the largest, most controversial **water** development projects undertaken anywhere. Over the next 50 years 30 major **dams**, 135 medium-sized dams and 3,000 smaller dams are to be built on India's Narmada River and its tributaries. The bulk of outside financing for the project is supplied by the **World Bank**. When completed, the goal is to irrigate 50,000 square kilometres and generate 2,700 megawatts of electricity.

Over 20 million people live in the Narmada Basin and Hindus consider the river to be holy. The project will submerge 3,500 square kilometres of forest (11% of the forest in the Narmada valley) plus 200 square kilometres of cultivated **land** and

Against the current

Workers carry materials for building the Sardar Sarovar Dam in Gujerat, part of India's ambitious Narmada valley project for irrigation and hydro-electricity which will displace some 1.5 million people. NARMADA VALLEY PROJECT

NASSER, GAMAL ABDEL (1918-1970)

Egyptian military leader and politician. The son of a postal worker, Nasser graduated from the Royal Military Academy. Following his service during the 1948-49 Palestine War, he returned to the Academy as a lecturer. He then became leader of the Free Officers organization which ousted King Faruq in 1952 and established the Revolutionary Command Council. Following a power struggle, a new Egyptian constitution was announced in 1956 and Nasser was elected President.

Once in power Nasser became increasingly concerned with political and economic independence for Egypt. When the United States refused to sell his country arms, he approached Czechoslovakia. The Americans responded by cutting **aid** for the proposed Aswan Dam and persuading the **World Bank** to do the same. Nasser nationalized the Suez Canal and accepted aid from the Soviet Union in retaliation.

The resulting Suez War in 1956 further alienated Nasser from the West. He became leader of the **Non-Aligned Movement** and in 1958 he was elected head of the short-lived United Arab Republic, a merger of Egypt and Syria.

In 1967 Israel threatened Syria for allowing Palestinian forces to operate from its **soil**. Nasser responded by closing the Straits of Tiran to Israeli shipping, a move which sparked the 1967 Arab-Israeli War. Eventually he was forced to accept a UN Security Council Resolution calling for the peaceful co-existence of Israel and the Arab states in order to make the Israelis withdraw from Egyptian territories occupied during the war. But Nasser remained the most senior Arab leader and after the **Palestine Liberation Organization** and Jordanian army clashed in 1970, they turned to Nasser for mediation. He died from a heart attack during the negotiations.

some 400 square kilometres of grazing land. An estimated 40% of the land to be irrigated is susceptible to waterlogging and **salinization** and up to 1.5 million people will be

displaced by the dams. Many do not have title to land and thus will receive no compensation.

The World Bank temporarily suspended a $450 million loan for the first 2 dams (Sardar Sarovar in Gujarat and Narmada Sagar in Madhya Pradesh) pending a full review. In 1990 Japan also withdrew its support.

Despite growing national and international pressure and warnings that the project could endanger public health, including the spread of **schistosomiasis**, authorities have confirmed that the project will go ahead. During the 1990s, protests and court actions slowed construction. Thousands of people complained about terrible living conditions at resettlement sites. And others who were given infertile land after being relocated have returned to their original villages. In addition, 2 further World Bank studies have raised serious doubts about the project's finances and cost-effectiveness.

NATIONALISM
Devotion and loyalty to one's country or nation, such that national interests are placed above all others. Nationalism is a modern phenomenon dating from the mid-18th century. Increasing commerce, **capitalism** and industrialization created the need for a well-defined, unified state where the middle classes could participate in government. Common language and geography are the most important factors determining whether people can coherently form a nation. Religion, culture, **race**, politics and historical factors are also important. Nationalism may take many different forms and nationalist movements can arise in ethnic, racial or cultural communities which exist under the political control of others.

At the end of the 19th century, nationalist movements in Europe became more aggressive and reactionary which culminated in World War I. Thirty years later, after World War II, nationalist fervour in most of Europe had dissipated and the continent moved towards internationalism and unity. In part, this was due to the awareness of increasing interdependency, reinforced by international organizations such as **NATO**, the EEC and others.

In Africa and Asia, nationalism grew predominantly as a reaction against the colonial powers. Neutrality and non-alignment also became widely adopted as a means to counter **colonialism** and domination by foreign economic and political powers. With the break-up of the Soviet Union and the erosion of **communism** in Eastern Europe, nationalist forces emerged in many of the ex-communist states. Nationalism continued to reassert itself throughout the 1980s and 1990s. In France and Germany right-wing nationalists blamed immigrants and foreigners for high **unemployment** and growing social tensions. A vicious kind of nationalism was also evident in ex-Yugoslavia as age-old hatreds erupted between Serbs, Croats and Muslims.

NATIVE AMERICANS
(see also Indigenous Peoples)
Also called Indians or Native People, Native Americans are members of any of the indigenous peoples of the Western hemisphere. Native Americans are thought to have descended from Asian Mongoloid ancestors, nomadic hunters who migrated over the Bering Strait land bridge into North America about 30,000 years ago. Hundreds of such peoples spread throughout North, Central and South America. In North America, societies based on hunting, gathering and small-scale agriculture spread from the west coast to the eastern woodlands. Despite the widely differing environments in which they lived, all had similar economies and lifestyles. Hunting was a major source of meat and hides. In addition, groups established themselves in desert and scrub lands in the west, following primarily a nomadic, hunter-gatherer lifestyle and living in caves and natural rock shelters. In the hotter and drier southwest, several societies took up agriculture and began cultivating **maize** around 2000 BC, often using **irrigation** to raise their yield. From 1050-1300, the Pueblo culture in what is now Arizona and New Mexico developed the first dwellings using stone masonry and mud adobe.

Indians first reached Central America a little over 10,000 years ago, but quickly established farming communities. Agriculture enabled groups to develop their small settlements into towns and this led to the appearance of arts, crafts and trade in such goods as pottery and farming equipment. A mixture of agriculture, trade and religion facilitated the development of the Maya and the later empire of the Aztecs.

Native American civilizations in South America also began a little under 10,000 years ago in southern Chile and the south-central plains.

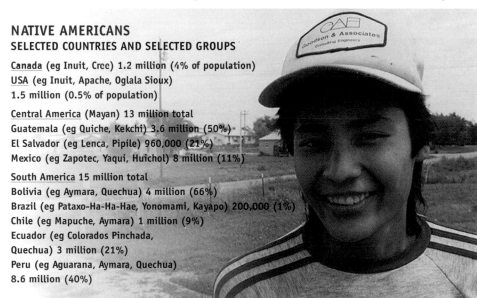

NATIVE AMERICANS
SELECTED COUNTRIES AND SELECTED GROUPS

Canada (eg Inuit, Cree) 1.2 million (4% of population)
USA (eg Inuit, Apache, Oglala Sioux)
1.5 million (0.5% of population)

Central America (Mayan) 13 million total
Guatemala (eg Quiche, Kekchi) 3.6 million (50%)
El Salvador (eg Lenca, Pipile) 960,000 (21%)
Mexico (eg Zapotec, Yaqui, Huichol) 8 million (11%)

South America 15 million total
Bolivia (eg Aymara, Quechua) 4 million (66%)
Brazil (eg Pataxo-Ha-Ha-Hae, Yonomami, Kayapo) 200,000 (1%)
Chile (eg Mapuche, Aymara) 1 million (9%)
Ecuador (eg Colorados Pinchada,
Quechua) 3 million (21%)
Peru (eg Aguarana, Aymara, Quechua)
8.6 million (40%)

The Gaia Atlas of First Peoples, by Julian Burger, Gaia Books 1990.

Proud dancers
Two young Sioux take a rest from a pow-wow (dance) on Cheyenne River Reservation, South Dakota. These increasingly popular gatherings help keep native people in touch with their past.
NATIVE AMERICANS

In the densely-forested interior, tribes grew larger practising a form of shifting agriculture. Today in the **tropical forests** of **Amazonia**, this lifestyle is still followed by groups such as the **Yanomami** indians.

Elsewhere along the coasts and along major rivers, cultivation began of crops such as corn and beans. This was coupled with civilizations becoming organized and complex, based on military and ritualistic leadership and incorporating centralized government and class systems. The best example is the Inca civilization that flourished until the arrival of European colonizers in the 16th century. The effects of the European invasion were catastrophic. Millions died from imported diseases; millions more were murdered or worked to death. Native cultures and religions were decimated. Those closest to major transport routes fared worst, the least accessible fared best.

In South America, the remotest of Indian peoples maintain many aspects of their traditional way of life even today, although they are under constant threat. With the Spanish conquistadors came Roman Catholicism, agricultural tools and European growing techniques. **Plantations**, **cattle** ranches and mines took Indian **land** and Indian labour. As commercialization and industrialization grew, native communities were forced more and more into isolation if they were to preserve their tradition lifestyles and cultural integrity.

In North America, the Spanish tried to convert Indians to **Christianity**, while the French who were interested in establishing trade, tried to relocate them. The British initially recognized Indians' legal title to their land, though in practice Native Americans had to fight for every scrap. In the US the Indian Removal Act of 1830 marked the end of this policy, especially when gold was discovered in California in 1848. By the late 1880s most Indian peoples in the US had been herded onto reservations and the Dawes General Allotment Act of 1887 confiscated around 35 million hectares of Native American land.

In Canada a series of treaties gradually accomplished the same results. However, across Canada today, Indian people are challenging the legal bases of many of these treaties and there is a vigorous battle over land claims and native self-government taking place in many parts of the country.

NATURAL GAS

A naturally-occurring mixture of gaseous hydrocarbons consisting mainly of **methane**. It is obtained from underground reservoirs and is often associated with **oil** deposits. Like oil it originates in the natural decomposition of animal matter. One major advantage of natural gas is its comparative cleanliness; burning gas produces only half the **carbon** dioxide (CO_2) produced by burning **coal**. It is a relatively cheap and effective fuel and is generally expected to be the fastest growing fuel source over the next decade, although in comparison to other fossil fuels such as coal, it is in short supply. Of the world's 86 trillion cubic metres of recoverable reserves, 35 trillion are in Russia and other states of the former Soviet Union, 11 trillion are in Iran and 5.8 trillion are in the US.

During the 1980s annual global production was around 1.9 trillion cubic metres. The Soviet Union (770 billion cubic metres), the US (472 billion) and Canada (85 billion) were the largest producers. During the early 1990s natural gas replaced **nuclear power** and coal to become the preferred fuel for power stations. Gas-fired electric plants cut carbon emissions by half, nitrogen oxide emissions by 90% and sulphur emissions by 99%, and cost half as much to build as coal-fitted plants.

Russia and the other ex-members of the USSR produce a third of the world's gas. Russia's gas reserves are controlled by GAZPROM, the world's largest monopoly.

NEO-COLONIALISM

A condition of economic dependency when the ability of politically-independent **Third World** countries to

Colonialism is dead – long live neo-colonialism!
Congo (former Zaire) may be an independent state but the transnational corporations have ways of keeping tight hold on people's wallets and their hopes: 'Dallas – the American Dream'.
NEO-COLONIALISM

control their own development and destiny is compromised and constrained by the actions of Western states, **transnational corporations** or international financial agencies.

NEW INTERNATIONAL ECONOMIC ORDER (NIEO)

This is a term introduced in 1974 to describe a comprehensive programme for radically restructuring the world economy in the interests of **developing countries** and global equality. The concept was coined by the nations of the **South**, specifically members of the Group of 77 and the **Non-Aligned Movement**. The NIEO was based on ideas of national sovereignty and the right of states to choose their own style and method of economic development. Its main documents were the Declaration and Programme of Action passed by the UN General Assembly in 1974, and the Charter of Economic Rights and Duties of States, adopted by the General Assembly later the same year.

The NIEO was adopted by the Group of 77 in 1976 and called for: a more equitable deal on commodity prices; a massive increase in **Third World** manufacturing; and a substantial infusion of financial resources from the West. The most significant component of the NIEO is the Integrated Programme on **Commodities** (IPC), an attempt to restrict the supply of Third World commodity exports in order to avoid gluts and maintain a stable income for producers. Unfortunately, the IPC has received little support from Northern industrial countries and its impact has been minimal.

NEWLY INDUSTRIALIZING COUNTRIES (NICs)

A term used to describe **developing countries** that are relatively far along the path to industrialization. Examples include India, Brazil, Taiwan, South Korea and Thailand. These countries are also sometimes referred to as the Advanced Developing Countries.

NITROGEN CYCLE

The process through which nitrogen, an essential element for plant growth and the formation of animal tissue, passes through the ecosystem. The earth's atmosphere contains a great deal of nitrogen but it cannot be used by most organisms in a gaseous form.

Nitrogen in the air is converted (or fixed) to ammonia naturally by the action of lightning and cosmic radiation. The ammonia can then be converted into nitrogen-containing compounds that can be used by plants.

Certain **soil** bacteria can also carry out this fixing process. Bacteria convert atmospheric nitrogen to nitrites then to nitrates which can then be used by plants to

NEHRU, JAWAHARLAL (1889-1964)

Indian politician, first Prime Minister of an independent India. Born into a well-educated family, he was the eldest of 4 children. He was educated at home before going to public school in England where he later qualified with degrees in natural science and law. He returned to India, married and had a daughter, Indira, who would later become Prime Minister using her married name Indira Gandhi.

He was a staunch nationalist and yearned for India's independence. In 1921, his political activities caused him to be arrested for the first time. Over the next 24 years he was to spend a total of 9 years in jail. He was elected President of the Congress Party in 1929 and presided over the historic Lahore party meetings that proclaimed independence as India's main goal. **Mahatma Gandhi** recognised his potential and he was soon seen as Gandhi's natural successor.

Nehru was in Europe in 1936 and when he returned home the rival Muslim League lost support in provincial elections and appealed to him to form a Congress-Muslim League coalition. Nehru refused. The clash hardened into a conflict between Hindus and Muslims that would eventually lead to the partition of India and the creation of Pakistan.

Following the Congress Party's 'Quit India' resolution in 1942, both Gandhi and Nehru were arrested. He was released in 1945 and after 2 further years of campaigning, India was granted independence. Although Gandhi refused to accept partition, Nehru reluctantly accepted and the states of India and Pakistan emerged in 1947 with Nehru as Prime Minister of an independent India.

During his 17 years in office he espoused democratic **socialism** and secularism. His policies reflected his desire to modernize India and bring it into line with technological and scientific advancements. He cleverly imported modern ways of thinking and working and adapted them to India's needs and conditions. He also reformed some of India's ancient laws, for example changing the Hindu civil code enabling widows to enjoy equality in matters of inheritance.

He was internationally respected and generally followed a path of nonalignment. Throughout his term Nehru was dogged by the troubles in Kashmir, a problem rooted in the Hindu-Muslim divide of India and Pakistan.

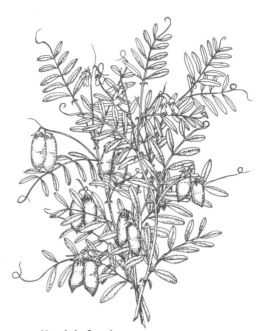

Health food
Protein-packed lentils are also good for the soil. NITROGEN CYCLE

make amino acids and proteins. Some species of nitrogen-fixing bacteria live on the roots of a specific group of plants called **legumes** which include peas, beans and certain trees. The presence of these plants greatly increases the nitrogen content of the soil and improves fertility.

Nitrogen in the form of inorganic compounds (nitrites and nitrates) is absorbed by plants and turned into organic compounds such as proteins. The plants containing the proteins are then eaten by herbivores and the nitrogen-containing compounds are released during digestion.

This process is repeated when herbivores are eaten by carnivores and so on up the food chain. The nitrogen is returned to the soil, either through excreta or when an organism dies. The micro-organisms responsible for decomposing dead tissue return the nitrogen to the soil in its inorganic form.

NITROGEN OXIDES

Nitrogen oxide and other oxides of nitrogen (NOx) are commonly formed during the combustion of fossil fuels and are vented from power stations and in exhaust fumes from vehicle engines. Nitrogen oxide acts as a catalyst in the formation of **ozone** at ground level. This low-level, tropospheric ozone is thought to damage trees and vegetation, contribute to the formation of smog and cause breathing difficulties, particularly among asthmatics.

In the stratosphere, oxides of nitrogen contribute to the destruction of the protective ozone layer. In the upper atmosphere 1 molecule of nitrogen can destroy 10 ozone molecules, with the result that NO_x account for about 6% of all **global warming**. On a per capita basis, the US (74 kilograms), Canada (69 kg) and Luxembourg (57 kg) release the most nitrogen oxides.

NOMADS

Peoples who live in no fixed place but wander periodically with their goods and possessions. Their movements are governed by the seasonal availability of food, pasture, trade or **employment**.

Transhumance is a form of pastoral nomadism in which livestock are moved seasonally between mountain summer pastures and lower-lying winter pastures or between wet-season and dry-season grazing areas. Pastoral tribes in Africa, goat herders in the Andes mountains in South America and Caribou herders in Scandinavia are

NKRUMAH, KWAME (1909-1972)

Ghanaian nationalist leader. Born into a professional family in the colony of the Gold Coast (now Ghana), he became a teacher before becoming interested in politics. He went to college in the United States, reading the works of **Marx**, **Lenin** and the black American leader Marcus Garvey and became president of the African Students Organization of North America. Later he was invited to serve as the Secretary-General of the United Gold Coast Convention (UGCC) a group working for independence in the Gold Coast. When rioting broke out in 1948, Nkrumah and several colleagues were arrested by the British. He formed the Convention Peoples' Party in 1949 dedicated to achieving immediate self-government, through a campaign of 'positive action' involving non-violent demonstrations, strikes and non-cooperation. In the Gold Coast's first general election in 1951 Nkrumah was elected to Parliament. He was released from prison to become government leader and Prime Minister the following year.

The Gold Coast achieved independence in 1957 and Nkrumah became the new nation's first Prime Minister. A year later he began to tighten his grip on power legalizing imprisonment without trial of anyone regarded as a security risk. At the same time he spent money on new roads, schools and health facilities and his popularity rose. In 1960, he became President of the Republic of Ghana and assumed sweeping legislative and executive powers. His administration became involved in grandiose development projects and Ghana was soon crippled by foreign debts.

His Second Development Plan in 1959 was abandoned 2 years later with a budget deficit of over $125 million. During this time he turned to the communist states for support. In 1962, Nkrumah declared Ghana a one-party state and assumed the position of Life President of both nation and party. Economic woes continued and shortages of food and goods became common. In 1966, the army and police staged a successful coup while Nkrumah was visiting China and he went into exile in Guinea.

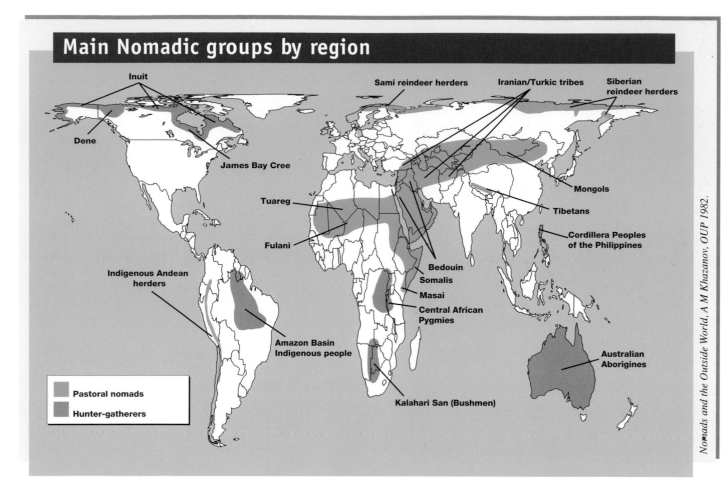

Main Nomadic groups by region

Inuit
Dene
James Bay Cree
Sami reindeer herders
Iranian/Turkic tribes
Siberian reindeer herders
Tuareg
Fulani
Mongols
Tibetans
Cordillera Peoples of the Philippines
Bedouin
Somalis
Masai
Central African Pygmies
Indigenous Andean herders
Amazon Basin Indigenous people
Australian Aborigines
Kalahari San (Bushmen)

Pastoral nomads
Hunter-gatherers

Nomads and the Outside World, A M Khazanov, OUP 1982.

amongst the 30-40 million pastoral nomads in the world today.

For thousands of years traditional hunter-gatherers, such as the Australian **Aborigines**, the **San Bushmen** people of the Kalahari desert or the **Inuit** in the Canadian Arctic, existed in small family groups that spent anywhere from a few days to a few weeks in a particular vicinity before moving on. In Europe traders, tinkers, entertainers and gypsies travelled widely and freely seeking work. However, nomadism is now being stamped out in most parts of the world. In Africa the artificial boundaries drawn up to form national frontiers take no heed of traditional migration patterns of many nomadic tribes, who now find themselves unable to cross international borders to carry on their traditional lifestyle.

Also, as the human population increases, there is less **land** available where nomads can wander. In addition, most authorities try to persuade nomadic people to settle in one spot so that they have access to modern medical facilities and other social services – and so that they can be taxed.

In certain parts of the world, notably in Africa, a nomadic lifestyle is the best means of existence in fragile environments. Well-digging programmes in the **Sahel** have caused pastoralists to stop moving their herds, leading to subsequent overgrazing on land that is already marginal.

Bans on movements to new areas of grassland and burning prior to grazing have increased the habitat for **tsetse** flies and reduced the nutritional quality of dry-season grass. Moving of herds traditionally allowed pastoralists to exploit fodder sources elsewhere when the rains failed.

The prevention of transhumance has also proved environmentally damaging throughout much of Africa where conditions are unsuited to intensive **cattle** ranching.

NON-ALIGNED MOVEMENT (see also G77)

A theory originated by **Jawarhalal Nehru**, Prime Minister of India from 1947 to 1964, which opposed **colonialism**, **neo-colonialism** and **imperialism**. The theory was adopted in 1961 at a 25-nation conference held at Belgrade. Delegates were mainly from Asia and Africa with India and Egypt playing leading roles. Initially, countries in the Non-Aligned Movement saw themselves as separate from both the Soviet and American power blocs.

However in 1979, under Cuban President Fidel **Castro**'s leadership and with the backing of Ethiopia and Vietnam, the non-aligned movement moved towards a 'natural' alliance with the Soviet Union. Since the break-up of the Soviet bloc, the movement refers to nations who are not members of the Western European/North American power bloc. The governments of the non-aligned group press for more

Nitrogen Cycle – Non-Aligned Movement

Signs of the times

Aid agencies like these in Burkina Faso try to shore up the gap between rich and poor: but people in countries like Ghana, Haiti, Venezuela, former Zaire and Zambia are poorer than they were in 1960. NON-GOVERNMENTAL ORGANIZATIONS

generous **terms of trade**, development **aid** from the relatively rich **North** and non-intervention in the **South**'s affairs. A central tenet is the need for a **New International Economic Order** (NIEO). The movement's membership grew as more countries gained their independence and it now has 111 members.

NON-GOVERNMENTAL ORGANIZATIONS (NGOs)

Also referred to as voluntary agencies. These are private organizations of a charitable, research or educational nature that are concerned with a wide range of social, economic and environmental issues – everything from the arms race, violence against women, **global warming** and **human rights**

to food security and gay rights.

They may act on an international, national or local scale. Some raise money from the public and from governments to help fund development projects in the **Third World** or to assist in disaster relief. Others attempt to educate the public and campaign on major global issues or to lobby governments and international agencies to change public policies.

There are now tens of thousands of NGOs world-wide, representing millions of supporters. The NGO movement is becoming increasingly involved in decision-making at both the national and international level. For example, NGOs are now actively involved in hammering out the agenda at major UN meetings.

NORTH

An unofficial and loosely-defined term used to describe those countries above a dividing line, drawn by the

Brandt Commission, which differentiates the better-off countries of the 'North' from the less-developed nations of the 'South'. The North refers to the wealthier, industrialized countries in Europe and North America together with Japan, Australia and New Zealand.

NORTH AMERICAN FREE TRADE AGREEMENT (NAFTA)

In 1992, Mexico, Canada and the United States joined in a comprehensive free trading arrangement that promised unrestricted trade and investment between the countries. NAFTA will create the largest market in the world in a combined economy of $6.5 billion, covering some 380 million people. Supporters, including most of the major corporations, claimed the agreement would benefit all 3 countries, each excelling in its own area of comparative advantage. NAFTA was not without its critics. Many Americans and Canadians feared NAFTA would simply push companies across the Mexican border in search of cheaper wages. Mexicans, on the other hand, feared their domestic industry would be swallowed up and their agricultural sector destroyed. Anticipation of NAFTA's negative effects sparked the **Zapatista** uprising in Chiapas on the treaty's January 1, 1994 implementation date. By the end of

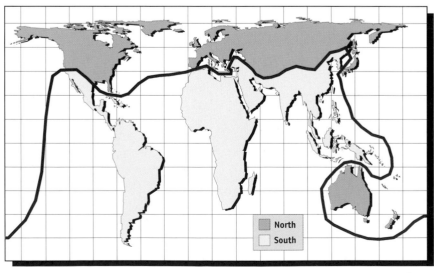

1994, Chile was also discussing the possibility of joining an extended version of NAFTA.

NORTH ATLANTIC TREATY ORGANIZATION (NATO)

A mutual defence alliance formed in 1949. The treaty was signed by Belgium, Canada, Denmark, France, Iceland, Italy, Luxembourg, the Netherlands, Norway, Portugal, the United Kingdom and the United States. It provided for the collective defence of member states against a perceived threat posed by the Soviet bloc. All member states are bound to protect and aid any member state against attack. NATO also seeks to encourage economic and social co-operation among signatory nations. Greece and Turkey joined in 1952, the Federal Republic of Germany in 1955 and Spain in 1982.

Both the Supreme Allied Commanders in Europe and the Atlantic are Americans. In 1960, a permanent multinational Allied Mobile Force (AMF) was established to provide a rapid response in the event of an invasion of any member nation. NATO has been beset with problems since its inception.

The presence in Europe of nuclear weapons under US control has caused considerable tension. The costs of the pact and what proportion individual nations should pay also proved to be a matter of discord, as did the problem of standardization of weapons. The role and effective future of NATO as an organization was thrown into doubt in 1990 following the collapse of the

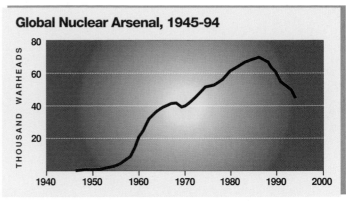

Global Nuclear Arsenal, 1945-94

Vital Signs 1995/96, Worldwatch Institute, Earthscan.

opposing **Warsaw Pact**, the reunification of Germany, the democratization process in Eastern Europe and the signing of the Conventional Forces in Europe (CFE) Treaty. Under the terms of the treaty, the 16 NATO members and the 6 Warsaw Pact states formally confirmed that they no longer regard each other as adversaries. NATO members and 22 eastern European states then formed the North Atlantic Co-operation Council (NACC) in 1991.

NUCLEAR ARMS

There are 5 acknowledged nuclear powers: the United States, Russia, France, China and the United Kingdom. Since 1945, these countries have manufactured some 128,000 nuclear warheads and spent more than $5 trillion on nuclear weapons. Following agreements to curb the arms race, the number of warheads in the world fell to 41,000 by 1995, a 9% decrease from the previous year. The US and Russia between them control 97% of all nuclear weapons.

By the time the Strategic Arms Reduction Treaties (START I and II) take effect in the year 2003, both these 2 countries will still have 3,000 warheads – enough to wipe out the Earth's **population** several times over.

In 1995, the **Nuclear Non-Proliferation Treaty** was extended indefinitely. However, there is still

Bombed out
Devastated Hiroshima, Japan, after the first atomic bomb (nicknamed 'Little Boy') was dropped by a US B-29 bomber, on 6 August 1945. NUCLEAR ARMS

Non-Aligned Movement – Nuclear Arms

cause for concern over proliferation. Although South Africa announced in 1993 that it had dismantled its arsenal of 6 warheads, nations like India, Pakistan and Israel also have limited nuclear arsenals or have the capacity to produce nuclear weapons. The US is also planning to create a reserve 'stockpile' of warheads and Russia may do the same with some of the 12,000 warheads it holds in storage.

NUCLEAR ENERGY

The energy produced through changes in atomic structure, either via nuclear fission or nuclear fusion. The energy liberated in fission occurs when a heavy atomic nucleus, such as uranium, splits into two or more parts.

The total mass of the parts is less than the mass of the original nucleus. The difference in mass is equivalent to the energy which is required to bind the original nucleus together. In a fusion reaction two lighter nuclei, such as hydrogen and deuterium, collide and combine to form a stable nucleus, such as helium. As the nucleus formed is lighter than the sum of the two component nuclei, energy is given off. The fusion process is the basis of the hydrogen bomb.

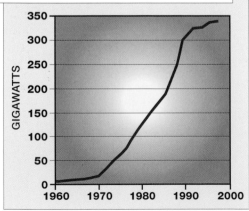

World Electrical Generating Capacity of Nuclear Power Plants, 1960-1996

Vital Signs 1997/1998, Worldwatch Institute, Earthscan.

NUCLEAR NON-PROLIFERATION TREATY

A 1970 treaty intended to stop the spread of nuclear weapons. Nuclear nations are obliged to destroy their nuclear arsenals in a gradual manner and non-nuclear nations must refrain from developing nuclear capabilities. Three permanent members of the UN Security Council (Britain, Russia and the United States) signed the Treaty in 1968. China and France added their names in 1992. In 1994, representatives of 174 nations agreed to extend the Treaty indefinitely.

NUCLEAR POWER

In nuclear power stations, the energy produced by fission reactions is harnessed to produce heat at a controlled rate. The heat is used to create steam which in turn drives a turbine and produces electricity. Both use natural uranium which contains less than 1% of the fissionable U-235 isotope. The rest is made up of U-238.

If a nucleus of **uranium**-235 is struck by a neutron, a U-236 nucleus is formed. This immediately splits into 2 parts and 2 or 3 more neutrons are liberated in the process. These neutrons will cause further splitting of nuclei and a chain reaction will build up. In a *thermal* reactor, the chain reaction is prevented by use of a moderator which slows down the neutrons. In a *fast breeder* reactor, the core is surrounded by natural uranium. Neutrons escape into the surrounding blanket, collide with U-238 to eventually form the fissionable **plutonium** isotope Pu-239. More Pu-239 is formed than is used to enrich the fuel in the core.

Fast breeder reactors are 50 times more economical in uranium usage than thermal reactors, although they operate at extremely high temperatures and require liquid metal coolants. The majority

Deadly mushroom
The number of nuclear warheads worldwide is down from the peak of 69,480 in 1968 to 49,910 in 1994.
NUCLEAR NON-PROLIFERATION TREATY

of commercial reactors are of the thermal type.

The world's first commercial-scale nuclear reactor began to operate in Britain in 1956. By the end of the 1980s, 435 nuclear reactor plants around the world were producing 17% of the total supply of electricity. In 1988, 114 further plants were under construction, 16 were on order and 96 were at the planning stages. During 1989, 10 new nuclear power plants were connected to national electricity grids. At the end of the year, 319,000 megawatts of electricity were being produced by nuclear power plants – 9,000 megawatts more than in 1988. Global nuclear capacity reached 340,000 megawatts in 1995, a slight increase over the previous year.

The history of the nuclear power industry has been fraught with problems and major accidents. The three most serious and well publicized have been: **Chernobyl** in the Soviet Union in 1986 (caused by a leak from a non-pressurized boiling-water reactor); at **Three Mile Island** in the United States in 1979 (a pressurized-water reactor leaked radioactive matter due to a combination of mechanical and electrical failure as well as operator error); and in the United Kingdom in 1957 when fire destroyed the core of a reactor at Windscale (Sellafield), releasing waves of radioactive fumes into the air.

The chequered history of the nuclear-power industry, including potentially catastrophic accidents and the huge costs of building and **decommissioning** plants, has undermined public confidence in the technology.

From 1970-87, the construction of 149 nuclear plants was cancelled, adding to the 58 that had been retired between 1956-87. In 1995 no new reactors were being built and globally only 34 reactors were still under construction. Two more reactors closed in 1995, raising the decommissioned total to 84. The average length of operation of these retired facilities was 17 years. Orders for only 2 new nuclear reactors were confirmed in 1995. Both were from China for French-designed technology sold with huge subsidies from the French Government.

NUCLEAR TEST BAN TREATY

A treaty signed in 1963 banning nuclear testing on the ground, in the atmosphere, in space and under **water**. The signatories were the Soviet Union, the United Kingdom and the United States, although many other countries agreed to adhere to the terms of the Treaty. It made no attempt to control or limit the stockpiling of nuclear weapons and was therefore rejected as ineffectual by both China and France.

From 1945-1989, there were 1,819 recorded nuclear tests. Tests have been carried out on every continent, an average of 1 test every 9 days. The US, Russia and China carry out tests at isolated sites within their mainland territory. Britain makes use of the US testing site in Nevada, while France has 2 test sites in French Polynesia in the Pacific Ocean. Despite global condemnation, France carried out a series of nuclear tests in the South Pacific in 1994. Tahitians were incensed by the tests and French riot troops had to be flown to the region to quell the violent protests that the tests provoked.

NYERERE, JULIUS (1922-)

Tanzanian politician. Son of a chief of the Zanaki people. Following schooling in the colony of Tanganyika, he attended university in Britain. He graduated with a degree in history and economics and returned home to teach. He entered politics and quickly became president of the Tanganyika African Association in 1953, transforming the organization into the Tanganyikan African National Union (TANU) which campaigned for social equality and racial harmony.

In 1955, with Tanganyika under UN Trusteeship, he visited UN headquarters in New York to press for independence. It was not until 5 years later that he managed to finally agree terms with Britain. Tanganyika attained self-government status and Nyerere became chief minister. His country finally gained full independence in 1961 and he assumed the post of Prime Minister. The following year Tanganyika joined Zanzibar to become the Republic of Tanzania, with Nyerere as President.

His policies were dedicated to the creation of an egalitarian socialist society based on co-operative agriculture. He collectivized village farms, introduced mass **literacy** campaigns and established free and universal education. He also intended Tanzania to become economically self-sufficient. Nyerere described this overall vision as *ujamaa*, a Swahili word meaning literally 'familyhood'.

In essence, Tanzania became a one-party state. He was re-elected for 3 more terms before he resigned in 1985. Nyerere was also a prime mover behind the Pan-African movement and in 1963 helped found the **Organization of African Unity**. He campaigned strongly against white minority rule in South Africa, Zimbabwe and Namibia and became a key figure in African events during the 1970s.

Although well regarded by Western **aid** donors, Nyerere's socialist policies failed to boost economic development substantially. When he resigned in 1985, Tanzania was still one of the world's poorest nations with a per capita income of $250. Agriculture remained at subsistence levels, food was scarce and the country's infrastructure was poor. Overseas aid accounted for a third of the nation's budget. Nonetheless, Tanzania had one of the highest literacy rates in Africa and the country was politically stable and markedly free of economic inequalities.

N**uclear Arms – Nyerere**

Organic Farming

Rabbits are usually thought of as a scourge to farming – but not here in the Philippines where this organic farmer collects rabbit dung to spread as fertilizer.

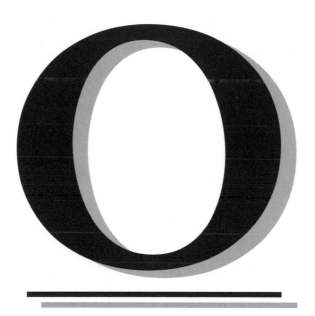

Bold indicates a cross-reference

OCEAN POLLUTION

Most waste and contaminants produced by human activities eventually find their way into the oceans. Each year billions of tonnes of silt, sewage, industrial waste, chemicals and **oil** pour into the world's seas. The flow of chemicals and metals into oceans due to human action far exceeds natural levels. Some pollutants such as plastic and oil are visible; others like **pesticides** are hidden. However the impact of ocean pollution is global. The circulation of ocean currents means that pollution is found even in **Antarctica**. **DDT** is regularly found in the bodies of penguins.

Sewage is a major source of ocean pollution, causing **eutrophication** and encouraging the spread of disease. Untreated sewage contains a cocktail of pathogenic organisms such as viruses, bacteria and protozoa which can cause **typhoid**, dysentery and a wide range of other diseases. Contrary to popular belief, pathogenic organisms can survive for a year or more in salt **water**.

Marine litter is also a significant problem, especially plastics. The **fishing** industry, where equipment is increasingly made of synthetic materials is a major contributor. More than 150,000 tonnes of fishing gear is lost each year.

Spills of crude oil cause widespread and lasting damage to marine flora and fauna. Around 32.2 million tonnes enter the oceans each year; nearly half of this is from oil spills and shipping. The rest comes primarily from industrial discharges.

Many synthetic, long-lasting and highly **toxic chemicals** also find their way into the oceans. These include pesticides, industrial chemicals such as **polychlorinated biphenyls** and tributyl tin, which is regularly applied to the underside of boats as an anti-fouling agent. Ordinary metals also cause widespread pollution. Concentrations of the metals build up in organisms as they pass up the marine food chain and they can eventually reach concentrations dangerous to humans.

From 1946 radioactive waste was regularly dumped at sea until the practice was outlawed under the 1982 London Dumping Convention. Several other global and regional treaties have been signed to help curb ocean pollution. These include the 1976 Barcelona Convention which established a plan to clean up the Mediterranean and which initiated a Regional Seas Programme and the 1973 International Convention for the Prevention of Pollution from Ships (**MARPOL**).

OGALLALA AQUIFER

The largest source of fossil **groundwater** in the United States, the Ogallala aquifer stretches from South Dakota to Texas. Expansion of agricultural production in the Great Plains of the US has been dependent on **irrigation**, most of which was supported by over-exploitation of the waters in the Ogallala.

From 1944-78 irrigated **land** in the area rose almost four-fold, from 21,000 square kilometres to 80,000 square kilometres. Approximately 20% of all irrigated cropland in the US is fed by **water** from the Ogallala. Since 1940, over 500 cubic kilometres of water have been withdrawn from the aquifer, far in excess of renewal.

Depletion has brought water reserves in some states

No barrier to pollution

Australia's Great Barrier Reef, from a 1911 painting. Today the delicate balance of life in a coral reef is disturbed by pollution from sewage, oil spills and toxic chemicals. **OCEAN POLLUTION**

down to half their normal level; underground supplies may last only a few more decades. If current trends continue, it is estimated that 20,000 square kilometres of land will be lost from production by the year 2,000. The irrigated area in the 6 states that rely most heavily on the Ogallala shrunk by 15% between 1978 and 1984. Between 1982 and 1992 farmers lost 3 times more irrigated hectares than they gained. By pumping groundwater faster than it is being renewed, the US joins China, India, Iran, Libya, Pakistan and Saudi Arabia in depleting their water reserves for short-term gain.

OIL

Crude petroleum is a thick, dark green oil that occurs in permeable underground rock. It is derived from the remains of living organisms that died millions of years ago. Under heat and pressure the organic material changed into oil which became trapped in underground reservoirs. The modern oil industry began in 1859 when oil was discovered in Pennsylvania. Petroleum cannot be used in its crude form and has to be refined by fractional distillation, in which the components of the oil are separated according to their boiling points. Blending of the final products can produce fuels such as gasoline, kerosene and aviation fuel, as well as a range of chemicals for other uses.

In the 1960s, oil replaced **coal** as the world's biggest source of industrial energy. Consequently the price and control over supply gained major political importance. In 1961 the **Organization of Petroleum Exporting Countries** (OPEC) was set up to protect the interests of major oil exporters, mainly Middle Eastern nations. The rise of OPEC ended the era of cheap energy, ruined the price-setting power of the so-called 'Seven Sisters' oil

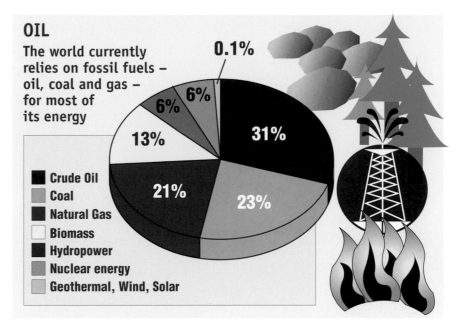

OIL
The world currently relies on fossil fuels – oil, coal and gas – for most of its energy

- **Crude Oil**
- **Coal**
- **Natural Gas**
- **Biomass**
- **Hydropower**
- **Nuclear energy**
- **Geothermal, Wind, Solar**

31%
23%
21%
13%
6%
6%
0.1%

The Future of Energy Use by R Hill, P O'Rourke and C Snape, Earthscan 1995.

companies (Exxon, Standard Oil, Texaco, Mobil, Gulf, Royal Dutch Shell and British Petroleum) and eventually precipitated the so-called 'energy crisis' of the 1970s. OPEC tripled oil prices from 1973-74 and again from 1978-80, as they tried to make-up for 14 years of frozen prices.

As a result the industrialized nations, which were heavily dependent on oil, entered a lengthy economic recession. Oil output fell by 10% during the following decade as non-oil producing countries tried to cut their energy demands or find alternate sources of energy.

Since then, various factors have combined to stabilize the situation, notably the discovery of new oil reserves in the North Sea and elsewhere. Global production of crude oil was 275 million tonnes in 1938. By 1960 it had risen to 1.05 billion tonnes, rocketing to 2.28 billion tonnes by 1970, before peaking at 3.1 billion tonnes in 1979.

Following OPEC's oil price hike, world-wide consumption declined, but consumption began to rise again in 1986. By 1988, global production of crude oil was again over the 3 billion tonne mark with the Soviet Union (624 million tonnes), the US (409 million tonnes) and Saudi

Arabia (255 million tonnes) being the largest individual producers. By 1995, production had risen to 3.03 billion tonnes and was set to surpass the 1979 peak. Most new production was in **developing countries** outside the Middle East that had encouraged exploration by multinational oil companies.

Oil is the world's major fuel, supplying about 30% of global energy; more than a billion people depend on it for transport, heating and other vital tasks.

However, burning fossil fuels like oil and **natural gas** is also a major source of atmospheric pollution. Oil is the main energy source of industrial society and its use is coming under increased scrutiny and criticism.

Public scepticism about the oil industry was fuelled by tanker **disasters** such as the **Exxon Valdez** and Sea Empress. Recently, Royal Dutch Shell also outraged people around the world by its attempts to dump the Brent Spar oil exploration platform at sea and by its collaboration with the Nigerian military regime in Ogoniland. The company did little to prevent Nigerian authorities from executing Ogoni activist Ken Saro-Wiwa and his colleagues.

World reserves of oil are suffi-

Strolling along the corniche
The oilfields of Dubai (United Arab Emirates) lie in the coastal area with its sand-dunes and off-shore coral islands. OIL

cient to meet prevailing demand for a further 40 years. Almost 60% of known reserves are in the Middle East. The world's recoverable **resources** of crude oil in 1990 were estimated at around 94 billion tonnes. Saudi Arabia (23 billion tonnes) and Kuwait (10 billion tonnes) have the largest national reserves.

OIL PALM

A tree native to the tropical lowland forest areas of West Africa. Now cultivated on **plantations** in South America, Indonesia, Malaysia and throughout Southeast Asia as the source of palm oil. Several varieties exist, each producing a distinctive fruit. The trees are grow tall (up to 15 metres) and produce large, fleshy fruits which contain a white kernel with a hard black shell. Oil palm trees reach full maturity between 8-10 years after which harvesting is a continuous operation.

Palm oil is used in the manufacture of margarine and cooking fats, glycerine, oil paints and polishes. It is also used in soups and stews and is a major source of vitamin A. The kernel yields another type of oil which is used in soap manufacture. One hectare of palms normally produces about 800 kilograms of palm oil and 100 kilograms of kernel oil.

The trees have a number of other uses too. The leaves and fibres are used to make brooms and mats, and the bark is used to make baskets. The shells and fibre of the fruits are

Greasing palms
Wielding his long pruning pole, a worker trims an oil palm on a plantation in Ivory Coast. The palm nuts yield oils used in margarine, polish and soap, while fronds provide fibre for matting. OIL PALM

used as a fuel. A highly-nutritious 'palm wine' can also be made. The residue left after oil-extraction can be used as livestock fodder. In many plantations **cattle** are raised under the tall palm trees as they maximize the productivity of the **land** and keep weeds and other shrubs at bay. Around 5 million tonnes of palm oil are produced annually with Malaysia producing almost half the total. Nigeria and Indonesia are the world's other major producers.

OLIGARCHY

Government by a select few, especially despotic power wielded by a small and privileged group for corrupt or selfish purposes. Most oligarchies have emerged when a ruling grouping or caste is set above society by reasons of heredity, religion, kinship, economic status or language.

ONCHOCERCIASIS

Also known as River Blindness, onchocerciasis affects much of West and Central Africa and parts of Latin America and the Middle East. It is a disease of the skin and underlying connective tissue caused by a parasitic worm. Fibrous nodular tumours grow around the adult worm in the skin; these may take several months to appear after infection. The skin becomes inflamed and itches and if secondary bacterial infections occur, the nodules degenerate into abscesses. The migration of larvae produced by the worms into the eye can cause total or partial blindness – hence the name River Blindness. The disease is transmitted through the bite of Black Flies which breed in rivers. Where onchocerciasis is endemic, vast tracts of fertile **land** along river banks becomes useless.

The **World Health Organization** (WHO) says 18 million people in 34 countries, mostly in tropical Africa, suffer from the disease. A new drug (ivermectin) provides effective treatment and has been available since 1987. It is hoped that the disease will be eliminated as a public health problem by the year 2000.

ORAL REHYDRATION SALTS (ORS)

Dehydration as a result of persistent diarrhoea has killed well over 150 million children since 1950. Around 750 million children suffer from diarrhoeal diseases annually and at least 10,000 infants under the age of

Which hand?
In this case, you are safe both ways: this farmer in the Philippines is strictly organic!
ORGANIC FARMING

Oral rehydration

Chart showing percentage of all cases of diarrhoea in children under five years old treated with oral rehydration salts or recommended home fluids.

ORS % use rate 1990-1996
(selected countries)

Turkmenistan	98
Somalia	97
Ethiopia	95
Liberia	94
Panama	94
Mozambique	83
El Salvador	69
Ecuador	64
Egypt	43
Eritrea	38
Mali	31
Iran	37
Sri Lanka	34
Nepal	27
Niger	20
Senegal	18

The State of the World's Children 1997, UNICEF.

5 die every day as a result of dehydration and **malnutrition** caused by diarrhoea.

Oral rehydration salts could prevent 70% of these deaths. ORS are an inexpensive, carefully balanced mixture of **sugar** and salt which is mixed with **water** and given orally to sick children. Using contaminated water to mix the salts can introduce other diseases so parents and health workers are advised to boil water first.

From 1983-93 the use of ORS more than tripled and the lives of a million children were saved each year. By 1993, oral rehydration therapy was being used for treatment in almost half the developing world.

Researchers have also discovered that feeding infants water in which rice has been boiled has a similar effect to rehydration salts.

Each ORS packet costs less than 10 cents (US) and normally 2 packets mixed with boiled water are sufficient to cure dehydration caused by diarrhoeal diseases. Nevertheless, in 1990 less than a third of all children suffering from diarrhoea were receiving ORS therapy. In Africa only a quarter of all children have access to ORS treatment.

ORGANIC FARMING

Organic farming means growing crops without using human-made chemical **fertilizers**, herbicides and **pesticides**, and using instead animal and composted manure and natural additives. Natural fertilizers put organic matter back into the ground, improving fertility and helping prevent erosion.

Since the 1970s, organic farming has been a high-growth industry and output has climbed steadily. In the **European Union**, the area of **land** given over to organic cultivation quadrupled between 1987 and 1993, while the number of organic farmers doubled. In the US, sales of organic farm products more than doubled from 1990 and 1994. The 'organic' label is now routinely applied to a variety of items, including personal care products and clothing made from natural fibres like **cotton**.

Organic farming is much kinder to the environment than modern, industrial farming. In Europe, governments are subsidizing farmers who convert from high-tech farming. Even though organic produce is 20-100% more expensive than conventionally-grown food, consumer demand is increasing.

In India, farmers see organic

production as a way to reduce costs by avoiding expensive **agrochemicals**. Latin American farmers believe organically-grown food will help them enter the lucrative US market-place. Peasant organizations in Mexico are exporting organically-grown **coffee**, sesame seeds, beans, **bananas**, vanilla and vegetables direct to major customers in the US. In Japan consumers can purchase goods directly from organic farmers either individually or in **co-operatives**.

Although organic produce currently accounts for less than 2% of the food sold in most industrial countries, the potential is great. In Japan, 3.5 million customers buy organic produce regularly and in the US, 24% of shoppers buy organic produce at least once weekly. Expansion of organic farming is limited only by the availability of organic nutrients at the farm level. For example, most urban organic waste is not currently returned to the land.

ORGANIZATION FOR ECONOMIC CO-OPERATION AND DEVELOPMENT (OECD)

An intergovernmental organization of 25 industrialized countries which was established in 1961 and is based in Paris. The OECD attempts to co-ordinate the economic policies of member states.

It replaced the Organization for European Economic Co-operation, which was established in 1948 to promote economic recovery in Europe under the **Marshall Plan**. When Canada and the United States joined in 1961 the scope of the organization was extended to include development policies and overseas **aid**.

The OECD aims to achieve the highest levels of sustainable **economic growth** and **employment** and a rising standard of living in member countries; to contribute to sound economic expansion in all

A yen for economic growth
The bustling stock exchange in Tokyo. Japan is a member of the OECD or 'Rich countries' club' which aims to achieve high economic growth for its member states. OECD

member as well as non-member nations; and to further the expansion of world trade in accordance with international obligations. **The Development Assistance Committee** (DAC) serves solely to improve the flow of resources to the **Third World**.

Member countries are: Australia, Austria, Belgium, Canada, Denmark, Finland, France, Germany, Greece, Iceland, Ireland, Italy, Japan, Luxembourg, Mexico, Netherlands, New Zealand, Norway, Portugal, Spain, Sweden, Switzerland, Turkey, the United Kingdom and the United States. The **European Union** is also regarded as a 'special' member.

ORGANIZATION FOR SECURITY AND CO-OPERATION IN EUROPE (OSCE)

Formerly the **Conference on Security and Co-operation in Europe**. The OSCE aims to create a forum for discussion of mutual defence among member states and to review implementation of the Helsinki Agreement. Fifty-two European states are members and the former Yugoslav state of Macedonia is an observer.

ORGANIZATION OF AFRICAN UNITY (OAU)

Founded in 1963 in Addis Ababa, the OAU's aims are to promote unity and co-operation among African countries; oppose **colonialism**; mediate territorial disputes between member states; and discourage attempts to change frontiers that cut across tribal areas. The OAU also attempts to co-ordinate efforts to raise living standards throughout Africa via improvements in the economic, cultural and political spheres.

It helped co-ordinate member policies towards **apartheid** in South Africa and has taken a leading role in promoting environmental-improvement policies throughout the continent. The OAU's 53 members include all states in Africa plus Western Sahara, over which the OAU remains split.

Throughout its history the organization has been beset with disputes. In 1982, divisions amongst member states prevented the summit meeting from being held.

A summit meeting which governs OAU activities is held annually. And a permanent Standing Committee and permanent Secretariat is maintained in Ethiopia. The OAU operates through a number of specialized commissions dealing with economic, social, technical, scientific, cultural and defence co-operation. The OAU's Joint African and Mauritanian Organization (OCAM) was founded in 1962 and works for African solidarity in Francophone Africa.

ORGANIZATION OF AMERICAN STATES (OAS)

Originally established in 1890 to encourage friendly relations between countries in the Americas, the Organization of American States has been known by several names, including the International Union of American Republics (1890-1910) and the Pan-American Union. (1910-1948).

The OAS was formed in 1948 'to foster mutual understanding and co-operation between all American republics'. In fact, the Organization has largely been a tool of the United States, allowing Washington to pursue its economic and political interests in Latin America under the guise of regional decision-making. It is based on the principle of the Monroe Doctrine of 1823 which has formed the backbone of American foreign policy in the region for most of the past 200 years.

This Doctrine carved out spheres of influence, warning European powers not to intervene in the Americas and in return the US would refrain from intervention in Europe. In 1962, Cuba was expelled from the OAS because of its decision to base missiles from the Soviet Union on the island.

OAS members include the United States, Canada and 34 South and Central American countries and Caribbean states. Some people feel that the Organization should be controlled by its Latin American member states.

ORGANIZATION OF PETROLEUM EXPORTING COUNTRIES (OPEC)

Established in 1960 in Baghdad to co-ordinate the price and supply of **oil** from the world's major oil-producing states. It was formed to represent the interests of the 11 chief oil-exporting nations (Abu Dhabi, Algeria, Indonesia, Iran, Iraq, Kuwait, Libya, Nigeria, Qatar, Saudi Arabia and Venezuela) in dealings with the major Western-based transnational oil companies.

OPEC also used its clout to strengthen and improve the position of **Third World** countries by forcing the developed world to provide them with technology and to open up Northern markets to Third World exports.

OPEC has been based in Vienna since 1965 and is the only example of a cartel dealing with a primary resource that has met with comparative success. In 1973, it decided to double the price of crude oil and has continued to manipulate the supply of oil and control its price ever since. The OPEC oil price hike in the 1970s triggered a world-wide recession while generating huge revenues for OPEC member states. Some of these sums were donated or recycled to poorer **developing countries**. However, the 'oil crisis' led to the introduction of extensive energy-saving programmes throughout the industrial world and intensified the search for alternative sources of energy. It also sparked a boom in oil exploration outside OPEC countries.

In the 1980s, OPEC's dominant position was undermined by reductions in demand for oil in the industrialized countries and by

Oiled up
Kuwait is one of the 12 oil-exporting (OPEC) countries. During the 1991 Gulf War some of its wells went up in flames, causing widespread pollution. OPEC

East is east

'Orientalism' portrays the East as exotic and idle, rather than as a hive of industry, and this false perception was used to justify colonialism. ORIENTALISM

rising oil production in non-OPEC nations, notably from North Sea oil controlled by Britain and Norway. These factors contributed to a sharp fall in the world oil price and forced OPEC members to cut production. OPEC now has 12 members: Algeria, Gabon, Indonesia, Iran, Iraq, Kuwait, Libya, Nigeria, Qatar, Saudia Arabia, United Arab Emirates and Venezuela.

ORIENTALISM

A term used by the US-based Palestinian academic and critic Edward Said to describe the vision of Arabic and Asian peoples in the literature of the colonial powers. Orientalism paints the East as exotic and idle, a world of ethereal fragrances and spices rather than of action and industry. Said claimed that this false perception coloured Western views of the East and became an intellectual justification for **colonialism** and exploitation. Literature, he said, spread this stereotype throughout Western culture and politics.

OZONE

A pale blue, condensed, gaseous form of oxygen which is both unstable and toxic. It is one of the main components of ground-level smog which damages trees and vegetation and causes respiratory problems in humans. In the stratosphere it provides a barrier against ultraviolet (UV) light and stops other harmful, high-energy solar radiation from penetrating to the earth's surface. Exposure to UV light is closely linked with the incidence of melanoma, the most common form of skin **cancer**.

During the 1980s global attention was drawn to the fact that industrial chemicals, notably **chlorofluorocarbons** (CFCs), were gradually destroying the protective ozone shield. As a result, experts predict that both skin cancer and eye cataracts will increase significantly over the next 40 years. Aquatic organisms, especially marine phytoplankton and zooplankton and the larval stages of certain **fish** are also extremely sensitive to even small increases in UV radiation.

Ground-level Ozone: Ozone is a major constituent of photochemical smog at ground level, which is synthesized from car exhausts in the presence of sunlight. Ultraviolet light is scattered by air molecules and dust particles causing it to take zig-zag paths. Short wavelengths are scattered more than longer wavelengths.

In summer or at low latitudes when the air is dry and dusty a combination of scattering and extra ozone could explain why UV light is lower in the **North**. In the **South** there is less ground-level ozone since the air is generally cleaner. This may result in an increase of UV light reaching the ground south of the equator. In the northern hemisphere the lower-atmosphere concentration of ozone has been increasing by about 1% annually.

Stratospheric Ozone: The ozone layer in the upper atmosphere (the stratosphere) is from 20 to 50 kilometres above the earth. Ozone forms as the result of the dissociation by solar UV radiation of molecular oxygen into single atoms, some of which then combine with intact molecules to form ozone. Ozone absorbs UV radiation and thus protects the earth's surface from its potential dangers.

Over the past 10-15 years ozone in the upper atmosphere has declined by several per cent. The depletion is most marked south of the equator, especially over the polar area. In the cold still air of the Antarctic, clouds form containing nitric acid and water ice.

These stratospheric clouds drain nitrogen out of the air, leaving behind chlorine in the active form of its oxide. This directly destroys ozone in the spring when the sunlight returns, causing destructive photochemical reactions.

It is believed the same process is occurring outside the polar regions, with drops of sulphuric acid (from industrial pollution) taking the place of the ice crystals. In the northern Arctic, the layer of ozone is also thinning but less severely.

This is partly because the stratosphere above the North Pole is warmer than over the South Pole and partly because air above the Arctic mingles with other air flows and is not so isolated from the rest of the atmosphere during the winter months. Many industrial pollutants with the potential to destroy ozone, including chlorine and nitrogen compounds, never reach the stratospheric ozone layer.

They are trapped below this level and fall to earth as **acid rain**. However, the exhaust from supersonic aircraft and rockets, which do penetrate the ozone layer, are particular destructive.

A single flight of the US Space Shuttle emits 187 tonnes of chlorine compounds and 7 tonnes of nitrogen compounds before it reaches a height of 50 kilometres. It also produces 840 tonnes of other gases that remove ozone molecules from the atmosphere on a one-to-one basis. As few as 300 flights could destroy the ozone layer entirely.

Several attempts have been made by the global community to protect the stratospheric ozone shield, most notably the **Montreal Protocol**. The major stumbling block has been who should pay for implementation. The US, along with other **developed countries**, finally agreed in 1990 to contribute to a $230 million fund to pay for ozone-friendly technology for **developing countries** and Eastern Europe – mainly to allow these countries to replace their production of ozone-destroying chlorofluorocarbons with safe alternatives.

Throughout the 1990s ozone depletion worsened considerably. In 1995, the ozone hole over **Antarctica** was the largest and longest-lasting on record, having exceeded 20 million square kilometres for 7 years in a row.

ORTEGA, DANIEL (1945-   )
Nicaraguan **guerrilla** leader and politician. Ortega began life as the son of a peasant farmer. On graduating from university he became a member of the **Sandinista National Liberation Front** (FSLN) and went underground. By 1967 he was in charge of the FSLN's urban campaign against the ruling Somoza family. Later that year he was arrested and imprisoned. Seven years later he was released as part of a prisoner exchange for some high-level hostages that the FSLN had kidnapped. Ortega and his fellow prisoners were exiled to Cuba where he underwent several months of intensive guerrilla training.

After returning to Nicaragua, Ortega campaigned for support from a variety of businesses and political groups against the Somoza regime. A full-fledged civil war followed from which the Sandinistas emerged victorious in 1979. Ortega was appointed co-ordinator of the Sandinista military junta in 1981 and in 1984 was elected President of Nicaragua. US efforts to destabilize the Sandinistas, whom they viewed as a socialist menace, paid off in 1990 when Ortega was defeated in his bid for re-election by one of Nicaragua's wealthy élite, Violeta Barrios de Chamorro.

Pollution Trading

Billowing clouds of smoke spew out of factory chimneys at a steel works in India, dispersing their sulphur-laden fumes on local people, food and water.

P LO – Qaddafi

Bold indicates a cross-reference

PALESTINE LIBERATION ORGANIZATION (PLO)

The PLO held its first congress in East Jerusalem in 1964 and adopted the Palestine National Charter which called for a democratic and secular state in Palestine as it had been constituted under the former British mandate.

After Egypt's defeat in the 1967 Arab-Israeli war the PLO's importance increased and it changed its charter to allow for armed struggle. In 1968 **Yasser Arafat** became leader. Following the 1973 Arab-Israeli war the PLO agreed to a Palestinian state in the Israeli Occupied Territories as an interim stage toward full liberation. The **Arab League** and the **United Nations** General Assembly both recognized the PLO as the representative of the Palestinian people and reaffirmed Palestinian rights to **self-determination**.

In 1975 a UN Security Council resolution agreed with this view but the resolution was vetoed by the US. By the late 1970s, the PLO had an army of 10,000 troops and commanded 23,000 armed **guerrillas**, with an annual budget of $500 million mostly supplied by oil-rich Arab states.

The PLO was forced to leave its base in Beirut when Israel invaded Lebanon in 1982. Its new headquarters in Tunis was bombed by the Israelis in 1985. In 1988, 70 countries granted the PLO full diplomatic status. The same year Arafat was named President of the State of Palestine and renounced the use of violence. He also accepted the idea of Palestinian self-determination in co-existence with Israel. His decision to side with Iraq during the invasion of Kuwait lost the PLO many friends and brought the Organization close to bankruptcy when money from the Arab oil states dried up.

Israel's Labour Government lifted a ban on contact with the PLO in 1993 and peace talks took place in Norway. The accord called for mutual recognition, and for limited Palestinian autonomy in the Gaza Strip and Jericho. Arafat returned from Tunis in 1994 to administer the two territories.

PANAMA CANAL

A canal across the Isthmus of Panama which connects the Atlantic and Pacific Oceans. Over 82 kilometres long, it is one of the two most strategic artificial waterways in the world. Construction began at the end of the 19th century by the French Panama Canal Company but excavations were halted in 1889 due to a combination of the firm's bankruptcy and diseases like **malaria** and **yellow fever** which killed off hundreds of construction workers.

In 1903, the United States was granted construction rights by the newly-independent Panamanian Government and the Canal was officially opened in 1914, allowing ships to sail from the Atlantic to the Pacific without having to travel around South America, cutting 8,000 nautical miles from the voyage. Under the terms of the 1903 treaty the US acquired sovereignty in perpetuity over the Canal Zone, a region extending 5 kilometres on either side of the Canal. In return Panama received $10 million and an annuity. The Panama Canal Treaty of 1977 agreed that the Canal should revert to Panamanian sovereignty by the year 2000. Panama assumed jurisdiction over the Canal Zone in 1979. Tolls from

Canal cruise

Anti-submarine cruisers sweep majestically through the Panama Canal, 1915. The short-cut trimmed 8,000 nautical miles from the (former) round-the-Horn voyage. PANAMA CANAL

the Canal bring in $350 million annually, 8% of the country's **Gross National Product** (GNP).

Deforestation along the length of the Canal now threatens its existence. As **soil erosion** speeds up, sediment accumulates in the Canal and dredging costs increase. There are plans to build a similar inter-ocean canal through Nicaragua.

Petroleum products, grains and **coal** are among the main **commodities** shipped via the canal. Although ships can pass in opposite directions, the Panama Canal is already too small, and can only accommodate relatively small ships of up to 30,000 tonnes. A 1984 study estimated that the cost of enlarging the Canal to allow passage for larger ships would be in the region of $40 billion, while the cost of building a new canal through Nicaragua is likely to cost only a quarter of this.

PARAQUAT

A yellow, water-soluble compound widely used as a broad-spectrum weedkiller. It adheres strongly to **soil** particles and so is not free to poison other plants. Consequently, new crops can be planted soon after spraying. Furthermore, it has an advantage over other weedkillers of being quickly degraded by soil organisms. Farmers in many countries use paraquat instead of ploughing to prepare the soil for sowing, many referring to it as 'the chemical machete'.

However, paraquat differs from most other herbicides in that it is highly toxic to mammals and humans. Less than a teaspoon can be fatal if swallowed and the chemical is also absorbed through the skin. It generally concentrates in the lungs and also causes kidney damage, usually with fatal results. Treatment for paraquat poisoning involves the use of activated charcoal or some other adsorbing material but it is only effective if it is carried out

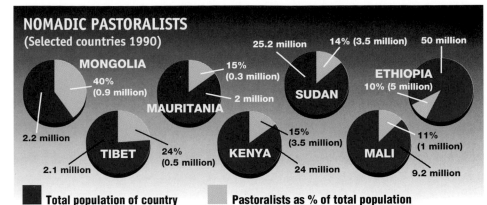

NOMADIC PASTORALISTS
(Selected countries 1990)

MONGOLIA — 40% (0.9 million) — 2.2 million

TIBET — 24% (0.5 million) — 2.1 million

MAURITANIA — 15% (0.3 million) — 2 million

KENYA — 15% (3.5 million) — 24 million

SUDAN — 25.2 million — 14% (3.5 million)

ETHIOPIA — 50 million — 10% (5 million)

MALI — 11% (1 million) — 9.2 million

■ **Total population of country**   ■ **Pastoralists as % of total population**

Nomads at the Crossroads, UNESCO.

immediately after ingestion of the toxin. There is no other treatment available. Where it is used intensively paraquat can drain into rivers poisoning **fish** and other wildlife.

The British company ICI is the major producer and exporter of paraquat, but there are also producers in the US, Japan, Brazil, India and Malaysia. The chemical is one of ICI's biggest-selling products and is used widely on Third World **plantations**.

PARIS CLUB

Also known as the Group of 10. An international forum of foreign **aid** donor and recipient governments which began in the 1950s. The Paris Club provides a place where payment terms on loans from official bilateral creditors can be renegotiated if recipient governments have trouble meeting their obligations. It has no fixed membership nor any firm institutional structure. During the 1980s, it was actively engaged in finding solutions to major **debt** crises being faced by many cash-strapped **developing countries**.

PASTORALISM

A way of life intimately linked to animal husbandry, usually involving periodic or seasonal movements with livestock in search of pasture. Pastoralists roam the world's rangelands, extensive tracts of arid and semi-arid lands that are essentially

No place to roam
Pastoralist Masai, pictured here in Kenya, used to roam freely across East Africa with their cattle herds. Now their ranges are being reduced by encroaching farms and game parks. PASTORALISM

unsuited to rain fed crops, forestry or **urbanization**. Without **irrigation** these lands are best used for livestock grazing or left as wilderness.

More than 200 million people use rangelands and 30-40 million of them are wholly dependent on livestock. The majority of the world's pastoralists live in Africa (55%), Asia (29%), the Americas (15%) and in Australia (1%). In northern Africa, pastoral populations make up 10-25% of the population, and in Sudan, Somalia and Chad the figure is higher. Their economic contribution is substantial. Live animals and meat make up 80% of Somalia's total agricultural exports.

Few pastoralists have control of the **land** or **resources** along their traditional nomadic routes. In the **Sahel**, herders have no legal guarantees that their seasonal rangelands will remain open. In East Africa, the situation is similar – although the Masai in Kenya and Tanzania have managed to retain some of their land by dividing it into group ranches registered under national land laws. In Tanzania, the Barabaig herders have lost more than 400 square kilometres of their dry-season range to a mechanized **wheat** farm.

In the 1960s, the **World Bank** sought to transform subsistence pastoralism into commercial livestock rearing. From 1960 to 1980, $625 million was poured into Sub-Saharan Africa for livestock development projects. But by the end of the 1980s the results were so dismal that funds were stopped.

On the Central Asian plains, pastoralists live in the autonomous area created for them by China and the former Soviet Union. But only in Mongolia, where herders constitute the majority of the population, do they have effective control of grazing lands.

PEACE CORPS

A US Government-backed agency of volunteers founded in 1961 by President John Kennedy, who appointed his brother-in law as director. The purpose of the corps was to provide skilled professionals (teachers, agriculturalists, health specialists and technicians) to work in **Third World** countries and pass on skills needed to stimulate economic development.

The Kennedy administration saw the Peace Corps as a kind of Trojan Horse for American cultural and economic values and a way of countering the growing influence of **socialism** in the **developing countries**.

Peace Corps workers are mainly young volunteers prepared to spend at least 2 years abroad. The Corps grew from 900 volunteers scattered across 16 nations in 1961 to a peak of 15,556 spread around 52 countries in 1966. By 1989, budget shortfalls had reduced the number of volunteers to 5,100 working in 90 countries, including some in Eastern Europe. Similar state-supported organizations exist in France, Germany, Canada, Britain and elsewhere.

PEACEKEEPING

Peacekeeping operations have become a major focus of the UN in recent years. The organization spent less than $4 billion on peacekeeping during its first 40 years. But in 1993 alone, the peacekeeping bill amounted to $2.5 billion. UN troops have been active in numerous

UN PEACE-KEEPING OPERATIONS, 1997

UNFICYP Cyprus
UNIFIL Lebanon
MINURSO Western Sahara
UNMIH Haiti
UNOMIL Liberia
UNAVEM II Angola
UNMOT Tajikistan
UNPREDEP TFYR Macedonia
UNMIBH Bosnia-Herzegovina
UNMOP Croatia
UNTAES Croatia
UNOMIG Georgia
UNTSO Middle East
UNDOF Syria
UNIKOM Iraq/Kuwait
UNMOGIP India/Pakistan

THE PEACEKEEPERS

By early 1993 the UN was deploying four times the number of troops, 70 times more police and over 100 times the number of civilian personnel as in 1987 at nearly 10 times the annual cost

CONTRIBUTION OF FORCES TO UN PEACEKEEPING BY COUNTRY

Total number of troops as of 30 June 1994 = 67,352		
1. PAKISTAN	7,920	11.76%
2. FRANCE	6,050	8.98%
3. INDIA	5,340	7.93%
4. BRITAIN	4,072	6.05%
5. JORDAN	3,338	4.96%
6. BANGLADESH	2,935	4.36%
7. MALAYSIA	2,696	4.00%
8. CANADA	2,272	3.37%
25. UNITED STATES	868	1.29%
39. AUSTRALIA	67	0.10%

COST OF UN PEACE-KEEPING

$1,228m

$600m

1991   1997

● Payment by the UN helps poor countries like Pakistan and Bangladesh offset the cost of the large standing army they want to keep for local strategic reasons. France and Britain, meanwhile, contribute mainly to the force in Bosnia, which is in their sphere of interest.

United Nations

PERON, EVA (1919-1952)

Charismatic second wife of Argentinian President **Juan Peron**. After an undistinguished acting career she married Colonel Juan Peron in 1945. She participated in his election campaign that year and won the adulation of the Argentinian public, whom she called *los descamisados* – the shirtless ones. She was popularly known as Evita. Although never elected she acted as *de facto* minister of health and labour. She provided generous wage increases to **trade unions** who had supported her husband.

She started her own Eva Peron Foundation with resources from unions and businesses and from the state lottery. Funds were dispensed to build thousands of hospitals, schools, orphanages and homes for the elderly. She introduced compulsory religious education into all schools and was instrumental in passing the suffrage law. She was nominated for Vice-President in 1951 although she was dying of **cancer**. Following her death, her influence as a national symbol continued. In 1955 after her husband was deposed, her enemies stole her body and it was kept in secrecy in Italy for 16 years. In 1971, the Argentinian military Government relented and handed over her remains to Juan Peron who was then exiled in Spain. Peron eventually resumed the Presidency of Argentina but died in office in 1974. His third wife, Isabel, eager to gain the support of the masses, repatriated Evita's remains and installed them next to Juan's. Two years later, a new military junta opposed to Peronism removed the bodies. Evita's remains were then interred in her family's crypt.

PERON, JUAN (1895-1974)

Argentinian soldier and politician, founder of the Peronist movement. He entered military school at the age of 16 and made rapid progress through the ranks. He served in Italy in the late 1930s as a military attaché and saw Fascism first hand. In 1943, having returned to Argentina, he played a leading role in a military coup. By 1945 he was minister of war and vice-president. He was popular and respected in the military and began to amass huge popular support. Then one night in 1945 he was ousted from his posts and arrested. His soon-to-be wife, Eva, rallied vast numbers of workers in his support and he was released from custody. Later that night he addressed a crowd of 300,000 from the balcony of the presidential palace and promised to lead them to victory in the forthcoming election. A few days later he married his second wife, **Eva Peron**, who died in 1952.

In 1946 he was elected President and introduced a policy based on rapid industrialization to provide greater economic benefits to the working class. He also adopted a strong anti-US position, promoting what he termed a 'Third Position' between **communism** and **capitalism**. He dictated the political activities of the nation through his control of the army and was not averse to eliminating constitutional rights if necessary. He was re-elected with an increased majority in 1951 but was overthrown by a coup in 1955 stirred up by increased **inflation** and corruption. After fleeing to Paraguay, he settled in Spain and continued to work towards resuming power in Argentina. In 1973, Peronists won back the presidency and control of the legislature and he returned to his homeland in triumph. Later that year he was elected President in a specially-arranged poll. When he died in 1974 his widow, Isabel, was left to carry on the Peronist cause. But she was unpopular and was the victim of an armed forces coup in 1976.

hot spots around the globe including Cyprus, Rwanda, Somalia, former Yugoslavia and Haiti. Yet they have been criticized as much as they have been praised.

A major problem is their mandate. Since their role is peacekeeping, they are prevented from taking an active role in conflicts and may only act in defence. As development **aid** dwindles, there are likely to be more conflicts and more need of peacekeeping in the future. As a result, the nature of the UN's peacekeeping role needs to be reassessed and redefined. In Somalia, for example, $10 was spent on peacekeeping for every dollar of **food aid** delivered.

PEARSON COMMISSION

Lester Pearson (1897-1972) was a Canadian politician and diplomat. Following a posting as Ambassador to the United States (1945-46) he became a delegate to the **United Nations** and in 1951 Chair of the **North Atlantic Treaty Organization** (NATO).

He played a crucial role in helping to settle the Suez Crisis in 1956 and was awarded the Nobel Peace Prize in 1957, primarily for his role in helping to create the United Nations Emergency Force.

He was leader of Canada's Liberal Party from 1958 and Prime Minister from 1963 to 1968. He was appointed head of an independent commission set up in 1968 by the **World Bank** to improve the overseas **aid** system. The Pearson Commission set an aid target of 1% of **GNP** for **OECD** countries – a goal which few nations have met. In the 1980s the **Brandt**, Palme and **Brundtland Commissions** followed the path set by Pearson 20 years earlier.

PESTICIDES

Chemicals used to kill insects or other organisms harmful to cultivated plants or human health. Many

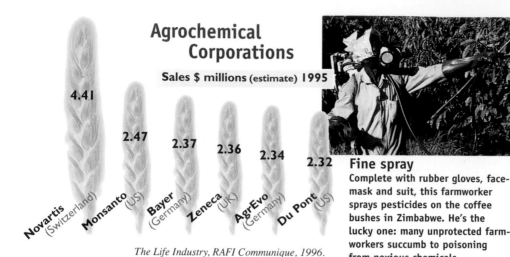

Agrochemical Corporations

Sales $ millions (estimate) 1995

4.41 — Novartis (Switzerland)
2.47 — Monsanto (US)
2.37 — Bayer (Germany)
2.36 — Zeneca (UK)
2.34 — AgrEvo (Germany)
2.32 — Du Pont (US)

The Life Industry, RAFI Communique, 1996.

Fine spray

Complete with rubber gloves, face-mask and suit, this farmworker sprays pesticides on the coffee bushes in Zimbabwe. He's the lucky one: many unprotected farm-workers succumb to poisoning from noxious chemicals.
PESTICIDE POISONING

pesticides are toxic to humans, livestock and wildlife as well as to the target pest. Some like parathion, **DDT** and **dieldrin** have caused widespread poisoning in humans and animals afterwards and their use in many industrialized countries has been prohibited or restricted. Globally, up to 40% of crops are lost to insects, pests, disease and weeds: more than 10,000 insect species are known pests. Of the 30,000 weed species, 1,800 are responsible for major economic losses.

For the past 40 years the control of plant pests and insects has been based on the extensive use of chemicals. These toxic pesticides have played a major role in the battle to maintain adequate food supplies: around 90% of pesticides are used for agricultural purposes.

Since the late 1940s pesticide use has increased 11-fold and led to enormous environmental and economic costs. World sales increased from $2.7 billion in 1970 to $28 billion in 1996. Eighty per cent of these deadly chemicals are used in **developed countries**. The UN **Food and Agriculture Organization** (FAO) says pesticide use in the **North** will need to grow by 4% annually to meet growing food demands. In **developing countries** pesticide use is likely to double during the next decade.

However, serious criticisms about the environmental and health consequences of pesticide use are now being raised. Less than 1% of the

chemicals applied to crops actually reach the pest. More than 99% seep into the ecosystem to contaminate **land**, **water** and air. Ecosystems have no natural mechanism for breaking down these human-made chemicals with the result that they usually persist in the environment.

Many of the pesticides used in the **Third World** such as DDT have already been banned in the North because they have been found to damage either human health or the environment. The bulk of pesticide production is controlled by companies in the North: 15 companies in 5 countries account for 90% of global production.

Despite 40 years of extensive pesticide use, world-wide crop losses from insects have almost doubled. The FAO reports that more than 1,600 insect species have developed **pesticide resistance**. Pesticides kill harmful insects but they also kill beneficial ones like bees. Losses from reduced pollination reach $4 billion annually in the US alone. Furthermore, rats have begun to develop resistance to the latest generation of pesticides, meaning that there may soon be no effective chemical to combat one of the world's most destructive pests.

PESTICIDE POISONING

Many **pesticides** are so persistent in the environment that millions of

people continue to ingest minute amounts of **toxic chemicals** like **DDT** and **dieldrin**. These chemicals are fat-soluble and are concentrated in the human body, often in mother's milk through which the toxin is passed on to new-born children. Direct consumption of foodstuffs treated with pesticides can also prove fatal. Over 500 people died in Iraq in 1971-72 from eating bread made with **wheat** which had been treated with a toxic fungicide.

Surprisingly little is known about the effect of pesticides on human health. And reliable data on poisonings is scarce. It is believed that nearly half of all poisonings and 90% of pesticide-related deaths occur in the **Third World**, even though these countries account for only 20% of global pesticide use. Misleading advertising and inadequate labelling, widespread **illiteracy**, lack of regulation and policing, and inadequate medical care all contribute to the toll.

The **World Health Organization** (WHO) estimates that 20,000 people in **developing countries** are killed annually as a result of pesticide poisoning and a further study reports that 25 million agricultural workers suffer some form of acute poisoning each year. The number of cases of **cancer** due to pesticide exposure will not be known for decades. The National Academy of Sciences in the US predicts up to a million cancer cases over the next 70 years due to pesticides.

Meanwhile, the **Food and Agriculture Organization** (FAO) Code for Safe Pesticide Use (adopted in 1985) continues to be widely ignored. The code details the responsibilities of manufacturers and governments in helping to prevent poisoning. It specifies warnings that manufacturers should print on their labels and what level and form of advertising is acceptable. In 1987 it was suggested the **FAO** code be strengthened by the inclusion of a **prior informed consent** (PIC) clause. PIC forces exporters to inform importing countries of the reasons why pesticides have been restricted or banned in the exporting nation and to provide detailed information of the hazardous properties of each pesticide. Most countries were in favour of the clause, but the 8 major pesticide manufacturing countries (the UK, the US, France, Canada, Germany, Belgium, Switzerland and Japan) opposed the move.

In 1989, the FAO finally agreed to toughen its code and introduced a 'Red Alert List' of more than 50 pesticides and chemicals that have been banned or restricted in 5 or more nations. However, critics argue that the new list excludes the most widely-used pesticides which cause the most poisonings.

PESTICIDE RESISTANCE

Many pests, especially those with a short life cycle, develop quick resistance to chemicals used to try and control them. Resistance has greatly accelerated since synthetic **pesticides** were introduced in the late

1940s. Insects, mites, ticks, fungi and rodents have all developed some degree of resistance to chemical and **biological control** agents. From 1970-1980, the number of arthropod pest species (mainly insects) showing resistance almost doubled and by 1990 the UN **Food and Agriculture Organization** (FAO) was reporting that 1,600 insect species had developed resistance to the most commonly-used insecticides. Many became resistant to a range of different pesticides. During the 1980s, rats and other rodent pests started to exhibit resistance to the so-called 'second generation' rodenticides, having developed resistance to 'first generation' compounds within 5 years of their introduction in the 1950s.

PHOSPHATES

Phosphorus-containing, naturally-occurring nutrients which are essential for healthy plant growth but which can cause serious environmental pollution in large quantities. Phosphate rock occurs as sedimentary deposits of phosphoric limestone,

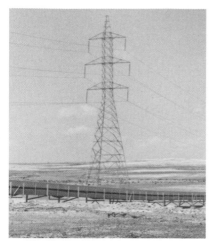

A long way to go
It might not look much but this is the world's longest conveyor belt (100 kilometres), carrying phosphates from the Boucraa mines to the coast in Western Sahara. **PHOSPHATES**

as guano which accumulates from bird droppings, and as an igneous mineral (*apatite*). Of the 3 principal **soil** nutrients (nitrogen, phosphorus and potassium), phosphorus is the least abundant.

At least 75% of phosphate rock is used as **fertilizer** and world consumption continues to rise. Around 130 million tonnes of phosphate are mined each year. The US (51 million tonnes), the Soviet Union (25 million tonnes) and Morocco/Western Sahara (19 million tonnes) are the main producers. Misuse of phosphate **fertilizers** can cause **eutrophication**. This occurs when phosphates and other nutrients accumulate in lakes, ponds or slow-moving rivers. The two main sources of phosphate pollution are caused by human activities. The first is run-off from agricultural **land**. Phosphates leak out of chemical fertilizers which are applied in amounts far greater than can be taken up by target crops. The second source is waste from human sanitation systems which enters waterways in the form of treated and untreated sewage. Sewage is a greater problem when it contains synthetic detergents which have a high phosphate content.

Phosphate fertilizer contributes to the large-scale transfer of phos-

How does your garden grow?

Corporations need to conduct field tests in order to check out how crops grow, and respond to chemicals. This involves potential risks to local populations and to the surrounding environment, as all these tests are experiments. Thousands of such tests have been taking place since 1987, mainly in the **US** and Britain, sometimes in great secrecy. They have also taken place in Argentina, Belize, Bolivia, Chile, Costa Rica, Cuba, Dominican Republic, Egypt, Guatemala, India, Morocco, Mexico, Peru, Puerto Rico, South Africa and Thailand, where there are fewer controls.

Types of field tests carried out in 14 OECD countries 1993-1994 (% of total)

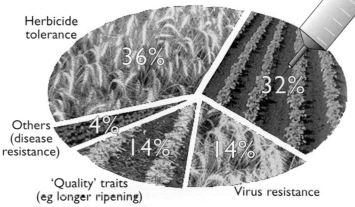

Herbicide tolerance **36%**

Insect resistance **32%**

Others (disease resistance) **4%**

'Quality' traits (eg longer ripening) **14%**

Virus resistance **14%**

From Green to Gene Revolution by R Steinbrecher, The Ecologist Vol. 26, No. 6.

PINOCHET, AUGUSTO (1915-   )

Chilean military leader. A career soldier appointed army commander by President **Allende** in 1973. Eighteen days later he planned and led the coup (backed by the CIA and the American company ITT) which deposed Allende. Appointed head of the military junta, Pinochet moved swiftly and ruthlessly to crush Chile's liberal and socialist opposition. More than 130,000 people were arrested in the following 3 years. Under Pinochet, Chile witnessed a reign of terror – thousands of people were kidnapped, sent to concentration camps, tortured and murdered.

In 1974, he assumed sole power, scrapping plans for a rotating presidency among junta members. Pinochet's push for a free-market economy at all cost led to a harsh reversal of Allende's socialist policies and a brutal elimination of left-wing views. Strict monetarist economic policies reduced **inflation** and caused exports of raw materials to boom between 1969-79. However, social services were cut dramatically and the gap between rich and poor widened.

A new constitution was adopted in 1981 which allowed Pinochet to serve another 8-years as President before a national referendum to approve the junta's rule. During his term, the economy performed well and Pinochet continued to exert strict control over opposition groups. He lost the 1989 plebiscite by a vote of 55% to 43%. Free elections were held the following year when a Christian Democrat, Patricio Aylwin, was elected. Pinochet then altered the constitution to diminish the power of the incoming President and retained his position as head of the armed forces.

phorus from land to ocean. In 1990, 30 million tonnes of phosphorus were washed into the world's oceans, the same amount as added to global cropland. Phosphorus flows only from land to sea, so the outflow is not recoverable and phosphate is already in short supply in many regions. Western Sahara in North Africa has the world's largest deposits.

PHOTOVOLTAIC CELL
(see Solar Cells)

PHYSICAL QUALITY OF LIFE INDEX (PQLI) (see also Alternative Economic Indicators)

A comparative measurement of a nation's general well-being, devised by the US Overseas Development Council. The index is based on three social indicators: **life expectancy** (at age 1), **infant mortality** and adult literacy rates. Each component is measured equally on a scale from 0 to 100. If life expectancy is 38 years, the country scores 0. If it is 77, it scores 100. The infant mortality scale ranges from 229 to 7 deaths per 1,000 live births. Literacy rates are taken as direct scores. Although there is some correlation between income and PQLI, there are significant variations. Sri Lanka, for example, has a low per capita income but a high PQLI.

PLANTATION

A large estate in a tropical or sub-tropical region that is cultivated predominantly by unskilled or semi-skilled labour under central direction. The term was used to describe the huge tracts of **land** used to grow export crops during the European colonization of the New World. A plantation is usually a self-sustained community, governed by the planter. Today many are run by managers appointed by the **transnational** companies that actually own the land. Since the 18th century hundreds of thousands of square kilometres of land throughout the tropics has been cleared for the cultivation of plantation crops like **tobacco**, **sugar**, **cotton**, **rubber**, **tea** and rice. Centuries ago plantations were dependent on huge armies of unskilled workers. But with the abolition of the slave trade, labour-intensive plantations began to disappear or become mechanised. Many were divided into smaller units to be run by tenant farmers. On others the land is worked by wage-labourers or share-croppers.

Chocolate source
Cocoa is a typical plantation crop, grown for export in countries such as Ivory Coast, Ghana and Brazil. PLANTATION

PLUTONIUM

A synthesized element not found in nature, plutonium was first produced in 1941. It is derived from uranium. By 1945 only a few kilograms had been made following research which had cost an estimated $2 billion. However this was enough for testing programmes and for the manufacture of at least two atomic bombs used during World War II.

Plutonium is made in nuclear reactors by bombarding uranium-

238 (U-238) with neutrons. The U-238 transforms to plutonium-239 by absorbing a neutron into its nucleus. Plutonium can then be extracted from the reactor fuel by a series of chemical reactions referred to as 'reprocessing'. It can be used as fuel either in conventional or thermal nuclear reactors or in fast-breeder reactors.

Countries that reprocess spent nuclear reactor fuel have large and ever-increasing stocks of plutonium and are facing problems of how to dispose of it. The United Kingdom has more than 30 tonnes stockpiled. No-one knows how much plutonium exists. However, nuclear reactors around the globe are thought to be producing over 70 tonnes annually, and may well be producing twice this amount by the year 2000.

The **International Atomic Energy Agency** (IAEA) has developed a system of registering plutonium. But the US alone is unable to account for 4,500 kilograms of enriched uranium produced since 1950. The risk of terrorists acquiring weapons-grade plutonium escalated after the break-up of the Soviet Union when it was suspected that lax security had made large quantities of the substance available for illegal trade.

POLIO

Polio is an infectious viral disease which affects the central nervous system and can lead to paralysis. It occurs in different forms, mostly attacking children. The virus is excreted in faeces, so the disease is found most often, though not exclusively, in areas with poor sanitation. However, epidemics can occur even in regions with good hygiene if people have not been immunized.

Symptoms begin 7-12 days after infection. In the milder form of the disease symptoms are muscle stiffness, general weakness and fever

Polio
Immunization for Polio is effective and it is hoped that the disease may be eradicated by the year 2000.

	Annual deaths (all ages) if no immunization	Prevented	Occurring	%
POLIO (cases of lifelong paralysis)	640,000	550,000	90,000	86

The Progress of Nations 1996, UNICEF.

– not unlike influenza. In severe cases, these symptoms may be followed by weakness and eventual paralysis, although the paralytic form of the disease is now uncommon. There is no treatment. Around a tenth of those infected with paralytic polio die. Vaccinated children develop lasting immunity to the disease.

Around 110,000 children a year, mostly in **developing countries**, are stricken with the disease. An estimated 10 million people have some degree of lameness as a result of having being infected during childhood.

The disease has been eliminated from 145 countries and the **World Health Organization** (WHO) hopes to eradicate polio by the year 2000. China's massive **vaccination** campaign reaches more than 100 million children and has been labelled the world's biggest public health campaign.

POLLUTER PAYS PRINCIPLE

A concept designed to ensure that polluters accept responsibility for their actions in order to protect the natural environment. In 1972, members of the **Organization for Economic Co-operation and Development** (OECD) adopted this principle which was later endorsed by the **European Community**. In 1989 the **United Nations Environment Programme** (UNEP) recommended that all governments adopt the

principle. Despite widespread lip service the concept has had almost no impact in practice.

POLLUTION TRADING

An idea first raised during discussions on global climatic changes in the late 1980s with the goal of allowing nations to meet stricter pollution-emission standards. The premise was that some factories in a country would be allowed to pollute above accepted emissions standards, so long as other factories in the same country fell below them, and total emissions were equal to or below levels that would have occurred if all factories had conformed to emission control levels. The notion first appeared following the US Clean Air Act amendments of 1990. These

Playing unsafe
Kids frolic in the River Pasig in Manila, Philippines – but the waters are heavily polluted by rubbish and waste from local factories. POLLUTER PAYS PRINCIPLE

set a cap on **sulphur dioxide** emissions and established a market for tradable emission permits. In 1992 several permit trades took place, at roughly half the costs that the buyer would have had to spend to install pollution controls.

Singapore also used the system, auctioning declining numbers of permits to allow the production or importing of **chloroflourocarbons**. Critics of the system point out that most governments give the permits to companies rather than sell them, effectively subsidizing industry for past emissions and making pollution-intensive **commodities** like electricity appear cheaper than they really are.

POLYCHLORINATED BIPHENYLS (PCBs)

A group of more than 200 chemicals first synthesized in 1881, and used on a commercial scale since the 1930s. Their high heat-resistance and low electrical conductivity make them valuable components in a variety of products. PCBs became widely-used in the production of fluorescent light bulbs, adhesives, hydraulic fluid, electrical transformers and capacitators. They are also used as 'plasticizers', improving the flame retardance of plastics and increasing resistance to chemical attack.

In the 1930s they were discovered to have toxic effects, but it was not until 1976 that the **European Community** banned the use of PCBs in unsealed equipment. As a result, the problem of what to do with PCBs in old, damaged equipment has yet to be solved. PCBs are extremely stable and can only be destroyed through incineration at temperatures above 1,200°C.

Incomplete combustion can lead to other, more toxic compounds like **dioxins**. PCBs can also be released through the incomplete incineration of waste plastics. Once PCBs enter the environment a process of bio-concen-

tration takes place. For example, in the North Sea concentrations of PCBs in seawater are .000002 parts per million (ppm) in seawater and 160 ppm in marine mammals. As an indication of how widespread the problem has become, high levels of PCBs have been found in the body fat of killer whales and polar bears in remote parts of the Arctic.

POPULATION

The global population doubled between 1950 and 1987 and is now well over 5 billion. The pace of population increase has been a major concern. It took over 100 years for the human population to double from 1.25 to 2.5 billion, but only 37 years for the next doubling. Medium level projections by the UN predict that the human population will hit 6 billion by 1999 and 8 billion by 2025, finally stabilizing at 10 billion towards the end of the next century.

Surprisingly, world population growth began to slow dramatically in the early 1990s. At the beginning of the decade, population was growing by 90 million people annually. By 1995, the annual growth was about 87 million. The average growth rate during those 5 years was 1.48% – well below what most analysts had forecast.

The cause was a decline in fertility. In 1950 women world-wide had an average 5 children. By 1995, the average was 2.9 children. If this trend continues, the population of many countries will stabilize in the next century. Europe's population is already stable and expected to decline. China's population should stabilize within 40 years, by which time India will have become the world's most populous nation with 1.6 billion inhabitants. Many countries, particularly resource-poor nations with high population growth rates, are faced with an increasing

PEOPLE PRESSURE

World population continues to rise by about 87 million people a year – the baby that breaches the six-billion barrier will be born early in 1999.

But these facts mask a hopeful trend – the average annual growth rate in world population has been steadily declining since the early 1960s, from 2.2 per cent down to its current 1.5 per cent. The empowerment and education of women has now been accepted as a key contribution to reducing population growth – but dividing the wealth and resources of the world more fairly would be even more crucial.

Average annual growth rate in world population, 1960-1996

US Census Bureau in Vital Signs 1997/1998, Worldwatch Institute, Earthscan.

dilemma. How to satisfy the **basic needs** of their people? Feeding the global population has been recognized as a major problem for decades. The world has over 8 billion hectares of **land** suitable for agricultural which works out to about 1.6 hectares per person. But the distribution of this land does not match up with where people live. In some parts of the world not enough food is produced, while in other regions there are surpluses.

Over the last 40 years the amount of cropland per person has actually fallen by a third. However, **fertilizer** use has jumped 5-fold and as a result global food supplies have slightly increased. In Europe the problem of human numbers was lessened partly by the plague which wiped out a quarter of the population in the Middle Ages and by mass emigration. From 1846 to 1930, 50 million Europeans left the continent for North and South America, Australia, New Zealand and parts of Africa.

The main question for the future is: what standard of living will be sustainable for a population of 8 to 10 billion? Historically, national living standards have only increased when population replacement levels have been reached.

Ecologist Arthur Westing says the current world population must be halved if an 'affluent' Western standard of living is to become commonplace. On the other hand, if a per capita **Gross National Product** (GNP) based on the global average was the goal, around 70% of the world's population could be supported. Countries with a per capita GNP near the global average include Greece, Malta and Gabon.

But even if there was world-wide agreement over which standard of living should be the global goal, serious problems of social justice and equity would need to be resolved: including the growing concentration of land ownership, a highly unequal distribution of wealth and income, and the

question of access to and benefit from natural **resources**.

POTATO

The potato was first cultivated around 200 AD in the Peruvian and Bolivian Andes. More than 150 varieties are now grown. The best varieties can yield up to 40 tonnes per hectare. In the vegetable's ancestral home in South America as many as 60 varieties can be found at market places.

The potato was introduced into Europe in the late 16th century. It quickly became an important part of the diet of many nations, especially in poor communities. By the end of the 17th century it was a major crop in Ireland and quickly spread into continental Europe, especially Germany. The Irish economy and diet rapidly became dependent on the new arrival. But in 1846 a potato blight invaded Europe, wiping out the Irish harvest, causing widespread **famine** which killed millions and forced millions more to emigrate in search of food.

Potatoes are now a valuable staple food throughout the world, especially in Europe, and new blight-resistant strains have been

developed. They are good energy foods and are highly nutritious, containing more protein than many cereals or other root and tuber crops. In addition they are a source of iron, vitamins B and C. Potatoes will grow at high altitudes where **maize** does not grow well, commonly producing twice as much protein and 25% more starch. In cool, dark conditions, potatoes can be stored for several months. Potato cultivation is expanding in many **developing countries**. But overall only 15% of global production is in Asia, Africa and Latin America. Worldwide, almost 300 million tonnes are produced each year. Poland and China are the largest growers.

POVERTY

A lack of money or material possessions such that a person is unable to meet the **basic needs** necessary for survival. The definition of poverty varies depending on the social context and what is held to be an 'acceptable' standard of living. In modern industrial societies the total output of goods and services is theoretically great enough to provide everyone with a reasonable standard of living. The fact that poverty still

Poverty stricken

Hundreds of millions of people who lack the basic resources needed to make a decent home are left without one – and their number is growing. The proportion of poor people in the world has fallen slightly, but with a rising world population their total number is increasing fast.

◆ During the 1980s average incomes were reported to have fallen by 10% in most of Latin America and 20% in Sub-Saharan Africa. In many urban areas wages have fallen by as much as 50%.
◆ A recent summary of studies on the incidence of poverty in individual developing countries reveals levels regularly in excess of 50% of the population.
◆ Inequality between rich and poor has grown as fast in the North as in the South: average real wages in the US have not increased at all for the past 10 years.
◆ One in three children in Britain lives below the poverty line.

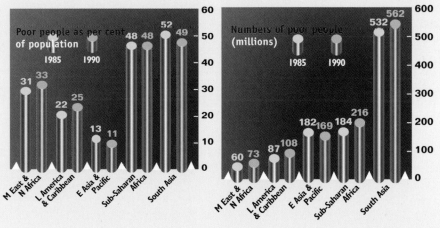

Poverty in the Developing World

The State of the World's Children 1994, UNICEF; Our Planet Our Health, WHO; The Incidence of Poverty in Developing Countries, ILO; The Joseph Rowntree Trust.

exists in the West is more a question of distribution, social justice and lack of political will than of available wealth. According to the UN the number of people living in poverty worldwide rose to more than 1.3 billion by the mid-1990s – approaching 1 in 5 of the world's **population**.

PRECAUTIONARY PRINCIPLE

A term coined at the Bergen conference in Norway in 1990, attended by the United States, Canada and 34 nations from Eastern and Western Europe. The meeting was held as a follow-up to the findings of the **World Commission on Environment and Development** (WCED). The basic agreement was that the global community must take action to stave off potential large-scale environmental **disasters** such as **global warming**, without waiting for scientific proof about their cause or extent.

Furthermore, wealthier nations must help poorer countries to protect their environment for the good of the global community. The precautionary principle has since been applied to protection of the North Sea and has also been adopted by the **United Nations Environment Programme**, the Barcelona Convention for the Mediterranean and the Nordic Council.

PRIMARY HEALTH CARE

In 1978 an international conference on Primary Health Care (PHC) in Alma-Ata called for 'Health For All by the year 2000'. PHC was defined as providing a basic level of care, attention and advice to all people throughout the world. It was built on the principles of social justice and equity, self-reliance and community development.

In 1981 members of the **World Health Organization** (WHO)

decided that progress should be measured against a set of targets. Two of these targets were a **life expectancy** of 60 years and an **infant mortality rate** below 50 per 1,000 live births. By 1995 the number of countries satisfying the first of these criteria had risen from 98 to 120. Similarly, countries meeting the infant mortality guideline had risen from 77 to 103. Most **developed countries** are approaching full PHC though there is still much ground to cover in the **Third World**. Inequities are highlighted by comparison of life expectancies which vary between 50 years in poorer countries to over 70 where health care systems are efficient and widely available.

Literacy and **poverty** rates correlate directly with health indicators. Improving literacy rates raises health awareness and general welfare. Yet the number of illiterate women in **developing countries** is growing and the literacy gap between men and women is also widening. Poverty, a leading factor in the creation of poor health, is also on the increase: an estimated 1.3 billion struggle to survive on less than the equivalent of a dollar a day.

PRIMARY PRODUCTS
(see also Commodities)

Any agricultural product or mineral, in natural or unprocessed form, which enters into international trade. Primary products are mainly produced by **developing countries** for sale to industrialized nations where most of the processing occurs. As a result, developed nations play a major role in setting the prices for primary products which they do not actually produce.

Many **Third World** countries have become dependent on a few primary products for the bulk of their export earnings.

A **United Nations Conference on Trade and Development**

Pineapple poll
Pineapples are valuable 'primary products' for countries like Malawi and the Philippines, but increasingly countries try to 'add value' by canning or processing them before export. PRIMARY PRODUCTS

(UNCTAD) survey of 84 developing countries found that 43 were dependent on primary **commodities** for at least 90% of their total export revenue. More than 80% of these countries depended on a single commodity for at least 75% of their export earnings. Agricultural products are especially sensitive to vagaries of climate which can directly influence production and export earnings. Paradoxically, increased production is not beneficial either, since over-supply forces world prices down. The price of **tea**, jute and **rubber** fell by 60% or more between 1960-81, while the price of **bananas**, palm oil and **sisal** declined in real terms by around 40%. For the past 20 years the real prices of common primary products all showed a significant drop on the world market.

PRIOR INFORMED CONSENT (PIC)

A principle used to regulate the movement of **toxic chemicals**, nuclear waste or other hazardous substances. Before any exporting country can despatch a shipment it must have the importing country's consent, usually in writing. Prior to this, the exporting country must have first provided the importing country with full and detailed information on the content and nature of the intended export, allowing the recipient nation to make a full assessment of the risks involved.

PRIVATIZATION

Private ownership of property or enterprises formerly owned by the state. The term is the opposite of 'socialization' and is identified with the brand of conservatism favoured in Britain under Prime Minister Margaret Thatcher in the 1980s.

Since then privatization has achieved almost a cult status with free-enterprise oriented economists and has become a central part of the structural adjustment policies enforced on cash-strapped **Third World** nations by the **World Bank** and the **IMF**. The rationale is that state-owned enterprises are inherently inefficient and that market discipline is needed to iron out those inefficiencies. In many instances this is true. In 1991 in China, almost a third of state-run enterprises operated at a loss. And in Tanzania during the 1980s, half the state-owned industries consistently made losses. But state-owned enterprises are not necessarily inefficient. They can be run more easily in the public interest by conscientious management and be used as tools of public policy when profitability is not the only criteria for success.

From 1980-91, nearly 7,000 state enterprises were privatized, mostly in the former East Germany and other former centrally-planned economies. Over 1,400 state-owned enterprises in developing nations were also sold off, almost 60% of them in Latin America. But privatization is not a panacea. There are often high social costs including **unemployment**, decreased public services and higher costs to consumers. The privatization process often resembles a cut-price sale of potentially highly-profitable essential industries to favoured groups or individuals.

PRODUCER CARTELS

A group of independent companies, individuals or countries which have banded together to exert a restrictive or monopolistic influence on the production or sale of a commodity or group of **commodities**. The most common examples of this influence are price fixing, output control and the division of markets. The main reasons companies use for establishing cartels is protection from 'ruinous' competition. Cartels distort the market system and usually result in higher consumer prices. They also maintain inefficient firms and prevent the introduction of cost-saving technologies or systems that could result in lower prices. Business cartels in most industrialized countries are illegal, breaching laws controlling monopoly and anti-trust legislation. Nevertheless informal cartels exist and continue to multiply. In the developing world, producer cartels have emerged around specific commodities like **bananas** and **coffee**. But their impact has been minimal.

PROSTITUTION

The provision of sex, usually to individuals other than a spouse or friend, in exchange for some form of payment. The definition is hard to pin down since prostitution varies according to the values adopted by different societies. Prostitutes may be of either sex and may hire their bodies for homosexual or heterosexual activity. However, it is mostly women who provide a service for male clients. In general prostitutes are reviled by society. They are punished under the law, while their clients rarely face the same degree of attention.

Prostitution came under strict control in Europe in the 16th century following a widespread epidemic of venereal disease, coupled with stricter sexual morality

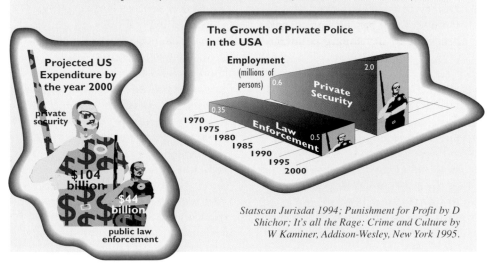

Privatizing police

◆ In Canada between 1971 and 1991 the number of police officers increased by 41% and the number of private security guards increased by 126%. By 1991 private security forces outnumbered police by about 2 to 1.

◆ In the US two major companies account for 50% of private contracts to run prisons.

Projected US Expenditure by the year 2000

private security

$104 billion

$44 billion

public law enforcement

The Growth of Private Police in the USA

Employment (millions of persons)

Private Security

0.6

2.0

0.35

1970
1975
1980
1985
1990
1995
2000

Law Enforcement

0.5

Statscan Jurisdat 1994; Punishment for Profit by D Shichor; It's all the Rage: Crime and Culture by W Kaminer, Addison-Wesley, New York 1995.

Poverty – Prostitution

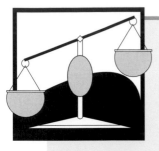

Prostitution & the Law

IRAN

Policy: The 1925 Penal Code stated that prostitution was not a crime in itself, but that it was a crime to advocate it, to aid or abet a woman to enter prostitution or to operate a brothel. The current regime believes that execution – by firing squad or stoning – is a fitting penalty.

Practice: Execution is common. Some Iranian feminists regard *mut'a*, a form of temporary marriage where the woman has few rights, as akin to prostitution. Under *mut'a*, it is possible to be 'married' for as little as half an hour.

KENYA

Policy: No legal definition of prostitution in the Penal Code. But it is illegal to live off the earnings of prostitution.

Practice: Prostitution is increasing in urban areas as many rural migrant women fail to find other employment. Police regularly harass prostitutes. Researchers on AIDS and prostitution report that any woman who is single and has multiple male sex partners is considered to be a prostitute, whether or not money changes hands.

NEW ZEALAND/AOTEAROA

Policy: Prostitution is not illegal, but soliciting, brothel-keeping, living off the earnings of a prostitute and procuring are. Conviction can result in a prison sentence of up to five years.

Practice: Sex workers must use elaborate precautions to disguise the real nature of their work. This provides a major impediment for HIV/AIDS education in the sex industry.

THAILAND

Policy: It is illegal under the Criminal Code to work as a prostitute or to live off the earnings of a prostitute.

Practice: Prostitutes operate as 'entertainers'. Sex tourism, including sex with children, is common, though the majority of clients are local.

UK

Policy: Prostitution itself is not illegal, but soliciting, pimping and kerb-crawling are, making it effectively against the law. Most prostitutes have spent periods of time in jail, charged with soliciting.

Practice: Conviction means that they are banned from certain jobs and from travelling to certain places (such as the US) for the rest of their lives.

INDIA

Policy: Illegal. There is a plethora of laws against the sex trade, including one in 1985 to ban *devidasis*, or temple prostitutes.

Practice: Organized networks for buying and selling women and girls exist despite the legislation. *Devidasis* continue to be sold to the temples. Any sexual intercourse outside socially acceptable unions is likely to be regarded as prostitution.

BRAZIL

Policy: Not illegal. It is illegal to operate an hotel or a house for prostitution purposes, to live off a prostitute's earnings or to exploit a child for the purposes of prostitution.

Practice: Prostitutes are tolerated. Transvestites are generally arrested for offending public morals. Male prostitution is either subsumed under female or categorized as homosexuality.

CANADA

Policy: Not an offence *per se* in the Criminal Code. Private transactions are legal, but soliciting, pimping and brothel-keeping are illegal under federal law.

Practice: Some cities use municipal by-laws relating to loitering and public nuisance against prostitutes. Prostitutes' rights organizations have been working to repeal the prostitution laws and to empower prostitutes to improve their working conditions.

Information supplied by **Priscilla Alexander**, consultant to WHO; and **Mr A de Graaf Stichting** of an Amsterdam-based information centre.

---

which accompanied the Protestant Reformation. Today in the majority of Western nations prostitution is quietly tolerated, with only occasional efforts to prevent it. In countries such as the Netherlands and Germany, prostitution has been legalized in specific locations accompanied by strict health and welfare checks. Health hazards have always included venereal diseases but now also include **HIV** and **AIDS**.

China claims, unconvincingly, that prostitution no longer exists within its borders. In fact, the trade continues to flourish openly through most of Asia. Female prostitutes tend to be poor and lacking in skills to support themselves. Consequently, for many such women prostitution is the only opportunity they have to make money. Female prostitutes are often manipulated by 'pimps' or work in a brothel managed by a supervisor. Homosexual male prostitution and the use of children for prostitution has become increasingly common over the past 3 decades.

PROTECTIONISM

The practice of protecting domestic markets and industries by restricting or prohibiting competition from abroad, usually through tariffs or quotas or any other mechanism to restrict the flow of imports. Protectionist policies have been implemented by most countries, even though mainstream economists and government officials trumpet the benefits of **free trade**. Some Keynesian economists argue that import controls raise national income (since there is less domestic spending) and so will eventually lead to more purchases from abroad and a higher level of imports. They argue that import controls benefit both home markets and international trade and that other states need not resort to retaliatory trade barriers.

Economic depressions, recessions and wars traditionally result in increased protectionism, while peace and prosperity have the opposite effect. In 1913, customs duties were low throughout the Western world and few quotas were in place. After World War I customs tariffs were introduced throughout most of Europe. During the Great Depression of the 1930s, record **unemployment** sparked an epidemic of protectionist measures, causing global trade to shrink greatly. In the UK, protectionism decreased during the 19th century after the nation had become an industrial power in Europe.

The US too was protectionist until it had become the major world industrial power. Tariffs in the US reached their maximum during the Great Depression of the 1930s when 59% of the value of imports was collected as duty. Following World War II, the US along with 22 other nations signed reciprocal trade agreements in the form of the **General Agreement on Tariffs and Trade** (GATT). By 1990, over 100 nations were partners to the accord. Many of the members did reduce their tariffs and quota systems. However, the GATT agreements only limited protectionist measures; they did not eliminate them and **developing countries** always seemed to be the biggest losers.

PYRETHRUM

Flowering plants of the genus *chrysanthemum* which are commonly grown for ornamental purposes in temperate regions and commercially for the production of biological **pesticides** in Africa. Pyrethrum (or pyrethrin) is a potent insecticide derived from the flower heads of the *cinerariaefolium* variety.

This plant grows best on well drained, fertile soils above 2,000 metres where annual rainfall averages at least 1,000 millimetres a year. The plants reach peak yields about 3 years after planting. Flowers are picked by hand and yields of around 300 kilograms per hectare are average.

Potent pesticide
White-flowered insecticidal pyrethrum grows alongside tea and maize on a Kenyan farm. This plant packs a punch of pyrethrins – used in mosquito repellents. PYRETHRUM

Pyrethrum was the first widely-used biopesticide. It has several advantages over synthetic insecticides. It is relatively safe to use near food or humans; it has a repellent as well as deadly effect on insects; it breaks down rapidly in the environment; and insects do not seem to be able to develop resistance to it. As a result, it is now commonly used in household aerosols and as a powder in grain-storage warehouses. However, pyrethrins do kill non-target organisms and natural enemies of some pests.

QADDAFI, MUAMMAR-EL (1942-   )
Controversial Arab leader. The son of a Bedouin farmer who graduated from university in Libya in 1963 and later from the country's military academy. A devout Muslim and committed Arab nationalist, Qaddafi overthrew Libya's King Idris in a 1969 coup and seized control of the country. He then became Commander-in-chief of the armed forces and Chairman of Libya's Revolutionary Command Council. The following year he ordered all US and British bases in Libya closed. In 1973 he nationalized all foreign-owned petroleum assets, expelled the native Italian and Jewish communities and outlawed alcohol and gambling. He made several unsuccessful attempts to unify Libya with other Arab nations and from 1974 onward followed a path of Islamic **socialism**, documented in his *Green Book* (1976).

He was implicated in several abortive coup attempts in Egypt, the Sudan and Chad. His government also financed subversive, revolutionary and terrorist groups around the world, including the Black Panthers in the United States and the Irish Republican Army. His agents were held to be directly or indirectly responsible for the assassination of opponents abroad and for numerous terrorists acts in Europe and elsewhere. His alleged support of terrorists caused the US to take drastic military action, with the assistance of Britain and other nations. In 1986 a group of US-controlled, British-based warplanes bombed several sites in Libya, narrowly missing Qaddafi, but killing or wounding several of his children. Despite this action, which several countries condemned, Qaddafi has maintained his policies and continued his verbal campaign against the United States.

Rice
Women harvesting rice in Sri Lanka. Rice is the cereal that directly
feeds most people in the world – other grains like wheat and maize
are often fed to animals which in turn become food for people.

Race– Rural Development

Bold indicates a cross-reference

RACE

A concept used to classify humans according to origin and consistent physical traits. Discrimination based on such ideas is referred to as racism. In the past the idea of racial subdivisions had some scientific backing, with specific physical characteristics providing the basis for four distinct races: Negroid, Caucasian, Asian and Mongoloid. However, contemporary science has shown that all people come from common genetic stock and the genetic differences within so-called races are greater than those between them

Race is often discussed in the West in terms of the continued disadvantage and persecution wrought on people of colour by whites. But the fact remains that it is a very ill-defined term which can include criteria such as skin colour, other physical features, language, religion, ideas of nationhood and culture. Race problems are created by and maintained by those privileged by racism even though the disadvantaged are usually blamed.

Racist thinking thrives in times of crisis when defining groups of people in terms of their otherness can provide convenient scapegoats for wider problems. Conservative governments frequently disguise failures of economic policy by claiming that foreigners have 'stolen' jobs.

In the colonial heyday racial classification was used to justify the inhuman treatment of 'inferior' races. Nineteenth century science claimed that Africans were similar to apes. An estimated 30 million Africans perished when they were shipped as slaves to the New World. During the Nazi occupation of Europe over 6 million Jews were systematically murdered when German leader Adolf Hitler blamed them for his country's economic and political woes, which compounded Germany's humiliating defeat in World War I.

The Western idea of the nation state has often fuelled racism by propounding the notion of building ethnic unity within a single strong nation. Often this means that the dominant group's values are identified as 'national' values and any difference is punished. Since World War II about 40 ethnic groups have been the victims of 'ethnic conflict'. The death toll exceeds the combined deaths in international, colonial and civil wars. The current world-wide crisis of **indigenous peoples** testifies to the unfriendliness of the nation state to minorities. Minority communities can suffer racially motivated attacks, higher rates of **unemployment**, low-paid work, poorer standards of health care and education and higher levels of imprisonment.

RADIOACTIVITY

The atoms of certain elements are unstable and may easily lose part of their nuclear material. These elements are liable to transform into other similar elements by spontaneously ejecting or 'radiating' various particles or energy waves from their atomic nuclei. These particles or energy waves can damage or destroy living cells.

Radioactive decay takes different forms (alpha, beta or gamma) depending on what particles are lost from the nucleus. All are potentially hazardous. Alpha radiation does not penetrate human tissue to any depth but causes damage when ingested. Beta particles are around 2,000 times smaller than alpha particles.

They can travel through a centimetre of living tissue but still cause most damage when ingested. Gamma radiation, in electromagnetic wave rather than particle form, can easily penetrate skin and is far more dangerous. It requires a thick layer of a dense material such as **lead** or concrete to provide an effective barrier.

Almost 40 years after the first commercial nuclear reactor began operating, there is still no safe and acceptable means of dealing with radioactive waste. The 84,000 tonnes of radioactive waste stored in 1990 was forecast to more than double by the year 2000.

RAPE

Sexual intercourse without consent, predominantly applied to describe sexual attacks on women who are

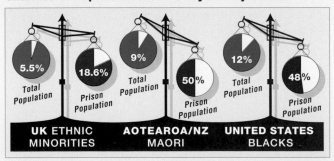

IMPRISONMENT and EXILE

Belonging to the 'wrong' racial group increases the chances of imprisonment and asylum rejection.

5.5% Total Population
18.6% Prison Population
UK ETHNIC MINORITIES

9% Total Population
50% Prison Population
AOTEAROA/NZ MAORI

12% Total Population
48% Prison Population
UNITED STATES BLACKS

● Most of the world's 15 million refugees come from the South and seek refuge in neighbouring countries. One person in 10 was a refugee in Malawi in July 1993, compared to one in 5,000 in the UK. The rate of asylum refusal on appeal in the UK has risen from 14% to 72%.

Home Office Statistics Bulletin 9/91; NEMDA; The Gaia Atlas of First Peoples by Julian Burger 1990; Bureau of Justice Statistics in New Statesman 1/4/94; WUS Update, June 1994.

'No bail for rapists!'
Rape is prevalent in South Africa, and strong slogans trumpet the actions called for by these women demonstrating in Johannesburg. RAPE

the main victims of sexual crimes. Women who have suffered rape are haunted by it throughout their lives as it exposes them to unwanted pregnancies, sexually-transmitted diseases and major psychological trauma. Young girls are universally the main target of child sexual assaults. Studies in several countries have found that a third of all women were sexually abused during childhood. In the US, it is estimated that 15-20% of all women are rape victims. Comparative studies in cities in **developing countries** found rates of 10%.

Ethnic conflicts during the early 1990s brought the crime of mass rape during war to public attention. In 1993 a **European Community** investigation found more than 20,000 Muslim women were raped during the conflict in Bosnia. Many had been held in 'rape camps', where they were forced to bear the children of the Serbian soldiers responsible.

The health care costs of rape can be extremely high. The **World Bank** says that 19% of all diseases contracted by women aged 15-44 in industrialized countries can be linked to domestic violence or rape.

Women's groups have long campaigned to have **gender** issues incorporated into international **human rights** legislation.

In 1993 the World Conference on Human Rights adopted the Vienna Declaration which stipulated that violence against women was a violation of human rights. The UN General Assembly has also passed the Declaration on the Elimination of Violence against Women which includes an official UN definition of gender-based abuse.

REAGAN, RONALD WILSON (1911-   )
American politician. Son of a shoe vendor, he initially worked as a radio announcer before a long career as a Hollywood film actor of limited success. He served as President of the Screen Actors Guild during which time he attempted to combat alleged Communist influences in the US motion picture industry. When his movie work started to dry up he became a travelling spokesperson for the General Electric Company. He entered the national political arena as Governor of California from 1967-74. He fought 2 unsuccessful campaigns for the Republican presidential nomination before succeeding, serving as President from 1981-89.

Throughout his tenure he adopted 'supply-side' economics, regularly increasing defence spending and lowering **taxes**. He followed a hard line towards the Soviet Union and against left-wing forces in Central America, especially Nicaragua. His administration sanctioned US intervention in Lebanon and Grenada. The US invasion of Grenada and covert Central Intelligence Agency (CIA) operations in Nicaragua were approved despite opposition from Congress. An aggressive foreign policy was highlighted by his sanctioning of a destructive long-range bombing raid on Libya. His Strategic Defence Initiative (popularly known as Star Wars) involved a military use of outer space and proved to be increasingly controversial. It was also one of the most expensive research and development programmes ever proposed.

In 1986 it was revealed that his administration had been shipping arms to Iran to buy the release of American hostages in Lebanon. It also became known that senior officials on the National Security Council had diverted some of the profits from the Iranian arms sales to the US-backed groups fighting against the Sandinista government in Nicaragua.

His summit meeting with Soviet leader Mikhail Gorbachev in 1988 led to the signing of the Intermediary-Range Nuclear Forces Treaty, curbing medium-range nuclear weapons. He survived an assassination attempt in 1981 and retired from the presidency after two terms of office. He had little knowledge or interest in world affairs but his acting skills made him one of the best 'communicators' of all American presidents. His final years in office were hampered by worsening Alzheimer's disease.

Natty dreadlocks

The distinctive Rastafarian look, popularised by Bob Marley, is a part of the lifestyle that dates back to the 1950s 'Back to Africa' movement.
RASTAFARIANISM

RASTAFARIANISM

A quasi-nationalist, politico-religious movement among the black population in the West Indies. Rastafarianism originated in the mid-1950s and can be traced to the 'Back to Africa' movement led by Marcus Garvey in the early years of the century. The movement became most prominent in Jamaica thanks to the exposure given to it by the musician Bob Marley. Followers believe Ras Tafari (the title and surname of the former Emperor **Haile Selassie** of Ethiopia) to be a semi-divine being. He is seen as champion of the black **race**, protector of African civilization and representative of the form of **Christianity** closest to the gospels and indigenous to Africa. According to Rastafarians, blacks are the Israelites reincarnated and have been subjected to the evil white race as divine punishment for their sins. They will be redeemed by repatriation to Africa. Followers typically sport dreadlocks and beards, wear beret-like hats called 'tams', adopt a vegetarian diet and smoke marijuana as part of their lifestyle.

RECYCLING

The reclamation of potentially useful material from household, agricultural and industrial waste. Humans produce around a billion tonnes of waste each year. Farmers have for centuries recycled organic waste into compost or low-cost animal feed or **fertilizer**. However, recycling of manufactured goods is a recent innovation. The goal is to reduce pollution and save energy and costs while slowing down the rate at which non-renewable **resources** are depleted.

Several countries around the world now have active recycling programmes for consumers and for industry. In Europe, glass recycling doubled to about 2.7 million tonnes during the 1980s. By the mid-1990s, the Netherlands, Austria, Canada, Germany and Iceland were all recovering more than 75% of glass while Switzerland was recycling nearly 85%. Recycling of **aluminum/aluminium** cans in the US grew from 24,000 tonnes in 1972 to 510,000 in 1982; 55% of all aluminum cans in that country are now recycled. This compares to 65% in Canada, 42% in Japan and 13% in Europe. It is estimated that 80% of aluminum could be recycled and the global trade in aluminum scrap is now worth $600 million.

One tonne of recycled newsprint saves a tonne of wood, equivalent to almost a dozen trees. Globally, only 25% of newsprint is recycled, yet recycling half of the world's paper would meet over 70% of global demand for new paper and save 8 million hectares of forest.

In **developing countries** like Egypt and Brazil, recycling is well advanced but only because thousands of poor people earn a living by recycling materials dumped at public waste-disposal sites.

In Canada, when municipal authorities in Victoria, British Columbia introduced a garbage tax of almost $2 a bag in 1992 (along with a recycling programme), household waste dropped 18% within a year.

Industry has also been forced to develop recycling programmes. In the US the recycling of industrial solvents is expected to reach a value of $1 billion by the year 2000. In the former German Democratic Republic an estimated 30 million tonnes of industrial wastes were being recycled each year in the early 1980s, providing 12% of the raw materials needed for industry. In Hungary, 29% of all industrial wastes were being recycled by 1985. In some European nations waste exchange networks have been established with over 150 waste products listed in the exchange scheme. The European steel industry re-uses scrap metal and **copper** with energy savings of 50% and aluminum with energy savings of 90%. It requires

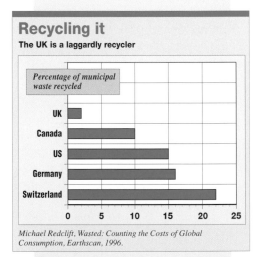

Recycling it
The UK is a laggardly recycler

Percentage of municipal waste recycled

Michael Redclift, Wasted: Counting the Costs of Global Consumption, Earthscan, 1996.

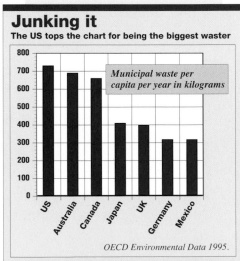

Junking it
The US tops the chart for being the biggest waster

Municipal waste per capita per year in kilograms

OECD Environmental Data 1995.

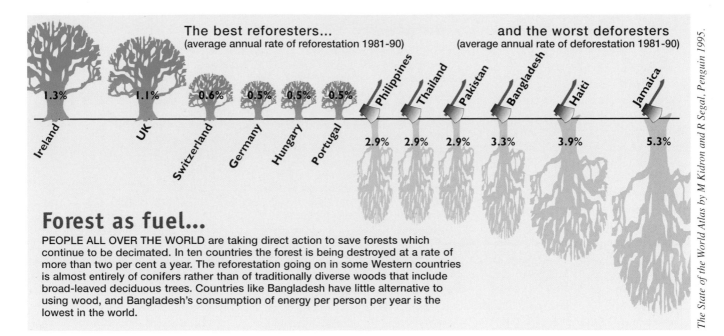

The best reforesters...
(average annual rate of reforestation 1981-90)

and the worst deforesters
(average annual rate of deforestation 1981-90)

Ireland 1.3%
UK 1.1%
Switzerland 0.6%
Germany 0.5%
Hungary 0.5%
Portugal 0.5%

Philippines 2.9%
Thailand 2.9%
Pakistan 2.9%
Bangladesh 3.3%
Haiti 3.9%
Jamaica 5.3%

The State of the World Atlas by M Kidron and R Segal, Penguin 1995.

Forest as fuel...

PEOPLE ALL OVER THE WORLD are taking direct action to save forests which continue to be decimated. In ten countries the forest is being destroyed at a rate of more than two per cent a year. The reforestation going on in some Western countries is almost entirely of conifers rather than of traditionally diverse woods that include broad-leaved deciduous trees. Countries like Bangladesh have little alternative to using wood, and Bangladesh's consumption of energy per person per year is the lowest in the world.

20-25 times more energy to make aluminum by smelting **bauxite** than it does to melt and produce 'new' aluminum from scrap. The energy required to recycle **copper** is only a tenth that used to refine new copper. And energy savings when steel is made from scrap amount to 47%. In Japan, where automation is used to sort both household and industrial waste, recycling of raw materials has tripled in recent years.

As concern for the environment spreads, especially in the industrialized countries, the value of recycling has become more accepted. Unfortunately, recycled materials are sometimes overlooked in favour of artificially cheap raw materials. In Germany, some reports suggest that only 3% of glass, paper, plastic and tin collected is in fact recycled.

Recycling is not only good for the environment, it also creates jobs. At least 30,000 people are involved in recycling aluminum in the United States, twice the number employed in primary aluminum production.

REFORESTATION

Managed programmes to replace forests that have been harvested or destroyed. By the 1990s, 20 million hectares of **land** were being reforested each year, with China (4.6

million hectares) and the former Soviet Union (4.5 million hectares) in the lead. Reforested **plantations** in the tropics cover a relatively small area. In Africa reforestation offsets a mere 10% of the trees lost to logging. Brazil, with massive **deforestation**, was replanting on average half a million hectares of forests throughout the 1980s.

The majority of reforestation schemes are carried out with one eye on future commercial logging, including many so-called 'social forestry' initiatives in the **Third World**. These were intended to provide villagers with **fuelwood** and other **resources** but often ended up providing local industry with trees for pulp. The choice of fast-growing trees such as **eucalyptus** and leucaena led to the degradation of soils, loss of nutrients and lowering of **water** tables in areas already under pressure as a result of previous forest depletion.

Successful reforestation projects are either run by the local population or are based on the active participation of different interest groups from the local community.

South Korea is a model example. In 1970 the country was denuded of trees. Hillsides were eroded and land had lost the capacity to retain water. Initial attempts at reforestation

failed. The key to success was the participation of villagers. Every hectare planted with fuelwood trees was matched by half a hectare planted with chestnuts. The production of mushrooms, fibre, bark, resins and other non-wood products was encouraged. In 1978, these products were generating an income of $100 million for the 2 million families involved in the programme. And by the mid-1990s, nearly 70% of South Korea was covered by trees.

Replacing forests with new trees has been promoted as way to lock up **carbon dioxide** (CO_2) and so reduce the **greenhouse effect**. Like all vegetation, trees absorb CO_2 from the atmosphere through photosynthesis. The Dutch Government has taken a global lead in this respect and intends to plant over 250,000 hectares of **tropical forests** at a total cost of $460 million.

REFUGEES

People who flee their own country for political or economic reasons, or to avoid war and oppression. In 1995 the number of refugees around the world was estimated at 27.4 million. About 40% of these were in Africa and 35% in Asia. Many nations now use legislation or screening procedures to limit refugees.

In Afghanistan some 5.9 million people fled to neighbouring Iran or Pakistan to avoid the recent civil war. In Southern Africa a million Mozambicans fled to Malawi, Zimbabwe and South Africa in order to escape civil conflict. In Ethiopia around 1.1 million people sought refuge in Sudan and Somalia to escape the wars raging in Tigray and Eritrea. In Southeast Asia at least 1.2 million people have fled from Vietnam since 1975. Civil war in Liberia during the late 1980s and Iraq's invasion of Kuwait in 1990 created new refugee hotspots. The conflict in Bosnia-Herzegovina added over 2 million more to the list.

By the early 1990s a new trend had begun to emerge: fewer refugees were crossing international borders while the number of displaced persons within countries was dramatically increasing. Afghanistan remained the greatest single source of refugees with 2.6 million Afghans living in Iran, Pakistan, India and other surrounding states. The second largest source was Rwanda with 1.8 million citizens living in neighbouring countries. By contrast, Bosnia and Herzegovina had 2.7 million internally-displaced people and Liberia 1.5 million. Africa with 11.8 million refugees was the continent with the greatest number of refugees.

Over the past few decades refugees have also been fleeing environmental damage. There are an estimated 10 million environmental refugees worldwide. During the drought in the early 1970s nearly a million people were forced to leave Burkina Faso and a further 500,000 left Mali. In fact, the degradation of agricultural **land** is currently displacing more people than any other factor. An estimated 50 million people live off land that is rapidly deteriorating. Soon they will be unable to meet their **basic needs** for food and fuel and will add to the environmental refugee total. Poisoning of

UNHCR By Numbers 1995.

Refugees

Political repression, war, hunger and environmental degradation force increasing numbers of people to flee their homes.

At the end of 1995 some 27 million people qualified for international assistance as official refugees. Of these nearly three million were from Afghanistan and just over two million from Rwanda. The number of people 'displaced' within their own countries by destitution, war or environmental degradation doubles this figure. An estimated two million people are homeless in the former Yugoslavia.

Oceania 51,200
Europe 1,876,400
Latin America 109,000

Estimated number of refugees January 1995

Africa 6,752,200
Asia 5,018,000
North America 681,400

land by toxic wastes, pollution and natural **disasters** caused by human activities are also increasing the flow of refugees. A projected rise in sea level caused by **global warming** could produce a further 50 million environmental refugees by the middle of the next century.

RENEWABLE ENERGY

The sun provides the earth with energy in the form of **electromagnetic radiation**. Without it, surface temperatures would plummet and plants and animals would not be able to survive. Of the small amount of solar energy intercepted by the earth, 30% is reflected back into space. The remainder is absorbed by the atmosphere, by **water** and **land**, and by living organisms.

The world's **population** has become dependent on 'unrenewable' fossil fuels like **coal**, petroleum and **natural gas**, all of which originate from the sun. But most 'renewable' forms of energy also harness solar energy. Solar panels trap the sun's heat directly and **photovoltaic cells** can turn the sun's energy directly into electricity. Solar energy is also used by plants to manufacture simple sugars, using **carbon dioxide** in the air or water. These compounds are then converted into more complex, organic molecules. When wood is burned for heat and light, the sun's energy is released.

The sun also evaporates water from oceans, lakes and rivers. The sun effectively lifts the water and this

is exploited by hydroelectric installations. As the water falls back to the sea it is used to drive turbines. The energy contained in wind and waves is also derived from the sun. As the earth's surface heats up it causes differences in atmospheric pressures which forces the air to move. The wind propels the water in the world's oceans to form waves. The rise and fall of ocean tides is also affected by the sun, although it is primarily due to the moon's gravitational pull. Tides are highest when the earth, moon and sun are aligned.

The solar energy absorbed by the earth in a year is equivalent to 20 times the energy stored in all of the world's reserves of recoverable fossil fuels. The earth's core is also heated by the decay of naturally-occuring radioactive elements such as uranium and thorium. This heat can be extracted either by drilling into natural aquifers of hot water or by forcing water under pressure through hot rock. Renewable sources such as **biomass** and **hydro-electric power** already provide 19% of the total energy consumed worldwide. However, if just .005% of the solar energy reaching the earth could be tapped from renewable sources like wind turbines, solar collectors, hydropower and wave-energy converters, it would supply more energy in a year than could be obtained by burning the same reserves of coal, **oil** and gas combined.

Unfortunately, renewable energy sources tend to be dispersed and intermittent and the electricity they produce is usually hard to store. Nevertheless within a few decades the contribution of all renewable sources to global energy production is expected to exceed that of **oil** and its derivatives.

REPRODUCTIVE RIGHTS

Reproductive rights of women include: the right to plan one's family; the right to assistance in preventing and overcoming infertility; and the right to full and timely knowledge about all aspects of reproductive health and sexuality.

RESOURCES

The most severe consequence of unfettered **economic growth** is the depletion of the planet's natural resources. Some resources like **coal, oil, soil** and **fossil groundwater** take thousands or even millions of years to form, and so are not replaceable once consumed. Such resources are termed 'non-renewable' and include energy sources like wood, coal, oil and **natural gas**.

Other sources of energy (the sun, the tides and the wind) are termed 'renewable' because human use will not deplete them to any significant degree. Resources such as forests, **fish**, plants, animals and freshwater are part of a natural cyclical system. These resources are potentially 'renewable', but only if they are

RENEWABLE POTENTIAL

RENEWABLE ENERGIES HAVE A TREMENDOUS POTENTIAL WHICH IS BARELY BEING USED.

◆ **WIND:** Land-based turbines could provide 20,000 terawatt-hours of electricity per year – or twice as much as the world consumed in 1987.

◆ **BIOMASS:** More than 50 Third World countries would be able to produce as much energy from the residues generated by sugar production as they use now via imported oil.

◆ **HYDRO:** Less than 5% of the world's small-scale hydropower potential has been exploited so far.

used in a sustainable fashion, where the rate of depletion is no greater than the rate of regeneration. If the current logic of economic growth at any cost continues, the reserves of most non-renewable resources will soon be exhausted – including some that are crucial to the survival of humankind.

RESPIRATORY INFECTIONS

More than 4 million children, mostly in **developing countries** and most of them under 5 years of age, die each year from acute respiratory infections – primarily pneumonia. Every child develops up to 8 respiratory infections a year, most of these minor infections of the upper respiratory tract. However the incidence of life-threatening lower respiratory-tract infections is far higher amongst children in developing nations. This is due to a variety of factors – including poor nutrition, low birth-weight, inadequate sanitation and lack of medical facilities. Pneumonia in children cannot be prevented by vaccines but it can be cured with a standard, inexpensive antibiotic treatment for as little as $4 per child. Other respiratory diseases like pertussis (whooping cough) and the lung complications brought on by **measles** can be prevented by vaccines at a cost of less than $2 per child.

Over half of all visits to health service facilities are related to acute respiratory infections in children. This tremendous strain on medical staff and health-care facilities is especially serious in the **Third World**. The tragedy is that the burden could easily be alleviated with a relatively small, well-planned and cost-effective investment.

RICE

An annual cereal grass consisting of 24 species, 2 of which are extensively cultivated. *Oryza sativa* is the most important and was probably native to India. It is now grown in tropical, subtropical and warm-temperate regions throughout the world. It is the main cereal crop and staple food for more than half of the world's **population**, most notably for the people in Southeast Asia where 90% of the world's rice is produced and consumed.

There are now thousands of **high-yielding varieties** (HYV) of rice which were developed through plant-breeding techniques. Although most varieties are grown in standing **water**, 'upland' types can be grown on dry **land** where rainfall is heavy. Virtually no rice grows where precipitation is under 100 centimetres annually. Most varieties tolerate high temperatures and humidity and can produce up to

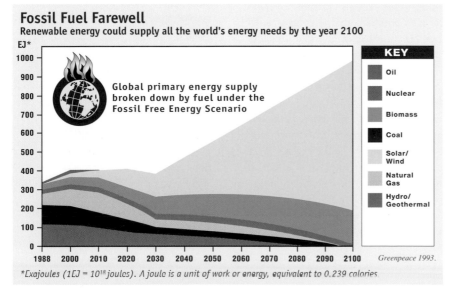

Fossil Fuel Farewell
Renewable energy could supply all the world's energy needs by the year 2100

Global primary energy supply broken down by fuel under the Fossil Free Energy Scenario

KEY
- Oil
- Nuclear
- Biomass
- Coal
- Solar/Wind
- Natural Gas
- Hydro/Geothermal

Greenpeace 1993.

Exajoules (1EJ = 10^18 joules). A joule is a unit of work or energy, equivalent to 0.239 calories.

River green paddy
Most rice in Bangladesh grows in the fertile delta region formed by the rivers Meghna, Ganges and Brahmaputra. RICE

3 crops per year under continual cultivation systems. The combination of HYV seeds with **irrigation** and large quantities of **fertilizers** and **pesticides** saw rice yields in **developing countries** rise by 1.9% annually between 1961 and 1980. In nations like the Philippines and Indonesia yields increased by over 3% a year. However, the dependence on HYV rice is not without problems.

The damaging impact of huge quantities of **agrochemicals** on the environment in Asia is already being felt. And the loss of diversity and disappearance of locally-adapted rice strains could prove disastrous. In Indonesia alone, 1,500 local varieties of rice have disappeared in the past 15 years and nearly 75% of the rice planted today descends from a single maternal plant. By the year 2005, India may be using fewer than 10 rice varieties. In addition, the need for irrigation water to satisfy the burgeoning needs of cities may severely curtail rice harvests in future since rice is predominantly grown on irrigated land.

Seedlings are transplanted into flooded paddy fields which can be drained where necessary to allow mechanical harvesting of the crop.

In developing countries harvesting is done most commonly by hand. Milling which removes the outer husk of the grain produces brown rice; white rice (which is deficient in vitamin B) is produced when both the husk and the underlying bran are removed. Global production is around 480 million tonnes annually and is steadily increasing. China (176 million tonnes), India (122 million tonnes) and Indonesia (47 million tonnes) are the world's largest producers.

RINDERPEST
A contagious viral disease, also known as 'cattle plague', which affects **cattle** and certain wild animals throughout much of Asia and Africa. Rinderpest is native to India. Once the virus was introduced into Africa in 1890 it spread rapidly, killing local cattle and decimating herds of antelopes, buffaloes and giraffes which had no immunity. Symptoms occur 3 to 9 days after infection and include loss of appetite, fever, mouth ulcers, dysentery and severe weight loss. Among livestock at least 90% of acute cases are fatal. In chronic cases

mortality rates are much lower, but in all cases productivity is seriously reduced. Compulsory slaughter of all infected herds or **vaccination** programmes are usually employed to control outbreaks of the disease.

RUBBER
A synthetic or natural organic polymer that is tough and elastic. Raw rubber had few uses until 1770 when a chemist coined the name after observing how good it was for erasing pencil marks. Natural rubber is made from latex, a milky fluid collected from rubber trees. The rubber tree (*Hevea brasiliensis*) is native to Brazil but is now widely cultivated throughout Southeast Asia. Seeds were originally shipped from Brazil to the UK in 1876. From there the seeds went to British colonies in Asia where large tracts of **land** were given over to **plantations**. Rubber trees yield latex after the sixth year of growth. When the bark is cut, the fluid flows and can be easily collected using containers which are strapped to the tree. The latex is processed with acids and the resulting rubber is then pressed into

Tapping wealth
A deft slice with the knife and milky latex runs down the tree into the little cup, in this photo from early 20th-century Malaya. Rubber plantations brought vast wealth to companies like Goodyear, Firestone and Dunlop, but not to workers. RUBBER

sheets and air dried.

Charles Goodyear invented the process of 'vulcanization', in which rubber is mixed with sulphur and heated. The product is more resilient and consistent in its properties than ordinary rubber. Vulcanized rubber is used to make a huge range of products, including hoses, conveyor belts, insulation for electric cables and tyres for **automobiles** and **bicycles**.

A variety of synthetic rubbers are also made from petrochemicals. Styrene-butadiene rubber is the most common of the manufactured rubbers. It is often mixed with natural rubber to improve its resilience. Despite the combined efforts of scientists and researchers around the world, there is currently no environmentally sound and effective means of disposing of synthetic rubber compounds.

Of the global total of 4.8 million tonnes of natural rubber produced annually, most comes from Southeast Asia. Thailand (1.7 million tonnes), Indonesia (1.4 million tonnes) and Malaysia (1.1 million tonnes) produce over half of the global supply. Some 10 million tonnes of synthetic rubber are also produced each year, with the states of the former Soviet Union (2.5 million tonnes), the United States (2.3 million tonnes) and Japan (1.3 million tonnes) producing the bulk of the total.

RHODES, CECIL JOHN (1859-1902)

English financier and politician. The son of a rural vicar, he was despatched to South Africa at the age of 16 to work on a **cotton** farm with his brother. The farm failed and along with thousands of others he left for the diamond fields of Kimberley. For 8 years he divided his life between South Africa and Britain. He graduated from Oxford University in 1881.

He then entered the political arena standing for election to parliament in the Cape Colony. He won the seat and held it for the rest of his life. His persistence in mining finally made him some money and he formed De Beers Consolidated Mines. By 1891 the company controlled 90% of the world's diamond production. Rhodes then bought a large stake in the Transvaal gold mines. Both companies stimulated his desire for expansion northwards into the uncharted African interior, which brought him into dispute with many other imperial powers, including the Germans, Belgians and Portuguese. Mineral wealth, communications and white settlement were his objectives.

In 1885 he met Paul Kruger, the Boer president of the Transvaal. Both wanted to extend their power and control in Southern Africa, and would be at loggerheads for the rest of their lives. In 1889 Rhodes obtained a charter for his new British South Africa Company to develop the territory to the north which was named Rhodesia in his honour. This led to major conflicts with the people of present-day Zimbabwe.

He became Prime Minister of Cape Colony in 1890, pursing segregationist policies, but was forced to resign in 1896 after supporting an abortive and misconceived raid into the Transvaal. Rhode's zeal for economic expansion and infrastructural development made a lasting impact in the region. He devoted most of his fortune to fund scholarships at Oxford University for young men from the colonies, the United States and Germany.

RURAL DEVELOPMENT

Around 60% of the world's **population** live in rural areas, mostly in the developing world. It is a generally believed that the larger the rural population, the poorer the country. Historically, farming communities have had significantly higher birth rates than urban societies. Their populations have also tended to be younger, to live in large families and to include a slighter higher percentage of males.

In industrialized nations, the countryside has been massively depopulated. In the US only 6.7% of people worked in agriculture, fisheries or forestry in 1970 and the number continues to decline. The mass exodus to the cities which followed industrialization led to huge slums and urban **poverty** in the late 19th and early 20th century. Today the same process is taking place in the **Third World**. For example, in China rapid industrialization in the 1980s and 1990s led some 120 million people to urban centres in search of work.

However, in most parts of the south rural populations continue to grow. The number of smallholders and **landless labourers** is now over 200 million. Without a chance to make a decent living these millions will be consigned to a life of poverty, forced to exploit and exhaust what little **land** they have in order to survive in the short-term.

The backbone of any rural development programme must be **land reform**. But this must be reinforced by a system to distribute agricultural inputs, credit and all support services. Smallholders must also be involved in the planning of agricultural policies. In addition there need to be opportunities for work outside of agriculture (for example in storage and packaging, small-scale manufacturing or environmental management) in order to provide income for those who may still be landless.

Rice – Rural Development

Shifting Cultivation

Golden flames leap from the blaze, twigs crackle in the heat, smoke billows skywards as the forest burns in Amazonia, Brazil. This 'slash and burn' method clears the land for farming, or for cattle.

S

Bold indicates a cross-reference

SAHEL

A semi-arid region of western and north-central Africa extending from Senegal eastward to the Sudan. It forms a transition zone between the dry Sahara to the north and the humid savannah to the south. The vegetation of the Sahel consists of low-growing grass, taller herbaceous plants, thorny shrubs, **acacia** and baobab trees, all of which act as forage for the region's extensive livestock. The terrain is chiefly savannah with little cover. At least 9 months of the year are dry, rainfall occurring in a short season and totalling 100-200 millimetres. Crops like **millet** and **groundnuts** are grown. However, overstocking and poor farming practices exacerbate the tendency toward **desertification**. In the 1960s and 1970s **soil erosion** and desertification became extreme, mainly due to the ever-increasing demands of a burgeoning human population and the resultant explosion in livestock numbers.

Urban dwellers stripped more and more trees for **fuelwood** and **land** was increasingly cultivated in an unsustainable fashion. The already poor **soil** was then eroded by wind and rain, leaving the region arid and barren. In 1968, a prolonged drought hit the Sahel. By the early 1970s nearly all crops had been wiped out and 70% of **cattle** had perished. In 1972, virtually no

SADAT, ANWAR (1918-1981)
Egyptian politician. A graduate of the Cairo Military Academy, he plotted with the Germans to oust Britain from Egypt but was arrested. Later he joined Gamal Abdel Nasser's Free Officers organization and took part in a coup which deposed the Egyptian monarchy in 1952. Following Nasser's election as President in 1956 Sadat twice held the post of Vice-President, finally succeeding **Nasser** in 1970.

During his term he decentralized and diversified the economy and moved Egypt away from the Soviet camp and toward increasing alliances with the United States. He led the Egyptian campaign in the 1973 war against Israel and despite defeat came out of the war with his reputation enhanced – he was the first Arab leader to actually retake territory from Israel. Afterwards, he worked towards peace. In 1977 he paid a historic visit to Israel to try and reconcile the 2 countries. He shared the Nobel Peace Prize with Israel's **Menachem Begin** in 1978 for their efforts in formulating the **Camp David Agreement** and subsequent peace treaty. Opposition to the peace treaty grew following an economic crisis in Egypt and Sadat's suppression of dissent. He was assassinated by Islamic fundamentalists in 1979.

rain fell and the Sahara had advanced 100 kilometres south. An estimated 100,000 people died during this drought and **famine**.

In times of normal rainfall the desertified area shrinks back to its original borders. Severe drought and famine struck again from 1983-85 and the desertification process began afresh, despite several large **reforestation** and anti-desertification programmes.

SALINIZATION

The process through which salt concentrations in the **soil** build up. In areas of regular rainfall salts are flushed out of the soil into underlying **groundwater** or carried away to the sea. However, where rainfall is low and evaporation rates high, such as in the arid tropics, soils tend to have a high salt content. Salts can comprise up to 12% of soil in the worst-affected areas. Salts inhibit roots, limiting plant growth.

They build up in the top few centimetres where roots are most active and in severe cases form a salt crust

on the **land** surface. **Irrigation** of land which is used year after year without fallow periods is now a major cause of salinization. Land must be well drained or water-table levels rise bringing the salt in the soil

Salt of the earth
A farmer coaxes water along the channel to his vegetable plot in Mali. In dry areas, water evaporates fast and leaves salts in the soil which stunt growth.
SALINIZATION

to the surface where it is concentrated by evaporation. The **United Nations Environment Programme** (UNEP) reports that 30-80% of irrigated land in the world suffers to some degree from salinization. Tens of thousands of hectares are now too salty to support plant life and 22 million hectares are thought to be waterlogged, allowing salt concentrations to build up. Estimates now suggest that as much land is being *taken out of* production as a result of salinization and waterlogging as is being *brought into* production through irrigation.

Between 1950 and 1970 the global total of land under irrigation doubled. Just under 20% of the world's cropland is now irrigated and salinity is a serious problem on 20-30 million hectares. Moreover, the process of salinization is increasing at a rate of 1-1.5 million hectares annually.

Salinization is becoming acute in China, India and other parts of Asia where the **Green Revolution** was based on the use of irrigated land and high-yield cereal varieties. Northern Africa, Australia and the United States are also experiencing increasing levels of salinity.

In the Colorado Basin in the US, the annual salt build-up of 10 million tonnes causes crop losses of over $113 million. This figure may reach $270 million a year by 2010. Salt build-up is thought to be reducing crop yields by 30% in Egypt and Pakistan.

Globally, around 20 million hectares of land is thought to be naturally saline, mostly in **wetlands** and coastal areas in arid regions. Figures suggest that about 30% of the world's potentially arable land is affected by salt. Although salinized soils can be rehabilitated by draining away excess **water** and flushing out the salts with freshwater, both methods are extremely expensive operations and not widely employed.

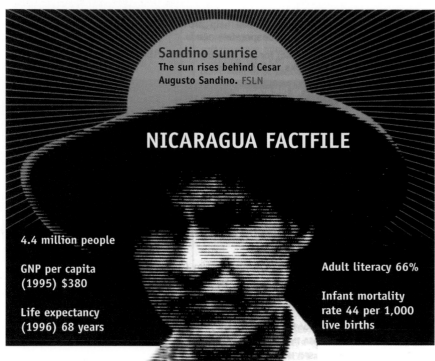

Sandino sunrise
The sun rises behind Cesar Augusto Sandino. FSLN

NICARAGUA FACTFILE

4.4 million people

GNP per capita (1995) $380

Life expectancy (1996) 68 years

Adult literacy 66%

Infant mortality rate 44 per 1,000 live births

World Development Report 1997, World Bank; The State of the World's Children 1997, UNICEF.

SANDINISTA NATIONAL LIBERATION FRONT (FSLN)

The FSLN deposed President Anastasio Somoza Debayle of Nicaragua in 1979, ending 46 years of dictatorship by the Somoza family. The FSLN was founded in 1962 by Carlos Fonseca Amador, Silvio Mayorga and Tomas Borge Martinez and named after Cesar Augusto Sandino, a Nicaraguan resistance leader during the US occupation of 1927-33. Dedicated to the overthrow of the Somoza family, the FSLN gathered widespread popular support and carried out regular attacks on the Nicaraguan National Guard from bases in Honduras and Costa Rica. Somoza's forces fought back and Fonseca and Mayorga were killed. The FSLN then split into 3 groups with differing views about how to achieve their aim.

The revolution of 1978-79 reunited the Sandinistas under the leadership of brothers Daniel and Humberto Ortega. With 5,000 fighters and widespread popular support they defeated the National Guard and overthrew Somoza. A National Directorate was set up to lead the FSLN and set policy for the junta headed by **Daniel Ortega**. Humberto Ortega created the 50,000-strong Sandinista army, mainly to help fight off counter-revolutionary forces (known as the 'contras') who were based in Honduras and armed and financed by the United States. The resignation of several non-Marxist members of the leadership pushed the FSLN and the country further to the left. Belligerent American opposition to the Sandinistas made Nicaragua increasingly dependent on support from the Soviet Union and Cuba. The Sandinista Government confiscated Somoza's land and nationalized the country's main industries. However, small and medium-sized enterprises were allowed to continue operating as before and there was no centralized planning. Having opted for multi-party elections, the FSLN won 60 of 96 seats during 1984 elections and a new National Assembly was created with Daniel Ortega appointed as

President. However, American support for the 'contras' increased and Washington cut nearly all trade with the country. With the economy in shreds and the nation torn apart by civil war, Nicaraguans voted the Sandinistas out of power in 1990.

SCHISTOSOMIASIS

Also known as **bilharzia**. A debilitating parasitic disease thought to affect over 200 million people in tropical countries. At least 1 billion people are at risk, especially those whose daily activities bring them into contact with untreated **water** through swimming, **fishing**, irrigated farming, washing and bathing in streams or ponds. The disease comes from a species of water snail which acts as a host to the first larval stage of flukes of the genus *schistosoma*. When these larvae leave the snail in their second stage of development, they are able to pass through human skin, become sexually mature and produce vast quantities of eggs which then pass to

Picture of health
This Indian girl looks healthy but water-borne parasitic diseases like bilharzia lurk in many tropical countries, affecting 200 million people. SCHISTOSOMIASIS

the human intestine or bladder. The release of the spiked eggs causes **anaemia**, inflammation and the formation of scar tissue. Diarrhoea, dysentery, enlargement of the spleen and cirrhosis of the liver may also

SEA-LEVEL RISE – Major cities at risk from sea-level rises

FOSSIL FUELS (oil, coal and gas) currently provide the world with most of its energy. But burning these fuels is the primary source of carbon dioxide emissions, the main cause of global warming. At this rate the global temperature is set to rise 3-4 °C by 2100, causing a rise in sea levels of 66 cms and the disruption of the world's climate. The low-lying Maldive islands, in the Indian Ocean, would disappear entirely.

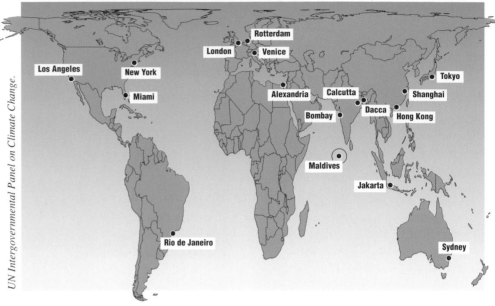

UN Intergovernmental Panel on Climate Change.

occur. Numerous eggs then pass out of the body in urine or faeces to continue the cycle.

The disease contributes to **malnutrition**. The listlessness and fatigue it causes translate into loss of productivity. Seventy-four **developing countries** report the disease regularly and at least 200,000 people die from schistosomiasis each year. Praziquantel, a drug developed in the 1990s can cure it but the problem lies in the high rate of re-infection. **Pesticides** to control the snail hosts are effective but more expensive.

SEA-LEVEL RISE

Sea **water** expands when warmed with polar ice caps and inland glaciers melting as temperatures rise. In 1985 experts concluded that **global warming** of between 1.5°C to 4.5°C would result in a rise in sea level of 20-140 centimetres. A rise of one metre would affect over 300 million people in low-lying coastal areas. Island states such as the Maldives and Kiribati could disappear altogether. A rise of only

50 centimetres would displace 16% of Egypt's population and in the southern United States, the Gulf of Mexico would creep 53 kilometres inland. The cost of protecting people and investments from encroaching waters, as estimated by the International Panel on Climate Change (IPCC), would exceed $20 billion a year.

Computer models on climate change, global warming and sea-level rise are mostly guesswork at present but they are steadily improving. A revised estimate in 1990 predicted that a warming of 1.5°C-4.5°C would cause ocean levels to rise from 14-24 centimetres by 2030. The increase would be caused by thermal expansion of the oceans and by melting alpine glaciers. By 1996, sea level increases of 15-94 centimetres were being forecast with a best estimate of 50 centimetres.

Over 118 million people living in coastal areas will be threatened if this prediction comes about. In Bangladesh 25,000 square kilometres or 17% of the country would be inundated. Vietnam would need to build 4,700 kilometres of dykes to protect its coasts. And some 5 million square kilometres of coastal areas around the world would eventually be threatened. These areas make up a third of the earth's total cropland and are home for over a billion people.

SECOND WORLD
(see also Third World)
An infrequently used term to describe the industrialized, predominantly communist nations that formed the former Soviet Bloc.

SEDIMENTATION
When **soil** particles settle in **water** they form a sediment and the process is referred to as sedimentation. As much as 30 billion tonnes of soil is estimated to be carried from the **land** by rivers into the world's oceans each year. Only 9 billion tonnes of that comes from natural processes. The rest is a result of human activities.

When forests are chopped down or land paved over, erosion and silt loads increase. Silt prevented from moving downstream by a dam restricts water flow, builds up on the river bed and may eventually cause

SCHUMACHER, EF (1911-1977)
Economist and philosopher. Born in Germany, he attended university at Oxford where he became sceptical of orthodox growth-centred economics and recognized the need to build caring and environmentally sustainable economies. Following a teaching job in the United States, he worked in business, farming and journalism before re-entering academia as an economist in the mid-1940s.

He was the originator of the concept of 'intermediate technology' (IT) for **developing countries** and founder of the Intermediate Technology Development Group in the UK. His thoughts and philosophy of economic development were summed up in his best-selling critique of Western economic orthodoxies, *Small is Beautiful*. He became a regular advisor to governments throughout the world on problems of **rural development**.

flooding. It can also foul hydro-electric **dams**.

In river deltas and other low-lying areas where embankments have been built to prevent flooding, the river bed can quickly rise and the threat of flooding is magnified. A single breach of the right bank of the Brahmaputra in Bangladesh during the floods of 1988 swamped 1,000 square kilometres of land.

Sedimentation is particularly acute in China where **deforestation** and massive agricultural schemes have led to vast amounts of soil being eroded. The Sanmexia Dam was commissioned in 1964 and closed the same year when silt rendered the dam unusable. Where the Yellow River crosses the plains, embankments have been constructed to prevent flooding and the river bed has risen 5 metres above ground

level. A breach in the embankment could have catastrophic consequences.

Some 250,000 tonnes of soil are washed off Nepal's deforested hillsides each year and a similar amount from the Himalayan foothills in India. As a result, a huge area of shallow water is building up in the Bay of Bengal covering some 5 million hectares. When the land breaks the sea surface, India and Bangladesh will probably fight over ownership, though most of the soil originated in Nepal.

SEED BANKS
Also known as gene banks or germplasm banks, seed banks are repositories of seeds or plant tissue obtained from a wide range of primitive strains and wild crop varieties. The seeds are stored as a future resource to help maintain genetic diversity.

Different varieties will survive for varying lengths of time in storage. For example, **wheat** seed will remain viable for a few hundred years. But on average a gene bank needs to grow out all its seeds every 10 years.

Seed banks have brought the commercial and political problems of **biotechnology** to global attention. In 1984, the International Undertaking on Plant Genetic Resources was adopted by the **Food and Agriculture Organization** (FAO), with only the United States voicing a protest. Members agreed that all germplasm,

Still waters run shallower
Serene waters of the Cabora Bassa Dam in Mozambique hide the build-up of silt or 'sedimentation' that is going on beneath the surface. SEDIMENTATION

Sandinistas – Seed Banks

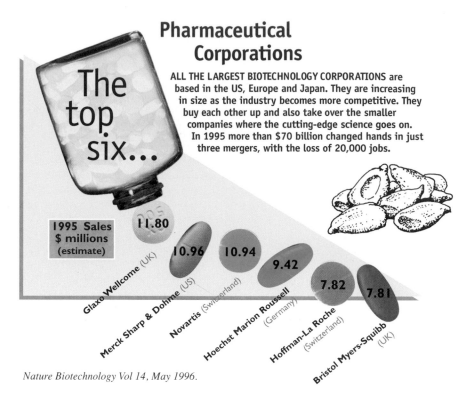

Pharmaceutical Corporations

ALL THE LARGEST BIOTECHNOLOGY CORPORATIONS are based in the US, Europe and Japan. They are increasing in size as the industry becomes more competitive. They buy each other up and also take over the smaller companies where the cutting-edge science goes on. In 1995 more than $70 billion changed hands in just three mergers, with the loss of 20,000 jobs.

The top six...

1995 Sales $ millions (estimate)

- 11.80 — Glaxo Wellcome (UK)
- 10.96 — Merck Sharp & Dohme (US)
- 10.94 — Novartis (Switzerland)
- 9.42 — Hoechst Marion Roussell (Germany)
- 7.82 — Hoffman-La Roche (Switzerland)
- 7.81 — Bristol Myers-Squibb (UK)

Nature Biotechnology Vol 14, May 1996.

including seeds improved by biotechnology should be freely available to all. But the accord did not last long. Ethiopia, Taiwan, India and Brazil soon prohibited the export of germplasm from specific crops and the US refused to allow some gene bank seeds to be sent to Nicaragua.

The International Board for Plant Genetic Resources (IBPGR) is responsible for running the world's gene banks. The IBPGR is part of the Consultative Group on International Agricultural Research (CGIAR) which is controlled by the industrialized nations. Around 60 gene banks have been established, a third of which are in the developing world. Nonetheless, **developed countries** hold over 90% of known genetic plant-material stocks, while the **Third World** holds only 33%. This is despite the fact that the Third World actually donated over 90% of all the material that is held in gene banks.

The reasons for the conflict over seeds and germplasm are clear. By 1989, the global seed business was worth $13 billion a year. Plant breeding was dominated by a small number of multinational petro-

chemical and pharmaceutical companies. In the industrialized world, legislation designed to protect plant breeders ('Plant Breeders Rights') gave patent-like control to these companies over any new varieties that they might develop – including those produced

from gene-bank material originally supplied by **developing countries**. An extension of the patent laws to the Third World would give the companies control over new seeds developed from seeds originating in the Third World. And the use of genetically-engineered seeds would soon become unavoidable if those same companies ceased to offer traditional varieties for sale.

In response, developing countries have pressed for 'Farmers Rights', so farmers in the **South** who have developed strains through years of cultivation can also be rewarded. One way to facilitate this would be through the creation of a World Gene Fund which could support the **conservation** and development of seed **resources** within the Third World.

In 1996 it became clear that seed banks were so badly underfunded that global stocks of countless seed varieties were threatened. Seeds stored in refrigerators were not being re-grown often enough to stop them from dying. Human and mechanical failure was also destroy-

SELASSIE, HAILE (1892-1975)

Ethiopian emperor, also known as Ras Tafari. Haile Selassie's father, Lij Tafari, was a politically progressive adviser to Emperor Menelik II. When the emperor died in 1913, his grandson Lij Yasu succeeded to the throne. However, his liking for **Islam** made him unpopular. Lij Tafari, with the backing of the Christian population, deposed Lij Yasu in 1916 and named Ras Tafari as his heir apparent. Ras Tafari, also a progressive, became a focus for those who wanted to modernize Ethiopia. In 1923 Ethiopia joined the **League of Nations**. The following year Ras Tafari visited Britain, the first Ethiopian leader to travel abroad.

He was crowned Emperor in 1930 and assumed the name Haile Selassie (Might of the Trinity). When Italy invaded Ethiopia in 1936 he was forced into exile in Britain. With British backing he was restored to the throne in 1941 and took steps to maximize his authority and modernise Ethiopia by improving social and economic conditions. In 1960, opposition to his absolute rule began to surface but was quickly silenced. He played a pivotal role in helping to establish the **Organization of African Unity** in 1963 and ruled until 1974. With **famine**, high **unemployment** and political stagnation gripping the country he was deposed by the military and spent the remainder of his life under house arrest in his palace.

ing whole collections, such as when a cold-storage unit broke down at the International Centre for Research in the Semi-Arid Tropics (ICRISAT) in India. Workers at Olomouc in the Czech Republic planted 800 varieties of onions, leeks and related species to regenerate the collection, but then found there was no money to harvest the crop. Similar problems arose in the United States and Russia. It is estimated that $3 billion is needed to maintain these critical genetic resources.

SELF-DETERMINATION

The process by which a group of people who perceive themselves as a nation form their own state and government. After World War II the **United Nations** adopted self-determination as one of its main goals. The UN charter specifies 2 meanings of the term. First, a state is held to have the right to choose freely its own political, economic, social and cultural systems; second, self-determination is defined as the right of any people who define themselves as a nation to constitute themselves in a state or otherwise freely decide the form of association within an existing state.

SHARIA LAW

Islamic law. The word 'sharia' is Arabic for 'way' or 'road'. It is based on the concept of obligation rather than right and comes from divine revelation in the *Quran*, and prophetic practice (or 'sunna') as recorded in the *Hadith*. Sharia completely governs the individual and the social life of the believer. It prescribes not only religious duties but covers every aspect of life. All human actions are divided into 5 categories: obligatory, recommended, indifferent, undesirable or prohibited. (Sunni and Shia Muslims have different interpreta-

Stark stumps and green shoots
Green shoots of pineapples and rice signal new life from the charred earth, cleared by burning the vegetation and trees, at this homestead in Indonesia. SHIFTING CULTIVATION

tions of what is obligatory.)

Instructions are given on how the obligatory and recommended functions are to be performed. The law also minutely details all bodily functions and prescribes how these should be performed to keep the body pure. There is also an all-encompassing code of social behaviour. Sharing these common codes has meant that wherever they live, all Muslims exhibit common behaviour patterns. Sharia law covers marriage, divorce and inheritance. Among other things it forbids usury, the visual depiction of living beings, drinking of alcohol and eating of pork. It also prescribes penalties and punishment for crimes. Although many Islamic states exist none are governed exclusively by Sharia law – not even rigid theocratic states like Iran.

SHIFTING CULTIVATION/SLASH and BURN AGRICULTURE

A cultivation system that preserves **soil** fertility by rotating the **land** being farmed rather than the crop. A

plot of land is cleared and cultivated for a short period of time. It is then abandoned and allowed to revert to its natural state as the cultivator moves to another plot of land. One such system is 'slash and burn' agriculture, which leaves only stumps and large trees after the natural vegetation has been cleared and the area burned. The system is usually used by root crop farmers in **developing countries**, especially in **tropical forests** and by upland-rice farmers on forested hillsides in Asia. Areas of forest are cleared and burned for planting. This releases most available nutrients, allowing them to be returned to the soil as ash in a form that is quickly and easily used by other plants.

Slash and burn agriculture is an ecologically-sound method of farming common in the tropics. Some 250 million farming families around the world, mainly in developing countries, practice shifting cultivation. It is the only sustainable way of farming in rainforests due to the low fertility of the soil, though it is often criticized because it requires extensive amounts of land and population growth is rapidly reducing the amount available. Some critics say that it degrades the fertility of forests soils. But it remains the only ecologically sound means of cultivation of land in many tropical areas since it requires neither complex soil conservation techniques nor expensive agro-chemicals. However, increasing human numbers and social pressures limiting access to land have resulted in fallow periods declining or disappearing altogether. When this happens, slash and burn and shifting cultivation become distinctively destructive means of farming, giving the land no time to recover its fertility.

SHINING PATH

A revolutionary movement (known in Spanish as *Sendero Luminoso* or Shining Path) which uses guerrilla tactics and violent terrorism in the name of Maoism. Founded in 1970, it took its name from the founder of Peru's Communist Party, Jose Carlos Mariategui who claimed that 'Marxist-Leninism will open the shining path to revolution'.

The founder and leader Abimael Guzman Reynosos was a philosophy teacher who adopted China's Cultural Revolution as a model. He advocated revolution through terror and violence and hoped to win widespread peasant support and organize Peru's native people to help overthrow the country's Spanish-speaking élite. Sendero's violence failed to convince the peasantry and brought bloody reprisals against innocent villagers by the Peruvian military.

By 1992 Sendero's campaign of terror had caused 25,000 deaths and brought serious disruption to the nation's economy. Guzman was eventually captured by police in Lima in 1992 and was sentenced to life imprisonment.

SICKLE-CELL ANAEMIA

◆ Each year about 200,000 babies of African, Mediterranean and Asian descent are born with the disease.

◆ About 20,000 people die each year from sickle-cell anaemia.

◆ Deaths can be greatly reduced through early diagnosis.

Normal shape of red blood cell

Sickle-shaped cell

SICKLE-CELL ANAEMIA

A condition arising from an abnormal form of haemoglobin, the oxygen-carrying pigment of red blood cells. The disease was identified in 1910. It is hereditary and not contagious, affecting only people of African, Mediterranean and Asian descent.

When blood is deprived of oxygen the abnormal haemoglobin crystallizes and distorts the red cells into a sickle shape. These misshapen cells are removed from the blood in the spleen, eventually leading to anaemia. The deformed cells have a restricted capacity for carrying oxygen.

They cluster together and form blockages which cause intense pain, heart and lung seizures and blindness. About 20,000 people each year die from the disease and many others succumb to secondary infections. About 200,000 babies are born with the condition each year. Of those that survive through childhood, few live beyond the age of 40.

Those less severely affected do survive and 'carry' the disease. These individuals tend to have a built-in resistance, which may explain why sickle-cell anaemia is retained in the population. There is no satisfactory treatment. However, deaths can be reduced by up to 90% if the disease is diagnosed before the age of 4 months.

SINGLE MARKET

An economic area within which persons, goods, services and capital have unrestricted freedom of movement. This entails the elimination not only of customs and immigration barriers, but also of technical, tax, legislative and other obstacles.

SISAL

A plant of the agave family, the fibre of which is used for a variety of purposes. Sisal is native to Central America where its fibre has been used for centuries. The plant stems grow to about 1 metre in height with lance-shaped leaves forming a dense rosette. The plants grow best in well-drained soil in moist climates and are propagated from rhizomes (underground stems) of mature plants. Sisal matures 3-5 years after

Sisal sentinels

Sisal plants stand silent vigil in a Zimbabwean field. This crop, originally from Central America, is used to make nautical ropes and twine. SISAL

planting. Plants yield good-quality fibre for 7-8 years, producing about 300 leaves during the period. Initial harvests are about 70 leaves per plant, falling to an annual average of around 20. Fibre is produced from the leaves by crushing. Originally this was done by hand but is now done by passing the leaves through mechanized rolling machines.

The fibre is highly valued for its strength and durability and resists deterioration in saltwater. Because of this it is used extensively for making ropes for marine and shipping use. It is also used to make mats, brushes and hats. Commercial interest in the plant began when the first mechanized grain harvester was designed in the 1880s. This stimulated a massive demand for good quality, reliable twine. Plantations of sisal were quickly established in Tanzania and the Bahamas. By the 1940s it was widely cultivated in Angola, Mozambique, Taiwan, Brazil, Indonesia and elsewhere. Tanzania and Brazil are the world's largest producers.

SLAVERY

A condition in which a person is effectively owned and controlled by another. A slave was considered property in law and was deprived of most of the human rights ordinarily held by free people. Generally speaking slaves were of a different race, ethnicity, nationality or religion from their owners. Most were taken from their own society against their will.

The greater the difference between slave and owner, the worse the conditions for the slave and the fewer the human rights enjoyed. The degree of social isolation and maltreatment were usually worse in situations where the slave was black and the owner white.

Slavery has existed in various forms for centuries and probably began when humans opted for a

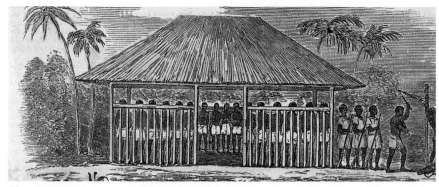

Short stay
A *barracoon* or slave lodge in Sierra Leone, pictured in 1849, where slaves were held before shipment to the plantations of the Americas. SLAVERY

pastoral rather than hunter-gatherer lifestyle. Enslavement usually arose through capture in battle, kidnapping, punishment for criminal acts, payment for debt, direct sale by a parent or guardian or by transfer from one master to another. As societies evolved from subsistence-level agriculture to a market-type where surpluses were produced, the status of slaves declined drastically.

Modern mass slavery began in the 15th century when the Spanish conquered the New World. Native Indians were put to work in the mines and fields established by the Spanish, but quickly died from disease and dreadful working conditions. To solve this problem, the Spanish began importing slaves from Africa in 1517. The first slaves were despatched to the West Indies and Brazil where sugar plantations had been started.

The first African slaves in North America landed in Virginia aboard a

Dutch ship in 1619. The English had established plantations of sugar, tobacco and cotton in the new colony and thousands of slaves were required. The number of slaves in Virginia quickly rose to 2,000 by 1681. By the mid-19th century the slave population in America was more than 4 million.

By then public opposition to slavery was spreading. The Anti-Slavery Society, founded in Britain in 1823, achieved freedom for slaves in British colonies by 1833 and France abolished slavery in its West Indian colonies in 1848.

In the northern US, slavery was banned in 1787, though it remained in the South where it became a cause of the American Civil War. The US finally put a stop to slavery in 1865. In 1980, Mauritania became the last country to officially abolish slavery. Slavery is no longer legally recognized or accepted by any of the world's governments.

SMITH, ADAM (1723-1790)
Scottish social philosopher and political economist educated in Scotland and at Oxford University in England. Smith's major work was *An Inquiry into the Nature and Causes of the Wealth of Nations* (1776). In it he analyzed the impact of competition in determining an economic system based on self-interest and completely transformed the subject of political economy. Smith suggested that there were great potential gains from trade and exchange and he praised the virtues of competition, rejecting the primacy of agricultural production in favour of manufacturing. He staunchly defended the concept of laissez-faire economics and argued that a market economy left to its own devices has a natural tendency toward equilibrium.

SMALLPOX
◆ So far only one killer disease, smallpox, has been eradicated by vaccine, saving approximately 5 million lives each year.

SMALLPOX

The only disease of major global significance to be eradicated by human action. Smallpox is an infectious viral disease marked by a skin rash that leaves permanent pitted scars. Symptoms are transmitted by direct contact and begin 8-18 days after infection. The initial symptoms of fever, prostration, severe headache and backache are followed by a rash. Secondary infections often prove fatal. There is no specific treatment but an attack of the disease, particularly during infancy, usually confers immunity. The development of a vaccine and widespread **immunization** programmes led to the eradication of the disease.

In 1967, smallpox was endemic in 31 countries. In that year alone between 10-15 million people were stricken with the disease. Of these, some 2 million died and millions of survivors were left either blind or disfigured. A global campaign in which 250 million people were vaccinated then took place and the disease disappeared. The last known case of smallpox was detected in Somalia in 1979.

SOCIALISM

A system of social organization where private property and the distribution of income are subject to control by society rather than being determined by individuals pursuing their own self-interest or by the market forces of **capitalism**. The term can also be applied to political movements which strive to establish this system.

Socialism comes in many variants. Some socialists advocate that all industries should be nationalized, while others claim that only the largest or most important should be owned and controlled by the state. Some socialist doctrines call for complete central control, others allow for more decentralization and still others for a directed manipulation of a market economy.

The word 'Socialism' was first coined about 1830 to describe ideas proposed by Fourier and Saint-Simon, who were French, and Robert Owen, British. Fourier described an economic unit and a community of people voluntarily joined in productive labour and contented living. Saint-Simon placed greater emphasis on the duty of the state to co-ordinate production. In contrast, Owen advocated a co-operative, competi-

Motherland calling!
Toidze's 1941 *Your Motherland Calls to You* is a brilliant example of the Soviet heroic poster. SOCIALISM

tion-free system designed to improve the welfare of all concerned.

In 1848, **Karl Marx** and Friedrich Engels authored the *Communist Manifesto*. In it they took the best of several forms of socialism and built a 'scientific' rather than 'utopian' model in which society would take control of all means of production. They used the word 'communism' to describe the classless society and in 1847 formed the Communist League, to distinguish it from the many socialist parties that existed at the time.

Twentieth-century socialism retained a rich diversity ranging from the strictly state-controlled example of the Soviet Union to the less centralized Yugoslavian model, where factory workers were involved in both governance and profit sharing. A brand of mild socialism was adopted in the welfare states of Sweden, Denmark and Britain – countries where socialist parties won political power and enacted policies aimed at bringing a reasonable standard of living to all members of society. Even non-socialist countries like the US adopted elements of national welfare.

In 1987, the era of *perestroika* (restructuring) began which saw the collapse of the Communist societies in the Soviet Union and Eastern Europe, all of which moved towards democratic free-market economies.

SOFT LOAN

A loan generally made as a form of **aid** or assistance to a developing nation. Soft loans are so-called because they carry a rate of interest significantly below the going market rate for a loan of similar risk.

SOIL

Soil is formed mainly through the weathering of bedrock, a natural and time-consuming process. The type of soil differs according to the rock from which it came. There are five main soil types: clay, sand, loam, peat and calcareous or chalky soil which is derived from limestone. All

Stonewalling
Stone lines or 'diguettes' like this one in Burkina Faso are a cheap and easy way to conserve water and soil. SOIL

soils contain organic matter, minerals and millions of living organisms. The depth of soil varies according to the prevailing climate, contour of the **land** and rainfall. Soil washed off mountains builds up in valleys and may be deep and very fertile. In general, though, it is the top few centimetres of precious topsoil that supports the food and fibre crops upon which the world depends. Soil formation occurs at a rate of about 1 millimetre every 100 years, or around 150 kilograms per hectare. Once removed it is only replaced very slowly. Since 1945 the per capita amount of productive cropland in the world has fallen by a third as topsoil has been lost or exhausted through overuse.

A 1990 **UN** report on global land degradation found that between 1945 and 1990 more than 15% of agricultural land was degraded to a point beyond restoration. With even modest yields, the lost land could have fed 1.5 billion people. Nearly two-thirds of it was in Africa and Asia. Recent increases in food production have largely been due to artificial replenishment of soil nutrients. For example **fertilizer** use has increased five-fold since the mid-1940s. During this period many of the world's farmers, notably those in the industrialized nations, have been mining the soil and growing food in a unsustainable manner.

The use of chemical fertilizers tends to degrade and exhaust topsoil, making it more prone to erosion. Organic fertilizer is better, organic farms having been shown to lose up to 4 times less soil per year than those using inorganic fertilizers. But it is not a long-term solution. Fallow periods, crop rotations and **intercropping**, all of which allow the soil to regenerate, have been abandoned in pursuit of profits and intensive cultivation of a single crop.

In many **developing countries**, agriculture is the mainstay of the economy and supports the majority

CRUMBLING EARTH

The world is losing seven million hectares of fertile land each year due to soil degradation, an area nearly as large as Ireland. Overgrazing is the single most prominent cause of soil damage.

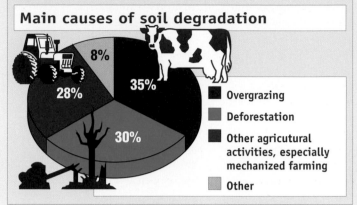

Main causes of soil degradation

- 8%
- 35%
- 28%
- 30%

- ■ Overgrazing
- ■ Deforestation
- ■ Other agricultural activities, especially mechanized farming
- ■ Other

The State of the Environment Atlas by Joni Seager, Penguin 1995.

of people. Yet the pursuit of an 'industrial' agriculture and the production of **cash crops** results in peasants being ejected from arable land. In addition, pastoralists are being forced to give up their traditional nomadic lifestyle and become sedentary farmers, placing extra stress on already impoverished soils.

Human action has caused the loss of vast amounts of irreplaceable soil at rates far in excess of replacement levels. On steep slopes in Ethiopia losses of 296 tonnes per hectare have been recorded.

In India the annual harvest depletes the soil of 18.5 million tonnes of nutrients while only 10 million tonnes, made up of organic waste and fertilizers, is replaced. Yet the country must somehow double its food output on this land if it is to feed its 1 billion citizens in the next few years.

SOIL EROSION

The surface layer of productive topsoil can be eroded from **land** by wind or **water**. Erosion is determined by a combination of climate, topography, **soil** type and vegetation cover. Humans can make it worse by stripping away vegetation. Soil lost to wind and water ranges from 5-10 tonnes per hectare annually in Africa, Europe and Australia to 10-20 tonnes per hectare in North, Central and South America and nearly 30 tonnes per hectare in Asia. About half the world's croplands are so badly managed that they are losing topsoil at the rate of 7% per decade seriously reducing fertility with possibly catastrophic consequences in the long-term.

Wind erosion: One of the key causes of **desertification**, wind erosion occurs when soil is left bare of vegetation. It is most severe in

Scaled heights

Trees and plants have been stripped from these Nepalese hills, leaving bare earth at the mercy of wind and rain. SOIL EROSION

Smallpox – Soil Erosion

arid and semi-arid lands exposed to overgrazing by livestock. Over 20% of Africa north of the equator and 35% of land in the Middle East is susceptible to erosion by wind. Top soil is stripped away and land, buildings, machinery and fences can be fully or partially buried or damaged. In extreme conditions up to 150 tonnes of soil can be blown from a hectare of land in an hour. Between them Africa and Asia lose almost a billion tonnes of soil annually through wind erosion.

The 'dust bowls' in the American west in the 1930s were caused by wind erosion and millions of hectares of productive land were lost. A single storm lasting 4 days in 1934 was reported to have blown away 300 million tonnes of soil.

Water erosion: Water erosion occurs wherever steep land is farmed or where sloping land is left exposed for any length of time. The UN **Food and Agriculture Organization** (FAO) estimates that about 25 billion tonnes of soil are lost to water erosion each year: 11% of Africa north of the equator is subject to water erosion as is 17% of the land in the Middle East and 90 million hectares of land in India.

Two of the world's major rivers, the Yangtze in China and the **Ganges** in India, transport around 3 billion tonnes of soil annually. Soil is washed into rivers where it can silt-up reservoirs and prevent hydro-electric plants from operating. It is also washed into coastal waters where it can destroy **fishing** grounds. Some estimates have placed the annual global loss of soil as high as 75 billion tonnes.

SOLAR CELLS

Solar cells, also called photovoltaic cells, convert sunlight directly to electricity and are rapidly becoming a viable source of electric power. Although they are manufactured from silicon, the second most abundant element in the earth's crust, they are still relatively expensive. However, as the technology becomes more efficient supporters believe solar electricity will compete directly in price with grid electricity. In 1994, a US-based manufacturer developed a triple-junction solar cell capable of generating power at 10-12 cents per kilowatt/hour. The goal is to produce electricity at 4 cents per kilowatt/hour by the year 2020, a price comparable to electricity produced by new **coal** or **natural gas** power plants.

When the solar cell industry began to flourish in the 1970s, the major **oil** companies initially lobbied strongly against it. They then proceeded to buy out most of the independent producers as well as the research and development organizations. By 1983 the 4 largest photovoltaic manufacturers controlled half the global market and were wholly owned by major **oil** companies. From 1990-1994, global shipments of solar cells jumped by more than 50% and the world market stood at close to $1 billion.

SOLAR POWER

The use of the sun's energy to provide heating or to generate electricity. A vast amount of solar energy falls on the earth each year. It can be harnessed to produce heat, cause chemical reactions or generate electricity. It can also be used directly: the most common and simplest method is the heating of **water** flowing through flat-plate panels exposed to the sun's rays. The panels are usually made of a blackened metal plate covered by glass. The rise in temperature of the exposed water is fairly small but it reduces the need for energy to produce hot water for space heating. Mirrors can also be used to concentrate the sun's rays to boil water in so-called solar furnaces.

The resulting steam can be used to drive a turbine, as at Odeillo in France where 20,000 mirrors are used to produce a temperature of 3,500°C. Because solar radiation at the earth's surface is diffuse, both types of collectors must have a large surface area: about 40 square metres to serve an average person for 1 day. Solar radiation can also be converted into electrical energy through the use of a solar or photovoltaic cell.

At present these **solar cells** are used mainly in small-scale operations, powering remote monitoring equipment in desert regions or in spacecraft and satellites. However, the potential for solar energy is enormous. Each day the earth receives 200,000 times the world's electricity-generating capacity in the form of solar energy.

Solar harvest
The sun can produce at least 1,000 times more usable energy than we currently need

♦ In OECD – or Western industrialized countries – the usable solar harvest is 170 times more than needed

♦ In the CIS – former USSR countries – the ratio is 400

♦ In the South – or Majority World – it is 950

OECD: 170 x need

CIS: 400 x need

SOUTH: 950 x need

Solar Power, Understanding Global Issues, 1996; Unlocking the Power of our Cities, Greenpeace, 1995.

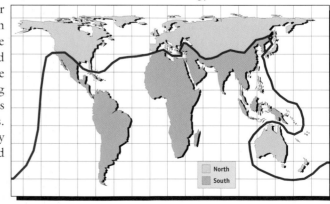

North
South

SOUTH

A term used to refer to those countries with low per capita incomes, also known as the 'less developed' countries or the **Third World**. The terms **North** and South are widely used to denote the 'rich' nations of the industrialized world and the 'poor' nations of the developing world. In the South/North demarcation formulated by the **Brandt Commission** in 1980, the 2 'rich' countries south of the equator, Australia and New Zealand, are considered part of the **North**.

SOUTH-EAST ASIA TREATY ORGANIZATION (SEATO)

A collective defence organization formed to protect south-east Asian countries from possible communist aggression. Analogous to the **North Atlantic Treaty Organization** (NATO). The SEATO treaty was signed in Manila in 1954 by Australia, France, New Zealand, Pakistan, the Philippines, Thailand, the United Kingdom and the United States. No joint action was ever taken under SEATO, although American, Australian, New Zealand, Filipino and Thai forces all fought in the **Vietnam War** during the 1960s. The organization was phased out in 1977 and replaced by the trade-oriented Association of South-East Asian Nations (ASEAN).

SOUTHERN AFRICAN DEVELOPMENT COMMUNITY (SADC)

An organization set up to promote regional co-operation and to fight racial discrimination, while lessening economic dependence on South Africa. The group's first conference was held in Lusaka in 1980. Membership included all the 'Front-Line' states bordering South Africa. Following that country's transition to democratic rule in 1992, South Africa became an integral member of the organization. Other members are Angola, Botswana, Lesotho, Malawi, Mozambique, Namibia, South Africa, Swaziland, Tanzania, Zambia and Zimbabwe.

SOUTH PACIFIC FORUM

Established in 1971 on the initiative of Fiji to provide a forum for political consultation between heads of government of the independent and self-governing countries of the South Pacific, Australia and New Zealand. Since its inception the members of the forum (Australia, Cook Islands, Fiji, Kiribati, Marshall islands, Micronesia, Nauru, New Zealand, Niue, Papua New Guinea, Solomon Islands, Tonga, Tuvalu, Vanuatu and Western Samoa) have been particularly concerned with the problem of nuclear testing in the region. The 1985 Treaty of Rarotonga established a South Pacific Nuclear Free Zone, but France refused to sign the treaty. The UK and the US agreed to abide by the terms set out in the treaty but also refused to sign.

THE PACIFIC – A VERY SPECIAL PLACE

The Pacific Ocean is the earth's largest single geographical feature and contains:

◆ three-quarters of its active volcanoes
◆ an estimated half of its remaining fish
◆ four-fifths of its islands
◆ a quarter (1,200) of its languages – 700 in Papua New Guinea alone
◆ enough water to swallow every landmass – and still leave room for another continent the size of Asia

The South Pacific region contains the earth's:

◆ highest ratio of ocean to land – 1 square *metre* of land per 10 square *kilometres* of ocean
◆ highest proportion of endemic species per unit of land area or per human inhabitant
◆ deepest marine trench – the Marianas Trench (at 11,000 metres almost half as deep again as Mount Everest is high)
◆ most diverse oceanic island chain – the Solomon Islands
◆ highest rate of deforestation – Western Samoa
◆ first nuclear-free constitution – Palau

SPECIAL DRAWING RIGHTS (SDR)

The accounts of the **International Monetary Fund** (IMF) are maintained in SDR units. SDRs were created in 1970 and were intended to replace gold and national currencies in settling international transactions. They are issued to members of the Fund from time to time in proportion to their quotas. SDRs are not money; they are potential overdraft facilities. Their value derives from their convertibility to foreign exchange. They can be exchanged through the IMF for national currencies or held by a country as a reserve asset. They are not used commercially and are only traded between central banks and the **Bank of International Settlements**.

Members of the IMF have the right to draw on the fund to finance balance-of-payments deficits. SDRs, unlike normal loans, do not have to be repaid and therefore form a permanent addition to a country's reserves. They function as an international reserve currency and supplement its holdings of gold and convertible currencies. SDRs are a composite currency unit computed as a weighted average of the 5 most widely-traded international currencies: the dollar (US), yen (Japan), deutschmark (Germany), franc (France) and pound sterling (United Kingdom). Their advantage over gold and other reserve currencies is that their supply can be controlled and their worth is not so closely tied to gold deposits or dependent on the US balance-of-payments or strength of the US dollar.

SPECULATION, FINANCIAL

Buying and selling of something with a view to making a profit as a result of price changes. The specula-tor makes no contribution to the economy, either as a producer or a distributor. Moreover, the specula-tor not only profits from instabilities, he or she may also cause or encourage them.

STOCKHOLM CONFERENCE

Common name for the UN Conference on the Human Environment, held in 1972 and attended by representatives from 113 nations. The Stockholm Conference is considered to be a major landmark in the development of global environmental concern. The Conference resulted in the formation of the **United Nations Environment Programme** (UNEP), an important monitoring and watchguard body. However, UNEP's ability to force environ-mental change has been limited by its reluctance to criticize those gov-ernments which provide the bulk of its funding.

STOCKHOLM PEACE RESEARCH INSTITUTE (SIPRI)

An organization established in 1966 by the Swedish government to carry out scientific research into all aspects of peace and security. SIPRI special-izes in **disarmament** and **arms control**; military technology; a co-operative security system for Europe; Russia's security agenda; preventive diplomacy; military spending; international **peacekeep-ing**; chemical and biological weapons; and nuclear testing and

weapons proliferation. Its activities and reports have become the basis for other projects such as those implemented by the Independent Commission for Disarmament, commonly referred to as the Palme Commission.

STRATEGIC ARMS LIMITATION TREATY (SALT)

The **League of Nations**, the fore-runner of the **United Nations**, first attempted to introduce a programme to reduce armaments in 1930.

After World War II and the massive build-up of arms that followed, US President Lyndon Johnson proposed a Strategic Arms Limitation Treaty (SALT) with the Soviet Union in 1967. Agreement was delayed by Soviet intervention in Czechoslovakia but the first SALT I treaty finally came into force in 1972.

An updated SALT II treaty was approved but never ratified. Several further agreements were made between the US and the Soviet Union to try and reduce the number of intermediate range nuclear weapons, strategic arms and weapons in outer space. The Intermediate Range Nuclear Force Treaty (INF) of 1987 was the first to actually require weapons to be removed and destroyed.

STREET CHILDREN

A term applied to young children who, for one reason or another, are forced to either live or work on the streets. In **developing countries** an estimated 100 million children between 5 and 18 spend most of their lives in the streets. Many actually live at home but are forced out to earn money to help support their family. The work they do is menial and low-income: begging, shining shoes, **prostitution**, selling newspapers and cigarettes or

Why aren't they in school?

Children not in school are likely to be working and one in five of the world's children aged 6 to 11 is not attending school – around 140 million.

● The proportions of children out of school are much higher in South Asia and Sub-Saharan Africa, where enrolment in primary school is still very low. In Latin America enrolment is higher but many more children than elsewhere drop out early.

● The single biggest reason why the world has not succeeded in delivering universal primary education to all its children is that it has not invested enough resources in decent schooling. Sub-Saharan Africa currently pays $12 billion in servicing its debts – yet just $2 billion would be enough to offer all the region's children a place in school.

The State of the World's Children 1997, UNICEF.

cleaning windscreens. The remainder live full time on the streets, trying to exist as best they can with little or no adult support.

The work of street children may be dangerous, but their meagre income is crucial to the survival of millions of families in the **South**. In a survey of Jamaican street children, a third were the only working

Mean streets
A child in Thailand faces another day shining shoes, selling cigarettes or his body on the streets of Bangkok – he's one of 100 million or so street kids in the world.
STREET CHILDREN

member of their household.

The common response to the proliferation of street children try and institutionalize street kids: to put them in homes, schools or residential facilities where their welfare can be improved. However, in some countries street children are the target of torture and murder by so-called 'death squads' – vigilante groups whose answer to increasing street-crime is to kill children living rough. Over 5,000 children in Brazil have been killed by such death squads, some of which were believed to be private security forces. Similar killings were reported in South Africa, Colombia, Haiti, Guatemala and Thailand.

In 1986, **UNICEF** called for an international **non-governmental organization** (NGO) to look out for the welfare of street kids. This led to CHILDHOPE, an NGO which seeks to address the needs of street children and serve as an international centre to co-ordinate services for them. At the same time street children in Brazil organized the Movement for Street Boys and Girls, an advocacy group with significant political and social power, with a membership of more than 80,000 street kids.

STRUCTURAL ADJUSTMENT LOAN

Large loans made by the **World Bank** and the **IMF** to **Third World** countries which carry strict financial and budgetary obligations. In 1992, nearly 75% of the World Bank's $22 billion budget went into Structural Adjustment Programme (SAP) loans.

The required 'reforms' are intended to open up the recipient economy to private investment and to make the country more competitive in the global economy. They usually include reducing barriers to foreign imports and the promotion of 'free market' policies while relaxing state controls. Recipient governments must also direct spending away from social services like education and healthcare towards export businesses and **debt** servicing. Governments are generally forced to privatize public industries and, on occasion, to devalue local currencies. They may also postpone plans for economic self-sufficiency and instead focus on their area of 'competitive advantage'.

As a result of the imposition of SAPs, real wages fall, **unemployment** rises and the price of imported manufactured goods places them out of the reach of most of the local population. The theory is that more exports will eventually create more wealth which will 'trickle-down' (see **Trickle-Down Development**) to the poor. In fact, the poor suffer directly from structural adjustment: they tend to lose jobs, income and public services and see their cost of living rise.

SUGAR

A sweet, crystalline substance obtained from various plants and available in several forms. Sugar production is believed to have begun in India around 5,000 years ago.

It is grown essentially as a luxury in the human diet, but every country has developed a taste for it. The Western world consumes huge quantities – around 50 kilograms (kg) – per person annually although consumption is declining. In parts of Africa, such as

You should insist on **TATE & LYLE'S PACKET SUGAR**

because it is the best and purest sugar obtainable. Every packet of Tate and Lyle's sugar is guaranteed full net weight and to be of uniform high quality. Obtainable in Cube, Granulated, Caster and Preserving.

Also ask for

LYLE'S GOLDEN SYRUP

It is a food of very great nutriment and yields the full muscular energy of pure sugar. Give your children plenty of bread spread with Lyle's Golden Syrup.

SEND FOR THIS BOOK NOW!

free Write now for the interesting recipe book "SOME EVERYDAY DISHES." Post free on request from Dept. G.H.1, TATE & LYLE LTD., 21, Mincing Lane, London, E.C.3

C.F.H.

Egypt, average consumption is 30 kg per person and rising. World consumption has risen by 1 million tonnes a year over the last century. Recent growth in **population** and incomes in Latin America, the Middle East and Asia has sparked a demand for soft drinks and processed foods, so consumption in these regions has increased significantly. Sugar is one of the most politically and socially sensitive of all crops. All commercially-produced sugar used to come from sugar cane which is grown on large-scale **plantations** in tropical and subtropical regions. By-products from the processing of sugar cane, such as molasses and bagasse have a variety or uses including fuels, animal food-stuffs and paper making.

In the past, sugar was intimately associated with the slave trade and, later, indentured labour. In some parts of the world, cane plantation workers are still low paid and have little **employment** protection. The general decline in the global sugar

SUGAR PRODUCTION	
EU	16.8 million tonnes
India	15.0 million tonnes
Brazil	12.0 million tonnes
Cuba	4.0 million tonnes

Every last drop
Distillery workers in Dominica feed the crusher with sugar-cane, squeezing out the sweet juice to make rum. SUGAR

trade over the last 20 years led to 60,000 small-scale sugar growers in the Philippines losing their livelihood and has had a similar effect elsewhere in the Third World. Declining sugar prices are largely due to policies adopted by industrialized countries.

To compete with cane sugar, Europeans began to grow sugar beets – mainly in Western Europe and the ex-Soviet Union. Sugar beet is not economically competitive with sugar cane but tends to be grown as an import-substitution crop. In the mid-1970s, the European Community was importing a million tonnes of sugar annually. Now, due to subsidized sugar beets, the EC exports up to 5 million tonnes at reduced prices, depressing the price of sugar on the world market in the process.

There are around 100 major sugar-producing countries which means there is global overproduction and depressed markets. This is despite efforts to impose export quotas and stabilize prices. Sugar prices have been drifting downwards

for several decades and only 20% of all sugar is sold at world prices. Many importing countries pay above the world benchmark for sugar from favoured nations.

Some countries like Brazil are faced with over-production and depressed prices. So they put their sugar crop to other uses – like converting it to alcohol for use as a fuel. Around 10 billion litres is fermented from sugar in Brazil and many vehicles, especially taxis, have been converted to run on the alcohol-based fuel known as gasohol.

Around 118 million tonnes of sugar are produced annually. The European Union is the biggest producer (16.8 million tonnes) while India (15 million tonnes) is the leading producer in the developing world. Brazil produces 12 million tonnes, some of which is destined for gasohol production. Cuba, which produces 4 million tonnes annually, is facing major difficulties. The island nation used to sell half its sugar to the USSR at 10 times the world prices. But with the break-up of the Soviet Bloc that

lucrative market has now dried up.

Recently, artificial sweeteners and those made by genetically-engineered organisms have begun to have a major impact on the global sugar market. Prices will continue to fall as long as the glut of over-production continues.

SULPHUR DIOXIDE
One of the most widespread atmospheric pollutants in industrialized countries, sulphur dioxide (SO_2) is released into the atmosphere chiefly through the combustion of sulphur-containing fossil fuels. SO_2 is a corrosive gas and a major cause of acid rain. It is emitted by natural sources, such as volcanoes and decaying organic matter as well as through human activities.

Global emissions of SO_2 have been rising for 100 years – from less than 10 million tonnes in 1860 to around 150 million tonnes in the mid-1980s. Burning fossil fuels release approximately 70 million tonnes of sulphur per year while another 70 million tonnes are released naturally. A further 10 million tonnes come from industry.

The environmental impact of SO_2 emissions was first recognized in the 1970s. Following international pollution-control agreements, several countries managed to reduce their emissions in the period 1970-85 by switching to cleaner fuels for power plants. Using low-sulphur coal and low-sulphur oil is the quickest way to reduce SO_2 emissions, but supplies of both are limited.

It is also possible to remove sulphur from fossil fuels but it's expensive – around $30 for a tonne of heating oil for example. The cost of removing sulphur raises the price of electricity by 15%. Various advanced 'fluidized bed' technologies, in which coal is burned more efficiently, also allow sulphur emissions to be reduced by the addition of limestone or dolomite to

SUKARNO, ACHMED (1901-1970)

Indonesian nationalist and politician. Son of a poor schoolteacher, he was skilled at languages and later became interested in mysticism which may explain his tremendous popular following later in life. He graduated as a civil engineer in 1927 and soon became involved in the Indonesian independence struggle. He was arrested for his nationalist activities and spent 2 years in jail followed by nearly 14 years in exile (1929-1942).

When the Japanese invaded in 1942, he welcomed them as liberators, using his position to press the Japanese for independence. In 1945 he announced the doctrine of 'Pantjasila' which was to become the country's guiding ideology based on nationalism, internationalism, democracy, social prosperity and belief in God.

He declared Indonesia's independence later the same year and the Dutch reluctantly transferred sovereignty to Sukarno in 1949. The Indonesian independence movement was an important example for other Third World countries and Sukarno was one of the main leaders of the pro-Third World movement. In 1955, the city of Bandung played host to a meeting of heads of government, giving rise to the Non-Aligned Movement. In 1956, he dismantled parliamentary democracy and introduced a dictatorial reign of 'Guided Democracy' based on his interpretation of Pantjasila. His personal excesses incensed many and he narrowly avoided several assassination attempts.

Sukarno launched nationalist development programs and created a state petroleum company. In 1965 he nationalized all Indonesian oil deposits. With inflation driving up the cost-of-living to record highs, Sukarno broke with both the Soviet Union and the United Sates and withdrew from the United Nations. Later that year, he was implicated in a attempt to oust a number of top military officers opposed to his rule. In September of the same year a small force of soldiers led by General Suharto seized power under the pretext of 'stemming the communist tide'. The bloody coup left nearly 700,000 dead and another 200,000 imprisoned. In 1966 Sukarno was forced to delegate his power to Suharto who took over as president in 1968.

the bed mixture. In 1988 the European Community (EC) passed the Large Combustions Plant Directive through which member nations were obliged to cut SO^2 emissions by 57% by the year 2003. During the 1980s, Austria cut its SO^2 emissions by 75%, Germany by 67%, Sweden by 60% and Norway by 57%. Progress has been good because most of the emissions can be controlled simply by regulating power generation. Overall, European SO^2 emissions fell 40% from 1980-1993. Nonetheless, surveys of acid rain damage in the early 1990s found more than 25% defoliation in Germany's forests, 55% in Poland's forests and 28% in Norway's.

In 1980, two-thirds of global sulphur emissions were in Europe and North America. On a per capita basis, Canada (119 kilograms/kg), the US (81 kg) and Germany (71 kg) are the worst polluters. As cleaner technologies were adopted in these regions, sulphur emissions in developing countries began to form a greater percentage of the global total. Around 75% of China's energy needs are currently met by burning high-sulphur 'brown' coal using old-fashioned technologies.

SUSTAINABLE DEVELOPMENT

Ultimately, all economic development depends on the earth's natural resource base. It is the primary biological production generated by photosynthesis that sustains the human race and virtually every other life form. Maintaining this biological productivity is therefore the key to sustainability. It is also crucial that the needs of the present are met without compromising the ability of future generations to meet their needs. That is why sustainable development implies limits. To be 'sustainable', development must meet human needs without depleting resources or irrevocably damaging the systems which produce those resources. Under present conditions, organic matter equivalent to 40% of the primary production of the earth's ecosystems is being consumed by humans. If the world population doubles humans will devour as much biological material as is produced each year. At this level of exploitation the quality of the environment and, consequently, of human life will quickly decline. The World Commission on Environment and Development defines sustainable development as a 'process of change in which the exploitation of resources, the direction of investments, the orientation of technological development and institutional change are all in harmony and enhance both current and future potential to meet human needs and aspirations'.

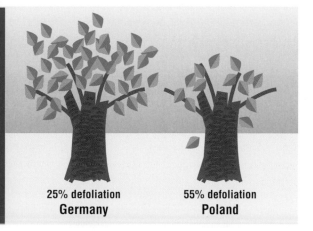

Leafless trees and acid rain

Although European SO^2 emissions fell by 40% between 1980 and 1993, trees are still being damaged.

25% defoliation
Germany

55% defoliation
Poland

Traditional Medicine

Fly-whisk at his feet, this Tuareg traditional healer sets out his treatments of ground roots and herbs in Bamako, Mali.

Bold indicates a cross-reference

TAXES

A levy placed by the state on the property or income of its citizens and corporations. Societies need to address common needs and problems like roads, sewers, street lighting, schools, wildlife **conservation** and public health. These have to be paid for from the public purse and taxes are the means through which this money is raised. Militant free marketers believe wealth is the creation of individual initiative and that the wealthy owe little to those around them. Yet in a sense all wealth is common wealth since individual wealth-creating efforts are founded on a social apparatus which is the creation of millions of people and scores of generations.

Food and manual labour were the original form of wealth. Peasants were forced to pay a tithe from their harvests or to serve as soldiers or builders for those who controlled the state. As trade increased, it became easier to levy taxes on the sale of **commodities** like salt, especially as there were fewer taxpayers involved. Sales taxes remain an important source of cash for governments today, accounting for about 20% of all revenues. Yet, sales taxes are 'regressive' taxes: they have a greater impact on the poor than the rich. Part of the justification for taxation in the modern world is to wipe out inequalities in the distribution of wealth. This is called 'progressive' taxation: when the rich pay a proportionately greater share of

TAX TALK – A GLOSSARY

● **PROGRESSIVITY**
The phrase used to describe the steepness of the tax rate as you move up the income scale. A rate of 19% on the lowest taxable incomes and a rate of 28% on the highest is not very progressive while a low rate of 15% and a high rate of 65% is.

● **TAX INCIDENCE**
Who ends up actually paying a tax. If landlords or businesses have the ability to pass on taxes in the form of price and rent hikes the tax incidence falls on someone else.

● **TAX EXPENDITURES**
Indirect government spending – the result of not collecting taxes. For example tax breaks on mortgages and other interest costs are available to taxpayers in many countries although companies and large investors profit most from this loophole. This type of government spending by not collecting tends to escape public scrutiny.

● **DIRECT AND INDIRECT TAXES**
Direct taxes are geared to the individual's income, profit or wealth and are to some extent based on ability to pay. Indirect taxes are levied on particular goods (as with taxes like the VAT or GST), imports or exports (a favourite Third World form of taxation) or sin taxes on alcohol, gasoline and tobacco – regardless of the individual's ability to pay.

● **TAX HAVENS**
Low-tax jurisdictions like Switzerland, Panama and Hong Kong, where companies and some wealthy individuals arrange to maintain their investments or maintain branches so their profits can surface in a low-tax environment.

● **BASE AND RATE**
The tax base is the income or economic activity that is subject to tax and the rate indicates how much tax is due from each source. Some tax systems have high rates but have a narrow base, allowing for example, generous deduction of business expenses. Other tax systems have a wide base with few exemptions and lower rates.

● **TAX SHELTERS**
A way in which the taxpayer can park their income in a particular kind of investment such as retirement savings used by many or tax-exempt foundations for the wealthy few. The theory is that this parked income will be taxable at some later date that is more advantageous to the taxpayer.

their income in taxes than the poor.

Through the ages, the costs of **war** have soaked up a huge amount of tax money. In the United Kingdom, income tax from the period 1799-1815 was used mostly to pay for the Napoleonic wars. In the US, income tax was used to pay for the Civil War in the 1860s. Taxes on income, profits and sales became the normal form of taxation in Western nations by the mid-1940s.

In **developing countries**, most people and businesses do not earn enough to justify the expense of computing incomes and profits. In India, for example, 75% of government revenue comes from taxes on imports, exports and sales and the wealthy largely escape paying taxes. The difference in personal taxation between the 'developed' and 'developing' worlds is stark. In 1994 the German Government raised 50 times as much revenue per citizen as the Indian Government.

Globally, taxation raises $7.5 trillion annually, equivalent to around a third of all economic output. Most of that comes from charges on production. In ancient times, only basic

necessities such as food were taxed. Since farmers needed to feed their families, they would not produce less simply because they knew they would have to pay a tithe. Today, most taxes on productive activities such as work and commerce tend to discourage the activities they tax and drastically affect economies and living standards. This contradiction has stimulated thinking around environmental or 'green' taxes which tax 'bads' instead of 'goods'. Studies in Britain and the US found that replacing existing taxes on **employment**, incomes and profits ('goods') with taxes on energy use ('bad') can yield a 3-fold dividend: better overall national economic performance; higher levels of **employment**; and a cleaner environment.

In 1993 the European Commission encouraged member governments to levy 'green' taxes on energy and water use and on emissions of carbon gases. The idea was to reduce both resource consumption and pollution. By the late 1990s, environmental-protection taxes were found in many countries including the UK, the Netherlands and China. In Western Europe these taxes led to 35% reduction in **sulphur dioxide** emissions.

Since their introduction, taxes have been used by the powerful to protect themselves. That is still the case today. Many industrialized nations, supporters of free-market systems, impose heavy tariffs on goods produced in the developing world in order to protect their own industries and workers. There are many ways by which the wealthy avoid paying taxes.

Tax havens, transfer pricing by corporations, currency speculation – all these make it difficult for the tax collector to track down funds. **Capital flight** hits **Third World** countries hard, given their limited ability to keep track of sophisticated dealings. Ultimately, there must be a series of international tax agreements effectively outlawing tax havens if capital is to be prevented from playing one country off against another in an effort to minimize the money going into the public purse.

TEA

The dried leaves and shoots of an evergreen shrub (*camellia sinensis*) which yield a beverage when infused with **water**. The drink has a stimulating effect due to its caffeine content (about 3.5%). Native to parts of India and China, the tea plant has 3 major varieties (China, Assam and Cambodia) and numerous hybrids.

Fingertip touch

In the blazing sunlight, the deft fingers of a Sri Lankan tea-picker pluck the shiny tender green leaves from the top of the bush. Tea is one of the most popular drinks in the world, but tea-pickers earn very little for their labours. TEA

Tea is a valuable, labour-intensive export crop which is grown at 1,500-2,200 metres altitude on well-drained **soil** in areas with an annual rainfall of around 1,400 millimetres. Young leaves are plucked by hand when the plant is about 5 years old.

Black tea is made from dried leaves, broken up to release the essential oils and allowed to ferment before the moisture is removed in ovens. Green tea is steamed and quickly dried before fermentation can occur. About half of the total annual production of tea is consumed in the countries of origin, the rest is exported.

The world's leading exporting nations are India which produces 744,000 tonnes and Sri Lanka where annual production is around 244,000 tonnes. Most of the tea grown in China (about 588,000 tonnes) is drunk at home. India, China and the United Kingdom are the world's main tea drinking nations.

Asian countries produce 75% of the world's tea. However, a handful of European and American firms control 90% of the tea traded on the world market. Sri Lanka earns more than half its export earnings from tea and thus suffers most from fluctuations in the global market. Over the last decade the price of tea has fallen by 25% in real terms. The demand of European and North American consumers for cheap tea and the stranglehold of **transnational corporations** on the global market means

that tea is vastly underpriced. Consequently, workers on **plantations** in Asia and East Africa are poorly paid with few rights.

Third World tea producers in 1993 formed the International Tea Committee (ITC). Member states account for 75% of global production but the ITC is not a policy-making or negotiating body. Its activities are limited to data collection on production and consumption.

TEHRI DAM

A controversial dam project in the Himalayas in northern India. It is the first of a series of **dams** planned for the Bhagirathi and Bhilangana, major rivers that feed the **Ganges**. If completed the 260-metre high dam will be the highest in India and the seventh highest in the world.

The 'rock-fill' dam system will generate an estimated 2,400 megawatts of electricity and irrigate 660,000 hectares of **land**. However, the reservoir behind the dam will flood the town of Tehri and 23 other villages and force the resettlement of over 70,000 people. In addition, 1,000 hectares of cultivable land and 1,000 hectares of forest will disappear under **water**.

The dam has been sited in an area that has a history of intense seismic activity and critics of the scheme claim the weight of the impounded water (around 3.2 billion tonnes) will trigger earthquakes. Engineers claim the dam will operate for up to 100 years while opponents say the build-up of silt could render the dam useless in 25 years. With the forced relocation of the townspeople imminent, the Indian Government has yet to undertake a full, independent review of the project.

TERMS OF TRADE

A phrase used to describe the ratio between export prices and import prices, calculated as the unit value of

TERMS OF TRADE*
*How much you earn for what you export, compared with what you pay for imports (selected countries).

Mozambique, Tanzania and Bangladesh export mainly primary commodities (like coffee, sisal and jute). Thailand and Brazil have increasingly moved from primary commodities to manufactured goods.

EXPORT EARNINGS ($ million)			COST OF IMPORTS ($ million)	
1980	1995		1980	1995
281	169	MOZAMBIQUE	800	784
511	639	TANZANIA	1,250	1,619
793	3,173	BANGLADESH	2,600	6,496
6,510	56,459	THAILAND	9,210	70,776
20,100	46,506	BRAZIL	25,000	53,783
21,900	52,692	AUSTRALIA	24,400	61,280
226,000	584,743	US	257,000	770,852

World Development Report 1997, World Bank.

a nation's exports over the unit value of its imports. This ratio can then provide an indication of the 'purchasing power' of a country's exports. An improvement in the terms of trade means that export prices have increased compared to imports, or import prices have fallen compared to exports. When terms of trade are falling, fewer foreign products can be purchased with the income generated by exports. Most **Third World** nations are primary producers, dependent on the export of agricultural **commodities** like **coffee**, **sugar** and **cocoa**. The prices of these commodities are determined by market forces beyond the control of the producing country. These prices fell dramatically during the 1980s. In 1992 terms of trade for most commodity-dependent nations reached their lowest point this century.

TERRORISM

Terrorism is 'the use of violence on non-combatant, unarmed, defenceless individuals in the name of religious, national or political aspirations'. The phrase was first used during the French Revolution to describe the Jacobin 'Reign of Terror' (1793-1794) and was meant to describe any violent act perpetrated against civilians by those in power, to inspire fear for political reasons. Since then the exact definition has become blurred. Terrorism was widely used in anti-colonial struggles after World War II in countries like Palestine, Kenya, Cyprus, Algeria, Angola and Mozambique. The 1960s and early 1970s saw a proliferation of terrorist groups who received global media attention. In Western Europe the most notorious of these was Germany's Red Army Faction (or Baader-Meinhof Gang). In Latin America, especially during the 1960s and 1970s, radical political groups used terrorism as a means of advancing their cause while right-wing vigilante groups murdered and terrorized thousands of civilians in an effort to crush political opponents.

Today, terrorism is used largely by ethnic and religious minorities in search of national **self-determina-**tion – examples include the **PLO** (Palestine), IRA (Ireland), ETA (Spain) and the Tamil Tigers (Sri Lanka). In recent years new 'single issue' groups (animal liberationists, environmentalists and anti-abortion campaigners) have occasionally resorted to terrorist tactics. In addition, state-sponsored terrorism continues in an effort to repress political dissidents and enforce social conformity. Over 50 **Third World** governments could be accused of state terrorism with Algeria, Guatemala, Liberia and Indonesia among the worst offenders.

THIRD WORLD

A term applied collectively to the nations of Africa, Asia, Latin America (including the Caribbean) and Oceania (excluding Australia and New Zealand) which are industrially underdeveloped and economically weak. Although Third World countries comprise about 80% of the world's **population**, they are responsible for less than 30% of global industrial production. The term 'Third World' was first coined by French demographer Alfred Sauvy in 1952. *Tiers Monde*, an academic quarterly launched in Paris in 1956, used the term to suggest a parallel between the *Tiers Monde*

Violent deaths in Northern Ireland

Total deaths in The Troubles 1969 - 1993
3,284

Perpetrated by:

Loyalist paramilitary **27.7%**

British forces **10.9%**

Republican paramilitary **58.6%**

Others (includes: hunger strikers, riot victims, unattributed murders) **2.8%**

CIVILIANS KILLED BY: Loyalist paramilitaries – 871 (95.7% of their victims); Republican paramilitaries – 829 (43.1% of their victims); British forces – 203 (56.9% of their victims).

Republican paramilitary groups (particularly the IRA) have been responsible for more than half the killings, but Loyalist paramilitaries count a far higher proportion of civilians among their victims.

Bear in Mind These Dead: An Index of Deaths from the Conflict 1969-1993 by Sutton, Beyond the Pale, Belfast 1993.

THANT, U (1909-1974)
Burmese diplomat who served as acting Secretary-General of the **United Nations** following the death of **Dag Hammarskjöld** in 1961. U Thant then held the post in his own right from 1962-71. He played an important negotiating role in resolving the US-Soviet crisis over the installation of Soviet missiles in Cuba in 1963 and was later responsible for the controversial decision to withdraw UN Peacekeeping forces from the Egypt-Israel border in 1967 during the Arab-Israeli War.

(the world of the poor countries) and the *Tiers Etat* (the third estate or common people of the French Revolutionary era), a group of people deprived of privileges.

During the 1950s the world's nations divided roughly into three groups. The North American/European 'Western bloc' (or **First World**) and the Soviet-led 'Eastern bloc' (or **Second World**) had most of the world's economic and military power and were engaged in a tense ideological competition. The Third World countries in Latin America, Africa, southern Asia and the Pacific had just broken free of colonial rule and were concerned with their own position rather than the tug-of-war between East and West. Today the term Third World has less meaning following the break-up of the Soviet Union and many refer to the **South** (as opposed to the industrial nations of the **North**) or the Majority World instead.

THREE GORGES PROJECT
The Three Gorges hydro-electric project in China, first proposed over 30 years ago, involves construction of the world's biggest **dam** (2 kilometres long and 175 metres

high). Located on the Yangtze River the dam is designed to produce 14,700 megawatts of electricity. Supporters say it will supply much-needed electricity, make the river navigable for ocean-going vessels and prevent flooding (the last major flood in 1954 reportedly killed 330,000 people). Opponents disagree.

They note that the Yangtze is one of the most silt-laden rivers in the world, carrying 450 million tonnes of sediment annually and that silt build-up would soon block hydro-electric production altogether. The dam's reservoir would flood 10 cities and partially flood 8 others. Over 440 square kilometres (32,000 hectares) of farmland would be drowned and 1.2 million people would have to be resettled. Some 80 **fish** species and wetland habitats would be threatened and rare Chinese river dolphins and alligators would face extinction. The weight of dammed **water** could also trigger earthquakes. Successive Chinese governments have backed the scheme and a 1987 Canadian study for the **World Bank**, which considered financing the project, concluded that the dam was 'technically, financially and economically achievable'. In 1989 intense

Shape of things to come
With colourful red and yellow hard-hats, building workers toil on the construction of China's ambitious – but controversial new dams. THREE GORGES PROJECT

criticism by more than 100 Chinese scientists along with stiff opposition by Western environmentalists forced the Chinese Government to shelve the plan. But within a year Chinese authorities began to look at the scheme again. In 1992, despite widespread opposition, the National People's Congress gave the final green light. The total bill for the project is put at between $17-75 billion. The World Bank eventually abandoned the scheme when research revealed that silt build-up would destroy the dam's turbine within 10 years. Nevertheless, construction is now underway, scheduled for completion in 2009. In 1996, Japan decided to offer loans and trade insurance to any Japanese company wanting to work on the project. And the Chinese Government has imposed a 2% electricity tax to help fund the scheme.

THREE MILE ISLAND
(see also Nuclear Power)
Located on the Shenandoah River in the US state of Pennsylvania, the island is the site of a **nuclear power** station containing 2 Pressurized Water Reactors (PWR). In 1979, several water-coolant feed pumps in the facility failed; although the reactor closed itself down, emergency **water** supply lines were blocked. The nuclear reaction in the fuel core continued and, compounded by human error, the heat built up to a point where the uranium fuel itself may have begun to melt. The likelihood of a massive explosion and subsequent release of vast amounts of **radioactivity** forced the evacuation of people within a 8-kilometre radius.

It was 2 years before workers could go back inside the plant and clean-up costs – originally estimated at $1 billion – are still rising. When the reactor is finally decontaminated the building will be entombed in concrete. More than 2,000 people

Meltdown!
Under a leaden sky, the Three Mile Island nuclear power plant looks dull and safe – but in 1979 the reactor faltered and almost caused a mighty nuclear explosion.
THREE MILE ISLAND

are seeking damages from the companies that either owned, operated or supplied materials to the plant. In 1996, the US Supreme Court ruled that the claimants are entitled to sue for both punitive and compensatory damages.

TIDAL POWER

The use of natural tides to drive turbines and generate electricity. Large tidal flows are needed to make the process economically viable, so schemes are usually restricted to bays or estuaries on ocean coasts. Although capital costs for tidal power are high, operating costs are low. The units generate large amounts of power and have long working lifetimes. There are 6 tidal power stations now operating: 3 in China, 1 in the Soviet Union, 1 in Canada and 1 in France. The first, biggest and best-known installation was built in 1961 across the Rance estuary in France, with 24 large, reversible turbines, each capable of generating 10,000 kilowatts, in a **dam** 750-metres long. The turbines operate on both ebb and flow tides and produce 500 million kilowatt/hours per year. Although

tidal power appears to be a non-polluting and sustainable source of energy, little is known about possible long-term environmental effects.

TILAPIA

The 100 species of tilapia are freshwater fishes of the Cichlid family. Most tilapia are large-headed, deep-bodied **fish** which grow up to 30 centimetres in length. They are 'mouth breeders' – hatching fertilized eggs in their mouths. Tilapia are important as food in many **Third World** countries where they are eaten directly or sold in local markets. They occur in large numbers in the lakes and rivers of Africa with major fisheries in Lakes Victoria, Chad and Nyasa. They are also found in Latin America, India, China and parts of the Middle East. In some places, tilapia are the only food source containing animal protein. As they eat almost any vegetation or insect they are excellent candidates for **fish farming** and form the backbone of inland **aquaculture** in many **developing countries**.

TOBACCO

The most commonly-used and widely-distributed drug in the world is one which damages both the natural environment and human health. Its use is legal in all countries even though it is potentially lethal. The leaves of the tobacco plant (*nicotiana*) are used for making cigars, cigarettes, snuff and chewing wads. Climate greatly affects the quality of the leaves and optimum growth occurs where the temperature is between 18-27°C. Although tobacco originated in tropical America, the bulk of world production occurs outside the tropics. The world's major producers are China (2.3 million tonnes), the US (604,000 tonnes) and Brazil (454,000 tonnes).

Tobacco is one of the world's

most important crops. It accounts for 1.5% of total agricultural exports and generates an estimated $3 billion in annual profits. It is also the Third World's eighth largest agricultural export earner. The crop has no nutritional value and yet is grown in countries where **hunger** is rife. It ruins **soil**, taking out 11 times more nitrogen, 36 times more phosphorus and 24 times more potassium than most food crops. It also requires huge inputs of nutrients, **fertilizer** and **pesticides**. After harvesting, leaves are dried in the sun or in hot air for up to 2 months and then fermented for 4-6 weeks. Around half of all tobacco is flue-cured over wood fires – an extremely wasteful process. Over a million hectares of open forest are stripped yearly for this purpose and 55 cubic metres of wood are burned for every tonne of tobacco cured.

Tobacco smoke consists of tar droplets, various gases including carbon monoxide, and nicotine. Nicotine is one of the most addictive drugs known. Each cigarette is believed to shorten the life of a regular smoker by 5 minutes. As smoking increases, the chances of heart disease, lung and mouth **cancer**, strokes, bronchitis and other life-threatening conditions rise. Tobacco-related diseases kill an estimated 3 million people annually making tobacco the largest single preventable cause of death. Rising awareness of the dangers of smoking, coupled with a government-imposed suppression of advertizing, has led to a decrease in consumption of around 1% per year in **developed countries**. In the developing world, governments do not always have the power or the will to control transnational tobacco companies. Consequently tobacco consumption in the **Third World** is rising by over 2% yearly. In some Caribbean and Latin American cities more than half of all young people smoke.

Tobacco is estimated to cost the

Ratio of heart attack rates: smokers versus non-smokers of the same age

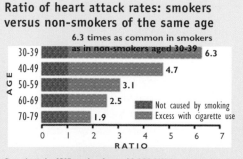

6.3 times as common in smokers as in non-smokers aged 30-39

AGE	RATIO
30-39	6.3
40-49	4.7
50-59	3.1
60-69	2.5
70-79	1.9

Not caused by smoking
Excess with cigarette use

Based on the ISIS study of over 10,000 UK heart attacks, British Medical Journal, 19 August 1995.

world some $200 billion annually in increased health-care costs – a sum that could easily double the current health budget of all **developing countries**.

TOBIN TAX

A tax on foreign exchange transactions, proposed as a means of reducing the destabilizing influence of financial markets and raising funds to finance the UN system. It is named after Professor James Tobin, the 1981 Nobel Prize winner in economics who first proposed it in 1992. World-wide transactions in currency markets are estimated at around $1 trillion daily. A tax of 0.5% would yield $1.5 trillion annually.

Governments would benefit by having more control over national monetary policy since influence from currency speculators would be reduced. In addition, all states would benefit from the additional revenues. The main barrier to the plan is the political power of the finance sector whose supporters and apologists work hand-in-glove with national politicians and bureaucrats.

TOKYO ROUND

The sixth Round of multilateral trade negotiations under the **General Agreement on Tariffs and Trade** (GATT), launched in Tokyo in 1973. The Tokyo Round set out to reduce or eliminate both tariff and non-tariff barriers and secure additional trade benefits for **developing countries**. Negotiations began in earnest in 1975 when the American Congress passed a Trade Bill empowering the US to participate. The fruits of the discussion were implemented in 1980 and provided only marginal benefits to **Third World** countries.

TOURISM
(see also Eco-Tourism)

Tourism has become one of the world's leading industries. It grew by more than 40% during the 1990s and continues to expand. International tourism leapt from 25.3 million people in 1950 to 286 million in 1980. By the early 1990s, nearly 600 million tourists were criss-crossing the globe and the business was worth more than $200 billion. The global interchange of people should soon exceed earnings from sales of **oil**.

Tourism is already the largest industry in the world in terms of **employment** with 1 in every 16 workers owing their job to it. The International Air Transport Association predicts that passenger numbers will continue to grow at around 7% annually. Tourists spent an estimated $77 billion in the US in 1995, but Europe still makes more from tourism than any other region. France is the perennial top destination, attracting over 60 million people each year.

Developing countries, particularly in Asia, are also increasing their share of the international tourist trade and now receive a fifth of the total. Recently Cuba announced plans to make tourism its number one foreign exchange earner and India is seeking to more than double hotel occupancy over the next decade, a move which will create at least 250,000 jobs.

Nonetheless, the long-term cultural, social and environmental impact of tourism remain unknown. The social systems and physical or cultural resources of many developing countries have a limited **carrying capacity**, able to accommodate only a restricted number of newcomers before they begin to fray at the edges.

TOXIC CHEMICALS

Toxic chemicals are substances which are poisonous to humans and wildlife. Ten million synthetic chemicals are now registered and

World's Top 10 Tourism Destinations

Rank	Country	International Tourist Arrivals (thousands)	Market Share % of World Total
1	France	61,500	10.39
2	United States	44,791	7.57
3	Spain	41,295	6.98
4	Italy	35,500	6.00
5	China	26,055	4.40
6	United Kingdom	25,800	4.36
7	Mexico	21,732	3.67
8	Hungary	20,670	3.39
9	Poland	19,420	3.28
10	Canada	17,345	2.93

World Tourism Organization, 1997.

almost 80,000 are in common use around the world. In 1989 the **Organization for Economic Co-operation and Development** (OECD) announced plans to investigate 1,500 of these. Little is known about the impact of these substances on the environment, even though they account for 95% of all chemicals used. The OECD will first examine 147 so-called 'mystery' compounds about which virtually no toxicological information exists. Seventy of these are produced in quantities exceeding 10,000 tonnes annually. Until recently the most common way to get rid of them was to dump them in landfill tips.

The movement of **hazardous waste** across borders has been prohibited under the Basle Convention and national policies are also beginning to appear to monitor and curb toxic wastes. In the United States, where 265 million tonnes of toxic waste are produced annually, the Emergency Planning and Community Right-to-Know Act resulted in the creation of the Toxics Release Inventory. This is an annual record of about 300 toxic chemicals which are released into the environment by some 24,000 industrial plants.

TRADE UNIONS

An association of workers in a particular trade, set up for the self-protection of the employees, originally in response to the conditions of industrial production in the 18th century. Trade unionism originated as a movement in Britain, Europe and the United States. Unions were initially prohibited as a conspiracy to restrain trade but were eventually legalized after decades of organizing by working people. Unions were first legalized in Britain in the Trade Union Act of 1871.

They soon began to turn their attention to improving pay and working conditions. This was met with increasing hostility from employers. Without the right to withdraw their labour, trade unions had little power to confront their bosses. In Britain, the Trade Disputes Act of 1906 finally gave unions the right to strike.

The earliest unions were small, formed among skilled workers and it was not until much later that the idea of creating general mass-participation unions, embracing large numbers of skilled and semi-skilled workers was adopted.

In general, the strength and power of the labour movement is strongest in times of economic prosperity and weakest when **unemployment** is high and wages are falling. The principles and practices of trade unionism are now embedded in most Western countries, although the rise of the global economy may be a serious threat to their future survival. Within communist countries, trade unions were not free to take industrial action. They were perceived as devices to air grievances within the framework of democratic centralism, without disrupting the process of production.

TRADITIONAL MEDICINE

More than 80% of people in **developing countries** use traditional practitioners and local medicinal plants as their primary form of health care. In the industrialized countries interest in alternative and holistic forms of medicine has also been booming over the past few decades. Acupuncture has been used in China for thousands of years. It is simple and cheap with minimal side-effects and is being used increasingly in the developed world. By 1990, there were 88,000 acupuncturists working in Europe and some 20 million people around the world were thought to be using acupuncture to improve or maintain their health.

In Canada, 42% of people use some form of alternative treatment such as herbal medicines, acupuncture or homeopathy to supplement or replace conventional treatments. In the United States nearly a third of the population uses alternative medical treatments. In the Netherlands and Belgium people are willing to pay extra health insurance for alternative medicine and 74% of

TRADE UNIONS

TRADE-UNION MEMBERSHIP declined during the right-wing ascendancy in countries like Britain during the 1980s. But it is now surging in international terms as civil societies become stronger in newly democratic countries, particularly in Africa and Eastern Europe.

MEMBERSHIP OF FREE TRADE UNIONS

127 million — 1995
87 million — 1987

The State of the World Atlas by M Kidson and R Segal, Penguin 1995.

Eye of newt...
Or skull of monkey, jaw of crocodile and carapace of turtle as seen here at the Akodessewa fetish and herbalist market in Togo. TRADITIONAL MEDICINE

Britons would like to see alternative medicine as part of their health service.

Despite the widespread use of plant-based medicines and therapies, only a small number of plant species (around 5,000) have been studied for their possible medical use. Nonetheless, a quarter of all non-prescription drugs dispensed in the US between 1986-90 contained compounds extracted from natural products, mostly plants.

Micro-organisms have produced more than 3,000 antibiotics; snakes and leeches provide anticoagulant drugs; and most anti-cancer drugs come from coral. Medicines like aspirin, quinine and digitalis which are derived from natural products are worth about $40 billion annually.

TRAGEDY OF THE COMMONS

A phrase introduced by a US biology professor Garrett Hardin to describe a process of environmental degradation caused by excessive self-interest at the expense of the common good. The original process was first described by William Forster Lloyd (1794-1852). He looked at the impact of the actions of individual herders on common grazing **land**. He concluded that since the land is open to all and owned by none, each herder will try and keep as much

stock as possible on the land. This will cause no problems until the **carrying capacity** of the land is reached. All the benefits from adding an animal go to the individual while the overgrazing created by each extra animal is shared by all.

Each person sharing the commons is driven to increase their herd size without limit. The tragedy is that everyone suffers in the end as the commons is destroyed by what appear to be rational acts of self-interest.

Hardin used the 'tragedy of the commons' theory to argue in favour of strict population control policies in the **Third World**. His approach was also applied specifically to Africa where nomadic herders were blamed for ignoring the environmental consequences of their huge herds. As a result government planners in East Africa and elsewhere attempted to institute a system of private land ownership so herders could assume direct responsibility for their actions. The move was a disaster, worsening environmental degradation and driving **nomads** to the cities.

TRANSMIGRATION

The transmigration programme in Indonesia is the world's largest effort to relocate people from one

region to another in the same country. It is a government-led initiative to encourage Indonesians from the overpopulated, fertile islands of Java and Bali to resettle on the outlying, underpopulated, tropical-forested islands of Sumatra, Kalimantan and Irian Jaya. Indonesia has a marked imbalance in its population, with over half its 200 million people living on Java, where the soils are especially fertile.

Between 1984 and 1990 the Indonesian Government planned to resettle 750,000 families, representing some 3 million people in all. The original plan was to move a further 65 million by the year 2008. The programme has come under constant criticism for the devastation that it is causing to **tropical forests** on the outlying islands and for the social disruption of local people and the migrants themselves.

Over 10% of the world's tropical forests are in Indonesia but they are being rapidly decimated by commercial logging and the resettlement scheme. At least 1.2 million hectares of tropical forest were razed annually between 1980-90.

It costs about $9,000 to move each family to the outer islands and the bulk of the financing is provided by the **World Bank**. So far $800 million out of a proposed investment of $1.5 billion has been spent.

The transmigration programme has become a source of major conflict in Irian Jaya where indigenous groups

Right of way
Goats take to the streets in Kenya, voraciously grazing roadsides and rubbish dumps – and any garden plants that are not safely fenced. TRAGEDY OF THE COMMONS

WORLD'S TOP 12 Transnational Corporations, 1997		
GLOBAL 500 RANK	COMPANY	REVENUES $ MILLIONS
1	General Motors Corporation	168,369
2	Ford Motor Company	146,991
3	Mitsui & Co., Ltd.	144,943
4	Mitsubishi Corporation	140,204
5	Itochu Corporation	135,542
6	Royal Dutch/Shell Group	128,174
7	Marubeni Corporation	124,027
8	Exxon Corporation	119,434
9	Sumitono Corporation	119,281
10	Toyota Motor Corporation	108,702
11	Wal-Mart Stores, Inc.	106,147
12	General Electric Company	79,179

Fortune 500

have been fighting for independence since Indonesia annexed the region in 1962. They see the resettlement programme as an attempt by the Indonesian Government to defuse the independence movement by swamping Irian Jaya with millions of ethnically-different and culturally-separate peoples from Java.

TRANSNATIONAL CORPORATIONS (TNCs)

Transnationals (sometimes called multinationals or MNCs) are major business corporations which have subsidiaries, investments or operations in more than one country. According to the **United Nations**, TNCs are associations which 'possess and control means of production or services outside the country in which they were established'. Some TNCs are viewed as threats to national sovereignty exerting undue influence to achieve their corporate goals or of sacrificing

human and environmental well-being in order to maximize profits. Annual sales of some TNCs exceed $100 billion, far greater than the exports and imports of most **Third World** nations.

In 1992, the top ten TNCs announced combined sales of $342 billion and employed 2.7 million people. Five of the top twelve are based in the US. Transnationals often control whole areas of business through 'vertical' and 'horizontal' integration, monopolising 94% of global **agrochemicals** sales for example. They are also responsible for many of the world's worst human-made ecological **disasters**, including the deadly chemical leak in **Bhopal**, India and the massive **oil** spill off the Alaskan coast by the **Exxon Valdez** tanker.

TREATIES OF ROME

Two treaties signed in Rome in 1957 by representatives of Belgium, France, Italy, Luxembourg, the Netherlands and Germany. The treaties led to the European Economic Community (EEC) and the European Atomic Energy Community (EURATOM), which both came into being in 1957. The goal of the treaties was to create a common market permitting the free movement of individuals, goods, services and capital – with the long-term goal of European union.

The treaties also called for the establishment of a European Investment Bank and a European Social Fund. Trade between the signatory nations was made duty-free by stages; the last tariffs were abolished and a **customs union** established in 1968. The 6 nations eventually agreed to merge into the **European Community** in 1967. The same year the Common Agriculture Policy (CAP) came into force. By 1990, several other nations had signed the Rome Treaties and the Community had expanded to 12 nations. The original countries were joined by the UK, Denmark, Ireland, Greece, Spain and Portugal. Applications for membership had been also received from Austria, Turkey, Morocco, Cyprus, Malta and several Eastern European nations.

TRICKLE-DOWN DEVELOPMENT

Theory of economic development in which investment and resources poured into government coffers, industry and high-technology projects are supposed to create wealth which will eventually 'trickle down' to improve the lives of the poor. Forecasts made during the 1960s that this approach would alleviate **poverty** in the **Third World** have proved false. In reality wealth has stayed in the hands of a small élite, mainly those close to, or related to, those in power. The wealthy have a lifestyle similar to their counter-parts in the industrialized nations while the majority still live in conditions of poverty and suffering.

TROPICAL FORESTS

Tropical forests lie roughly 10 degrees north and south of the equator and are almost entirely in **developing countries**. They cover almost 1.8 billion hectares and include evergreen rain forests as well as moist, deciduous and dry zone ecosystems. They cover 6% of the earth's **land** surface, yet comprise half the planet's wood and house 70-90% of the earth's living organisms.

Some 25% of pharmaceutical drugs are derived from rainforest plants. Tropical forests also play a vital role in regulating the local and global climate by storing carbon (some 1.5 billion tonnes) that would otherwise be released into the atmosphere. In addition, thousands of communities depend on the forests for their survival. And many of those have evolved ways of living in sustainable harmony with their environment.

Huge tracts of forest are being destroyed in Latin America, Southeast Asia and Africa to expand cropland, establish **cattle** ranches and extract timber. The ecological impact is disastrous. Severe **soil erosion** chokes rivers and watercourses and leads to flooding. Thousands of plant and animal species become extinct. Population resettlement schemes in Brazil and Indonesia have directed and encouraged people to colonize forest land.

As much as 5 million hectares of tropical forest has been converted by these landless peasants into cropland, much of which quickly loses its fertility. Some 200,000 hectares of Indonesian rainforest is converted to cropland each year. In Latin America, 20 million hectares of tropical forest has been replaced by cattle ranches. In Africa, the continent's last remaining forest people, the Pygmies, are losing their forest homeland, as are the Penan in Malaysia and the **Yanomami** in Brazil.

TROPICAL FORESTRY ACTION PLAN (TFAP)

Launched in 1985 by the **World Bank**, the **United Nations Environment Programme** (UNEP), the **Food and Agriculture Organization** and the World Resources Institute. The objective of TFAP is to review the state of forests in every tropical country in terms of their contribution to national economic development, the needs of local people and the environment. These national reviews are meant to allow governments to decide their own priorities in forest **conservation** and development and to secure the support and co-operation of **aid** donors.

Following the basic premise that **deforestation** cannot be solved in isolation from other aspects of development planning, the TFAP aims to co-ordinate efforts to save the world's **tropical forests** and improve the lot of the rural poor by identifying and promoting ways in which forests can be exploited in a sustainable manner. Since 1986, national sector reviews have been completed in 20 countries and are underway in another 34.

Since its inception critics have complained that the TFAP is a smoke screen whose purpose is to promote logging and deforestation. They claim that the rights of forest people are being overlooked because national 'action plans' are dominated by the commercial forestry and timber industries. Critics also charge that the TFAP ignores the causes of landlessness, itself a major cause of deforestation and the main reason why more and more forest is being converted to farm **land**.

In 1990 **non-government organizations** (NGOs) succeeded in changing the TFAP so its objectives are now 'conservation and **sustainable development** of forestry **resources** in the interests of the country concerned and the global community'. The new Tropical Forestry Action Programme was to be strengthened by the World Forestry Convention proposed for adoption at the UN Conference on Environment and Development (UNCED) in 1992. It was favoured by the **North** but strongly opposed by developing nations in the **South**. UNCED then abandoned its plans and proposed instead that forest cover should be expanded through **plantations** and sustainably managed forests.

TRYPANOSOMIASIS

A collection of debilitating, long-lasting diseases caused by infestation with microscopic single-celled trypanosoma organisms. Included in this group are sleeping sickness in humans and *ngana* in **cattle**, both found in Africa and transmitted by **tsetse** flies. In the Americas, the incurable **chagas disease** is a form of trypanosomiasis spread by triatomine

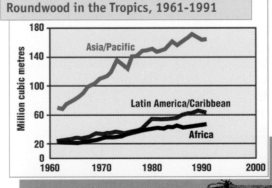

Production of Non-coniferous Industrial Roundwood in the Tropics, 1961-1991

FAO in Vital Signs 1997/1998, Worldwatch Institute, Earthscan.

Tip-toe tsetse
Scourge of the African tropics, the tsetse fly transmits deadly organisms to cattle and humans alike: only indigenous wild animals can resist its bite. TSETSE

bugs. At least 140 million people are affected by these diseases, mainly in the tropics.

African trypanosomiasis (sleeping sickness) is a severe, often fatal disease. Some 55 million people in tropical regions of Africa are at risk and it is a major barrier to human development on the continent. Ngana disease effectively renders commercial livestock production impossible over 10 million square kilometres of high-rainfall **land** in Africa.

Every year 30,000 new cases of human trypanosomiasis are reported; the disease kills 20,000 people and 3 million animals every year. The few effective drugs all have serious short-comings. Consequently, efforts to combat the disease have been directed at controlling the tsetse fly. In 1990 a new drug, Ornidyl, was found to act quickly and have few side effects. However, the drug is expensive and well beyond the reach of those who most need it.

TSETSE

The tsetse is a large bloodsucking fly which lives in tropical Africa and belongs to the genus *glossina*. There are several species which feed on humans and other warm-blooded animals, generally living close to river banks or on the edge of savannahs, their preferred habitat. The fly transmits sleeping sickness (**try-panosomiasis**) to humans and a disease called ngana to **cattle**. Indigenous wild animals are largely immune.

The fly has been a serious barrier to livestock production in much of Africa and has prevented farmers from using vast areas of arable **land**. The tsetse is also extremely difficult to control. The fly spends most of the day resting in the shade under branches and leaves. Aerial application of **pesticides** must be combined with intensive ground-level spraying.

A multi-million dollar scheme has been proposed to clear the tsetse fly from 38 African countries. This could free up more than 18 million square kilometres of new land for agricultural production. Critics fear the scheme will lead to uncontrolled settlement, overgrazing and **soil** degradation while environmentalists argue that strict land-use plans should be incorporated in any tsetse control programme. Dangerous toxic chemicals have traditionally been used in the war against the tsetse. More than 300,000 square kilometres in Africa have regularly been sprayed with **DDT**, **dieldrin** and lindane. Conservationists believe safer, odour-baited traps should be used. Cost-effective traps for several species of tsetse fly have now been developed, costing as little as $10 each. These can kill 5,000 flies daily and require little maintenance.

TUBERCULOSIS (TB)

An infectious disease caused by the bacillus *mycobacterium tuberculosis*. The illness is characterized by the formation of nodular lesions or tubercles in body tissues. The bacillus is easily inhaled and a primary nodule is quickly formed. The body's natural immune system may heal it at this stage and when this happens a lasting immunity develops. Other people may become infected but show no signs of illness. They act as carriers of the disease, transmitting the bacillus by coughing and sneezing. The highly-

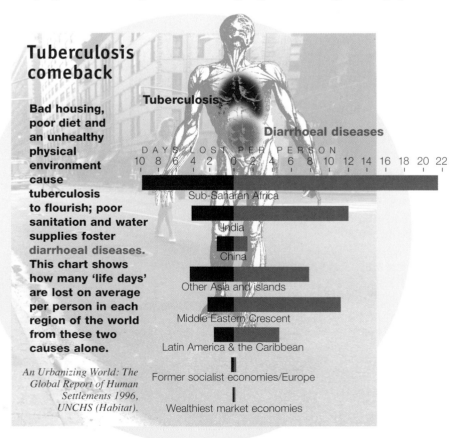

Tuberculosis comeback

Bad housing, poor diet and an unhealthy physical environment cause tuberculosis to flourish; poor sanitation and water supplies foster diarrhoeal diseases. This chart shows how many 'life days' are lost on average per person in each region of the world from these two causes alone.

An Urbanizing World: The Global Report of Human Settlements 1996, UNCHS (Habitat).

Tuberculosis

Diarrhoeal diseases

D A Y S   L O S T   P E R   P E R S O N
10 8 6 4 2 0 2 4 6 8 10 12 14 16 18 20 22

Sub-Saharan Africa

India

China

Other Asia and islands

Middle Eastern Crescent

Latin America & the Caribbean

Former socialist economies/Europe

Wealthiest market economies

infectious bacterium can remain dormant in the body for years. Symptoms include fever, night sweats, weight loss and spitting of blood. Tuberculosis is curable with antibiotics, and a vaccine gives protection to those who have not already developed immunity to the disease.

There are 8.9 million new cases of TB each year, mostly in the **developing countries**. An estimated 3 million people die from tuberculosis every year and another 1.7 billion people are infected with the TB bacillus. TB has made a startling comeback in the industrialized nations in recent years. In the US the number of cases declined steadily for 32 years until 1984, but is now on the increase. One reason for the resurgence is the spread of the **human immuno-deficiency virus** (HIV) which by weakening the immune system increases the likelihood of infection with the TB bacillus. According to the **World Health Organization** (WHO), 95% of tuberculosis patients could be cured in 6 months using antibiotics costing less than $30 per patient.

TUNDRA

Tundra is cold, treeless ground found in polar regions (Arctic tundra) or high mountains (alpine tundra). In the polar regions, winters are long, dark and very cold and there is little precipitation throughout the year. The flora and fauna have evolved to survive in these conditions. Trees cannot survive due to permafrost, a layer of permanently frozen **soil** up to 450 metres deep. On top of this, another thin layer of soil alternates between freezing and thawing.

Permafrost is found only in Arctic tundra, but both Arctic and alpine tundra have the freeze-thaw layer. Vegetation is greenish brown. Along foggy, moist coasts, grassy swards develop. In drier inland areas,

TUTU, DESMOND (1931-)
A South African cleric noted for his strong opposition to **apartheid**. Desmond Tutu was ordained in 1960 and became the first black General Secretary of the South African Council of Churches (an organization with a membership of over 12 million) in 1978. In 1984 he was appointed Anglican Bishop of Cape Town and later that same year he was awarded the Nobel Prize for peace for his tireless efforts to combat racial segregation in South Africa. In 1988 the South African Government clamped down on anti-apartheid activists and Archbishop Tutu and other religious leaders were arrested. Following a brief detention he continued to campaign for democracy and was a leading figure in the eventual fall of the apartheid regime. He retired as Archbishop in 1996 and subsequently chaired the Truth and Reconciliation Commission.

spongy turf and lichen heaths are common, producing mossy bogs. Tundra stretches in a continuous belt across northern North America and Eurasia covering 10% of the earth's surface. In these Arctic regions extremely long periods of light and darkness are normal. Consequently plants have developed biological rhythms based on changes of temperature rather than light, with a growing season of 2-4 months.

TUPAMAROS

A left-wing, urban **guerrilla** group from Uruguay. The group was named after Tupac Amaru, a Peruvian indian revolutionary who opposed Spanish rule in Peru in the 18th century. Founded in 1963 by Raul Sendic, the Tupamaros began by robbing banks and businesses and distributing the proceeds to the poor. In 1968, they began to intensify their efforts, breaking into arsenals, setting fire to buildings and assassinating politicians and police.

These activities reached their peak in the early 1970s. A coup in 1973 installed a military government which targeted the Tupamaros, killing 300 and imprisoning a further 3,000. When democratic rule returned to

Uruguay in 1985 most of those jailed, including Sendic, were released. The Tupamaros then reorganized themselves into a political party.

TYPHOID

There are 16 million cases of typhoid fever a year and more than 600,000 deaths. Eighty per cent of these are in Asia and most others are in Africa and Latin America. The disease is transmitted through faeces-contaminated food or **water**.

Salmonella typhii, the bacterium responsible for causing the disease, has developed resistance to commonly-used antibiotics. As a result new resistant strains have caused outbreaks in India and Pakistan. Without effective antibiotic treatment typhoid kills 10% of those infected.

The disease is characterized by an infection of the digestive system causing high fever, a rash and possible inflammation of the spleen and bones. Safe drinking water, hygienic food-handling and adequate sanitary facilities are essential for prevention of infection. A vaccine exists but it does not give complete protection and patients who survive take several months to recover.

Unemployment

Jobless plumbers and 'electricistas' – electricians – ply their trades in Mexico City. Thirty-seven per cent of Mexico's population is in the official workforce, but many more work 'informally' in backyards, little shops and on the streets.

UV

Unemployment – Vietnam War

UV

Bold indicates a cross-reference

UNEMPLOYMENT

Globally, at least 120 million people of working age are unemployed. Another 700 million more are 'under-employed', mostly working but not earning enough to meet their **basic needs** or those of their families. The global labour force is projected to grow by around 1 billion during the next 20 years, with most of the increase in **developing countries**.

UNITED NATIONS (UN)

An association of independent countries whose aim is to promote international peace, security and co-operation. It replaced the **League of Nations** in 1945. Current member-ship is 184 countries. The Holy See, Switzerland and the Palestine Liberation Organisation hold observer status. All UN members are represented in the General Assembly.

The Charter of the United Nations was drafted by the international community in San Francisco in 1945 and its headquarters are located in New York. It has 6 principal sections: General Assembly, Security Council, Economic and Social Council, Trusteeship Council, **International Court of Justice** and General Secretariat.

Member states contribute funds according to their own resources, following an assessment of what their contributions should be as calculated by the General Assembly. The UN finances a variety of **aid** programmes through its own agencies and other international bodies. However, UN activities are restricted by available funds, with many nations failing to pay their dues. The total amount owed by member countries in 1990 stood at $660 million. The US was the largest debtor, owing a total of $521 million. The organization has 6 working languages: English, French, Russian, Spanish, Chinese and Arabic.

The UN General Assembly: Meets annually and is composed of one representative from each of the member states. Special sessions can be convened at the request of the Security Council (see below) or a majority of members. Each has a single vote so the Assembly is the one major forum where the **South** can outvote the **North**. Major decisions taken by the Assembly require a two-thirds majority.

UN Security Council: When the UN Charter was adopted the composition and role of the Security Council reflected the political strengths of the era. Five permanent members were elected to the Council: China, France, the Soviet Union, the United Kingdom and the United States. The other 10 members of the council (increased from 6 in 1965) serve a term of 2 years and retiring members are ineligible for re-election. Only the permanent members have the power of veto. The power of the veto has meant that the Security Council could recommend no action over events such as the Soviet intervention in Hungary (1956), the Suez Canal Crisis (1956), Soviet intervention in Afghanistan (1979), US action in Grenada (1983) and the US bombing of Libya (1986).

UN Secretariat: Based at UN Headquarters in New York, the Secretariat is composed of the Secretary-General who is the chief administrative officer of the UN appointed by the General Assembly,

UN Birth

Standing rigid as the flag poles which surround them, the men in suits pose at the solemn occasion of signing the United Nations Charter in 1945. UNITED NATIONS

THE MEMBERS

UN membership embraces virtually the whole world but continues to expand – due in the 1960s to decolonization and more recently to the arrival of smaller nation-states, especially after the break-up of the USSR.

● The Swiss voted against joining the UN in a referendum in 1986; Serbia and Montenegro have been debarred from taking up the former Yugoslavian seat at the UN and have to reapply.

United Nations

and an international staff appointed by the holder of the post. There have been 7 Secretary-Generals: **Trygve Lie** (Norway) 1946-53; **Dag Hammarskjöld** (Sweden) 1953-1961; **U Thant** (Burma) 1961-71; **Kurt Waldheim** (Austria) 1972-1981; **Javier Perez de Cuellar** (Peru) 1982-91; Boutros-Boutros Ghali (Egypt) 1992-1996; and Kofi Annan (Ghana) appointed in 1997.

UNITED NATIONS CENTRE FOR HUMAN SETTLEMENTS (UNCHS)

UNCHS, also known as Habitat, acts as the secretariat to the inter-governmental policy-making body, the Commission on Human Settlements. The Commission meets bi-annually and has a membership of 58 countries, each selected for a 4 year term. UNCHS was established in 1978, 2 years after the UN Conference on Human Settlements in Vancouver.

It is based in Nairobi and is the UN agency responsible for co-ordinating all activities in the field of human settlements. It is charged with co-ordinating the 'Global Strategy for Shelter by the Year 2000' initiative and for implementing the Agenda 21 programme on **sustainable development**.

The Commission operates 8 working sub-programmes: Global issues and strategies; National Policies and Instruments; Integrated Settlements Management; Financial Resources; Land Management; Infrastructure Development; Housing Production; and

Construction. Its research, training and technical co-operation are intended to help members formulate and implement national shelter strategies.

UNITED NATIONS CHILDREN'S FUND (UNICEF)

Originally established in 1946 by the General Assembly of the UN to co-ordinate relief work in war-torn countries. The acronym UNICEF is retained from the original title, UN International Children's Emergency Fund. The agency is based in New York and Geneva. Almost all of its **aid** is devoted to long-term programmes, chiefly for maternal and child welfare, child nutrition and education.

It provides and co-ordinates basic services for children, mothers and community development and promotes the concept of global interdependence and respect for other cultures. The Fund is financed entirely by voluntary contributions from governments, private groups and public and individual donations. There are at least 41 separate UNICEF National Committees, and Liaison Offices exist around the world.

UNITED NATIONS CONFERENCE ON TRADE AND DEVELOPMENT (UNCTAD)

Launched in the early 1960s in response to growing **Third World** demands for greater economic development through trade, UNCTAD is scheduled to meet every 4 years but

its work continues between sessions through the Trade and Development Board and various standing committees, all based in Geneva. It deals with a wide range of issues including: monetary reform and **debt** problems; technology transfer; the 'brain drain'; shipping and flags of convenience; commodity agreements and tariff preferences.

UNCTAD conferences serve as the main international forum for dealing with **North/South** economic issues and all UN member states may participate, along with **non-governmental organizations** (NGOs) and intergovernmental organizations.

The first meeting in Geneva in 1964 agreed in principle that industrialized nations should aim to transfer 1% of national income to **developing countries**. The second Conference in New Delhi in 1968 increased the **aid** target to 1% of **Gross National Product** (GNP) and agreed on a general system of preferences for exports of manufactured and semi-manufactured goods from developing countries.

The third UNCTAD meeting in Santiago, Chile (1972) looked mainly at trade in primary **commodities** and developed a case-by-case timetable for negotiations and discussions of a 'Common Fund' for financing buffer stocks.

The following conferences in 1976 (Nairobi), 1979 (Manila), 1983 (Belgrade), and 1987 (Geneva) dealt primarily with **protectionism** and adopted over 20 major resolutions in an attempt to promote freer trade. The 1996 Conference was held in South Africa.

The outcome of many of UNCTAD's meetings have been compromises which have failed to satisfy the majority of developing countries. UNCTAD has 187 members, all member states of the UN plus the Holy See, Switzerland and Tonga.

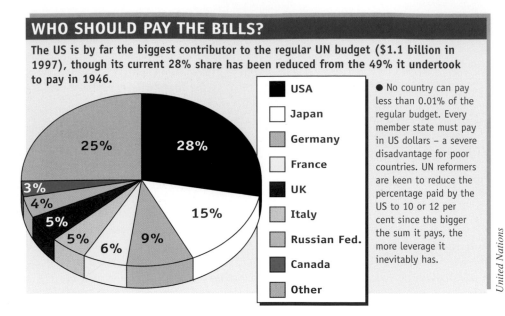

United Nations

WHO SHOULD PAY THE BILLS?

The US is by far the biggest contributor to the regular UN budget ($1.1 billion in 1997), though its current 28% share has been reduced from the 49% it undertook to pay in 1946.

Legend:
- USA
- Japan
- Germany
- France
- UK
- Italy
- Russian Fed.
- Canada
- Other

Pie chart values: 28%, 25%, 3%, 4%, 5%, 5%, 6%, 9%, 15%

● No country can pay less than 0.01% of the regular budget. Every member state must pay in US dollars – a severe disadvantage for poor countries. UN reformers are keen to reduce the percentage paid by the US to 10 or 12 per cent since the bigger the sum it pays, the more leverage it inevitably has.

UNITED NATIONS DEVELOPMENT PROGRAMME (UNDP)

UNDP was established in 1965 and has a membership of 36 nations from all parts of the globe. The agency serves as the central planning, funding and co-ordinating body for all forms of technical and scientific co-operation carried out under the UN system.

It orchestrates activities between specialized UN agencies, governments and bilateral donors. UNDP and its associated 'special funds' provide assistance in agriculture, education, health, **employment**, fisheries, industry, science and technology, and transport and communications. It is also concerned with promoting the **New International Economic Order**, donor 'round tables' for the **Least Developed Countries**, women in development, liberation movements and the activities of **non-governmental organizations** (NGOs) in **developing countries**.

The Programme has field offices in 112 nations and serves 152 countries and territories. UNDP offers assistance in the form of experts, training and a small amount of equipment. It also organizes resource surveys, prepares studies to facilitate investment and helps establish technical, training and research institutions. It does not itself provide capital for development projects.

UNITED NATIONS EDUCATIONAL SCIENTIFIC AND CULTURAL ORGANIZATION (UNESCO)

Established in 1946 to promote international understanding through education, science and culture. Its work includes raising **literacy**, improving facilities for teacher training and promoting co-operation in scientific research programmes. It also assists in the application of natural sciences, technology and social sciences to development, promoting and preserving all aspects of culture and encouraging the spread of modern communications.

UNESCO is based in Paris and has 182 members and 3 associate members. It is also concerned with the media, **human rights**, geological and environmental sciences, the preservation of cultural heritage, and the promotion of peace and international understanding.

UNITED NATIONS ENVIRONMENT PROGRAMME (UNEP)

UNEP was established in 1972 following the UN Conference on the Human Environment held in Stockholm. Its mandate is to review the state of the global environment and to help safeguard the planet for present and future generations by ensuring that all environmental problems of international significance are addressed by the global community. It has 58 members and was the first UN agency with headquarters in a developing country (Nairobi, Kenya).

The agency has identified environmental health, terrestrial ecosystems, environment and development, oceans, energy and natural **disasters** as priorities.

It operates a worldwide surveillance system (EARTHWATCH) which is intended to avert impending environmental crises. The system has three major components: the **International Register of Potentially Toxic Chemicals** (IRPTC), the International Referral System (INFOTERRA) and the Global Environmental Monitoring System (GEMS).

UNEP also administers the United Nations Environment Fund, which is supported by voluntary government contributions and is used to finance specific environmental assessment and management projects.

UNITED NATIONS FUND FOR POPULATION ACTIVITIES (UNFPA)

Originally established in 1967 as a Trust Fund of the UN Secretary-General, UNFPA was placed under the administration of the **United Nations Development Programme** (UNDP) in 1969 and in 1972 transferred to the authority of the General Assembly. The UNDP Governing Council remains the controlling body of UNFPA, subject to the policies and conditions established by the UN's Economic and Social Committee (ECOSOC). UNFPA is supported by voluntary contributions from over 90 governments and not from the general UN budget. It directly manages a third of all population assistance to **developing countries**.

It also helps governments obtain information on the growth, make-up and movement of their populations; promotes awareness and research into the relationship between **popu-**

lation and economic and social development; provides expert advice on population policy; and supports **family planning**, education and training programmes. UNFPA provides assistance at the request of governments and supports only non-coercive population policies. It upholds every nation's right to determine its own population policies as well as the rights of all couples and individuals to decide freely and responsibly the number and spacing of their children. UNFPA does not regard abortion as a means of family planning, but it has attracted criticism from several governments for its position on the **abortion** issue.

UNITED NATIONS GROUPS

To ensure a balanced representation of regional interests in UN committees and agencies, the UN has an arrangement whereby UN-member countries are divided into 4 groups. Each group has been allocated a set number of seats on the Trade and Development Board of UNCTAD

Killing fields
Civil war erupted in Rwanda in 1990 leading to one of the worst massacres of the century; the UN mission to Rwanda (UNAMIR) arrived in 1993 but seemed powerless to stop the slaughter.
UNITED NATIONS

and on the Industrial Development Board of the **United Nations Industrial Development Organization** (UNIDO). Group A consists of African and Asian countries. Group B comprises Western European, North American and other fully-industrialized nations. Group C contains Central and South American Countries. Group D is made up of Eastern European and former Communist-Bloc countries. Members of groups A and C are sometimes referred to as the Group of 77.

UNITED NATIONS HIGH COMMISSIONER FOR REFUGEES (UNHCR)

The agency was established in 1951 to continue work originally begun by the International Refugee Organization. UNHCR provides protection and assistance on a social and humanitarian basis to **refugees** who are not considered nationals by the countries in which they seek asylum. It aims to help with their voluntary repatriation or their assimilation within new national communities. With a membership of 47 nations, its programmes are financed by voluntary contributions from governments, private agencies and institutions.

UNITED NATIONS INDUSTRIAL DEVELOPMENT ORGANIZATION (UNIDO)

Set up in 1965 and based in Vienna, UNIDO has 166 member states. The agency's purpose is to promote the industrialization of **developing countries** and to co-ordinate UN activities in this area. It deals with all aspects of establishing factories and managing projects, regional and local industrial planning, institutional infrastructure development, technology transfer and investment promotion. UNIDO derives the bulk of its technical co-operation

Home from home
After the 1993 escalation of war in Sudan thousands fled to northern Uganda where UNHCR helped them settle, usually in *tukuls* like this – thatched grass and mud huts. UNHCR

funds from the **United Nations Development Programme** (UNDP), supplemented by voluntary member contributions.

UNITED NATIONS RELIEF AND WORKS AGENCY (UNRWA)

Established by the General Assembly in 1949 to supervise relief activities for Palestinian **refugees** in the Middle East. UNRWA promotes resettlement and now helps channel **resources** and funds to all countries in the region. It caters to the needs of millions of registered refugees, helping to arrange for basic shelter, food, health and welfare services and educational facilities in Jordan, Lebanon, Syria and the occupied West Bank and Gaza Strip. It has a membership of 10 countries and is financed from voluntary contributions.

UNITED NATIONS UNIVERSITY (UNU)

Based in Tokyo, the University has no campus. Instead it supports individual researchers in a wide range of academic and research institutions in 32 countries around the world. The five major research areas are: peace and conflict resolution; the global economy; **hunger**, **poverty** and environmental **resources**; human and social development; and science, technology and the information society. The UNU also produces academic publications and journals, a regular series of reports and newsletters and a collection of audio-visual materials.

UNIVERSAL DECLARATION OF HUMAN RIGHTS

Declaration drafted by the United Nations Commission on Human Rights and adopted by the UN General Assembly in 1948. The 30-article declaration contained general definitions of the main civil and political rights: including the right to life, liberty and security of person; freedom of movement; freedom from arbitrary arrest, detention or exile; the right to a fair and public hearing by an independent, impartial tribunal; freedom of thought, conscience and religion;

and freedom of peaceful assembly and association.

It also specified many economic, social and cultural rights: including the right to social security, work, and education. The declaration was to be a common standard of achievement for all peoples and all nations. It was adopted by unanimous vote (6 members of the Soviet Bloc, Saudi Arabia and South Africa abstained).

UNIVERSAL POSTAL UNION (UPU)

Originally founded in 1874 as the General Postal Union, the organization became a specialized agency of the UN in 1948. The UPU is based in Switzerland and now has 189 members. It aims to ensure the integrated organization and development of postal services around the world and will provide technical help as requested by member countries.

Speaking out
The Universal Declaration of Human Rights was adopted by the UN general Assembly in 1948. UNIVERSAL DECLARATION

URANIUM

The heaviest naturally-occurring element. Uranium is a silvery-white radioactive metal with several radioactive isotopes. It is now primarily used as a fuel in **nuclear power** plants. In nature it is thinly dispersed and costly to extract.

Natural uranium contains a mixture of 3 isotopes: U-238 (99%), U-235 (0.7%) and U-234 (0.006%). Contemporary commercial nuclear power reactors use the isotope U-235 although 'fast breeder' reactors are capable of using U-238 which is more abundant. Nuclear fuel is fre-

quently 'enriched' by increasing the concentration of U-235. Like the **plutonium** produced in nuclear fuel reprocessing plants, enriched uranium tends to go missing. In the US, 4,500 kilograms of enriched uranium has disappeared since 1950. Uranium has been found in many countries and it is considered to be one of the most strategically-important minerals. There are an estimated 1.5 million tonnes of recoverable reserves. The biggest are in Australia, Canada, South Africa, Niger and the United States. Global production is in the order of 37,500 tonnes annually.

Uranium is usually found on marginal lands which are unsuitable for agricultural use. In the US, half of all uranium is on **land** owned by **Native Americans**. Similarly, in Australia over 70% of the country's known deposits are in areas of importance to **Aboriginal** culture.

URBANIZATION

Over the last 50 years as rural migration has increased and **population** levels have risen, cities have expanded dramatically. Between 1950 and 1980 the world's urban population almost tripled. In 1950, only 29% of the world's population were city dwellers. By 1995, 45% of the global population was living in cities, some 2.5 billion people. By the year 2005 it is estimated that half the world's population will be city dwellers.

Urbanization rates are growing fastest in the **Third World**, by over 3% a year. In the period 1970-80, 320 million people swarmed into Third World cities and that figure may swell to a billion by the year 2000. In China alone, more than 100 million people have left their farms to search for a better life in the nation's booming urban areas.

In 1995, 66% of the world's city dwellers lived in **developing countries**. In the Western industri-

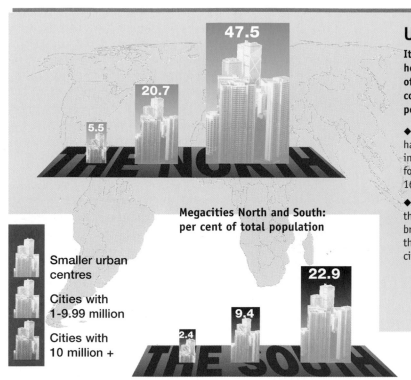

47.5

20.7

5.5

THE NORTH

**Megacities North and South:
per cent of total population**

Smaller urban
centres

Cities with
1-9.99 million

Cities with
10 million +

22.9

9.4

2.4

THE SOUTH

Urban Living

It is often assumed that millions of people are homeless because they have migrated to the slums of Southern 'megacities'. But such cities still comprise a very small proportion of the total population, both North and South:

◆ In 1975 Mexico City was projected by the UN to have a population of 31.6 million by the year 2000 – in 1994 the projection was reduced to 16.4 million; for Cairo the projections have been reduced from 16.4 million to 10.7 million.

◆ For most of the past 2,000 years the largest cities in the world have always been in Asia and Africa: only briefly during the 19th century and the beginning of the 20th were more than half of the world's 10 biggest cities in Europe and North America.

D Satterthwaite, IIED, London.

---

alized countries, urban populations grew by 2% annually from the 1920s to the 1960s. It is estimated that they will grow by only 0.8% in the 1990s.

Urbanization in the industrialized world took many decades, allowing economic, social and political systems to evolve gradually to cope with associated problems. In the Third World today the process is far more rapid and is taking place against a backdrop of high population growth and low incomes. In 1950, only 1 city in the developing world (Buenos Aires) had a population over 4 million. In 1960, there were 8 cities of that size. By 1980, there were 22 such cities in the developing world, 6 more than in the **developed countries**. By the year 2000 there will be an estimated 61 cities with a population of 4 million people or more in Third World – compared to only 25 in the industrialized countries.

Housing, **water**, sanitation, power and other services need to be provided for all city dwellers. Food has to be grown and transported in vast quantities, **employment** and

health care also need to be provided. The planning, co-ordination and resources necessary to accomplish all this are often unavailable to governments in many developing countries.

With both housing and **land** scarce, new city dwellers are often forced to live in slums or shanty towns where they have little access to safe drinking water or proper sanitation facilities. Over the coming decades, city governments will have to balance the ever-growing needs of urban dwellers with the protection of natural **resources** and the local environment. Roads, factories, houses and shops will be needed in the expanding cities, which in turn will require vast tracts of land. In Egypt, 4,000 square kilometres of fertile land in the Nile Valley were lost to urban expansion from 1955-75, more than was brought into new agricultural production.

Even if migration from the rural areas in developing countries is halted, natural population growth will ensure that urbanization remains a major problem for decades to come.

URUGUAY ROUND

The eighth series of four-year negotiations held under the **General Agreement on Tariffs and Trade** (GATT). This Round dealt with agriculture in far greater depth than any of the previous rounds. The reduction of import barriers and schemes to discourage the use of government export subsidies formed a major part of the talks. (Countries in the **North** spend $290 billion annually on measures to protect their farmers and guarantee artificially high prices for agricultural exports.)

A major focus was how to improve export earnings for **Third World** countries dependent on a single agricultural commodity. The talks also dealt with service industry issues, trade-related investment issues and trade-related intellectual property rights. The aim was to lower tariffs and other barriers to Third World exports. However, the US and the **European Community** could not reach agreement over cuts in subsidies to European farmers and the talks ended in deadlock in 1990.

In addition, many Third World nations were annoyed they were not being compensated for adopting trade liberalization measures as part of the structural adjustment programmes being forced on them by multilateral lenders. For example, Mexico's maximum import tariffs were reduced by 80% during the Uruguay Round. And manufactured exports from **developing countries** faced 50% more barriers in the Northern markets countries than in the mid-1980s. The Uruguay Round finally wound up in Morocco in 1993. When the final accord was signed by representatives of the 125 nations in attendance, the GATT itself was replaced by the **World Trade Organization**.

VACCINATION

Also known as **immunization**. The introduction of inactivated, disease-causing micro-organisms (vaccine) into the body to stimulate the formation of antibodies to the organisms, without producing the disease. This is an effective means of inducing immunity from future attacks of the disease. The first vaccination, against **smallpox**, was carried out in 1798. Vaccine is now routinely used to prevent life-threatening diseases such as **polio**, diphtheria, tetanus and **tuberculosis**. It is also used to protect people travelling to areas where diseases such as **yellow fever**, **cholera** and **typhoid** are endemic. Vaccines are

It won't hurt...
The cow (vacca in Latin) stands ready as its cells vaccinate a child against smallpox in Paris, 1898. VACCINATION

usually given by injection but some can be taken orally. Globally, vaccination is co-ordinated through the UN's **Expanded Programme of Immunization** (EPI).

VACCINE-PREVENTABLE DISEASES

Every year at least 46 million infants around the world are not fully immunized against the 6 major childhood killer diseases – **polio**, tetanus, **measles**, diptheria, pertussis (whooping cough) and **tuberculosis**. About 2.8 million children die as a result of these diseases and another 3 million are disabled, mostly in the developing world.

Vaccines exist to immunize children against these diseases but it is lack of money to purchase, store and administer the vaccines that is the problem. According to the **World Health Organization** (WHO), the **Expanded Programme of Immunization** (EPI) has increased the level of **immunization** of the developing

world's children from 5% to over 80%. It costs only $10 to vaccinate a child against all 6 diseases. The WHO reports that for less than a billion dollars, or the cost of 20 modern military planes, the world could control all these illnesses. In total, 1.8 billion people are infected with vaccine-preventable diseases.

VAVILOV CENTRES

Specific geographic regions where the genetic stock of our most commonly-cultivated crop plants originated. Named after Nikolay Vavilov, the Russian plant geneticist who discovered them. Vavilov travelled widely from 1916-33, amassing a vast collection of 50,000 kinds of wild plants and 31,000 **wheat** varieties which he brought back with him to the Soviet Union. He concluded that a cultivated plant's origin would be in the region where wild relatives of the plant showed the greatest adaptability. Eventually, he proposed 13 world centres of plant origin, which became known as the Vavilov Centres. In an era of widespread monocropping and genetic uniformity in our main food and fibre crops, the Vavilov Centres have become crucially important. They offer a valuable pool of new wild genes which can be introduced into genetically-uniform crops in the event of crippling diseases or pests. Environmentalists are concerned that these rich centres of biodiversity will be destroyed by **population** pressures and industrial development thus threatening future food supplies.

VIETNAM WAR

A war between Communist North Vietnam and Western-supported South Vietnam which lasted from 1954 to 1975. The conflict was a protracted yet unsuccessful venture by South Vietnam and the United States to prevent the Communist

The Progress of Nations 1996, UNICEF.

Vaccination

● Two hundred years after the discovery of vaccine by Edward Jenner, immunization can be credited with saving approximately 9 million lives a year worldwide. A further 16 million deaths a year could be prevented by effective vaccine programmes.

● Only smallpox so far has been eradicated, but polio is almost gone and measles could also be extinct. Vaccines have brought seven major diseases under some control – smallpox, diphtheria, tetanus, yellow fever, whooping cough, polio and measles.

north from absorbing the south. Following an unresolved struggle between the nationalist Viet Minh and France, the colonial ruler of Vietnam, a dividing line was drawn across the 17th parallel in 1954. It was agreed that general elections would be held in 1956, under the supervision of an International Committee. When the Prime Minister of South Vietnam, supported by the US, refused to hold the elections, the North decided to unify the country by force rather than political means. From then on, **guerrilla** warfare was waged by the northern-based Viet Cong. The North received direct support from China and took full advantage of weak governments in Laos and Cambodia to move arms and soldiers into South Vietnam from the west.

From 1961 on, the South was helped directly by the US, which had been providing South Vietnam's government with large-scale **aid** since 1954. By 1962, there were 11,000 US military advisers in

Bomb blitz
North Vietnamese women assess the damage after an attack on Haiphong by US B-52 bombers. VIETNAM WAR

Fighting for survival
Vietcong troops training in 1967. Around 900,000 North Vietnamese fighters were killed. **VIETNAM WAR**

South Vietnam and President Kennedy authorized them to fight if they were attacked.

Following the Tonkin Gulf incident in 1964, in which 2 US ships were reputedly attacked by North Vietnamese forces, the United States intervened directly in the war. By 1965, US aircraft were regularly bombing North Vietnam, often indiscriminately. South Vietnamese troops were also supported by contingents from Australia, New Zealand, the Philippines, South Korea and Thailand. By 1968 there were an estimated 500,000 Americans troops in the war.

Opposition in the US to the War grew as the death toll mounted. Peace marches and civil disobedience spread across the country and US President Johnson then began to negotiate a peace settlement with the north. Increasingly frustrated, Johnson announced in 1968 that bombing of the North would cease and that he would not seek re-

election. Further peace efforts in 1969 scaled down the conflict, but it flared into life again following the US bombing of North Vietnamese forces in Cambodia the following year.

A massive Communist offensive in 1972, coupled with continuing domestic opposition to American involvement, forced the US to find a peaceful solution to the War. These initiatives eventually led to the Paris Agreement in 1973 and US troop withdrawal. The North finally defeated the South in 1975 after all US aid had been withdrawn. Following the Communist victory, the north and south re-united in 1976.

The War marked the first ever military defeat for the United States. Of the 2.5 million US troops that fought in the War, 350,000 were either killed or injured. South Vietnam lost 700,000 and the North 900,000 troops. In addition, over a million civilians lost their lives. The total cost of the War was estimated at more than $200 billion.

Wind Power
White arms reaching up against the blue sky, the windmills hum to the
breeze on their hill at Altamont Pass, California.

W

W

Bold indicates a cross-reference

WALDHEIM, KURT (1918-   )

An Austrian diplomat who served in France and Canada before becoming Austria's representative to the **UN** from 1964-68. Following a stint as Austrian Foreign Minister from 1968-70 he returned as the nation's UN representative in 1970. He succeeded **U Thant** as Secretary-General in 1971, serving in the post until 1981. He was then elected President of Austria in 1986. But his tenure was marred by repeated accusations of involvement in war crimes when he was an army officer in World War II. The US Department of Justice barred him from the United States on the grounds of being a suspected war criminal and he was not invited to attend the UN's 50th anniversary celebrations in New York.

WAR

Since the end of World War II there have been at least 170 armed conflicts around the world and many civil wars. In the 1950s there were an average 9 outbreaks a year. By the 1980s the number had risen to 16. From 1945 to 1989, an estimated 22 million people were killed in wars, including millions of civilians and nearly 2 million children. Paradoxically, it is safer to be a soldier than a civilian in a conflict zone. The costs of modern warfare are astronomical. For example, the US and its allies spent billions on the 1991 **Gulf War** and they will have to find nearly three times as much again to pay for the medical and pension costs of their wounded soldiers. On the other side, rehabilitation costs in Iraq following the war were estimated at close to $200 billion.

In addition to destroying human life, most wars decimate farming and food production. World War II caused agricultural productivity in Europe to fall by 38%. The environmental impact of war is also beginning to be recognized. As weapons become more deadly, so does the impact on the ecosystem. The widespread use of defoliants, napalm and herbicides in the **Vietnam War** destroyed 1,500 square kilometres of **mangrove** forest and damaged a further 15,000 square kilometres of **land**.

Natural **resources**, notably minerals, are being depleted at increasing rates to fuel military development. Up to 12% of metals like aluminum, **copper**, **lead**, iron ore, nickel, platinum, silver, tin and tungsten are used for military purposes. The military accounts for at least 5% of the global consumption of petroleum.

Another problem is the potentially disastrous impact of the so-called 'remnants' of war. Since the end of World War II, 14.9 million land mines and 73 million bombs, shells and hand grenades have been recovered in Poland alone. During the wars in Indochina, 2 million bombs and 23 million artillery shells were thought not to have exploded. After the 1973 war between Egypt and Israel, Egypt discovered 8,500 non-exploded devices and cleared 700,000 **landmines**.

WARD, BARBARA (1914-1981)

British economist and conservationist. She graduated from Oxford University and worked as a university lecturer and journalist. She was active in the arts and wrote several significant books on the subjects of **ecology** and political economy, including *Spaceship Earth* (1966) and *Only One Earth* with René Dubois (1972).

The latter was commissioned as a report for the UN Conference on the Human Environment and was a synthesis of knowledge and opinion from the world's leading experts in many fields as well as information from the general public. She was Professor of International Economic Development at Columbia University (1968-73) before becoming president of the International Institute for Environment and Development in 1973.

WARSAW PACT

An alliance between the Soviet Union and the Communist states of Eastern Europe which was established after the Federal Republic of Germany became a member of the **North Atlantic Treaty Organization** (NATO) in 1955. The Pact was a military treaty between the USSR, Bulgaria, Czechoslovakia, East Germany, Hungary, Poland and Romania. It was officially based in Moscow, headed by the Soviet army's

Gateway to communism
The Brandenburg Gate seen behind the Berlin Wall – one of the starkest symbols of the Cold War period, when the Warsaw Pact was formed. WARSAW PACT

highest ranking officer. Albania was a member until 1968. After the fall of Communist governments in Eastern Europe in the late 1980s and the reunification of Germany, the Warsaw Pact soon fell apart. In 1990, Warsaw Pact nations reached an agreement with NATO stating that they no longer regarded each other as adversaries. That move signalled the total collapse of the Pact and it was officially dissolved in July, 1991.

WATER

Water is essential to life. It is a renewable, but limited resource. Only 3% of all the water on earth is freshwater. Most of that is locked up

SPRING OF HOPE

Two decades ago less than half the people of the developing world had access to safe, clean water. Now more than two-thirds have this most fundamental resource.

1975 40%

1995 70%

The State of the World's Children 1998, UNICEF.

in ice caps and glaciers (77%) or in **groundwater** (22%). The rest is found in lakes, rivers and streams.

About 40,000 cubic kilometres of water fall to the ground every year as part of the natural water cycle. Much of this is lost in floods or held in lakes or in the **soil** itself. Still, about 2,000 cubic kilometres is readily available, more than enough to satisfy the needs of the world's **population**. Every human being requires a minimum of 5 litres of water daily for basic survival. Average consumption varies from 5.4 litres a day in Madagascar to 500 litres a day in the United States.

In total, about 73% of freshwater around the world is used for agriculture, 21% by industry with just 6% left over for public use. Water-use patterns differ from region to region. In the rich world, industry accounts for 40% of water use, while in the **developing countries** the bulk of freshwater is used for crop **irrigation**. Overall irrigation is projected to rise two-fold and industrial use four-fold by the end of the century.

The availability of freshwater varies according to geography. For example, citizens of Iceland have 654,000 cubic metres each while people living in Bahrain have no renewable water **resources** whatso-

ever. Per capita water use is greatest in Turkmenistan, Tajikistan, Uzbekistan and other Central Asian countries that were former members of the Soviet Union.

As the demand for water increases, the supply of freshwater will become increasingly important and contentious. There are at least 200 rivers whose waters are shared by 2 or more countries. Already the waters of the **Ganges**, the Euphrates and the Zambezi have been the subject of heated international conflict. In 1997, **UNEP** forecast that 3 billion people were likely to face the prospect of severe water shortage within 50 years.

WATERBORNE DISEASE

Name given to a group of diseases transmitted to humans by bacteria, insects and other organisms that live or breed in **water**. Most of the world's deadliest diseases are in this group: including **cholera**, amoebic dysentery, **typhoid**, **hepatitis**, all diarrhoeal diseases, infections of the intestinal tract, trachoma, scabies, **leprosy**, **malaria**, river blindness, **yellow fever**, **schistosomiasis**, **dengue fever** and elephantiasis. The **World Health Organization** (WHO) estimates that 80% of all illnesses in the developing world stem from lack of safe water and adequate sanitation. These water-linked diseases kill at least 25,000 people each day yet they can all be significantly reduced by providing clean, safe water and adequate sanitation. In 1996 a quarter of the population in the developing world did not have access to safe water and more then two-thirds lacked adequate sanitation.

WEALTH DISTRIBUTION

Both wealth and income, on a global, national and individual basis are distributed unevenly and, many would argue, unjustly. Since 1900, the value of goods and services produced each year has risen 20-fold and the use of energy 30-fold. But not everyone has shared in the bounty. The difference between rich and poor continues to grow. There are over 200 billionaires and perhaps 3 million millionaires in the world. But 100 million people are **homeless** and 1 billion people, mostly in the developing, world live in **poverty**.

World-wide, the richest fifth of the **population** receive more than 60 times the income of the poorest fifth. And this ration has doubled over the last 40 years. In general, the industrialized countries with 20% of the global population receive three-quarters of world income. The 75% who live in **developing countries** get 20%; while the remaining 5% goes to people in the former Eastern bloc. Similar divisions exist within nations as well as between them. Among some of the world's most populous countries (China, the former Soviet Union and Japan) income distribution is relatively equitable, with the richest fifth of households in the nation receiving 3 to 4 times as much as the poorest fifth. In Brazil, the gap is much worse, the richest fifth earning 28 times as much as members of the poorest fifth.

RICHER AND POORER
Share of global income 1960 and 1993

85%

70%

Ratio richest:poorest **30:1**

Ratio richest:poorest **61:1**

2.3%

1.4%

Poorest 20% / Richest 20% — **1960**
Poorest 20% / Richest 20% — **1993**

Human Development Report 1996, UNDP.

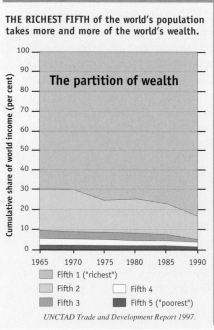

THE RICHEST FIFTH of the world's population takes more and more of the world's wealth.

The partition of wealth

Cumulative share of world income (per cent) — 1965, 1970, 1975, 1980, 1985, 1990

Fifth 1 ("richest")
Fifth 2
Fifth 3
Fifth 4
Fifth 5 ("poorest")

UNCTAD Trade and Development Report 1997.

WESTERNIZATION

Importing and accepting customs and institutions typical, or believed to be characteristic, of the West. It is usually used to describe the inexorable, often unintended process through which a capitalist economy and a consumer society take root wherever they are not deliberately avoided or eliminated. The process brings with it customs and habits which the majority of the population appear unable to resist.

In many societies the Western way of doing things is perceived to be more modern and glamorous than the way things are traditionally done. With that perception comes a burgeoning demand for consumer goods. This is testament to the value and impact of modern mass communications, advertising and propaganda.

Westernization can also be used to describe a more deliberate adoption of the Western model, as illustrated by the actions of **Kemal Ataturk** who insisted that the Western way of doing things was essential if Turkey was to change its social and political systems and structures and adopt a more modern lifestyle.

WETLANDS

Wetlands such as marshes, swamps, bogs and fens are amongst the most fertile and productive ecosystems in the world. They can produce up to eight times as much plant matter as an average **wheat** field. Wetlands cover 6% of the Earth's **land** surface and are found in all countries and in all climates.

They are important breeding grounds for **fish** and other wildlife. But they also help maintain the global **water** cycle and act as a filtering system to clean up polluted water, encouraging plant growth and improving water quality. They protect coastlines from erosion and act as barriers against storm surges, thus guarding inland areas from flooding as well as providing people with a wide range of staple food plants, fertile grazing lands and fuel.

Throughout the world, the need for more agricultural land has led to wetlands being drained for cultivation. For example, from 1950-1970 185,000 hectares of wetlands were lost each year in the US. All **dams** and barrages built for **irrigation** and hydropower generation reduce downstream wetlands, destroying fish breeding grounds and removing coastal protection.

Wetlands are the only ecosystem which is protected by a specific international convention. Under the RAMSAR Convention (adopted in

WETLANDS
● Wetlands cover 6 per cent of the earth's land surface and are highly productive ecosystems. They include swamps, marshes, mangrove forests and wet prairies.
● Canada has the largest known area of wetland marsh with 127 million hectares. Brazil, with 30 million hectares, comes second.
● Major threats come from construction development such as housing, roads and airports; demand for fresh water; agricultural development and pollution.
World Resources 1995.

THE **A** TO **Z** OF WORLD DEVELOPMENT

Ramsar, Iran) over 200,000 square kilometres of wetlands have been preserved though this is just a small portion of the global total. In 1996, RAMSAR revealed that the US states of Ohio and California had lost 90% of their wetlands. When the US was first colonized, it boasted 90 million hectares of wetlands. Since then 50 million have been degraded or destroyed. A survey also found that France has lost 67% of its wetlands, Italy 66%, Greece 63% and the Netherlands 55%.

WHALING

The hunting of whales began in the 15th century and became widespread in both hemispheres during the 18th and 19th century. The first species to attract the attention of hunters was the Right whale, so-called because it was slow, easy to catch and a good source of oil and whalebone. Victorian desires for stiff, whalebone corsets probably drove the Right whale close to extinction, although population estimates prior to the 1900s are not reliable. By the mid-1800s, Sperm whales were being hunted for their oil which was used in lamps. In addition, the Bowhead and Grey whales were hunted for both oil and whalebone. In 1872, a cannon-fired harpoon was developed which was capable of killing the faster species such as Blue, Fin and Sei, mainly for use as pet food. Each species was hunted until numbers dwindled, then attention was switched to another species. Since 1900 whaling has been concentrated in the Antarctic where whales congregate in summer to feed. Traditionally, whale carcasses were taken to **land** for processing into meat, fats, oils and other chemicals. The introduction of large 'factory' ships by the Soviet Union and Japan, meant that whales could be caught and processed at sea. This increased whaling efficiency to a point where many of the world's great whales were threatened with extinction. Today, several species – the Blue, Humpback, Bowhead and Northern Right – are officially recognized as 'endangered'.

Figures for numbers of whales are a matter of conjecture and fierce debate, mostly between whaling and non-whaling nations. Various local populations have become 'extinct', but individuals from the same species surface elsewhere. In 1989, killed by Japan's whaling fleet for 'scientific' reasons sold for $10.6 million wholesale.

Pressure from the US and consumers in Europe, led by Greenpeace, resulted in Iceland suspending its whaling activities for 2 years. The boycott reportedly cost the Icelandic **fishing** industry around $50 million in lost exports. Both Japan and Norway are also reluctant to abandon their lucrative whaling industries and in fact

In at the kill
Orca, the Latin name for whales, means mythical monster, but the name is more normally applied now to the (actually rather gentle) 'killer whale'. WHALING

the **International Whaling Commission** (IWC) estimated that there were 120,000 Fin whales, 14,000 Blue whales and 10,000 Humpback whales still surviving. The IWC set a moratorium on whaling beginning April 1988 to which all countries adhered – although Iceland, Norway and Japan began to operate 'scientific' whaling programmes, ostensibly killing whales to gather data on whale populations. Opponents claimed that scientific whaling was merely a front for normal whaling activities. Whale meat from the 1988 'scientific' catch was selling in Japanese stores in 1989 for $51 per kilogram. In 1990, 600 tonnes of meat from the 300 Minke whales

Norway increased its quota of Minke whales in both 1996 and 1997. Japan, too, is likely to start commercial whaling again soon.

Although the IWC was set up to promote sustainable whaling it has become the main forum for international anti-whaling protests. It is in dire financial straits with several member nations years behind in paying their dues.

WHEAT

A cereal grass belonging to the genus *triticum*, originally native to western Asia but now widely cultivated throughout subtropical and temperate regions. Wheat was amongst the first cultivated plants

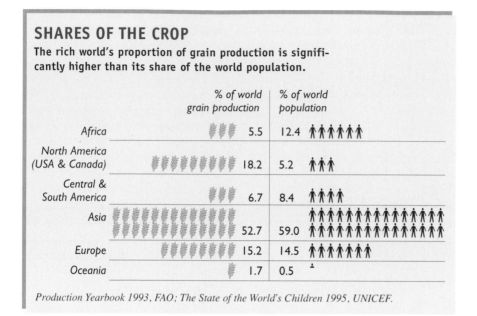

SHARES OF THE CROP

The rich world's proportion of grain production is significantly higher than its share of the world population.

	% of world grain production	% of world population
Africa	5.5	12.4
North America (USA & Canada)	18.2	5.2
Central & South America	6.7	8.4
Asia	52.7	59.0
Europe	15.2	14.5
Oceania	1.7	0.5

Production Yearbook 1993, FAO; The State of the World's Children 1995, UNICEF.

and about 820 million people around the world currently live on wheat-based diets. Many different varieties have been developed. Wheat is ground to produce flour and to make pasta, and is also important in the brewing industry. The world now grows more wheat than any other cereal and it is the most important cereal in international trade. After robust increases averaging 2.3% annually from 1950-1984, yields rose just 1.8% over the next decade. In 1989, 537 million tonnes of wheat were produced, 29 million tonnes more than the previous year. But since then there has been virtually no growth.

Wheat has become a major, but contentious component of **food aid** in recent decades. Although it helps ward off starvation, it also disrupts internal markets for peasant agriculture and creates a taste for a cereal that is not commonly grown in recipient nations.

Wheat does not grow well in tropical and semi-tropical climates without the addition of vast quantities of expensive chemicals. As a direct result of food aid programmes, the **Third World** is consuming more and more imported wheat and less and less traditional, locally-produced crops.

Wheat consumption in **developing countries** is growing 6 times faster than that of native crops.

In addition, there are no trading agreements to stabilize prices so wheat prices rise and fall according to supply. In terms of high demand (often during **famine** and food shortages) prices arc upwards and food import bills for **developing countries** also escalate.

Global annual wheat production is more than 530 million tonnes: China (95 million tonnes), the former-Soviet Union (88 million tonnes) and the United States (65 million tonnes) are the largest producers.

WILDLIFE TRADE

By the early 1990s, the global trade in wildlife and in products derived from wild plants and animals was worth more than $5 billion annually – double the 1984 total. The populations of hundreds of species of animals, including elephants, rhinoceros, tigers, crocodiles, turtles, whales, walruses and seals, have been severely reduced as a result of hunting and poaching.

Large **land** animals have been among the hardest hit. For example,

the demand for rhinoceros horn has seen the rhino population fall by 70% since 1970. Hundreds of tigers are killed each year in India, mainly to satisfy the demand for Chinese traditional medicines. In parts of the former Soviet Union poaching and illegal trade in **endangered species** is widespread. Snow leopards and lynx are killed for their skins and there is a thriving trade in rare amphibians and reptiles.

Trade in 675 species of wildlife, or products derived from them, is officially banned by the **Convention on International Trade in Endangered Species of Wild Fauna and Flora (CITES)**. Trade is also strictly regulated for another 30,000 species.

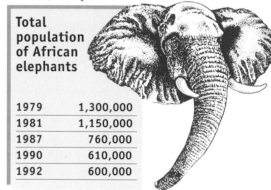

Total population of African elephants	
1979	1,300,000
1981	1,150,000
1987	760,000
1990	610,000
1992	600,000

Monitoring of the global wildlife trade is done by the Trade Records Analysis of Flora and Fauna in

Mammoth task
Its posterior bristling like a pincushion, this elephant seeks to dodge the spears and outrun its hunters in an 1857 engraving. WILDLIFE TRADE

Commerce (TRAFFIC), an international network co-ordinated by the **World Conservation Union**'s Conservation Monitoring Centre. The illegal trade in endangered or protected species is worth $1.5 billion annually, about 30% of the total trade in wildlife and wildlife products. Most of the illegal trade is in Southeast Asia, Japan, Africa and Latin America. However, there are now major efforts underway in Africa and Asia to try and curb the illicit business.

WIND POWER

Wind has been used to fill sails and power grain mills and **water** pumps for centuries. However, the use of wind to generate electricity is more recent. The main advantages of wind power are that it is non-polluting (since it uses no fuel) and that peak output (on cold, windy days) often coincides with peak demand. The other advantage, of course, is that wind is completely free.

The major disadvantage of wind-power is that production is unpredictable. Wind farms also require large tracts of **land** and generally need to be built on open ground some distance from the cities where power is needed most.

Nevertheless, wind power is one of the most rapidly developing of all the so-called alternative sources of energy. The average size for a wind-generator at the beginning of the 1980s was 25 kilowatts. It is now near 200 kilowatts and the production cost per kilowatt has fallen from $3,000 to less than $1,000 over the same period. Some manufacturers have gone so far as to guarantee that electricity will be produced costing less than 5 cents per kilowatt/hour. At this rate it would be one of the cheapest forms of electricity, competitive with **oil** and well below the cost of **nuclear power**. In the US, wind farms are already sound com-

World solar and wind energy capacity in megawatts, 1980-95

Vital Signs 1996/1997 Worldwatch Institute, Earthscan.

■ Sun   ■ Wind

mercial investments. A recent **World Bank** study identified 13 **developing countries** (Jordan, India, Pakistan, China, Mauritania, Morocco, Chile, Sri Lanka, Jamaica, Syria, Yemen, Romania and Tanzania) as having good potential for wind-energy developments. India has the most ambitious programme with plans to install 5,000 megawatts by the year 2000.

Wind power provides less than 1% of the world's electricity, but there is a huge potential for increase. Generating capacity jumped 22% in 1994 alone and installed capacity rose to 3,700 megawatts per year. The annual world-wide market for wind power is estimated at about $1 billion.

WORLD BANK (see International Bank for Reconstruction and Development)

WORLD COMMISSION ON ENVIRONMENT AND DEVELOPMENT (WCED)

An independent commission established by the UN General Assembly in 1983 to produce recommendations for a 'global agenda for change'. The WCED was to examine and analyze the interlinked issues of environmental deterioration and human development. Guidelines for concrete and realistic action were proposed – in particular a strategy to promote **sustainable**

development by the year 2000.

The WCED was chaired by Gro Harlem **Brundtland**, then Prime Minister of Norway, and was composed of 21 prominent political figures and leaders in environment and development from around the world. With a budget of $6 million the Commission travelled to 10 countries on 5 continents, hearing evidence from government officials, scientists, industrialists, **non-governmental organizations** (NGOs) and the general public. Seventy-five studies written by experts also formed part of the Commission's research.

The Commission's report, *Our Common Future* (1987), described 22 new principles to help achieve sustainable development. These were to be incorporated into national laws specifying the rights and duties of citizens and the state.

The report concluded that huge increases in expenditure will be needed to repair environmental damage, control pollution and to invest in sustainable development. In one of its few really innovative recommendations, the Commission

Future imperfect
Mining for uranium has destroyed mangroves in Rum Jungle, Australia, ruining the habitat of fish and shellfish too. WCED

Conserving stocks
Fish ponds like this one in Java, Indonesia, allow fish to be farmed sustainably. They can also give a watery home to ducks and rice, providing meals for the family.
WORLD CONSERVATION STRATEGY

suggested that these funds should be raised by levying **taxes** on the use of the 'Global Commons', including 'parking charges' for geo-stationary communications satellites and taxes on revenues from sea-bed mining and ocean **fishing**.

WORLD CONSERVATION STRATEGY
In 1976, the **Worldwide Fund for Nature** (WWF), the International Union for the Conservation of Nature (IUCN), known as the **World Conservation Union**, and the **United Nations Environment Programme** (UNEP) agreed on the need for a global **conservation** strategy. More than 700 scientists and 450 government agencies from over 100 countries contributed information and advice which resulted in the publication of the *World Conservation Strategy* in 1980. The document outlined the main aims of conservation: maintenance of essential ecological processes; preservation of bio-diversity; and careful, sustainable use of the earth's natural **resources**.

An updated version, *Caring For The World: A Strategy For Sustainability* (1991), stressed the need to protect the earth's vitality and diversity as the core of a sustainable lifestyle. It called for all nations to adopt a far-reaching strategy to safeguard their own natural bio-diversity and to protect at least 10% of each of the main ecological regions within their borders by the end of the century.

WORLD CONSERVATION UNION (IUCN)
The IUCN is an independent, international organization representing a wide-ranging network of governments, **non-governmental organizations** (NGOs), scientists and other **conservation** experts working together to promote the protection and sustainable use of the world's natural resource base. More than 778 national governments, state authorities, private nature conservation organizations and international conservation groups from 125 countries are members. The IUCN promotes scientifically-based action towards the sustainable use and conservation of natural **resources**. The IUCN also plays an important role devising special measures to prevent species from becoming endangered or extinct. As part of its activities, the IUCN monitors the status of ecosystems and wildlife throughout the world. It co-ordinates action by governments, intergovernmental bodies and NGOs and provides assistance and expert advice.

It has 6 specialized commissions that rely on the work of 3,000 experts. There are commissions on threatened species; protected areas; **ecology**; environmental planning and policy; law and administration; and environmental education. It also produces specialised publications such as the *Red Data Book* (listing all endangered animal species), the *UN List of National Parks and Protected Areas*, the *World Conservation Strategy* and *Caring for the Earth: A Strategy for Sustainable Living*. It is funded through contributions from the **Worldwide Fund for Nature** (WWF), grants from governments, membership fees, donations from UN agencies and other independent foundations.

WORLD COUNCIL OF CHURCHES (WCC)
A group of over 335 Protestant and Orthodox Christian churches from more than 100 countries. The WCC is a product of the ecumenical movement and was founded in Amsterdam in 1948. Now based in Geneva, membership includes almost all Christian Churches including Anglican and other Protestant denominations, as well as Orthodox and Old Catholics. There is also increasing support from the Roman Catholic Church. The Vatican has never been a full Council member, but has always co-operated with the WCC and sent observers to meetings. The WCC has no authority over its members but helps to co-ordinate common action in the cause of Christian unity. The Council's policy of support for liberation

movements and social justice causes in the **Third World** has been controversial and has been opposed by right-wing Christian fundamentalists.

WORLD COURT (see International Court of Justice)

WORLD FOOD COUNCIL (WFC)

The Council was established by the UN following a recommendation from the World Food Conference (1974) and is composed of 36 ministerial-level members from differing nations. Based in Rome, the Council aims to keep under review major problems and policies affecting the world food situation, stimulate food production, improve food trade and to put into action the recommendations of the World Food Conference.

WORLD FOOD PROGRAMME (WFP)

The WFP attempts to stimulate and advance economic and social development through the provision of **food aid**. The programme was established in 1963 and is based in Rome. It operates as a specialized programme of the **Food and Agriculture Organization** (FAO), to which governments can pledge food or money.

The WFP concentrates on those most in need and the majority of its projects are designed to increase food and agricultural production and promote **rural development**, particularly in low-income, food-deficit countries. A significant part of WFP resources and activities are devoted to improving nutrition in the most vulnerable groups: the poor, children and pregnant or nursing mothers.

The Programme supplies food aid at the request of governments and is administered by the Committee on Food Aid Policies and Programmes of the **FAO**. Since its inception, the WFP has shipped over $7.5 billion in food to more than 250 million people.

Typically, labourers are given food rations for their work, usually in agricultural or rural development projects. Money which the government saves on food imports is then used to fund other development

Tipping the scales
A bouncing baby weighs in at the clinic in Burkina Faso: basic food and healthcare are essential for infant growth. **WFP**

projects. The WFP also provides food **aid** to areas where the food is in short supply due to war or natural **disasters**. Contributions of food and money from more than 131 countries are channelled through the WFP. The agency now handles 25% of global food aid and has become a major funder of agricultural and rural development projects in over 100 countries.

WORLD HEALTH ORGANIZATION (WHO) (see also United Nations)

The WHO was founded in 1948 and was the first specialized agency of the **United Nations**. The organization works to help control disease and improve general standards of health and nutrition through international co-operation. Its overall goal is 'the attainment by all peoples of the highest possible level of health'.

The WHO is based in Geneva and has 189 members. It supports programmes to eradicate diseases; undertakes, co-ordinates and finances epidemiological research; trains health workers; strengthens national health services; and suggests international health guidelines and regulations. It also sponsors research, promotes improved standards of teaching and training in the health and medical professions and can provide

---

FEAST AND FAMINE

The rich world has a glut – of food and obese citizens. In the US about a third of the population is overweight – $33 billion is spent each year in attempts to lose weight. In the poor world millions subsist on an amount of food that is simply inadequate for good health. An estimated 190 million children under the age of five are chronically malnourished.

The State of the World's Children 1997, UNICEF.

THE FEAST
Countries with highest daily supply of calories per head as % of requirements* 1988-90

Ireland	157
Greece	151
Belgium	149
Bulgaria	148
France	143
Spain	141
Italy	139
US	138
Hungary	137
Singapore	136
Aotearoa/NZ	130
UK	130
South Africa	128
Australia	124

THE FAMINE
Countries with lowest daily supply of calories per head as % of requirements* 1988-90

72	Afghanistan
73	Chad
73	Ethiopia
77	Mozambique
80	Angola
81	Somalia
82	Central African Republic
82	Rwanda
83	Sierra Leone
84	Burundi
84	Bolivia

Shocking as they may be, these figures are only averages. There are hungry people in rich countries and those who can afford more than they need in poorer ones, which makes the contrast between greed and need even more dramatic.

* An adequate adult calorie intake is between 2,350 and 2,600 calories per day, depending on climate and kinds of work performed.

emergency and disaster **aid**. Most of the agency's work deals with health issues in the developing world. The supranational activities of the WHO proceed solely on the basis of national government co-operation.

In addition to regular funding through the UN system, the WHO operates a Voluntary Fund for Health Promotion (VHFP) which has a balance of $55 million. More than a third of the WHO's operating budget is now sustained through contributions to the VFHP from donor governments, international agencies, foundations and individuals.

WORLD INTELLECTUAL PROPERTY ORGANIZATION (WIPO)

A specialized agency of the **UN** based in Geneva with 147 member states. WIPO was set up in 1974 and aims to promote co-operation in the recognition and enforcement of international agreements on industrial property: trademarks, patents, inventions and industrial designs. It also has a similar role with regard to copyright of literary, musical and artistic works.

WORLD SUMMIT FOR CHILDREN

A 1990 meeting in New York at which government leaders and representatives from 72 nations signed the World Declaration on the Survival, Protection and Development of Children. The Summit was initiated by Canada, Egypt, Mali, Mexico, Pakistan and Sweden, but attracted barely half of all UN members.

The Summit called for concerted global action to protect the rights and improve the lives of children. The goals included a reduction in infant deaths by a third and a halving of the **maternal mortality** rate. In a subsequent report **UNICEF** estimated that it would cost $20 billion annually if the targets set by the World Summit were to be achieved by the end of the decade.

WORLD TOURISM ORGANIZATION (WTO)

A **UN** agency established in 1975 with the aim of promoting **tourism** globally as a means of contributing to economic development, peace and international understanding. The organization has 121 member countries and 4 associate members.

WORLD TRADE ORGANIZATION (WTO)

The WTO is the legal and institutional foundation of the multilateral trading system. At the conclusion of the **Uruguay Round** of the **General Agreement on Tariffs and Trade** (GATT) in Morocco in 1994, it was agreed to dissolve GATT into the WTO. GATT dealt largely with trade in merchandise goods whereas the WTO will cover trade in goods,

Trade-off
Peruvian coffee grower Gregorio, on a visit to Britain, watches as an advert for fair-traded Cafédirect takes shape on the screen. WORLD TRADE ORGANIZATION

services and in ideas or intellectual property.

The WTO is a permanent institution with a Ministerial Council as its highest authority, composed of one representative from each member state. A General Council will sit annually with representatives from all members. Two thirds of the 128 member countries are from the developing world. WTO will operate by consensus, but a one-country-one-vote system is also in place if consensus cannot be reached. The General Council will also sit as a dispute settlement body to resolve trade disputes, including authorizing retaliatory measures. There is also a trade policy review body to conduct regular reviews of trading policy in member states. The essential functions of WTO are to administer and implement multilateral trade agreements; to act as a forum for multilateral trade negotiations; to try and resolve trade disputes; to oversee national trade policies; and to co-operate with all other agencies in trade-related matters.

Critics argue that the WTO is an attempt by global corporations and their supporters to dismantle national social standards and environmental regulations in the name of **free trade**. According to the WTO, any attempts to protect domestic

WORLD METEOROLOGICAL ORGANIZATION (WMO)

A UN agency established in 1951 with the aim of standardizing international meteorological observations and improving the exchange of weather information. Its chief activities are the World Weather Watch programme which co-ordinates facilities and services provided by members and a research and development programme focusing on climate change. The organization has 175 members and is based in Geneva.

industries, consumers, workers or the environment may be challenged as barriers to free and open trade. In its first trade dispute judgement the WTO ruled that the US Clean Air Act, which set different standards for US and imported gasoline, was discriminatory.

WORLD WIDE FUND FOR NATURE (WWF)

Formerly known as the World Wildlife Fund (WWF). The organization changed its name to the World Wide Fund for Nature in 1989 but retained the acronym. It still uses its original name in Canada and the United States. WWF is based in Switzerland with 23 national branches on 5 continents. It is dedicated to the **conservation** of **endangered species** and their natural habitats. Since 1961 WWF has financed conservation projects around the globe as well as remaining a major contributor to the budget of the International Union for the Conservation of Nature (**World**

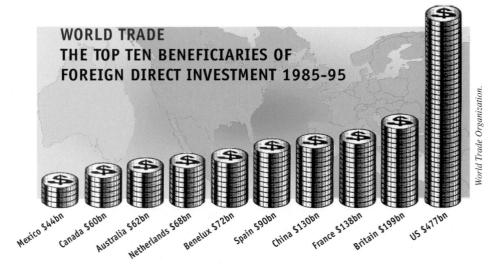

WORLD TRADE
THE TOP TEN BENEFICIARIES OF FOREIGN DIRECT INVESTMENT 1985-95

Mexico $44bn · Canada $60bn · Australia $62bn · Netherlands $68bn · Benelux $72bn · Spain $90bn · China $130bn · France $138bn · Britain $199bn · US $477bn

World Trade Organization.

Conservation Union). WWF has more than 5.2 million members. It is dedicated to the conservation of the natural environment and the ecological processes essential to life on earth, and to create awareness of threats to the natural environment. WWF has channelled over $130 million to 5,000 projects in over 130 countries. It has served as a catalyst for conservation action and provided a link between conservation needs, the scientific resources necessary to meet them and the authorities whose partici-

pation or action is needed. WWF works in conjunction with government and **non-governmental organizations** but it has also adopted a crucial and pioneering role in bridging the gap between the conservation movement and the business community. In 1990, WWF underwent major restructuring after it was discovered that WWF International had investments in multinational companies whose activities it was campaigning against. Long identified with efforts to save particular species, WWF's new mandate is to focus on **sustainable development**, pollution control and reducing wasteful consumption.

Shark's tooth
A shark devours prey under the gaze of a diver on Australia's Great Barrier Reef — one of the world's richest natural habitats. **WWF**

W HO – WWF

Zapatistas

The Zapatista movement surprised the world when it mobilized 2,000 peasants in 1994 to protest at Mexico's joining the North American Free Trade Agreement.

Xenotransplantation – Zionism

Xenotransplantation – Zionism

Bold indicates a cross-reference

XENOTRANSPLANTATION

Transplanting animal organs into humans. Most organs transplanted into humans come from donors who are 'brain stem dead' but on life-support systems. The increasing success rate of organ transplants has sparked an international trade in body parts. Western brokers offer poor people in **developing countries** money or consumer goods in exchange for their kidneys or corneas.

The growing demand has also stimulated research into xenotransplantation. Pigs are being genetically engineered to produce organs that will fool the human immune system into reacting to the organs as if they were human.

Xenotransplantation could create a global transplantation boom, enabling kidney transplants to jump ten-fold. Heart, lung and liver transplants could show even greater increases. Potential revenue from xenotransplants could be as high as $5 billion annually within 15 years. One pharmaceutical company has already earmarked $1 billion for research into the area.

However, critics warn that xeno-transplantation could lead to new pandemics as animal diseases are transmitted to humans. In 1995, a group calling themselves Doctors and Lawyers for Responsible Medicine wrote to the UK Government calling for a immediate cessation of xenotransplantation.

YANOMAMI

Indigenous people of South America who live in remote forest areas along what is now the border between Brazil and Venezuela. Their

> ### Threats
> ● Individual prospectors can be as damaging to indigenous peoples as multinational companies. In Brazil it is the *garimpeiros*, small-scale gold miners, who are most active on Yanomami land.
>
> ● Since 1987 over 50,000 miners have poured in, clearing forests, destroying the soil, diverting rivers and polluting them with mercury.

contact with the outside world up until the early part of the 20th century was minimal. In the 1960s there were estimated to be 20,000 Yanomami.

They practise **slash-and-burn** agriculture and live in small, scattered communal groups, clearing the forest around their dwellings where the women grow plantains, **cassava** and **maize** and collect berries and nuts. The men hunt monkeys, deer, fowl and armadillos.

They also grow **tobacco** and **cotton**. Dogs are kept for hunting and security. The way of life of the Yanomami was first threatened in the early 1900s when thousands of gold miners invaded their tradition-al lands. The miners have shot and killed the Indians, polluted local rivers and **water** courses, deforested large areas, and brought unfamiliar diseases. A single **malaria** epidemic is thought to have killed 15% of the Yanomami people.

In 1990-91, under heavy

YANGTZE RIVER

ECO-SYSTEM: Known as the 'Long River' or 'The River of Golden Sand', the Yangtze is the longest river in Asia. It rises in the Tanglha mountains very near Tibet and flows through Szechwan and Hunan to enter the Yellow Sea near Shanghai. Some of its 600 million annual tons of mud and silt is deposited on its fertile delta and Chongming Island at the river's mouth. The Yangtze has 700 tributaries and its drainage basin covers 20% of China's total land area. One in 13 people on the planet live in its basin.

THREATS: The Yangtze's dangerous floods have drowned 330,000 people this century alone. For centuries a system of dykes held back floods – some as ancient as the eighth century are still in working order. The Three Gorges Dam will be the world's biggest and is projected to control flooding and provide energy-inefficient Chinese factories with hydro-power. It will cost between $17-75 billion, take 10 years to complete and flood a million people from their homes. Some 300,000 farmers will lose their land and controversies rage on the dam's effectiveness in controlling floods and on long-term social and ecological costs.

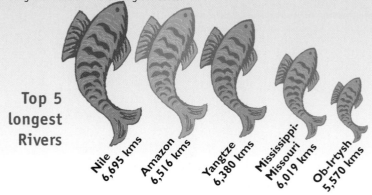

Top 5 longest Rivers

Nile 6,695 kms · Amazon 6,516 kms · Yangtze 6,380 kms · Mississippi-Missouri 6,019 kms · Ob-Irtysh 5,570 kms

Encyclopedia of the World's Great Rivers, Rand-McNally, New York 1980.

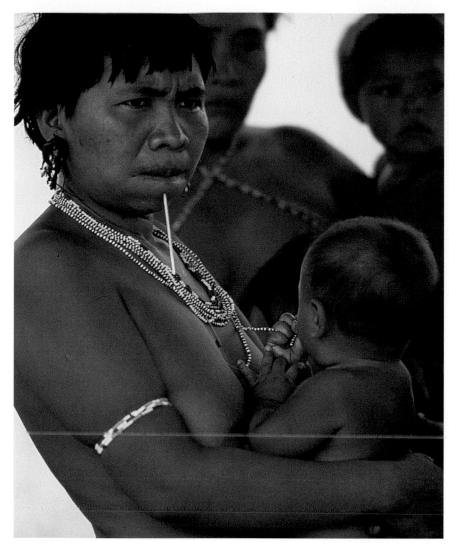

Mother love
The Yanomami live in the rich Amazonian forests of Brazil, but their way of life is threatened by deforestation, mining and construction. YANOMAMI

the heart. It can also harm the liver, causing jaundice (thus the name 'yellow fever'). Death may result from heart or liver failure.

Although yellow fever frequently proves fatal without medical help, recovery from a first attack confers subsequent immunity. There is no specific treatment once the disease has developed. But two kinds of vaccine, the first developed in 1951, can successfully immunize people and have played a major role in limiting the range of the disease.

Nonetheless, yellow fever is increasing in all endemic areas. In South America, the number of cases has been rising steadily recently.

In Africa, the disease reached epidemic proportions in 1986-87 when more than 5,300 cases were reported. The **World Health Organization** (WHO) estimates that 200,000 people yearly come down with yellow fever and more than 20,000 of them die.

pressure from the international community and **human rights** organizations, the miners were expelled from Yanomami lands. Then in 1991, the Venezuelan Government allocated an amount of forest the size of Austria as a permanent homeland for the Yanomami. The Brazilian Government followed suit. But miners have continued to invade Yanomami **land** while local authorities charged with policing the area turn a blind eye.

YELLOW FEVER
A once widespread viral infection transmitted to humans by the *aedes aegyptii* **mosquito**. Medical care,

coupled with campaigns to reduce mosquito numbers, significantly reduced the range of the disease which is mainly confined to tropical rainforest regions of Africa and South America.

However, in common with other mosquito-transmitted diseases, yellow fever is now on the increase. The largest number of new cases in 40 years was reported in 1990. In 1992, Kenya reported its first ever epidemic. And in 1995, Peru reported the highest number of cases ever in the Americas.

After an incubation period of up to 14 days the yellow fever patient develops a chill, headache, aching muscles and a fever. In severe cases the virus can attack the kidneys and

ZAPATA, EMILIANO (1879-1919)
Mexican revolutionary leader who championed the cause of agrarian reform. A peasant of Indian blood, he led a **guerrilla** revolt against the dictator Porfirio Diaz and successive governments from 1911 onwards under the slogan *Tierra y Libertad* (Land and Liberty). By late 1911 he controlled the state of Morelos where he carried out extensive **land** reforms, driving off estate owners and distributing their land to the peasants. In 1919 he was tricked into an ambush and assassinated.

'And they said we did not exist!'
Stirring words from the Zapatista Army of National Liberation (named after Mexican revolutionary hero Emiliano Zapata) roused Chiapas peasants for the uprising in 1994. ZAPATISTAS

ZAPATISTAS

A **guerrilla** group which staged a rebellion against the Mexican Government on New Year's Day 1994. The Zapatista National Liberation Front (FZLN) adopted the name of the legendary Mexican guerrilla leader **Emiliano Zapata**. Their cause was supported by the **indigenous people** of Chiapas State in southern Mexico and other Mexicans who opposed the country's decision to join the **North American Free Trade Agreement**.

The Government despatched the army to deal with the uprising but failed to subdue the FZLN. The Zapatistas quickly became a potent force, making use of sophisticated electronic communications technologies to spread their message to the outside world. However, the low-intensity war against the FZLN made conditions worse for the people of Chiapas. In 1996, some 27,000

people were on the edge of starvation as a result of the army's activities, which reportedly included the torture and murder of dozens of villagers. The US Government provided the Mexican Government with over $100 million worth of equipment and training to help wage their campaign against the Zapatistas.

ZIMBABWE AFRICAN NATIONAL UNION (ZANU)

In 1953, Southern Rhodesia united with Nyasaland (now Malawi) and Northern Rhodesia (now Zambia) to form the Central African Federation of Rhodesia. Within the region, the African nationalist movement, spearheaded by the National Democratic Party (NDP), struggled to achieve independence. Eventually the NDP was banned and split into 2 groups – the Zimbabwe

ZIA, BEGUM KHALEDA (1945-)

A Bangladeshi politician and member of the Bangladesh National Party (BNP). She was elected Prime Minister of Bangladesh in 1991 after General HM Ershad was forced to step down as leader. Begum Zia was the widow of **Ziaur Rahman**, who had served as the country's President from 1975 until he was assassinated during a coup attempt in 1981.

After the 1991 election Begum Zia announced her intention to establish a parliamentary democracy. This was approved by all parties and Begum Zia became head of the new parliamentary regime. She sought to facilitate greater **economic growth** and foreign investment in Bangladesh. Zia faced a turbulent opposition campaign by political groups opposed to the rule of the BNP. Opposition parties boycotted the February 1996 elections and subsequently staged a series of strikes, transport blockades and violent demonstrations. In March 1996 Begum Zia handed over power to a caretaker government.

African People's Union (ZAPU) led by Joshua Nkomo and the Zimbabwe African National Union (ZANU) led by Ndabaningi Sithole and later by **Robert Mugabe**.

Following the break-up of the Federation in 1963 the white, Rhodesian Front Government of Ian Smith declared unilateral independence from Britain. ZAPU and ZANU then waged **guerrilla** war against Smith's regime from bases in Zambia and Mozambique. After 10 years in which thousands died and

Fruit of Zimbabwe
A woman and her son selling watermelons by the roadside near Bulawayo. ZIMBABWE

millions more were uprooted, the white minority finally agreed to multiracial elections in 1980.

Robert Mugabe's ZANU party won easily and Mugabe became Prime Minister and soon established a one-party, Marxist-oriented state. A multi-party system was re-adopted in 1990, but with little real opposition. Several opposition parties boycotted the 1995 elections and ZANU won

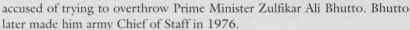

ZIA ul-HAQ, GENERAL MOHAMMED (1924-1988)
Pakistani general and politician. Zia received his commission in 1945 from the Royal Indian Military Academy. Following service in the military in Pakistan, he was appointed president of the military courts that tried several Army and Air Force officers accused of trying to overthrow Prime Minister Zulfikar Ali Bhutto. Bhutto later made him army Chief of Staff in 1976.

The following year he led the bloodless coup which deposed Bhutto who was later charged with murder. He appointed himself chief martial law administrator in 1977 and assumed the Presidency in 1978 when Fazal Elahi Chaudhry resigned. Earlier in 1979, he had refused world-wide appeals to commute Bhutto's death sentence for conspiracy to murder and had executed the charismatic and still popular former leader. Zia banned all political parties, prohibited labour strikes and imposed strict press censorship. When the Soviet Union invaded neighbouring Afghanistan in 1979, his response was a huge military build-up financed by the United States. He kept martial law in place and tried to 'Islamicize' Pakistan's political and cultural life. He was killed in a plane crash in 1988.

all but 2 parliamentary seats.

In the same year, Ndabaningi Sithole, now head of the ZANU-Ndonga party and one of only 2 non-ZANU MPs was arrested in connection with an alleged plot to assassinate Mugabe. This happened shortly after Sithole announced that he would run against Mugabe in the 1996 presidential election.

ZIONISM
A Jewish nationalist movement which emerged in the 19th century following a tide of European **nationalism** combined with virulent anti-Semitism. The movement was formally established in 1897 at the first Zionist Congress in Basel. The aim was to build a Jewish homeland in Palestine on the basis of 'Biblical rights'.

Since the birth of Israel in 1948, the Zionist movement has continued to encourage Jewish immigration to Palestine and to express support for the new state of Israel. In 1991, following a joint request from Israel and the United States, the UN General Assembly revoked a resolution which defined Zionism as a 'form of racism and racial discrimination'. The resolution had been passed in 1975 with widespread support from both the **Third World** and the Soviet bloc. It had been seen as a show of support for Palestine when the **Palestine Liberation Organization** was granted UN observer status that year.

ZIAUR RAHMAN, MUHAMMED (1936-1981)
Bangladeshi politician and army officer. He fought against Pakistan in the 1971 war and became army chief of staff in 1975, the same year he founded the Bangladesh National Party (BNP). Following the assassination of Bangladesh's first prime minister Sheikh Mujibur Rahman in 1975, martial law was declared and Ziaur Rahman became chief martial law administrator. He assumed the Presidency in 1977 after his position had been confirmed by a referendum, but was assassinated in 1981.

ABOUT THE AUTHORS

ANDY CRUMP

As an ecologist, teacher, writer, photographer and videographer, Andy Crump has lived and worked in the Pacific, Africa, Europe and North America. His work in academia, for non-governmental organisations and for various agencies of the UN system has also taken him to various parts of Asia and Latin America. He has been observing and reporting on diverse attitudes, differing life values, scientific and technological advancements and social development – and the often bizarre aspects of these – for over 25 years. With the guiding philosophy that people everywhere should be free to make up their own minds and take their own decisions, and that we should be armed with as much information as we can obtain in order to base those decisions on sound foundations, he has striven to contribute and disseminate his observations and knowledge as widely as possible. As a result, his work has appeared in media ranging from newspaper and magazine articles, books, exhibitions, photographs, to television programmes and interactive educational packages at the World Health Organization in Geneva.

WAYNE ELLWOOD

Wayne joined the **New Internationalist** magazine in 1977 as an editor. He set up the **NI** office in Toronto and played several roles in the early years in addition to his editing one: fund-raising, marketing and accountancy. He has travelled widely in the Third World including Zimbabwe, Liberia, Malaysia, Thailand, Indonesia, India, the Philippines and most recently Cuba.

BIBLIOGRAPHY

Statistical Yearbook *UN.*
Country Human Development Indicators *UNDP.*
Human Development Report 1996, 1997 *UNDP/Oxford University Press.*
Social Indicators of Development *World Bank/Johns Hopkins Press.*
The State of the World's Children 1996, 1997, 1998 *UNICEF/Oxford University Press.*
World Development Report 1996, 1997 *World Bank/Oxford University Press.*
World Health Report *World Health Organization.*
World Development Indicators *World Bank.*
Yearbook of Labour Statistics *International Labour Office.*
International Trade Statistics Yearbook *UN.*
Statistical Yearbook *UNESCO.*
Record of World Events *Keesings Worldwide LLC.*
World Factbook *Central Intelligence Agency (USA).*
International Yearbook & Statesmen's Who's Who *Reed Information Services.*
Geographic Distribution of Financial Flows to Aid Recipients *OECD/Development Assistance Committee.*
Green Globe Yearbook *Oxford University Press/Fridtjof Nansen Institute.*
Environmental Data Report *United Nations Environment Programme/Basil Blackwell.*
World Labour Report *International Labour Office.*
World Economic Outlook *International Monetary Fund.*
Production Yearbook *Food and Agriculture Organization.*
World In Figures *Profile Books/Economist.*
Europe in Figures *EUROSTAT (1995).*
Encyclopaedia Britannica *Encyclopaedia Britannica Inc.*
Guinness Concise Encyclopaedia – Ian Crofton (Ed.) *Guinness Publishing (1993).*

Websters International Encyclopaedia – Michael D. Harkavy (Ed.) *Trident Press International (1994).*
Dictionary of Environment and Development – Andy Crump *Earthscan (1991).*
Dictionary of the Middle East – Dilip Hiro *Macmillan (1996).*
Dictionary of Economics – Jae K. Shim & Joel G. Siegel *John Wiley & Sons (1995).*
Dictionary of International Trade – Jerry M. Rosenberg *John Wiley & Sons (1994).*
Dictionary of Political Thought – Roger Scruton *Macmillan (1996).*
Dictionary of Politics – David Robertson *Penguin (1993).*
Cambridge Biographical Dictionary – David Crystal (Ed.) *Cambridge University Press (1996).*
Concise Science Dictionary *Oxford University Press (1996).*
State of the World – Lester Brown et. al. *Earthscan.*
Vital Signs – Lester Brown et. al *W.W. Norton & Co.*
World Guide – Instituto del Tercer Mundo *New Internationalist Publications (1997).*
Third World Guide – Instituto del Tercer Mundo *New Internationalist Publications (1993/94, 94/95).*
Beyond the Limits – D.H. Meadows, D.L. Meados & J. Randers *Earthscan (1992).*
Gaia Atlas of Planet Mangement – Norman Myers (Ed.) *Gaia Books Ltd. (1994).*
Women and the Environment – Annabel Rodda *ZED Books (1993).*
Women and Health – Patricia Smyke *ZED Books (1991).*
Women and Human Rights – Katarina Tomasevski *ZED Books (1993).*
Earth Summit 1992 – Joyce Quarrie (Ed.) *Regency Press (1992).*
Caring for the Earth *Earthscan.*

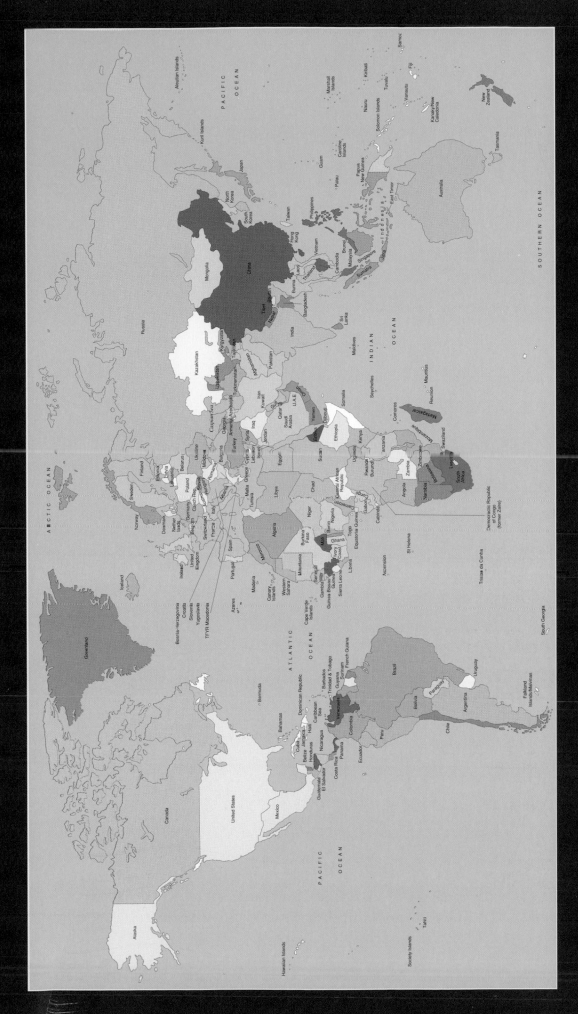

Countries of the World

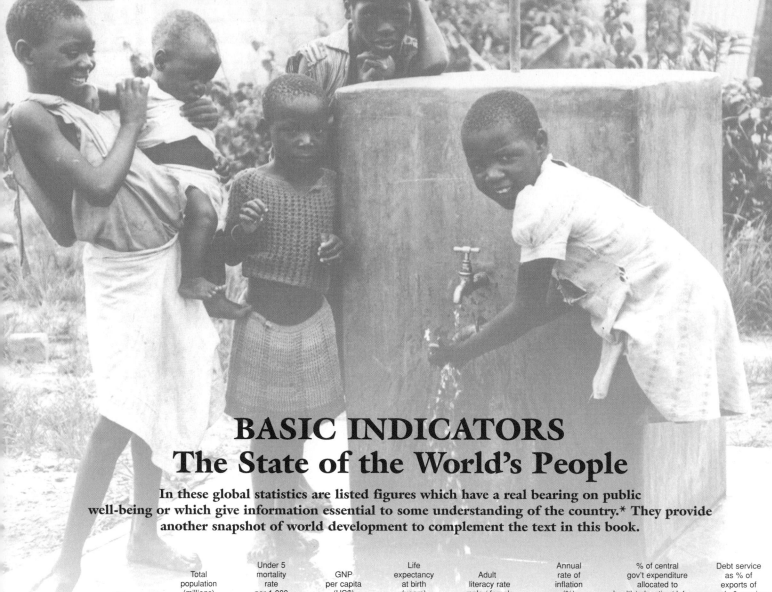

BASIC INDICATORS
The State of the World's People

In these global statistics are listed figures which have a real bearing on public
well-being or which give information essential to some understanding of the country.* They provide
another snapshot of world development to complement the text in this book.

	Total population (millions) 1996	Under 5 mortality rate per 1,000 1996	GNP per capita (US$) 1996	Life expectancy at birth (years) 1996	Adult literacy rate male / female 1995	Annual rate of inflation (%) 1985 - 95	% of central gov't expenditure allocated to health/education/defence 1990 - 96	Debt service as % of exports of goods & services 1970/1995
Afghanistan	20.8	257	250	45	47 / 15	–	– / – / –	– / –
Albania	3.4	40	670	71	– / –	27	6 / 2 / 7	– / 1
Algeria	28.8	39	1600	68	74 / 49	23	– / – / –	3 / 37
Angola	11.2	292	410	47	56 / 29	170	6 / 15 / 34	– / 15
Argentina	35.2	25	8030	73	96 / 96	256	2 / 5 / 7	22 / 26
Armenia	3.6	30	730	71	100 / 99	183	– / – / –	– / 1
Australia	18.1	6	18720	78	– / –	4	13 / 8 / 7	– / –
Austria	8.1	6	26890	77	– / –	3	14 / 10 / 2	– / –
Azerbaijan	7.6	44	480	71	100/ 99	279	– / – / –	– / 1
Bangladesh	120.0	112	240	57	49 / 26	6	5 / 11 / 10	0 / 15
Belarus	10.3	18	2070	70	100/ 99	309	2/ 18 / 4	– / 2
Belgium	10.2	7	24710	77	– / –	3	2 / 12 / 5	– / –
Benin	5.6	140	370	54	49 / 26	3	6 / 31 / 17	2 / 13
Bhutan	1.8	127	420	52	56 / 28	8	8 / 10 / –	–/ 10
Bolivia	7.6	102	800	61	91 / 76	18	6/ 19 / 8	11 / 26
Bosnia- Herzegovina	3.6	17	–	73	– / –	– / –	– / – / –	– / –
Botswana	1.5	50	3020	52	81 / 60	12	5 / 21 / 12	1 / 4
Brazil	161.1	52	3640	67	83 / 83	875	5 /3 / 3	12 / 29
Bulgaria	8.5	19	1330	71	99 / 98	46	3 / 4 / 6	– / 11
Burkina Faso	10.8	158	230	46	30 / 9	3	7 / 17 / 14	4 / 17
Burundi	6.2	176	160	46	49 / 23	6	4 / 16 / 16	4 / 22
Cambodia	10.3	170	270	53	80/ 53	71	– / – / –	– / 2
Cameroon	13.6	102	650	56	75 / 52	2	5 / 18 / 9	3 / 17
Canada	29.7	7	19380	79	– / –	3	5 / 3 / 6	– / –
Central African Rep.	3.3	164	340	49	69 / 52	4	– / – / –	5 / 3

BASIC INDICATORS

	Total population (millions) 1996	Under 5 mortality rate per 1,000 1996	GNP per capita (US$) 1996	Life expectancy at birth (years) 1996	Adult literacy rate male / female 1995	Annual rate of inflation (%) 1985 - 95	% of central gov't expenditure allocated to health/education/defence 1990 - 96	Debt service as % of exports of goods & services 1970/1995
Chile	14.4	13	4160	75	95 / 95	18	12 / 15 / 9	19 /15
China	1232.0	47	620	69	90 / 73	9	0 / 2 / 12	0 / 10
Colombia	36.4	31	1910	71	91 / 91	25	5 / 19 / 9	12 / 27
Congo	2.7	108	680	51	83 / 67	2	– / – / –	11 / 11
Congo, Dem. Rep.	46.8	207	120	53	87 / 68	–	1 / 1 / 4	5 / 6
Costa Rica	3.5	15	2610	77	95 / 95	18	21 / 17 / –	10 / 15
Côte d'Ivoire (Ivory Coast)	14.0	150	660	51	50 / 30	4	4 / 21 / 4	7 / 18
Croatia	4.5	11	3250	72	98 / 97	–	15 / 7 / 21	– / 2
Cuba	11.0	10	1170	76	96 / 95	–	23 / 10 / –	– / –
Czech Rep.	10.3	7	3870	73	– / –	12	17 / 12 / 6	– / 8
Denmark	5.2	6	29890	75	– / –	3	1 / 9 / 4	– / –
Dominican Rep.	7.9	56	1460	71	82 / 82	26	10 / 12 / 5	4 / 16
Ecuador	11.7	40	1390	70	92 / 88	46	11 / 18 / 13	9 /21
Egypt	63.3	78	790	65	64 / 39	16	2 / 12 / 9	26 / 21
El Salvador	5.8	40	1610	69	74 / 70	15	8 / 13 / 8	4 / 13
Eritrea	3.3	120	100	50	– / –	–	– / – / –	– / –
Estonia	1.5	16	2860	69	98 / 98	77	17 / 9 / 3	– / –
Ethiopia	58.2	177	100	49	46 / 25	6	5 / 14 / 20	11 / 20
Finland	5.1	4	20580	76	– / –	4	3 / 11 / 4	– / –
France	58.3	8	21000	79	– / –	3	16 / 7 / 6	– / –
Gabon	1.1	145	3490	55	74 / 53	5	– / – / –	6 /13
Gambia	1.1	107	320	46	53 / 25	9	7 / 12 / 4	1 / 11
Georgia	5.4	29	440	73	100 / 99	310	– / – / –	– / 4
Germany	81.9	6	27510	76	– / –	3	17 / 1 / 7	– / –
Ghana	17.8	110	390	57	76 / 54	29	7 / 22 / 5	5 / 15
Greece	10.5	9	8210	78	98 / 95	15	7 / 9 / 9	9 / 17
Guatemala	10.9	56	1340	66	63 / 49	19	11 / 19 / 15	7 / 11
Guinea	7.5	210	550	46	50 / 22	17	3 / 11 / 29	– / 13
Guinea-Bissau	1.1	223	250	44	68 / 43	63	1 / 3 / 4	– / 30
Haiti	7.3	134	250	54	48 / 42	15	– / – / –	5 / 14
Honduras	5.8	35	600	69	73 / 73	14	10 / 19 / 7	3 / 32
Hungary	10.1	12	4120	69	99 / 99	20	8 / 3 / 4	– / 31
India	944.6	111	340	62	66 / 38	10	2 / 2 / 14	21 / 23
Indonesia	200.0	71	980	64	90 / 78	9	3 / 10 / 7	7 / 23
Iran	70.0	37	1033	69	78 / 59	24	9 / 16 / 6	– / 19
Iraq	20.6	122	1036	61	71 / 45	–	– / – / –	– / –
Ireland	3.5	7	14710	76	– / –	3	14 / 13 / 3	– / –
Israel	5.7	9	15920	77	97 / 93	17	9 / 13 / 18	3 / –
Italy	57.2	7	19020	78	99 / 98	6	11 / 8 / 4	– / –
Jamaica	2.5	11	1510	74	81 / 89	28	7 / 11 / 8	3 / 17
Japan	125.4	6	39640	80	– / –	1	2 / 6 / 4	– / –
Jordan	5.6	25	1510	69	93 / 79	7	8 / 16 / 21	4 / 21
Kazakhstan	16.8	45	1330	68	100 / 99	307	– / – / –	– /3
Kenya	27.8	90	280	54	86 / 70	13	5 / 19 / 6	6 / 23
Korea Dem. Peo. Rep.	22.4	30	970	72	– / –	–	– / – / –	– / –
Korea Rep. of	45.3	7	9700	72	99 / 97	7	1 / 21 / 17	20 /3
Kuwait	1.7	14	17390	76	82 / 75	-1	6 / 11 / 25	– / –
Kyrgyzstan	4.4	50	700	68	99 / 95	172	– / – / –	– / 7
Lao Peo. Dem. Rep.	5.0	128	350	53	69 / 44	23	– / – / –	– / 8
Latvia	2.5	20	2270	68	100 /100	73	6 / 15 / 3	– / 1
Lebanon	3.1	40	2660	69	95 / 90	46	– / – / –	– / 16
Lesotho	2.1	139	770	58	81 / 62	13	13 / 21 / 6	1 / 17
Liberia	2.2	235	490	48	54 / 22	–	5 / 11 / 9	8 / –
Libya	5.6	61	5540	65	88 / 63	–	– / – / –	– / –
Lithuania	3.7	18	1900	70	100 / 99	151	7 / 7 / 2	– / –
Madagascar	15.4	164	230	58	60 / 32	18	6 / 11 / 5	32 / 7
Malawi	9.8	217	170	41	72 / 42	22	7 / 12 / 5	8 / 22
Malaysia	20.1	13	3890	72	89 / 78	3	6 / 22 / 13	4 / 3
Mali	11.1	220	250	47	39 / 23	5	2 / 9 / 8	1 / 7
Mauritania	2.3	183	460	53	50 / 26	7	4 / 23 / –	3 / 19
Mauritius	1.1	23	3380	71	87 / 79	9	9 / 17 / 2	3 / 5
Mexico	92.7	32	3320	72	92 / 87	37	3 / 27 / 4	24 / 19

BASIC INDICATORS

	Total population (millions) 1996	Under 5 mortality rate per 1,000 1996	GNP per capita (US$) 1996	Life expectancy at birth (years) 1996	Adult literacy rate male / female 1995	Annual rate of inflation (%) 1985 - 95	% of central gov't expenditure allocated to health/education/defence 1990 - 96	Debt service as % of exports of goods & services 1970/1995
Moldova, Rep. of	4.4	32	920	68	98 / 99	–	– / – / –	– / 5
Mongolia	2.5	71	310	65	89 / 77	52	4 / 7 / 12	– / 9
Morocco	27.0	74	1110	66	57 / 31	5	3 / 18 / 14	8 / 39
Mozambique	17.8	214	80	47	58 / 23	52	5 / 10 / 35	– / 15
Myanmar/Burma	45.9	150	220	59	89 / 78	26	4 / 12 / 37	18 / 15
Namibia	1.6	77	2000	56	78 /74	10	10 / 22 / 7	– / –
Nepal	22.0	116	200	56	41 / 14	12	5 / 14/4	3 /8
Netherlands	15.6	6	24000	78	– / –	2	15 / 11 / 4	– / –
New Zealand/Aotearoa	3.6	7	14340	77	– / –	4	16 / 15 / 4	– / –
Nicaragua	4.2	57	380	68	65 / 67	962	13 / 15 / 6	11 / 57
Niger	9.5	320	220	48	21 / 7	1	– / – / –	4 / 9
Nigeria	115.0	191	260	52	67 / 47	33	1 / 3 / 3	4 / 22
Norway	4.3	6	31250	77	– / –	3	4 / 7/ 7	– / –
Oman	2.3	18	4820	70	71 / 46	0	6 / 13 / 35	– / 8
Pakistan	139.9	136	460	63	50 / 24	9	1 / 2 / 31	22 / 29
Panama	2.7	20	2750	74	91 / 90	2	18 / 17 / 5	8 / 8
Papua New Guinea	4.4	112	1160	57	81 / 63	5	8/ 15 / 4	1 / 10
Paraguay	5.0	34	1690	69	94 / 91	25	7 / 22 / 11	12 / 8
Peru	24.0	58	2310	68	95 / 83	399	5 / 16 / 11	12 / 13
Philippines	69.3	38	1050	68	95 / 94	10	3 / 16 / 11	8 / 16
Poland	39.0	14	2790	71	99 / 98	92	– / – / –	– / 6
Portugal	9.8	7	9740	75	92 / 87	11	9 / 11 / 6	7 / 16
Romania	22.7	25	1480	70	99 / 97	69	8 / 10 / 7	0 / 4
Russian Federation	148.1	25	2240	65	100 / 99	149	2 / 2 / 12	– / 8
Rwanda	5.4	170	180	36	70 / 52	11	5 / 26 / –	1 / 28
Saudi Arabia	18.8	30	7040	71	72 / 50	3	6 / 14 / 36	– / 1
Senegal	8.5	127	600	51	43 / 23	4	– / – / –	4 / 12
Sierra Leone	4.3	284	180	37	45 / 18	62	10 / 13 / 10	11 / 27
Singapore	3.4	4	26730	77	96 / 86	4	7 / 23/ 29	1 / –
Slovakia	5.3	11	2950	71	– / –	11	– / – / –	– / 6
Slovenia	1.9	6	8200	73	100/ 99	–	– / – / –	– / 3
Somalia	9.8	211	110	48	36 / 14	75	1 / 2 / 38	2 / 7
South Africa	42.4	66	3160	65	82 / 82	14	– / – / –	– / 5
Spain	39.7	5	13580	78	98 / 96	6	6 / 4 / 3	– / –
Sri Lanka	18.1	19	700	73	93 / 87	12	6 / 10 / 15	11 / 11
Sudan	27.3	116	310	54	58 / 35	63	– / – / –	11 / 0
Sweden	8.8	4	23750	78	– / –	6	– / 5 / 6	– / –
Switzerland	7.2	5	40630	78	– / –	3	20 / 3 / 6	– / –
Syria	14.6	34	1120	68	86 / 56	16	3 / 9 / 28	11 / 3
Tajikistan	5.9	76	340	67	100 / 100	147	– / – / –	– / –
Tanzania	30.8	144	120	51	79 / 57	32	6 / 8 / 16	1 / 16
TFYR Macedonia	2.2	30	860	72	– / –	–	– / –	– / 7
Thailand	58.7	38	2740	69	96 / 92	5	8 / 22 / 14	3 / 3
Togo	4.2	125	310	50	67 / 37	3	5 / 20 / 11	3 / 5
Trinidad and Tobago	1.3	17	3770	73	99 / 97	7	– / – / –	5 / 16
Tunisia	9.2	35	1820	69	79 / 55	6	6 / 17 / 6	18 / 17
Turkey	61.8	47	2780	68	92 / 72	65	3 / 12 / 10	16 / 27
Turkmenistan	4.2	78	920	65	99 / 97	381	– / – / –	– / 4
Uganda	20.3	141	240	41	74 / 50	66	2 / 15 / 26	3 / 18
Ukraine	51.6	24	1630	69	98 / 99	363	– / – / –	– / 2
United Arab Emirates	2.3	18	17400	75	79 / 80	–	7 / 17 / 37	– / –
United Kingdom	58.1	7	18700	77	– / –	5	14 / 5 / 8	– / –
United States	269.4	8	26980	76	– / –	3	19 / 2 / 17	– / –
Uruguay	3.2	22	5170	73	97 / 98	71	6 / 7 / 7	22 / 22
Uzbekistan	23.2	60	970	68	100 / 100	239	– / – / –	– / 3
Venezuela	22.3	28	3020	72	92 / 90	38	10 / 20 / 6	3 / 17
Vietnam	75.2	44	240	67	97 / 91	88	– / – / –	– / 4
Yemen	15.7	105	260	57	53 / 26	–	5 / 21 /30	– / 5
Yugoslavia	10.3	22	–	72	99 / 97	–	– / – / –	– / –
Zambia	8.3	202	400	43	86 / 71	92	14 / 15 / –	6 / 24
Zimbabwe	11.4	73	540	49	90 / 80	21	8 / 24 / 17	2 / 20

BASIC INDICATORS

	Total population (millions) 1996	Under 5 mortality rate per 1,000 1996	GNP per capita (US$) 1996	Life expectancy at birth (years) 1996	Adult literacy rate male / female 1995	Annual rate of inflation (%) 1985 - 95	% of central gov't expenditure allocated to health/education/defence 1990 - 96	Debt service as % of exports of goods & services 1970/1995
Regional summaries								
Sub-Saharan Africa	576.1	**170**	501	51	66 / 47	20	5 / 14 / 10	6 / 11
Middle East and North Africa	318.2	**65**	1710	65	70 / 47	14	6 / 15 /21	12 / 13
South Asia	1267.7	**119**	345	61	63 / 36	10	2 / 3 / 16	17 / 22
East Asia and Pacific	1797.8	**54**	1043	68	91 / 76	9	2 / 12 / 14	6 / 7
Latin America and Caribbean	479.1	**43**	3271	69	88 / 85	406	5 / 11 / 5	13 / 21
CEE/CIS* and Baltic States	474.6	**36**	2086	68	98 / 96	139	4 / 7 / 10	– / 9
Industrialized countries	838.7	**7**	25926	77	98 / 96	3	12 / 4 / 9	– / –
Developing countries	4577.7	**97**	1101	62	79 / 62	141	4 / 11 / 12	11 / 13
Least developed countries	594.5	**171**	220	51	60 / 38	30	5 / 13 / 15	6 / 14
World	5752.3	**88**	4812	63	81 / 66	32	11 / 6 / 10	11 / 12

*Central & East European/Commonwealth of Independent States

Definitions of the indicators

Under-five mortality rate – Probability of dying between birth and exactly five years of age expressed per 1,000 live births.

GNP per capita – Gross national product (GNP) is the sum of gross value added by all resident producers, plus any taxes that are not included in the valuation of output, plus net receipts of primary income from non-resident sources. GNP per capita is the gross national product, converted to United States dollars using the World Bank Altas method, divided by the mid-year population.

Life expectancy at birth – The number of years newborn children would live if subject to the mortality risks prevailing for the cross-section of population at the time of their birth.

Adult literacy rate – Percentage of persons aged 15 and over who can read and write.

The State of the World's Children 1998, UNICEF/Oxford University Press.

> *The list does not include the less populous countries (those with fewer than one million people).

PHOTO REFERENCE

A

2 Aral Sea, Uzbekistan *Ben Ares/Panos Pictures*. **4** Aborigines, Australia *Derek Roff/Camera Press*. **8** Crop spraying *WHO/USIS*. **11** Traffic, London UK *Tim Ridley/Panos Pictures*; Salvador Allende *Christian Belpaire/Camera Press*. **13** Amazon *P Kaipiainen/Camera Press*. **14** Idi Amin *Photonews/Camera Press*. **15** Antartica *Edward A Wilson/Mary Evans Picture Library*. **17** South African kids *Troth Wells/New Internationalist*; Prawn Farm, Bangladesh *Peter Barker/Panos Pictures*. **18** Cory Aquino *Paul Raffaele/Camera Press*. **19** Yasser Arafat *Gavin Smith/Camera Press*. **21** Aswan Dam, Egypt *Camera Press*. **22** Kemal Ataturk *Camera Press*. **23** Aung San Suu Kyi *Benoit Gysembergh/Camera Press*.

B

24 Buddha, Burma *Claus-Dieter Brauns/Camera Press*. **26** Matoke (green bananas), Uganda *Penny Tweedie/Panos Pictures*. **27** Bob Geldof *D Stone/Camera Press*; Hastings Banda *James Soullier/Camera Press*; Sirimavo Bandaranaike *Camera Press*. **28** Menachem Begin *WB/Camera Press*. **29** Bhopal demonstration, India *David Dahmen/Panos Pictures*. **30** Steve Biko *IDAF/Camera Press*. **31** Passenger Pigeon illustration *Edith Looker*. **32** Leaving Ireland after the potato famine 1845. **35** Borehole, Burkina Faso *Claude Sauvageot*; Norman Borlaug *UN/FAO*. **36** BSE cow *Tom Hanley/Camera Press*. **37** Willy Brandt *Vario Press/Camera Press*. **37, 38** Baby feeding, Burkina Faso *Claude Sauvageot*. **39** Bushmen (San) *Vierentia Beukes/Camera Press*; Chief Buthelezi *David Channer/Camera Press*.

C

40 Cocoa pod in Grenada *Lennox Smillie/Camera Press*. **42** Amilcar Cabral *Peter Larsen/Camera Press*. **43** Tram in Prague, Czech Republic *Trygve Bolstad/Panos Pictures*. **44** Italian worker in German car factory *Harry Redl/Camera Press*. **47** Fidel Castro *Ivan Meacci/Camera Press*; Cassava plant *John Miles/Panos Pictures*. **48** Dinka cattle camp *Hutchison Library*. **50** Gulf War – Iraqi prisoners of war *Camera Press*. **53** Statue of Christ, Betancuria, Fuerteventura *Troth Wells*. **54** Coal miners, Nigeria *Mike Wells/Camera Press*. **56** Berlin Wall 1975 *Camera Press*. **57** Famine in India 1897 *Topani in Le Petit Journal/Mary Evans Picture Library*. **58** Commonwealth education ministers, Gaberone, Botswana 1997

Commonwealth Secretariat. **60** Masai, Nairobi, Kenya *Troth Wells*. **62** Family Planning poster, Burkina Faso *Claude Sauvageot*; illustration *Alan Hughes*. **64** White rhinos in Kenya *Fred Hoogervorst/Panos Pictures*. **65** Great Barrier Reef, Australia *John Miles/Panos Pictures*. **66** Cotton plant, Uzbekistan *Marcus Rose/Panos Pictures*. **67** Javier Perez de Cuellar *Ralph Crane/Camera Press*; Chinese child *Claude Sauvageot*.

D

68 Desertification in the Sahel *Jeremy Hartley/Panos Pictures*. **69** The Dalai Lama *Michael Blackman/Camera Press*. **71** DDT and pesticides, Mali *Betty Press/Panos Pictures*. **73** Barclays Bank 'debt' advert *Dexter Tiranti*. **75** Logging in Kalimantan, Indonesia *Chris Stowers/Panos Pictures*. **77** Deng Xiaoping *Camera Press*. **78** Western Sahara desert *Chris Brazier/New Internationalist*. **79** Globe illustration *Bill Sanderson*. **81** Anti-drug hoarding in Belize City *Neil Cooper/Panos Pictures*.

E

82 Gorrilla in Virunga National Park, Rwanda *Victoria Keble-Williams/Panos Pictures*. **84** UK poster on East Timor. **86** Kuwaiti women *Penny Tweedie/Panos Pictures*. **88** Worker **89** North American Mastodon illustration *Edith Looker*. **90** LL Zamenhof *Mary Evans Picture Library*; Beer bottles in China *Trygvre Bolstad/Panos Pictures*. **91** Sasnia graves, Bosnia *Robert Rajtic/Camera Press*. **92** Eucalyptus leaves, Uganda *Crispin Hughes/Panos Pictures*; European flag *Y-M Quemener/Camera Press*. **93** Butter mountain *Camera Press*. **95** Exxon Valdez oil spill clean-up *Heidi Bradner/Panos Pictures*.

F

96 Fishing in Bangladesh *Shahidul Alam, Drik Picture Library*. **98** Family Planning poster, Burkina Faso *Claude Sauvageot*; Famine in India 1900 *Mary Evans Picture Library*. **100** Fish drying, Ghana *Crispin Hughes/Panos Pictures*. **102** Food Aid *UN*. **103** Paulo Freire *John Taylor/World Council of Churches*. **104** Milton Friedman *Jean Regis/Camera Press*; Frelimo freedom fighters, Mozambique *Camera Press*.

G

106 Banks of the Ganges, Varanasi, India *TS Nagarajam/Camera Press*. **108** JK Galbraith *Karsh/Camera Press*. **109** Indira Gandhi *Camera Press*; Mohandas Gandhi in London, 1930s *Bassano/Camera Press*. **110** Bob Geldof

Andy Nicholls/Camera Press; Gay Rights march, South Africa *Eric Miller/Panos Pictures*. **111** Indian woman *Alan Hughes*. **113** Apples *Troth Wells*. **114** Cooling towers *UN*. **115** Miners in South Africa *David Ransom/NI*. **118** Cassava in Ibadan, Nigeria *Bruce Paton/Panos Pictures*. **119** Women in groundnut field, Kenya *Troth Wells/NI*. **120** Che Guevara *Prensa Latina/Camera Press*; Mao poster and junk *Frank Fischbeck/Camera Press*. **121** Clearing mines in Kuwait after the Gulf War *Nick Wildman/Camera Press*.

H

122 Slums and high rise buildings, Mumbai (Bombay), India *Ron Gilling/Panos Pictures*. **124** Amazon deforestation, Brazil *Michael Harvey/Panos Pictures*. **126** Soybeans Ibadan, Nigeria *Bruce Paton/Panos Pictures*; Priest and bridegroom, Malaysia *Dexter Tiranti*. **127** Ho Chi Minh *Camera Press*. **128** Homeless, London *Liam Ryan/Camera Press*. **130** Saddam Hussein *Imapress/Camera Press*; **131** Tucurui hydro-electric dam, Brazil *Michael Harvey/Panos Pictures*.

I

132 Yanomami indians, Brazil *P Kaipiainen/Camera Press*. **135** Sioux indian and cradle, USA *Alan Hughes*. **136** Yanomami child, Brazil *P Kaipiainen/Camera Press*. **137** Workshop in Tunisia *Amedeo Vergani*; Computer class *Guy Mansfield/Panos Pictures*. **138** Cochineal on prickly pear plant *Troth Wells*; Intercropping, South Africa *W Beinart*. **139** Rice illustration *Steve Weston*. **140** Nuclear power plant, Brazil *Michael Harvey/Panos Pictures*. **143** Making watering cans, Uganda *Nick Robinson/Panos Pictures*. **145** Woman walking on logs, Kalimantan, Indonesia *Chris Stowers/Panos Pictures*; Palestinian card. **146** Egyptian shaduf *Mary Evans Picture Library*. **147** Mosque in Nairobi, Kenya *Troth Wells*; Elephant hunt engraving c 1860 *Mary Evans Picture Library*.

JKL

148 Landmines, Angola *Trygve Bolstad/Panos Pictures*. **150** JR Jayewardene *Govt of Sri Lanka*; Muhammad Ali Jinnah *Camera Press*. **151** Kenneth Kaunda *Paul Conklin/Camera Press*; Jomo Kenyatta *Anthony Howard/Camera Press*. **152** Martin Luther King *Karsh/Camera Press*; Korean War *Camera Press*. **154** Cambodia *UN*. **156** Lee Kuan Yew

F/T/Camera Press; **157** Painting of Lenin by A Gerasimov *Camera Press.* **159** Locust swarm 1891 *Mary Evans Picture Library.*

M

160 Mosquito *Hans Pfletschinger/Camera Press.* **162** Maize illustration *Steve Weston.* **163** Malaria poster, Ghana *Bruce Paton/Panos Pictures.* **164** Nelson Mandela *Stewart Mark/Rota/Camera Press.* **165** Michael Manley *Lennox Smillie/Camera Press.* **166** Mao Zedong *Camera Press.* **167** Ferdinand Marcos *Veronica Garbut/Camera Press;* Ship in Malaysia *Dexter Tiranti.* **168** Karl Marx illustration *Alan Hughes.* **169** Mau Mau, Kenya *Cyril Mathews/Camera Press;* Robert McNamara *Camera Press;* Margaret Mead *Penguin Books.* **170** Golda Meir *Eli/Kaminer/Camera Press.* **171** Mercury, Philippines *Chris Stowers/Panos Pictures;* **172** Egyptian and Bangladeshi workers in Kuwait *Penny Tweedie/Panos Pictures.* **173** Margaret and Denis Thatcher *Guardian.* **174** Monsoon in India *JL Whimper/Mary Evans Picture Library.* **175** Hosni Mubarak *Imapress/Camera Press;* Testing for malaria, Thailand *Marcus Rase/Panos Pictures.* **176** Robert Mugabe *Norman Sagansky/Camera Press.*

N

178 Bosnia, exodus from Tuxla, July 1995 *Paul Harris/Camera Press.* **180** Narmada dam in India *Roderick Johnson/Camera Press;* Gamal Abdel Nasser *Camera Press.* **181** Sioux youth , USA *Alan Hughes* **182** Sioux, USA *Alan Hughes;* Cigarette advertising, Kisangani, Democratic Republic of Congo *Marc Schlossman/Panos Pictures.* **183** Jawaharlal Nehru *Baron/Camera Press.* **184** Lentils illustration *Steve Weston;* Kwame Nkrumah *Ian Russell/Camera Press.* **186** NGO signs, Burkina Faso *Jeremy Hartley/Panos Pictures.* **187** Nuclear bomb devastation, Japan *USAF.* **188** Nuclear explosion *USAF.* **189** Julius Nyerere *Norman Sagansky/Camera Press.*

O

190 Farmer with organic fertilizer, Mindanao, Philippines *Sean Sprague/Panos Pictures.* **192** Australia Great Barrier Reef, 1911 *Mary Evans Picture Library.* **194** Women in Dubai *Amedeo Vergani;* Oil Palm, Ivory Coast *Paul Harrison/Panos Pictures.* **195** Organic pesticides, Philippines *Ron Giling/Panos Pictures.* **196** Stock Exchange, Tokyo *Chris Stowers/Panos Pictures.* **197** Oil lake pollution, Kuwait *Penny Tweedie/Panos Pictures.* **198** Scene from a play, Japanese print *Mary Evans Picture Library.* **199** Daniel Ortega *Ivan Meacci/Camera Press.*

PQ

200 Steel works, India *Fram Petit/Panos Pictures.* **202** Panama Canal, ca 1915 *Mary Evans Picture Library.* **203** Masai, Kenya *Troth Wells/New Internationalist.* **204** Peacekeepers *UN* **205** Juan and Eva Peron *Camera Press.* **206** Coffee spraying, Zimbabwe *D Reed/Panos Pictures.* **207** Phosphates conveyor belt, Western Sahara *Hugues De Wurstemberger.* **208** Augusto Pinochet *Juan Pablo Lira/Doce/Camera Press;* Cocoa plantation, Uganda *Jim Holmes/Panos Pictures.* **209** Children in polluted river, Manila, Philippines *Ron Giling/Panos Pictures.* **212** Pineapple, Africa *Guy Mansfield/Panos Pictures.* **215** Muammar Qaddafi *Tessa Colvin/Camera Press;* Pyrethrum on smallholding, Kenya *Troth Wells.*

R

216 Women in paddy field Kegalla district, Sri Lanka *Amedeo Vergani.* **219** Anti-rape march, Johannesburg, South Africa *Giséle Wulfsohn/Panos Pictures;* Ronald Reagan *Gely/Imapress/Camera Press.* **220** Rastafarian, Jamaica *Lennox Smillie/Camera Press.* **224** Rice fields, Bangladesh *Shahidul Alam/Drik Picture Library;* Rubber plantation, Malaya, early C20 *Mary Evans Picture Library.* **225** Cecil Rhodes by Mortimer Menpes *Mary Evans Picture Library.*

S

226 Forest in Brazil *Marcos Santilli/Panos Pictures.* **228** Anwar Sadat *Leif Skoogfors/Camera Press;* Irrigation, Mali *Jeremy Hartley/Panos Pictures.* **230** Bathtime, India *Claude Sauvageot.* **231** Cabora Bassa dam, Mozambique *Trygve Bolstad/Panos Pictures.* **232** Seeds illustration *Steve Weston;* Haile Selassie *Marian Kaplan/Camera Press.* **233** Slash and burn in Indonesia *Jeremy Hartley/Panos Pictures.* **234** Sisal, Zimbabwe *David Reed/Panos Pictures.* **235** Slave house, Sierra Leone, 1849 *Mary Evans Picture Library;* Adam Smith by John Kay, 1790 *Mary Evans Picture Library.* **236** Soil conservation, Burkina Faso *Jeremy Hartley/Panos Pictures.* **237** Soil erosion, Himalayas, India *Jeremy Hartley/Panos Pictures.* **239** Pacific island *David Ransom/NI.* **240** Street-kid, Thailand *Jean-Léo Dugast/Panos Pictures.* **242** Squeezing sugar-cane, Dominica *Amedeo Vergani.*

T

244 Tuareg traditional healer, Bamako, Mali *Betty Press/Panos Pictures.* **246** Banknotes *Susanne Schmuck/Deutsche Bank.* **247** Tea leaves, Sri Lanka *Jean-Leo Dugast/Panos Pictures.* **248** Cocoa sack, Ghana *Crispin Hughes/Panos Pictures.* **249** Three Gorges Dam project, China *NCNA/Camera Press.* **250** Three Mile Island nuclear power station, USA *Williy Spiller/SE/Camera Press.* **251** Tobacco, Nicaragua *Jon Spaull/Panos Pictures.* **252** Worker *UN* **253** Traditional medicine market, Togo *Anders Gunnartz/Panos Pictures;* Goats, Kenya *Troth Wells.* **254** Cigarette advertisement, Cameroon *Sean Sprague/Panos Pictures.* **255** Loading logs, Burma *Jean-Leo Dugast/Panos Pictures.* **256** Tsetse fly *Oxford Scientific Films/Camera Press.* **257** Archbishop Desmond Tutu *Camera Press.*

UV

258 Jobless advertise their trades, Mexico City *Ron Gilling/Panos Pictures.* **260** Signing the UN charter, 1945 *Camera Press.* **263** UNHCR resettling refugees, Uganda *Crispin Hughes/Panos Pictures;* UN tank, Rwanda *Trygve Bolstad/Panos Pictures.* **264** Universal Declaration of Human Rights *UNESCO.* **266** Smallpox vaccination, Paris 1893 *Mary Evans Picture Library.* **267** Vietnam war photos *Leclerc/Camera Press.*

W

268 Wind farm, USA *Sean Sprague/Panos Pictures.* **270** Kurt Waldheim *Camera Press.* **271** Brandenburg Gate, Berlin *Camera Press.* **273** Killer whale *Jeff Foott/Camera Press.* **274** Elephant hunt, 1857 *Mary Evans Picture Library.* **275** Mangrove, Australia *Penny Tweedie/Panos Pictures.* **276** Fishpond, Indonesia *Jeremy Hartley/Panos Pictures;* illustration *Edith Looker.* **277** Clinic, Burkina Faso *Claude Sauvageot.* **278** Lake Tanganiyka *JC Callow/Panos Pictures;* Fair traded coffee *David Ransom/NI.* **279** Great Barrier Reef, Australia *L and B Cropp/Camera Press.*

XYZ

280 Zapatistas, Mexico 1993 *Liam Bailey/Camera Press.* **283** Yanomami, Brazil *P Kaipiainen/Camera Press;* Emiliano Zapata *Mary Evans Picture Library.* **284** Zapatistas, Mexico 1993 *Liam Bailey/Camera Press.* **285** Watermelon sellers, Zimbabwe *Troth Wells;* Zia ul-Haq *Nick Fogden/Oxfam;* Ziaur Rahman *Camera Press.*

288-291 Malaysia *Dexter Tiranti;* Zambia *Black/UNICEF;* Sri Lanka *ILO;* Turkey *ILO.*

Also from New Internationalist Publications:

The World Guide 2000
An alternative reference to the countries of our planet

The World Guide, published regularly since 1979, is a major reference work which, with its highly informative and easy-access alphabetical format, has become an essential addition to libraries, schools and outward-looking homes everywhere. The book contains a comprehensive profile of every country, including its history, politics, economics, environment and social setting, with key facts and indicators on literacy, trade, employment, schooling, health, communications and energy use. These issues are supported by charts, statistics and maps. While including everything that is found in a conventional reference work, the Guide offers in addition a wealth of development information, unavailable elsewhere, and challenges the Euro-centric perspective of the world and subsequent priorities on which such works are usually based.

The World Guide is researched and edited by the Third World Institute in Uruguay in collaboration with a range of development and campaigning organisations in the South. The work prioritises the facts and issues that are central to the lives of people in Africa, Asia, the Middle East and Latin America & the Caribbean. **The World Guide** contains more than 600 pages of global information with over 250 maps, 650 diagrams, 10,000 references and an easy-to-use index. It divides into 85 pages on special development themes accompanied by 520 pages with country-specific information plus map, and also includes a large fold-out colour world map 420 mm x 270 mm (16" x 10 1/2").

Special development themes include:

Demography	**Labour**	**Childhood**	**Habitat**
Food production	**Overseas Aid**	**Debt**	**Communications**
Refugees	**Social Development**	**Health**	**Deforestation**
Education	**Women**	**Trade**	**Arms**
Indigenous people	**Global Warming**	**Water**	**Transnational Corporations**

Contact details: New Internationalist Publications, 55 Rectory Road, Oxford OX4 1BW, UK.
e-mail: jol@newint.org OR your national distributor.

'The World Guide provides detailed information on all countries and a committed Latin American perspective on virtually every Third World issue. As a reference book it is indispensable for all concerned with North-South relations.'
Willy Brandt, former Chancellor of West Germany.

'It contains the naked portrait of reality.'
Eduardo Galeano, author of the historical trilogy on Latin America — Memory of Fire.

'Offering a Third World perspective, this amazing reference work would sit well in the libraries of schools and colleges ... To find such a diversity of opinions and wealth of data adds much ... you could read this for hours.'
Times Educational Supplement, United Kingdom.